Executive Compensation Answer Book

Third Edition

Bruce Overton

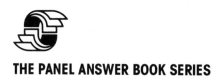

THE PANEL ANSWER BOOK SERIES

Copyright © 1998

by
PANEL PUBLISHERS
A division of Aspen Publishers, Inc.
A Wolters Kluwer Company

1185 Avenue of the Americas
New York, NY 10036
(212) 597-0200

ISBN 1-56706-393-4

Printed in the United States of America

About Panel Publishers

Panel Publishers derives its name from a panel of business professionals who organized in 1964 to publish authoritative and timely books, information services, and journals written by specialists to assist business professionals in the areas of compensation and benefits management, pension planning and compliance, and human resources, as well as owners of small to medium-sized businesses and their legal and financial advisors.

Titles available from Panel Publishers on related topics include:

Books

      Officer Compensation Report
      The Pension Answer Book*
      Pension Distribution Answer Book*
      Pension Investment Handbook
      401(k) Answer Book*
      Estate and Retirement Planning Answer Book*
      Nonqualified Deferred Compensation Answer Book*

Journals and Newsletters

      Journal of Pension Benefits
      Journal of Deferred Compensation
      Compensation & Benefits Management
      Pension Plan Administrator

Companion volume of Forms & Worksheets also available

PANEL PUBLISHERS
A division of Aspen Publishers, Inc.
Practical Solutions for Business Professionals

iii

SUBSCRIPTION NOTICE

This Panel product is updated on a periodic basis with supplements to reflect important changes in the subject matter. If you purchased this product directly from Panel Publishers, we have already recorded your subscription for this update service.

If, however, you purchased this product from a bookstore and wish to receive future updates and revised or related volumes billed separately with a 30-day examination review, please contact our Customer Service Department at 1-800-234-1660, or send your name, company name (if applicable), address, and the title of the product to:

PANEL PUBLISHERS
A Division of Aspen Publishers, Inc.
7201 McKinney Circle
Frederick, MD 21701

Introduction

The *Executive Compensation Answer Book, Third Edition* has been extensively revised, updated, and expanded to bring subscribers the most authoritative, current information on the full spectrum of executive compensation issues. The areas in which the *Third Edition* provides practical guidance range from base salary to incentive plans, from small company considerations to board of directors' compensation. New and critical issues addressed in this *Third Edition* include:

- Complete description of the Financial Accounting Standards Board Ruling #123 on accounting for stock plans in both private and public companies
- A summary of the Securities and Exchange Commission's new clarifications of Section 16 on stock transactions by public company "insiders"
- A discussion of the impact that Section 162(m) will have on the deductibility of executive pay in public and private corporations
- Detailed examples of executive agreements, executive severance agreements, and rabbi trust agreements
- An updated appendix on trends in executive compensation
- A discussion of total compensation strategies used in small entrepreneurial companies
- Up-to-date descriptions of "cafeteria" shareholder proxies used in public companies
- Examples of economic-value-added incentive compensation plans and shareholder value incentive compensation plans

The *Executive Compensation Answer Book, Third Edition* also contains two entirely new chapters on the following topics:

- Economic value-added with implementation strategies
- Trends in executive compensation, including total cash compensation, long-term compensation, and compensation for outside directors

The *Executive Compensation Answer Book, Third Edition* offers authoritative, practical guidance on how companies can structure executive compensation programs that not only help to recruit, retain, and motivate quality executives, but also ensure that those companies receive the best return possible on their compensation dollar. The *Third Edition* provides straightforward answers to such significant questions as the following:

- How can a company assess the advantages and disadvantages of particular types of executive compensation plans?
- How can a company set performance standards that assess whether the compensation system is actually rewarding performance?
- What are the effects of various executive stock ownership plans—including restricted stock purchases, discounted stock options, premium stock options, and reload options?
- What techniques can companies use to determine how much pay they should provide to executives?
- How can companies comply with ERISA requirements for nonqualified plans?
- How can companies comply with Section 16 SEC regulations that define which executives involved in "insider" stock ownership transactions are subject to reporting requirements?
- How can companies calculate the dollar value of long-term incentive plans?

The questions and answers covering these and many other key issues give subscribers an overview of the intricacies of developing and administering executive compensation programs. The pages that follow are filled with examples and practice pointers illustrating the concepts presented. The author hopes that the *Third Edition* will be of significant value as both a reference tool and a practice-based guide to executive compensation.

Bruce Overton
November 1997

How to Use This Book

The *Executive Compensation Answer Book, Third Edition* uses clear, precise language and avoids technical jargon wherever possible. The question-and-answer format, with its breadth of coverage and plain-language explanations, effectively conveys the complex and essential subject matter of executive compensation and makes the material readily accessible.

To provide additional assistance in locating related topics, the *Third Edition* makes use of an extensive system of cross-referencing.

Detailed Listing of Questions. The detailed listing of questions that follows the table of contents at the front of the book is designed to help the reader locate specific areas of immediate interest. This listing functions as a detailed table of contents and provides the specific question that you are researching as well as the page number on which the answer appears.

Question Numbers. The questions are numbered consecutively within each chapter.

Glossary. Because the executive compensation area is replete with technical terms that have specific legal meanings, a special glossary of terms is provided following the question-and-answer portion of the book. Expressions not defined elsewhere, and abbreviations used throughout the book, are defined in the glossary, which is arranged in alphabetical order.

Index. At the back of the book is a detailed key-word index that is provided as a further aid to locating specific topical information. All references in the Index are to question number rather than to page number.

The *Executive Compensation Answer Book, Third Edition* is intended to provide you with a comprehensive set of answers to the issues you face when designing or evaluating your company's executive compensation philosophy. By using it in conjunction with Panel's highly acclaimed executive compensation survey report *Officer Compensation Report: The Executive Compensation Survey for Small to Medium-Sized Businesses*, you can compare your compensation practices with the actual pay practices of other companies within your industry to ensure that your company receives the best return on its compensation investment.

The Editors
November 1997

About the Author

BRUCE OVERTON is a partner in the human resource consulting firm of HR Management Inc., located in Atlanta, Georgia. Mr. Overton also has consulting experience with Sibson & Company Inc. His company experience includes 12 years with RJR Nabisco, Inc., where he served as their top compensation executive and as Vice President, Personnel. In that capacity, he oversaw worldwide personnel policy, staffing, and compensation programs for 120,000 employees. He has published numerous articles on personnel and compensation issues and is past Chairman of the Board and Life Member of the American Compensation Association.

Contents

List of Questions   xxiii

CHAPTER 1

Fundamental Concepts of Executive Compensation .   1-1

      Total Compensation Issues   1-2

      Base Salary   1-12

      Incentive Plans   1-14

      Tax Considerations   1-21

      Accounting Considerations   1-29

CHAPTER 2

Private Versus Public Company Considerations   2-1

      General Considerations   2-2

Stock-Based Plans 2-4

S Corporations 2-8

SEC Regulations 2-12

Proxy Rules 2-19

CHAPTER 3

Base Salary 3-1

Establishing Base Salary 3-2

Job Evaluation 3-3

Salary Increases 3-9

Salary Banding; Other Increases 3-10

CHAPTER 4

Annual Incentives 4-1

General Considerations 4-2

Plan Design 4-10

Performance Measures 4-23

Performance Standards 4-30

Funding Incentive Plans 4-33

Contents

CHAPTER **5**

Long-Term Incentive Plans   5-1

    General Considerations   5-2

    Plan Comparisons   5-12

    Compensation Philosophy   5-21

    Plan Design   5-23

    Stock Options   5-26

    Omnibus Plan   5-29

    Tax Considerations   5-30

    Exercising a Stock Option   5-36

    Plan Administration   5-41

CHAPTER **6**

Purchase Plans   6-1

    General Considerations   6-2

    Incentive Stock Options   6-4

    Nonstatutory Stock Options   6-11

    Discounted Stock Options   6-18

    Premium Stock Options   6-21

Option Reloads 6-24

Book Value Purchase Plans 6-26

Convertible Debentures 6-29

Junior Stock Plans 6-33

Performance-Based Stock Options 6-34

CHAPTER 7

Appreciation and Full-Value Plans 7-1

Appreciation Plans 7-2

Full-Value Plans 7-13

Performance Unit Plans 7-22

Performance Share Plans 7-24

CHAPTER 8

Combination Long-Term Plans 8-1

General Considerations 8-1

Performance Share/Stock Option Plans . . . 8-3

Restricted Stock/Stock Option Plans 8-8

SAR/Stock Option Plans 8-11

Contents

CHAPTER **9**

Executive Benefit Plans   9-1

    General Considerations   9-2

    Nonqualified Retirement Plans   9-3

    Funding Arrangements   9-17

    Insurance-Related Nonqualified Deferred
    Compensation Plans   9-20

    Split-Dollar Life Insurance   9-23

    Executive Disability Income Insurance . . .   9-26

    ERISA Considerations   9-27

    Top-Hat Plans or SERPs   9-28

    Excess Benefit Plans   9-33

    Nonqualified Plans in Nonprofit Organiza-
    tions   9-37

    Tax Considerations   9-39

CHAPTER **10**

Perquisites and Other Benefits   10-1

    General Considerations   10-2

    Reimbursement   10-3

Memberships and Other Common Perquisites 10-5

Employment Agreements 10-9

Severance Agreements 10-12

CHAPTER 11

Building a Total Compensation Strategy 11-1

General Considerations 11-2

Compensation Factors 11-3

Benefit Factors 11-6

Other Factors 11-9

Determining the Mix 11-10

Developing a Total Strategy 11-14

Approval and Implementation 11-15

Examples of Strategy Statements 11-17

CHAPTER 12

Small Company Considerations 12-1

General Considerations 12-2

New Venture Businesses 12-10

Contents

CHAPTER **13**

Board of Directors' Compensation 13-1

    General Considerations 13-2

    Outside vs. Inside Directors 13-3

    Compensation Methods 13-6

    Other Benefits 13-8

CHAPTER **14**

Executive Compensation in the Not-For-Profit
   Organization 14-1

    General Considerations 14-1

    Base Salary 14-6

    Annual Incentives 14-7

    Long-Term Incentives 14-9

    Perquisites 14-10

CHAPTER **15**

Special Early Retirement Programs 15-1

CHAPTER **16**

U. S. Executives Working Overseas 16-1

    General Considerations 16-2

Tax Considerations 16-9

Special Compensation 16-16

CHAPTER 17

Executive Compensation in the Public Sector 17-1

CHAPTER 18

Compensation for Temporary Executives 18-1

CHAPTER 19

Economic Value-Added 19-1

General Considerations 19-1

Implementation 19-6

CHAPTER 20

Trends in Executive Compensation 20-1

Total Cash Compensation 20-1

Long-Term Compensation 20-5

Outside Directors 20-8

Regulations 20-9

APPENDIX A

IRS Model Rabbi Trust Arrangement A-1

Contents

APPENDIX **B**

Sample Compensation Agreements B-1

APPENDIX **C**

Sample Severance and Noncompetition Agreement .   C-1

APPENDIX **D**

Sample Employment Agreements D-1

APPENDIX **E**

Sample Shareholder-Approved Annual Incentive
   Compensation Plan E-1

        Fortune Brands, Inc. Annual Executive In-
        centive Compensation Plan E-2

APPENDIX **F**

Sample Compensation Plan for Outside Directors . . .   F-1

        Dupont Stock Accumulation and Deferred
        Compensation Plan for Directors F-1

APPENDIX **G**

Sample Proposal to Increase the Number of Shares
   Used in an Executive Compensation Plan G-1

        Proposal to Amend the 1992 Executive
        Long-Term Incentive Plan by Increasing the
        Number of Shares Available for Issuance . .   G-1

APPENDIX **H**

Sample Proposal of Shareholder-Approved
   Performance-Based Compensation Plan as Defined
   under Section 162(m) of IRS Regulations H-1

   Amendment to the Incentive Compensation Plan for Officers of the Boeing Company   H-2

   Attachment 1 . . . .   H-5

   Incentive Compensation Plan for Officers
   and Employees of The Boeing Company
   and Subsidiaries (As Amended and Re-
   stated) H-5

INDEX IN-1

List of Questions

Chapter 1 Fundamental Concepts of Executive Compensation

Total Compensation Issues

Q 1:1	What is total remuneration?	1-2
Q 1:2	How does base salary meet the needs of executives as well as the company?	1-2
Q 1:3	How do annual and long-term incentives meet the needs of executives and the company?	1-2
Q 1:4	How do benefits and perquisites satisfy executive needs?	1-3
Q 1:5	How do companies express the value of all elements of executive compensation?	1-3
Q 1:6	What is total cash compensation?	1-5
Q 1:7	What is total compensation?	1-5
Q 1:8	What are some of the factors that affect total compensation?	1-5
Q 1:9	How does the type of executive responsibility affect total compensation?	1-6
Q 1:10	How does level within the organization affect an executive's total compensation?	1-6
Q 1:11	How does the type of industry affect an executive's total compensation?	1-8
Q 1:12	How do supply and demand factors influence total compensation?	1-8
Q 1:13	How does company size influence total compensation? .	1-9
Q 1:14	How does company performance affect total compensation?	1-10

Q 1:15   Does executive performance affect total compensation? .   1-11

Base Salary

Q 1:16   Does geographic location affect an executive's base salary?   1-12
Q 1:17   How is base salary related to the other components of total
          compensation for executives?   1-12
Q 1:18   How can base salary be used to determine the mix of total
          compensation?   1-13

Incentive Plans

Q 1:19   What is the rationale for having an incentive plan?   1-14
Q 1:20   Are annual incentive plans appropriate for all types of organi-
          zations?   1-15
Q 1:21   What characteristics identify organizations for which annual
          incentive plans are feasible?   1-15
Q 1:22   How can companies deal with executives' focusing on the
          short run at the expense of long-term performance in their
          efforts to receive high annual payout?   1-16
Q 1:23   What is the typical relationship between annual and long-
          term incentives?   1-16
Q 1:24   What are some basic guidelines for incentive plan design?   1-17
Q 1:25   Typically, who is eligible for incentive plan participation? .   1-17
Q 1:26   How do executive compensation programs differ in emerg-
          ing or start-up companies?   1-19
Q 1:27   How does corporate philosophy affect the method of com-
          pensation chosen?   1-19
Q 1:28   What are the objectives of long-term incentive plans? . . .   1-20
Q 1:29   What is the difference between annual incentive plans and
          long-term incentive plans?   1-21
Q 1:30   Are stock plans considered incentive plans?   1-21

Tax Considerations

Q 1:31   What are the general tax implications of different forms of
          compensation?   1-21
Q 1:32   What is unreasonable compensation?   1-22
Q 1:33   What happens if an executive's compensation is deemed
          unreasonable?   1-23
Q 1:34   What were the clarifications to Code Section 162(m) issued
          by the IRS in early 1996?   1-23

Q 1:35   Should executive compensation plans be changed in re-
          sponse to congressional "caps" on executive pay? . . .   1-25
Q 1:36   What is ordinary income?   1-26
Q 1:37   What are capital gains?   1-26
Q 1:38   What was the rationale for favorable capital gains treatment?   1-26
Q 1:39   How do tax rates affect executive compensation planning?   1-27
Q 1:40   What is the effective tax rate?   1-28
Q 1:41   What is the marginal tax rate?   1-28
Q 1:42   What is the alternative minimum tax?   1-28

Accounting Considerations

Q 1:43   What are the general accounting implications of the different
          forms of compensation?   1-29
Q 1:44   What accounting statements contain compensation ex-
          penses?   1-30
Q 1:45   What is the accounting for stock awards?   1-30
Q 1:46   How does APB 25 compare to FAS 123?   1-32
Q 1:47   What changes in APB 25 have been implemented by the
          FASB under FAS 123?   1-32
Q 1:48   What stock plans are included in FAS 123?   1-33
Q 1:49   How is the fair value calculation done under the new FAS
          123?   1-34
Q 1:50   How do some of these fair value determination models work?   1-35
Q 1:51   What are the disclosure requirements of FAS 123?   1-37
Q 1:52   What are the current FASB guidelines on earnings per share
          calculations that are effective until December 1997? . . .   1-37
Q 1:53   What are the new FASB guidelines on EPS calculations that
          are to be used in company financial statements issued after
          December 15, 1997?   1-38
Q 1:54   How should companies respond to the new FASB regula-
          tions being considered for stock options?   1-39

Chapter 2   Private Versus Public Company Considerations

General Considerations

Q 2:1   What is a public or publicly traded company?   2-2
Q 2:2   What is a private or privately held company?   2-2
Q 2:3   What is a closely held company?   2-2

Q 2:4   Is a privately held company always considered closely held as well? **2-3**

Q 2:5   Do executive compensation programs in privately held companies differ from those in publicly traded companies? .   **2-3**

Stock-Based Plans

Q 2:6   Do privately held companies use stock-based capital accumulation programs to structure their executive compensation arrangements? **2-4**

Q 2:7   What are the most common forms of long-term incentives in private companies? **2-4**

Q 2:8   Are there problems with using stock plans in private companies? **2-4**

Q 2:9   What is an example of a buy-back agreement? **2-6**

Q 2:10   Is there a negative effect if a privately held company does not provide long-term incentive plans? **2-7**

S Corporations

Q 2:11   What is a Subchapter S corporation? **2-8**

Q 2:12   How does a company elect to become a Subchapter S corporation? **2-8**

Q 2:13   Does electing S corporation status have an impact on executive compensation? **2-9**

Q 2:14   Does the issue of unreasonable compensation affect publicly traded companies differently from privately held and S corporations? **2-10**

SEC Regulations

Q 2:15   What is the Securities Act of 1933, and how does it affect executive compensation? **2-12**

Q 2:16   What is the Securities Exchange Act of 1934, and how does it affect executive compensation? **2-13**

Q 2:17   How can a company avoid application of the 1933 Act? .   **2-13**

Q 2:18   What are the basic SEC Section 16 rules? **2-14**

Q 2:19   What were the major changes in SEC Section 16 rules effective May 1, 1991? **2-14**

Q 2:20   What are the most significant effects of the new Section 16 rules from a compensation perspective? **2-16**

Q 2:21   What actions are needed in order to give certain transactions the benefits of SEC Rule 16(b)3? **2-18**

Q 2:22 What are the other clarifications of SEC Section 16(b)3 issued in May 1996? **2-18**

Proxy Rules

Q 2:23 What are the shareholder proxy and the proxy statement? **2-19**

Q 2:24 How do the SEC proxy reporting requirements affect executive compensation? **2-20**

Q 2:25 What is the compensation committee of the board and what role does it play in executive compensation? **2-22**

Q 2:26 What are the regulatory base and effective dates for the SEC proxy reporting rules of 1993? **2-23**

Q 2:27 What disclosure information charts must now be included with proxy statements? **2-23**

Q 2:28 What other executive compensation information must be disclosed in the proxy statement? **2-25**

Q 2:29 How should public companies determine the future value of stock options and its effect on executive compensation? **2-26**

Q 2:30 How can companies reduce negative media/shareholder reaction to major stock option exercises by executives in years when company earnings are flat or down from previous years? **2-27**

Q 2:31 How will the new requirement for a company performance comparison graph affect the amount of executive compensation awarded? **2-28**

Q 2:32 How have the new SEC proxy reporting rules generally changed the treatment of executive compensation? . . . **2-28**

Chapter 3 Base Salary

Establishing Base Salary

Q 3:1 How is an executive's base salary set? **3-2**

Q 3:2 How do companies decide on salaries or salary ranges for executives? **3-2**

Job Evaluation

Q 3:3 What is job evaluation? **3-3**

Q 3:4 How does the ranking system work? **3-3**

Q 3:5 How does a classification system work? **3-5**

Q 3:6	How does the point factor approach work?	3-5
Q 3:7	How does factor comparison work?	3-6
Q 3:8	How do companies establish labor market values for executive positions?	3-7
Q 3:9	How do most companies position their executive base salary and annual incentive against labor market competitors?	3-8
Q 3:10	Are there reasons for paying base salaries above or below a competitive average?	3-9

Salary Increases

Q 3:11	Do merit increases motivate executives?	3-9
Q 3:12	How can companies reduce the inflationary impact of annual base salary increases?	3-10

Salary Banding; Other Increases

Q 3:13	Are there alternatives to base salary ranges and merit pay for executives?	3-10
Q 3:14	What are some positive company experiences with salary banding?	3-12
Q 3:15	What are some negative company experiences with salary banding?	3-13
Q 3:16	What have been company experiences with economic pay increases?	3-13

Chapter 4   Annual Incentives

General Considerations

Q 4:1	How is short-term or annual incentive defined?	4-2
Q 4:2	How prevalent are annual incentive plans?	4-3
Q 4:3	What is the rationale for having an annual incentive plan?	4-3
Q 4:4	How is eligibility in annual incentive plans typically determined?	4-4
Q 4:5	Which forms of payment are typically used in an annual incentive plan?	4-5
Q 4:6	Are annual incentive plan payments pensionable compensation?	4-7
Q 4:7	What is the tax impact of annual incentive plans on the executive?	4-7

Q 4:8   What is the accounting treatment for annual incentive plans?   **4-8**

Q 4:9   Is shareholder approval required for annual incentive plans?   **4-9**

Plan Design

Q 4:10   What are the key issues in the design of an annual incentive program? **4-10**

Q 4:11   What are the basic plan designs for annual incentive plans?   **4-11**

Q 4:12   How does a profit sharing plan operate? **4-11**

Q 4:13   What are the advantages of a profit sharing plan? **4-12**

Q 4:14   What are the disadvantages of a profit sharing plan? . . .   **4-12**

Q 4:15   How does a growth or improvement plan operate? **4-13**

Q 4:16   What are the advantages of a growth or improvement plan?   **4-14**

Q 4:17   What are the disadvantages of a growth or improvement plan? **4-14**

Q 4:18   How does the target performance plan work? **4-14**

Q 4:19   What are the advantages of a target performance plan? .   **4-16**

Q 4:20   What are the disadvantages of a target performance plan?   **4-16**

Q 4:21   How does a peer company performance plan operate? . .   **4-16**

Q 4:22   What are the advantages of a peer company performance plan? **4-17**

Q 4:23   What are the disadvantages of a peer comparison plan? .   **4-18**

Q 4:24   What are the key features of a matrix plan? **4-18**

Q 4:25   What are the advantages of a matrix plan? **4-19**

Q 4:26   What are the disadvantages of a matrix plan? **4-19**

Q 4:27   What is a discretionary plan? **4-19**

Q 4:28   What are the advantages of a discretionary plan? **4-20**

Q 4:29   What are the disadvantages of a discretionary plan? . . .   **4-20**

Q 4:30   Are executives categorized as U.S. expatriates included in annual incentive compensation programs? **4-20**

Q 4:31   Do companies with international operations include local national executives in incentive compensation plans? . .   **4-21**

Q 4:32   Can incentive compensation plans be utilized in new ventures/start-up businesses? **4-21**

Q 4:33   How can annual incentives for executives be distinguished from those for mid-level managers? **4-22**

Q 4:34   How can short-term incentive plans be integrated with executive compensation plans during a merger of two companies? **4-23**

Performance Measures

Q 4:35 What types of performance measures are commonly used in annual incentive plans? **4-23**

Q 4:36 What are some examples of quantitative performance measures? **4-24**

Q 4:37 What financial performance measures are commonly used in annual incentive plans? **4-24**

Q 4:38 What is earnings per share and how is it calculated? . . . **4-25**

Q 4:39 What is return on assets and how is it calculated? **4-25**

Q 4:40 How is return on equity calculated? **4-26**

Q 4:41 How is return on capital calculated? **4-26**

Q 4:42 What non-financial performance measures are commonly used in annual incentive plans? **4-26**

Q 4:43 What is the difficulty of using performance measures in annual incentive plans? **4-27**

Q 4:44 How does a company decide whether the incentive programs should be based on group or individual performance? **4-28**

Q 4:45 How do performance measures vary by group or organizational level? **4-28**

Q 4:46 What performance measures work best for a manufacturing organization? **4-29**

Q 4:47 What performance measures work best in financial institutions? **4-29**

Q 4:48 Which performance measures are best for a service company? **4-30**

Performance Standards

Q 4:49 What are the basic methods of comparing performance in annual incentive plans? **4-30**

Q 4:50 How does the look forward approach to performance comparison work? **4-30**

Q 4:51 How does the peer group approach to performance comparison work? **4-31**

Q 4:52 How does the look back approach to performance comparison work? **4-31**

Q 4:53 How does the percentage of profits approach to performance comparison work? **4-31**

Q 4:54 May performance maximums be set for annual incentive plans? **4-31**

Q 4:55   Do companies typically establish a threshold performance level in annual incentive award plans? **4-32**

Q 4:56   How can you determine whether your performance standards are appropriate? **4-33**

Funding Incentive Plans

Q 4:57   How do companies determine the size of award appropriate in annual incentive compensation plans? **4-33**

Q 4:58   What factors drive the amount of annual incentive amounts paid to executives? **4-34**

Q 4:59   How does the pool method operate when used in determining incentive funds? **4-35**

Q 4:60   Are there advantages to the pool method? **4-36**

Q 4:61   Are there disadvantages to the pool method? **4-36**

Q 4:62   How is the participant method used in determining incentive pools? **4-36**

Q 4:63   Are there advantages to the participant method? **4-37**

Q 4:64   Are there disadvantages to the participant method? **4-37**

Q 4:65   Do incentive plans have maximums or caps on incentive payments? **4-37**

Chapter 5 Long-Term Incentive Plans

General Considerations

Q 5:1   What are long-term incentive plans? **5-2**

Q 5:2   What are the characteristics of long-term incentive plans? **5-2**

Q 5:3   How is eligibility for participation in long-term plans determined? **5-2**

Q 5:4   How prevalent are long-term incentive plans? **5-3**

Q 5:5   What is the rationale for having a long-term incentive plan? **5-5**

Q 5:6   What should be considered in selecting a long-term incentive plan? **5-5**

Q 5:7   What are the principal types of long-term incentive plans? **5-7**

Q 5:8   What new forms of long-term incentive are currently emerging? **5-8**

Q 5:9   What is economic value-added? **5-9**

Q 5:10   How do economic-value-added plans work? **5-10**

Q 5:11   What is shareholder value? **5-11**

Q 5:12   How do shareholder value plans work? **5-11**

Q 5:13   What is a long-term performance plan? **5-12**

Q 5:14   What is a stock option plan? **5-12**

Plan Comparisons

Q 5:15   What is the advantage of a stock option plan over a long-term performance plan? **5-12**

Q 5:16   What are the advantages of a stock option plan over a restricted share plan? **5-13**

Q 5:17   What is the disadvantage of stock options compared to long-term performance plans? **5-13**

Q 5:18   Are there disadvantages to using stock options as compared to restricted stock? **5-14**

Q 5:19   Under what circumstances is a performance plan the best type of long-term incentive for a company to select? . .   **5-15**

Q 5:20   Under what circumstances are stock-based plans the best form of long-term incentive for a company to select? . .   **5-15**

Q 5:21   How can companies get executives to own stock? **5-16**

Q 5:22   What are the advantages of shareholder value/economic value plans over stock plans? **5-16**

Q 5:23   What are the advantages of shareholder value/economic value plans over performance plans? **5-17**

Q 5:24   What are the general rules regarding taxation of long-term incentive plans? **5-18**

Q 5:25   What are the basic accounting issues for a long-term incentive plan? **5-18**

Q 5:26   How does the Black-Scholes option pricing model work? .   **5-20**

Compensation Philosophy

Q 5:27   How should a corporate compensation philosophy be utilized in plan design? **5-21**

Q 5:28   What is the primary disadvantage of long-term performance plans? **5-22**

Plan Design

Q 5:29   How do companies typically determine the amount of the long-term incentive payout or grant? **5-23**

Q 5:30   How does the salary multiple approach work in determining the size of long-term incentive awards? **5-24**

Q 5:31   How does the targeted income approach work in determining the size of a long-term incentive award? **5-25**

Stock Options

Q 5:32   What are the different types of stock options? **5-26**

Q 5:33   What is the typical exercise period for a stock option? . .   **5-26**

Q 5:34   What is the rationale behind using stock-based plans? . .   **5-28**

Q 5:35   Under what conditions are stock options effective? **5-28**

Q 5:36   In what cases are stock options ineffective? **5-28**

Q 5:37   How do companies determine the number of shares to reserve for stock option plans? **5-29**

Omnibus Plan.

Q 5:38   What is an omnibus plan? **5-29**

Tax Considerations

Q 5:39   How does the tax doctrine of constructive receipt affect a long-term incentive plan? **5-30**

Q 5:40   What are some of the conditions that create a substantial risk of forfeiture in a long-term incentive plan? **5-31**

Q 5:41   What are some of the conditions that do not create a substantial risk of forfeiture in a long-term incentive plan? . .   **5-32**

Q 5:42   What is the general tax effect of a stock option? **5-32**

Q 5:43   What is the general tax effect of a stock appreciation right?   **5-33**

Q 5:44   What is the general tax effect of a restricted stock grant? .   **5-33**

Q 5:45   What is the general tax effect of a performance plan award?   **5-34**

Q 5:46   How does the constructive receipt doctrine affect deferred compensation? **5-34**

Q 5:47   What is the economic benefit theory? **5-35**

Q 5:48   What is a Code Section 83(b) election? **5-35**

Exercising a Stock Option

Q 5:49   What are the different ways an employee can pay the exercise price of a stock option? **5-36**

Q 5:50   How do the Section 16 rules of the SEC affect stock plans and the way employees can pay for stock? **5-37**

Q 5:51   What is a cashless option exercise? **5-37**

Q 5:52 What is Regulation T, and what is its effect on executive compensation? **5-38**

Q 5:53 What is a stock swap? **5-38**

Q 5:54 What is a pyramiding stock swap exercise? **5-39**

Tax Considerations

Q 5:55 What is the tax treatment of a stock swap or pyramiding exercise? **5-39**

Q 5:56 Are there drawbacks to a pyramiding exercise or stock swap? **5-40**

Plan Administration

Q 5:57 What is needed to institute a long-term incentive plan? . . **5-41**

Q 5:58 What is needed to amend a long-term incentive plan? . . **5-41**

Q 5:59 What information about a long-term incentive must be disclosed in a company's proxy statement? **5-42**

Q 5:60 How should long-term incentive compensation plans be handled during a merger of two companies? **5-43**

Q 5:61 How should deferred compensation be integrated during a merger of two companies? **5-44**

Q 5:62 What is an example of integration of deferred accounts? . **5-45**

Chapter 6 Purchase Plans

General Considerations

Q 6:1 What is a purchase plan? **6-2**

Q 6:2 What are the different types of purchase plans? **6-2**

Q 6:3 What are the fundamental differences between different types of purchase plans? **6-2**

Q 6:4 How are stock option exercise prices set? **6-2**

Q 6:5 How long is the typical option exercise period? **6-3**

Incentive Stock Options

Q 6:6 What is an incentive stock option? **6-4**

Q 6:7 What is the tax treatment for an ISO? **6-5**

Q 6:8 What is the effect of the alternative minimum tax on the tax treatment of an ISO? **6-7**

Q 6:9 What is the accounting impact of an ISO? **6-8**

Q 6:10   What approach is used in calculating the fully diluted earnings per share for an ISO?   6-9
Q 6:11   How prevalent are ISOs?   6-10
Q 6:12   What are the advantages of an ISO?   6-10
Q 6:13   What are the primary disadvantages of an ISO?   6-11

Nonstatutory Stock Options

Q 6:14   What is a nonstatutory stock option?   6-11
Q 6:15   How prevalent are nonstatutory stock options?   6-12
Q 6:16   What is the accounting treatment of a nonstatutory stock option?   6-12
Q 6:17   How does a company calculate dilution with a nonqualified stock option?   6-13
Q 6:18   What is the tax treatment of a nonstatutory stock option? .   6-14
Q 6:19   What are the advantages of nonqualified stock options? .   6-15
Q 6:20   What are the disadvantages of the nonqualified stock option?   6-16
Q 6:21   Can features be added to nonstatutory stock options to offset the withholding burden?   6-16
Q 6:22   How do ISOs compare with nonstatutory stock options? .   6-17

Discounted Stock Options

Q 6:23   What is a discounted stock option?   6-18
Q 6:24   How prevalent are discounted stock option plans?   6-19
Q 6:25   What is the tax treatment for a discounted stock option? .   6-19
Q 6:26   What is the accounting impact of a discounted stock option?   6-19
Q 6:27   What are the advantages of a discounted stock option plan?   6-20
Q 6:28   What are the disadvantages of a discounted stock option plan?   6-20
Q 6:29   How deeply can discounted stock options be discounted?   6-21

Premium Stock Options

Q 6:30   What is a premium stock option?   6-21
Q 6:31   How is the premium established on a premium stock option?   6-22
Q 6:32   How prevalent are premium stock options?   6-23
Q 6:33   What is the accounting impact of a premium stock option?   6-23
Q 6:34   What is the tax treatment for a premium stock option? . .   6-23
Q 6:35   What is the advantage of a premium stock option?   6-24
Q 6:36   What is the disadvantage of a premium stock option? . . .   6-24

Option Reloads

Q 6:37 What is an option reload plan? 6-24
Q 6:38 What is the accounting impact of a reload option? 6-25
Q 6:39 What is the tax treatment of a reload option? 6-25
Q 6:40 What are the advantages of an option reload provision? . 6-26
Q 6:41 What are the disadvantages of an option reload plan? . . 6-26

Book Value Purchase Plans

Q 6:42 What is a book value purchase plan? 6-26
Q 6:43 What is the accounting impact of a book value purchase
        plan? 6-27
Q 6:44 What is the tax treatment for a book value purchase plan? 6-27
Q 6:45 What are the advantages of a book value plan? 6-28
Q 6:46 What are the disadvantages of a book value plan? 6-28
Q 6:47 For what type of companies does a book value plan make
        sense? 6-28

Convertible Debentures

Q 6:48 What is a convertible debenture? 6-29
Q 6:49 Is shareholder approval required to issue convertible deben-
        tures? 6-30
Q 6:50 What is the accounting impact of a convertible debenture? 6-30
Q 6:51 What is the tax treatment for a convertible debenture? . . 6-31
Q 6:52 What is the earnings per share impact of a convertible de-
        benture? 6-31
Q 6:53 What are the advantages of a convertible debenture pro-
        gram? 6-32
Q 6:54 What are the disadvantages of a convertible debenture pro-
        gram? 6-32
Q 6:55 For what type of company does a convertible debenture plan
        make sense? 6-32

Junior Stock Plans

Q 6:56 What is a junior stock plan? 6-33
Q 6:57 What are the advantages of a junior stock plan? 6-33
Q 6:58 What are the disadvantages of a junior stock plan? 6-33
Q 6:59 How prevalent are junior common stock plans? 6-34

Performance-Based Stock Options

Q 6:60	What are performance-based stock options?	6-34
Q 6:61	What are the advantages of performance-based stock options?	6-34
Q 6:62	What are the disadvantages of performance-based stock options?	6-35
Q 6:63	What are the tax consequences of performance-based stock options?	6-36
Q 6:64	What is the accounting treatment of a performance-based stock option?	6-36
Q 6:65	What is an indexed stock option?	6-37

Chapter 7 Appreciation and Full-Value Plans

Appreciation Plans

Q 7:1	What are appreciation plans?	7-2
Q 7:2	What are examples of appreciation plans?	7-2

Stock Appreciation Rights

Q 7:3	What is a stock appreciation right?	7-2
Q 7:4	How do the Section 16 rules affect SARs?	7-4
Q 7:5	How prevalent are SARs?	7-5
Q 7:6	Should the SAR be eliminated now that the cashless exercise is possible?	7-5
Q 7:7	What is the accounting impact of an SAR plan?	7-5
Q 7:8	What is the tax treatment for an SAR plan?	7-7
Q 7:9	When do SARs typically vest?	7-8
Q 7:10	What are the advantages of an SAR plan?	7-8
Q 7:11	Are there disadvantages to using SARs?	7-9
Q 7:12	For what type of company does an SAR make sense? . .	7-10

Book Value Appreciation Rights

Q 7:13	What is a book value appreciation right?	7-10
Q 7:14	What is the accounting impact of a book value appreciation right?	7-11
Q 7:15	What is the tax treatment for a book value appreciation right?	7-11
Q 7:16	What are the advantages of book value appreciation rights?	7-12
Q 7:17	Are there disadvantages to book value appreciation rights?	7-12

Full-Value Plans

Q 7:18 What are full-value plans? 7-13
Q 7:19 Why would a company choose to implement a full-value plan
        rather than a purchase plan? 7-13

Phantom Stock Plans

Q 7:20 What is a phantom stock plan? 7-14
Q 7:21 Are dividends paid on phantom stock? 7-15
Q 7:22 How prevalent are phantom stock plans? 7-16
Q 7:23 What is the accounting impact for a phantom stock plan? 7-16
Q 7:24 What is the tax treatment for a phantom stock plan? . . . 7-16
Q 7:25 What are the advantages of a phantom stock plan? 7-17
Q 7:26 Are there disadvantages to a phantom stock plan? 7-17
Q 7:27 When do phantom stock units typically vest? 7-18
Q 7:28 For what type of company does a phantom stock plan make
        sense? 7-18
Q 7:29 What is a shadow stock plan? 7-18

Restricted Stock Grants

Q 7:30 What is a restricted stock grant? 7-18
Q 7:31 How prevalent are restricted stock grants? 7-19
Q 7:32 What is the accounting impact of a restricted stock grant? 7-19
Q 7:33 What is the tax treatment for a restricted stock grant? . . . 7-20
Q 7:34 How does a Section 83(b) election affect a restricted stock
        grant? 7-20
Q 7:35 What is the typical vesting period for a restricted stock grant? 7-21
Q 7:36 What are the advantages of a restricted stock grant? . . . 7-21
Q 7:37 Are there disadvantages to a restricted stock grant? . . . 7-21
Q 7:38 For what types of companies do restricted stock grants make
        sense? 7-21

Performance Unit Plans

Q 7:39 What is a performance unit plan? 7-22
Q 7:40 How are performance measures established for a perform-
        ance unit plan? 7-22
Q 7:41 What is the accounting impact of a performance unit plan? 7-22
Q 7:42 What is the tax treatment of a performance unit plan? . . . 7-23
Q 7:43 What is the typical award period for a performance unit plan? 7-23
Q 7:44 What are the advantages of a performance unit plan? . . . 7-23

Q 7:45   Are there disadvantages to instituting a performance unit plan? **7-23**

Performance Share Plans

Q 7:46   What is a performance share plan? **7-24**

Q 7:47   What is the tax treatment of a performance share grant? .   **7-24**

Q 7:48   What is the accounting treatment of a performance share?   **7-24**

Chapter 8 Combination Long-Term Plans

General Considerations

Q 8:1   What is a tandem plan? **8-1**

Q 8:2   What is a parallel plan? **8-2**

Q 8:3   Are there advantages to creating tandem or parallel combination plans? **8-2**

Q 8:4   Are there disadvantages to tandem and parallel combination plans? **8-2**

Q 8:5   What compensation combinations are the most common in combination long-term plans? **8-3**

Performance Share/Stock Option Plans

Q 8:6   What are combination stock option and performance plans?   **8-3**

Q 8:7   What is the accounting impact of combination performance share and stock option plans? **8-4**

Q 8:8   What is the tax treatment for combination performance share and stock option plans? **8-6**

Q 8:9   Are there advantages to a combination plan of performance shares and stock options? **8-6**

Q 8:10   Are there disadvantages to the combination performance share and stock option plan? **8-7**

Q 8:11   For what type of company does a combination performance share and stock option plan make sense? **8-7**

Restricted Stock/Stock Option Plans

Q 8:12   What is a tandem restricted stock/stock option plan? . . .   **8-8**

Q 8:13   Can a parallel grant be made of restricted shares and stock option shares? **8-9**

Q 8:14   What is the accounting impact of a combination restricted stock/stock option plan? **8-9**

Q 8:15   What is the tax treatment for a combination restricted stock/stock option plan? **8-10**

Q 8:16   What are the advantages of a combination restricted stock/stock option plan? **8-10**

Q 8:17   What are the disadvantages of the combination restricted stock/stock option plan? **8-11**

Q 8:18   For what type of company does a restricted stock/stock option plan make sense? **8-11**

SAR/Stock Option Plans

Q 8:19   What is a tandem SAR/stock option plan? **8-11**

Q 8:20   What is a parallel SAR/stock option plan? **8-12**

Q 8:21   How prevalent are SAR/stock option plans? **8-13**

Q 8:22   What is the accounting impact of combination SAR/stock option plans? **8-13**

Q 8:23   What is the tax treatment of combination SAR/stock option plans? **8-14**

Chapter 9   Executive Benefit Plans

General Considerations

Q 9:1   Why are executive benefit plans so important? **9-2**

Q 9:2   How do traditional benefit programs fail executives? . . .   **9-3**

Q 9:3   How do these executive benefit programs fit into overall compensation? **9-3**

Nonqualified Retirement Plans

Q 9:4   What is deferred compensation? **9-3**

Q 9:5   What are the three primary approaches for deferring compensation? **9-3**

Q 9:6   What is a nonqualified deferred compensation plan? . . .   **9-4**

Q 9:7   How does a nonqualified deferred compensation plan differ from a qualified plan? **9-4**

Q 9:8   What do nonqualified deferred compensation plans typically provide? **9-5**

Q 9:9 What is the rationale for creating nonqualified deferred compensation plans for executives? **9-5**

Q 9:10 What changes did the Omnibus Reconciliation Act of 1993 (OBRA) add to the regulatory limits of qualified plans? . **9-6**

Q 9:11 What are the typical objectives of the executive in deferring income under a nonqualified deferred compensation plan? **9-7**

Q 9:12 What are the typical objectives of the company in providing a deferral program? **9-7**

Q 9:13 Who can generally benefit under a nonqualified deferred compensation plan? **9-8**

Q 9:14 Are there different types of nonqualified deferred compensation plans? **9-8**

Q 9:15 How are nonqualified and qualified plans treated for tax purposes? **9-10**

Q 9:16 What is an example of the tax treatment on company contributions to a nonqualified plan? **9-10**

Q 9:17 What is an example of the tax treatment on company contributions to a qualified plan? **9-11**

Q 9:18 Are contributions to a funded plan treated differently than contributions to an unfunded plan? **9-12**

Q 9:19 What questions need to be answered by a company in determining the appropriateness of a deferred compensation plan? **9-12**

Q 9:20 When are deferred compensation arrangements subject to FICA and FUTA taxes? **9-13**

Q 9:21 What are the general ERISA requirements for a nonqualified deferred compensation plan? **9-14**

Q 9:22 What are the general reporting and disclosure requirements for a nonqualified deferred compensation plan? **9-14**

Q 9:23 What are the general participation, vesting, and funding requirements for a nonqualified deferred compensation plan? **9-15**

Q 9:24 What are the general fiduciary issues for a nonqualified deferred compensation plan? **9-15**

Q 9:25 Is plan termination insurance needed for a nonqualified plan? **9-15**

Q 9:26 Is a nonqualified deferred compensation plan a security subject to SEC registration? **9-15**

Funding Arrangements

Q 9:27 What is a rabbi escrow agreement? **9-17**

Q 9:28 What is a rabbi trust? **9-17**

Q 9:29   What is a secular trust?   9-19

Q 9:30   What are the major distinctions between a secular trust and a rabbi trust?   9-19

Q 9:31   Can life insurance also be used by an employer to fulfill its promise to an employee?   9-19

Insurance-Related Nonqualified Deferred Compensation Plans

Q 9:32   How is life insurance used by an employer to fulfill its promise to an employee?   9-20

Q 9:33   Can life insurance other than COLI be utilized to fund nonqualified deferred compensation programs?   9-21

Q 9:34   What is the difference between COLI and "retail" life insurance contracts?   9-22

Q 9:35   What are the advantages of using employee-owned life insurance to fund nonqualified deferred compensation benefits?   9-22

Split-Dollar Life Insurance

Q 9:36   What is split-dollar life insurance?   9-23

Q 9:37   How is split dollar treated under ERISA?   9-23

Q 9:38   How does the policy splitting occur?   9-23

Q 9:39   Must the executive actually pay his part of the premium? .   9-24

Q 9:40   How is the policy split accomplished?   9-24

Q 9:41   What happens when the executive retires?   9-24

Q 9:42   What are common split-dollar applications?   9-24

Q 9:43   What problems do executives experience in group term life insurance plans?   9-25

Q 9:44   Why is split dollar effective in replacing group term coverage?   9-25

Q 9:45   Why is split dollar useful in estate planning?   9-25

Q 9:46   How can split dollar enhance a nonqualified retirement plan?   9-26

Executive Disability Income Insurance

Q 9:47   How does an executive disability income insurance plan work?   9-26

Q 9:48   What legal framework should exist to minimize taxation of executive disability plans?   9-26

Q 9:49   How are benefits taxed to the executive?   9-26

Q 9:50   How are premiums taxed to the executive and the employer?   9-27

Q 9:51 Are executive disability premiums more expensive than LTD? **9-27**

Q 9:52 Do executive disability income plans have to be funded by the employer? **9-27**

ERISA Considerations

Q 9:53 For purposes of ERISA Title I, is a nonqualified deferred compensation plan generally considered funded or unfunded? **9-27**

Q 9:54 What is the difference between a funded and an unfunded plan? **9-28**

Q 9:55 For purposes of ERISA Title I, are plans affected by whether or not they are considered funded or unfunded? **9-28**

Top-Hat Plans or SERPs

Q 9:56 What is a top-hat plan? **9-28**

Q 9:57 Why would an employer establish a top-hat plan? **9-29**

Q 9:58 Does an employer inadvertently create a top-hat plan that is subject to ERISA requirements when it provides benefits to one executive under an employment contract? **9-30**

Q 9:59 How does the employer pay the benefits provided by a top-hat plan? **9-30**

Q 9:60 Can employer assurances be made that future benefits will be paid without subjecting employees to current taxation? **9-30**

Q 9:61 Are top-hat plans subject to the requirements under Title I of ERISA? **9-32**

Q 9:62 Is a top-hat plan a funded or unfunded plan for purposes of Title I of ERISA? **9-32**

Q 9:63 Are contributions to an unfunded top-hat plan treated differently than contributions to a funded top-hat plan? **9-32**

Q 9:64 What is an example of a supplemental executive retirement plan? **9-33**

Excess Benefit Plans

Q 9:65 What is an excess benefit plan? **9-33**

Q 9:66 What is the main difference between a SERP and an excess benefit plan? **9-34**

Q 9:67 How does a plan qualify as an excess benefit plan? **9-34**

Q 9:68 Why would an employer establish an excess benefit plan? **9-34**

Q 9:69 Are there benefits to establishing an excess benefit plan? **9-35**

Q 9:70 Are there limitations in establishing an excess benefit plan? **9-35**

Q 9:71   Is an excess benefit plan subject to the ERISA Title I requirements? **9-36**

Q 9:72   Is an excess benefit plan subject to the participation, vesting, and funding requirements imposed by Title I of ERISA? . **9-36**

Q 9:73   Is an excess benefit plan subject to the reporting and disclosure requirements imposed by Title I of ERISA? **9-36**

Q 9:74   What is an example of an excess benefit plan? **9-37**

Nonqualified Plans in Nonprofit Organizations

Q 9:75   What is a Code Section 457 deferred plan? **9-37**

Q 9:76   What is an example of a Code Section 457 plan? **9-38**

Tax Considerations

Q 9:77   How are employers who establish funded excess benefit plans treated for tax purposes? **9-39**

Q 9:78   How are employees who benefit from excess benefit plans treated for tax purposes? **9-39**

Q 9:79   Are contributions made pursuant to a nonqualified deferred compensation plan includable in an employee's income under the constructive receipt doctrine? **9-39**

Q 9:80   Are contributions made pursuant to a nonqualified deferred compensation plan includable in the employee's income under the economic benefit doctrine? **9-40**

Q 9:81   How does Code Section 83 tax property transfers to an employee in exchange for the performance of services? **9-40**

Chapter 10   Perquisites and Other Benefits

General Considerations

Q 10:1   What is an executive perquisite? **10-2**

Q 10:2   What is the tax treatment of executive perquisites? **10-2**

Q 10:3   What is the accounting treatment of executive perquisites? **10-3**

Reimbursement

Q 10:4   What expenses can a company generally reimburse an executive for without creating income to the executive? . . **10-3**

Q 10:5 What are the special rules relating to the reimbursement of travel expenses? **10-4**

Q 10:6 What are the special rules relating to the reimbursement of entertainment expenses? **10-4**

Q 10:7 How common are expense accounts and how are they treated for tax and accounting purposes? **10-5**

Memberships and Other Common Perquisites

Q 10:8 How common are club membership payments and how are they treated for tax and accounting purposes? **10-5**

Q 10:9 How common are company car programs, and how are they treated for tax and accounting purposes? **10-5**

Q 10:10 How common are home offices, computers, and car phones, and how are they treated for tax and accounting purposes? **10-6**

Q 10:11 Can a hiring bonus be provided as a perquisite? **10-6**

Q 10:12 Is supplemental life insurance a taxable perquisite to the executive? **10-7**

Q 10:13 What is split-dollar life insurance? **10-7**

Q 10:14 Can a company take out additional insurance on an executive with itself as the beneficiary? **10-8**

Q 10:15 Are company planes and first class air travel common perquisites? **10-8**

Q 10:16 What is the financial planning perquisite? **10-8**

Q 10:17 How common is it to offer low-interest or interest-free loans to executives? **10-9**

Employment Agreements

Q 10:18 What are the advantages of giving an executive an employment agreement? **10-9**

Q 10:19 Are there disadvantages of giving an executive an employment agreement? **10-10**

Q 10:20 What is an example of an executive employment agreement? **10-10**

Q 10:21 How enforceable is a contractual agreement with regard to a fixed term of employment? **10-11**

Q 10:22 How enforceable is a noncompetitive agreement? **10-12**

Severance Agreements

Q 10:23 Is severance compensation an employee perquisite? . . . **10-12**

Q 10:24   What is a golden parachute? **10-13**

Q 10:25   What is an example of a golden parachute provision? . . .   **10-13**

Q 10:26   What constitutes a change in control? **10-14**

Q 10:27   Why do companies provide golden parachutes? **10-15**

Q 10:28   Are there criticisms of golden parachute programs? **10-15**

Q 10:29   What penalties has the government imposed on golden parachutes? **10-15**

Q 10:30   What is an excess parachute payment? **10-16**

Q 10:31   Is there any way to avoid the negative tax impact of the excess parachute payment? **10-16**

Chapter 11   Building a Total Compensation Strategy

General Considerations

Q 11:1   What is a total compensation strategy? **11-2**

Q 11:2   What elements of executive compensation are included in a total compensation strategy statement? **11-2**

Q 11:3   What are the business purposes of a total compensation strategy? **11-2**

Compensation Factors

Q 11:4   What factors determine a total compensation strategy? . .   **11-3**

Q 11:5   How does a company's philosophy affect its total compensation strategy? **11-3**

Q 11:6   How can a company's mission or vision statement affect its total compensation strategy? **11-4**

Q 11:7   How can a company's business plan affect a total compensation strategy? **11-4**

Q 11:8   How can a company's life cycle affect its total compensation strategy? **11-5**

Q 11:9   How do internal factors affect a company's total compensation strategy? **11-5**

Q 11:10   How do external factors affect a company's total compensation strategy? **11-6**

Benefit Factors

Q 11:11   What benefit programs should be included in a total compensation strategy statement? **11-6**

Q 11:12 How can health care plan benefits and costs affect a total compensation strategy statement? **11-7**

Q 11:13 How can retirement benefits affect a company's total compensation strategy statement? **11-7**

Q 11:14 How can life insurance and disability insurance affect a company's total compensation strategy statement? . . . **11-8**

Q 11:15 How can capital accumulation plans affect a company's total compensation strategy statement? **11-8**

Other Factors

Q 11:16 Can total compensation strategies vary by company business unit? **11-9**

Q 11:17 Can total compensation strategies be developed for international businesses? **11-10**

Determining the Mix

Q 11:18 How can a company determine the proper mix of executive compensation elements in a total compensation strategy statement? **11-10**

Q 11:19 How should companies define competitive labor markets? **11-11**

Q 11:20 Should all companies establish a total compensation strategy to pay at the 50th percentile of labor market competitors? **11-12**

Q 11:21 How can a company decide on the type of short-term incentive? **11-12**

Q 11:22 How can companies decide on the best type of long-term incentive? **11-13**

Developing a Total Strategy

Q 11:23 What should be included in a total compensation strategy statement? **11-14**

Approval and Implementation

Q 11:24 Who should approve a total compensation strategy? . . . **11-15**

Q 11:25 How should a total compensation strategy be communicated to executives? **11-15**

Examples of Strategy Statements

Q 11:26   What is an example of a total compensation strategy statement for a small company? 11-17

Q 11:27   What is an example of a total compensation strategy statement for a large company? 11-18

Q 11:28   What is an example of a total compensation strategy statement in an entrepreneurial, high-growth company? . . . 11-19

Chapter 12   Small Company Considerations

General Considerations

Q 12:1   How does the mix of executive compensation elements differ in small companies? 12-2

Q 12:2   How do small companies with less sophisticated business performance measures establish annual incentives? . . 12-3

Q 12:3   How can small companies with a small human resources staff determine appropriate compensation levels? 12-3

Q 12:4   What form of long-term incentive is most appropriate for small companies? 12-3

Q 12:5   How can small companies attract high-quality people without offering competitive base salary and bonus amounts? . 12-5

Q 12:6   How can small companies offer competitive executive retirement plans without incurring significant costs? 12-6

Q 12:7   When and how do family-owned companies provide stock to non-family members? 12-7

Q 12:8   What total compensation strategies are used in small companies? 12-7

Q 12:9   How do small, high-growth companies establish competitive values on executives when their companies are doubling in size every one or two years? 12-8

Q 12:10   Are design issues for annual incentive compensation plans different in the small company? 12-9

Q 12:11   How are executive benefits and perquisites different in the small company? 12-9

New Venture Businesses

Q 12:12   How is incentive compensation structured in new venture businesses? 12-10

Q 12:13   How are base salary and benefits structured in new venture
           businesses?   12-11

Chapter 13 Board of Directors' Compensation

General Considerations

Q 13:1   How does a company choose the members of its board of
           directors?   13-2
Q 13:2   What is the role of a company board of directors?   13-2

Outside vs. Inside Directors

Q 13:3   Why would a company choose to have outside directors?   13-3
Q 13:4   What are the typical compensation elements for directors?   13-4
Q 13:5   Are inside directors compensated specifically for their activi-
           ties as directors?   13-5
Q 13:6   How much do outside directors receive for their services?   13-5

Compensation Methods

Q 13:7   How is director income taxed?   13-6
Q 13:8   What methods are used in deferring compensation for direc-
           tors?   13-6
Q 13:9   In what types of performance-based plans do directors par-
           ticipate?   13-6
Q 13:10   How are stock options used in compensating directors? .   13-7
Q 13:11   How do the Section 16 rules apply to directors' options? .   13-8
Q 13:12   Do companies provide "regular" stock plans for directors?   13-8
Q 13:13   Can tandem SARs/stock options be granted to directors?   13-8

Other Benefits

Q 13:14   What other benefits are typically provided to directors? . .   13-8
Q 13:15   Do companies provide retirement benefits for their directors?   13-9
Q 13:16   Can Keogh plans be utilized by outside board members?   13-9
Q 13:17   Can Keogh plans be utilized by insider board members? .   13-9
Q 13:18   What are some new trends in board of director compensa-
           tion?   13-9
Q 13:19   Do outside directors get perquisites?   13-10

Chapter 14 Executive Compensation in the Not-For-Profit Organization

General Considerations

Q 14:1   What is a not-for-profit company? **14-1**

Q 14:2   How does the mix of executive compensation elements differ in a not-for-profit company? **14-2**

Q 14:3   How do the business objectives of executive compensation plans differ in a not-for-profit company? **14-2**

Q 14:4   Does the size of the organization affect executive compensation in a not-for-profit organization? **14-4**

Q 14:5   Does the type of not-for-profit organization affect the level of executive compensation? **14-4**

Q 14:6   Does geographical location affect executive compensation in the not-for-profit company? **14-5**

Q 14:7   What is the impact of recent legislation on not-for-profit organizations? **14-5**

Base Salary

Q 14:8   How are base salary ranges established in not-for-profit companies? **14-6**

Q 14:9   Are merit increases to base salary used in not-for-profit companies? **14-7**

Annual Incentives

Q 14:10   What is the prevalence of annual incentive plans in not-for-profit companies? **14-7**

Q 14:11   Does the size of the annual incentive award in the not-for-profit company differ from that in the for-profit company?   **14-8**

Q 14:12   What performance measures are typically used in the annual incentive plans of not-for-profit companies? **14-8**

Q 14:13   How is eligibility determined for annual incentive plans in not-for-profit companies? **14-8**

Q 14:14   What regulations guide incentive compensation plans for the not-for-profit company? **14-9**

Long-Term Incentives

Q 14:15   What types of long-term incentive plans are prevalent in not-for-profit companies? **14-9**

Perquisites

Q 14:16 What types of perquisites are prevalent in not-for-profit companies? 14-10

Q 14:17 What are the requirements of a SERP for executives in a not-for-profit organization? 14-10

Chapter 15 Special Early Retirement Programs

Q 15:1 What are special early retirement programs? 15-1

Q 15:2 Why do companies offer special early retirement programs? 15-2

Q 15:3 Do companies offer special severance programs with special early retirement programs? 15-3

Q 15:4 What are the typical severance benefits used with a special early retirement program? 15-3

Q 15:5 How do companies fund the costs of these programs? . . 15-3

Q 15:6 What, if any, are the negative consequences to companies that implement special early retirement programs, and how can these consequences be handled? 15-4

Q 15:7 Are there any negative consequences to employees who accept a special early retirement program? 15-4

Q 15:8 What are the ERISA implications of a special early retirement program under a qualified plan? 15-5

Q 15:9 Do companies require employees who elect a special early retirement to sign non-compete and/or non-litigation agreements? 15-7

Q 15:10 Do companies provide medical benefits with a special early retirement program? 15-7

Chapter 16 U. S. Executives Working Overseas

General Considerations

Q 16:1 What is an executive expatriate? 16-2

Q 16:2 What are the typical elements of an executive expatriate compensation package? 16-2

Q 16:3 What is a foreign service premium? 16-3

Q 16:4 What is a hardship allowance? 16-3

Q 16:5 What is a cost of living allowance? 16-3

Q 16:6 What is a housing allowance? 16-5

Q 16:7 Do executive expatriates receive reimbursement of any home sale or other relocation costs when they take an overseas assignment? 16-6

Q 16:8 What is a home rental program? 16-8

Q 16:9 What is an education allowance? 16-8

Q 16:10 What is language training? 16-8

Q 16:11 What is home leave? 16-9

Tax Considerations

Q 16:12 What is tax equalization? 16-9

Q 16:13 What is tax-free income? 16-11

Q 16:14 What is spendable income? 16-12

Q 16:15 What are foreign earned income exclusions? 16-13

Q 16:16 How can executive expatriates avoid taxes when on overseas assignment? 16-14

Q 16:17 Can an executive expatriate avoid capital gains tax on the sale of a home while on overseas assignment? 16-16

Special Compensation

Q 16:18 Are executive expatriates protected against currency fluctuations? 16-16

Q 16:19 What is a completion bonus? 16-17

Q 16:20 Can stock options be granted to executive expatriates? . . 16-17

Q 16:21 What are free-standing stock appreciation rights? 16-18

Q 16:22 Can long-term bonus plans be used for executive expatriates? 16-18

Q 16:23 Can annual incentive plans be used for executive expatriates? 16-19

Q 16:24 What kind of medical benefits are provided to executive expatriates? 16-19

Q 16:25 What happens to an executive expatriate's pension plan while on overseas assignment? 16-20

Q 16:26 How are life insurance and disability established for executive expatriates? 16-20

Q 16:27 What perquisites are provided to executive expatriates? . 16-20

Q 16:28 What is done for executive expatriates upon repatriation? . 16-21

Q 16:29 What special compensation is provided to an executive expatriate who takes a second overseas assignment? . . . 16-21

Q 16:30   What are the elements of a net to net compensation pro-
           gram? **16-22**

Q 16:31   What are the typical elements of a modified home country
           balance sheet compensation program? **16-24**

Q 16:32   Is there a checklist of issues that should be considered by a
           company and/or executive in developing an executive ex-
           patriate compensation program? **16-24**

Chapter 17   Executive Compensation in the Public Sector

Q 17:1   What is the driving philosophy behind executive compensa-
           tion in the public sector versus that in the private sector?   **17-1**

Q 17:2   How is base salary different in the public sector organization
           than in the private sector organization? **17-2**

Q 17:3   Are job evaluation systems used for executive positions in
           public sector organizations? **17-3**

Q 17:4   Can merit increases to base salary work for executive posi-
           tions in public sector organizations? **17-4**

Q 17:5   What are the advantages and disadvantages of tenure-based
           pay increase systems? **17-5**

Q 17:6   Why do public sector organizations prefer a tenure-based
           pay increase system? **17-6**

Q 17:7   Are salary ranges used in the public sector? **17-6**

Q 17:8   Are annual incentives used in public sector organizations?   **17-7**

Q 17:9   Are long-term performance plans or stock award plans used
           in public organizations? **17-8**

Q 17:10   Are insured benefits in the public sector better than those in
           private companies? **17-8**

Q 17:11   Are retirement plans in the public sector better than those in
           private companies? **17-9**

Q 17:12   Can supplemental retirement plans be used in public sector
           organizations? **17-9**

Q 17:13   Are public sector organizations subject to Title VII of the Civil
           Rights Act of 1964, the Fair Labor Standards Act, Americans
           with Disabilities Act, Age Discrimination in Employment Act,
           or other such regulations? **17-10**

Q 17:14   Do public sector executives have perquisites? **17-10**

Q 17:15   How can compensation plans be used to attract high-quality
           executives into the public sector? **17-10**

Chapter 18 Compensation for Temporary Executives

Q 18:1   What is a temporary executive?   18-2
Q 18:2   Are temporary executives independent contractors?   . . .   18-2
Q 18:3   What are the advantages and disadvantages of being an independent contractor to the executive?   18-3
Q 18:4   What are the advantages and disadvantages of independent contractors to a company?   18-3
Q 18:5   What is the difference between a short-term and long-term temporary assignment?   18-4
Q 18:6   What is outsourcing?   18-4
Q 18:7   What are other alternatives to outsourcing?   18-5
Q 18:8   How do temporary executives obtain an assignment? . . .   18-5
Q 18:9   How is base salary determined for temporary executives?   18-5
Q 18:10   Are temporary executives provided with incentive compensation?   18-7
Q 18:11   Are temporary executives provided with stock awards? . .   18-8
Q 18:12   Are temporary executives provided with perquisites? . . .   18-8
Q 18:13   What insured benefits are provided to temporary executives?   18-8
Q 18:14   Are temporary executives provided with retirement benefits?   18-8
Q 18:15   Are temporary executives subject to federal regulations on equal pay, age, etc.?   18-9
Q 18:16   Can temporary executives be placed on an overseas assignment?   18-9
Q 18:17   Can temporary executives be converted to full-time status?   18-9

Chapter 19 Economic Value-Added

General Considerations

Q 19:1   What is the definition of economic value-added?   19-1
Q 19:2   Why are companies using economic value-added?   19-2
Q 19:3   What are the disadvantages of economic value-added? .   19-3
Q 19:4   How do companies use EVA plans?   19-4
Q 19:5   Can executives really have an impact on the cost of capital?   19-5
Q 19:6   Can EVA be used in divisions or SBUs?   19-6
Q 19:7   Can EVA be correlated to shareholder value?   19-6

Implementation

Q 19:8   What steps are required to implement an EVA plan? . . .   **19-6**

Q 19:9   Can stock options be linked to EVA? **19-7**

Q 19:10   How do companies link EVA to executive compensation?   **19-8**

Q 19:11   How are EVA plans communicated to executives? **19-9**

Q 19:12   Can EVA plans apply to non-executives? **19-9**

Q 19:13   What is an example of a successful EVA plan? **19-9**

Q 19:14   What is an example of an unsuccessful EVA plan? **19-10**

Chapter 20 Trends in Executive Compensation

Total Cash Compensation

Q 20:1   How are base salary levels changing for executive positions
in large companies? **20-1**

Q 20:2   Is the $1 million cap on the deductibility of executive pay
having any influence on the base salary levels of the top five
officers in public companies? **20-2**

Q 20:3   How are base salary levels for executives changing in small
companies? **20-2**

Q 20:4   Are there any new ideas in base salary administration for
executives? **20-3**

Q 20:5   How are annual bonus levels changing for executives? . .   **20-3**

Q 20:6   How are bonus payout schedules changing? **20-4**

Q 20:7   What changes are occurring in the mix of base salary and
annual incentive for executive positions? **20-5**

Long-Term Compensation

Q 20:8   How are stock award levels changing for executive positions? **20-5**

Q 20:9   Does the use of performance-based stock options continue
as a trend? **20-6**

Q 20:10   Have non-compete clauses been used in stock award plans?   **20-7**

Q 20:11   Are economic value-added plans continuing as a trend? .   **20-7**

Outside Directors

Q 20:12   How are remuneration levels changing for outside directors?   **20-8**

Q 20:13   Are retirement plans still prevalent for outside directors? .   **20-8**

Q 20:14   Do outside directors still receive stock awards? **20-9**

Regulations

Q 20:15   How have companies reacted to FAS 123 on the accounting
for stock options? **20-9**

Q 20:16   How do executive compensation levels compare to company
performance graphs that are displayed, per SEC regulations, in public company proxies? **20-10**

Q 20:17   What is the new bill in Congress that is intended to further
limit the tax deduction companies can take on stock op-
tions? **20-11**

Q 20:18   Will the proposed changes in capital gains tax rates affect
executive compensation? **20-11**

Q 20:19   Will more executives be subject to the alternative minimum
tax if ISO use increases due to a lower capital gains tax?   **20-12**

Chapter 1

Fundamental Concepts of Executive Compensation

The growth and development of a company can be greatly assisted if quality executives can be secured and retained. Efficiently designed executive compensation programs are an important ingredient in a company's ability to recruit and retain an executive team. A typical executive compensation package consists of a base salary, annual incentives, long-term incentives, benefits, and perquisites. The cost to the company and the value to the executives of long-term incentives and executive benefits continue to grow. The design of executive compensation packages is driven by competitive practices, tax and accounting rules and regulations, and company values and strategies. This chapter addresses the fundamental concepts in executive compensation.

Total Compensation Issues   1-2
Base Salary   1-12
Incentive Plans   1-14
Tax Considerations   1-21
Accounting Considerations   1-29

Total Compensation Issues

Q 1:1 What is total remuneration?

Total remuneration is generally defined as a combination of five factors:

- Base salary
- Annual incentives
- Long-term incentives
- Benefits
- Perquisites

Each of the elements of the total remuneration package meets a different executive need as well as a company need.

Q 1:2 How does base salary meet the needs of executives as well as the company?

Base salary supports the executive's lifestyle, providing the cash to meet day-to-day expenses. From the company's point of view it is a fixed cost for services rendered. It also can represent the minimum rate that the company is willing to pay for a given job.

Q 1:3 How do annual and long-term incentives meet the needs of executives and the company?

Annual incentives supplement base salary and provide lump-sum payments to executives based on their achievement of annual goals (which are generally stated in the company's annual business plan). These incentive payments can also be provided on a monthly or quarterly basis. Annual, quarterly, or monthly incentives provide the company with an excellent means of motivating executives to achieve specific and critical company goals. The term "annual incentive" has the same meaning as the term "annual bonus."

Long-term incentive programs (i.e., plans that have an award period of two years or more) provide executives with the wherewithal to accumulate capital and build an estate. They can serve as a significant means of retaining key executive talent. Long-term incentives are provided in the form of cash payments or stock payments; therefore, significant rises in stock prices can result in quite significant amounts of compensation. The term "long-term incentive" has the same meaning as the term "long-term income."

Q 1:4   How do benefits and perquisites satisfy executive needs?

Benefit programs provide financial security in the case of death, disability, sickness, or retirement, while perquisites, such as club memberships, first-class air travel, company cars, financial planning, supplemental retirement, and supplemental insurance, are special entitlement programs made available to a select group of executives.

Q 1:5   How do companies express the value of all elements of executive compensation?

Elements of the total compensation package can be expressed as a percentage of base salary. This analysis can be represented by the following:

Total Compensation as a Percentage of Base Salary	$100,000 Base Salary	$250,000 Base Salary
Base Salary	100%	100%
Annual Incentives	30%	40%
Annual Value of Long-Term Incentives	35%	50%
Benefits	30%	30%
Perquisites	10%	15%
Total Compensation	205%	235%

Companies also express the mix of executive compensation elements as a percentage of total compensation. This is shown in Chart 1-1.

Chart 1-1. Total Mix of Executive Compensation for CEO Position

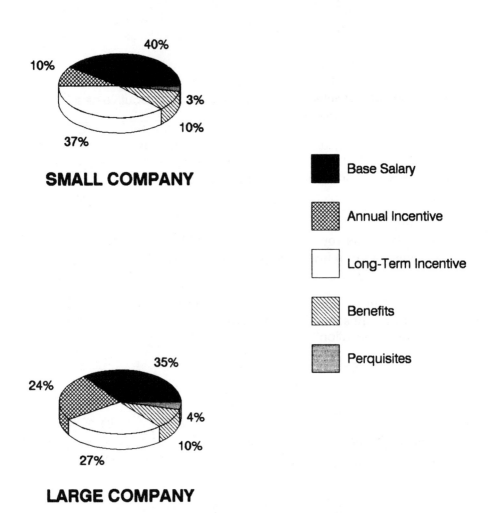

SMALL COMPANY

LARGE COMPANY

Source: Management Performance International, Inc.

Q 1:6   What is total cash compensation?

Total cash compensation (also known as total direct compensation) is the sum of annual base salary plus annual payments from any short-term incentive compensation plan. This can be measured by using targeted or actual annual short-term incentives plus base salary. Most companies establish executive compensation levels by reviewing their own business needs and by reviewing competitive total cash compensation practices using *actual* short-term incentive amounts paid, not *targeted* amounts.

Q 1:7   What is total compensation?

Total compensation is the sum of annual base salary plus annual payments from any short-term incentive compensation plan plus annual payments (or the annualized value of potential payments) from any long-term incentive or stock award plan.

Q 1:8   What are some of the factors that affect total compensation?

The following six factors have some impact on executive compensation:

- Job responsibility
- Level of job within the organization
- Type of industry
- Supply and demand factors in the labor market
- Size of organization
- Company and executive performance

All other factors being constant, job responsibility and organizational size have the most significant impact on the total compensation for any executive.

Q 1:9   How does the type of executive responsibility affect total compensation?

The executive's necessary skills and responsibilities and expected achievements have a significant effect on total compensation. For example, a vice president of finance typically receives a higher total compensation package than a vice president of human resources because most companies consider the human resources position less complex and easier to learn and the finance position more critical to the success of the business operation. Functional responsibilities in a job therefore have a direct impact on an executive's total compensation.

In most companies the chief executive officer's (CEO's) compensation is the foundation upon which the balance of a company's compensation practices and pay levels are based. The compensation for executives who report to the CEO will show a constant pattern; their compensation is expressed as a percentage of the CEO's. It is thus extremely important to establish a proper value for the CEO and to consider the relationship between the compensation of this CEO and other executives in the organization. Chart 1-2 presents average compensation of executive positions as a percentage of average CEO base salary and total compensation, as reported in *The Officer Compensation Report, 1997* (Panel Publishers). (*The Officer Compensation Report* offers comprehensive annual labor market data on top executive positions in small and medium-sized companies.)

Q 1:10   How does level within the organization affect an executive's total compensation?

The closer an executive's position is to the top position in the organization (usually the CEO), the more likely that the total compensation will be higher.

Example. The Vice President of Engineering in Company A reports to the Chief Operating Officer, who in turn reports to the Chief Executive Officer. The Vice President of Engineering in Company B reports directly to the Chief Executive Officer. Assume that both companies have the same sales volume and the same number of employees. The Vice President of Engineering for Company B (who is closer in reporting structure to the CEO) will receive a higher

Chart 1-2. Average Officer Compensation as a Percentage of Average CEO Compensation

	Percent of Average Base Salary 1996 (Bonus Ineligible)	Percent of Average Base Salary 1996 (Bonus Eligible)	Percent of Average Bonus 1996 (Bonus Eligible)	Percent of Average Total Direct Comp 1996 (For Bonus Eligible Execs who received bonuses)
CEO/Pres	100	100	100	100
COO	90	68	61	67
Fin/Acctg Exec	63	52	37	47
Sales/Mktg Exec	58	50	37	46
Mfg/Prod Exec	53	45	32	41

base salary, a greater bonus eligibility, a more lucrative capital accumulation plan, and probably have access to more perquisites. Part of this is caused by the organizational-level salary differentials that most companies attempt to maintain. Part of it is also caused by the organizational perspective that the closer an executive is to the CEO in reporting relationship, the more impact that executive has on the company's performance and, therefore, the greater his or her compensation should be.

Q 1:11   How does the type of industry affect an executive's total compensation?

The industry in which an executive is employed has an impact on the total compensation of the executive for two main reasons. First, executives generally are compensated more highly in industries where companies tend to have larger sales volume or assets (see Q 1:13). Industries with larger companies, such as petroleum manufacturing and energy, will therefore generally provide higher compensation packages than industries like health care and banking, which traditionally compensate executives at a lower rate.

Second, companies with higher profit margins tend to have higher total executive compensation packages. For example, an executive in the pharmaceutical industry would tend to be paid at a higher rate than an executive in another consumer product company because the higher profit margins in this industry drive higher amounts of total compensation.

Planning Tip. One way to determine the industry for comparison is to find out which companies your current executives were hired from, and which companies hire your former executives.

Q 1:12   How do supply and demand factors influence total compensation?

Because executive talent is a free market commodity, its price varies according to the classic laws of supply and demand. At various times during the past 30 years financial executives have been more in demand than marketing executives, while at other times during that same period, the reverse has been true. This demand occurs not only in the general economy and specific industries, but also in the life cycle of a given company. For example, companies in a growth cycle tend to recruit executives heavily, while companies in a mature or declining cycle do not recruit as heavily.

When executives are in high demand, total compensation increases in order to attract them. This can have a compounding effect on the compensation levels of longtime company executives, whose compensation should stay equitable with that of newly hired executives. Companies in a recruiting mode need to project these associated costs so that this can be budgeted and planned in advance.

Q 1:13   How does company size influence total compensation?

Two CEOs with similar responsibilities can have two totally different total compensation packages based entirely on the size of the organization. The executive in a company that has greater sales volume typically receives higher total cash compensation than the executive in a smaller company. Companies believe that because such executives have a greater magnitude of accountability, they should be more highly paid. This reality is reflected in the labor market and in all surveys of executive compensation.

Example. Consider the case of a CEO in a $10 billion company versus the CEO of a $1 billion company. The CEO in the company with the significantly higher sales volume, the $10 billion company, will be more highly paid. Taking this point further, assume that the CEO in the $10 billion company has a division president who manages a $1 billion business. Compare the compensation of such a division president with that of a chief executive officer of a $1 billion company. The CEO will be more highly paid than the division president because this individual reports directly to the board of directors, not to a corporate CEO. The issue of accountability, the fact that there is one less reporting level, has a direct impact on total compensation (see Q 1:10).

Company growth, acquisition, or divestiture can compound the difficulty of determining executive compensation. For example, whenever a corporation decides to divest itself of poorly performing companies, should it reduce CEO salary because company size has decreased? Or, if the CEO acquires a new subsidiary company with a large revenue (but perhaps no profits), does the company automatically increase CEO salary?

The answer to both of these questions is no, not at the time. If acquisitions and divestitures continue, however, over time this will affect the level of total compensation, because company size is a major influence on executive pay.

Numerous charts in *The Officer Compensation Report* show how CEO compensation varies by company size (i.e., the larger the company, the higher the total compensation).

Q 1:14   How does company performance affect total compensation?

Corporations, consulting firms, academic institutions, and the media have actively tried for years to correlate executive pay with company performance. Every spring, the media publishes executive compensation data on public companies to support this correlation.

Annual incentive plans, if properly designed, call for incentives to rise and fall with company performance. Clearly this is the intent of any executive compensation program. Most studies relating total cash compensation to performance will show that annual incentives are usually slightly higher in successful firms than in unsuccessful firms (of course, surveys vary in their definitions of successful and unsuccessful firms). Performance can, however, be difficult to evaluate. Consider the case where a company with a 2 percent profit margin increases that profit margin to 3 percent. Contrast this with a similar company in a similar business that increases its profit margin from 10 percent to 15 percent. Both companies have achieved increases of 50 percent in their profit margins. Some would argue that executive compensation increases in each company should be the same, because performance was the same. Others would argue, however, that executive compensation increases in the company that increases its profit margin from 10 percent to 15 percent should be significantly higher because profit percentages are higher.

Most companies resolve this difficulty by using two main criteria to set performance goals with their boards of directors: (1) improvement over the prior year and (2) positive comparison to similar companies. These two dimensions of performance can be useful criteria to support increases in an executive's total compensation. Moreover, they provide a solid link between executive and company performance and executive total compensation.

Long-term income programs also correlate positively with company performance because they are based on the appreciation of a company's stock value. Therefore, payments to executives from a long-term stock award program will increase, as will the appreciation in company stock held by shareholders. Since executive performance can affect stock price, there can be a correlation between executive pay and company performance as measured in stock price.

Not all components of executive compensation are tied to performance. Base salary, benefits, and perquisites serve other purposes such as financial security and supporting a day-to-day standard of living.

Q 1:15   Does executive performance affect total compensation?

As is the case with company performance (see Q 1:14), executive performance, as measured in short- and long-term incentive plans, can also affect total compensation.

Example. Executive A in Company A receives a stock option to purchase 1,000 shares at $5 per share. Executive B in Company B also receives a stock option to purchase 1,000 shares of stock at the same price. The stock in Company A increases to $10 per share, while the stock in Company B increases to $15 per share. If both executives exercise their rights to purchase these shares, Executive A has received a value of $5,000 ($5 per share × 1,000 shares), while Executive B has a value of $10,000 ($10 per share × 1,000 shares).

The effect of executive performance on total compensation can also be illustrated by the huge stock grants that have been made to some CEOs in the past few years. One example is the CEO of Coca-Cola, Roberto Goizueta, who received an outright grant of

1.2 million shares of Coca-Cola stock worth, at the time, $80 million. At the shareholders meeting, Mr. Goizueta pointed out to great acclaim that during his term as CEO the total value of the company stock had risen $500 million. Jumbo stock grants have also been made to Michael Eisner of Disney and Lee Iacocca of Chrysler, to name a few.

Base Salary

Q 1:16 Does geographic location affect an executive's base salary?

Surprisingly, no. For example, it is generally argued that it costs more to live in New York City than in Atlanta, Georgia. A comparison of compensation levels for comparable positions in comparably sized organizations shows, however, that pay premiums for New York City are less than 10 percent over Atlanta, substantially less than the approximately 30 to 40 percent cost-of-living differential that exists between the two cities. (Although surveys show little noticeable geographic difference in total compensation for executives, this is not the case for lower-level management positions and nonexempt or hourly positions.)

It should be noted, however, that executives do receive substantial relocation benefits whenever they are asked to move from a low cost-of-living area to a high cost-of-living area. As mentioned in Question 1:12, executives in high demand will often be provided with large base salary increases as well as front-end hiring bonuses, and special benefits and perquisites, to attract them to a company. This is another reason that geographic pay differentials are not a major factor in executive base salary.

Q 1:17 How is base salary related to the other components of total compensation for executives?

Since annual incentives and in some cases long-term incentives can be targeted as a percentage of base salary, total cash compensation as well as total compensation can vary significantly between executive jobs with significant differences in base salary.

Example. An executive with a base salary of $100,000 might typically have a targeted annual bonus award of 25 percent of base, or $25,000, and a targeted annual long-term incentive award of 30 percent, or $30,000. Thus the level of base salary in most companies is used to drive the amount of total compensation.

For this reason, most companies will provide executive base salary amounts that are very close to targeted competitive levels.

Q 1:18 How can base salary be used to determine the mix of total compensation?

Since base salary is used as the foundation for the annual and long-term incentive portions of total compensation, it will have a direct effect on the mix of total compensation (i.e., annual bonus and long-term incentive).

Example. A company desires a total compensation strategy that will provide an executive with amounts of annual bonus and long-term incentive that will equal annual base salary. If this executive has a base salary of $200,000, then the targeted annual bonus could be 50 percent ($100,000), and the targeted annual award from the long-term incentive could also be 50 percent ($100,000), for a total of $200,000. The mix of total compensation meets company objectives.

In establishing the mix of total compensation, companies will typically deviate from average competitive total compensation by 10 percent. Assume a typical annual incentive for a CEO of 40 percent of base salary when the annual base salary is $200,000 (Company C). Further, assume that the annualized long-term incentive plan has a goal of providing 50 percent of base salary. The executive in Company A who is paid a lower base salary of $180,000 (10 percent below the competitive labor market) has a significantly lower total compensation than the executive in Company B who is paid a base salary of $220,000, or 10 percent above the competitive labor market.

Total Compensation Element	Company A	Company B	Company C
Base Salary	$180,000	$220,000	$200,000
40% Annual Incentive	72,000	88,000	80,000
50% Long-Term Incentive	90,000	110,000	100,000
Total Compensation	$342,000	$418,000	$380,000

Planning Tip. When establishing base salary, companies should consider the desired level and mix of total compensation. The mix of base salary, annual incentive, and long-term incentive can vary provided the total compensation remains competitive.

Incentive Plans

Q 1:19   What is the rationale for having an incentive plan?

There are several reasons why companies have incentive plans. Incentive payments have proved to be one of the most effective ways to motivate executives to focus on specific corporate performance objectives. These plans also help companies gain a comparative advantage or avoid a comparative disadvantage in terms of recruiting and retaining employees; many companies today offer some sort of incentive plan to their executives, especially in cases where base salary levels are perceived as below the market rate. As a variable form of compensation, incentive payments are reduced or eliminated as corporate performance declines; this affords a measure of safety to the company. Also, the use of incentive payments may benefit the company's cash flow either because payments are deferred until the end of a year or because they are made in company stock.

Another rationale for having incentive plans is that if executives can make decisions and judgments that affect year-to-year company results, it makes sense for these executives to have a significant part of their current earnings dependent upon the achievement of these results.

Q 1:20 Are annual incentive plans appropriate for all types of organizations?

No. In small organizations where results are not always measurable, annual incentive plans are difficult to implement and manage. They are usually not appropriate for rapidly growing companies either, because it is difficult for these companies to set realistic goals on a year-to-year basis. The lack of an annual incentive plan in fast-growth companies can typically be offset, however, by lucrative long-term plans.

Q 1:21 What characteristics identify organizations for which annual incentive plans are feasible?

Several characteristics identify those companies and/or industries for which incentive plans are more feasible:

1. Numerous short-term decisions affect company profits. In this case, executives tend to be motivated to achieve short-term profits, and their success can be judged in a relatively short time (i.e., one year or less). This is important because profit is a common performance measure in short-term incentive plans. Executives want to earn money from short-term incentive plans, so they tend to go for short-term profit.

2. The organization is decentralized. Executives have clearly defined areas of profit and loss responsibility and individuals, not committees, have the authority to make decisions and implement them.

3. The accounting and economic data used to evaluate performance are available and accessible. Too often, this characteristic is overlooked.

4. The management team is goal-oriented. This management attitude emphasizes executive focus on specific business activities that will produce overall success for the company.

5. Base salary is set below market level, but annual incentives are used to compensate for the variance.

Q 1:22   How can companies deal with executives' focusing on the short run at the expense of long-term performance in their efforts to receive high annual payout?

Annual incentives can create an overemphasis on short-term performance. For example, if the executive has no long-term objectives, or if current long-term objectives give executives the opportunity to achieve short-term results at the expense of, or in lieu of, long-term results, then these objectives should be changed. Companies should provide short-term incentive plan objectives that are integrated with long-term incentive plan objectives.

Planning Tip. One plan design method of ensuring that executives do not overemphasize annual performance is to make sure that the sum of the annual rewards over a period of time is less than the probable long-term plan payout. Consider a CEO who is currently earning a base salary of $200,000 and is eligible for an annual incentive plan payment of 50 percent of that base and is also eligible for a long-term plan that will pay out in five years.

Year	Base*	Annual Incentive
1992	$200,000	$100,000
1993	214,000	107,000
1994	228,980	114,490
1995	245,008	122,504
1996	262,158	131,079

*Assume 7% annual salary adjustment.

The long-term plan should be designed so that if performance expectations are met both on an annual and long-term basis, the long-term plan should pay out at least $575,073 (sum of annual incentive payouts) and probably 150 percent of that amount, or $862,609. With such a large long-term payout, the financial incentive will weigh toward the long term.

Q 1:23   What is the typical relationship between annual and long-term incentives?

Most companies both small and large will focus on the long-term performance of their executives. Therefore, most executives receive compensation from long-term incentive plans that is equal to or greater (on an annualized basis) than that received from the annual incentive compensation plan.

For example:

	Base Salary	Bonus %	Long-Term %
Executive A	$100,000	25%	25%
Executive B	$200,000	30%	35%
Executive C	$300,000	40%	50%

Q 1:24 What are some basic guidelines for incentive plan design?

Obviously, all incentive plans must be tailored to the company's policies and to its financial and operating circumstances. To help focus on these issues, many companies develop a written compensation philosophy statement (see Chapter 11, "Building a Total Compensation Strategy Statement," and Q 1:27). This statement, which documents the values and the unique operating circumstances of the company as they relate to the compensation of executives, can be used as a guide in the development of incentive programs. For example, if a company's compensation philosophy states that the organization values teamwork and group performance, it clearly would be inappropriate to develop an incentive program emphasizing individual performance.

Q 1:25 Typically, who is eligible for incentive plan participation?

There is a great variance between companies and within industries on what percentage of executives participates in an annual incentive plan. As a rough rule of thumb, 1 percent of employees in an organization are eligible to participate. Two principal factors affecting the extent of eligibility in incentive plans are whether the company is capital-intensive or people-intensive, and whether the company is centralized or decentralized. Highly capital-intensive industries have proportionately fewer individuals eligible for incentive plans than people-intensive industries. Centralized companies also have fewer individuals eligible for incentive plans than decentralized companies.

Companies should consider two primary criteria when determining eligibility for incentive plans. First, they should include those executives who can make decisions that affect the results of the company overall or its business units in a significant way. Second, companies should also consider competitive practices. If there are executive positions that normally participate in incentive plans in other organizations, then these positions must be closely scrutinized for participation.

While eligibility may be somewhat arbitrary, it is typically based on one or more of the following criteria:

1. Salary level, for example, "all employees who earn $60,000 or more per year";

2. Salary grade, for example, "all employees who are in compensation grade 20 or higher";

3. Organizational level, for example, "all executives who report directly to the chief executive or chief operating officer";

4. Combination approaches, for example, "all executives who are in grade 20 or higher and report directly to the chief executive or chief operating officer."

Each of these approaches has distinct disadvantages. Salary level favors those disciplines with high market worth and may not reflect potential impact on company performance. Salary grade cutoff favors the market value considerations that went into designing the salary structure, and puts pressure on the job evaluation program to evaluate many jobs at the minimum grade level required for eligibility in the annual incentive plan. Finally, the organizational level approach can result in the inclusion of executives with relatively minor responsibilities and the exclusion of those executives who have substantial organizational impact.

Planning Tip. Most companies are now using a combination of two or more criteria to guide incentive plan eligibility. For example, a job must be evaluated in job level 10 and report to the president. (Question 4:51 also includes a discussion of incentive plan design issues.)

Q 1:26 How do executive compensation programs differ in emerging or start-up companies?

Stock-based plans are a common component of an executive compensation program in both young and mature companies. Stock-based plans are even more crucial to start-up and emerging companies because many start-up companies and emerging companies cannot offer competitive base salary and benefits to executives. In addition, annual incentive plans that pay out in cash can be large cash drains to a start-up company.

The start-up or emerging company can, however, offer something that the mature company may not be able to offer: a chance for the executive to build wealth through stock ownership, if and when the company succeeds. This is particularly common in the field of high technology where it is common for stock-based compensation to be a significant part of the total package. Often this package is offered not only to executives, but to other key managers and technical staff as well.

Q 1:27 How does corporate philosophy affect the method of compensation chosen?

A company's philosophy includes a number of statements on company values, beliefs, and principles that should guide the development of executive compensation plans.

For example:

- Is the organization risk-oriented or risk-averse?
- Does the organization focus on individual achievement or teamwork?
- What performance measures relate directly or indirectly to the company's values and beliefs?

These internal organizational values, expressed in a compensation philosophy statement, should be as important as competitive issues in determining the appropriate design of an executive compensation program.

Planning Tip. Distribute your company's corporate compensation philosophy annually to your top executives and members of the board of directors in order to generate a discussion of current and/or new executive compensation plans and how they can be a tool to support the company's philosophy.

Q 1:28   What are the objectives of long-term incentive plans?

Companies use long-term incentive plans for the following reasons:

1. *Encourage executives to increase shareholder value.* Some companies believe that their primary purpose is to deliver financial returns to shareholders. Long-term incentive plans are an excellent tool for getting executives to focus on this business objective, particularly if shareholder value is the performance measure used in the long-term incentive and/or if stock is the main vehicle in the long-term plan.

2. *Motivate executives to achieve the long-term goals of the company.* These goals might be increasing company net worth, or more specific business goals like the development or introduction of a new product or service, the construction of a new facility, research projects, the acquisition or divestiture of a profit center, etc.

3. *Retain executives.* The retention of key executives is a critical human resource issue in most companies. This retention is achieved by offering substantial opportunities for gains in personal capital and net worth to the executive. The degree of gain is typically performance-based and therefore dependent upon achieving goals or increasing stock/shareholder value.

4. *Make executives owners/entrepreneurial owners of the business.* Companies achieve this primarily with stock options and stock award plans. Companies also encourage a feeling of entrepreneurial ownership in their executives by planning and investing in long-term business strategies with executives and by sharing in the profitability of business success with executives. An example is the development and introduction of a product expansion in a consumer product company or the expansion of a menu item in a food service company. Both have been done by companies jointly with executives (and with

executive investment) by making them part of the entire process.

Q 1:29   What is the difference between annual incentive plans and long-term incentive plans?

Annual or "short-term" incentive plans typically cover a company's 12-month fiscal year. Some companies use 6- or 18-month periods that relate directly to their executive measurement periods. An example is a company in the fashion industry where success is measured every six months. They use two six-month periods in their annual/short term incentive plan.

Long-term incentive plans cover a two- to three-year or greater period. Stock plans typically have a 10-year award period, but vest after three to four years, while performance plans typically correspond to the company's strategic planning period, i.e., a three-to-four-year period.

Q 1:30   Are stock plans considered incentive plans?

Yes, in practice, companies consider stock plans to be incentive plans because they "incent" executives to increase stock price. Also, the Internal Revenue Service (IRS) states in its clarifications of Internal Revenue Code (Code) Section 162(m) that stock plans are considered "performance-based" plans and they can be excluded from compensation amounts subject to the $1 million cap on the tax deductibility of executive compensation for a public company's top five executives.

Tax Considerations

Q 1:31   What are the general tax implications of different forms of compensation?

As a general rule, amounts paid by companies to their employees as compensation are tax-deductible to the companies, as long as certain requirements are met:

1. The compensation must be an ordinary and necessary business expense.
2. The compensation must be reasonable in amount.
3. The compensation must be paid in the taxable year that the company takes a tax deduction.

The timing of the compensation deduction to the company may vary from the time that the services were rendered, although in all cases it will be at the same time that an executive incurs an ordinary income tax obligation.

Example. Executive A earns compensation in 1994, and receives this compensation in 1994. The executive incurs an ordinary income tax obligation in 1994, and the company can also take a tax deduction from the revenue base on which it calculates its corporate tax in 1994.

Executive B earns compensation in 1994, but defers receipt, in accordance with tax laws, to 1996. The executive incurs an ordinary income tax obligation in 1996, and the company can also take a tax deduction in 1996.

Q 1:32   What is unreasonable compensation?

In order to be tax-deductible to the company, the compensation package of key executives must be reasonable. The Internal Revenue Service determines reasonableness using a number of key factors, including:

- Compensation paid to executives in similar jobs in similar organizations
- Executive qualifications, such as previous experience and academic credentials
- Size and complexity of the business
- Executive duties

The IRS will also take into account the nature of the compensation in determining whether it is reasonable. Incentive compensation, which is usually compensation that is contingent on the company's future performance, can generally be given in amounts that would be considered unreasonable if paid to the executive in the form of salary.

This is because the executive is risking part of his or her compensation based upon the company's performance and should be entitled to a greater reward based on that performance.

Questions regarding the reasonableness of compensation most often arise in connection with payments made to shareholder-executives of a closely held corporation (see Q 2:14), especially where those shareholder-executives own a substantial part of the stock of their employer. This is because it is unclear in this situation whether the compensation is actually a disguised distribution of profits rather than true compensation. Therefore, the IRS closely scrutinizes situations where compensation or bonuses are proportionate to the amount of stock owned and/or where the company is generating profits but paying nominal or no dividends to its shareholders.

Q 1:33 What happens if an executive's compensation is deemed unreasonable?

If the IRS determines that the compensation paid to an executive, including deferred and incentive compensation, is unreasonable, the alleged excess will not be deductible to the company unless the company is able to prove that the compensation is in fact reasonable. The executive would, of course, be taxed on the amounts received, whether or not deductible by the company.

Where the IRS disallows a compensation deduction, the company will typically have to pay back taxes and, in some cases, a penalty. In small, private companies, this can become a major financial hardship.

Q 1:34 What were the clarifications to Code Section 162(m) issued by the IRS in early 1996?

These clarifications are:

1. The definition of public company was expanded to include affiliate or subsidiary companies unless these companies are publicly owned and report as a separate corporation. Private companies that become public during a fiscal year have relief in that the $1 million limit does not apply to the compensation plans for the top five executives that were in effect prior to the

initial public offering (IPO), provided that these compensation plans were described in the IPO prospectus.

Public companies having contracts with the top five executives prior to the 1993 regulations may keep them in effect and still have relief from the $1 million limit even if these contracts include non-performance-based compensation.

2. With respect to the top five executives, the regulations now state that any officer who retires during the fiscal year is not included in the $1 million limit; therefore, if a retiring CEO received a non-performance-based retirement payment from a supplemental retirement plan in the fiscal year, the company would not be subject to the deduction limit on these payments because the retiring CEO is not covered on the top five that year.

3. All "applicable compensation" is included in the company's calculation for the top five executives. Exceptions to applicable compensation are as follows:

   a. Contributions to a tax qualified plan (e.g., defined retirement, 401(k))

   b. Commission-based compensation

   c. Performance-based compensation

To qualify for performance-based compensation, companies must meet the following:

1. Compensation plans must be written, approved by shareholders, and administered by non-employee directors.

2. Goals in compensation plans must be in writing, and must use objective measurement criteria.

3. The achievement of goals must be certified by the outside directors who administer the plan.

Performance-based compensation does not generally include base salary, but can be in the form of annual incentive. The new regulations contain an unusual provision on annual incentives: Whenever an individual executive is paid a percentage of a bonus plan, then the sum of all individual executive bonus percentages cannot exceed 100 percent of the pool; if one executive's portion of the bonus pool is decreased, then another person's cannot be increased. This seems most illogical.

Stock options are specifically identified as being performance-based, along with all long-term performance plans. Any long-term compensation plan that started prior to December 20, 1995 is exempt from the limit of $1 million on the company's tax deductibility.

Restricted stock is specifically identified as not being performance-based.

To date, based on a review of public company proxies, there has been full adherence to the provisions of Code Section 162(m).

Q 1:35   Should executive compensation plans be changed in response to congressional "caps" on executive pay?

This refers to the $1 million limit on the pay of some executives, recently implemented by the IRS. The Revenue Reconciliation Act of 1993 established this limitation, and it was adopted by the IRS in Code Section 162(m).

Under this ruling, public companies can no longer deduct the expense of executive compensation for their top five executives if the total compensation of any individual executive is $1 million or more. The Securities and Exchange Commission also requires public companies to comment on their adherence to Code Section 162(m) during their discussion of executive compensation in each year's proxy report to shareholders; therefore, in addition to the potential loss of a tax deduction, public companies might also face negative reaction from shareholders, employees, and the media if executive compensation does not qualify for a tax deduction. The perception is that compensation is excessive. Moreover, shareholders could decide to file a lawsuit that might charge members of the board of directors with waste or mismanagement of company assets/revenue.

There is some concern by company executives that these considerations will in turn limit the pay of other executives. To date this has not been the case. A review of 200 company proxies in early 1997 shows that all companies are commenting on Code Section 162(m), and all have executive compensation plans that allow a tax deduction.

The new regulations permit flexibility as to type of compensation that is offered to executives. Specifically, the new regulations exclude performance-based pay in the calculation of compensation that is subject to the $1 million cap. The IRS has stated that stock plans are performance-based. Long-term performance plans and annual bonus plans are also typically performance-based, because award levels are determined based on the achievement of predetermined goals.

Most compensation experts believe that companies will continue emphasizing stock plans and performance-based long-term and short-term incentive plans; therefore, total compensation opportunities should not go down because of caps on the deductibility of executive compensation.

Q 1:36   What is ordinary income?

Ordinary income is earned income subject to the ordinary income tax that does not qualify as capital gains. The current ordinary income tax rates range from 15 percent to 39.6 percent, depending on taxable income and filing status (e.g., single, married).

Q 1:37   What are capital gains?

Capital gains are gains from capital assets (e.g., real estate, stock). Currently the capital gains tax of 28 percent is slightly lower than the ordinary income tax rate for most executives.

Q 1:38   What was the rationale for favorable capital gains treatment?

The capital gains treatment had been intended to encourage risk-taking by investors. In addition, the favorable capital gains tax rate recognized that appreciation in value over a long period should not be taxed in full in the year of the income receipt. There was a substantial reduction in tax rates provided by the Tax Reform Act of 1986 (TRA '86). At that time, Congress concluded that it was no longer necessary to provide preferential treatment for capital gains, and it established a capital gains tax rate at the same rate as ordinary income tax, 28 percent. Then in 1993, Congress passed the Omnibus

Budget Reconciliation Act, which left the capital gains tax rate at 28 percent, but raised the maximum ordinary income tax rate to 39.6 percent in 1994.

Q 1:39   How do tax rates affect executive compensation planning?

Capital gains is a more favorable tax to an executive. The only form of executive compensation that offers capital gains tax on all values received is the incentive stock option (ISO) (see discussions at Questions 5:32 and 6:6). If held for one year after purchase, the ISO defers tax until the shares of stock are sold and offers capital gains on the entire spread (option price versus sales price). The ISO is an excellent means of providing executives with tax-effective compensation, particularly if higher tax rates prevail in future years, which most experts believe will happen.

Another way to offer tax-effective compensation opportunities for executives is to allow for income deferral, with the expectation that the executive's ordinary income tax bracket at retirement will be lower than his or her current ordinary income tax level. The primary forms of income deferral, discussed in Chapters 9 and 10, are non-qualified income deferral plans and life insurance plans.

Many executives ask for compensation programs that are tax-effective, meaning that they provide the executive with capital gains tax (at 28 percent) rather than ordinary income tax (at 39.6 percent). Cash compensation is always taxed at ordinary income tax rates; therefore, it has no tax advantage to the executive.

Stock, which is a capital asset, is subject to capital gains tax rates after being held for one year. Therefore stock awards, when earned, can provide capital gains tax rates to the executive.

There is one exception to this rule. Incentive stock options, discussed in subsequent chapters of this book, can under certain circumstances provide executives with capital gains tax treatment before ownership occurs. This means that as a stock award increases in value (i.e., appreciates in price), this value, when received by the executive, is taxed at capital gains rates. (See Chapters 5 and 6.)

In concept, tax rates should not be a factor in executive compensation planning; however, it is one of many practical considerations in the selection of executive compensation plans and plan provisions. During 1997, both republicans and democrats have drafted tax-cut packages that contain a lower capital gains tax (democrats, 18%; republicans 20%). But both political parties have other complex additions to their 1997 tax reform packages. It is predictable that if capital gains goes to or around 20 percent, the use of incentive stock options in company executive pay plans will increase.

Q 1:40   What is the effective tax rate?

The effective tax rate is the rate the executive pays on all of his income, typically measured as adjusted gross income. For example, if the executive's adjusted gross income was $200,000 and the amount of tax was $40,000, the effective tax rate is 20 percent ($200,000 divided by $40,000).

Q 1:41   What is the marginal tax rate?

The marginal tax rate is the rate the executive pays on the next dollar that is earned. That rate can be used to calculate the net value of an increase in compensation. For example, if an executive with a salary of $200,000 is to receive an increase of 5 percent or $10,000, and if this executive is at a marginal tax rate of 28 percent, then the net value of the salary increase to the executive is $7,200 ($10,000 – $2,800).

The marginal tax rate is also used to determine the value of a tax deduction to the executive. For example, if an executive's marginal tax rate is 28 percent, a $1,000 deduction saves the executive 28 percent in taxes or $280 ($1,000 × 28%).

Q 1:42   What is the alternative minimum tax?

The alternative minimum tax (AMT) is a second method of calculating an executive's tax liability. The AMT is sometimes called the add-back tax, because its calculation involves adding back adjustments and deductions that are allowed under the ordinary income tax calculation. The AMT is designed to ensure that all high-income executives bear at least a minimum level of the federal tax burden. An executive must use the AMT calculation to determine taxes due when primary sources of income are tax-sheltered or subject to favorable tax treatment. Such situations may occur when a large portion of income has been realized through stock option gains or certain tax-sheltered investments, or where a large portion of income has been protected by tax shelters.

The AMT requires that an affected executive calculate her tax liability under AMT rules, and then calculate tax liability under ordinary income tax rules. The executive then pays the higher of the two tax obligations. The 1995 AMT rate is 28 percent.

Accounting Considerations

Q 1:43 What are the general accounting implications of the different forms of compensation?

Unlike tax laws, which establish a taxable event when compensation is paid, accounting regulations, established by the Financial Accounting Standards Board (FASB), require companies to accrue compensation costs on accounting statements as they are earned; therefore, a company may not be able to take a tax deduction (from the revenue base used to calculate annual corporate taxes) for executive compensation earned in a given year. The same company will be required, however, under FASB regulations to reduce revenue reported in the same year by that same amount of executive compensation. For example: An executive earns a $30,000 bonus in 1994, but, in accordance with tax regulations, defers receipt of this bonus to 1996. The company must deduct $30,000 from its accounting statements for the year 1994. The company does not get to take a tax deduction for this same amount until 1996. Therefore, companies keep two sets of financial statements, one for tax purposes and one for accounting purposes.

Q 1:44   What accounting statements contain compensation expenses?

Both the income statement (profit and loss statement) and the balance sheet statement contain compensation expenses. The income statement reflects company revenues and expenses over a fixed period—a fiscal year, which is any 12-month period. The income statement documents all sources of company income, as well as all company expenses, including compensation expenses, in order to arrive at a net income or a net loss for the period. Included under operating expenses (also known as selling, general, and administrative costs) are compensation expenses and cash payments earned by an executive, as well as accruals for long-term cash payments that companies expect to pay to executives in the future (long-term incentive payments are accrued and charged to the income statement during the period in which they are earned).

At the end of the period of the income statement, any accrued compensation expenses are transferred to the balance sheet and carried as a liability. The balance sheet reflects company assets, liabilities, and equity or net worth. The sum of liabilities and equity will always equal the sum of total assets.

Q 1:45   What is the accounting for stock awards?

Companies may select one of two ways to establish the accounting treatment of stock awards (both stock option grants and full-value stock grants). The first is to follow APB 25, and the second is to follow FAS 123.

The Financial Accounting Standards Board continues to allow companies to select APB 25, created by its predecessor organization the Accounting Principles Board (APB). Under APB 25, companies must accrue compensation costs for stock awards based on the measurement principle. The measurement principle states that compensation costs will be determined on the measurement date, when two factors are known: (1) the number of shares that the executive is eligible to receive and (2) the price per share to be paid by the executive.

The compensation cost for stock awards is calculated as the difference on this date between the value of the stock award (the number of shares multiplied by their current market value) and the cost of the shares to the executive (the number of shares multiplied by the price per share to be paid by the executive).

Example: APB 25. A company grants an executive the right to purchase 1,000 stock option shares at $20 per share, which is the current market value. The accounting charge to the company's income statement is zero, calculated as follows: The value of the shares can be determined on the date of grant, and that amount is $20,000 (1,000 shares × the $20 fair market value). The cost to the executive can also be determined on this date, and is $20,000 (1,000 shares × the $20 option price to the executive). $20,000 − $20,000 = $0.

If that company granted an executive the right to purchase 1,000 stock option shares at a price of $15 per share, when the fair market value is $20 per share, the company must accrue a charge to its income statement of $5,000. The value of the shares on the date of grant is $20,000 (1,000 shares × $20). The cost to the executive on this date is $15,000 (1,000 shares × $15). $20,000 − $15,000 = $5,000.

Under the new ruling by the FASB known as FAS 123, a company may elect to establish a "fair market value" of a stock award at the time of grant and accrue this cost on the company's income statement over the period that the stock award vests. The FASB suggests that companies use a stock pricing model to establish the "fair value." (See Q 1:49 as to the specific criteria such a stock pricing model should meet.) If a company does not select FAS 123, it must include a footnote in its financial statements that shows the earnings per share (EPS) impact that would have occurred if the stock award had been assigned a fair value that was charged to the company's earnings.

Example: FAS 123. A company grants an executive the right to purchase 1,000 stock option shares at $20 per share, which is the current market value. The accounting charge to the company's income statement is $7 per share or $7,000 (1,000 shares × $7), which must be accrued over the vesting period of the stock option.

The fair value of $7 per share was determined by reducing the executive's option price of $20 by the present value of that price, discounted back from the expected exercises/purchase date to the date of grant. This amount was further reduced by the present value of the expected stream of dividends over the expected term of the grant. (See Q 1:46.)

Many large human resource consulting firms and CPA firms offer computer discs with an option pricing model such as Black-Scholes. These are most valuable in calculating a fair value for stock awards. Every executive compensation administrator should have one.

Q 1:46   How does APB 25 compare to FAS 123?

The following chart compares key features of the two accounting regulations with an impact on stock awards.

Provision	APB 25	FAS 123
1. Date for measuring compensation cost	Date that stock price and number of shares are known	Date of grant
2. Definition of measurement	Market value minus amount to be paid by executive	Fair value as determined by an option pricing model
3. Accrual period	Vesting period	Vesting period
4. Impact on income	Footnote	Charged as statement expense

Q 1:47   What changes in APB 25 have been implemented by the FASB under FAS 123?

FAS 123 significantly changes the accounting for stock plans in 1996. Under FAS 123, both private and public companies must select either APB 25 or FAS 123 as the basis for determining the charge to company earnings on any awards from a stock plan. If companies decide to use FAS 123, they must establish a "fair value" of the stock grant and charge their income statement with this fair value over the vesting period of the stock award.

Acceptable option pricing models such as Black-Scholes (see Q 5:26), the binomial option model, and the minimum value method have been identified by FASB as acceptable methods for determining fair value.

Companies that elect to continue using APB 25 are required to show the impact that a fair value measure of any stock award grant would have on its earnings per share. This impact is to be shown as a footnote to the income statement.

An important caveat to this choice is that whatever alternative a company may select for the reporting of stock options must also be used for the reporting of other forms of long-term incentive, such as performance plans, SARs, and other variable awards.

FAS 123 also requires expanded disclosure of company practices on the accounting for stock award plans.

For companies that elect to use FAS 123, the effective date for implementation is in fiscal years beginning after December 15, 1995. For companies that elect to continue using APB 25, the effective date for implementation is in fiscal years beginning after December 15, 1994.

Q 1:48   What stock plans are included in FAS 123?

Stock plans are defined in FAS 123 as including stock options, performance-based stock options, stock appreciation rights, performance shares, restricted stock, stock purchase plans, and any other equity award to employees. Employee stock ownership plans (ESOPs) are not included in FAS 123.

Companies that use multiple forms of stock awards for executives have a challenging decision on the election of accounting methods, because a company must choose one accounting for all stock plans. For example, if a company provides executives with both stock options and performance shares, it cannot choose APB 25 for the stock options and FAS 123 for the performance shares.

Example. A company grants an executive 1,000 stock option shares at $20/share when the current market value of the shares is also $20. The same executive is also granted 1,000 performance shares when the company's stock price is $20.

Under previous accounting regulations, the company would apply APB 25 to the stock options and have no charge to earnings because they were granted at the current fair market value. The company would then use FAS 28 and establish a charge to earnings for the actual amount earned from the performance shares, i.e., $20,000 (1,000 shares × $20) or greater if the stock price goes up during the award period.

Under current accounting regulations, the company must choose either FAS 123 or APB 25 for both grants. Clearly the company would like to use APB 25 for the stock option because it will result in no charge to earnings. The company would prefer FAS 123 for the performance shares, because the charge to earnings will be less than $20,000. Under Black-Scholes or most any other option pricing model, the charge to earnings is less because in calculating the fair value the company is able to calculate a discounted present value and further discount for the value of dividends. The actual charge depends on the assumptions used. Unfortunately, the company cannot use APB 25 for the stock options and FAS 123 for the performance shares.

Companies with multiple forms of stock grant will want to do some in-depth analysis of the impact that these new accounting regulations will have on current and future year costs to the income statement.

Q 1:49   How is the fair value calculation done under the new FAS 123?

FAS 123 requires that the following assumptions be used in determining the fair value of a stock award:

1. The expected life of the stock award;

2. The expected volatility of the company's stock price (public companies only);

3. The expected dividend yield of company stock during the expected life of the stock award;

4. The risk-free interest rate during the expected life of the stock award;

5. The current price of the stock award;

6. The price that the executive will pay for the stock.

The FASB has stated that a company can use any stock model in establishing the fair value of a stock grant as long as it meets these criteria. One exception noted by the FASB is that private companies may use the less complicated minimum value method for establishing the fair value of a stock award. Most large companies have already started using the Black-Scholes option pricing method, and most small companies are using the minimum value method. Another alternative is the binomial stock price model.

Both the binomial models and Black-Scholes take into account the statistical probability of stock volatility or the extent to which a company's stock price will increase or decrease in the future. Small or private companies do not have to factor-in stock volatility; therefore, they have no need to use Black-Scholes or the binomial methods.

Q 1:50   How do some of these fair value determination models work?

The minimum value method is calculated by taking the present value of the executive's purchase price of the stock grant and adding the present value of expected dividends (if any), and then subtracting this from the current price of a company share of stock.

Example: Minimum Value Method.

Present value of executive's option price	$30
Present value of expected dividends	0
Current stock price	$40
Fair value per share ($40 – $30)	$10

The calculation of fair value under both Black-Scholes and the binomial models is much more complicated. Following are some examples of Black-Scholes:

Example: Black-Scholes.

Black-Scholes

Purchase Price	$40
Expected Life	5 Years
Volatility	1.25
Dividends	3%/Year
Risk-Free Rate of Return	7%
Fair Value	$11.50

Black-Scholes Without Volatility

Purchase Price	$40
Expected Life	5 Years
Volatility	-0-
Dividends	3%/Year
Risk-Free Rate of Return	7%
Fair Value	$7

Black-Scholes Without Dividends or Volatility

Purchase Price	$40
Expected Life	5 Years
Volatility	-0-
Dividends	-0-
Risk-Free Rate of Return	7%
Fair Value	$9

Planning Tip. The previous examples show that:

1. The higher the dividend, the lower the fair value.
2. The higher the volatility, the higher the fair value.
3. The lower the fair value, the lower the charge to the company's income statement.

These examples illustrate the type of analysis companies will need to conduct in order to make an informed decision on the accounting impact of stock award plans.

Q 1:51   What are the disclosure requirements of FAS 123?

All assumptions used in calculating fair value by a company must be disclosed in the company's financial statements. This disclosure must include:

1. A description of the accounting method chosen by the company for all stock grants.

2. A description of the assumptions used in calculating the fair value amount to be accrued on the income statement, shown as a footnote on the income statement.

3. A description of the stock plan, to include the type of award, the terms of the award, the vesting provision, and the number of shares authorized under the plan.

4. For stock options, the weighted average fair value of all stock options granted during the year. If the option exercise price is different than the current market value of the stock, then the fair value of all stock option grants must be reported separately for each grant that year.

5. For stock options, the number of shares and the weighted average option exercise price for all shares granted, forfeited or expired, and exercised.

6. For other stock grants, the weighted average fair value at the date of grant.

These disclosures are similar to those required by the Securities Exchange Commission on executive compensation.

Q 1:52   What are the current FASB guidelines on earnings per share calculations that are effective until December 1997?

Under FAS 123, companies (private or public) are required to report the earnings per share impact of stock award plans. The current definitions of primary EPS and fully diluted EPS are to be modified in company financial statements issued after December 15, 1997.

Currently, both of these calculations are defined as earnings divided by common shares outstanding. Also in both, common shares outstanding include "common stock equivalents," which are calculated using what is called the treasury stock method. This treasury stock method assumes that stock options not yet exercised, but that have appreciated value (i.e., the current market price is greater than the purchase price of the stock option), must be included in the EPS calculation. This is accomplished by assuming the stock option had been exercised, and taking the proceeds from the option purchase (and in the case of a non-qualified stock option, also taking the hypothetical value of the company's tax deduction equal to the appreciated value in the stock option/the executive's taxable income) and buying shares of company stock at the current market price. In performing this calculation the number of shares that can be purchased is obviously less than those granted in the stock option because this calculation is only done if stock price increases. The shortfall in shares is referred to as common stock equivalents. The common stock equivalents at the beginning of the year and at the end of the year are averaged and the average common stock equivalents are included in the EPS calculation. Primary earnings per share includes these common stock equivalents from stock options and those from convertible shares, while fully diluted EPS is more comprehensive and includes all of this plus common stock equivalents from other potential derivatives or securities that could also become outstanding shares in the future.

Q 1:53 What are the new FASB guidelines on EPS calculations that are to be used in company financial statements issued after December 15, 1997?

The new methods of calculating earnings per share are referred to as "basic earnings per share" and "diluted earnings per share." Basic EPS does not include any common stock equivalents and is simply net income divided by common shares outstanding, using a weighted average common shares during the reporting period.

The fully diluted EPS calculation method is essentially the same method as the old fully diluted described in Q 1:49, and it therefore does include common shares equivalents using the treasury stock method.

Companies are required to report both basic and diluted earnings per share. Obviously, the FASB wants to show investors the potential dilutive impact of company stock option plans (or other share equivalents) in these new calculations.

Q 1:54 How should companies respond to the new FASB regulations being considered for stock options?

Most companies will clearly choose the continued use of APB 25; however, the footnote requirement is expected to be quite burdensome, because it will require pro-formas that display how a fair market value would have affected net income and earnings per share, plus the assumptions used to compute the fair market value. Still, this alternative does not require companies to deduct the fair market value from their reported net income (except as a "what if" footnote).

One company response to these new regulations can be to make a special large grant of stock options (jumbo grant) to take advantage of current accounting regulations that do not require an expense charge to company earnings. This will need to be done with the knowledge that jumbo or front-end grants mean that no additional long-term awards will be made for a few years.

Another response by companies would be to accept the fact that stock options are a compensation cost for labor services rendered. Accept them as a reward for services rendered just as a bonus payment, and accept the charge to earnings as is done with bonus payments. If an executive position adds value and profitability to an organization, then one could argue that a company should provide appropriate compensation, including stock option grants, and absorb any associated costs. This response suggests that the issue is one of appropriate rewards for productivity rather than cost.

Planning Tip. The longer the vesting period in stock award plans, the less the annual accrual to a company's income statement for stock award plans. For example, if a company needs to accrue $100,000 for a long-term stock award plan, the annual accrual for a plan with three-year vesting is $333,333, while the annual accrual for a plan with five-year vesting is $200,000.

Chapter 2

Private Versus Public Company Considerations

Privately held and closely held companies have unique organizational characteristics that typically require a significantly different approach to executive compensation. Frequently, an executive compensation plan that is effective and appropriate in publicly traded organizations will be neither effective nor appropriate in a privately held company. The use of stock-based plans, for instance, so common in publicly traded companies, is less extensive in private companies. Furthermore, in small start-up companies, annual incentive plans that are so common in large organizations are difficult to make effective. This chapter compares the different approaches of private companies and public companies to executive compensation program design as well as general plan design and competitive practices. It also provides information on the regulations of the Securities and Exchange Commission that apply to public companies. The regulations in SEC Section 16 have direct impact on the design and reporting of executive compensation in public companies.

General Considerations 2-2
Stock-Based Plans 2-4
S Corporations 2-8

SEC Regulations   2-12
Proxy Rules   2-19

General Considerations

Q 2:1   What is a public or publicly traded company?

A company is publicly traded if it has a class of equity securities that is registered under the Securities Exchange Act of 1934 (the 1934 Act) and, as a result, is subject to the ongoing disclosure and reporting requirements of the 1934 Act.

Equity securities must be registered under the 1934 Act if either a public offering of those securities is made under the Securities Act of 1933 (the 1933 Act) or if the company in question has more than $3 million in total assets or more than 500 shareholders of any one class of its equity securities.

Q 2:2   What is a private or privately held company?

A company is privately held if none of its equity securities are registered under the 1934 Act.

Q 2:3   What is a closely held company?

A closely held company is one in which management and ownership are substantially the same. The term "closely held corporation" is derived from the fact that the company's stock is "held closely" by a few individuals. Such companies are frequently referred to as "close corporations" or "family corporations."

Q 2:4   Is a privately held company always considered closely held as well?

No, although these terms are often incorrectly used interchangeably. A closely held company will always be a privately held company, because in a private company it is possible to limit the shareholders; however, in a public company public shares cannot be held by a few "close" individuals. Anyone can own shares in a public company.

A privately held company will not necessarily be closely held, because some of the shareholders may be very independent.

Q 2:5   Do executive compensation programs in privately held companies differ from those in publicly traded companies?

In many cases they do, because the underlying motivations of executive compensation programs differ from public to private companies. A public company's primary motivation in instituting a compensation program is to offer executives enough compensation to retain them and motivate them to work their hardest toward achieving the company's strategic interests. This motivation exists already for owner-executives of a small private company because they already have a substantial stake in the company's stock ownership and, therefore, in ensuring that the company achieves its strategic interests. As a result, many small private companies will concentrate on rewarding their owner-executives for their efforts through perquisites. In large privately held companies, the business value and underlying motivations of executive compensation programs are similar, because most executives are not owners.

Another difference between private and public companies is that, in privately held companies, base salaries for executives appear to be somewhat higher, but total cash compensation (salary plus bonus) is lower. This reflects the limited cash available and the career caps that exist in some private companies that are family-owned. The career caps reflect the fact that in many privately held companies the top positions are available only to the family members of the primary owners.

Where annual incentive plans are used in privately held companies, they do not significantly differ in design from those in publicly traded companies. However, privately held companies tend to place more emphasis on internally set performance objectives rather than external performance measures such as earnings per share, peer comparisons, and cash flow. Book value growth appears frequently as a performance measure for private companies.

Stock-Based Plans

Q 2:6   Do privately held companies use stock-based capital accumulation programs to structure their executive compensation arrangements?

Yes, but not as frequently as public companies. Some owners do not wish to grant options widely to their nonowner employees because they do not want a substantial increase in the number of owners. If a privately held company does use a stock-based capital accumulation program, it tends to distribute more shares to fewer executives than would be the case in a publicly traded company. Furthermore, the private company would certainly be well advised to keep the number of shareholders comfortably below the 500 number, which would prevent triggering reporting requirements under the 1934 Act.

Q 2:7   What are the most common forms of long-term incentives in private companies?

As shown in Chart 2-1, the most frequently used long-term incentives in closely held companies are book value plans (see Q 6:42), performance units plans (see Q 7:39), and phantom stock plans (see Q 7:20). If stock-based plans are offered, they are almost always accompanied by buy-back provisions.

Q 2:8   Are there problems with using stock plans in private companies?

There are several reasons stock option plans and stock-based plans are used less frequently in privately held companies. One

Chart 2-1. Privately Held Company Long-Term Incentive Plan

Book Value	24%
Stock Options	12%
Phantom Stock Plans	26%
Performance Plans	16%
Combination Plans	8%
Other	14%
	100%

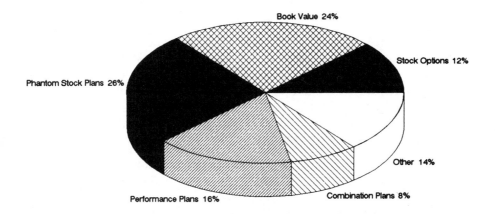

Source: Management Performance International, Inc.

reason, as stated in Q 2:6, is that an executive compensation plan that uses stock eventually results in a minority shareholder position for a number of executives, with all the rights that this position entails, including the right to vote stock, review financial records, and attend shareholder meetings. This may not be appealing to the majority owners, both because their ownership becomes diluted and they have additional people to answer to. In addition, this minority ownership can lead to an unfriendly minority shareholder if the executive is terminated or leaves the firm to join a competitor, although this problem may be avoided through the use of restrictive buy-back agreements.

Such agreements typically obligate executives to sell their stock back to the company or the majority shareholder following termination of employment, or allow currently employed executives to liquidate their investment. Restrictive buy-back agreements also typically allow the buy-back to take place over a reasonable span of time to avoid the cash burden to the company owners that could result from an obligation to purchase the stock immediately.

Privately held companies may also avoid the use of stock-based plans so as not to have to value the stock to establish the purchase price. A private company must hire an outside party to determine the value of its shares. As a result, the buy-back agreement usually stipulates a formula price or method by which the purchase price is to be determined at the time of sale, at specified intervals during the award period, and at the end of the award period.

Planning Tip. Phantom plans can be exactly like those used by publicly traded companies, with an exception: Executives are able to sell their shares only to the company, which is typically enforced by granting the company a right of first refusal. The company may also want to specify financing terms as part of the repurchase agreement, permitting it to settle the executive's interests over a number of years to minimize the impact of an immediate cash drain.

Q 2:9   What is an example of a buy-back agreement?

An executive may be awarded company shares with the following provisos:

1. The executive may sell the shares if one of the following events occurs:

   a. Death, disability, or early or normal retirement

   b. Voluntary termination or involuntary termination if other than for cause

   c. The completion of ten years of service after stock ownership occurs

2. If the executive then wishes to sell such shares, she must first offer the company the opportunity to purchase all of the shares. The purchase offer period will extend for 75 days after one of the events occurs. If the company does not exercise its right to buy the shares by then, the executive may sell or transfer ownership at any time.

3. If the shares are sold to the company after a public offering has been completed, the price per share will be the average high and low trading price of the shares on the effective date of the sale as reported on the stock exchange. If the shares are sold to the company prior to a public offering, the price will be calculated as of the last stock valuation conducted by the company. These valuations are conducted by the company each quarter of the fiscal year. In all cases, the executive will be eligible for a payment per share equal to the price at the time of sale minus the price he paid at the time ownership occurred.

Q 2:10   Is there a negative effect if a privately held company does not provide long-term incentive plans?

Yes. In not providing long-term incentive programs, privately held companies are denying themselves an important tool to recruit, retain, and direct executive talent. They are also probably paying more than is necessary in fixed cash compensation. In addition, they are losing the opportunity to put executives in the same boat as the owners.

Virtually all types of privately held companies can offer meaningful capital accumulation plans to key executives, the most prevalent type of which is a cash-based, long-term phantom stock plan (see Q 7:20).

S Corporations

Q 2:11 What is a Subchapter S corporation?

The Internal Revenue Code (the Code) permits shareholders of certain privately held companies to elect to be taxed as though the shareholders were carrying on their activities as partners. In such a case, the shareholders are taxed directly on the earnings of the company in proportion to their ownership of stock. As a result of this election, the shareholders avoid the double taxation of corporate earnings (first, at the corporate level on the company's earnings and, second, at the individual level when those earnings are distributed to the shareholders in the form of dividends) by passing the tax obligations through to themselves.

Q 2:12 How does a company elect to become a Subchapter S corporation?

A corporation becomes a Subchapter S corporation (S corporation) by filing an S corporation election under Code Section 1362(a). That election may only be made by a corporation that meets all of the following eligibility requirements:

1. It must be a corporation organized under the laws of the United States.
2. It cannot have more than 35 shareholders.
3. Its shareholders must be individuals, estates, or certain trusts.
4. It cannot have more than one class of stock.

Furthermore, certain types of companies are ineligible for S corporation treatment regardless of whether they meet the above criteria. Such companies include financial institutions, insurance companies, and members of a group determined to be "affiliated" under Code Section 1504(b). Generally, the most significant implication of the affiliated group prohibition is that an S corporation may not have a subsidiary unless another person or entity holds at least 20 percent of the total voting power and also holds a value equal to at least 20 percent of the total value of the subsidiary's stock, or unless that subsidiary is in fact inactive.

Q 2:13 Does electing S corporation status have an impact on executive compensation?

Yes. An S corporation must be careful in implementing a stock-based plan because it risks losing its S corporation status if it violates one of the eligibility requirements (see Q 2:12). The number of executives entitled to participate in such a plan must be limited because the number of shareholders of an S corporation is limited. The plan must be monitored to ensure that it does not, by design or unintentionally, create a second class of stock.

The events that create a second class of stock are not always clear. The use of restricted shares may constitute a second class of stock where shares that are issued are subject to such substantial conditions or restrictions that they are deemed to not have the same rights to corporate assets as other, unrestricted company stock. Certain restrictions can, however, be imposed without creating a second class of stock. Such restrictions include:

1. Requiring the executive to obtain corporate consent prior to selling the shares to a third party

2. Requiring the executive to resell the shares to the company at a specified price, even if that price is less than the fair market value of the shares

3. Providing that the executive will forfeit the shares if she quits or is fired for good cause

Typically, an S corporation will choose to avoid the problems associated with stock-based plans by using related devices such as stock appreciation rights (SARs) and phantom stock plans (see Qs 7:3 and 7:20).

The election of S corporation status also has an impact on the adoption of other nonqualified deferred compensation vehicles such as rabbi trusts or corporate-owned life insurance, although these vehicles are rarely used by S corporations because they have little value to the owner-executive of an S corporation. They are of little value because the S corporation is not a tax-shielding entity like a regular corporation. The owner-executives are currently taxed, like partners, on the income held by the company or paid in the form of insurance premiums.

A positive dimension of S corporation status can be the category of income received by executives. Direct compensation (salary, bonus, etc.) is of course taxable to the executive, a tax deduction to the company, and subject to FICA payment by both executive and company. Dividends are also taxable to the executive; however, they are not a tax deduction to the company, nor are they subject to FICA for the executive or the company. The income category of dividends can therefore represent a substantial savings in FICA payments to the S corporation and the executive.

One caution on this strategy is that an S corporation cannot categorize all income as dividends just to avoid FICA tax. There must be a logical basis for the company to distinguish between direct compensation and dividends. For example, a professional services company may pay its executives a fixed salary and target bonus as direct compensation in anticipation of expected revenue and net income. An unusually profitable year might then result in a substantial dividend due to the unusual level of company success.

The Small Business Job Protection Act of 1996 (SBJPA) has modified a number of S Corporation shareholder eligibility rules, which will be discussed in a future supplement.

Q 2:14   Does the issue of unreasonable compensation affect publicly traded companies differently from privately held and S corporations?

Technically, no; in practice, yes. The requirement that compensation be reasonable applies universally to all companies. There is nothing in the Code or corresponding treasury regulations that limits the application of unreasonable compensation issues to privately held companies. In practice, however, it is almost exclusively the privately held company that is challenged on this issue. The reason for this seemingly selective application is that there is far greater potential for and likelihood of abuse in the case of a privately held company, where the owner-executives typically have the power to fix their own compensation and to control the company's dividend-paying policy. Furthermore, the requirement that a publicly traded corporation disclose the profit it earns each year, as well as the compensation it pays to its top executives, acts as a natural barrier against the payment of excessive salaries.

S corporations, although privately held, are generally exempt from this special scrutiny because there is no reason for the owner-executives to try to classify dividend payments as compensation unless the compensation in question is of a type (e.g., retirement plan contributions or deferred compensation) that affects the company's tax situation and the tax deductibility of compensation. The S corporation and the C corporation can easily trigger an unreasonable compensation issue: The owner-executive can classify dividends as salary in order to obtain a tax deduction for the company. If the IRS believes this to be the case, it can declare the salary unreasonable, in which case the salary becomes classified as dividends, and the company loses its tax deduction. This is very serious to a C corporation because it loses the tax deduction and pays a higher tax, and the owner-executive still pays tax on the dividend payments as he would if it were salary. In an S corporation, corporate income is taxed as ordinary income to the executive; therefore, no reason exists to reclassify income from dividends to salary.

This is in contrast to another strategy in which the owner-executive classifies salary as dividends to avoid (1) payment by the company and by the individual executive of FICA and FUTA (federal unemployment) taxes, and (2) federal withholding tax requirements that are applicable to compensation payments (see Q 2:13). This will not raise an unreasonable compensation issue from the IRS; however, the IRS may raise the issue that salary payments may have been misclassified to avoid taxation. Owner-executives are wise to seek advice and counsel from tax attorneys or CPAs on these complex issues.

When the IRS makes a determination of unreasonable compensation, it is presumed to be correct; therefore, the burden of proving that the payments are reasonable falls on the company and the owner-executive. In any compensation arrangement between a privately held company and its owner-executives, it is also assumed that arm's-length bargaining did not occur, which increases the likelihood that compensation will be found to be unreasonable. Each case is decided, however, on its own facts, a practice generally seen as more favorable to the executive and the company because it gives more latitude to each company. Unfortunately, as a result, there are no firm guidelines or precedents to rely upon in analyzing a reasonable compensation issue, because each company, executive, and situation is different.

> **Planning Tip.** An important strategy in any unreasonable compensation claim by the IRS is for the company or owner-executive to present labor market information on typical (reasonable) total compensation payments made to similar executives in similar companies over an extended period of time (e.g., five to ten years). The next step is to compare total compensation actually paid to the executive over this period to competitive total compensation that would typically have been provided over the same period of time.

SEC Regulations

Q 2:15   What is the Securities Act of 1933, and how does it affect executive compensation?

The 1933 Act sets forth the principal federal rules governing the issuance and sale of securities in the United States. The 1933 Act governs the sale by a company of shares of its stock to the public.

Under the 1933 Act, every offer and sale of a security must be registered with the Securities and Exchange Commission (the SEC) unless the offer and sale are exempt from registration. There is a "private offering" exemption for offerings not made to the general public as well as an exemption for certain offers and sales of securities by private companies that are made pursuant to employee benefit plans or contracts with its employees, consultants, or advisors. Rule 144 under the 1933 Act allows the executive of a public company to hold securities that have not been registered under the 1933 Act, also known as "restricted securities," for a minimum of two years, at which time the executive may resell the shares to the public subject to the volume limitation and other manner-of-sale requirements of Rule 144. After the securities have been held for three years, they may be transferred without regard to the volume limitations.

Q 2:16   What is the Securities Exchange Act of 1934, and how does it affect executive compensation?

The 1934 Act contains the reporting rules that must be followed by a company whose shares are held by the public. The basic principle is that everyone who buys and sells shares of the company's stock must have access to the same information concerning the company at the same time. This principle prevents certain categories of people, referred to as "insiders," from profiting at the public's expense from any information that they have gained solely by reason of their position with the company. Therefore, a publicly traded company must file quarterly and annual statements containing audited financial statements and must notify the public of any material changes in its business or operations. Furthermore, the publicly traded company's executive officers and directors are prohibited from buying or selling shares of company stock if they have any material information that has not yet been disclosed to the public.

The 1934 Act's primary effects on executive compensation arise from the fact that the company must disclose the compensation paid each year to its most highly compensated employees and from the presumption set forth in Section 16 and the rules promulgated under that Section that an insider who buys and sells stock in a six-month period is trading on inside information.

Q 2:17   How can a company avoid application of the 1933 Act?

The 1933 Act applies to the sale of stock to the public. In order to avoid the requirements of the act a company must remain private and not offer its shares to the public. A company thereby avoids the extensive disclosure requirements outlined in Question 2:16. These include insider restrictions on the purchase and sale of stock (buy and sell transactions cannot occur within six months of each other) and the required registration with the SEC of any such stock sale or purchase. The act also requires that executive compensation for the top five highly compensated executives be disclosed to the public. These regulations, which have recently been modified by the SEC, are discussed in Questions 2:23 through 2:32.

As noted in Question 2:15, a company can also avoid application of the 1933 Act by utilizing its principal exemption for private offerings—that is, sales of stock that are made without an offering to the general public. This exemption is available to both publicly traded companies and privately held corporations.

Q 2:18   What are the basic SEC Section 16 rules?

Section 16 of the 1934 Act is designed to minimize the unfair use of inside information, which is information that is not available to the public. This is accomplished through the interaction of Section 16(a), which defines an "insider" and states that an insider must promptly disclose all transactions in company stock, and Section 16(b), which states that any profits made by an insider from transactions involving a purchase and sale of company stock within any six-month period must be returned to the company. Any combination of purchase and sale within the six-month period will result in a violation of Section 16(b) (known as the short-swing trading violation), regardless of how long the shares being sold have been held or whether the executive in fact possessed material nonpublic information. The amount of profit earned will be calculated by the method producing the highest recovery for the company: The highest sale price will be matched with the lowest purchase price in the period.

Because certain stock transactions are not likely to result in abuse of insider information, Section 16(b)3 exempts these transactions from Section 16 coverage. These include stock transactions within certain employee benefit plans that allow executive participation. Section 16(b)3 also allows insiders to exercise a stock appreciation right, for cash, during the "window period," which is the third through the twelfth working day following the release of quarterly earnings. The SEC recently provided additional interpretations of Section 16, an analysis of which follows in Questions 2:18 through 2:20.

Q 2:19   What were the major changes in SEC Section 16 rules effective May 1, 1991?

The new Section 16 rules changed the definition of an insider to include directors, executive officers, and holders of 10 percent or more of the outstanding shares of a company's stock. The term "executive officers" includes "presidents or vice presidents who are in charge of a principal business unit, division, or function, and other persons who perform similar policy-making functions." [Note 33 to Release No. 34-28869] Specifically included in this category are the company's principal financial officer and principal accounting officer or controller. Executive officers of parent or subsidiary companies can also be considered executive officers of the company itself if they perform the described functions. The new definition is narrower than the previous definition, which subjected all officers, regardless of policy-making function, to the reporting requirements and potential liability of Section 16.

The definition of 10 percent owner has changed in some minor respects; it is now tied directly to the definition provided in Section 13(d) of the 1933 Act. Essentially, the opportunity, directly or indirectly, to profit or share in the applicable transaction, or the right to vote or direct the voting of shares, constitutes ownership of the shares.

The new Section 16(a) reporting requirements are similar to the old ones. Under the new requirements, an insider files a Form 3 at the time he or she becomes an insider, setting forth the number of shares of company stock he owns (including shares held by his or her spouse, children, and any other relative living in his household), as well as the number of shares he or she is then entitled to acquire upon the exercise of any option or other right. Any changes are then reported on a Form 4 within the first ten days of the month following the month in which the transaction takes place, except for the changes that are exempt from Section 16(b) liability, which may be voluntarily reported immediately but otherwise are to be reported on the first Form 4 that the insider is otherwise required to file or on a Form 5 filed within 45 days after the end of the year. An important new sanction contained in Section 16(a) is the obligation of the company to report, in the annual information that it provides to its shareholders, not only any violations by any of its insiders of the short-swing profit rules of Section 16, but also any lapses or mistakes in the filing of the disclosure reports.

One of the most significant changes to Section 16(b) involves the treatment of the acquisition and exercise of options and other derivative securities. Under the new rules, the granting of a stock option, warrant, or other convertible security is deemed to be a purchase event for purposes of Section 16(b). The subsequent exercise of the option, warrant, or conversion of the convertible security is not a purchase event for the purposes of Section 16(b).

Rule 16(b)3 continues to provide guidelines for certain employee benefit plans, including stock option plans, where participation is not deemed to be subject to the abuse of insider information. As long as these plans meet the Section 16(b)3 guidelines, grants of options and other securities will not be deemed to be purchases of the securities for purposes of Section 16(b), although they will be subject to Section 16(a) reporting requirements.

Q 2:20   What are the most significant effects of the new Section 16 rules from a compensation perspective?

The revised rules exempting the exercise of stock options from consideration as an insider purchase event under Section 16(b) allow an insider to exercise an option and sell shares of stock (to pay for that exercise) simultaneously. Thus many compensation devices designed to provide the executive with cash to exercise his or her options, such as the stock appreciation right, are no longer needed.

From a corporate perspective, executive compensation plans may have to be amended in order to comply with the revised Section 16 exemption requirements. There are two other important implications of these changes for both insiders and companies:

1. If an insider exercises a stock option before six months has expired since the date of grant (the purchase event) and immediately sells the shares (a sale event), a violation of Section 16(b) has occurred.

2. If an insider sells owned shares (a sale event), and is then provided with a stock option grant (a purchase event) within six months, then a violation of Section 16(b) may have occurred if the option shares were not issued under a "16b-3 plan." Under such a plan, stock option shares are granted by "disinterested parties" (outside members of a company's board of directors who typically are members of the board compensation committee) under a plan approved by shareholders.

Example 1. Executive A, an insider, receives a stock option grant of 1,000 shares at a purchase price of $15 per share on May 1, 1992. On August 1, 1992, the executive exercises the option. On September 1, 1992, the executive sells the shares at $25 per share. The executive has violated SEC Section 16 because the shares had not been held for six months from the date of grant (the purchase date of May 1, 1992) when they were sold on September 1, five months after the purchase date. As an insider, Executive A is required to hold shares for six months before a sale event can occur after a purchase event.

Example 2. Executive B, an insider, sells previously owned shares (a sale event) on February 1, 1992. On May 1, 1992, this same executive is provided with a stock option grant of 1,000 shares, with an option price of $15 per share. The new stock option shares are non-16(b)3 stock option grants. As a result, Executive B has violated SEC Section 16 because a purchase event (the granting of the new stock option shares) has occurred within six months of a sale event (the sale of shares on February 1, 1992). If, however, those stock option shares had been 16(b)3 plan shares, this executive would not have violated SEC Section 16, because the stock option shares granted on May 1, 1992, (a purchase event) would not be matched against shares sold on February 1, 1992.

Example 3. Executive C, an insider, sells previously owned shares on February 1, 1992. This same executive is provided on May 1, 1992, with a stock option grant of 1,000 shares, at an option price of $15. These stock option shares are 16(b)3 plan shares. On August 1, 1992, C exercises the right to purchase these shares, and then sells these shares on September 1, 1992. As a result, C has violated SEC Section 16 because the sale event on September 1, 1992, occurred within six months of the purchase event (the granting of the stock option shares on May 1, 1992).

Example 4. Executive D is provided with a stock option grant of 1,000 shares on May 1, 1992, at an option price of $15 per share. These stock option shares are 16(b)3 plan shares. On August 1, 1992, the executive exercises the stock option at $20 per share. On November 1, 1992, the executive sells these shares (a sale event) at $25 per share. Executive D has not violated Section 16 of the SEC regulations because six months have transpired between the sale date of the shares (November 1, 1992) and the purchase of these shares (the grant date of May 1, 1992).

Q 2:21   What actions are needed in order to give certain transactions the benefits of SEC Rule 16(b)3?

In May 1996, the SEC issued new regulations on this subject. Under SEC Rule 16(b)3, a stock plan qualifies for an exemption to Rule 16(b) if it meets the following criteria: Executives must be granted stock options by a group of non-employee directors. The term "disinterested party" has been changed to "non-employee director"; this new definition excludes former company officers who become outside directors, consultants, lawyers, bankers, and others who earn more than $60,000 from the company, and any person employed by the company who earns more than 5 percent of the gross revenue.

The requirement for shareholder approval has also been eliminated; however, shareholder approval is still required by other regulatory organizations such as the stock exchanges (if stock is part of the plan), and the IRS, which in Code Section 422 requires companies who have incentive stock options to have shareholder approval.

If a stock option plan meets these basic requirements, grants made under the plan to insiders as defined in Section 16(a) will be exempt transactions under Section 16(b) as long as the insider holds the stock security for six months from the date of grant (the purchase event). Thus a stock option granted to an insider is not deemed to be a purchase that will be matched to a sale (Section 16(b) provision) as long the insider does not sell the stock option shares for six months after the grant.

Q 2:22   What are the other clarifications of SEC Section 16(b)3 issued in May 1996?

In addition to the clarifications noted in Q 2:21, the SEC also stated the following:

1. Stock transactions from qualified plans are exempted from Section 16(b) six-month buy/sell matching. A qualified plan is defined as an excess benefit plan or stock purchase plan. An

ERISA excess plan is included in this definition; however, a supplemental 401(k) plan is not included.

2. Cashless exercises for insiders are still not exempt from Section 16(b) buy/sell matching; however, the exercise of an SAR for cash is exempt. This is a glowing inconsistency in that both the cashless exercise and the cash-based SAR produce the same result to the insider. The window period requirement has also been eliminated for insiders. Previously the SEC required insiders to exercise SARs for cash only during the window period, which is the 3rd to 12th working day after release of quarterly earnings.

3. Stock options can now be transferred to children, trusts, and charities by an insider. Previously this was not possible.

4. Exemptions of discretionary transactions have been added to Section 16(b)3. There are four categories of exemptive relief that are just being clarified as this book goes to press.

In summary, the SEC has significantly liberalized its Section 16 regulations. The rationale is that misuse of Section 16(b) and its requirement that insiders be prohibited from making a buy/sell or sell/buy transaction within six months is generally at the expense of the company rather than open market participants, who are the primary group that the SEC is trying to protect.

Proxy Rules

Q 2:23 What are the shareholder proxy and the proxy statement?

A shareholder's proxy authorizes its holder to vote on behalf of the shareholder at the annual shareholders' meeting. In voting "by proxy," the shareholder instructs the company as to how his votes should be recorded on any business issue on the shareholders' meeting agenda, which is mailed to all shareholders in the proxy statement. This proxy method was developed because of the difficulties involved if shareholders had to vote directly on all corporate matters discussed at the annual meeting of shareholders, including the annual election of directors. The Securities Exchange Act of 1934 regulates the solicitation of proxy votes by public companies by requiring that the shareholder be furnished with enough information to make an informed decision on all voting issues. Section 14 of the act specifies that no proxy may be solicited unless it is preceded or accompanied by a proxy statement.

The contents of the proxy statement will vary each year, depending upon the issues to be discussed at the meeting. If a proxy is sought for approval of the election of specified directors, the proxy statement must disclose specific information about them, including their backgrounds, company committee service, and company shares owned. When the company seeks approval for new executive compensation plans, or new or additional shares of stock to be used in executive compensation programs, the proxy statement must include information on the plans being presented for approval (e.g., copies of the plan text, or a version of the current plan with proposed amendments clearly marked). Sample compensation plans presented to shareholders for consideration at an annual meeting are provided in Appendix B at the back of this supplement.

Each national stock exchange (e.g., NYSE, NASDAQ) also requires shareholder approval of any executive compensation plan that will pay awards in stock. Public company shareholders must therefore approve the specific amounts of stock to be used in executive compensation plans. The shares are expressed as a percentage of total shares outstanding.

The annual company proxy statement is also used to disclose compensation paid to the company's most highly compensated officers, and the methods used to determine amount of pay and benefits. Proxy statements also include amounts of compensation and benefits provided to nonemployee outside directors.

Q 2:24   How do the SEC proxy reporting requirements affect executive compensation?

The SEC has issued new reporting rules for companies to use in summarizing executive compensation in proxy statements (see Qs 2:23–2:32). These requirements are generally believed to act as a control on the level of executive compensation. Because disclosures of executive compensation must be made more clear and concise and the reasoning behind executive compensation programs must also be explained in more detail, shareholders could use this information at any time to initiate a court action challenging the amounts and types of compensation provided to executives, just as the IRS can challenge compensation as being unreasonable. Such a shareholder suit could be extremely embarrassing to a corporation, especially when publicized by the media. Shareholder challenges to compensation are actually quite rare, and are almost never successful, since executive compensation levels are determined by a disinterested group of outside, nonemployee directors of the company and the primary holders of company shares of stock are typically pro-management people and/or organizations.

Challenges to executive pay can also come from the media, as they can from a group of dissident shareholders or from hostile takeover groups. The media has, in recent years, developed numerous methods to compare executive compensation pay levels to company performance, and has been quick to point out any inconsistencies. The new SEC proxy recording requirements therefore include specific comparisons of company pay to company performance so that this key relationship is visible and easy to understand.

Tables of the top five executives' pay clearly identify current and historical levels of pay. Details of this information are discussed in Q 2:25. Now, the media and all investors can compare this to company performance charts discussed in Q 2:26. High performance should correlate to increases in pay, while low performance should correlate to no increases in pay. But of even greater significance is that board compensation committees must prepare a narrative explaining the basis for executive pay.

Most believe that this will have a major effect on company outside directors who determine executive compensation, typically those on the company's compensation committee of the board of directors (see Q 2:25), and that they will be much more interested and dutiful in fulfilling their responsibilities for establishing executive pay and benefit levels and programs.

Q 2:25 What is the compensation committee of the board and what role does it play in executive compensation?

The compensation committee is a specially designated committee of nonemployee members of the board of directors who are considered disinterested parties since they do not benefit personally from any compensation decisions by the committee. This is a requirement of the SEC. Board compensation committees typically perform the following types of duties and responsibilities:

1. Approve levels of executive compensation and benefits;

2. Approve executive compensation and benefit programs;

3. Review executive and nonexecutive compensation and benefit policy and program design strategy;

4. Approve individual grants of stock options, including the number of shares, the price per share, the award period, and other similar design issues relevant to stock award plans;

5. Approve the specific type of long-term incentive plan to be used for company executives (e.g., stock options, restricted stock, performance shares).

In fulfilling these responsibilities, members of a compensation committee represent the shareholders in assuring the appropriateness and equity of executive pay and in ensuring that executive compensation programs attract, motivate, and retain executives within the company so that company goals beneficial to shareholders are achieved. In this capacity, board compensation committees are both extremely powerful and function in a "fishbowl," in that all of their decisions are subject to the evaluation, scrutiny, and audit of all shareholders, as well as the media. Moreover, during corporate restructuring, such as a merger, acquisition, or recapitalization, board compensation committees are asked to deal with many difficult compensation issues such as golden parachutes, the disposal of compensation programs that are no longer needed, and maintaining the equity of executive pay plans where only some executives receive buyouts from existing compensation programs. In some cases, they significantly influence the determination of future company ownership via their approval of executive compensation programs that involve equity/ownership in the company. As a result, in recent years many board compensation committees have turned more extensively to survey data and outside compensation consultants in order to enhance their contribution to executive compensation decisions.

An example of this from an actual company proxy statement is as follows:

Example. The compensation for the top five officers consists of base salary, annual bonus, long-term bonus, share options, and other benefits. Studies are conducted periodically by an outside consulting firm of 24 companies in the electronics field, 19 of which are in the S&P Electronic Subgroup Index shown in the performance graph on the previous page. This study uses regression analysis techniques that relate our company's size and performance to those in other companies, and the compensation committee considers the results of these studies in determining appropriate compensation levels for the CEO.

Q 2:26 What are the regulatory base and effective dates for the SEC proxy reporting rules of 1993?

The 1993 SEC proxy reporting rules are contained in revisions to Item 402 of Regulation S-K of the Securities Exchange Act of 1934 and to the registration statements under the Securities Act of 1933. These revisions were approved for use with any new registration statement under the Securities Act filed on or after January 1, 1993, and on any new proxy statement filed after January 1, 1993, except that proxy or information statements filed with respect to the annual election of directors by registrants whose current fiscal year ends on or after December 15, 1992, are required to comply with the new provisions whenever filed. Small businesses (less than $25 million) are required to comply with the new rules for any new 1933 Act registration statement, any new 1934 Act registration statement or periodic report, and any new proxy or information statement filed on or after May 1, 1993.

Q 2:27 What disclosure information charts must now be included with proxy statements?

These new SEC rules modify the compensation disclosure rules by establishing new charts on the top five company executives to be recorded in proxy statements. These charts are:

1. A summary chart of base salary, annual bonus, stock awards, other forms of long-term income, and other annual compensation (i.e., the cost of providing perquisites and personal benefits, tax gross-ups, discounts on purchases of company stock, and any other preferential interest or dividend payments provided to executives). This information must cover the top five executives for the past three years.

2. A table on stock option/SAR grants made during the last fiscal year. While this essentially repeats some of the information in the summary compensation table, its coverage is more extensive. Companies are required to estimate the future value of stock options either by using assumptions of company stock appreciation at both 5 and 10 percent yearly increases in value over the term of the option, or by using another recognized option evaluation technique such as the Black-Scholes method (see Q 5:26). A similar table is to be provided for long-term incentive plans (performance units/performance share plans) showing the number of shares, the performance period, and estimated future payouts using threshold, target, and maximum payout levels.

3. A special table on the aggregated stock option/SARs exercised during the last fiscal year for each of the five executives. This table is to include the number of shares acquired or exercised during the last fiscal year, the actual value realized by the individual executive, the number of unexercised options or SAR shares at the end of the fiscal year, and the number and value of both exercisable and nonexercisable shares at the end of the fiscal year.

4. A table of estimated retirement benefits for the executives named in the summary compensation table. This table is also to show annual retirement benefits payable to executives at various levels of credited earnings under the company's qualified pension plan, and to indicate whether supplemental retirement plans are provided to participating executives (the top five and the other levels represented). The respective years of service credited for pension plan purposes to each of the top five executives is also to be designated.

Q 2:28   What other executive compensation information must be disclosed in the proxy statement?

Executive compensation information that must be disclosed in the proxy statement includes the following:

1. The compensation committee of the board must submit a report indicating the members of the committee and discussing the committee's strategies in determining executive compensation and benefits, including the extent to which such compensation is performance-related and the performance measures considered. Specifically, this portion of the proxy statement must include a discussion of the CEO's compensation, and how the specific level of pay and benefits for this position was established by the committee. The specific stock or long-term incentive awards provided to the CEO and the rationale for these awards is also to be included in this report.

2. Compensation committee "interlocks" are also to be disclosed. Interlocks are members of the compensation committee who also serve as a partner of a major company supplier, law firm, or financial institution, or a CEO of another company for which the company CEO serves on the Board compensation committee.

3. A performance graph must be prepared comparing the company's total shareholder return against a performance indicator of the overall stock market as published by the Standard & Poor's 500 index or other similar index. A second performance graph is also to be prepared, comparing total shareholder return for that company against a selected group of peer companies, again using some form of recognized industry index or similar published index relevant to that company's industry or line of business. Total shareholder return is generally understood to mean stock price appreciation plus dividends paid during each fiscal year shown by the graph. These graphs are to reflect the five-year cumulative shareholder return.

4. Employment contracts and arrangements are to be discussed for the company CEO and other top four executives shown in the proxy statement. This includes special severance or change of control agreements for these executives, as well as special severance benefits to other key management employees.

5. Pay of outside directors is to be summarized in the proxy statement, although individual director amounts need not be specified. Director fees, retainers, stock awards, retirement plans, deferral arrangements, and even charitable/legacy programs are included in this section of the proxy statement.

6. An option/SAR repricing report on all executives included in the proxy statement must be provided. This describes the events triggering the option repricing, the options currently being repriced, and similar actions taken during the last 120 months, and includes a ten-year option/SAR table showing the name, date, number of option/SARs repriced, market price at the time of repricing, exercise price at the time of repricing, new exercise price, and length of the original option term remaining on the date of repricing. Obviously, the SEC is trying to discourage companies from repricing stock options and SARs, since this alternative is not available to other shareholders.

These new SEC executive compensation reporting rules are likely to drive a number of design changes in company executive compensation programs, particularly annual incentives (see Chapter 4) and long-term incentives (see Chapters 5 through 8).

Q 2:29 How should public companies determine the future value of stock options and its effect on executive compensation?

In response to the new SEC proxy reporting rules, approximately 60 percent of all companies project stock growth at 5 to 10 percent per year during the option award period using an SEC-suggested method. The remaining 40 percent of all companies use the Black-Scholes option pricing model (see Q 5:26).

These stock growth projections serve only to predict the future compensation of the top five executives in the company. The stock appreciation actually realized by the executives when they complete a purchase and subsequent sale of the stock options can be unpredictable. Historically, some companies have had no stock growth over the entire stock award period, while other companies have had 100 percent or greater growth.

Despite the difficulty of projecting stock growth, public companies should recognize that the new SEC regulations give them reason to weight the top executives' total compensation package in favor of stock options or similar stock grants. If future compensation of top executives is related to stock growth (whatever that growth may be), then there will be little media criticism of executive compensation because as the executive gains from stock appreciation so does the shareholder.

Q 2:30   How can companies reduce negative media/ shareholder reaction to major stock option exercises by executives in years when company earnings are flat or down from previous years?

The following alternatives are available:

1. Communicate the importance of stock option exercise timing to the executive. Prior to the 1990s, the timing of stock option exercises was rarely an issue in executive compensation administration because CEO compensation was neither a major topic of media analysis, discussion, and articles nor as available for public scrutiny. Companies must now sensitize executives to and train them on this issue. While this alternative places new requirements on the executive, it allows more positive acceptance and cooperation from the media and more responsiveness from executives.

2. Establish minimum exercise provisions for each stock option grant. Assume that an executive receives a 10,000-share stock option grant. The stock options vest 20 percent per year or 100 percent after five years, and the award period of the stock option is ten years. A company could require the executive to exercise a minimum of 20 percent of those stock option shares each year from Year 6 through Year 10.

3. Require approval by a board compensation committee (see Q 2:25) on all stock option exercises by the company's top five executives. This will obviously serve to increase executive focus on the issue of stock option timing, although it does take away flexibility.

4. Provide more flexible post-termination/retirement exercise provisions for the top five executives. A company could allow a

retiring executive to exercise vested stock options for a three-to five-year period after retirement, at which point the exercise transaction would not be included in company proxies.

Q 2:31   How will the new requirement for a company performance comparison graph affect the amount of executive compensation awarded?

The new SEC proxy reporting rules call for the development of a performance graph that compares company stock performance to a broad index of stock growth in other companies and stock perform-ance of a relevant peer group (see Q 2:28). Company stock perform-ance graphs have an even greater impact than the stock growth charts. If the graphs show low company stock performance relative to the broad market or peer group index, any increases in total cash compensation (salary plus bonus) or in total compensation (total cash plus long-term incentive) could raise numerous questions from shareholders and the media. Therefore, companies must ensure that there is a correlation between the stock performance graphs and actual total cash compensation provided and reported on the top five executives in each year's annual proxy. For example, if a stock performance graph shows a 5 percent decline in the company's position, actual total cash compensation should also show some decline from the previous year, or the company's board compensa-tion committee should provide a good reason why lower compensa-tion should not follow lower performance. This would be the logic of the shareholders, media people, and other investors who review company stock performance graphs.

This issue is of critical importance, and many board compensation committees will want to analyze the graphs each time they are asked to make key executive compensation decisions. These regulations could further be a catalyst toward improving the correlation of executive compensation and performance in public companies.

Q 2:32   How have the new SEC proxy reporting rules generally changed the treatment of executive compensation?

Company proxies show full compliance by public companies to these new proxy reporting rules. The following results are obvious from reading and reviewing these proxies:

1. The purpose and business value is confirmed for each element of executive compensation, and the company's total compensation strategy (see also Chapter 11) is clarified.

2. Board compensation committee members have increased their involvement in the review and approval of executive compensation and benefit programs. Communication among those who develop and administer executive compensation programs within the company, outside consultants who advise the company, and board compensation committee members has created a clear rationale for executive compensation programs as displayed in 1993 proxies to date.

3. Company performance measures have been evaluated and confirmed; moreover, their use in executive compensation programs is very clear since the performance graphs required by the new proxy rules put a definite focus on the comparison of executive pay versus company performance as measured in total shareholder return.

4. More frequent monitoring of executive compensation programs by company management and board compensation committee members is expected to occur during the year to ensure that the pay for performance comparisons reported in the proxy are being followed and achieved within the company. Any increase in executive compensation when company stock price and/or performance decreases would produce a significant negative shareholder and media response.

5. The company strategies developed for the executive pay programs must have continuity and staying power; board compensation committee members will not be willing to make constant program changes each year, simply because these changes have to be explained in the proxy.

It is clear that the new proxy reporting rules, and subsequent access to the details of public company executive compensation programs, will be a major factor in executive compensation program design for many years to come.

Chapter 3

Base Salary

Base salary represents the single largest element of the total compensation package, which consists of salary, annual and long-term incentives, benefits, and perquisites. Base salary is still the principal method of compensating executives. Because annual and long-term incentives are frequently developed as a percentage of base salary, an inappropriate base salary can have a compounding effect on the total executive pay plan. From a business standpoint, the ideal base salary is the one that, at the lowest cost to the company, leaves the executive in a posture of aggressive contentment—content enough not to seek other opportunities, but aggressive in the desire to earn the incentive portions of the total compensation package. This chapter provides information on how companies establish internally equitable and externally competitive base salaries.

Establishing Base Salary	3-2
Job Evaluation	3-3
Salary Increases	3-9
Salary Banding; Other Increases	3-10

Establishing Base Salary

Q 3:1   How is an executive's base salary set?

Base salary is the amount of fixed cash compensation that is paid to an executive on a periodic basis that represents income that is not at risk. The board of directors of the company typically sets the base salary of the chief executive officer (CEO) using market data obtained by the board. There is a growing tendency, because of board liability concerns, to use outside consultants to provide competitive compensation data from several independent sources for this purpose as well. The company's compensation specialist frequently collects all such appropriate competitive practices information.

The other executive salaries are normally established by the CEO, who may or may not present this information for approval to the board of directors. The CEO receives the market data and either formally or informally reviews the executive's performance.

Q 3:2   How do companies decide on salaries or salary ranges for executives?

Two approaches are typically used to peg the value of an executive position. Internal equity is determined by some form of job evaluation process and attempts, without any external reference, to determine which executive positions have more value to the corporation. External equity is determined by some method of data collection to establish what similar companies are paying for similar positions. The process of establishing external equity is referred to as market pricing. These two approaches, which are generally used in combination, often give conflicting rankings of positions and therefore act to counterbalance each other. Using either formal statistical techniques or a more subjective management decision process, a dollar value range is then assigned to each executive position. Typically, clusters of similarly valued positions are assigned to one salary range.

It is important to note, however, that in some industries base salary may be set at significantly lower levels than indicated by either the internal or external equity approach (see Q 3:10). Where this is the case, bonuses are often used to compensate for the variance (see Chapters 4 and 5).

Job Evaluation

Q 3:3 What is job evaluation?

Job evaluation is the process that establishes a position's internal relative worth to a company by measuring a position's duties against a predetermined yardstick. Job evaluation measures job worth in an internal sense rather than in an economic or social one.

A company establishes the economic worth of a position by looking outside the organization to see what the market is paying for a position; social worth is a function of the external perception of the importance of the contributions of a specific person or occupation. The internal concept of job worth involves the scope of responsibility or difficulty of assignments. Market worth, social worth, and internal value are not identical and may not correlate.

This lack of correlation is one of the difficulties of job evaluation. As a result, there are hundreds of different methods of job evaluation, and all of them measure job responsibilities against a different pre-established yardstick. They differ in (1) whether they measure the whole job or elements of the job and (2) how they assign values to the steps on the yardstick.

The four basic approaches to job evaluation are:

- Ranking system
- Classification system
- Point evaluation
- Factor comparison system

Q 3:4 How does the ranking system work?

In this approach, the chief company executive, usually with the help of the chief human resource executive, simply ranks one executive position against another. The CEO compares the two positions

Chart 3-1. Job Evaluation Methodology for Executives

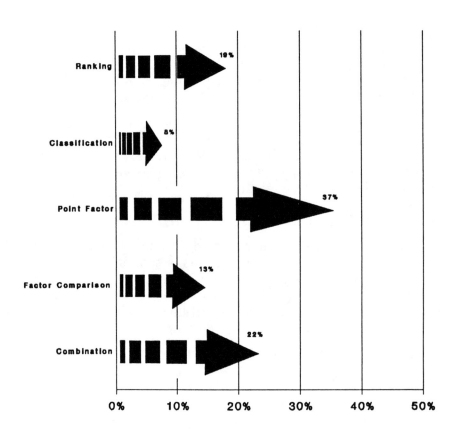

Source: Miller Mason & Dickenson, 1991

and decides which is more difficult or important. A third position is compared to the first two and so on until all jobs have been ranked. The advantage and disadvantage of this approach is its simplicity.

Q 3:5 How does a classification system work?

In a classification system, each job is measured against a predetermined scale whose various categories define the overall value of the positions. The CEO, or a committee of company employees, typically compares each job against the scale and assigns each executive position to the grade that best describes the position.

Q 3:6 How does the point factor approach work?

The point factor system, which is the most widely used approach to job evaluation, measures a position against a series of factors (e.g., administrative responsibility, technical expertise, financial impact), with each factor having a scale of points for the degree that each applies to a specific job. A company can choose the degrees for each factor and assign points on a scale based on relative value to the company. The scale defines values and degrees of each factor. Many companies use plans developed by consulting firms that have predetermined factors and factor values for each degree.

Example. One such plan assesses the following job factors:

1. *Administrative Responsibility.* Degree of managerial responsibility over people and/or business functions, and the degree of human relations knowledge required in the job
2. *Technical Expertise.* Depth and breadth of skill and knowledge of a business function(s) required in the job
3. *Financial Impact.* Magnitude of the impact that the job has on company operations

The first factor, administrative responsibility, is assigned factor degrees as follows:

Independence of Action	*Scope of Management*				
	Minor Individual Contributor	*Moderate Department Level*	*Diverse Multi- Department*	*Complex Multi- Function*	*Corporate Management*
1. Follows established procedures	30	60	90	120	150
2. Wide variety of decisions	60	90	120	150	180
3. Decides from general policies	90	120	150	180	210
4. Complex problems requiring creative judgment	120	150	180	210	240

Q 3:7   How does factor comparison work?

The factor comparison job evaluation approach is similar to the point factor approach except that it ranks positions based on selected factors, without definitions or values for the various degrees. The CEO would analyze and rank all positions in terms of one factor, then all positions in terms of the second factor. Only after all positions are evaluated are the points assigned for each factor. The points are added to get the positions' overall relative value.

Example. The following chart highlights the same job factors as in Q 3:6, but rather than assigning factor degrees, the company assigns points as follows:

Points	*Factor*		
	Administrative Responsibilities	*Technical Expert*	*Financial Impact*
60	Research Fellow	—	—
90	—	—	Research Fellow
120	Director Finance	Director Finance	—
150	—	VP Marketing	Director Finance
180	VP Marketing	Research Fellow	VP Marketing

Q 3:8   How do companies establish labor market values for executive positions?

Market pricing is the name of the process used by companies to value the "outside" or labor market value of executives. Companies can use labor market comparisons either to establish the value of points used in a job evaluation plan or simply to value executive jobs directly from the market pricing process. Pricing executive positions is a critical activity. The first step in this process is for a company to establish a list of competitive companies by determining the previous employers of current company executives and determining the companies that provide similar products and/or services (see Q 1:11).

The next step is to establish a match between the responsibilities of the company's executive positions and the responsibilities of similar positions in competitor companies. This process will be kept manageable by using market pricing only for "benchmark jobs" (jobs that are common to most companies, easy to define, and represent various company functions and organization levels). Matches should not be based on job titles and will rarely reflect education and experience for executive jobs. (For non-executive jobs, education and experience can, however, be very relevant. For example, in major job families like engineers, research associates, or accountants, base salary surveys will frequently show a direct relationship between salary and level of education and number of years of experience. This is not used for executive jobs because the more relevant factor that drives the value of a job is the degree of responsibility.) When matching executive jobs, the key six to eight major responsibilities in each executive position should be identified, with matching positions having at least 75 percent of the same responsibilities. Data should be collected on base salary and annual incentives (i.e., total cash compensation) for each of these positions.

Many surveys are available for use in market pricing positions. A number of companies also conduct their own customized surveys throughout competitor companies to establish the labor market value of executive positions. It is important to note, as well, that a company's compensation philosophy may affect market pricing. For example, if a company has a high-growth, high-risk pay philosophy and views its labor market as "leadership" or "innovative" companies, then this could affect the selection of competitor companies.

Once labor market data is gathered, companies use it to either value job evaluation points and then convert points to a salary range or they use the data directly in establishing a salary range for each position.

Q 3:9 How do most companies position their executive base salary and annual incentive against labor market competitors?

Once a company has "market priced" total cash compensation, (see Q 3:8), it must decide on a market value from the survey. Consider a CEO salary survey of five companies:

Company	Base Salary	Annual Incentive	Total Cash Compensation
A	$180,000	45%	$261,000
B	$170,000	50%	$255,000
C	$230,000	35%	$310,500
D	$200,000	40%	$280,000
E	$220,000	40%	$308,000

The median base salary is $200,000, while the median total cash compensation is $280,000.

It is not appropriate to determine a company's base salary position without considering annual incentive because some competitors may structure their compensation packages differently; for instance, some companies pay a lower base but higher bonus than competitors, and vice versa. This can be countered by establishing the position of both pay elements at the same time; this is usually done by using the median survey base salary to establish a company's salary range midpoint and the median survey annual incentive to establish the company's target annual incentive. The company must decide how competitive its executive compensation should be with the median survey amounts. If the median (50th percentile) survey data are not consistent with the company's pay philosophy, then another market value should be utilized (see also Q 3:12).

Q 3:10 Are there reasons for paying base salaries above or below a competitive average?

Yes. If an executive's base salary is 10 percent above or below the average competitive base salary as reported in a salary survey, then that executive's base salary is competitive. The best survey data are accurate at plus or minus 10 percent, and most companies establish salary ranges for executives that are plus or minus 20 percent from competitive data to allow for performance and job tenure differences among executives.

A company may need to pay a high base salary if it has no annual incentive or long-term incentive plans. If other aspects of a company make it unattractive as an employer, it may have to pay a premium base salary. For example, if the company is experiencing financial difficulties or if it is in a geographically isolated area, it may have to pay a premium to attract executives. A company in a slow- or no-growth environment may have to pay a premium to compensate for limited career promotion opportunities.

The other extreme of high base-paying companies are high-growth companies that offer low base salaries in exchange for substantial long-term compensation and career movement opportunities. In high-growth companies, promotions and promotional salary adjustment can compensate for lower competitive salaries.

Salary Increases

Q 3:11 Do merit increases motivate executives?

Some companies have concluded that merit increases do not motivate executives. This is a recent trend. The logic behind this conclusion is that executives are motivated instead by annual and long-term incentives, which can be substantial in comparison with the standard merit increase of 4 or 5 percent.

As a first step in implementing this concept, companies establish equity in the base salaries of their executives (a one-time salary adjustment may be necessary to achieve this). They then provide annual salary adjustments to all executives equal to the average annual increase (if any) in executive salary ranges.

Other companies have eliminated annual base pay increases altogether and added their equivalent value to the targeted or potential amount of the annual incentive. These companies will provide a general adjustment to base salaries, but this will be a discretionary amount every two to three years.

Q 3:12   How can companies reduce the inflationary impact of annual base salary increases?

Most companies do not like to be perceived as average in the way they pay executives. Thus a number of companies pay at the 75th percentile of labor market competitors (see Q 3:9). This compensation strategy creates two significant problems. One obvious problem is that many companies are paying more than is necessary. The second problem is less obvious: as more companies pay at the 75th percentile, the median salary increases, and companies chase an ever-increasing target. This can be circumvented by the following actions:

1. Pay below the 75th percentile of competitors.
2. Pay all executives an "economic" increase approximately equal to the average salary range adjustment and then allow for a "merit" increase to 20 percent of the executive population (one of five employees, i.e., high performers).
3. Use "lump sum" merit increases (that are not added to base salary but paid as a one-time bonus) periodically in lieu of regular merit increases.
4. Establish an "expected level of performance" for executives in the merit increase plan and communicate to them that the merit increase norm is that associated with the expected level of performance. Such terminology (normal increase rather than average increase) is easier to communicate and more flattering.

Salary Banding; Other Increases

Q 3:13   Are there alternatives to base salary ranges and merit pay for executives?

Yes. Two new ideas have been implemented in a number of large, progressive companies: range banding and economic pay increases.

Range Banding. Range banding represents the combining of two or more salary ranges into a broader range or "band." The banding of executive job classifications produces fewer and broader salary ranges or bands. Bands are different from salary ranges in that they include a number of executive jobs and job families and they do not have a midpoint, only minimums and maximums.

Companies use banding to enhance the career mobility of executives. Banding allows for lateral job movement of executives within the company (thus supporting career development moves) and puts less emphasis on single incumbent job equity. Annual or group incentives, long-term incentives, and perquisites can also be the same for a given band, which may facilitate administration. Another advantage of banding is that executive teamwork is easier to achieve, because many executives are in the same salary range, rather than in different or competing salary ranges.

The disadvantage of banding is that it can be difficult to determine which executive jobs to assign to one band. Numerous jobs must be assigned, and labor market information on the value of an executive job to the company can frequently indicate that one job would be very low in one band or very high in another band. Another disadvantage to banding is that it requires strong performance management systems, because typical salary administration guides are not as meaningful (e.g., midpoints, merit increase guides).

Economic Pay Increases. Under this salary program, merit pay and salary ranges are eliminated. A job rate is established for each executive job. The concept and strategy is that executives should not be in training for their jobs, and therefore broad salary ranges are not necessary. The market rate for the executive job is the executive's job rate. Salary increases are given annually equal to some economic factor such as the average increase in the overall labor market. Executives are motivated and challenged to achieve company business objectives through other executive compensation programs such as short- and long-term incentives. The advantage of the economic pay increase is that executives can be more objective in determining budgets and salary increases for nonexecutive employees, since executives are not included in the merit increase program. Moreover, administrative effort by managers and human resource staff is significantly reduced. The disadvantage is that executive salaries have little upward movement under an economic pay increase system, other than promotions.

Q 3:14 What are some positive company experiences with salary banding?

This idea is becoming prevalent. Most surveys will indicate that 20 to 35 percent of surveyed companies are using broad banding. Positive experiences indicate that, where implemented, the concept results in greater employee focus on career development, and it encourages broader skill/managerial development by executives in order to enhance their salary growth within the band. Executives in particular respond to the less-structured environment and flexibility that surround the use of broad bands, in that they place more emphasis on performance measurement (i.e., goal setting and goal evaluation) within the annual bonus plan (variable pay), rather than merit pay (fixed pay). This is beneficial to both the executive and the company.

The banding concept seems to work best in organizations that are going through a cultural change, or a change in strategic direction, because this new approach to salary administration is a tool for the company to use in effecting change.

Example. Company A has consolidated three divisions into two divisions and has sold a fourth division. In addition, the company has offered all employees a one-time special early retirement program, which was accepted by some executives. A number of executive jobs have had significant changes in responsibilities. In response to these facts, the company has updated all executive job descriptions and has replaced current salary ranges with salary bands that group numerous executive jobs into the same band. The impact of this action will be to:

1. Reduce executive concern over whether new job responsibilities are higher or lower in the hierarchy of executive jobs

2. Increase the company's ability to modify executive job responsibilities after the restructuring (due to continuing changes in the strategic direction of the business) without affecting the status or hierarchy of executive job grades, since most future changes will not affect the executive's assigned salary band

Q 3:15 What are some negative company experiences with salary banding?

On the negative side, some organizations are not ready for the renewed focus on performance management that is associated with broad banding. The wider salary ranges associated with salary banding require new definitions of promotions and new merit increase guidelines. Executives therefore need to be trained in these new policies.

There is also a requirement for new methods for market pricing jobs (see Q 3:8), because many jobs are grouped into one salary band rather than individual salary ranges. Career paths for executives must be analyzed before companies determine the number of salary bands.

Salary bands have not faced any test of time; that is, banding has not yet been used over an extended period. One concern is that with fewer promotions (which means fewer base pay increases) and ongoing inflation (which keeps the bands increasing), executives will not be able to progress through the salary band. Some companies would not view this as a problem; however, their executives may not agree.

A final negative is the question of "if there is not any problem with current salary ranges, then why change to salary bands"?

Example. A company is going through a cultural change from a paternalistic environment to a risk-oriented environment. It decides to implement salary bands for its executive jobs.

After all jobs are assigned to a new salary band, the company finds the need to define future promotions. It separates each executive band into four segments; however, the previous number of salary ranges in each band equaled four. Each salary band segment is similar to one of the former salary ranges! Has the company really changed its salary ranges?

Q 3:16 What have been company experiences with economic pay increases?

This idea is not as prevalent as salary banding. Only a few companies have tried using economic increases, with some positive results:

1. When economic pay increases are used only for executives, and merit pay increases are used only for nonexecutives, the executives do a better job of administering merit pay systems for nonexecutives, simply because executives do not participate in the merit pay system.

2. Because economic pay systems do not require goals, the focus of each executive's effort is more clear, because the executive does not have merit pay goals and annual incentive plan goals.

On the negative side, where economic pay increases are used, human resource departments are "pressured" to establish higher job rates for executive positions, and to establish high annual economic pay increases.

Chapter 4

Annual Incentives

The vast majority of companies provide annual incentive opportunities to their executive management team. While base salary remains the largest fixed element of an executive compensation package, the value of annual incentives to the total cash compensation package is growing. Companies use annual incentives to reward executives when company and/or individual performance meets company expectations. Key issues in the development of an annual incentive plan include the degree to which executive, business unit, or company performance determine annual incentive payout and the measures used to evaluate individual executive, business unit, and/or company performance. This chapter provides a comprehensive overview of annual incentive plans and addresses why companies use annual incentives, the types of incentive plans, the strengths and weaknesses of frequently used plans, and alternative solutions to the various incentive plan design issues.

General Considerations   4-2

Plan Design   4-10

Performance Measures   4-23

Performance Standards   4-30

Funding Incentive Plans   4-33

General Considerations

Q 4:1   How is short-term or annual incentive defined?

Annual incentive is a term that is frequently used interchangeably with short-term incentive. Short-term or annual incentive is usually defined as an incentive paid for performance over no more than one year. Short-term incentives can measure performance, and be paid over periods less than one year, e.g., quarterly or semi-monthly, depending upon company planning cycles. For example, the retail and advertising industries use short-term objectives of three to six months; however, short-term incentives (and total cash compensation) are usually measured over a fiscal year. Usually these programs pay out the earned amount in cash (some companies pay all or part in stock).

Short-term incentive plans can be formal or informal. If they are informal, there may be no written plan and no predetermined funding method or participant allocation rules. Some companies prefer not to establish a formal annual incentive plan and instead simply have a policy of paying out bonuses annually that are based on the company's performance, without any predetermined funding method or participant allocation rules. This allows a company, within the context of overall firm performance, to provide incentives and rewards to executives based on their own individual performance. The informal method is most often recommended for small companies where the cost of creating a formal program is not justified. However, an informal plan is also appropriate for any company that feels that flexibility is necessary to retain valued executives by increasing their proportionate reward, and by small companies that want to provide "contingent remuneration" (i.e., compensation that varies and is based on performance).

Most short-term incentive plans are designed to produce a payout for an executive that is either a specified percentage of base salary or a percentage of a total target amount to be paid if company objectives are met.

A typical annual incentive plan would provide incentive opportunities that vary by job level:

CEO	40–60 percent
VP	25–35 percent
Others	20 percent

The highest percentage potential is given to the highest ranking executive: He or she is assumed to have the most responsibility for ensuring that the company achieves its annual objectives. From a company perspective, it is desirable to have a higher amount of total cash compensation "at risk" and subject to performance achievement for the higher level executive. This is known as bonus progressivity (i.e., bonus amounts for executives progress higher as job responsibility increases). This is also desirable because higher level executives can make decisions that directly affect company success. Therefore, their total cash compensation should be contingent upon the success of these decisions (i.e., pay for performance).

The payment for short-term incentives is usually made at the close of the plan cycle. Voluntary or mandatory deferral is, however, occasionally used for all or part of the earned amount.

Q 4:2   How prevalent are annual incentive plans?

The vast majority of companies have an annual incentive plan. Industry surveys usually report that approximately 90 percent of companies surveyed (both large and small companies) have an annual incentive plan. Those few companies that do not have incentive plans believe that base salary (and performance-based salary adjustments) can effectively distinguish between levels of performance. Compensation surveys show that while base salaries are somewhat higher in non-bonus companies, the additional money does not compensate for the lack of an incentive opportunity.

Q 4:3   What is the rationale for having an annual incentive plan?

Most companies have an annual incentive plan in order to motivate executives to achieve annual company operating goals. A second reason for incentive pay, especially for companies with relatively small revenue, is that these plans make a part of the executive payroll a variable cost. The total cost of these payments can be a significant part of after-tax profits.

Another rationale for having annual incentive plans is that if executives can make decisions and judgments that affect company results for the year, then it makes sense for these executives to have a significant part of their current earnings dependent upon the achievement of these results.

A final, important, reason for having an annual incentive plan is to offer competitive compensation programs that can attract and retain executives. With over 90 percent of companies offering executives annual incentives, a company would be at a recruiting disadvantage without such a program. It is interesting to note, however, that while executives in the recruitment situation seem to be concerned about the existence of a program, they rarely question how much the plan paid out in the past, perhaps because of the expectation that such plans will pay off in the future.

Planning Tip. Because incentive plans can lose their effectiveness over time, plans should have a three-year expiration cycle. Every three years participation, performance goals, and payout should be reviewed and the necessary modifications or revisions made. Otherwise, plans tend to continue without reassessment or revision.

Q 4:4 How is eligibility in annual incentive plans typically determined?

Participation should be limited to those individuals who can substantially affect the performance measures used in the annual incentive plan. In practice, the eligibility levels of competitive organizations is often the deciding factor. If it is perceived that a position would be incentive-eligible in other companies, a company will often make it eligible for the incentive plan in order to establish annual incentive plan eligibility practices parallel to those in competitive organizations.

Incentive plan eligibility is typically expressed as a percentage of total employment. This percentage varies from 1 percent or less in very large companies, to up to 10 percent in very small companies.

There is an inverse relationship with respect to annual incentive plan eligibility: As company size increases, the percentage of executives in an annual incentive plan decreases. For example, the number of executives (as a percentage of total employment) eligible for annual incentive payments in a company with $100 million of sales will be approximately 5 percent; however, the number of executives (as a percentage of total employment) with annual incentive plan eligibility in a company with $1 billion of sales would be approximately 1 percent. This is because the number of executives (as a percentage of total employment) who can influence annual business results is greater in a small company where there are fewer organizational levels, fewer business systems, and less overall structure.

Companies also use a number of other factors to determine eligibility in an annual incentive plan. These include: base salary, job level, reporting relationship, job title, or any combination of these.

More specific techniques used to establish eligibility include:

1. Requiring senior executives to recommend jobs that they judge to be "critical" to business success;

2. Establishing a targeted award level for all management positions and a maximum pool of target award dollars that can be utilized by each department executive, and requiring each department executive to recommend eligibility up to the maximum amount of the target award pool; and

3. Using one of the previous factors (e.g., job level, reporting relationship, title) and allowing each recommending executive to add up to an additional 10 percent to the initial eligibility list.

Whatever method is used for determining eligibility, one consequence is certain: Eligibility will increase over time. There are few, if any, documented instances of companies where annual incentive plan eligibility has gone down.

Q 4:5 Which forms of payment are typically used in an annual incentive plan?

Annual incentive awards are paid in cash, stock, or some combination of the two. Cash awards are the most common, although a number of small companies will use stock, particularly where cash is scarce.

The issue of deferral is an important consideration in determining the form of payout. There are voluntary and mandatory deferrals. Most mandatory deferrals are short-term, while voluntary deferrals can be both short- and long-term. The following are examples of mandatory deferral:

Example 1. A $12,000 annual incentive award is earned by an executive, for whom one of two mandatory deferral schedules is arranged: $4,000 is paid in the year earned, $4,000 is paid after one year, and $4,000 after two years. This method allows the company to meet retention or "golden handcuff" objectives. Executives do not usually favor such a mandatory deferral method since, in their view, the annual incentive must be "earned twice."

Example 2. In the second case, the deferral schedule calls for $6,000 to be paid in cash and $6,000 to be provided in the form of restricted stock, with one-half of the shares vesting after one year and the other half vesting after two years. This alternative has the advantage of making the executive a stockholder; the arrangement could also call for 100 percent of the restricted shares to be vested upon any involuntary termination in order to avoid the inference that such an award must be earned twice.

Voluntary deferral can be arranged in any number of ways. For example, the executive might arrange for regular installment payments to commence after a designated deferral period. This could provide an excellent means of funding a known future expense such as a child's college education. An annual incentive award might also be deferred until retirement, allowing an executive to build supplemental retirement funds. Here are some examples of voluntary deferral:

Example 1. An executive wishes to defer annual bonus earned during the upcoming fiscal year. An irrevocable election form is signed by the executive asking the company to defer any earned amounts for five years (which happens to be when the executive's oldest child will start college). A $12,000 bonus is earned, and the company advises the executive, then has the executive choose, from a number of alternatives, one or more funds where the deferred amount is invested during the deferral period.

Example 2. An executive wishes to defer annual bonus earned during the upcoming year until retirement. The same procedure is followed as described in Example 1, except that the deferral period is until the executive's retirement. This is known as a voluntary long-term deferral. In contrast, Example 1 is a voluntary short-term deferral.

When deferrals are permitted as part of any annual incentive plan, the form of payment and the method of deferral must be specified in accordance with the doctrine of constructive receipt, outlined in Qs 5:39 and 5:40. Most deferrals as described in this question represent unfunded liabilities for a company, meaning that the company acknowledges its obligation to pay the deferred amounts per the executive's deferral agreement. If the company goes into bankruptcy, however, these deferred funds are available to creditors. For this reason, some companies will establish secular trusts to secure the payment of deferred funds. (See Qs 9:22 and 9:23.)

A similar situation exists if a company is sold. The new owner may decide to cancel deferred funds. For this reason, many companies will establish a rabbi trust to secure the promise to pay these funds in the future. (See Q 9:23.)

Q 4:6 Are annual incentive plan payments pensionable compensation?

Most surveys will show that at least two-thirds of all companies, large or small, include annual incentive plan payments as pensionable compensation in qualified or nonqualified retirement plan packages. Total cash compensation (base salary plus annual incentive) tends to be used by executives to establish a basic standard of living; therefore, any pension amount should be a percentage of total cash compensation.

Q 4:7 What is the tax impact of annual incentive plans on the executive?

For a cash-basis company, annual cash incentive payments are deductible as and when the payments are actually made to the employee. For an accrual-basis company, amounts paid in cash to employees are deductible as and when the obligation to make the payments accrues (that is, when the liability for payment is fixed and definite and not subject to indeterminable future events). An exception to this rule is made for the deduction of bonus payments by accrual-basis companies, if a full or partial payment is made up to 2½ months prior to the end of the fiscal year. This is an important factor for a company to consider, particularly if substantial amounts of annual incentives are paid, because if a company can take a tax deduction in the year in which the annual incentive amounts have been accrued, it can not only reduce the amount of taxes paid in that year but it will further improve its cash flow position.

Executives recognize income from annual bonus payments in the year in which payment is received. For example, if an executive defers an annual incentive compensation plan, there is no taxable event until the deferral period has expired (provided the deferral was made in compliance with constructive receipt; see Q 9:53). Whenever an executive defers income under these circumstances, the company cannot take a tax deduction until the year in which the payment is received.

Planning Tip. Companies need to consider the cost effect of allowing executives to defer annual incentive amounts earned. Accounting regulations require that annual incentives be booked as an expense when they are earned; however, for purposes of calculating the company's taxes, a deduction cannot be taken for these annual incentive amounts until they are paid.

Annual incentive compensation must also comply with Internal Revenue Service regulations on reasonableness (see Qs 1:31 and 1:32). Companies cannot use annual incentive compensation as a disguised distribution of profits or they lose the deductibility of these payments.

Q 4:8 What is the accounting treatment for annual incentive plans?

Like salaries, cash incentive payments are typically accrued as expenses for the accounting period in which the related services are performed. For example, annual incentive compensation payment amounts are charged to the income statement in the year in which they are earned.

Any accrued but unpaid incentive payments are shown in the liability section of the balance sheet. For example, a company using an incentive compensation plan must accrue these expenses each year on the income statement and then transfer this future liability to the balance sheet, if not fully earned in one fiscal year.

> **Example.** An executive is provided with a short-term incentive compensation opportunity of $20,000 to be earned over a 12-month period. The company will be required to accrue one-quarter of this targeted amount ($5,000) each quarter on the income statement. At the end of the year, $20,000 will have been accrued on its income statement. Any difference between what has been accrued and what is actually paid is reconciled. Had the incentive award period in this example been 15 months rather than 12 months, then the company would have accrued one-fifth of the targeted award, or $4,000 each quarter. At the end of the fiscal year (four quarters), $16,000 would have been accrued, and this amount is then transferred to the liability section of the balance sheet. In Year 2, an additional $4,000 is charged to the income statement and the balance sheet. Upon payment of the incentive amount in Year 2, the actual payment is reconciled to the accruals, and the total amount of liability on the balance sheet is reversed.

While this is how accounting accruals are generally conducted for a short-term incentive compensation plan, the Financial Accounting Standards Board has modified some accounting regulations. For example, amounts accrued each year can be adjusted based on the anticipated level of the final payment. For these reasons, human resource professionals dealing with incentive compensation plan design, whether annual or long-term, should coordinate both accounting and tax implications with the company's financial department.

Q 4:9 Is shareholder approval required for annual incentive plans?

Shareholder approval is required for annual incentive plans only if the plan design or payment uses company stock; however, many companies do seek shareholder approval in order to maintain positive relations with their shareholders.

Plan Design

Q 4:10   What are the key issues in the design of an annual incentive program?

There are many important issues to address in the design and/or review of an annual incentive program. Some of these issues are:

1. What is the appropriate incentive plan payout level? What should the target payout be if the business objectives are achieved?

2. Which executives should be eligible for the annual incentive program? Where do executive incentive plans end and middle management incentive plans begin? What jobs have measurable performance goals? What jobs are critical to company success?

3. What is the appropriate measure of business performance? What financial measures, quantitative measures, or nonfinancial measures should be used to evaluate performance? What is the level of performance that should be established for payment of the standard or target incentive amount?

4. What is the appropriate leverage to be used in the payout schedule? How much should an executive receive for exceeding the established objectives, and how much should the executive be penalized for not achieving the established objectives?

5. What is the method of incentive fund accrual? What is the appropriate threshold level (minimum performance level) in both performance and amount of payment?

6. How should company performance, business unit performance, and individual performance be weighted when establishing performance measures (see Qs 4:34 and 4:40)?

7. What will be the form of payment? Will deferral of earned payments be permitted?

Q 4:11 What are the basic plan designs for annual incentive plans?

The basic plan designs for annual incentive plans are:

- Profit sharing plans
- Growth or improvement plans
- Target performance plans
- Peer company comparison plans
- Matrix plans
- Discretionary plans

Q 4:12 How does a profit sharing plan operate?

Under a profit sharing plan, the company pays a predetermined percentage of company or division profits as a cash bonus to selected participants. There usually is not a performance threshold level such as an earnings target or return on stockholder equity.

Example. Company A has a profit sharing plan. It allocates 7 percent of after-tax profits to a pool to be shared among its 12 executives. This amount is allocated among executives in the following manner:

CEO	25 percent
COO	13 percent
CFO	8 percent
Other 9 executives	6 percent

At the end of the fiscal year, sales were $36 million. After-tax profits were $5 million. The pool would be $350,000 ($5M × 7%). The incentive would be distributed as follows:

CEO	25 percent
COO	13 percent
CFO	8 percent
Other 9 executives	6 percent

At the end of the fiscal year, sales were $36 million. After-tax profits were $5 million. The pool would be $350,000 ($5M × 7%). The incentive would be distributed as follows:

CEO	0.25 × $350,000 = $87,500
COO	0.13 × $350,000 = $45,500
CFO	0.08 × $350,000 = $28,000
Other 9 executives	0.06 × $350,000 = $21,000

Q 4:13   What are the advantages of a profit sharing plan?

There are several distinct advantages to a profit sharing plan, including:

1. The plan is easily understood by participants.
2. No incentive plan payouts occur unless the company or division is profitable.
3. Incentive plan payouts increase in direct proportion to profits.

Q 4:14   What are the disadvantages of a profit sharing plan?

The primary disadvantage of the profit sharing plan is that incentive plan payouts are open-ended, which could possibly result in large windfalls.

Example. The facts are the same as in the example at Q 4:12 except that over time the plan was not changed but, through acquisition and growth, the company became a $120 million revenue company. Assume that there was $12 million in after-tax profits. The bonus pool would have increased to $840,000 (7% × $12M). The incentive payments would have increased as follows:

CEO	0.25 × $840,000 = $210,000
COO	0.13 × $840,000 = $109,200
CFO	0.08 × $840,000 = $ 67,200
Other 9 executives	0.06 × $840,000 = $ 50,400

Bonuses would have increased more than 100 percent, but operating performance would have declined. The profit margin of $5 million compared to $36 million (from the example in Q 4:12) is approximately 14 percent; however, the profit margin of $12 million compared to $120 million is 10 percent, or a decline of approximately 30 percent.

The other disadvantage of a profit sharing plan is that the amount of capital needed to produce the profit does not play a role in measuring performance.

Q 4:15 How does a growth or improvement plan operate?

Typically a company selects one or more performance factors (net earnings, earnings per share (EPS) or sales growth are commonly used; see Q 4:37). The incentive pool is created based upon improvement over the prior year's results. The average of several prior years may be utilized to minimize year-to-year variations. A percentage of increased profits, revenues, or sales growth is typically used to create the pool.

Example. Company C has a growth or improvement plan in which its executives share as follows:

CEO	25 percent
COO	13 percent
CFO	8 percent
Other 9 executives	6 percent

Company C's after-tax profits during the prior three years averaged $5 million, and Company C decides to allocate to the pool 50 percent of its after-tax profits in excess of $5.5 million, an increase of 10 percent over the prior three-year averages. If profit is below $5.5 million, the incentive plan will not provide a payout. If Company C's after-tax return hits $6.2 million, the pool, therefore, is $350,000 (0.7 million × 0.50). The distribution would be:

CEO	0.25 × $350,000 = $87,500
COO	0.13 × $350,000 = $45,500
CFO	0.08 × $350,000 = $28,000
Other 9 executives	0.06 × $350,000 = $21,000

Q 4:16 What are the advantages of a growth or improvement plan?

The distinct strength of this type of plan is that it pays an incentive only if there is improvement. This plan is ideal if a company believes that base salary compensates an executive for managing the firm and incentive plans reward the executive for additional effort and improvement, in performance. Since the plan focuses on improvement there is no need for accurate forecasting of business conditions and performance targets.

Q 4:17 What are the disadvantages of a growth or improvement plan?

There are several drawbacks to these types of plans. Improvement over past results is not always an appropriate performance measure for the future. In some years, performance of a company can be outstanding if it maintains prior year profit levels.

Example. The facts are the same as in the example at Question 4:15 except that the economy fell into a major recession and Company C saw its product demand evaporate; however, through cost cutting and new products, Company C achieved a $5 million after-tax profit, even when its competitors were losing money. Under the growth or improvement plan, none of the executives would have received a bonus.

Conversely, in some years, improvement over past results may not indicate good management performance. For example, a company's 10 percent growth rate may indicate poor performance in a high-growth industry where demand is increasing at a 25 percent rate. Executives could be receiving a bonus even if they substantially underperformed against their competitors. In periods of cyclical or fluctuating profits, executives can be rewarded for the same improvement over and over.

Q 4:18 How does the target performance plan work?

Under the target performance plan, the company establishes "targeted" performance levels based on projected business results during the plan year. The company has the choice of setting aside either a fixed percentage of executive salaries (or range midpoints) or a fixed percentage of after-tax profits in the incentive pool for awards when the target is reached; it also has the choice of which results to measure for purposes of the plan (see Q 2:28). The incentive pool then increases to a maximum performance level or decreases to a minimum or threshold performance level. This approach is widely used and is easily adopted to individual business units.

Example. Company D has a target performance plan. The following performance goals are established to determine incentive payments (as a percentage of executive base salary):

After-Tax Returns

Position	Minimum Percentage (10%)	Target Percentage (14%)	Maximum Percentage (18%)
CEO	25	50	60
COO	20	40	48
CFO	15	30	36
Others	12.5	25	30

If the target of a 14 percent increase in the chosen performance factor is achieved, the payout would be as follows:

Title	Base Salary	Percentage	Payout
CEO	$200,000	50	$100,000
COO	160,000	40	64,000
CFO	125,000	30	37,500
Executive 1	110,000	25	27,500
Executive 2	88,000	25	22,000
Executive 3	88,000	25	22,000
Executive 4	76,000	25	19,000
Executive 5	75,000	25	18,750
Executive 6	70,000	25	17,500
Executive 7	68,000	25	17,000
Executive 8	68,000	25	17,000
Executive 9	65,000	25	16,250

If the performance level fell between the defined targets—for example, 12 percent—the incentive payments could be extrapolated or only the lower target amount paid out.

Q 4:19   What are the advantages of a target performance plan?

A target performance plan clearly establishes the criteria for generating the incentive pool based on the projected business results, and accrues incentive funds based on the level of performance achievement. If the pool is based upon participant salaries, it automatically increases in relation to new participants. Shareholder interest can be protected by the way the minimum performance level is established and how the maximum level is capped. The shareholder can be assured of a minimum performance before bonuses are paid.

Q 4:20   What are the disadvantages of a target performance plan?

The primary disadvantage of this type of plan is that it is difficult to estimate targeted performance accurately. Targets must be established each year, which requires accurate forecasting of company results, external business conditions, and competition in order to establish accurate target, minimum, and optimistic objective performance levels.

Q 4:21   How does a peer company performance plan operate?

The company selects one or more financial measures and a group of competitor companies to be compared against. A targeted incentive pool is created for these competitors. The targeted incentive pool for the company can be established by using a percentage of participant salaries/midpoints or of profits. At the end of the performance period, actual performance of the company is compared to the average performance of the peer group. An increasing pool is provided to company executives as relative performance of the company exceeds peer company performance.

Example. Hospital A has identified bed occupancy (the percentage of hospital beds that are utilized over the year) as the prime objective next year. During the current year, bed occupancy was 76 percent. In the geographic area in which Hospital A competes, the average bed occupancy is 78 percent. The following matrix determines the payout as a percentage of executive base salary:

Bed Occupancy

Position	Average Percentage	2% Above Average	4% Above Average
CEO	40	48	52
CFO	30	36	39
COO	20	22	26
Others	15	16.5	19.5

If, during the next year, bed occupancy for the region was again at 78 percent and Hospital A improved its bed occupancy to 78 percent, the incentive payout would be from the first column average. But, assume that average bed occupancy for the region dropped to 60 percent and Hospital A's bed occupancy dropped to 70 percent. Despite this drop in bed occupancy, Hospital A would pay the highest level of bonus (the third column) because Hospital A's bed occupancy was more than 4 percent above the average.

Q 4:22 What are the advantages of a peer company performance plan?

This plan is clearly performance-based. It insulates the company's performance from uncontrollable market conditions since these conditions should, in theory, affect all companies to the same degree. The need for accurate forecasting is therefore unnecessary. The peer company performance type of plan reinforces the shareholder interest. Investors who choose to invest in a given industry want to invest in the company that outperforms the other companies in that industry, the company that has the best returns in the industry.

Q 4:23 What are the disadvantages of a peer comparison plan?

The greatest difficulty with this plan is related to comparison factors. Data may not be available for all competitors. Peer comparison plans are most common among companies in industries that are easily defined and produce uniform and easily available financial data. Banking and hospitals are two industries that meet these criteria and frequently use peer comparison plans.

Q 4:24 What are the key features of a matrix plan?

With a matrix plan, the company establishes a two- or three-dimensional performance matrix for each group of executives covered, incorporating various performance measures and indicating the percentage of salary or after-tax profit payable at various performance levels. Frequently, these plans utilize two or more design features or two or more performance measures. Although primarily used in annual incentive plans, this plan design approach is also utilized in long-term incentive plans, such as performance unit plans (see Chapter 7).

Example. Company E has a matrix incentive plan. Its performance measures are sales growth and return on equity (ROE). The payout matrix for the corporate officers position is shown in Chart 4-1, which shows that if the sales growth target of 14 percent and ROE target of 8 percent are achieved, the participants would receive 100 percent of their targeted annual incentive. Performance below 10 percent sales growth or below 6 percent ROE would result in no incentive payment. The incentive payment is capped so that performance above 10 percent of ROE or 18 percent sales growth would still provide a maximum incentive payment of 130 percent of targeted incentive. Performance between the established points (for example, ROE of 7 percent and sales growth of 12 percent) would be 85 percent, per Chart 4-1.

ROE (%)	SALES GROWTH (in Percentages)								
	10	*11*	*12*	*13*	*14*	*15*	*16*	*17*	*18*
6	70	75	80	85	90	95	100	105	110
7	75	80	85	90	95	100	105	110	115
8	80	85	90	95	100	105	110	115	120
9	85	90	95	100	105	110	115	120	125
10	90	95	100	105	110	115	120	125	130

Chart 4-1

Q 4:25 What are the advantages of a matrix plan?

A matrix plan focuses an executive on two or three significant performance measures. This approach also facilitates the weighting of performance levels. For example, an ROE of 6 percent (minimum performance) would earn a payment of 90 percent of the targeted incentive award if sales growth was 14 percent (targeted performance). See Chart 4-1.

Q 4:26 What are the disadvantages of a matrix plan?

It is extremely difficult to estimate targeted performance of one performance measure, and even more difficult to do the same for two performance measures. Accurate forecasting is required of company results, competitive conditions, and economic conditions. In addition, a matrix plan "documents" the payout schedule, and does not permit any discretionary judgment or flexibility of the payment decision.

Q 4:27 What is a discretionary plan?

A discretionary plan is one in which a CEO or other senior executive in a company determines individual incentive compensation payments on a purely discretionary basis at the end of a designated annual incentive compensation award period. No fixed goals or profit percentages drives this determination of incentive awards. The plan concept depends upon the fairness of the decision-making executive (or a committee of executives) to allocate incentive compensation awards on an equitable basis and in direct relation to the contributions of each eligible executive.

Q 4:28   What are the advantages of a discretionary plan?

The primary advantage of this type of plan is that the executive determining the individual bonus amounts can evaluate all events that occurred during the incentive award period, and the contributions made by each individual, so that a fair and logical incentive award can be determined for each individual.

In addition, the award amount is discretionary: There are no cost parameters on the payments from the plan, nor are there any fixed business conditions or results that must be achieved or estimated.

Q 4:29   What are the disadvantages of a discretionary plan?

There is no level of expectation established with the incentive plan participant; therefore, there is no direct motivation for participants under this type of plan. The discretionary plan is also subject to any personal bias of the person or persons responsible for determining individual incentive amounts, and there is a tendency in the administration of these plans simply to increase the award payments during each new incentive award period, rather than varying incentive compensation payments based on measurable performance criteria.

Q 4:30   Are executives categorized as U.S. expatriates included in annual incentive compensation programs?

Yes. Most expatriate programs follow a policy of providing the U.S. expatriate on assignment overseas with the equivalent executive compensation program provided to counterparts working in the United States. Because the expatriate is part of an international business unit, this policy often requires modifications to plan performance measures and in some cases to the type of plan. Payment is also frequently arranged entirely or partially in the local currency. This is done as a convenience to the expatriate and also because local and U.S. tax laws make this cost-effective for both the company and the expatriate.

> **Example.** A U.S. expatriate executive is assigned to manage a company profit center in Europe. Typically, in the executive's newly assigned country, the amount of potential (targeted) annual bonus is 20 percent of base salary. This executive's current annual bonus potential is 25 percent. The company will normally keep the executive's total cash compensation "whole" by keeping the annual bonus potential at 25 percent. In addition, the company will typically pay a portion of any annual bonus earned in local currency. The amount paid in local currency will be equal to the after-tax/take-home amount of annual bonus, assuming that the bonus will most likely be spent in local currency.

Q 4:31 Do companies with international operations include local national executives in incentive compensation plans?

Incentive compensation practices vary by country, but where they are typically part of a company's total compensation program in a specific country, incentives are provided to local nationals. As a general rule, the amount of incentive compensation provided in non-U.S. countries is less than that provided in the United States. Therefore, total compensation strategies (discussed in Chapter 11) for executives are particularly important since non-U.S. business objectives and total compensation practices vary significantly from those in the United States.

Q 4:32 Can incentive compensation plans be utilized in new ventures/start-up businesses?

Yes. New ventures or start-up businesses will typically establish incentive compensation plans that are tied to "milestone" accomplishments rather than to accomplishments during a specific annual or quarterly period. Since the business plans for these companies cannot always be established annually, incentive payments are tied to certain critical accomplishments (milestones) that must be achieved if the new venture is to be successful. Since the timing of these critical accomplishments or milestone events cannot always be predicted with great accuracy, the incentive compensation plan should be modified to meet the unique business characteristics of new venture organizations. Generally, the size of the incentive award will also vary in accordance with the length of a milestone. For example, if a milestone is expected in a year and a half, targeted incentive compensation would also be equal to the annual award multiplied by 1.5.

Q 4:33   How can annual incentives for executives be distinguished from those for mid-level managers?

Many companies adopt middle management annual incentive programs that are extensions of the executive annual incentive program. Other companies will design completely different programs. In this case, companies need to ensure that middle management executives do not receive a low or zero bonus when executives receive high bonus amounts, and vice-versa. Performance measures should be similar even if plan design differs.

Companies typically design executive incentive plans for those individuals or executives in the company who are eligible for both annual incentive plans and long-term incentive plans (stock awards). This eligibility criteria helps to distinguish executive annual incentive plan eligibility from that of middle management.

Another clear distinction is through the development of a company's total compensation strategy (see also Chapter 11). Companies can identify a specific business purpose for each element of compensation, such as a targeted labor market pay level to be achieved by the company. This can be done for both executive jobs and nonexecutive managerial jobs. This type of activity helps to ensure that plan design and performance measures are integrated between executive jobs and middle-management jobs.

Q 4:34 How can short-term incentive plans be integrated with executive compensation plans during a merger of two companies?

Upon the merger of two companies, a choice must be made as to which company compensation plan will continue. A transition to a new plan may be in order. If eligibility will not be continued for some executives after the transition, such executives will typically be provided with a plan buyout amount equal to the last incentive award or the average of the last two or three incentive awards paid. This can be done at any time during or shortly after the new incentive award period.

Any existing short-term incentive plans should also be reviewed after the merger to determine whether changes are necessary. In addition, the performance measures used in any plan generally require change after a merger. All other administrative provisions (i.e., form of payout, deferral, plan approvals) should also be reviewed after a merger. A task force of representatives from both companies should be given the responsibility of reviewing alternatives against an established total compensation strategy (see Chapter 11) and then presenting them to the new CEO or other approving authority for final approval.

The task force does not always conclude that the buying company's annual incentive plan should be adopted. The acquired company may have a better plan. Real experience in these situations is that the plan that has paid more to the executives over the past few years gets first priority by any reviewing committee.

Performance Measures

Q 4:35 What types of performance measures are commonly used in annual incentive plans?

Performance measures commonly used in annual incentive plans fall into three general categories: quantitative, financial, and nonfinancial.

Q 4:36 What are some examples of quantitative performance measures?

The most common types of quantitative performance measures are:

- Market share
- Sales units
- Inventory turns
- Productivity ratios
- Customer satisfaction surveys
- Production volume
- Shipping errors
- Budget/expense levels

Q 4:37 What financial performance measures are commonly used in annual incentive plans?

Most companies rely on financial measures for their annual incentive plans. The most frequently used financial performance measures are:

- Target earnings
- Target sales
- Increases in profits or earnings per share growth
- Increases in sales
- Profit margin
- Return on capital
- Return on assets
- Return on equity

Target earnings are frequently used even though this performance measure may not reflect the effects of inflation on the company's performance. Other companies use financial ratios such as return on assets and return on equity. The shortcoming of these ratios is that they reflect an accounting value of the investment base, rather than current market value. Some executives believe that these shortcomings can be overcome by using some measure of "shareholder value," which in its most simple form consists of increases in stock price plus stock dividends. Shareholder value can also be any other financial measure that will drive stock price up, such as a favorable "market to book value" ratio, or a favorable ratio of ROE to the cost of capital. A few companies also use similar measures of "economic value-added." This is defined as any increases in the net worth of the company. No matter what financial performance is chosen, there is still a requirement for accurate measuring and forecasting, so that annual incentive payments motivate executives and assist the company in meeting its business goals.

Q 4:38　What is earnings per share and how is it calculated?

Earnings per share is a frequently encountered measure of profitability. This ratio is computed by dividing net income attributable to common stock by the average number of common shares outstanding. There are two types of EPS: fully diluted and primary. Both include common shares outstanding and common stock equivalents such as securities, convertible preferred stock, unexercised stock options that have an increase in value over the option price, and any other security that will enable the owner to become a common shareholder. Primary EPS uses year-end shares outstanding, while fully diluted EPS uses the average of the beginning and year-end shares outstanding for the year.

Earnings per share has been criticized as a measure of profitability because it does not consider the amounts of assets or capital required to generate that level of earnings. Two firms with the same earnings per share will not be equally profitable if one of the firms requires twice the amount of assets or capital to generate those earnings than does the other firm. Despite this limitation, EPS is a commonly accepted management performance criterion, and many believe that EPS directly influences stock price.

Q 4:39　What is return on assets and how is it calculated?

Return on assets is an effective way to assess management's performance in using assets to generate earnings. This measure is often called the return on investment and is calculated by dividing net income, however defined (typically net/after-tax income), by average total assets.

This measure is frequently used in financial institutions, where earnings returns on assets (cash) is a critical indicator of business success.

Q 4:40   How is return on equity calculated?

Most shareholders are more interested in the rate of return on common shareholder's equity than the rate of return on assets. To compute this financial measure, divide earnings, however defined (typically after-tax earnings), by the average shareholders equity. Equity includes par value of preferred stock, par value of common stock, capital contributed in excess of par value on common stock, and retained earnings.

Q 4:41   How is return on capital calculated?

Return on capital is generally measured by comparing earnings to the two primary sources of capital available for the company: long-term debt and equity issued in the form of company stock. Therefore, this formula has earnings plus interest on long-term debt in the numerator, with the sum of the company's long-term debt plus equity as the denominator.

Interest on long-term debt is added to the numerator to show the typical earnings number as a net income or after-tax earnings value, without any reduction for expenses (interest), incurred in obtaining the long-term debt. Since this value would already have built in a deduction of any expenses accrued and paid for the maintenance of long-term debt during that earnings period, it is only fair to add these earnings back to the numerator so that a fair return measure can be established against the two sources of capital in the denominator.

Q 4:42   What non-financial performance measures are commonly used in annual incentive plans?

Non-financial performance measures are also used by many companies, particularly in divisional business units. As with financial performance measures, quantitative measures are used most in large mature companies that have a great deal of historical information and computer systems support in order to gather and analyze the information required.

Non-financial performance measures include:

- Management development goals
- Equal employment opportunity/affirmative action goals
- Targeted completion of new facilities
- Organization consolidations
- Implementation of quality teams
- Achievement of product development goals
- Identification of acquisition candidates

The use of non-financial measures is increasing due to current business conditions that include mergers, acquisitions, divestitures, restructurings, and downsizings, all of which require a new focus of executive time and effort. Another reason for increased use of non-financial measures concerns current changes in the role of managers from directors of work to facilitators of work, a change that requires a corresponding change in executive behavior. Non-financial performance measures can be a tool in achieving this business objective. Companies using them need to be aware, however, that executives must exercise judgment on the degree of achievement. While some executives are not comfortable with this responsibility, many others welcome the challenge of evaluating the level of goal achievement—particularly since it offers the opportunity to look back on past achievements, rather than trying to look forward in times of uncertainty to estimate future performance.

Q 4:43   What is the difficulty of using performance measures in annual incentive plans?

Most companies use more than one performance measure, e.g., a financial performance measure and a nonfinancial performance measure, or two financial performance measures, in their annual incentive plans. This can increase the complexity and decrease the understanding of the plan. Multiple goals also make it more difficult to project targeted performance goals.

Companies cannot and should not attempt to direct all elements of the management function through the use of an annual incentive plan. To include all management performance measures in the annual incentive plan is an error because certain types of management performance do not correlate to an annual timetable. Examples of this are increasing shareholder value, or achieving other long-term business objectives that are best rewarded through the company's long-term incentive plan.

Q 4:44 How does a company decide whether the incentive programs should be based on group or individual performance?

The primary factor to consider is whether the company has the capability to measure corporate, division, department, or individual performance accurately. A company must also consider whether it is practical to establish performance targets for individual executives, given its culture (team vs. individual) and management style. For example, a company that focuses on team performance may not want to use individual executive objectives in its annual incentive plan. The setting of individual targets is time-consuming. Most companies initially establish incentives on group performance (corporate, divisional, or department) and use individual targets as an adjustment to group performance. This approach balances the organization's need for teamwork while recognizing the individual's contribution. Generally, this balancing is accomplished by calculating a portion of the incentive payout earned by formula, with the remainder based on the manager's evaluation of individual executive performance. Performance measures are typically weighted. For example:

1. Organization goals 50% + individual goals 50%; or
2. Corporate goals 50% + divisional goals 25% + individual goals 25%.

Q 4:45 How do performance measures vary by group or organizational level?

Corporate performance measures are typically financial—such as earnings per share, return on capital, return on equity, or net income. Divisions generally use quantitative measures such as sales volume, expense budgets, number of units sold, operating income, or market share. Individual performance measures are represented by such objective measures as completion of a complex project on time and within budget, identification of a significant number of potential customers, or customer satisfaction levels of 99.5 percent on all customer service calls. Performance measures should "build up the organization," so that individual goals contribute to divisional goals, which contribute to corporate goals.

Q 4:46 What performance measures work best for a manufacturing organization?

Most manufacturing companies are capital-intensive; thus, performance is commonly measured by some earnings return on capital. There are three primary sources of capital in a manufacturing company:

- Borrowed money (long-term debt)
- Money raised from stock sale (equity)
- Use of retained earnings (equity).

Long-term debt and equity are therefore factored into the earnings return measure. Return on capital is typically calculated as net earnings plus the after-tax interest on long-term debt, divided by long-term debt and equity.

Quantitative measures are also frequently utilized in manufacturing companies and include cost and expense issues such as reduction in operating expense or achievement of targeted cost of goods sold. Since manufacturing companies sell products rather than services, sales units, market share, and net sales are also quantitative performance measures.

Q 4:47 What performance measures work best in financial institutions?

Financial institutions manage cash, which is an asset. Therefore, return on assets is the most common performance measure, since it compares earnings to assets. Financial institutions also focus on net interest (interest received minus interest paid), total deposits, the percentage of nonperforming assets, and staff expenses as a percentage of total sales and general and administrative expenses (SG&A). These quantitative measures are used simply because success in each of these can drive success in the financial institution.

Q 4:48   Which performance measures are best for a service company?

Return on equity is the primary performance measure in a service company because increasing the net worth or equity of the company is a primary business goal. Service companies also use a number of quantitative and objective performance measures such as customer service ratings and quality of services ratings, because repeat business is critical to company success and quality measures drive repeat business.

Performance Standards

Q 4:49   What are the basic methods of comparing performance in annual incentive plans?

Once the performance measures have been chosen, the most critical aspect in the design of an annual incentive plan is the setting of performance standards. Although the specifics vary a great deal among types of companies and within industries, there are four main ways of establishing performance targets. They are:

- The look forward method
- The peer group method
- The look back method
- The percentage of profits approach.

Q 4:50   How does the look forward approach to performance comparison work?

In a look forward plan, actual performance is measured against targets that are established each year based on business plans. This approach is most prevalent in annual plans. Its obvious advantage is that it focuses on the annual business plan.

Q 4:51   How does the peer group approach to performance comparison work?

In the peer group approach, actual performance is measured against performance of a group of competitor companies. This approach focuses on the firm's relative performance against competitor firms. It is appropriate only where timely and accurate competitor information is available. It is frequently used in banks, saving and loans, and utilities. The basic assumption in this plan is that outside forces will have had a similar effect on the performance of both the company and the comparison group. A company that has performed better than the comparison group is assumed to have demonstrated above average performance.

Q 4:52   How does the look back approach to performance comparison work?

The improvement or look back plan compares a company's current performance with its prior performance. Look back plans are most often established by young, growth-oriented companies, where accurate forecasting is difficult. One weakness of this plan design is that improvement over prior performance may not be an indicator of good performance.

Q 4:53   How does the percentage of profits approach to performance comparison work?

In this approach, a fixed percentage of income is used to fund a bonus pool. This fairly common approach results in a bonus pool funding without reference to a business plan or economic conditions. The drawback to this approach is that these fixed percentages tend to stay in place for many years, and thus are not responsive to economic conditions, competitive practice, and targeted total cash compensation.

Q 4:54   May performance maximums be set for annual incentive plans?

Because it is believed that company performance is ultimately driven by outside influences rather than by executive performance, maximum levels are generally determined for executive performance.

For example, a natural disaster such as flood could create a boom in the construction industry, as could a competitor going out of business. In this case, the boom has nothing to do with executive performance. Surveys are readily available on this, and would indicate that these maximum levels are generally set at 150 to 250 percent over the targeted performance level.

Q 4:55 Do companies typically establish a threshold performance level in annual incentive award plans?

Most annual incentive plans are based on the achievement of certain performance levels that include a threshold or minimum performance level. If these threshold levels are not met, no incentive plan payments will be made. Some typical threshold levels used in incentive compensation plans are as follows:

1. *Competitor level.* Company performance must be above a minimum competitor performance level.

2. *Dividend payments.* Sufficient profits must be made to cover a targeted dividend payment to shareholders.

3. *Minimum return against an alternate investment.* The company's return on investment (e.g., return on equity, return on assets, return on capital) must be greater than alternate investment opportunities of shareholders such as short-term money market rates, certificates of deposit, or three-month treasury bills.

4. *Interest rate.* The company's return on investment must be at least equal to the prime interest rate level.

5. *Past performance.* Performance level must be at least equal to the previous year or to the average of the last three years.

The appropriateness of threshold levels is a critical motivating factor in incentive plan design. Thresholds should not be so low as to guarantee regular incentive plan payments, nor should they be so high as to be unattainable.

Q 4:56   How can you determine whether your performance standards are appropriate?

If performance standards are too high and are never or rarely achieved, resulting in no incentive payments, executives will perceive these standards as being unattainable and the incentives actually will become disincentives. If performance standards are too low and are always achieved, the incentive plan becomes part of the salary program.

A rule of thumb in establishing performance standards is that in a ten-year period there would be one or two years in which there are no incentive payments and there would be one or two years where incentive payments would be at the maximum level.

While incentive payments do fluctuate in companies, it is becoming increasingly rare for an executive who is a participant in an annual incentive plan to receive no incentive payment. If an executive is eligible for an incentive payment of up to 40 percent of base salary, but over a prolonged time span is always earning between 20 to 40 percent and never earns less than 20 percent, it makes more sense to build that 20 percent into the base salary and offer the remainder as a true variable incentive payment.

Funding Incentive Plans

Q 4:57   How do companies determine the size of award appropriate in annual incentive compensation plans?

Companies will typically measure total cash compensation (annual salary plus annual bonus) provided in competitor companies and then establish their own targeted levels of base salary and annual bonus. In addition, companies will establish a total compensation strategy as outlined in Chapter 11, which provides a guideline on the size of annual incentive awards and long-term incentive awards.

The size of incentive awards is scope-sensitive, meaning that as company size increases, the amount of incentive award increases. For example, the controller in a company with $100 million in sales might have a target incentive award of 20 percent of base salary, while the same job in a company with $1 billion in sales might have a target incentive award of 30 percent.

Q 4:58   What factors drive the amount of annual incentive amounts paid to executives?

Four factors determine the amount of incentive pay an executive receives:

1. The amount of the executive's base salary or salary range midpoint;
2. The level the executive occupies within the organization;
3. The industry in which the executive works;
4. The individual performance of the company.

Base Salary. Typically, the higher the base salary, the larger the incentive opportunity (both as a percentage of base and, of course, the amount). For example, a CEO earning $200,000 will probably be eligible for a larger incentive payment than a CEO earning $100,000. This is partly explained by the fact that base salaries are significantly affected by the size of the corporation.

Organizational Level. The CEO normally is eligible for the largest incentive opportunity. Typically, his or her direct reports are eligible for 70 to 80 percent of the CEO bonus (expressed as a percentage). For example, if the CEO's bonus target is 50 percent of base salary, his or her direct reports will be eligible for between 35 to 40 percent of their base salaries. The next reporting level typically is eligible to receive between 50 and 60 percent of the CEO's percentage.

Industry. The manufacturing and service industries tend to pay larger incentive amounts then do industries such as health care or insurance.

Individual and Company Performance. One normally would assume that the better the company performance, the larger the amount the executive would receive as incentive payment. In most cases this holds true when analyzing individual company plans and payout. When looking at one specific company, incentive payments will typically be larger in those years where performance was better.

Because many companies establish annual incentive payment targets based on prior years' performance, poorly performing companies tend to establish lower performance targets. For example, a company that is losing money may see breaking even as excellent management performance, worthy of incentive payments; however, another company that historically has made a 20 percent return on investment may establish its targets at 22 percent return on investment. In the long run it will be easier for a poorly performing company to improve performance (break even and pay a bonus) than it will for a higher performing company to improve its performance.

Q 4:59 How does the pool method operate when used in determining incentive funds?

The pool method is a popular means of determining an incentive payout. An overall incentive pool is calculated for all participants or a group of participants, and each individual award is determined as a share of the pool. The following table demonstrates the pool method:

Participant	Total Annual Incentive Pool	Pro-Rata Share of Annual Incentive Pool (%)	Target Annual Incentive	Individual Pro-Rata Annual Incentive Award
A		30	$ 30,000	$ 36,000
B		20	20,000	24,000
C		15	15,000	18,000
D		15	15,000	18,000
E		10	10,000	12,000
F		10	10,000	12,000
G	$100,000	100	$100,000	$120,000

*The actual total annual incentive award was 120 percent of the targeted amount.

Q 4:60   Are there advantages to the pool method?

Yes. The primary advantage to the pool method is that it correlates the aggregate payout and costs to the number of participants or level of performance. In addition, it allows the performance of the organization, business unit, or department drive annual incentive plan payments.

Q 4:61   Are there disadvantages to the pool method?

Yes. The pool method has two basic disadvantages:

1. Superior performance by one or more persons cannot be rewarded.

2. An increase in the number of participants can dilute the available incentive payment of existing participants, unless the annual incentive pool increases as well.

Q 4:62   How is the participant method used in determining incentive pools?

Each participant has an incentive opportunity that is not affected by the performance of other participants, although the individual's own award may be adjusted based on his performance. The total payout is simply the sum of individual participant awards, after adjusting the target fund by company (or business unit) performance, as can be seen in the following table:

Participant	Annual Incentive	Target Performance Rating (%)	Adjusted Company Annual Incentive	Individual Target Performance Rating (%)	Individual Annual Incentive Award
A	$ 30,000	120	$ 36,000	100	$ 36,000
B	20,000	120	24,000	100	24,000
C	15,000	120	18,000	120	21,600
D	15,000	120	18,000	80	14,400
E	10,000	120	12,000	120	14,400
F	10,000	120	12,000	80	9,600
	$100,000		$120,000		$120,000

Q 4:63 Are there advantages to the participant method?

Yes. The participant method makes it much easier to communicate the incentive opportunity to participants. Moreover, because individual performance has a direct effect on individual incentive payments, each participant is motivated to achieve goals established in the annual incentive award plan.

Q 4:64 Are there disadvantages to the participant method?

Yes. The major disadvantage of the participant method is that it can make the amount of funds allocated for the annual incentive difficult to control. A recommending executive can rate individuals in a manner inconsistent with that of other departments. The best way to control this is to use the performance of the business unit or company to determine the incentive pool for each department or group of executives, and then to require that individual executive awards equal the pool generated by that performance.

Q 4:65 Do incentive plans have maximum or caps on incentive payments?

Most incentive plans do cap the potential payout opportunities so that managers would not benefit by events that are beyond the control of management. In the view of many companies, performance that substantially exceeds budgeted targets is more a reflection of poor budgeting or non-company-related economic conditions than excellent executive performance.

The arguments against capping incentive payout are twofold. First, if the goal is to tie performance to payout, then if performance exceeds all expectations, the incentive payment should exceed all expectations. Second, if the executive is at risk on the downside (i.e., he or she could receive less or nothing), the executive should have the upside potential uncapped.

A cap on incentive plan payouts may be expressed as an absolute dollar limitation (either on contributions to the pool or on individual awards) or as a percentage or multiple of the projected maximum payout.

Chapter 5

Long-Term Incentive Plans

Long-term incentive programs, frequently called capital accumulation plans, are offered to executives by a majority of companies. In fact, participation in these plans traditionally determined those employees considered executives. Three basic plan designs are utilized when implementing a long-term incentive plan. The first, the purchase plan, requires an executive to make an investment. The second, the appreciation plan, grants the executive the right to receive the value of the appreciation in the employer's stock. The third, the full-value plan, grants the executive the full value of the company stock plus any appreciation that may result over a period of years. This chapter discusses general design and administration issues for long-term incentive plans. Chapter 6 deals specifically with purchase plans; Chapter 7 covers appreciation and full-value plans; and Chapter 8 deals with the effects of combining two different long-term plans.

General Considerations 5-2
Plan Comparisons 5-12
Compensation Philosophy 5-21
Plan Design 5-23
Stock Options 5-26
Omnibus Plan 5-29
Tax Considerations 5-30
Exercising a Stock Option 5-36

Tax Considerations   5-39
Plan Administration   5-41

General Considerations

Q 5:1   What are long-term incentive plans?

Long-term incentive plans or capital accumulation plans are long-term programs that give executives the opportunity to accumulate estate-building capital when the value of the company's stock increases or when long-term company objectives are met. Since stock options are the most prevalent type of capital accumulation plan, many individuals use the two terms interchangeably. Stock options are, however, only one approach to capital accumulation and long-term incentives.

Q 5:2   What are the characteristics of long-term incentive plans?

Long-term incentive plans usually are structured with a three- to five-year time frame; however, to provide continuous incentives, many companies make annual grants that may subsequently result in annual payments. Long-term plans are generally stock-based or use increases in stock prices as the basis for payout, because they are designed to create an interest in the executive that mirrors the interest of the company's shareholders. Payments are typically made in stock, cash, or a combination, and if the combination approach is used, sufficient cash is paid out or withheld to cover the executive's tax obligation for the stock and/or cash received.

Q 5:3   How is eligibility for participation in long-term plans determined?

Only those executives who can make decisions that affect a company's long-term results usually participate in long-term incentive plans. When this criterion is used, participation in long-term plans is usually limited to a handful of executives. Survey information regarding Fortune 500 companies shows, however, that the trend is to extend eligibility for long-term incentive plans to middle managers at salary levels beginning at approximately $75,000 in large companies and $60,000 in small companies.

Emerging and growth companies that may have cost and cash-flow problems tend to include larger numbers of executives in these programs to compensate for lower base salaries. They also use long-term plans, with their accompanying prospects of huge future payout, as a recruitment and retention tool. This offsets the fact that these same companies often provide total cash compensation that is less than that provided to similar positions in large companies. Surveys show that these small, entrepreneurial companies use three to four times the amount of stock, as a percentage of total common shares outstanding in the company, for their long-term incentive plans than do large companies. This is because long-term plans with stock do not require cash or a charge to earnings, as do short-term incentives.

Most companies use long-term plan participation as a motivator so that the executives selected for participation are given the message that they have been selected for membership in a special group. The criteria used in establishing eligibility for long-term incentive plans are the same as those used in short-term incentives. For example, typical criteria include base salary/salary midpoint, job grade, reporting relationship, and job title.

Q 5:4　How prevalent are long-term incentive plans?

The majority of publicly traded companies offer some form of long-term incentive for their executives. As shown in Chart 5-1, stock options are used more often than any other form of long-term incentive. During the past few years restricted stock has been the fastest growing long-term plan, particularly because it has the strongest retention value (see Q 5:5). Of greatest significance in Chart 5-1 is that the types of long-term income used by companies do not add up to 100 percent, indicating that most companies use more than one form of long-term incentive. (See Chapter 2 for a discussion of the prevalence of annual long-term incentives in private companies.)

Chart 5-1. Prevalence of Long-Term Incentives in Public Companies

Stock Options	94%
Restricted Stock Options	45%
Performance Plans	40%
SAR	66%
Other	27%

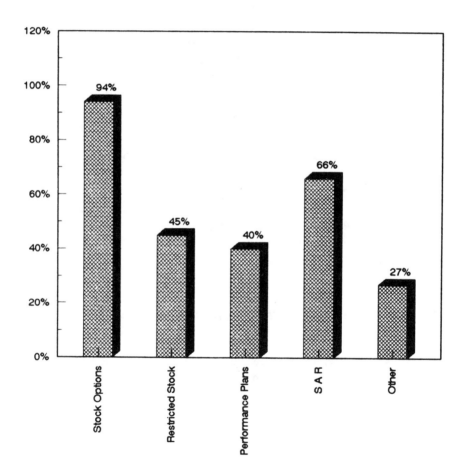

Source: Management Performance International, Inc.

Q 5:5   What is the rationale for having a long-term incentive plan?

Most companies provide long-term incentive plans primarily be-cause they believe offering an executive an ownership position or the potential for one will effectively motivate that executive to achieve the long-term goals of the company. A second reason is retention, or keeping the executive employed by the company, particularly during a company restructuring. This is achieved by adding "vesting require-ments" to long-term grants. For example, an executive is provided with the right to purchase 1,000 stock option shares at a fixed price. These rights might "vest" by 25 percent every four years, meaning that the executive can purchase 250 shares after Year 1, 500 shares after Year 2, 750 shares after Year 3, and 1,000 shares after Year 4. Given the fact that most stock option plans would have a total award period of ten years, this provides ample opportunity for the executive to exercise the right to purchase.

By providing annual grants of 1,000 shares as shown in the previous example, a number of vested and nonvested stock option grants will be ongoing, and any executive leaving the company would lose his nonvested shares.

A third reason for providing long-term incentive plans is to offer the executive significant opportunity for capital accumulation. If stock prices increase, this can be a significant factor in total compen-sation.

Q 5:6   What should be considered in selecting a long-term incentive plan?

In reviewing the numerous alternatives, there are some basic questions that, if evaluated honestly, will help determine the type of plan design that most effectively meets the employer's strategic compensation goals. The following list of key issues in capital accu-mulation is designed to outline questions that should be considered:

1. *Executive Investment.* Will the executive be required to make an investment, or will the executive participate in the plan without an investment?

2. *Ownership.* Will the objective of the program be to create ownership of stock by the executive, or is the intent to reward

the executive for improvement in stock price or some other financial measure?

3. *Company Impact.* What are the key long-term business factors in the company business plan? What company goals should a long-term incentive plan support? How will the company change in the next three to five years, and what long-term incentive plan can best support this anticipated change?

4. *Performance Factors.* What performance factor is indicative of company success? Is it stock price, or is it some other measure such as earnings per share (EPS) or return on equity? Is it important for executives to be motivated and rewarded based on company performance measures that they can directly influence, rather than stock price, which is subject to outside factors such as stock market performance or the state of the economy?

5. *Accounting and Tax Impact.* What are the tax, accounting, and financial impacts on the company and/or the executive?

   - The impact of the plan's tax treatment:
   - When will the taxable event occur for the executive and entitle the company to a corresponding compensation deduction in calculating its taxes?
   - What is the plan's effect on the executive's individual tax situation? Will it be ordinary or capital gains tax?
   - Will the executive be subject to a potential alternative minimum tax?
   - The impact of the plan on financial issues:
   - Is the payout chargeable as an expense against the company's income statement?
   - Must the payout be accrued as a liability on the company's balance sheet?
   - How important are income statement costs to the company?
   - What percentage of the shares outstanding will be required for the plan, and how much dilutive effect will the plan have on earnings per share?

6. *Payout Levels.* What level of payout should the executive receive when long-term objectives are achieved? How much capital accumulation is appropriate and fair to the company,

to the shareholders, and to the executive? What mix of short-term incentive and long-term incentive is desirable?

7. *Grant Frequency.* How often should long-term grants and/or awards be made?

8. *Corporate and Legal Restrictions.* What corporate and legal restrictions affect the company and/or the executive?

   • What is the impact of federal and state securities laws on the plan?

   • What considerations should be given to corporate insiders under SEC Regulation 16?

9. *Estate Building.* Is the long-term incentive plan intended to supplement retirement? How long will most participants be in the plan and how does this affect the amount of potential capital accumulation? If stock prices advance in the future as in the past, will the amount of capital accumulation be excessive?

10. *Eligibility.* Which executives have a direct effect on long-term performance? What is the eligibility in competitive companies? What will be the impact if eligibility is increased or decreased?

Q 5:7   What are the principal types of long-term incentive plans?

There are several variations on the long-term incentive plan, with stock options and stock appreciation rights (SARs) the most frequently utilized plan designs (see Qs 7:3–7:11; although SARs have recently lost much of their appeal as a compensation device). Performance share and performance unit plans are also commonly used, and restricted stock has recently had a resurgence in use. Most long-term incentive plans fall into four basic plan categories.

The first category includes plans that will provide the executive with stock provided that she makes an investment. These plans are the most common type of long-term incentive and are called purchase plans (see Chapter 6). Purchase plans include the following:

   • Nonqualified stock options
   • Incentive stock options

- Discounted nonqualified stock options
- Book value purchase plans

The second category includes plans that grant the executive the appreciation in the employer's stock over a certain period, but not the value of the stock itself. These plans, known as appreciation plans, include stock appreciation rights, phantom shares, and book value appreciation rights.

The third category of plans provides the executive with the full value of the share over a specified period, and in some cases also provides the executive with the appreciation in the value of the shares over this period. These plans are called full-value plans because the executive receives all of the benefits of the grant without having to make an actual investment. The plans include restricted shares, performance shares, and performance units.

Both appreciation and full-value plans are covered in detail in Chapter 7. Finally, there are combination plans, which utilize two or more plan types. These are discussed in detail in Chapter 8.

Q 5:8   What new forms of long-term incentive are currently emerging?

Three new long-term incentive awards are being considered by a number of companies in addition to the other forms of long-term incentive outlined in Q 5:7. These are:

1. *Performance-Based Restricted Stock.* Under this plan, the executive is granted full-value restricted shares with a performance-based restriction that will accelerate the vesting of restricted shares from a designated maximum period to a shorter time frame. For example, an executive is granted 1,000 restricted shares with a four-year time lapse restriction. A performance-based restriction is added to the provisions of the grant, such that if company earnings per share increase 15 percent after the first year, the restrictions will lapse one year earlier (i.e., after three years). If a 15 percent earnings per share growth is achieved during Year 2, the restrictions will lapse one additional year earlier (i.e., after the second year).

2. *Leveraged Stock Options.* This concept encourages an executive to purchase shares of company stock with personal funds. For every one share of stock that is purchased by the executive, the executive will receive four or five stock option shares. These stock option shares are above and beyond normal annual company stock awards. Thus the purchase of company shares by the executive is "leveraged" on behalf of the executive by the grant of the additional stock option shares. These leveraged stock options will typically carry the same plan provisions as the regular company stock option grants.

3. *Shareholder Value/Economic Value Plans.* These plans are based on the assumption that normal financial performance measures (e.g., earnings per share, return on capital, return on equity) do not accurately correlate with true shareholder value. True shareholder value is defined as increases in stock price plus dividends. Other performance measures should be used in long-term incentive plans, ones that will more accurately correlate to increases in shareholder value. A number of different shareholder value performance measures are being considered by companies. These shareholder value measures are not always found on company financial statements, but are defined by each company and utilized to motivate executives to achieve established goals in each of these areas, the theory being that such achievement will drive up company stock price.

Q 5:9   What is economic value-added?

Economic value-added (EVA) has many definitions. The most common ones are net earnings minus the cost of capital or return on capital divided by the cost of capital employed in the business. The earnings and return on capital numbers are easily identified in financial statements. The cost of capital is a little more difficult. Capital in a business is, of course, equity and borrowed money. Borrowed money has debt; long-term debt can also be identified on company financial statements. The cost of equity is more difficult to calculate. Most experts on this subject will say that this cost of equity is equal to what an investor could be earning elsewhere.

Therefore, to calculate cost of capital, companies need to add the value of all capital (e.g., buildings, equipment, investment in people and products or services), and apply a cost of capital to this value that is typically a hypothetical statistic determined by adding a typical investor return (e.g., T-bill interest of 6 to 7 percent) to a premium that is required to attract an investor to your company stock (e.g., 5 to 6 percent). The total cost of capital (e.g., 11 to 13 percent) is then multiplied by total capital and compared to pre-tax operating profit. To the extent executives increase pre-tax operating profit in relation to the cost of capital, they are adding "economic value" to a company.

Q 5:10   How do economic-value-added plans work?

The most common steps required for implementation of an EVA plan are:

1. *Select an EVA definition.* For example, when they established an EVA plan at Coca-Cola they used the following definition: NOPAT (net operating profit after tax) minus cash plus inventory plus [accounts receivable–accounts payable] plus non-current assets multiplied by cost of capital equals economic value-added. The current years EVA minus the prior years EVA equals the EVA that can be shared with all executives.

2. *Determine eligibility by evaluating who can impact EVA.* In most companies this is the executives; however, some companies include many other managers and/or all exempt employees.

3. *Design a payout schedule.* There are two dimensions to this decision. The first is to establish the targeted amount of annual incentive or annual plus long-term incentive to be paid each participant. The second is to analyze the companys business plans to determine potential growth in EVA. Analysis of the company's projected EVA based on business plans and targeted business performance in operating and/or strategic plans, plus a knowledge of competitive levels of annual/long-term incentive, are the two key facts required to develop the payout schedule. The potential increases in EVA, if business plans and targeted results are achieved, can be correlated to a company's targeted amounts of incentive to be provided to each executive, so that payout opportunities are properly estimated.

4. *Determine if EVA amounts earned will be paid in current cash and/or deferred.* In most EVA plans the executive participants will have a portion of earned awards paid currently (the amount that would parallel competitive levels of annual incentive) and a portion deferred until termination or retirement. Deferred amounts are eligible for the same investment alternatives that exist in a company's retirement plan or something similar to these investment alternatives with some additional investment choices like split dollar insurance or COLI. Non-executive participants are typically paid all in current cash.

Planning Tip. A unique feature typically found in EVA plans is that payout schedules do not have any maximum. The logic for this is that the higher the EVA, the higher the shareholder value. Like many sales incentive plans there is no need to have a maximum because as targeted performance levels are exceeded, everyone wins.

Q 5:11   What is shareholder value?

These definitions, like EVA, also vary. The simplest one is stock price increases plus dividends equals shareholder value. The more sophisticated definition is return on capital divided by the cost of capital. The later definition assumes that the correlation of these two measures will drive stock price and enhance shareholder value.

Q 5:12   How do shareholder value plans work?

Shareholder value plans work in the same way as performance plans, in that if an established goal is achieved, the executive will earn a long-term incentive and at the same time increase shareholder value.

Example. A company establishes a shareholder value measure of return on equity over the cost of equity. An increase in the ratio of these two measures will, it is believed, increase shareholder value. If return on equity is 16 percent and the cost of equity is 8 percent, the ratio is 2:0. If the company can increase this relationship to 2:1 or higher, investors will see that the true value of the company is increasing, and this factor will drive stock value up.

Shareholder value plans have the same advantages and disadvantages as other similar performance-based plans, and there are no guarantees that the stock market will react to the return on equity/cost of equity relationship, just as there is no guarantee that the stock market will relate to a favorable earnings per share or return on capital growth measure used in a performance plan. Some companies believe, however, that shareholder value plans provide a more accurate means to measure executive performance and its correlation to stock price.

Q 5:13 What is a long-term performance plan?

A long-term performance plan provides incentives to an executive if long-term business objectives are achieved. It is similar in design to a short-term incentive plan except the performance cycle is typically three to five years. Common performance plans are performance shares and performance units. These plans pay in cash, stock, or a combination of cash and stock.

Q 5:14 What is a stock option plan?

A stock option plan grants an executive the right to purchase a fixed number of company common shares, at a fixed price, over a specified period, after some vesting schedule is met. For example: An executive is granted a stock option on 1,000 shares, at $20 per share, over ten years, and this right vests at a rate of 25 percent per year. After four years, the executive is fully vested, and if the stock price has a market value of $35 per share at that time, the executive may purchase up to 1,000 shares at $20 per share.

Plan Comparisons

Q 5:15 What is the advantage of a stock option plan over a long-term performance plan?

A stock option plan involves no out-of-pocket cost to the company, but it does provide the company with positive cash flow when the executive purchases the stock. In addition, there is no accounting charge to the income statement if the stock option is granted at full market value; that is, the option exercise price is equal to the then-market value of the shares of company stock provided by the stock option. If the option is a nonqualified option the company receives a tax deduction upon exercise; however, this does not apply to an incentive stock option (ISO). Stock options also have the advantage of tying the executive's reward to what shareholders care most about—the price of company stock.

On the other hand, long-term performance plans require a charge to the company earnings (even though the company receives a tax deduction for this amount). If the long-term performance plan is paid in cash, the company incurs negative cash flow (that is, significant out-of-pocket cost). From a shareholder relations perspective, performance plans can pay out when stock price goes down.

Q 5:16   What are the advantages of a stock option plan over a restricted share plan?

The advantages stock option plans have over restricted share plans are the same as those outlined for stock option plans in Q 5:15. In contrast, restricted stock grants require an accounting charge to the income statement at the time of grant, based on the price of the share at that time. The company receives a tax deduction equal to the value of the restricted share at the time the restrictions lapse.

Restricted stock grants are not purchased by the executive. From a shareholder perspective, this can be a negative because executives can earn restricted shares during a time when the stock price has not changed.

Q 5:17   What is the disadvantage of stock options compared to long-term performance plans?

The major disadvantage of using stock options instead of long-term performance plans is that stock options have a dilutive effect on earnings per share. For example, if a company's earnings are $10 million and the number of shares outstanding is one million, then the company's EPS is calculated by dividing $10 million by one million, which equals $10 per share. If that company implements a new long-term stock option plan to add one million shares outstanding, the EPS calculation will, upon the exercise of all stock options (all other factors remaining the same), become $10 million divided by two million, which equals $5 per share. There has been significant dilutive effect on the EPS; this will be viewed negatively by both investment analysts and shareholders.

Other disadvantages of a stock option are that the executive must use personal funds to purchase the shares or borrow money to come up with the purchase price. If money is borrowed, the executive is at risk if the stock price goes down. Also, stock options are valuable only if share prices increase.

With respect to long-term performance plans, nothing is earned if goals are not achieved; however, the executive does not have to use personal funds or borrow money, since no purchase is required. Also, the performance plan is directly related to executive effort and to results as indicated by the company performance measure used in the plan. In contrast, stock options are subject to the vagaries of the stock market and do not necessarily correlate with executive performance.

Q 5:18 Are there disadvantages to using stock options as compared to restricted stock?

Stock options have a dilutive effect, as shown in Q 5:17, and they are only valuable to the executive if stock price increases. Executives must also purchase the stock option. In contrast, restricted shares require no executive investment and can have value to the executive even if the stock price goes down. While restricted shares also have a dilutive impact on the company's earnings per share, one can argue that executives are still motivated to raise company stock price so that the value of their restricted shares is higher at the time restrictions lapse. When this occurs, the company benefits from the tax deduction amount because this amount is equal to the value that the executive earns when the restrictions lapse, even though the company's accounting charge was equal to the lower value of the shares at the time of grant.

Q 5:19   Under what circumstances is a performance plan the best type of long-term incentive for a company to select?

In privately held companies, where ownership dilution is a concern, long-term performance plans are a good alternative to other incentive plans. Any public company that can measure long-term performance and wants to motivate executives to achieve long-term performance goals in the business plan would want to consider such a plan. In addition, any company whose stock is not traded very much and therefore has slow or erratic growth in stock price can also benefit from a performance plan.

Q 5:20   Under what circumstances are stock-based plans the best form of long-term incentive for a company to select?

The idea behind any long-term incentive plan is to motivate executives to do what is best for the company and its shareholders, and there is no better way to accomplish this than by making sure that the interest of both the executive and the shareholder is the same. This can be done by tying executive compensation to stock performance. In today's executive compensation environment, where public companies are under tremendous scrutiny by the media on potential excesses of executive compensation, stock plans, which directly align shareholder and executive interests, are an advantage. Consider the case of an executive who earns $10 million from a stock option over a five-year period. If the total increase in company stock price was $10 billion over that same period, media criticism of executive earnings can be completely neutralized.

Privately held corporations can also benefit from using stock-based plans as a way of gradually transferring ownership or voting control.

As a long-term incentive, the economic value to an executive of a stock-based plan can be duplicated through the use of a performance plan; however, stock options are less expensive to the company because they have no charge to the income statement. Restricted shares have a charge at the time of grant. Normally, this is better than when the restrictions lapse, provided that stock price increases.

Q 5:21   How can companies get executives to own stock?

The following alternatives are available:

1. Establish a minimum ownership requirement for executives. Companies using this alternative typically vary ownership levels by job level. For example, minimums could be set at 3,000 shares for an executive vice president, 2,000 shares for a senior vice president, and 1,000 shares for a vice president. Executives are typically given three years or more to accumulate minimum ownership positions.

2. Use reload options (see Q 6:37). These provide an additional ownership opportunity for executives by offering them new (reloaded) stock options every time they exercise an existing stock option share and retain ownership of those shares.

3. Grant restricted stock shares (see Q 7:31). These provide immediate ownership to executives; however, the executive must meet the restriction before he can take possession of the shares. In addition, companies can also require that executives continue ownership of restricted shares for a designated period after the restrictions lapse.

4. Provide leveraged stock options (see Q 5:8). Upon purchase of company shares the executive is given the right to purchase additional stock options in amounts equal to three to five times the number of shares purchased. Therefore the executive has "leveraged" the purchase of shares by obtaining the right to purchase a significant number of additional shares. Companies that use this alternative may also require the executive to retain ownership of the purchased shares for a designated period.

Q 5:22   What are the advantages of shareholder value/economic value plans over stock plans?

Advocates of shareholder value/economic value-added plans argue that these forms of long-term incentive motivate executives to increase the value of a company by meeting business goals that they control or significantly influence. The primary drivers of a company's stock price is shareholder value/economic value because if shareholders or potential shareholders see the company growing on these measures, they will continue to buy company shares and share price will respond by also growing. These measures are not subject to the vagaries of the stock market, and are therefore the best indicators of true value added to a company by executive performance.

Stock plan advocates argue that despite the vagaries of the stock market, it is the only true indicator of shareholder value, and therefore stock plans are the best form of long-term incentive. They produce a direct correlation of shareholders and executives because both own (or have the potential to own) shares. Measures of shareholder value/economic value-added cannot be exchanged for real dollars between owners/shareholders. Stock certificates can be exchanged for real dollars.

Q 5:23 What are the advantages of shareholder value/economic value plans over performance plans?

The advocates of shareholder value/economic value-added plans suggest that these plans use performance measures that cannot be manipulated by executives. Most traditional accounting measures can be manipulated by executives. For example, earnings per share goals can be easily met if executives buy back company shares, and thus lower the shares outstanding. Also, the traditional accounting measures in performance plans have goals that are negotiated between executives and the company chief executive officer and/or board compensation committee. Executives are motivated to negotiate low goals that they are assured to meet so that incentive payments are earned. This is not the case with economic value-added plans where typically the payout schedule has a targeted amount but no maximum; therefore, executives are always motivated to maximize their performance.

Advocates of performance plans suggest that because the measures used in these plans are directly controlled or influenced by executives, motivation is achieved. In shareholder value/EVA plans, executives do not directly influence cost of capital. Moreover, performance plans can be structured to pay out in company stock rather than cash and thus create more direct ties between executives and shareholders.

Q 5:24 What are the general rules regarding taxation of long-term incentive plans?

The company receives a federal income tax deduction at the time the executive incurs an ordinary income tax event. Plans that defer executive recognition of income will also defer the date on which a company may claim a tax deduction.

Capital gains tax applies to a corporate capital asset. Stock is a capital asset. Therefore, an executive who sells stock is subject to a capital gains tax. Companies receive no tax deductions from capital gains tax. The only form of long-term incentive that offers executives capital gains on shares of stock before they are owned is the incentive stock option (discussed in Chapter 6).

Q 5:25 What are the basic accounting issues for a long-term incentive plan?

The basic issue for accounting purposes is whether a given cost associated with a long-term capital accumulation plan will be expensed currently or whether it will be treated as a long-term capital expense that must be accrued as plan benefits are earned. Many believe that the Accounting Principles Board (APB) Rule 25 and Financial Accounting Standards Board (FASB) Rule 28 on long-term capital accumulation plan accounting treatment are contradictory and inconsistent.

APB Ruling 25 specifically states:

> Compensation for services that a corporation receives as consideration for stock issued through employee stock option, purchase, and award plans should be measured by the quoted market price of the stock at the measurement date less the amount, if any, that the employee is required to pay . . . if a quoted market price is unavailable, the best estimate of the market value of the stock should be used to measure compensation. The Measurement Date for determining compensation cost in stock option, purchase, and award plans is the first date on which are known both (1) the number of shares an individual employee is entitled to receive and (2) the option or purchase price, if any.

In contrast, FASB 28 states that stock appreciation rights and other "variable stock awards" as well as variable performance awards, where measurement dates cannot be established, will require that companies accrue cost over the period that the award is being earned.

Given these statements, consider for example that a stock option granted at market value has no charge to the company's income statement. The SAR produces a similar benefit to the executive but requires an accounting charge to the company's income statement.

The opposing point of view is that because an executive receives income from a stock option only after the executive sells the shares on the open market, the stock market, and not the company, is actually providing the executive with this income. In contrast, the SAR represents actual amounts paid to the executive by the company, and it is therefore appropriate that only this form and similar forms of long-term incentive require an accounting charge to the company's income statement.

Example 1. An executive is granted 1,000 stock option shares and at the time of grant the stock is trading at $20 per share, which is also the executive's option price. At the time of grant, under APB 25, the number of shares to be purchased by the executive and the purchase price are known. This amount is $20,000. Since the value of the option at the time of grant is $20,000, and the amount to be paid to the executive is $20,000, the company has zero charge to its income statement.

Example 2. An executive is granted 1,000 nonqualified stock option shares with an SAR on all the shares. At the time of grant, the stock is trading at $20 per share and the option price is also $20 per share. At the time of grant, the company must accrue during each quarter of the SAR award period the amount of stock appreciation per share, such that when the SAR is exercised the amount of actual compensation paid to the executive is equal to the amount that has been accrued on the company's income statement over the award period. If the executive received $15,000 in stock appreciation, then the company would have charged its income statement with $15,000.

Because of this debate, the FASB has been reviewing the accounting treatment of stock options for many years. In December 1995 the

FASB finally issued a new regulation that will, in the future, require companies to select APB 25 accounting treatment for stock awards or select the new Financial Accounting Statement (FAS) 123 which requires companies to calculate a "fair value" to all stock awards and charge this fair value to earnings over the vesting period of the stock award. This fair value will be measured by an option pricing model that meets criteria established by the FASB. If a company elects not to use FAS 123, it will be required to calculate the fair market value of any stock awards and show the earnings per share impact that would have occurred had this value been taken as a charge to earnings. This footnote must appear in the company's financial statements. For companies electing to continue the use of APB 25, the effective date of the new regulation is any fiscal year starting after December 15, 1994. If companies elect to use FAS 123, the effective date is any fiscal year starting after December 15, 1996.

One acceptable option pricing method is the Black-Scholes option model.

Q 5:26   How does the Black-Scholes option pricing model work?

The Black-Scholes option model considers the following:

- Current market price of the stock award
- Expected life of the stock award
- Volatility in the company stock over the expected life
- Risk-free rate of return over the expected life of the stock award
- Discounted present value of the amount that the executive will have to pay for the stock award
- Expected dividend over the life of the stock award

A simplistic explanation of the Black-Scholes formula is that the value of a stock award can be determined by calculating the difference between the current market price and the discounted present value of the purchase price to the executive, recognizing that both are adjusted for stock price volatility and the value of dividends. Unfortunately, the actual Black-Scholes formula is considerably more complicated. The good news, however, is that computer discs are available from human resource and CPA firms that facilitate the use of Black-Scholes in determining the fair value of stock awards.

Critics of Black-Scholes suggest that the key assumption in this option model is that the variance in the rate of return from stock price appreciation and short-term interest rates are constant over the expected life of the stock award. This, they claim, is unrealistic because significant economic events may alter returns from stock price appreciation during the expected life of the stock award. Moreover, the stock market is not always an orderly process whose variance can be statistically measured. The stock market is driven by emotion. Despite this debate, many large companies have already started using the Black-Scholes method to project company stock price for purposes of meeting the FASB "fair value" earnings charge and to meet public company reporting requirements on stock awards established by then Securities Exchange Commission.

A typical Black-Scholes calculation is shown below.

Example.

Current Market Value of the Stock Award	$40
Expected Life	10 Years
Volatility	1.25
Risk-Free Rate of Return	7%
Dividends	3% per year
Discounted Present Value of the Purchase Price on the Stock Award	$30
Fair Value	$10

Under FAS 123 the fair value calculated above would be accrued on the company income statement over the vesting period of the stock option.

Compensation Philosophy

Q 5:27 How should a corporate compensation philosophy be utilized in plan design?

A company's compensation philosophy or strategy statement should be the basis for designing any long-term incentive plan. These statements should provide a clear understanding of the organization's business and/or human resource goals so that the value and impact of its compensation programs can be established. The following information from the total compensation strategy statement (see Q 11:3) can provide guidance in the design of long-term incentive plans:

1. Competitive labor markets are defined and a targeted level of executive long-term incentive is established.

2. The company's culture and management style are defined. This helps determine whether long-term incentive plans should be decentralized for major company divisions or centralized at the corporate level. Information on the company culture can also determine the level of risk acceptable to the long-term incentive plan.

3. Key business performance measures are identified.

4. The statement identifies where changes in business goals should be supported by the long-term incentive compensation program, so that executive effort is focused on key business success factors.

5. The strategy statement states whether executive stock ownership is desirable within the company.

Planning Tip. Companies can no longer use the general philosophy of "to attract, retain, and motivate executives," or "to pay for performance." Total compensation strategy statements need to be very specific in today's business environment and should include a reference to the types of programs desired by the company (e.g., goal-based annual incentives, stock-based long-term incentives). These statements should also identify targeted compensation levels (e.g., 50th percentile, 70th percentile). Once established, these total compensation philosophy/strategy statements are useful guides in the design of executive compensation programs.

Q 5:28 What is the primary disadvantage of long-term performance plans?

Experience shows that many companies are unable to forecast accurately for a three- to four-year period. Strategic plans that typically run three to four periods are updated every year; however, long-term incentive plans that are objective-based cannot be adjusted every year. Therefore, companies must work to improve their accuracy in predicting business results to be achieved at the end of a three- to four-year period and then to tie compensation to these results. In addition, as market, financial, and other business conditions change over long-term performance periods, executives may become eligible for "windfall" bonuses or, conversely, become ineligible for bonuses because of unforeseen changes in the business environment.

Long-term performance plans can only be successful where management has a successful track record of long-term forecasting, or where management operates in a relatively stable business environment. For example, an aerospace company with large volume contracts every three to four years would not typically be affected by annual changes in cost of living or other measures of the economy. The same might also be true of a nonprofit organization. On the other hand, consumer product companies and advertising agencies typically must react immediately to changes in economic conditions, and in consumer habits or attitudes. Long-term forecasting is most difficult in these organizations.

Plan Design

Q 5:29 How do companies typically determine the amount of the long-term incentive payout or grant?

Two basic methods are used to establish the potential payout amount of the long-term plan. These two methods are the salary multiple approach (see Q 5:30) and the targeted income approach (see Q 5:31).

While these are the two most common methods used by companies to establish the payout or grant amount for long-term incentive plans, other companies choose to make their own decisions for each executive. In the absence of any predetermined formula or approach, companies make these individual decisions based typically on previous grant amounts and on current company performance. The advantage of this approach is that it gives the company total flexibility in providing long-term incentive awards while yearly grant increases satisfy the executive. The drawback to this approach is that companies focus their decisions on internal factors without regard to the realities of the competitive labor market. This could result in a significantly high or low reward to key executives.

Other companies use sophisticated computer modeling programs to predict stock price and/or company performance. The Black-Scholes method (see Q 5:26) is an example of a sophisticated stock price projection method.

Q 5:30 How does the salary multiple approach work in determining the size of long-term incentive awards?

The salary multiple approach is the easiest to explain and is used by companies who provide stock option grants. This approach expresses the total value of the stock option (number of shares multiplied by the price per share) as a multiple of the participating executive's base salary. For example, companies can survey the option value provided by competitive companies over a four-year period, and if that option value for a given group of executives is four times their salary, the option value provided by the company to those executives over a four-year period would be four times their base salary or salary range midpoint.

Example. An executive has a base salary of $100,000. The company stock price is $20 per share. The company has determined that, under the salary multiple approach, this executive should receive stock options that are four times the executive's base salary over the next four years. The total option value for this executive should be $400,000 ($100,000 × 4). If this company grants stock options every two years, then this executive should receive stock options with a value of $200,000 for each grant ($400,000 ÷ 2). With the stock trading at $20 per share, this executive would receive 10,000 stock option shares for each grant during the two-year period ($200,000 ÷ $20 = 10,000 shares).

The advantage of the salary multiple approach is that it provides a simple, easy to understand basis for determining the number of shares in a stock option grant. The drawback of this approach is that it measures option value (number of shares times stock price) rather than actual gain/income received by the executive. A second drawback is that company stock price continuously changes, and as stock price increases, the number of shares will decrease. For example, if the stock price in the example was $30 per share at the time the executive was to be granted the second stock option award, the number of shares provided to the executive would be 6,667 rather than 10,000 ($200,000 divided by $30 = 6,667 shares).

Q 5:31 How does the targeted income approach work in determining the size of a long-term incentive award?

Under performance plans, companies simply determine a targeted income level for their long-term incentive (see Chapter 11, "Building a Total Compensation Strategy"). Under this approach, targeted income levels are established for each executive position.

This is a little more difficult under a stock option plan. Under these plans, companies project stock price appreciation, and based on this projection provide the executive with a number of shares that will deliver the targeted amounts of appreciation over the stock award period.

Example. To project stock price, a company can use the following stock price formula: Stock price = stock multiple times earnings per share. Therefore companies can predict stock price appreciation as shown in the chart below.

Year	Stock Multiple	Earnings Per Share	Stock Price
1990	5	$2.00	$10.00
1991	5	$2.10	$10.50
1992	5	$2.30	$11.50
1993	5	$2.50	$12.50
1994	5	$3.00	$15.00

Total Stock Appreciation = $5.

Given these stock price projections, which estimate stock appreciation to be $5 over the stock option award period of four years, the company would then take its targeted long-term income for this position and divide it by the estimated stock appreciation. If the targeted income was $10,000, then the company would want to give this executive 2,000 shares ($10,000 ÷ $5 = 2,000 shares).

The advantage of the targeted income approach is that it enables companies to determine grant levels for both stock options and other long-term incentive grants (i.e., performance plans). The drawback of this approach is that it requires companies to estimate stock price, and while there are many methods for doing this (such as in the previous example), no method can realistically factor in the vagaries of the stock market and the fact that the stock market does not always respond directly to company earnings performance.

Stock Options

Q 5:32 What are the different types of stock options?

The two primary types of stock options are the statutory stock option, also known as the incentive stock option, and the nonstatutory stock option, known as the nonqualified stock option. The statutory regulations of the ISO are contained in the Internal Revenue Code (the Code) Sections 421 and 422, while the tax treatment for nonstatutory (i.e., nonqualified) stock options is governed by Code Section 83.

Each of these types of stock options has a different tax treatment. The statutory option or ISO may qualify for the capital gains tax. All nonstatutory/nonqualified stock options subject the executive to ordinary income tax until such time as the executive owns the shares, at which time the executive is in possession of a capital asset and will then be eligible for capital gains tax on future stock appreciation.

In 1994, there is a difference between the two tax treatments, with ordinary income tax rates at a maximum of 39.6 percent, and the capital gains tax rate at 28 percent. Because of these differences in tax rates, many believe that companies will utilize statutory stock options (i.e., ISOs) in the future to take advantage of the capital gains tax treatment.

Q 5:33 What is the typical exercise period for a stock option?

The typical maximum exercise period for a nonqualified stock option is ten years. The typical exercise period for an incentive stock option is five years, although statutory regulations allow for the ISO to run ten years. Because the ISO statutory requirements state that executives must exercise/purchase the ISO and then hold it for one year before realizing capital gain on the entire appreciation, companies have typically opted to have a shorter exercise period. Another reason for this practice is that when the ISO was first authorized there was a sequential exercise requirement, meaning that each ISO grant had to be exercised (in total) sequentially. For example, if an executive had two ISO grants, one in 1993 at $30 per share and one in 1994 at $20 per share, the executive would have to exercise all of the 1993 grants at $30 (after meeting all required vesting periods) before the executive could exercise the 1994 shares granted at $20. This additional complexity prompted companies to shorten the exercise period. Survey data show that companies have continued this practice even though there is no longer a sequential requirement for incentive stock options.

Companies should consider a number of good reasons for not following the typical practice of a ten-year exercise award period for nonqualified stock options. One reason is that the longer the option's term the greater the benefits to the executive holding the option, because the executive will have greater flexibility in determining when to exercise the stock option for tax and financial planning purposes as well as from a stock market timing point of view. Another reason is the benefits to the company: Executive retention is encouraged by the longer exercise period. Some companies have also elected to extend stock option exercise periods for those executives who reach retirement. Such an approach provides flexibility to the executive in determining when to exercise the stock option after retirement, when funds would typically be needed. The tax, financial planning, and market timing issues become extremely critical for an executive who has retired. An example of this is to allow an executive three years after retirement to exercise all vested stock options.

In contrast, there is a good reason for not shortening the exercise period. Most companies provide executives with multiple forms of long-term incentive (e.g., stock options, restricted stock, performance plans). It is also typical for companies to make long-term incentive awards annually. Therefore executives have numerous grants from numerous forms of long-term incentive at any given point of time. Extending the exercise period to ten years adds complexity to this issue. Shortening the exercise period is beneficial to executives as they try to manage these multiple forms of long-term incentive in their best interest.

Q 5:34   What is the rationale behind using stock-based plans?

It is much less expensive for the employer to use stock in compensating executives than it is to provide them with cash from a long-term incentive plan. While earnings are reduced whenever cash is provided, this is not true for stock. Stock does, however, have a dilution cost: Stock grants are common stock equivalents, thus diluting shareholder equity. It is commonly believed, however, that the dilution cost has significantly less impact on the company than charges to the income statement. A second logic for using stock-based plans is that if the company is achieving its goals, stock should be worth far more over time than its original grant value. The appreciation in the shares is not a "cost" to the company; the gain received by the executive is provided by the stock market at the time shares are sold. Therefore companies have good economic reason to use stock-based plans.

In addition, publicly traded corporations like to use stock-based plans because this enables them to place a large block of stock in "friendly hands," which makes takeover attempts more difficult. Privately held corporations can also benefit from using stock-based plans as a way of gradually transferring ownership or voting control.

Q 5:35   Under what conditions are stock options effective?

For a stock option plan to be effective, the company's stock must be consistently appreciating or have sufficient fluctuation from the grant price such that the executive is motivated to exercise the stock option when the market value is well above the option value. A stock option that has an option exercise price that is above the current market price is said to be "under water."

Q 5:36   In what cases are stock options ineffective?

Under certain circumstances, stock options may not be an effective executive incentive. Stock options in mature companies with poor stock price growth potential are effective neither as a retention nor as a motivational tool. Stock options in highly cyclical industries are not necessarily an effective motivational tool because much of the gain in the price of stock is due to circumstances beyond the executive's control, although such stock options may be an effective retention factor during the growth portion of the cycle.

In addition, if executives do not have sufficient cash resources to purchase stock options, their interests may not be tied to those of shareholders. Stock options are also ineffective during a corporate restructuring, sale, or recapitalization because they are not owned shares and the executive may not benefit from the corporate restructuring, sale, or recapitalization.

Q 5:37 How do companies determine the number of shares to reserve for stock option plans?

There is no formula consistently used to determine the number of shares to reserve for long-term plans; practice has shown, however, that three factors affect this number: industry, company size, and the company's life cycle (i.e., growth versus maturity).

In general, companies reserve between 5 percent and 10 percent of their outstanding shares for executive stock option plans over a five-year period. This equals from 1 percent to 2 percent per year of the shares outstanding. Small growth companies in a high-risk, start-up situation will usually allocate higher percentages to their executive stock option plans. The percentage of shares outstanding in these cases is three to four times that of a typical company.

Omnibus Plan

Q 5:38 What is an omnibus plan?

An omnibus plan is a long-term incentive compensation plan submitted to company shareholders for approval that includes every conceivable form of long-term incentive, both stock-related plans and nonstock-related plans. A rationale for such a broad-based plan is that shareholder approval for a new long-term plan will not have to be sought as business conditions change. These plans generally authorize the issuance of a number of shares to be used for any or all stock award plans.

For example, an omnibus plan can provide grants for nonqualified stock options, incentive stock options, discounted stock options, stock appreciation rights, restricted stock grants, performance shares, performance units, or reload stock options. Before any grant is made, a company's board compensation committee would review current business requirements and approve a recommendation from management on the right form of long-term incentive grant. At times, executives at different levels in the organization could receive different forms of long-term incentive.

One concern about omnibus plans is that they are too general and may not provide sufficient information to the shareholders who must approve them. This problem can be overcome if omnibus plans include limitations on the grants per executive and/or a minimum company performance that must be achieved before various long-term grants are provided. For example, an omnibus plan could include a statement as follows: "No executive can own more than 3 percent of the shares outstanding." The type of grant would not matter to the shareholders because the number of shares per executive is limited. Another example of a company protection statement in an omnibus plan might be: "No long-term incentive grant will be made in any given year unless shareholder dividends were paid in the previous year and company return on capital is at least 10 percent." This type of statement in the omnibus plan protects shareholder interests.

Tax Considerations

Q 5:39 How does the tax doctrine of constructive receipt affect a long-term incentive plan?

In Question 5:24, there is a general outline of the taxation on long-term incentive plans. Under the doctrine of constructive receipt, an executive will be subject to tax if he has unrestricted control in determining income to be received. For example, interest from a bank CD or savings account is taxable in the tax year it is credited to an individual's account, even though the individual does not take receipt of the money. Because the individual could have taken it, she is in constructive receipt, and an ordinary income tax is due in that tax year. Compensation payments constitute income to the executive and a deduction to the company (assuming they are taxed as ordinary income) in the year they are actually or constructively received. With cash-based plans, the timing is relatively clear. With stock-based plans, the timing depends largely on the terms of the stock award. Generally, a stock award granted to an executive as compensation is not included in that employee's income because under the doctrine of constructive receipt, it is subject to risk of forfeiture. Once an executive earns a stock award, or exercises a stock option, the executive no longer has any risk of forfeiture, and must report ordinary income that is equal to the difference between the fair market value of the stock and the amount, if any, paid for the stock. At this time, the company is entitled to a corresponding tax deduction.

Under constructive receipt, the Code states that property vests when it is not subject to a substantial risk of forfeiture. Code vesting is not the same as vesting in a long-term incentive plan. For example, under stock option plan vesting, the executive simply earns the right to purchase the shares, but until the purchase occurs there is risk of forfeiture.

Q 5:40 What are some of the conditions that create a substantial risk of forfeiture in a long-term incentive plan?

The most important condition that creates a substantial risk of forfeiture is that the company could be liquidated, and the executive would lose his stock award. Another condition might be that an executive's right to the stock is dependent upon future performance of the company. For example, under a performance plan grant an executive receives the opportunity to earn 1,000 shares of stock if company earnings per share increase 10 percent per year over the next four years. Since the executive may not earn the shares unless that goal is achieved, a risk of forfeiture clearly exists.

Q 5:41 What are some of the conditions that do not create a substantial risk of forfeiture in a long-term incentive plan?

These are extremely rare. For purposes of determining whether stock has substantially vested under the Code, a substantial risk of forfeiture may not exist merely because the executive must forfeit the shares of stock or stock options, if the company liquidates, if the executive is convicted of a crime and terminated for cause, or because the executive may accept a job with a competing firm. Companies are, however, quick to overcome these potential situations that would not create a substantial risk of forfeiture, by stating in their plan texts that any and all potential payments must be approved by the committee administering the plan. These committees are, in most cases, composed of outside members (nonemployees) of the board of directors, who have the authority under the plan to amend, modify, rescind, or change awards in any way.

Another example of a condition that may not create a risk of forfeiture is a restricted stock grant where the restriction is a clearly attainable performance restriction such as earnings growth of 1 percent per year for a company that has been historically earning 10 percent per year for the last ten years. The IRS could view this as a restriction that does not have any risk of forfeiture and thus declare that the executive is in constructive receipt and that the entire value of the shares is taxable.

Q 5:42 What is the general tax effect of a stock option?

There are three different times in the life of a stock option at which it may be taxable to the employee: (1) at the time it is granted, (2) at the time it is exercised, and (3) at the time the share of stock is sold.

Statutory Options. A statutory option is one that qualifies (as opposed to one that is "nonqualified") for special tax treatment (e.g., capital gains). An employee in compliance with the required statutory holding periods will incur no tax consequences upon the grant or exercise of the option under Code Sections 421 and 422 and will be taxed only when the stock is sold. This is the case for incentive stock options. An additional statutory requirement is that, upon exercise of the option, the share of stock must be held for one year before it is sold. If this provision is met, the difference between the value of the share at the time it is sold and the option price is taxed as capital gains.

Nonstatutory Options. For a nonstatutory or nonqualified option, the employee is not taxed at the time of grant, but there is a taxable event at the time of exercise. When the employee sells the share, the gain recognized (the difference between market price of the stock at the time of exercise and the market value of the stock at the time of sale) will be taxed as long-term capital gain if the share was held one year after the exercise date. Because the executive incurred a taxable event at the time of exercise equal to the difference between the exercise price and the option price, the future tax base of that share is the market value of the share at the time of exercise.

Furthermore, an executive exercising an option must satisfy state and federal withholding requirements at the time of exercise. She cannot delay the taxable event until the end of the tax year in which the exercise occurs.

Q 5:43   What is the general tax effect of a stock appreciation right?

For SARS (see Qs 7:3–7:7), there is no tax at the time of grant and no constructive receipt during the award period until the time of exercise. At that time, a taxable event has occurred and the executive must pay ordinary income tax. The company then receives a tax deduction because this income is taxed at ordinary income tax rates. An executive taking the SAR in cash must also satisfy federal and state withholding requirements. The same is true if the executive takes the stock appreciation right in shares of stock. This can be accomplished by having the company withhold the required amount for taxes from the value of the SAR and then delivering the remaining shares to the executive. These remaining shares would be subject to capital gains tax if held for one year from the date of exercise.

Q 5:44   What is the general tax effect of a restricted stock grant?

There is no tax at the time a restricted stock option is granted, and there is no constructive receipt during the restriction period because there is a clear risk of forfeiture. When the restrictions lapse, there is an ordinary income tax event to the executive equal to the number of shares times the market price of the shares at the time the restrictions lapse. The company gets a tax deduction equal to the same amount. Again, the executive must satisfy federal and state withholding requirements and may do so by having the company sell sufficient shares to meet withholding requirements.

Q 5:45 What is the general tax effect of a performance plan award?

There is no tax on either a performance share or a performance unit at the time of grant, nor is there any tax during the performance period, since the executive is not in constructive receipt of the performance grant. Once the performance grant is earned, however, there is an ordinary income tax event equal to the total value received by the executive(number of shares or units times the price per share or unit). The executive must satisfy both federal and state withholding requirements. Moreover, shares issued to the executive may be used to pay the withholding tax or the amount may be deducted from the cash award.

Q 5:46 How does the constructive receipt doctrine affect deferred compensation?

It is critical to structure deferred compensation plans so that the executive cannot be regarded as being in constructive receipt of the compensation before it is actually received as compensation. In designing deferred compensation plans, the following safeguards should be included:

1. If the executive's decision to defer compensation (rather than to receive it currently) is voluntary, then the executive should make the election before the services are rendered.

2. If the compensation is deferred to some specific or determinable future date, the executive should, as a general rule, not be given a unilateral election to defer it to a still later date once the services have been rendered. For example, if an executive has elected to defer compensation until age 65, the executive

should not have a unilateral second election to defer its receipt until some age beyond age 65.

3. Most companies will require executives to provide an "irrevocable election" to defer future compensation prior to the performance period of the incentive compensation plan or at least 12 months before the end of the performance period. For example, an executive makes an irrevocable election during the second year of a three-year performance plan to defer for five years any income earned from the plan. In this case, the doctrine of constructive receipt has been met by virtue of the executive's signing an irrevocable election prior to the time that the compensation is earned.

Q 5:47 What is the economic benefit theory?

Under the economic benefit doctrine, when an economic benefit has been granted, the executive may be taxed currently. Economic value can be cash or anything equivalent to cash.

Example. Executive A earns $20,000 under a company's incentive compensation plan. In accordance with a doctrine of constructive receipt, the executive defers that amount for a five-year period. However, during the third year of the deferral, the executive borrows $20,000 from the bank and uses the deferred income as collateral for the loan. This executive has received economic benefit from the $20,000, and under the economic benefit tax doctrine, the deferred amounts become immediately taxable.

Q 5:48 What is a Code Section 83(b) election?

Code Section 83(b) allows an employee to choose to be taxed immediately on the amounts received in connection with a substantially "nonvested" right, i.e., compensation that has not been constructively received (see Q 5:39). This is accomplished by having the executive file an election with IRS stating that she will pay ordinary income on the value as measured at the time of grant. Any future appreciation in the stock property will be treated as capital gain when sold. This election must be made within 30 days after the stock is received.

The most significant drawback of the Code Section 83(b) election is that if the executive does not receive the stock, he forfeits taxes previously paid and cannot take a tax loss. Balancing this against the fact that stock price can go up or down, the election of Code Section 83(b) is not so compelling.

Example. An executive is given 1,000 restricted shares with a three-year restriction period at a time when the current stock price is $20. Within 30 days, the executive elects under Code Section 83(b) to pay tax on the $20,000 grant value. Upon completion of the three-year restriction period, the executive takes possession of the shares but has no taxable event. Upon the future sale of these shares, the difference between the sale price and $20 per share is subject to capital gains (if the shares are held for one year under the current tax laws).

Exercising a Stock Option

Q 5:49 What are the different ways an employee can pay the exercise price of a stock option?

There are three primary ways for an employee to pay the exercise price of an option. The three ways are (1) by using cash, (2) by delivering already-owned stock, i.e., a stock swap (see Q 5:53), and (3) by a "cashless exercise." Cash is the easiest method. Where an executive delivers shares of already-owned stock, the market value of the stock is applied toward the exercise price. As an example, Executive C has an option to purchase 1,000 shares of Company D stock at an exercise price of $10 per share (1,000 shares × $10 = $10,000). If the then-current market price is $25 per share, Executive C can pay the exercise price by delivering 400 shares of stock already owned. (400 shares × $25 = $10,000). The cashless exercise is described in Question 5:51.

Until the recent revisions to the Section 16 rules (see next question), insiders were limited to the use of cash in order to exercise their options. Now, however, these techniques are available to all employees.

Q 5:50 How do the Section 16 rules of the SEC affect stock plans and the way employees can pay for stock?

Under Section 16 an insider is not allowed to purchase and sell shares of stock within a six-month period. Under prior rules, the exercise of a stock option was considered a purchase of the underlying shares and "matchable" with any other sale by the executive during the six months before or after the date of exercise. As a result, an insider could not pay the option price by tendering already owned shares because that tender would constitute a sale that would be matched against the purchase that existed by virtue of the exercise of the option.

The amended SEC Section 16 rules of May 1991 provide that the exercise of an option is not considered a purchase, but the granting of the option is considered a purchase event under Section 16. These new rules have significantly liberalized the use of options by insiders, by extending to them the possibility of paying for their shares through a stock swap, a cashless exercise, or by immediately selling shares after the exercise. These new rules have also lessened the need for a stock appreciation right and other techniques designed to provide insiders with the cash required to exercise their stock options. An important provision of the amended Section 16 is that stock options granted as Section 16(b)3 shares are not matchable with a purchase event created by the issue of different stock options under Section 16(b)3. This means that executives can sell previously exercised stock option shares as well as previously owned shares without being subject to the "matching" provision of Section 16.

Q 5:51 What is a cashless option exercise?

Federal Reserve Board Regulation T of the NASD rules permits broker-dealers to treat an option exercise notice as if it were stock and, as a result, to advance funds to the executive in order to pay for the exercise of the option. This is called the cashless exercise of stock options. It is called "cashless" because the executive can pay the option exercise price for the stock with the proceeds of the sale from the underlying shares. The process involves the executive's giving the company an irrevocable exercise notice that instructs the company to deliver the stock subject to the option to the executive's broker.

The executive signs a promissory note to pay the exercise price. The broker is then instructed to sell the shares and to deliver the proceeds to the company. The company is thus provided with the option exercise value, and the executive then receives the remaining value.

> **Example.** An executive has 1,000 stock option shares vested at an option price of $30. In order to exercise the option, the executive owes $30,000. The current market price of the stock is $50. The executive completes a request to the company to exercise these shares and instructs the company to provide the shares to the broker. The executive also completes a promissory note to pay the broker $30,000. The executive is liable for payment of $30,000. The broker then sells the 1,000 shares at the $50 stock price. From the $50,000 proceeds, $30,000 is paid to the company; the executive then has $20,000 of taxable income. The company will deduct minimum required federal and state withholding taxes and appropriate broker fees from the executive's $20,000 and then return the net proceeds to the executive.

Q 5:52 What is Regulation T, and what is its effect on executive compensation?

Regulation T affects executive compensation because it affects how an executive can finance the exercise of options or sale of stock through a brokerage account. Specifically, the amount a customer must deposit in a margin account and the amount the broker may lend are prescribed by the Board of Governors of the Federal Reserve Board by authority of the Securities Exchange Act of 1934 under Regulation T. Regulation T permits the cashless stock option exercise (see Q 5:51).

Q 5:53 What is a stock swap?

A stock swap is another name for the method of allowing an executive to deliver already owned stock, instead of paying cash, to exercise a stock option.

> **Example.** An executive has the right to purchase 1,000 shares of stock at an option exercise price of $30. The executive also owns outright 600 other shares of company stock with a current market

value of $50. The amount required to exercise the 1,000 stock option shares is $30,000 (1,000 × $30). The value of the shares owned by the executive is also $30,000 (600 shares × $50). The executive can swap 600 shares for the exercise of 1,000 shares, after which the executive will own 1,000 shares.

Q 5:54 What is a pyramiding stock swap exercise?

Pyramiding is an extension of a stock swap that involves a series of stock swaps enabling the executive continuously to exchange the value of stock owned to purchase a stock option.

Example. Executive A owns one share of stock with a market value of $50. The executive also has an option to buy 200 shares at an option price of $10 per share. The executive could turn in the one share worth $50 in order to exercise a portion of his option as to five shares at $10 per share. He would then surrender those five shares, valued at $250, to exercise his option as to 25 shares, which have a market value of $1,250 (25 shares at $50), and then surrender those 25 shares to exercise his option as to 125 shares, and then surrender nine shares to exercise his option as to the remaining 45 shares. At the end of the process, he would have 161 shares worth $8,050. (This example ignores for illustrative purposes the tax withholding requirement.)

Tax Considerations

Q 5:55 What is the tax treatment of a stock swap or pyramiding exercise?

The impact of a stock swap or pyramiding exercise depends on whether the stock option is nonqualified or a statutory/qualified option.

Nonqualified Option. With a nonqualified option, the exchange of already owned shares for the same number of shares is a tax-free exchange, i.e., the owned shares keep their current tax basis. The fair market value of any additional shares received is taxable income to the executive, and the new shares have a tax basis equal to that fair market value.

Example. An executive had the right to purchase a nonqualified stock option of 1,000 shares at $30 per share. The executive swaps 600 shares owned at a market price of $50 to exercise the right to purchase 1,000 shares. The 600 originally owned shares represent a tax-free exchange, and the tax basis on these shares remains the same. The 400 new shares with a current market value of $50 per share represent $20,000 (400 shares × $50) of taxable income, taxed at ordinary income tax rates. Therefore, the new tax basis for the 400 shares will be the current market price of $50.

Incentive Stock Option (Statutory Option). With a statutory stock option (incentive stock option) the exchange is tax-free if the option meets all statutory requirements. The executive will not be taxed at the time of exercise on the amount by which the value of the newly acquired shares exceeds the value of the shares already owned. The shares that are swapped keep their same tax basis. The new shares have a tax basis of zero.

Example. An executive is granted 1,000 incentive stock options at an option exercise price of $30. The executive swaps 600 shares at a market value of $50 to meet the exercise price of $30,000. The 600 original shares are a tax-free exchange, and the tax basis for these shares remains unchanged. The 400 new shares have a tax basis of zero. If those shares are held for the one-year holding period required of the incentive stock option and then sold, they will be subject to capital gains tax based on the sale price minus zero, their original tax basis.

Q 5:56   Are there drawbacks to a pyramiding exercise or stock swap?

Yes. Remember that any shares surrendered by an insider to the company to satisfy the exercise price are deemed to have been sold for purposes of Section 16, and are therefore matchable against any other purchases by that insider during the preceding and succeeding six months. Furthermore, if the plan is already in place and does not permit payment by stock, then the plan would have to be amended and certain formalities would have to be followed (see Qs 5:57 and 5:58).

The other major drawback of pyramiding is the requirement that companies take an accounting charge when options are exercised with shares that are not mature.

Plan Administration

Q 5:57   What is needed to institute a long-term incentive plan?

A company's board of directors normally has the right to authorize the issuance of any authorized but unissued shares for purposes of a long-term incentive plan. The board of directors, through their compensation committee, may either make grants of stock or adopt a formal stock plan and grant full value shares or options up to the number of authorized but unissued shares available for use in executive compensation plans. Any company whose shares are traded on a listed stock exchange must have its executive compensation plan approved by shareholders if the plan involves awards or payments of executive compensation in the form of stock traded on that exchange.

As a practical matter, regardless of stock awards or stock payments, a publicly traded company will want to obtain shareholder approval for a plan so that grants under the plan will meet SEC Section 16 requirements. A privately held company will often want to obtain shareholder approval as a courtesy to their owner-managers. Once a plan has been adopted and approved by shareholders, the board of directors (or a disinterested compensation committee of the board in the case of public companies wishing to qualify for Rule 16(b)3 exceptions to SEC Section 16 (see Chapter 11)) will make grants under the plan periodically and as needed in order to compensate executives.

Special rules apply to statutory or incentive stock option plans because they must meet certain conditions in order for the executive to receive preferred tax treatment (see Q 6:6).

Q 5:58   What is needed to amend a long-term incentive plan?

In general, any requirement necessary to adopt a plan is necessary to materially amend it. The Section 16 rules specifically provide that if the amendment is one which would "(A) materially increase the benefits accruing to participants in the plan; (B) materially increase the number of securities which may be issued under the plan; or (C) materially modify the requirements as to eligibility for participation in the plan" then shareholder approval would be required or the Rule 16(b)3 exemption would be lost.

Q 5:59   What information about a long-term incentive must be disclosed in a company's proxy statement?

Any new capital accumulation plan (short-term or long-term) that utilizes company stock must be approved by shareholders. This is a regulation of the stock exchanges where the stock is traded, although most companies would have these plans approved by shareholders anyway as a matter of good business principle and for purposes of protecting the plan administrators from potential lawsuits by unhappy shareholders who may simply not like the plan.

Any "material" amendment to a long-term plan would also be approved by shareholders. The term material is subject to prudent definitions but normally means any substantial change in the level or type of award, or the number of participants. Material changes that are submitted to shareholders would be described along with disclosures of the amounts of cash (or stock) that would have been set aside during the previous or current fiscal year, had the plan been in effect.

On an ongoing basis, the Securities Exchange Commission requires a public company to report the following information on the top five executives in its annual proxy:

1. A summary chart of cash compensation earned during the last three years

2. A table on stock option grants made during the last fiscal year plus an estimate of the future value of these stock awards

3. A special table on the stock options of these executives and the number and value of those awarded and exercised during the last fiscal year, plus the unrealized value of unexercised options and stock appreciation rights

4. A table of estimated retirement benefits including special supplemental retirement benefits

5. The composition of the board compensation committee and a discussion by the committee of CEO compensation, its philosophy, and how levels of pay are determined

6. Two performance graphs that compare company performance to outside standards

7. A description of employment contracts and any special severance arrangements for the top five executives

8. Outside director compensation programs (fees, retainers, consulting contracts, retirement plans, etc.)

9. A detailed report on any stock options that were repriced during the last fiscal year

These provisions of the SEC are described in more detail in Q 2:26 and Q 2:28. They are extremely comprehensive and were designed by the SEC to insure that all compensation of top officers and performance of the company was reported in one place and made available to shareholders (and to media personnel and other employees) so that any potential excessive total compensation would be clear.

Q 5:60 How should long-term incentive compensation plans be handled during a merger of two companies?

Companies that merge must first determine whether one of the existing long-term incentive plans will remain. Whether one of the plans is retained or a new plan developed, one or both of the companies will need to buy out existing long-term incentive awards. This is typically done by prorating existing awards based on the vested amount of any stock options or by using a prorated payment for any performance plans or restricted stock plans. For example, if the performance period or restriction period is four years and the merger occurs after Year 2, a 50 percent proration is applied to the plans and paid to the executive.

Key plan provisions should be reviewed in making a transition to a new long-term incentive plan after a merger. These include the following:

- Eligibility
- Size of awards
- Type of long-term incentive plan
- Frequency of grant
- Award period
- Vesting requirements
- Plan administration issues (e.g., approvals, administrating committee, form of payment)

The development of a total compensation strategy, as discussed in Chapter 11, is also an extremely valuable activity to undertake during a merger.

Q 5:61 How should deferred compensation be integrated during a merger of two companies?

There are three key issues to be evaluated in deferred compensation plans during a merger. These are:

1. Investment alternatives available to participants
2. Analysis of whether the plans are funded or unfunded and/or secured with a rabbi trust, secular trust, or some form of insurance
3. Plan administration

Conclusions on these issues can be used to determine future deferral provisions. In most cases, the acquiring company practices prevail. A better approach is, however, to establish a task force of both acquiring and acquired company representatives to: (1) identify current practices, (2) select and evaluate alternative solutions, (3) recommend a solution, and obtain approval, and (4) implement these approved provisions.

Rarely do two merged companies apply similar investment alternatives to deferred accounts, nor do they have similar wording in their plan text on the maintenance and security of individual accounts. In some cases, the merger raises questions on the level of risk that deferred accounts will not be paid, since the merger modifies the new company's financial strength. Full payout of all deferred accounts may need to be considered.

Q 5:62 What is an example of integration of deferred accounts?

Let's say, for example, that Company *A* merges with Company *B*, and Company *A* is the surviving company. Company *A* has 60 deferred accounts that are invested in company stock units or have the T-bill interest rate applied quarterly. Company *B* has 40 deferred accounts that are invested in: (1) a real estate investment trust, (2) mutual funds, (3) stock/equities fund, (4) company-owned life insurance, and (5) prime rate. Plan administration is done by each company's treasurer's department.

The companies form a joint committee to evaluate and recommend a future structure for all future deferred accounts. The committee concludes that since one company has only a few conservative investments and the other has numerous aggressive investments, a revised group of investment alternatives need to be established by using a "middle of the road" strategy. They select the following:

- Quarterly T-bill interest
- The stock/equities fund
- The mutual fund
- Company stock units

All other former investment alternatives went through a "buyout" and conversion to one of these four alternatives. Each participant was provided with full information and asked to make revised selections by an established date in the future, otherwise all deferred accounts would be converted into company stock units.

Plan administration was placed in the acquiring company's treasurer's department, and the primary individual in the acquired company that administered deferrals was transferred to the acquiring company to assist in administering all deferred accounts.

Both companies had unfunded deferred accounts, which remained that way.

Chapter 6

Purchase Plans

Purchase plans are the most frequently used long-term incentive plan design, and come in many forms. This chapter covers eight of them: incentive stock options, nonstatutory stock options, discounted stock options, premium stock options, option reloads, book value purchase plans, convertible debentures, and junior stock plans. These types of plans require executives to make an actual investment if they wish to own shares. The chapter examines the tax, legal, and financial implications of purchase plans, as well as their relative strengths and weaknesses.

General Considerations 6-2
Incentive Stock Options 6-4
Nonstatutory Stock Options 6-11
Discounted Stock Options 6-18
Premium Stock Options 6-21
Option Reloads 6-24
Book Value Purchase Plans 6-26
Convertible Debentures 6-29
Junior Stock Plans 6-33
Performance-Based Stock Options 6-34

General Considerations

Q 6:1   What is a purchase plan?

Purchase plans are capital accumulation plans that give the executive the opportunity to purchase stock at a future date.

Q 6:2   What are the different types of purchase plans?

The seven main forms of purchase plans, all of which are discussed in this chapter, are as follows:

- Statutory (incentive) stock option plans
- Nonstatutory stock option plans
- Discounted stock option plans
- Premium stock option plans
- Option reload plans
- Book value purchase plans
- Convertible debenture plans
- Junior stock plans

Q 6:3   What are the fundamental differences between different types of purchase plans?

Purchase plans are similar in that they provide a way for a company to compensate employees with stock. Purchase plans differ primarily in how they accomplish the goal of compensating employees with stock, the tax treatment of the specific transaction, and the amount of investment required of the employee.

Q 6:4   How are stock option exercise prices set?

The most common approach is to set an option exercise price at the market value of the share of stock at the time of grant. In using this standard approach, companies take the average selling price of the stock at the beginning of the day and at the end of the day, and use this as the fair market value at the time of grant.

Companies that use discounted stock options, which are stock options with an option exercise price that is below the market value at the time of grant, will typically use the same approach of averaging stock price on the date of grant, and then discounting this amount by a fixed dollar per share amount or percentage amount. Upon grant of this stock the executive immediately realizes the appreciation potential, but may still be subject to specific vesting requirements in the stock option.

Companies can also grant premium stock options, which are options with an exercise price that is above the current market value at the time of grant. Along the same lines, companies will establish the fair market value at the time of grant of the premium stock option and increase that amount by a fixed dollar amount, or by some specified percentage.

Example.

> Regular Stock Option Grant:
> Average fair market value at the time of grant = $10
> Executive exercise price = $10
>
> Discounted Stock Option:
> Fair market value at the time of grant = $10
> Executive exercise price = $5
>
> Premium Stock Option:
> Fair market value at the time of grant = $10
> Executive exercise price = $15

Q 6:5 How long is the typical option exercise period?

Most surveys on this subject show that nonqualified options typically have a ten-year exercise period while incentive stock options (ISOs) typically have a five-year exercise period. Junior stock plans and book value purchase plans typically have an exercise period that is three to five years.

Incentive Stock Options

Q 6:6 What is an incentive stock option?

ISOs were created by the Economic Recovery Act of 1981, and the requirements that apply to them were modified by the Tax Reform Act of 1986. As a result, ISOs are required to meet the statutory requirements of Internal Revenue Code (Code) Section 422, which provides the following:

1. The ISO must be granted only to an employee of the issuing company, its parent, or a subsidiary of the issuing parent.

2. The ISO must be granted pursuant to a plan that specifies the total number of shares that may be issued under options and the employees or class of employees that are eligible to receive options. The plan must be approved by the company shareholders within 12 months before or after the date that the plan is adopted.

3. The maximum exercise period for the ISO cannot exceed ten years. The executive eligible for the plan cannot own more than 10 percent of the total combined voting class of stock in the company.

4. The ISO cannot be transferable by the optionee during the optionee's lifetime.

5. The exercise price of the ISO cannot be less then the fair market value of the stock on the date of the grant.

6. The executive cannot sell shares exercised under an ISO program within two years from the date the option is granted, or within one year from the date the option is exercised or purchased.

7. An executive cannot exercise ISOs that have an option value (number of shares times option price at the time of grant) that exceeds $100,000 during any given calendar year. This $100,000 limitation is cumulative (i.e., if not used in one year, the following year it is $200,000).

8. The owner of an ISO who retires must exercise the option within three months of termination from active employment.

9. An ISO cannot be granted with a stock appreciation right (SAR) unless the SAR meets the requirements outlined in Question 7:4.

10. The terms of an ISO cannot be amended or changed in the future; otherwise, the ISO will be considered a new grant under Code Section 422.

In obtaining shareholder approval for an ISO plan, companies will typically quote all or a portion of these Code Section 422 statutory requirements in the proxy statement provided to the shareholders so that it is clear that the shareholders are approving the ISO plan that meets all statutory requirements.

Q 6:7   What is the tax treatment for an ISO?

An executive does not recognize income upon the granting of the ISO, because the executive is not in constructive receipt of any income and there is substantial risk of forfeiture. In addition, the executive does not recognize income or incur a taxable event upon the exercise or purchase of the stock option.

When an ISO share is sold by an executive who has held the share for one year per the statutory requirement, the executive will incur a capital gains tax liability on the entire spread, that is, the difference between the sale price and the option exercise price.

The company is allowed no tax deduction from the granting of an ISO, the exercise of an ISO, or the sale of ISO shares by the executive, because the executive has incurred capital gains tax rather than ordinary income tax. Companies will receive a tax deduction only when executives incur ordinary income tax.

If an executive sells or transfers shares that were acquired under the exercise/purchase of an ISO, but does so within two years of the date of grant of the ISO or within one year after purchasing/exercising these shares, then the executive has incurred a disqualifying distribution. He has then disqualified the option as an ISO and loses the favorable tax treatment of capital gains. In that event, the executive will realize ordinary income in the year of the disqualification in an amount equal to the difference between the price of shares on the date of sale and the option price. The company can, of course, be entitled to a tax deduction on the amount of ordinary income taxed to the employee in the year in which the employee realizes the income from a disqualifying disposition; however, it is difficult for companies to keep track of these disqualifying dispositions. Some will track this via their transfer agent, while others will require employees to inform them of any disqualifying disposition of an ISO.

Example 1. On July 1, 1993, Executive A was granted an ISO for 1,000 shares of Gable Company stock. The exercise price is $20, the current value of the stock on the date of grant. On November 1, 1995 (two years later) A exercised her option to purchase the 1,000 ISO shares when the current fair market value was $24, by paying the full purchase price of $20,000 ($20 × 1,000 shares).

In December 1997, A sells her 1,000 shares when the current market value is $28, and receives $28,000 ($28 × 1,000 shares). Because she has satisfied the holding period requirements by not selling the stock within two years of the date of grant and one year of the date of exercise, she is entitled to capital gain treatment on the full amount of the spread between the date of grant and the date of the sale, or $8,000 ($28,000 − $20,000).

Gable Company does not receive a tax deduction when the option is granted, exercised, or sold.

Example 2. On July 1, 1993, Executive B is granted an ISO for 1,000 shares of Gable Company stock. The exercise price is $20, the current value of the shares on the date of grant. On November 1, 1995, B exercised his option to purchase the 1,000 shares when the current fair market value was $24, by paying $20,000 ($20 × 1,000 shares). In December 1995, B sells his 1,000 shares at a current market value of $28 per share and receives $28,000 ($28 × 1,000 shares). Executive B has met the two-year holding period by not selling the stock within two years of the date of grant; however, he has not met the one-year holding period from the date of exercise and will therefore be required to pay ordinary income tax on the $8,000 spread [(market price − option price) × number of shares].

Gable Company will receive a tax deduction in 1993 equal to the $8,000 of income received by Executive B.

Q 6:8   What is the effect of the alternative minimum tax on the tax treatment of an ISO?

The owner of an ISO may be subject to the alternative minimum tax (AMT) in the year the ISO is exercised because proceeds from the exercise are preference income as defined by the Code and are subject to an AMT calculation. AMT income on the ISO is equal to the difference between the fair market value of the stock at the date of exercise and the exercise price of the option, multiplied by the number of shares. The AMT calculation is made in the same tax year as the regular ordinary income tax calculation, and the executive is required to pay the greater amount of the AMT or the ordinary income tax. Rarely does the AMT calculation produce a tax that is greater then ordinary income; however, this can occur when an executive exercises many ISOs.

In addition, at the time the executive sells the ISO shares, the executive will (assuming the shares were held one year or more) be required to pay capital gains tax on the difference between the sale price and the exercise price, regardless of whether the executive paid ordinary income tax or AMT during the year that the ISO was exercised.

Example.

	AMT Calculation	Ordinary Income Tax Calculation
Gross Income	$300,000	$300,000
Adjustments	$ 20,000	$ 20,000
Adjusted Gross Income	$280,000	$280,000
AMT Preference Income	$100,000	$ 0
Deductions	$ 25,000	$ 30,000
Exemptions	$ 0	$ 0
Taxable Income	$355,000	$250,000
Ordinary Income Tax (36%)		$ 90,000
Alternative Minimum Tax (28%)	$ 99,400	

The executive would pay a higher tax than the normal ordinary income tax, because the AMT was greater than the ordinary income tax. Also, when the shares from the ISO are sold, if held for one year from date of exercise, the executive would be subject to capital gains tax on the difference between the sale price and the exercise price. If the executive were to sell the shares in the same taxable year without holding them for another year, then the spread or gain to the executive (difference between sale price and exercise price) would automatically be taxed at ordinary income tax rates.

Q 6:9   What is the accounting impact of an ISO?

A company must decide whether to follow APB 25 or FAS 123 in determining the accounting impact of an ISO (see Q 1:45).

If it follows APB 25, the company does not recognize any expense in connection with the granting of the ISO, either at the time of grant or upon the exercise of the ISO, because APB 25 states that any compensation expense for a stock option will be established at the "measurement date." The measurement date is that time when two variables are known: the number of shares that can be purchased by the executive, and the price per share to be paid by the executive. Compensation expense shall be the difference between the fair market value of the shares on the measurement date and the amount paid by the executive. Since all ISO grants must be at the fair market value per the statutory regulations that apply to these grants, there will never be a charge to earnings on an ISO under APB 25.

> **Example.** An executive is granted 1,000 shares under an ISO program at a time when the fair market price is $20 since the executive has the right to purchase the 1,000 shares at $20, the provisions of the APB 25 measurement date have been met, and the company calculates its charge to earnings by taking the compensation value of $20,000 (1,000 × $20) and subtracts what the employee is required to pay, which is also $20,000 (1,000 × $20), thus resulting in an expense accrual against earnings of zero.

If the company selects FAS 123, the company under its provisions must calculate the "fair value" of the ISO at the time of grant and charge its earnings with this amount over the vesting period of the ISO. The fair value calculation is discussed in Q 1:49.

ISOs that have not been exercised are considered common stock equivalents and are factored into the determination of earnings per share (EPS) (see Q 6:16), and can have a dilutive cost impact on the company's EPS and balance sheet if the stock price appreciates.

Q 6:10 What approach is used in calculating the fully diluted earnings per share for an ISO?

Until December 15, 1997, the ISO effect on fully diluted and primary earnings per share is computed by using the higher of average stock price during the financial period versus year-end stock price. Under primary EPS, the ISO effect is computed by using common shares outstanding plus common stock equivalents if they are dilutive. Fully diluted EPS calculations use common shares outstanding, common stock equivalents, and all other securities that can be converted to common shares. FAS 123 establishes guidelines on EPS calculations for stock options.

Example. Assume 10,000 shares are granted at $5 per share on January 1. On December 31 of the first year, the company's stock has a value of $7.

Number of stock option shares	10,000
Initial value (10,000 × $5)	$50,000
Common stock equivalents at year-end ($50,000/$7)	(7,142)
Dilutive impact on common shares on Jan. 1	0
Dilutive impact on common shares at year-end	2,858
Average common share dilution for the year (Jan. 1 and year-end average = 2,858/2)	1,429

The ISO has greater dilution than the nonqualified stock option because the nonqualified stock option, which gives the company a tax deduction equal to the total appreciation (difference between market price at exercise and option/exercise price), is compensation to the executive and is factored into the earnings per share calculation.

Example. Assume that an executive has 1,000 nonqualified stock option shares with an option price of $20. The executive exercises the right to purchase these shares when the stock price is $30. The executive has $10 appreciation per share ($10 × 1,000 = $10,000). This is taxed at ordinary income rates to the executive and is a compensation expense to the company. The company can take a deduction of this expense (from company income) when calculating the amount of their corporate tax.

The definitions of earnings per share and dilution are changing on December 15, 1997. See Q 1:52 and Q 1:53.

Q 6:11   How prevalent are ISOs?

ISOs exist in the majority of publicly traded companies. They are currently the only form of long-term incentive that offers executives the benefit of lower capital gains tax treatment (than ordinary income tax) on stock appreciation that occurs prior to stock ownership, i.e., the exercise of the stock option. This unique feature of the ISO could make it an extremely popular form of long-term incentive during the 1990s. Appreciation from nonqualified stock options is taxed at ordinary income tax rates; however, under the ISO the executive can purchase the shares, hold them for one year and receive capital gains tax treatment on the entire spread or difference between sale price and purchase price.

Most surveys of executive compensation will show that 90 percent or more of all companies, public or private, use stock options. Shown as follows, 98 percent of large companies and 93 percent of small companies use nonqualified stock options while 67 percent of large companies and 52 percent of small companies use ISOs.

Plan Type	Prevalence in Large Companies	Prevalence in Small Companies
Nonqualified Options	98%	93%
ISO	67%	52%
Restricted Stock	45%	28%
Performance Shares	34%	18%
Other	12%	22%

Source: Management Performance Int'l, Inc. survey data

Q 6:12   What are the advantages of an ISO?

The ISO continues to make sense to the executive because of its financial planning feature; the ISO permits the executive to choose when the taxable event will occur with the stock option, because the ISO generates taxable income only when it is sold. Nonqualified stock options, on the other hand, generate a taxable event when they are exercised/purchased. Therefore the ISO provides the executive with the opportunity to defer income without taxation, and possibly defer income and receive lower taxation at the same time.

ISOs also make sense from the company's perspective whenever the company is at a low or zero effective tax bracket, and does not need a tax deduction. When this is the case, the ISO's lack of tax deductibility (its primary disadvantage) is negated.

As ordinary income tax rates increase, capital gains tax will be much more attractive to executives. The ISO is the only form of long-term incentive that offers capital gains tax treatment on the full appreciation received by the executive from a stock plan.

Planning Tip. Companies with ISOs may want to encourage executives to notify them of any disqualifying dispositions of an ISO so that the company can receive a tax deduction in the amount of the gain received by the executive.

Q 6:13 What are the primary disadvantages of an ISO?

From a company's perspective, the primary disadvantage of an ISO is the lack of a company tax deduction when the executive exercises the option, which can make this an expensive compensation program to the company.

From the executive's perspective, the ISO shares must be held for one year before they can be sold and capital gains tax treatment received. Company stock price could go down during this period and the executive gain could be eliminated. Of course the executive could sell the shares prior to the one-year period and disqualify the ISO, incurring ordinary income as an alternative to losing all of the appreciation that may have existed at the time of exercise. Another disadvantage of the ISO to the executive is the $100,000 limitation in option value (option price × number of shares) that can be exercised during any given year. Also, executives may be subject to an alternative minimum tax (see Q 6:8), which could produce a higher tax than normal ordinary income tax rates during the year that ISOs are sold.

Nonstatutory Stock Options

Q 6:14 What is a nonstatutory stock option?

A nonstatutory or nonqualified stock option is any option that has no statutory requirements like those of an ISO. On the one hand, this has significantly greater flexibility than the ISO, but on the other hand it does not qualify for favorable tax treatment (i.e., capital gains).

Q 6:15   How prevalent are nonstatutory stock options?

Nonstatutory or nonqualified stock options are the most common form of long-term capital accumulation program (see Q 6:11). As shown in Question 6:11, companies typically grant nonqualified stock options along with other forms of long-term incentive. No other form of long-term incentive is as popular or used as much as the nonqualified stock option because of its favorable accounting treatment (see Q 5:25 for current treatment, Q 1:43 for proposed treatment).

In recent years ordinary income tax rates have approximated capital gains tax rates; therefore, the qualified stock option (ISO) did not provide any substantial tax advantage to executives. Current increases in the ordinary income tax rate could increase the popularity of ISOs, although the flexibility of the nonqualified stock option (no statutory requirements, unlike the ISO) should keep it the most popular form of long-term incentive for years to come. If the Financial Accounting Standards Board (FASB) creates a charge to earnings for stock options, which it is considering for 1997, there could be less use of the nonqualified stock option; however, because many companies will still want executives to purchase stock ownership via the stock option, few believe that the stock option will become less popular under modified FASB accounting regulations.

Q 6:16   What is the accounting treatment of a nonstatutory stock option?

A company must decide to follow APB 25 or FAS 123 in determining the accounting impact of a nonqualified stock option (see Q 1:45).

Under APB 25, if a nonqualified stock option is granted at the current market price, the company has no charge to its earnings statement. APB 25 requires a "measurement date" when two things are known: the price per share to be paid by the executive and the number of shares that the executive can purchase; this measurement date exists at the date of grant. APB 25 goes on to state that any company earnings charge will be the difference between the compensation value of the stock option, to be measured by the number of shares times the fair market value per share, and employee value, which is the amount that the employee will pay for the shares, to be measured by the employee price per share times the number of shares. Since these are both the same on a nonqualified stock option granted at the fair market value, there is no charge to the company's earnings.

In the case of a discounted stock option, the company must recognize a compensation expense equal to the compensation value at the time of grant minus the employee value. For example, if a nonqualified stock option is granted at $5 below fair market value, the difference between compensation value and employee value is $5 and this must be charged to earnings.

If the company elects to follow FAS 123, then the company must under this accounting regulation take a charge to earnings based on the "fair value" of the option. For an example of the fair value calculation see Q 1:49. This charge must be accrued over the vesting period of the stock option.

Q 6:17 How does a company calculate dilution with a nonqualified stock option?

A company's earnings per share are diluted by both a nonqualified stock option and an incentive stock option. Accounting regulations state, until December 15, 1997, that all stock options are considered common stock equivalents and are thus factored into earnings per share calculations, if the price per share of the company's shares increases over the financial period represented by the EPS calculation. A stock option that has a market value below the option/exercise price has no dilution. An example of dilution under a nonqualified stock option is shown below:

Example. Assume 10,000 shares are granted at $5 per share on January 1. On December 31 of the first year, the company's stock has a value of $7 per share.

Number of stock option shares	10,000
Initial value (10,000 × $5)	$50,000
Market value at year-end (10,000 × $7)	$70,000
Incremental market value (10,000 × $2)	$20,000
Value of company tax deduction ($20,000 × 34%)	$ 6,800
Year-end value of shares to company ($50,000 + $6,880)	$56,880

Common stock equivalents at year-end ($56,800/$7)	8,114
Dilutive impact on common shares on Jan. 1.	0
Dilutive impact on common shares at year-end (10,000 – 8,114)	1,886
Average common share dilution for the year (Jan. 1 and year-end average = 1,886/2)	943

Note: Earnings per share and dilution definitions are changing as of December 15, 1997. These are described in Q 1:52 and Q 1:53.

Q 6:18   What is the tax treatment of a nonstatutory stock option?

For a nonqualified stock option, there is no taxable event at the time that the shares are granted. At the time of grant the options will be subject to substantial risk of forfeiture and thus are not currently taxed.

At the time of exercise, the executive is subject to ordinary income tax on the spread (i.e., the difference between the market price at the time of exercise and the exercise price paid by the executive). The company receives a tax deduction equal to the amount of income received by the executive (the spread). For example, if an executive exercises the right to purchase 1,000 shares at $20 per share when the current market value is $30, then the spread, or the amount of gain provided to the executive is $10,000 (1,000 shares × $10 stock appreciation). The $10,000 is ordinary income tax to the executive, and the company gets a tax deduction on the same amount of $10,000. Once the employee takes ownership of the shares, future gains will be taxed at capital gains tax rates. If the shares are held for one year or more, the employee would be taxed at the capital gains tax rate. If the shares are held for less than one year, any subsequent appreciation in the shares between the time they were purchased and the time they were sold would be taxed at ordinary income tax rates. Employees are eligible for the capital gains tax rate only if they hold the shares (capital assets) for at least one year.

Q 6:19 What are the advantages of nonqualified stock options?

Most companies find that the nonqualified stock option has significant appeal because of the great flexibility it provides in plan design. No statutory requirements need to be met, and the company can set an option price anywhere it wishes. Companies can also apply dividend equivalents to nonqualified stock options and provide dividend payments to executives who have nonqualified stock option shares, even if they are not yet owners of these shares. Companies use dividend equivalents as a means of allowing the executive to build cash to use in purchasing the stock options. When used, dividends are typically on a one-for-one basis.

Example. A company grants an executive a nonqualified stock option of 1,000 shares, which vests 25 percent per year. The award period is ten years. The company also assigns to the executive dividend rights for each share of stock. The company pays a $2.50 annual dividend on each share of stock, quarterly. The executive will be paid $.65 per share each quarter ($2.50 divided by 4). The total amount received by the executive each quarter is $650 (1,000 shares × $.65), which is $2,500 ($650 × 4) per year.

Companies can also attach stock appreciation rights (SARs) to nonqualified stock options as another means of providing the executive with cash that can be used to purchase other stock options. These are typically in the form of tandem or parallel rights. Tandem SARs with a stock option are an "either/or alternative," i.e., the executive can exercise one or the other, but not both. Parallel SARs with a stock option are mutually independent grants. The exercise of one has no impact on the exercise of the other.

Example: Tandem SAR with Nonqualified Stock Option. An executive is granted 1,000 nonqualified stock options with tandem stock appreciation rights on each stock option share. If the executive subsequently exercises 250 stock appreciation rights, then 750 shares remain to exercise as either a stock option purchase or a stock appreciation right.

Example: Parallel SAR with Nonqualified Stock Option. An executive is granted 1,000 nonqualified stock options with 1,000 stock appreciation rights in parallel to the stock option. If the executive subsequently exercises 250 SARs, there remain 1,000 nonqualified stock options and 750 stock appreciation rights.

There is also a significant cost advantage to nonqualified stock options if the company elects APB 25 and grants the option at the current market value. In this case, there is no charge to the income statement. In addition, upon exercise of a nonqualified stock option, the company gets the benefit of a tax deduction on the total appreciation (compensation) realized by the executive. Under an ISO, there is no tax deduction to the company since the taxable event is deferred until sale. If the ISO is held for one year, the executive receives capital gains tax when the shares are sold. This is why nonqualified stock options are the most common form of long-term incentive.

Q 6:20   What are the disadvantages of the nonqualified stock option?

With a nonqualified stock option, the optionee is taxed at the time that the shares are exercised, so there is no deferral of the tax as there would be with an ISO. The corporation is required to withhold minimum federal tax amounts from the spread recognized by the executive at the time that the stock option is exercised. This can result in an additional burden to the executive who must find the money to purchase the stock option and to pay the taxes on the spread to be realized upon purchase/exercise of that stock option.

Executives classified as insiders also have to consider the rules of Securities and Exchange Commission (SEC) Section 16(b), which prohibit an insider from conducting any simultaneous buy/sell transaction within a six-month period (see Q 2:18 and Q 2:19 for additional information on Section 16).

Q 6:21   Can features be added to nonstatutory stock options to offset the withholding burden?

Yes. The following three methods are most often used in dealing with the withholding and payment burdens:

1. The corporation can provide a cash bonus on exercise. (A variation on this method involves the use of a tandem stock option/stock appreciation right, discussed in Chapter 9.)

2. The corporation can withhold from the number of shares issuable upon exercise of the option that number of shares necessary to satisfy the withholding requirement, or can accept from the employee a larger number of shares of stock in a stock-for-stock exercise.

3. The company can offer a cashless exercise to the executive. These enable the executive to use the proceeds from a simultaneous purchase and sale of shares, to pay the purchase or exercise price. (See Q 5:51.)

Where an insider is involved, Section 16 has an impact if one of the first two methods is chosen. A cash bonus payable upon the exercise of an option, even if not a formal tandem stock option/SAR, and the decision to have issuable shares withheld, are each deemed to be SARs and subject to special rules: the exercise must be made during the "window period" or the withheld shares will be deemed to have been sold for purposes of Section 16 liability (see Q 7:4).

Q 6:22   How do ISOs compare with nonstatutory stock options?

The principal benefit of the ISO accrues to the executive who is entitled to capital gains treatment on the full value of the spread (difference between sale price and option exercise price) at the time of sale. The other remaining advantage of the ISO is that the executive can defer the taxable event until the sale of the underlying shares.

From the company's perspective, the loss of a tax deduction on an ISO makes it a more costly form of stock option than the nonqualified stock option, which provides the company with a tax deduction based on the spread at the time of exercise (market value at exercise minus option price paid by the executive at exercise).

Example. Assume, as shown below, that an executive receives one nonqualified stock option share and one incentive stock option share with a grant price of $20. If these shares were exercised when the stock price was $30 and sold when the stock price was $35 after one year, then with the assumed tax rates shown on the table, the total tax on the incentive tax option share, at $4.20, is less than the total tax on the nonqualified share of $4.50.

	Tax on Nonqualified	Tax on ISO
Grant Price $20	0	0
Exercise Price $30	$3.10*	0
Sale Price $35	$1.40**	$4.20**
	$4.50	$4.20

*Ordinary Income Tax equals 31%
**Capital Gains Tax equals 28%

Discounted Stock Options

Q 6:23 What is a discounted stock option?

Although a discounted stock option (DSO) is technically any nonstatutory option with an exercise price that is lower than the fair market value of the stock at the time of grant, the term usually refers to an option with an exercise price that is fixed at a substantial discount from the fair market value on the date of grant. Frequently, these plans are utilized for compensating outside members of the Board of Directors (see Chapter 13). Traditionally, a DSO has been used to encourage immediate ownership and to protect against drops in the market price. To reinforce the ownership element, the purchased stock is sometimes subject to some holding period and/or tenure restrictions. For example, the shares acquired under such a plan may not be sold for a certain period after the purchase or must be resold to the company at the discounted price if the executive terminates employment prior to a specified date.

Example. Executive A works for Gable Corporation, which grants her an option for 1,000 shares of its stock on August 18, 1988. The exercise price of the option is $5, which is one-half the market value of $10. On September 1, 1989, the current value of the stock is $14 and A decides to exercise her option and purchase 1,000 shares for $5,000. For 1989, A has $9,000 of reportable income, which is computed as follows:

Value of the stock ($14 × 1,000)	$14,000
Purchase price	(5,000)
Reportable Income	$ 9,000

Gable Corporation receives a corresponding $9,000 tax deduction. In October 1991, A sells the 1,000 shares at $20 per share and reports a $6,000 taxable capital gain; Gable is not entitled to a deduction for that gain.

The exercise price for discounted stock options is generally expressed as a fixed price, although it is more rarely expressed as a percentage of market value at the time of exercise. If the exercise price is allowed to vary with the market price, the executive is at a real disadvantage for purposes of the Section 16 rules, as she will not be deemed to have acquired the shares until the option is actually exercised.

Q 6:24   How prevalent are discounted stock option plans?

The discounted stock option is not frequently used as a long-term incentive compensation program for executives. It is not viewed favorably by shareholders, who have to pay full price for their shares.

Q 6:25   What is the tax treatment for a discounted stock option?

The tax consequences resulting from the grant and exercise of a discounted stock option are the same as those applicable to nonstatutory options in general. Absent a Code Section 83(b) election, the discounted option is not compensation to the executive when granted, but becomes income upon its exercise recognizable by the employee and deductible by the corporation.

Q 6:26   What is the accounting impact of a discounted stock option?

A company must decide to follow APB 25 or FAS 123 in determining the accounting impact of a discounted stock option. If it follows APB 25, the company must take an earnings charge equal to the amount of the discount. (See Q 1:42.) If it elects FAS 123, it must take an earnings charge equal to the "fair value" of the stock option. (See Q 1:49.)

Q 6:27 What are the advantages of a discounted stock option plan?

The primary advantage of a discounted stock plan is the "cushion" provided an executive if the stock price falls and the built-in appreciation or gain the executive receives is diminished. A discounted stock option is also a way to effectively defer compensation, as no taxable income will be generated to the executive (absent an 83(b) election) until the option is exercised. (See Chapter 13 for the advantages for the director's compensation deferral.)

Q 6:28 What are the disadvantages of a discounted stock option plan?

The most often voiced criticism of a discounted stock plan is that the executive receives a reward even if the stock price does not appreciate or does not depreciate more than the discount.

Under a discounted stock option plan, even decreasing stock prices can generate large rewards.

Example. Executive B received 10,000 discounted stock options as part of the recruitment process. The option price was $34 and the current stock price was $68. Three years later when B exercised the options, the stock price had declined to $52 per share. At that point, B still received $180,000 (($52 − $34) × 10,000) for "managing" the stock price down by $16 per share.

A second disadvantage is the requirement that the company must reflect the benefit provided to the executive in the discount of the exercise price at the time of grant of the option as compensation expense for accounting purposes even though it is not entitled to the corresponding tax benefit until the option is exercised.

Another potential problem with discounted stock options is the depth of the discount, because at some point the grant of a deeply discounted option becomes the transfer of the underlying shares. However, instead of granting an executive an option to purchase a small number of shares at a deeply discounted price, a company can give the same initial benefit to an executive by granting him an option to purchase a larger number of shares at a price that is not so deeply discounted.

Example. In the previous example, Executive B had received 10,000 discounted stock options with an exercise price of $34 versus the $68 market price; the value of the benefit granted to him at that time by the company was $340,000. If the company had granted him 25,000 options with an exercise price of $50, the immediate spread would have been $450,000. In that case, he would have received only $50,000 upon the sale of the underlying shares after the company's dismal performance during the three years he held them.

Q 6:29 How deeply can discounted stock options be discounted?

The Internal Revenue Service (IRS) has avoided issuing regulations on the point at which a deeply discounted option would be considered to be a "sham" option and recharacterized as a transfer of the underlying stock, taxable immediately as income to the recipient. Recently, an executive who received discounted options with an exercise price equal to the par value of the stock, $1, to purchase company shares whose appraised value was $143 per share, was hit with a huge tax liability when the IRS determined that the grant was in fact a transfer of the underlying shares.

As a practical matter, discounts of more than 50 percent begin to expose the company and the executive to this kind of recharacterization. A company considering deeply discounted stock would be wise to consider getting a private letter ruling from the IRS on the appropriateness of the discount.

Premium Stock Options

Q 6:30 What is a premium stock option?

A premium stock option permits an executive to purchase company stock at a price that is above the current market value of the shares. The premium attached to the stock option above the current market price is typically in an amount equal to the normally expected minimum growth of the company stock price, and therefore serves as a threshold amount that guarantees the company will perform at a minimum level. Therefore, the stock price must increase before the executive can benefit from the stock option.

Example. Executive C works for the Cable Corporation and on July 1, 1993, when the market value of company shares is $10, she is granted an option to purchase 1,000 shares of stock at an exercise price of $15 per share. The stock option grant has 25 percent vesting per year over four years, and the stock award period is ten years. At the completion of the fourth year C is fully vested and can exercise the right to purchase 1,000 shares at $15 per share. The assumption is that during the four years of vesting, the company stock price has gone well beyond $15 per share. Therefore shareholders, and the executive, will have benefitted. In addition the company will have retained the services of the executive during the same period. In summary, everyone wins.

Q 6:31   How is the premium established on a premium stock option?

There are several ways to establish the premium although the most common methods are the treasury bill (T-bill) and the peer-group methods. The T-bill method is intended to reflect the cost of capital so that an executive may, for example, receive a ten-year option for 1,000 shares at a $47.75 exercise price when the current market value is $38. Assuming that the T-bill return is seven percent, the $38 stock price might reach the $47.75 exercise price after five years, and the executive would have an additional five years to exercise the stock option. The rationale for this approach is that the executive should not profit unless the executive can make the company outperform a low-risk investment such as treasury bills.

The peer-group approach, which is most appropriate for publicly traded companies and those companies with easily identifiable competitors, focuses on relative performance against competitor firms. For example, consider an airline company stock that is traded at $80 that wants to establish the price at which an option would be exercisable after five years. It would multiply $80 (the current price) by the industry average stock price appreciation. If the industry average stock growth rate was 10 percent over five years, the exercise price would then be established at $88. The peer-group approach emphasizes that an executive should not be rewarded if her company's stock price does not at least out-perform the average rate of performance within its industry peer groups. As a result, in this example, if the company's stock price moved 20 percent upward to $96, which exceeds the predetermined average, the executive would exercise that option at $88 and would profit $8 per option. However, if the company stock price moved only 10 percent (the industry average), the executive could still exercise the option and purchase shares, although she would receive no immediate reward or gain.

Q 6:32 How prevalent are premium stock options?

Premium stock options are not common among companies, although several large companies have implemented these plans in the last year.

Q 6:33 What is the accounting impact of a premium stock option?

A company must decide to follow APB 25 or FAS 123 in determining the accounting impact of a premium stock option. If it follows APB 25, the company must take an earnings charge equal to the difference, if any, between the current fair market value at grant and the executive's option price. The executive's exercise price is typically greater than the current market value at the time of grant under a premium stock option; therefore, there will be no charge to earnings under APB 25. (See Q 1:45.)

If the company elects FAS 123, it must take an earnings charge equal to the "fair value" of the stock option at the time of grant. (See Q 1:49.)

Q 6:34 What is the tax treatment for a premium stock option?

There is no tax effect to the corporation or to the executive at the time a premium stock option is granted. The corporation is, however, entitled to a deduction equal to the amount that is taxable when the executive receives ordinary income equal to the spread between the option exercise price and the fair market value of the shares. Because the spread is taxable as ordinary income, the company is required to withhold taxes.

Q 6:35　What is the advantage of a premium stock option?

This type of plan appeals to companies that believe that an executive should only be rewarded if the company stock appreciates more than a certain amount, and/or if they believe that an increase in company stock should be achieved before a stock option has value to the executive. A premium stock option plan will pay out only if there is either an active market for the stock and the stock appreciates or company performance drives the stock price up.

Q 6:36　What is the disadvantage of a premium stock option?

From the executive's perspective, the premium stock option requires stock appreciation, and the stock market does not always respond to company performance; in fact, the vagaries of the stock market will, in some cases, drive the stock price down when company performance goes up.

On the other hand, an executive can use the performance characteristics of a premium stock option to justify higher than normal award levels (i.e., higher performance should equal a higher number of stock options).

From the company's perspective, the only disadvantage is that if the company stock price does not move or goes down when company performance goes up, then executives will not be motivated, and may leave the company.

Option Reloads

Q 6:37　What is an option reload plan?

Under an option reload plan, at exercise an executive will receive new options at the current market price for the same number of shares that were used to exercise the original option, and with the same terms of the original option.

Example. On July 1, 1993 an executive receives an option to purchase 1,000 shares of company stock at an option price of $25. In July 1995, 50 percent of the shares have vested, and the executive exercises the right to purchase 500 of these shares when

the current market price is $45. When the executive takes posses-
sion of these 500 shares, the company will issue to the executive
another 500 stock option shares with an option price at the current
market value of $45, with the same vesting period and with the
same stock award period as the shares just purchased.

Option reload plans are typically provided in addition to normal
annual or biannual grants of stock options or other forms of long-
term incentive. Most companies will require that executives hold the
underlying shares that they have exercised for a minimum period of
years in order to receive the reload stock options.

Option reload plans can be used in connection with both qualified
and nonqualified stock option plans. Naturally, the reload options for
a nonqualified plan would be nonqualified shares and for an ISO plan
would be ISO shares.

Q 6:38   What is the accounting impact of a reload option?

A company must decide to follow APB 25 or FAS 123 in determining the accounting impact of a reload stock option (see Q 1:45). If it
follows APB 25, the company must take an earnings charge equal to
the difference, if any, between the current fair market value at grant
and the executive's option price. If the company elects FAS 123, it
must take an earnings charge equal to the "fair value" of the stock
option at the time of grant (see Q 1:46).

Since the executive's reload option typically has the same terms
as the option that triggered the exercise and subsequent "reloading"
of the stock option, the accounting treatment of the reload option will
be the same as the accounting treatment of the original option.

Q 6:39   What is the tax treatment of a reload option?

The tax consequences of the reload option would be the normal
tax consequences of statutory or nonstatutory options, depending on
the type of option the reload option is deemed to be.

Q 6:40   What are the advantages of an option reload provision?

This feature can encourage stock ownership, particularly if the company requires an executive to keep the exercised shares that trigger the reload event.

A reload feature makes sense for virtually all companies with stock option plans (although see Q 6:41 for a caveat where ISOs are involved). Although allowing an executive to pay an option exercise price with already-owned shares allows him to end up with a larger number of shares after the exercise, he does not end up with the ownership level that the company wished to give him. Adding an option reload feature rectifies this situation.

> **Planning Tip.** A reload plan could include a requirement that the shares received upon the exercise of the original option be held for a certain period in order for the reload option to vest.

Q 6:41   What are the disadvantages of an option reload plan?

A company must be careful in granting a reload option in connection with the exercise of an ISO. If the ISO did not contemplate the granting of the reload option at the time of grant, the reload feature could modify the terms of the ISO, thereby disqualifying it for the preferred capital gains tax treatment. Companies must also be sure to establish limits on the use of the reload feature, otherwise they can easily run out of authorized shares.

> **Planning Tip.** Companies should establish a "sunset" provision to any reload option, indicating how long the reload feature will be in effect. A never-ending reload feature could be a significant drain on authorized shares and it can dilute earnings per share.

Book Value Purchase Plans

Q 6:42   What is a book value purchase plan?

A book value purchase plan grants an executive the right to purchase a fixed number of company book value shares at its current book value price, over a fixed period, after meeting a specified vesting provision. Book value is determined by dividing company equity by the number of shares outstanding, to get a book value price per share.

Example. On July 1, 1994, an executive is granted the right to purchase 1,000 book value shares at a price of $100, over a ten-year period. This right vests at 25% per year. The executive buys the shares six years later, when company book value is $140, thus receiving a $40,000 gain (1,000 shares times $140 – $100).

Obviously, these plans will typically require the executive to sell the book value shares immediately back to the company (since there is no market other than the company to sell the shares). Therefore, the company must accrue cash in order to buy the shares back from the executive. This is significantly different from stock option shares used by a public company where the shares are traded on a stock market. In this case, the public company does not have to accrue cash to buy the shares back from the executive.

Q 6:43 What is the accounting impact of a book value purchase plan?

The accounting treatment for a book value purchase plan is the same as that for a stock option. A company must decide to follow APB 25 or FAS 123 in determining the accounting impact of a book value purchase grant. If it follows APB 25, the company must take an earnings charge equal to the difference, if any, between the current fair market value at grant and the executive's option/exercise price on the book value share. Since the executive's exercise price is typically the same as the current fair market value at the time of grant under a book value purchase grant, there will typically be no charge to earnings under APB 25. (See Q 1:42.)

If the company elects FAS 123, it must take an earnings charge equal to the "fair value" of the book value share at the time of grant. (See Q 1:46.)

Q 6:44 What is the tax treatment for a book value purchase plan?

The tax treatment for a book value purchase plan is similar to that of an incentive stock option. There is no tax at the time of grant, to either the company or the executive. When the company repurchases the stock from the executive, it is not entitled to a tax deduction for the "loss" it has incurred by selling shares at a lower price than the repurchased price, nor for the conceptual compensatory element resulting from the increase in the value of the shares. The appreciation that the executive receives is taxed at the capital gains tax rate at the time the book value shares are sold back to the company; therefore, the company receives no tax deduction.

Q 6:45   What are the advantages of a book value plan?

Many publicly traded companies feel that compensating the executive on the actual increase in the company's book value rather than as a result of the vagaries of the stock market constitutes the primary advantage of book value plans. Privately held companies benefit from not having to perform costly and often inaccurate appraisals of their stock, as is the case with stock options.

Q 6:46   What are the disadvantages of a book value plan?

From the company's perspective, a book value plan achieves much the same compensatory goal as a phantom stock arrangement, yet is less advantageous from a tax point of view because the company is neither entitled to a deduction at the time of grant nor to any deduction, either for compensation or for a loss, at the time it repurchases the shares.

From the executive's perspective, while she is not penalized if the stock market value of the stock declines despite an increase in the company's book value, she receives no benefit from the market value of the shares.

Q 6:47   For what type of companies does a book value plan make sense?

Book value plans are helpful to a privately held company whose stock does not have an easily ascertainable market value, but wants to achieve the goals usually associated with stock-based plans. Although valuation of the stock can be obtained through the use of a professional appraiser, such a procedure involves additional expense to the company, and the results of the appraisal may not satisfy either the company or the executive.

A publicly traded company can benefit from a book value plan in that it can give an equity interest in the company to its executives yet tie their reward to the company's performance rather than the vagaries of the stock market.

Many companies use a separate, nonvoting class of stock for use in their book value plans, and those who base the repurchase price on a multiple of earnings use a nondividend class of stock for their book value plans. These approaches would, however, not be appropriate for an S corporation because of the one-class-of-stock restriction.

Convertible Debentures

Q 6:48   What is a convertible debenture?

A convertible debenture is a fixed income debt security that is sold at a fixed price to an employee. The debenture has a face value on which periodic interest is paid to the executive, and it is typically convertible into stock of the company at a later date such as after the executive has completed a specified period of employment or specific performance goals have been met. Most companies have traditionally included a provision in the plan that the conversion right will be terminated if the debenture is transferred in order to discourage executives from transferring the debentures.

Convertible debentures involve securities that have to be registered under federal and most state laws unless an available exemption exists and the availability of an exemption depends on the details of each offer or offering.

Example. On February 3, 1985, Executive A purchased a convertible debenture from Altoona Corporation that had a ten-year maturity, a face value of $10,000, and paid an annualized interest rate of 8 percent. The current market value of the stock was $25. The debenture allowed a conversion to Altoona stock if, after five years, A was still employed and the return on investment over the five-year period was at least 9 percent. The conversion ratio was

40 shares for each $1,000 face value of the debenture equivalent to a purchase price of $25 per share. Each year, A was to receive $800 interest on the debenture, which would be taxable income to A and deductible to Altoona Corporation.

In March 1990, Altoona corporation achieved or exceeded its 9 percent target rate of return and A was still an executive with the company. A's debenture therefore became convertible to 400 shares of stock. A elected to convert the debentures at the point when the market value of the stock was $36 per share. At the time of this conversion, neither A nor the company experienced any tax consequences.

In April 1991, A decided to sell his 400 shares of stock for the then-current market price of $39 per share. He had a gain of $5,600, which is computed as follows:

Proceeds from sale ($39 × 400 shares)	$15,600
Purchase price or basis	(10,000)
Gain	5,600

The sale of the stock has no impact on the company.

Q 6:49 Is shareholder approval required to issue convertible debentures?

Although shareholder approval is not generally required to issue convertible debentures, approval of the board of directors is required when a company issues a debt obligation; however, it is prudent to obtain shareholder approval to avoid the possibility of a shareholder lawsuit challenging the appropriateness of the debt issuance.

Q 6:50 What is the accounting impact of a convertible debenture?

The accounting treatment for a convertible debenture plan is the same as that for other stock awards. A company must decide to follow APB 25 or FAS 123 in determining the accounting impact of a convertible debenture grant. If it follows APB 25, the company must take an earnings charge equal to the difference, if any, between the current fair market value at grant and the executive's conversion price of the debenture share. Since the conversion of the debenture to company shares is typically a lateral and non-taxable event there is typically no accounting impact at that time. When the executive sells company shares (after holding for one year), the executive would pay capital gains tax.

If the company elects FAS 123, it must take an earnings charge equal to the "fair value" of the common share equivalent convertible debenture share at the time of grant. (See Q 1:46.)

Q 6:51   What is the tax treatment for a convertible debenture?

If the convertible debenture is purchased by the employee at its fair market value, no tax event occurs at that time. If the market value of the debenture is greater than the amount paid by the executive, then that excess is included in the executive's income, and deducted by the corporation as a compensation expense, in the year of purchase. There is no taxable event to the company or the employee when the debenture is converted; however, upon the sale of the underlying shares, the employee is taxed on the gain she is deemed to have incurred, which is the sale price of the shares less the amount she paid for the converted debenture.

Interest paid on the debenture prior to its conversion will be interest income to the executive and an interest deduction to the company. (For an example of how a convertible debenture works see Q 6:48.)

Q 6:52   What is the earnings per share impact of a convertible debenture?

If the debenture's cash yield at the date of issuance is two-thirds of the bank prime interest rate, then the debentures are treated as common stock cash equivalents. As a result, earnings per share are affected not only as a result of the compensation expense but also as a result of the additional number of outstanding shares.

Q 6:53   What are the advantages of a convertible debenture program?

The principal advantage of using a convertible debenture is that the executive invests money in the company, which closely ties the interests of the executive and the shareholders. A convertible debenture program also minimizes the executive's downside risk by providing a fixed obligation of the company to pay both principal and interest to the executive and, if the stock price declines, the executive would still receive his principal back at the time the debenture matures. Furthermore, because interest at the prevailing interest rate is typically paid on the amount invested in the debenture, if the executive chooses not to convert, that executive will get his money back with interest, so the executive does not suffer a lost opportunity cost.

Q 6:54   What are the disadvantages of a convertible debenture program?

The primary disadvantage of a convertible debenture is that in most states it has to be registered under both federal and state securities laws, and the time and expense involved in this process may make the program prohibitive. Another disadvantage is the lack of executive involvement in the company stock's down side. Finally, the requirement that the executive make a substantial capital investment in order to participate in the program may be a problem because interest on any debt used to finance the purchase of the debenture is not deductible to the executive.

Q 6:55   For what type of company does a convertible debenture plan make sense?

A convertible debenture plan makes sense for those companies whose compensation philosophy includes the belief that an executive should make a substantial investment in the company's future, but who also recognize that because of the substantial investment required of the executive, her participation in the company stock's down side should be minimized.

Junior Stock Plans

Q 6:56   What is a junior stock plan?

Junior stock is a class of stock having lesser voting, dividend, and liquidation rights than ordinary common stock. Under a junior common stock plan, an executive receives junior stock that becomes convertible at a favorable rate into common stock. Junior stock plans were popular in the 1970s until the SEC and FASB proposed a rule that would require the full spread at conversion to be treated as an expense item to be reflected in the profit and loss statement and chargeable against earnings. This change eliminated the effectiveness of junior common stock, and most organizations dropped their existing plans.

> **Example.** Executive E is an executive of Altoona Corporation. On January 1, 1988, he was granted and exercised an option to acquire 1,000 shares of Altoona's junior common stock at $1 per share. The junior stock converts to common stock if earnings per share reaches $12 by December 31, 1991. The current market value of Altoona Corporation shares is $10. On January 1, 1992, Altoona Corporation's earnings per share is $14 and E is still an executive with the company. Therefore, the junior common stock converts to regular common stock.

Q 6:57   What are the advantages of a junior stock plan?

The primary advantage of a junior stock plan, prior to the SEC and FASB changes, was that it provided the executive with capital gains treatment not only on the future growth in value of the common stock, but also on the initial spread between the acquisition cost of the junior common stock and the common stock value at the date of purchase of the junior common stock. This offered substantial leverage in providing low cost equity participation to executives. Tax reform changes coupled with the SEC and FASB rulings have stripped junior stock plans of these advantages.

Q 6:58   What are the disadvantages of a junior stock plan?

In addition to the lack of tax deductibility, three disadvantages of junior stock result from its use of a separate class of stock. First, the device is unavailable to the S corporation. Second, shareholder approval is likely to be required in order to authorize the new class of stock, unless such a class already exists. Lastly, the value to public companies of a second class of stock that would in all likelihood not be registered is limited, as the executive's ability to resell her shares is limited.

Q 6:59   How prevalent are junior common stock plans?

Junior stock plans were previously adopted by many high technology companies and other companies that anticipated high stock price appreciation. Since FASB ruled that a charge to earning is required at the time of exchange, these plans have all but disappeared.

Performance-Based Stock Options

Q 6:60   What are performance-based stock options?

Performance-based stock options are regular nonqualified or incentive stock options granted to executives at typical option award levels and award periods, except that the vesting of the option is dependent upon or affected by the achievement of specified performance goals of the company.

> **Example.** An executive is given the right to purchase 1,000 shares of company stock at $20 per share (current fair market value). The vesting in this grant occurs when company earnings per share increase from $3 to $4 per share.

Q 6:61   What are the advantages of performance-based stock options?

The primary advantage to the company is that the company performance goal must be achieved before the executive can realize any value from the stock option. Board compensation committee members have favorable opinions of this form of long-term incentive because it is performance-driven. Moreover, if stock price is the performance measure, then the executive will receive value from the stock option only if shareholders also receive the same value from stock appreciation.

From an executive's point of view, the performance measure is simply another "hurdle" or "qualifier" that must be met in order to exercise the stock option. Most companies will, however, use a performance measure that the executive can influence or directly control so that executive motivation and retention is realized from the performance-based option.

Q 6:62 What are the disadvantages of performance-based stock options?

There can be disadvantages to the executive and to the company if the performance measure is not achieved.

Example 1. A company establishes 10 percent average annual earnings per share growth as the performance measure that must be achieved before vesting occurs on a stock option grant. An executive is given the right to purchase 1,000 shares at $20 per share (current fair market value). During the award period, the company does not achieve the EPS goal, but company stock price increases to $25 per share. The executive cannot exercise the stock option because the performance measure was not met.

In this example, the EPS goal may have been realistic or unrealistic. In either case, the executive would be dissatisfied. This could be a disadvantage to the company if the executive loses motivation to perform or resigns. The company objectives of motivating the executive to achieve EPS growth and of retaining key executives were not achieved.

Example 2. A company establishes $5 stock price appreciation as the performance measure that must be achieved before vesting occurs on a stock option grant. An executive is given the right to purchase 1,000 shares of stock at $20 per share (current fair market value). During the award period the company stock increases to $24 per share. The executive cannot exercise the stock option because the performance measure was not met. The disadvantage to the company and the executive is the same in this example as in Example 1.

Planning Tip. Company performance goals in a performance-based stock option should be realistic and should not be structured to result in a go or no-go situation. It is better to have various levels of performance achievement so that executives can accrue eligibility to exercise a portion of the stock option as they meet the established performance levels.

Q 6:63   What are the tax consequences of performance-based stock options?

The tax impact to the company and to the individual executive for performance-based stock options depends upon whether the option is nonqualified or whether it is an incentive stock option. Nonqualified stock options have no taxable event at grant, and the executive is taxed at ordinary income rates on any stock appreciation at the time of exercise. The company receives a tax deduction equal to the amount of stock appreciation received by the executive.

With an incentive stock option, there is no taxable event at the time of grant, and upon exercise, the executive defers tax until sale. If the stock is held for one year or more before a sale, the executive is taxed at the capital gains tax rate. In this event, the company receives no tax deduction. If the stock is sold by the executive after less than one year, then the executive is taxed at ordinary income tax rates and the company does not receive a tax deduction. (See Qs 6:7 and 6:18.)

Q 6:64   What is the accounting treatment of a performance-based stock option?

The determination of the accounting treatment for this form of long-term incentive can be challenging. In most cases, the company accountants and CPA firm will conclude that the award is "variable," in which case FASB 28 applies, and the company must accrue the anticipated value over the award period. The anticipated value means that any stock price appreciation is calculated and multiplied by the percentage of vesting that has occurred at that point. The company will anticipate that the performance measure will be met.

It is possible, but unlikely, that company accountants and their CPA firm will conclude that the performance measures will be met without question, and the award is therefore not variable. In this case the company must decide to follow APB 25 or FAS 123 in determining the accounting impact. If it follows APB 25, the company must take an earnings charge equal to the difference, if any, between the current fair market value at grant and the executive's option price (when the performance goal is met). Since the executive's exercise price is typically greater than the current market value at the time of grant under a performance-based stock option, there will be no charge to earnings under APB 25. (See Q 1:42.)

If the company elects FAS 123, it must take an earnings charge equal to the "fair value" of the stock option at the time of grant. (See Q 1:46.)

Example. An executive is granted 1,000 stock options at $20 per share with a performance measure that requires an average annual increase in earnings per share of 10 percent over the next four years before vesting can occur. After one year the stock price increases to $25 per share.

This is a variable award plan, and the company will anticipate that the EPS goal will be achieved, charging its earnings with that $5 per share increase multiplied by 250 shares (one-fourth of the shares, since this is the first year of the four-year vesting period).

Q 6:65 What is an indexed stock option?

This is a form of performance stock option that has the option price "indexed" to some performance measure.

Example. An executive is given the right to purchase 1,000 shares of company stock at $20 per share (current fair market value). The vesting in this grant occurs in accordance with the following:

25 percent vesting when the stock price increases to $22
50 percent vesting when the stock price increases to $24
75 percent vesting when the stock price increases to $26
100 percent vesting when the stock price increases to $28

The accounting and tax treatment is the same as with a performance-based stock option.

Chapter 7

Appreciation and Full-Value Plans

Appreciation and full-value plans are forms of long-term incentive plans that provide the executive with a benefit interest that does not require any actual investment by the executive. The two most common types of appreciation plan are the stock appreciation right plan and the book value appreciation right plan. The two most common types of full-value plans are restricted stock grants and performance plans. This chapter addresses the tax, legal, and financial implications of appreciation and full-value plans, including the circumstances where these types of plans work best and their relative strengths and weaknesses.

Appreciation Plans   7-2
    Stock Appreciation Rights   7-2
    Book Value Appreciation Rights   7-10
Full-Value Plans   7-13
    Phantom Stock Plans   7-14
    Restricted Stock Grants   7-18
Performance Unit Plans   7-22
Performance Share Plans   7-24

Appreciation Plans

Q 7:1   What are appreciation plans?

Appreciation plans provide opportunities for capital accumulation over a long term (at least three to five years) by granting the eligible executive the right to receive the value of share appreciation. Appreciation is typically based on changes in the fair market value of shares of stock traded by public companies, or the appraised price of shares in private companies. Another approach is to measure appreciation based on changes in the book value of the company. These plans do not require the executive to make an investment.

Q 7:2   What are examples of appreciation plans?

The most prevalent types of appreciation plans are the stock appreciation right (SAR) and the book value appreciation right. Stock appreciation rights provide long-term income as company stock price increases while book value appreciation rights provide long-term income as company equity (book value) increases.

Stock Appreciation Rights

Q 7:3   What is a stock appreciation right?

An SAR is the right to receive the value of the appreciation of a specified number of shares of a company's capital stock over a specified period of time. An SAR plan can provide that the SAR be exercised by the employee, after a specified vesting period, or it may be structured with a specified maturity date. Payment of any applicable stock appreciation is determined at maturity if the executive is still employed by the company at that date.

Upon exercise or maturity of an SAR, the executive will receive the full appreciated value in any combination of cash, stock, or other consideration, as specified in the SAR agreement. Most companies using the SAR will pay some of the appreciated value in cash so that the executive's tax liability can be offset.

SARs may be issued as "stand alone" rights to the executive or they can be linked with other forms of long-term income, usually stock options. An SAR may be granted "in tandem" with a stock option or "parallel" to a stock option. In tandem stock options (see Q 8:19) the exercise of one stock appreciation share cancels one stock option share, and vice-versa. Under parallel SAR/stock option plans, the executive receives an award of both forms of long-term income and the exercise of one is separate from the exercise of the other.

Example 1: Tandem Stock Option/SAR. Executive A works for Alpha Corporation. She receives a nonqualified stock option of 1,000 shares and stock appreciation rights in tandem with a stock option also equal to 1,000 shares. The option price at the time of grant is $20 per share, which represents the current market price of the stock. There is a one-year vesting provision, and the award period is ten years. After five years, the stock has increased to $40 per share. A exercises her right to the stock appreciation in 500 shares and receives $10,000 (500 shares × $20 per share stock appreciation). A has 500 shares remaining, which she can exercise as either a stock option or an SAR. A could use the $10,000 she received from exercising the SAR to purchase 500 nonqualified stock option shares, since the cost to exercise is also equal to $10,000 (500 shares × $20 option price).

The income to A for exercising 500 SARs and 500 nonqualified option rights is as follows:

Event	500 Shares Stock Option	500 Shares SAR
Exercise value	$20,000[1]	$10,000[2]
Amount paid	$10,000	0
Income	$10,000	$10,000

[1] $40 × 500 shares = $20,000

[2] ($40 − $20) × 500 shares = $10,000

Example 2: Parallel Stock Option/SAR. Executive B is an executive with Bravo Corporation. He is granted a nonqualified stock option of 1,000 shares and a parallel SAR of 1,000 shares. The option price for both the stock option and the SAR at grant is $20 per share, which represents the current market price of the stock.

There is a one-year vesting period, and the award period is ten years. After five years the stock price has increased to $40 per share. B exercises his right to 500 stock appreciation shares that have a value of $10,000 (500 shares × ($40 − $20) = $10,000), and he exercises his right to purchase 500 nonqualified stock options, which also have an exercise price of $10,000 ($20 × 500 shares). The amount of income in the example is the same as in the previous example; however, B still has 500 remaining SARs and 500 remaining nonqualified stock option shares.

Q 7:4   How do the Section 16 rules affect SARs?

The SAR is considered to be a derivative security, subject to Securities and Exchange Commission (SEC) Section 16(a) reporting requirements for insiders and Section 16(b) limitations for insiders on the buying and selling of shares (see Qs 2:17, 2:18, and 2:19). Stock appreciation rights for non-insiders have considerably more flexibility because they are not subject to SEC Rule Section 16(b)3. This rule states that an insider can only exercise a stock appreciation for cash during a ten-day window period that begins on the third business day after the company releases its annual or quarterly financial information, and ends on the 12th day after release of this information. An insider's failure to comply with these requirements turns the exercise of the SAR into a sale of the underlying shares for purposes of Section 16 and is a potential violation of Section 16(b), which prohibits the insider from making a buy and sell transaction within a six-month period.

An insider may exercise an SAR for stock at any time, subject to the provisions of Section 16(b) (a buy/sell transaction cannot occur within a six-month period). SARs for stock can still be used by insiders because the May 1991 clarifications in SEC Section 16 provide for the granting of an SAR (in conjunction with a stock option) as a purchase event. This results in the insider being able to exercise a stock option with an SAR for stock, and subsequently to sell that share immediately if she wishes, provided the exercise-and-sell occurred six months after the date of grant. Insiders also have the flexibility to exercise an SAR for cash during the "window period."

Q 7:5 How prevalent are SARs?

The SAR is most commonly granted in tandem with a stock option plan (normally, a nonqualified stock option plan, because if an SAR were granted with an incentive stock option (ISO), the exercise of the SAR would disqualify the ISO and prevent the executive from receiving any of its favorable tax treatment; see Q 6:7). Most surveys will show that the use of SARs within large publicly traded companies has decreased from 60 percent in 1988 to 40 percent in 1993 and 20 percent in 1996. This is expected to decrease dramatically further because the cashless exercise (see Q 5:51) provides the same benefit as an SAR without the same accounting impact (see Q 7:7).

Q 7:6 Should the SAR be eliminated now that the cashless exercise is possible?

Under the cashless option exercise (see Q 5:51) the company and executive receive the benefit equal to that of an SAR without the company having to accrue expenses for this amount of compensation on its income statement. Appreciation payments from an SAR must be accrued on the company's income statement. Therefore, there is no reason for companies to use SARs, except possibly for insiders, and key executives as defined in Q 2:19. Insiders are subject to a six-month holding period between the purchase and sale (or sale and purchase) of stock. If stock options are granted to insiders who have a six-month or greater vesting period, the cashless exercise can be used for them as well. The granting of the stock option is considered a purchase event (per SEC regulations), and since the exercise and subsequent sale of the options would be at least six months later, the cashless exercise is allowed. The SEC regulation requires that the stock option granted to the insider with a cashless exercise provision be classified as a Section 16(b) stock option.

Q 7:7 What is the accounting impact of an SAR plan?

The SAR is considered to be a "variable plan award" in accounting terminology. The number of shares to be granted and or purchased by the executive, as well as the price of such shares, cannot be determined until the date of exercise. Therefore APB 25, which is used for stock options (see Qs 6:9 and 6:16), does not apply to the SAR.

Companies can elect to use either FAS 28 or FAS 123 to establish the accounting treatment of SARs. Under FAS 28, any company that grants an SAR must accrue the anticipated compensation during the award period on its earnings statement. This accrual is calculated by measuring the amount by which the company's current stock price exceeds the SAR grant price, multiplied by the number of shares that are vested. Changes in the market value of SARs between the date of grant and the date of exercise can thus create significant costs.

Example. 1,000 SARs are granted to an executive at $20 per share, with a four-year vesting period (25% per year). After Year 1 the price per share has increased to $25. The company would have to charge its income statement with $1,250, which is the first year's stock appreciation ($5) times 250 shares (1,000 shares × 25% vesting). The same calculation would be done for all subsequent years that the SAR is outstanding.

Under FAS 28, accruals for an SAR will go up and down over the award period. A final cost accrual is always calculated by the company when the SAR is exercised such that the total accrual over the SAR award period is equal to the amount paid to the executive. Accruals are entered into the income statement each year and then shown in the balance sheet as accrued liabilities.

Example: SAR Accruals.

Assumptions: 1,000 stock appreciation rights at $20/share.
Stock price after Year 1 = $25
Stock price after Year 2 = $20
Stock price after Year 3 = $25
Stock price after Year 4 = $30
SAR exercised after Year 4 at $30/share

	Year 1	Year 2	Year 3	Year 4
Income Statement	$5,000	($5,000)	$5,000	$ 5,000
Balance Sheet	$5,000	($5,000)	$5,000	$10,000
At Exercise				($10,000)

Under FAS 123, a company must calculate the "fair value" of the SAR at the time of grant and charge its earnings statement with this amount over the vesting period. Fair value calculations are discussed in Q 1:49.

Q 7:8 What is the tax treatment for an SAR plan?

The grant of an SAR is not a taxable event since the executive has no constructive receipt. The exercise of the SAR is, however, taxable because the executive recognizes income in an amount equal to the appreciation per share times the total number of shares exercised. For example, if an executive exercises 1,000 SARs that have appreciated $20 per share, that executive will incur a taxable income of $20,000.

Amounts received by an executive from an SAR are taxed at ordinary income tax rates, and are subject to federal and state withholding regardless of whether payments are in cash or in stock. If the total value of the SAR is paid in stock, then the cost basis for the shares will be the fair market value on the date of exercise of the SAR.

As noted in Question 7:7, the company charges the compensatory value of an SAR against its quarterly and annual income statements when an SAR is exercised (whether for cash or for stock). The company is also entitled to a compensation deduction equal to the total appreciation value received by the executive.

The tax consequences of an SAR are compared to those of a stock option in the following example:

Example. An executive exercises 500 SARs and 500 nonqualified stock options, both having a grant price of $20 and a fair market value upon exercise of $40.

Event		500 SARs, 500 Stock Options
Exercise value:	SARs:	$10,000 (500 × ($40 – $20)
	Options:	$10,000 (500 × ($40 – $20)
Taxes @ 40%:	SARs:	$4,000 ($10,000 × 40%)
	Options:	$4,000 ($10,000 × 40%)

Event	*500 SARs, 500 Stock Options*
Amount paid for stock options:	$10,000 (500 × $20)
Amount received if stock is sold:	$20,000 (500 × $40)
Net income:	$12,000 ($20,000 + $10,000 − $10,000 − $8,000)

Note. If this executive wanted to use net proceeds from the SAR ($10,000) to exercise 500 stock option shares (−$10,000), he would be able to, and would still have $20,000 remaining to use for taxes. Using a tax rate of 40 percent, the executive's total tax is $8,000, leaving a net gain of $12,000.

Q 7:9   When do SARs typically vest?

Typically, the vesting requirements of an SAR will be similar to those of other stock option grants. In the case of a SAR granted in tandem to a nonqualified stock option, the vesting of the SAR will mirror that of the stock option to which it is attached. The most common vesting provision for nonqualified stock options is 25 percent per year, or full vesting after four years. The most common vesting period for an incentive stock option is 100 percent after one year. The reason for this difference is that the statutory requirements of ISOs (i.e., one-year holding period after exercise) drive companies into using shorter vesting periods for ISOs. However, it would be unusual to attach an SAR to an ISO because its exercise would disqualify the ISO.

Q 7:10   What are the advantages of an SAR plan?

From the executive's point of view, SARs provide a cashless way to receive the benefits of stock appreciation without having to purchase the stock, as would be the case with a stock option. For insiders, subject to SEC Section 16 rules, the SAR has provided an excellent way to ensure the cash necessary to exercise stock options; otherwise, the executive would need to raise the money by borrowing funds or using amounts in personal savings accounts. By using the SAR, an insider can either exercise during the "window period" or purchase the shares with greater flexibility under the revised Section 16 rules (see Q 7:4).

SARs that are not attached to stock options (stand-alone SARs) are also used by many companies with international operations. Therefore, companies use the SAR for key foreign national executives as a means of providing long-term incentive in the total executive compensation package. The tax laws of many non-U.S. countries are, of course, different from those of the United States, and in some cases, the granting of a stock option can result in a taxable event outside of the United States. Appreciation received from the stand-alone SAR is taxed at normal income tax rates for the specific country where the executive is located, the taxable event occurring when the SAR is exercised (i.e., whenever the value is received).

> **Example.** A non-U.S. executive is given appreciation rights to 1,000 shares of company common stock. These rights vest 25 percent per year until there is full vesting after four years. The executive has ten years to exercise these rights. If the grant price of the shares was $20 per share, and if the executive exercises the right to the appreciation in all shares after six years when the stock price is $50 per share, then the company provides the international executive with $30,000 (1,000 shares × $30 [$50 – $20]).

Q 7:11   Are there disadvantages to using SARs?

Yes. The primary disadvantage of an SAR plan is its negative accounting consequence, which is that the company must take a charge to earnings during each quarter/year in which the SAR is outstanding. Thus the SAR is a costly form of long-term income. In reality the SAR provides the same net benefit to the executive as a stock option plan; however, with a stock option, the appreciation is "free" to the company (the company does not have to take a charge to earnings) and the executive also receives the money once the stock is sold. With the SAR, the company must pay the appreciation itself.

SARs do not normally fill company goals of encouraging stock ownership for executives. Most surveys will indicate executives exercise SARs for cash approximately 90 percent of the time, meaning that only 10 percent of the SAR's exercise result in stock ownership. Also, because they do not encourage stock ownership, SARs do not provide voting rights, dividends, or other rights associated with stock ownership.

A final disadvantage is that SARs have an "uncapped liability." If the company stock price continues to increase, then the accounting accrual for the appreciated value in the SAR will grow each year. In large companies this can amount to millions of dollars of expense that the company has accrued on both its income statement and balance sheet.

Q 7:12   For what type of company does an SAR make sense?

With the recent changes in SEC Section 16, which give insiders much greater flexibility in the exercise of stock options and associated SARs, there is virtually little reason for a company to use an SAR plan unless there is a significant need to deliver cash to executives so that they can (or are required to) use it to purchase company stock. This would typically apply only to a young company whose executives have low tenure with the organization and have not had an opportunity to build capital accumulation and or a stock ownership position.

Book Value Appreciation Rights

Q 7:13   What is a book value appreciation right?

A book value appreciation right is the right to receive the value of the appreciation in a specified number of book value shares. Book value is defined as equity divided by company shares outstanding. For example, if company equity is $10 million and the number of shares outstanding is two million, then the book value is $5 per share. Book value share appreciation rights are normally "stand-alone" rights granted to an executive and are not normally granted in tandem or parallel to stock options. They are particularly useful for private companies without publicly traded shares of stock. Some public companies also use book value appreciation units along with another form of stand-alone long-term incentive (such as a perform-ance plan).

Example. Executive A works for a private company. She is granted 1,000 book value appreciation rights at a time when the book value per share in the company is $5. The vesting period for these rights is one year, and the award period is five years. At the completion of the five-year period, the company's book value is $12 per share. A can then exercise her right to the book value appreciation shares, and in this case would receive $7,000 ($12 – $5 = $7 book value appreciation × 1,000 shares).

Few companies use book value appreciation rights. Surveys indi-cate that less then 5 percent of public companies and less than 10 percent of private companies use this form of long-term incentive.

Q 7:14   What is the accounting impact of a book value appreciation right?

A book value appreciation right is also considered to be a "vari-able plan award" in accounting terminology, meaning that this plan is governed by FASB Statement No. 28. A company must measure the appreciation in book value shares during each period for which it issues an income statement, and the amount by which the shares have increased must be accrued to the income statement. Changes in the book value of the shares between the date of grant and the exercise date of the book value right will continue to accrue on the company's income statement during the entire award period.

In summary, a book value appreciation right has the same ac-counting treatment as a stock appreciation right. Therefore the com-pensation expense of the book value appreciation right will fluctuate along with the company's book value per share.

Q 7:15   What is the tax treatment for a book value appreciation right?

There is no taxation upon the granting of a book value apprecia-tion, because the executive is not in constructive receipt of any value. Upon exercise of a book value share appreciation right, the executive would recognize ordinary income equal to the total amount of book value appreciation received (book value at exercise minus book value at grant). The book value appreciation share therefore has the same tax treatment as the stock appreciation right.

Again, payment of the book value appreciation share is a compensation deduction for the company in its calculation of taxable income. Any book value appreciation share payment to an executive is subject to federal and state withholding.

Q 7:16   What are the advantages of book value appreciation rights?

To the executive in a company that has significant potential for growth in net worth/equity, the book value appreciation right provides a cashless way to receive income as the book value share appreciates in value. Like the SAR, this form of long-term incentive offers the executive the opportunity for substantial capital accumulation without the need to raise money to purchase any book value shares.

Book value appreciation rights can be advantageous to executives in private companies in that they provide long-term income opportunities without diluting the private company stock holdings of current owners.

Q 7:17   Are there disadvantages to book value appreciation rights?

Yes. As with the stock appreciation right, the book value appreciation right is a costly form of long-term incentive in that it requires a charge to the income statement and can be an "uncapped liability" to the company. The book value right does not represent a true ownership position in private companies that do not have any publicly traded shares because book value shares do not carry voting rights and similar rights associated with stock ownership.

Full-Value Plans

Q 7:18 What are full-value plans?

Full-value plans are capital accumulation plans that grant the executive the full value of a company's stock over a long term (three to five years). Full-value plans can provide executives with the full value of a company share and/or the appreciation from a full-value company share. It is significant to note that full-value plans do not require the executive to make an investment.

There are three primary forms of full-value plans: phantom shares, restricted shares, and performance plans.

Q 7:19 Why would a company choose to implement a full-value plan rather than a purchase plan?

It is important for companies to consider full-value and purchase plans in full recognition of their current business needs. Both full-value and purchase plans can permit the executive to gain from the appreciation in the price of company's stock; however, while a full-value plan gives the executive the value of the underlying stock, the purchase plan requires the executive actually to purchase the value of the underlying stock. Therefore, the prospect of a full-value long-term incentive award would more strongly motivate an executive to remain with the company. For this reason many companies going through restructuring, with much uncertainty about the future, will choose full-value plans to retain their executives. In contrast, companies in significant growth periods may believe that an executive should make more of an investment in the organization. In such a case, purchase plans would typically be chosen over full-value plans. Increased media focus on the subject of executive compensation has further encouraged a company attitude that executives should make some amount of investment in the company with purchase plans, just like shareholders.

Still other companies blend both perspectives and provide executives with "stand-alone" full-value grants in addition to "stand-alone" purchase plan grants. This practice of multiple long-term incentive grants (i.e., two different grants from two different plans) is occurring in well over 60 percent of all large publicly traded companies. As shown in Chart 5-1, in fact, many companies use three different types of long-term incentive plan grants.

Phantom Stock Plans

Q 7:20   What is a phantom stock plan?

A phantom stock plan is a plan in which executives are granted "pretend" (or "phantom") shares of stock rather than real shares. Phantom stock is a right to the increase in value of "phantom" (rather than real) shares of a corporation's common stock or book value stock, over a specified period of time. The bonus is typically an amount equal to the difference between the fair market value of the shares of common stock on the date of grant and the fair market value of the stock at the later specified date, although the difference can be measured using book value or some other performance measure. Phantom stock plans are similar to SAR plans, except that participants often have no choice with respect to the specified date of exercise in the typical phantom stock plan. The award when the phantom stock is converted may be paid out in either cash or stock.

Example. Executive C is an executive with Gable Corporation. On August 28, 1986, C is granted 1,000 shares of phantom stock that have a book value at the time of grant of $10 per share. The plan will vest in five years. During the five years, Gable Corporation declares an 8 percent dividend. The plan credits additional shares to C's account for the dividend payments as follows:

Year	Book Value	Beginning Year	Additions From Dividends	End of Year
1989	$10.00	$1,000.00	$ 80.00	$1,080.00
1990	10.60	1,080.00	86.40	1,166.40
1991	11.30	1,166.40	93.31	1,259.71
1992	12.00	1.259.71	100.77	1,360.48
1993	12.80	1,360.48	108.84	1,469.32
1994	13.60	1,469.32	117.55	1,586.87

On August 29, 1994, C is credited with 1,586.87 shares. The appreciation value from the initial date of grant is $3.60, and C receives $5,712.73. Gable Corporation is entitled to a deduction of $5,712.73, which represents that amount that C reports as taxable income.

A phantom stock plan, like an SAR plan, is subject to SEC Section 16(a) reporting and Section 16(b) liability (see Qs 2:17–2:19), and should therefore fully comply with the Rule 16b-3 provisions so that grants under the plan will be exempt transactions. Even if rewards are payable only in cash, the phantom stock will, however, be deemed to be a derivative security and treated like an option for purposes of the Section 16 rules, if its value is "derived from the value of an equity security." If the value of the phantom stock is determined from a formula based on earnings per share and return on equity, it will be a derivative security because it derives its value from the components of an equity security.

From the company's perspective, the use of phantom stock achieves the goals of increasing the executive's economic interest in the company and permitting him to participate in its growth, and yet permits the existing shareholders to retain all voting and liquidation rights associated with their ownership of shares. From the executive's perspective, he can acquire these interests without laying out funds or being subject to an immediate tax.

Phantom stock plans are sometimes utilized as a mechanism for a deferred compensation arrangement. Under this scenario, the executive elects to have her deferred compensation expressed in phantom shares of a company's stock. This sort of phantom stock plan is discussed more in depth in Chapter 9.

Q 7:21   Are dividends paid on phantom stock?

Dividends may, but need not, be paid on phantom stock. Some companies choose to pay dividends based on the philosophy that they have provided the executive with an interest that mirrors the interest of a shareholder. Other companies focus on the increased compensation expense that they must recognize for financial accounting purposes and choose not to pay or accrue phantom dividends.

Dividends may either be accrued or actually paid on phantom stock. If dividends are to be paid out, they result in income to the executive without deduction to the corporation. If dividends are accrued, they may be either allocated to the executive and eventually paid out when the phantom stock is paid out, or they may be converted into phantom stock themselves. This latter method results in a compounding of the benefit, and provides a far greater benefit from holding phantom stock than actual shares of stock.

Q 7:22   How prevalent are phantom stock plans?

Phantom stock plans are not used frequently by publicly held corporations: Fewer than 5 percent of public companies utilize this capital accumulation method for rewarding their executives. Private companies use this method much more frequently, although it is impossible to gather any statistics because of the unavailability of public information.

Q 7:23   What is the accounting impact for a phantom stock plan?

Appreciation in the value of the units and any dividends paid or credited during the period are reported as a compensation expense to the company. A public company will accrue the expense and charge it against earnings on a quarterly basis.

Because no stock is typically issued, the only impact on earnings per share in any period is the amount of compensation expense recognized by the company for financial reporting purposes.

Q 7:24   What is the tax treatment for a phantom stock plan?

The executive has no income, and the corporation receives no tax deduction upon the grant of phantom stock units.

As long as the executive does not have the right to any distribution from his phantom stock, other than dividends payable on the stock, the executive will not be taxed on her phantom stock until the units are converted to actual cash or stock. Whether she receives cash or stock, the executive will be taxed at ordinary income rates. The company is entitled to a deduction for the amount it pays to the executive, including the value of the stock distributed, as and when the executive realizes income, even if that amount includes phantom dividends accrued on the phantom stock.

If the executive is entitled to draw upon his phantom stock units, he will be deemed to be in constructive receipt of the units and taxed immediately on their value. Therefore, the company should make sure that the units are not set apart for him or otherwise made available so that he may draw upon them.

If the executive receives stock as a result of the conversion, the appreciation in those shares will be taxed as a capital gain at the time she sells the shares, if held for one year.

Q 7:25   What are the advantages of a phantom stock plan?

A phantom stock plan allows the executive to participate in the growth of the value of the company without actually making him a shareholder and diluting the value of issued stock.

The executive receives the same value as with a grant of stock, and yet is not required to make an investment, so that she is not at risk if the company's performance falters. Furthermore, she is able to defer being taxed on the benefit, which she could not avoid with a grant of stock. From the company's perspective, unless the granted stock is restricted, phantom stock may have more of a "retaining" incentive as the executive receives no benefit unless he continues with the company.

Q 7:26   Are there disadvantages to a phantom stock plan?

Yes. The principal disadvantage is that the costs are fully charge-able for financial accounting purposes as expenses as and when accrued. For smaller companies, or companies in cyclical businesses, this may be especially troubling.

Phantom stock that is converted into cash can be a severe drain on the company's cash, and many companies may not have sufficient cash flow to meet this potentially large expense. Therefore many companies prefer to convert phantom shares into real shares of stock.

Q 7:27   When do phantom stock units typically vest?

The typical vesting period for phantom stock units is five years.

Q 7:28   For what type of company does a phantom stock plan make sense?

In a privately held corporation, there is more of an incentive to use phantom stock rather than a true stock-based compensation technique in order to avoid dilution to current shareholders, as well as more of a reason to pay out phantom stock conversions in cash rather than in stock (although this may not apply to a cash-poor privately held company). Privately held companies will prefer to use phantom stock plans based on the book value of the stock, which will generally be much more easily ascertainable than the market value for the same stock.

Q 7:29   What is a shadow stock plan?

A shadow stock plan is another name for a phantom stock plan.

Restricted Stock Grants

Q 7:30   What is a restricted stock grant?

Under a restricted stock grant (RSG), an executive is granted shares of stock that are subject to forfeiture unless certain conditions are met. The shares become available to the executive as the restrictions lapse, usually on the completion of a period of employment or based on the performance of the company. The executive receives dividends and has full voting rights on his shares of restricted stock.

> **Example.** On January 1, 1990, Executive A, an executive at Gable Corporation, receives, at no cost, an award of 1,000 restricted shares of Gable Corporation. The restrictions will lapse on January 1, 1994, as long as A is an employee of Gable Corporation at that time. If she leaves the company prior to that time, the shares revert back to Gable corporation. At the time of the award, the shares are worth $10 each and the $10,000 total cost must be amortized as a

compensation expense over the five-year period. On January 1, 1994, A is still employed by Gable Corporation and the restrictions lapse. At this time the shares are worth $18 each. Assuming that she had not made an 83(b) election, A would recognize $18,000 as income on January 1, 1994, and Gable Corporation will be entitled to the corresponding $18,000 tax deduction, even though this amount differs from the $10,000 compensation expense it had accrued on its books.

Q 7:31   How prevalent are restricted stock grants?

The volatility of the stock market makes restricted stock a popular capital accumulation device because the executive receives value even if the stock price falls—without having to make any personal investment under this type of plan. As a result, approximately half of the large publicly traded companies utilize restricted stock grants.

Privately held companies that offer RSGs usually attach two conditions to the grant. The first condition is that the executive receives the stock after all restrictions lapse, and the second condition mandates that the company has the right of first refusal if and when the executive wants to dispose of the stock.

Q 7:32   What is the accounting impact of a restricted stock grant?

The new FAS 123 and the existing APB 25 accounting regulations apply to a restricted stock grant. A company must select one of these regulations to calculate the earnings charge. Under APB 25, the compensation value at the time of grant is accrued as an expense to the company. This expense is determined by measuring the value of the shares at the time of grant (number of shares times stock price), minus the amount to be paid by the executive (typically zero on most restricted stock grants).

If a service requirement is the "restriction" or condition for vesting of the restricted stock, then the compensation value is accrued over the applicable service or restriction period; however, if the stock is forfeited, the compensation expense recorded in previous financial reporting periods can be reversed to reflect the amount of the forfeiture. Under accounting regulations, the appreciation in the value of the restricted shares from the date of grant to the date of vesting is not recognized as a compensation expense for accounting purposes even though the full value of the shares at vesting is a tax deduction to the company. The reason for the tax deduction to the company is that the tax regulations allow a company an expense deduction for compensation and the release of restrictions on a restricted stock grant represents taxable compensation to the executive.

On a company's earnings per share calculations, the earnings and the number of outstanding shares of the company's stock are diluted because, under a restricted stock grant, shares have been issued and earnings have been charged with an expense.

Q 7:33   What is the tax treatment for a restricted stock grant?

The value of restricted stock granted to the executive will be taxable to the executive and deductible by the company in the year in which it is no longer subject to a substantial risk of forfeiture (i.e., when the restrictions lapse).

As long as no Section 83(b) election has been filed, dividends paid on restricted stock prior to the time the executive's rights become substantially vested can be deducted by the company as a compensation expense.

Q 7:34   How does a Section 83(b) election affect a restricted stock grant?

If an executive makes a Section 83(b) election on a grant or restricted stock, he will be taxed immediately on the fair market value of the restricted stock at the time of grant. Dividends paid on the shares will be normal dividend income to the executive, which is not subject to withholding and not deductible by the company. In the event that the executive elects Section 83(b) treatment and later forfeits the subject stock, he will not be entitled to any refund for the taxes paid; he will, however, be entitled to treat the forfeiture as a sale of the stock at a loss (i.e., capital loss).

Q 7:35   What is the typical vesting period for a restricted stock grant?

Restrictions on RSGs generally lapse in three to five years. Restrictions may lapse all at once at the end of the vesting period or in annual installments during the vesting period.

Q 7:36   What are the advantages of a restricted stock grant?

A restricted stock grant program is attractive from the company's perspective, fulfilling the goals of turning management into stockholders, yet retaining them through the restrictions on transferability. Most companies believe that restricted stock is a strong motivation and retention mechanism for executives.

Q 7:37   Are there disadvantages to a restricted stock grant?

Yes. Restricted stock is often criticized as a "freebie" for management because most companies condition the vesting of the stock only on service and do not impose any additional performance requirements. Therefore an executive will receive a reward even where there is no improvement in a company's performance; yet, this is not the type of situation where a reward seems appropriate. Existing shareholders are diluted as a result of the grant of stock for which no purchase price—or only a nominal one—has been paid.

Q 7:38   For what types of companies do restricted stock grants make sense?

Restricted stock may be most useful and defensible as grants to high-potential middle managers and professional employees in order to recognize those individuals with unique skills and contributions who are not normally eligible to receive stock options. Furthermore, a company that has difficulties recruiting or retaining key contributors can use restricted stock grants as a recruitment bonus. Finally, restricted stock grants are especially attractive to private companies as the transfer restrictions ensure that outsiders will not be able to acquire shares of the company's stock.

Performance Unit Plans

Q 7:39 What is a performance unit plan?

A performance unit plan (PUP) grants the executive performance units, which can be earned based on the attainment of company performance targets over a specified period, generally three to five years. The plan will set goals for the company and establish a fixed value for the units. The reward for the executive is equal to the number of units earned times the fixed value of the performance unit. The reward may be paid in cash or stock or a combination of both.

Q 7:40 How are performance measures established for a performance unit plan?

The company must determine the goals to be used for a PUP, generally an EPS goal, return on capital, return on equity, or some combination of these financial measures. The company must also decide what compensation amount should be provided if goals are met, exceeded, or not met. The performance measure is generally determined based on the performance of a group rather than of an individual, and the members of the group share in the reward relative to their contributions. Many companies will establish a percentage midpoint as the target award for a performance unit grant.

Example. Company A decides that it will allocate 100 performance units to an executive. It establishes a value of $50 for the performance units. Company A will pay out 100 of the performance units if EPS growth averages 10 percent over a three-year period. Company A will pay 75 units if EPS growth is 8 percent over the award period, and it will pay 125 units if EPS growth is 12 percent over the award period.

Assuming that the 10 percent EPS growth is reached, the executive will receive 100 performance units at a value of $5,000 (100 units × $50 per unit).

Q 7:41 What is the accounting impact of a performance unit plan?

For financial accounting purposes, PUPs are treated as "variable plan awards" and thus are subject to the same accounting treatment as the stock appreciation rights. Therefore, the company will have to accrue the estimated compensation expense proportionately over the award period.

Q 7:42   What is the tax treatment of a performance unit plan?

The executive recognizes no taxable income at the time of grant of the performance units. Once performance units are earned, the executive has a taxable event at the ordinary income tax rates, and the company will receive a tax deduction equal to the value received by the executive.

Q 7:43   What is the typical award period for a performance unit plan?

A typical PUP award period will be equal to the period covered by the company's strategic plan, which is generally three to five years.

Q 7:44   What are the advantages of a performance unit plan?

The principal advantage of a PUP is that it provides an opportunity for long-term capital accumulation to the executive based on company performance on which the executive can have a direct effect, rather than on stock market performance, which the executive cannot directly influence. Performance unit grants are often provided in addition to stock options or other market-based forms of long-term income so that the executive is rewarded for both stock performance and the achievement of key company long-term business goals.

Q 7:45   Are there disadvantages to instituting a performance unit plan?

Yes. The primary disadvantage of PUPs is the difficulty of accurately establishing performance goals for a period of three years or more. Also, because these plans typically pay in cash, a substantial charge to earnings occurs when goals are achieved. This represents a negative accounting consequence, and this charge to earnings occurs throughout the entire award period.

Performance Share Plans

Q 7:46   What is a performance share plan?

A performance share plan operates similarly to a performance unit plan, except that the value of each performance share is tied to the value of a company's share of stock. Therefore a performance share plan provides a dual incentive to the executive to achieve the earnings goal established under the plan and to further influence company stock price, since the higher the stock price the higher the value of the shares earned at the end of the award period.

> **Example.** Company B decides to provide 100 performance shares to an executive. Company B will pay out the 100 shares if company EPS growth is 10 percent over the next three years. It will pay out 75 shares if company EPS growth is 8 percent, and it will pay 125 shares if company EPS growth is 12 percent over the period. Assume that the stock price at the time of grant is $50 per share. At the end of the award period, if the company achieved its target EPS growth of 10 percent, then the executive would receive 100 performance shares. If the stock price at the end of the award period is $70, then the value received by the executive is $7,000 (100 shares × $70 per share). The compensation expense to the company's income statement will also be $7,000, accrued over the three-year award period. The executive will be taxed on ordinary income tax rates based on the $7,000 of income, and the company will receive a $7,000 tax deduction.

Q 7:47   What is the tax treatment of a performance share grant?

The executive recognizes no income at the time of grant of the performance shares. Once a performance share is earned, the executive has a taxable event at the ordinary income tax rates, and the company will receive a tax deduction equal to the value received by the executive in the year payment is received.

Q 7:48   What is the accounting treatment of a performance share?

Companies can elect to use either FAS 28 or FAS 123.

Under FAS 28, any company that grants a performance share must accrue the anticipated compensation during the award period on its earnings statement. This accrual is calculated by measuring the amount by which the company's current stock price exceeds the SAR grant price, multiplied by the number of shares that would be earned at 100 percent payout of the performance share, multiplied times a prorated number of years of the award period. Companies can assume a payout that is greater or less than 100 percent if this represents the most likely payout level. Changes in both the payout level and the market value of performance shares between the date of grant and the date of exercise can thus create significant costs.

Under FAS 123, a company must calculate the "fair value" of the performance share at the time of grant and charge its earnings statement with this amount over the award period. Fair value calculations are discussed in Q 1:49.

Chapter 8

Combination Long-Term Plans

Tandem plans utilize more than one type of long-term incentive plan. Usually, tandem plans provide executives with a choice between two types of options or awards. Once the executive chooses one alternative, the other is canceled. Two of the most common tandem plan combinations are the phantom stock/stock option plan and the restricted stock/stock option plan. A third variation of the tandem plan is the contingent stock award plan, which requires the executive to purchase and hold one option before obtaining access to a second option or other award. This chapter covers the requirements for implementing tandem plans as well as suggestions on maximizing their effectiveness.

General Considerations 8-1
Performance Share/Stock Option Plans 8-3
Restricted Stock/Stock Option Plans 8-8
SAR/Stock Option Plans 8-11

General Considerations

Q 8:1 What is a tandem plan?

A tandem plan grants an executive a choice between two types of capital accumulation plans. By choosing or exercising one alternative the other is canceled. For example, an executive can be granted 1,000 stock option shares and 1,000 stock appreciation rights (SARs) attached to each of the nonqualified stock options. If the executive exercises 250 of the SARs, then the executive has 750 remaining of either nonqualified stock options or SARs.

Q 8:2 What is a parallel plan?

A parallel plan grants the executive two types of capital accumulation plans that are mutually exclusive and stand-alone. The choice or exercise of one alternative has no effect on the other type of grant. For example, an executive could be granted 1,000 stock option shares and 1,000 stock appreciation rights under a parallel plan. If the executive exercises 500 SARs, then the executive still has 500 SARs and 1,000 nonqualified stock options remaining.

Q 8:3 Are there advantages to creating tandem or parallel combination plans?

Yes. For example, combining a nonqualified stock option with a stock appreciation right results in a long-term incentive plan that does not require an executive to invest funds, and at the same time provides the executive with an opportunity to use cash from the SAR to purchase a nonqualified stock option.

Other combination plans can provide the executive with opportunities for stock appreciation and capital accumulation from a performance-based plan that is not subject to the vagaries of the stock market. From the company's point of view, combination plans offer the opportunity for a dual incentive, that is, incentive for the executive to increase stock price and achieve long-term company performance goals.

Q 8:4 Are there disadvantages to tandem and parallel combination plans?

Yes. The primary credo of the tandem and parallel plans is that they provide downside protection to the executive, which is a protection that the average shareholder does not receive. For example, if an executive is provided with 1,000 nonqualified stock option shares and 1,000 long-term performance shares, the executive could earn the performance share grants based on achieving long-term performance goals even if, at the same time, the stock price is flat. On the other hand, the executive could exercise the stock option grants if the stock price went up even if the long-term performance goals in the performance share plan were not met. Thus the executive is protected in a way that other investors are not. From the investors' perspective, this represents an "unlevel playing field": The executive can win when the investor loses.

Q 8:5 What compensation combinations are the most common in combination long-term plans?

Three combinations are used most frequently. These combinations are:

- Stock options and performance plans (performance shares or performance units)
- Restricted stock and stock options
- Stock appreciation rights and stock options

Performance Share/Stock Option Plans

Q 8:6 What are combination stock option and performance plans?

These plans grant the executive stock options and either a performance share plan or performance unit plan (see Qs 7:46 and 7:39, respectively). The stock option plan would normally have a vesting period equal to the performance award period in the performance plan (e.g., four years). Under a tandem plan, upon conclusion of the vesting and performance award period, the executive would choose one award or the other. Under a parallel plan, the executive would then have the right to purchase the stock options and would receive the performance plan award if earned. Under either tandem or parallel arrangements, the stock option plan would typically have an award period of ten years, meaning that after completion of vesting (e.g., during the fourth year), the executive would have an additional six years to exercise the stock option.

Example 1: Tandem Plan. An executive is granted 1,000 performance shares and 1,000 stock option shares. The performance shares have a four-year award period, during which time specific earnings per share growth is to be achieved. The stock option award has a four-year vesting period and following the 100 percent vesting after four years the executive may exercise the right to purchase the option any time up to ten years from the date of grant.

If, at the end of the four years, the executive elects to take the performance shares (if earned), then the stock options are canceled. If, at the end of the four years, the executive has not earned the performance shares or elects the stock option for other reasons, the performance shares are canceled.

Example 2: Parallel Plan. An executive is provided with 1,000 performance shares to be earned over a four-year period if specific earnings per share goals are achieved. The executive is also provided with a 1,000 share stock option award, with four-year vesting and a ten-year award period. These grants are mutually exclusive: the exercise of any number of stock options has no effect on the performance shares, and the earning of any performance shares has no effect on the stock options.

Q 8:7   What is the accounting impact of combination performance share and stock option plans?

Since the accounting treatment is different for performance shares and stock options, this should affect plan consideration. Under a parallel plan, the grants stand alone and the stock options and performance shares each receive their regular accounting treatment. For a stock option, the company must select the use of either FAS 123 or APB 25. (See Q 1:45.)

Under a tandem plan, the accounting treatment of the performance share would prevail. A performance share plan is a "variable plan award" and the company would have to elect the use of accounting regulation FAS 28 or FAS 123.

Under FAS 28, a company is required to accrue the estimated compensation expense proportionately over the performance share award period, with adjustments made for any increases or decreases in the market value per share of stock. At the time the executive earns the performance shares a final accounting for expenses would occur, and the total amount earned by the executive would equal the total amount accrued by the company as an expense. If the executive chose the stock option in lieu of the performance share, at the end of the vesting period, then no additional compensation expense would be accrued for the remaining period of the stock option award. Liabilities accrued for the performance share during its award period would be reversed from the liability portion of the balance sheet once the stock option was elected.

Under FAS 123, the company is required to calculate a "fair value" of the performance share at the time of grant and accrue this cost over the award period. The fair value calculation is discussed in Q 1:49.

Example: Tandem Performance Share and Stock Option Grant. A company provides an executive with a combination grant of 1,000 performance shares at $20 per share and 1,000 nonqualified stock option shares, also at $20 per share, the current fair market value. The performance shares have an earnings per share growth objective of 20 percent over four years. The nonqualified stock options vest at 25 percent per year or 100 percent after four years. These grants are tandem, meaning that the executive must choose one or the other after the four-year period.

The accounting treatment for the nonqualified stock option would be to use either FAS 123 or APB 25; however, since this is a tandem grant, the accounting treatment of the performance shares would prevail, since it is the most likely result from the grant. Therefore, for each of the four years, the company would calculate its earnings charge by multiplying the number of vested shares in the performance share grant, times any stock appreciation during the financial period being measured, minus any earnings charge to date. If in Year 1 the per-share appreciation was $5 and in Year 2 the per-share appreciation was $12, the accounting accrual on the company's income statement would be $1,250 in Year 1 and $4,750 in Year 2, calculated as follows:

Year 1: 1,000 shares × 25% (1 year ÷ 4 years) = $250 × $5 = $1,250.

Year 2: 1,000 shares × 50% (2 years ÷ 4 years) = $500 × $12 = $6,000 − $1,250 = $4,750.

Q 8:8 What is the tax treatment for combination performance share and stock option plans?

The executive recognizes no taxable event at the time of grant for either a tandem or parallel combination plan of performance shares and stock options. If, under either plan, a performance share plan is earned, the value of the performance share award is taxable income to the executive at ordinary income tax rates. The company receives a tax deduction equal to the amount of income received by the executive. If the executive should have elected to defer income from the performance share, then the taxable event and the company tax deduction would be deferred as well. On the other hand, if the stock option is exercised under either tandem or parallel grants, then the executive is taxed at ordinary income tax rates, on the spread in value between the option price and the exercise price, if the stock option is non-qualified. If an ISO is used, the tax may be deferred until sale, and if held for one year, the executive would pay capital gains tax. The company would be eligible for a tax deduction in the same amount as the spread. The executive is eligible for capital gains tax from the point at which ownership occurs.

Q 8:9 Are there advantages to a combination plan of performance shares and stock options?

Yes. The primary advantage is that such a combination allows the executive to make choices that are financially advantageous. A parallel plan offers greater flexibility to the executive: The executive determines when to exercise the stock option and influences company performance in achieving the earnings goal and subsequent payment of the performance share. Under a tandem plan, the executive has the opportunity to choose one plan or the other at the end of the award/vesting period.

From the company's point of view, these plans assist in retaining key executives and can provide a "dual incentive" for the executive to increase stock price as well as achieve company performance goals.

Q 8:10   Are there disadvantages to the combination performance share and stock option plan?

Yes. An accounting charge is required for the performance share, which is a significant cost element to the company. Under the tandem plan, this may be reversed at the end of the award period if the executive chooses the stock option; however, during the award period earnings have been reduced because of the accruals required for the performance share.

Executives must utilize their own cash to exercise stock options. Under a tandem plan, it is unlikely that the executive would elect the stock option if a performance share has been earned. Under a parallel plan, the executive can, however, utilize cash earned from a performance share award to purchase the stock option.

These types of plans can be criticized by the media and by shareholders for giving the executive downside protection (i.e., potential earnings from the performance share even if the stock price remains constant), which is a protection that shareholders do not have.

Q 8:11   For what type of company does a combination performance share and stock option plan make sense?

A parallel grant of these forms of long-term incentive makes great sense to both the company and the executive in that the performance plan can generate cash to purchase the stock options. Therefore any company that wishes to build executive stock ownership can require its executives to use the cash earned from a performance share plan to purchase stock under a stock option plan.

Restricted Stock/Stock Option Plans

Q 8:12   What is a tandem restricted stock/stock option plan?

A tandem restricted stock/stock option plan grants both restricted stock awards and nonqualified stock options. Under this type of plan, the participant is allowed to choose whether to keep the restricted stock or to exercise the options, which cancels the restricted stock award. Furthermore, vesting of the restricted stock would also cancel the related stock option.

Example. Gable Corporation provides its directors with an annual retainer fee of $36,000. One-half of the fee, or $18,000, is paid in cash and the remaining $18,000 is paid-in to a tandem restricted stock/stock option plan at a ratio between the restricted stock and the stock options of 3 to 1. One director receives 720 shares of restricted stock ($18,000/$25, the current market value) and 2,160 nonqualified stock options with an exercise price of $25. She receives annual dividends on the restricted stock until the restrictions lapse in five years, at which point she will receive the stock and the corresponding nonqualified options will be canceled. In the alternative, the director can exercise her options at any time before the restrictions lapse and forfeit the restricted stock.

The following table shows how much the stock price moves, thereby determining whether the restricted stock or nonqualified stock option is a more advantageous alternative.

Stock Price Appreciation (in %)	Value of One Restricted Share	Gain on Three Option Shares Above the Exercise Price	Excess Value of Options
0	$25.00	0.00	$(25)
20	30.00	15.00	(15)
30	32.50	22.50	(10)
40	35.00	30.00	(5)
50	37.50	37.50	0
60	40.00	45.00	5
70	42.50	52.50	10
80	45.00	60.00	15

Assuming a three-to-one ratio, the crossover point is at a 50 percent stock appreciation level. Above this point, the director should exercise her options, which cancel the restricted stock ownership.

Q 8:13 Can a parallel grant be made of restricted shares and stock option shares?

Yes. As a parallel grant, each form of long-term incentive stands on its own, and a company must follow all applicable tax and accounting regulations for each.

Example. A company grants an executive 1,000 restricted shares when the stock price is $20 per share, and provides the same executive with 3,000 stock option shares at $20 per share, the current fair market value. The restricted shares have a four-year restriction period, and the stock option shares vest at 25 percent per year. With respect to the restricted stock, the company would be required to take a charge to earnings equal to $5,000 per year for four years (1,000 shares × $20 per share divided by four years). The stock options would have no charge to earnings because they were granted at the current market value.

Q 8:14 What is the accounting impact of a combination restricted stock/stock option plan?

Since the accounting treatment is now the same for restricted shares and stock options, this should not affect plan design considerations. Under a parallel plan, the grants stand alone and the stock options and restricted shares each receive their regular accounting treatment. For a stock option, the company must select the use of either FAS 123 or APB 25. (See Q 1:45.)

Under a tandem plan, the accounting treatment of the most likely event would prevail. The restricted stock is the most likely choice by the executive. The company would have to elect the use of accounting regulation APB 25 or FAS 123.

The regulations of APB 25 would require that the company determine the earnings charge at the time of grant. This calculation is done by multiplying the number of shares by the price per share and then accruing this amount over the restriction period.

The regulations of FAS 123 would require the company to determine the "fair value" of the restricted shares and charge its earnings over the restriction period.

Q 8:15   What is the tax treatment for a combination restricted stock/stock option plan?

The tax treatment at the time of grant is similar for both forms of long-term incentive. The executive would not recognize income on either the restricted shares or the stock options at that time. If the nonqualified stock option is exercised, a taxable event would occur to the executive, and the executive would have to pay ordinary income tax on the spread between the option price and the exercise price. If the restricted stock award is exercised, the executive would also be required to pay ordinary income tax on the total value of the restricted shares at the time the restriction has lapsed. The company would also receive a tax deduction equal to the taxable income incurred by the executive. Once the executive takes possession of shares, future taxation would be at the capital gains tax rate. If held for one year, the shares would be eligible for capital gains tax once sold.

> **Example.** An executive takes possession of 1,000 restricted shares when the price per share is $40. The executive has $40,000 taxable income at ordinary income tax rates. The company has a $40,000 tax deduction in the same year.

If the executive's tax rate was 30 percent, then the ordinary income tax would be $12,000 ($40,000 × 30%). In this case, the executive could sell 300 shares to fulfill the tax obligation (300 shares × $40 = $12,000). The remaining 700 shares would be subject to capital gains tax and if held for one year or more would be subject to a maximum tax rate of 28 percent on any additional appreciation beyond the current value of $40 per share. If sold before one year, any share appreciation beyond $40 would be subject to the executive's current ordinary income tax rate (in this case 30 percent).

Q 8:16   What are the advantages of a combination restricted stock/stock option plan?

The primary advantage of this type of plan is that it gives executives an immediate ownership position through the restricted stock so that the participant can vote and receive dividends, but can also take advantage of appreciation in the company stock.

Q 8:17   What are the disadvantages of the combination restricted stock/stock option plan?

This type of plan is criticized because the restricted stock component is not available to the average company shareholder. At a minimum, if it has a typical time lapse restriction, this component rewards the executive for tenure, regardless of stock market performance. The executive would not be likely to invest in the stock option component if the stock price appreciates, because the restricted shares receive the share appreciation without any investment by the executive.

Q 8:18   For what type of company does a restricted stock/stock option plan make sense?

A company that wants to give immediate ownership to the executive while encouraging the executive to make an investment should consider a restricted stock/stock option plan. Also, a company that expects and/or wants to motivate executives to work toward significant growth in its stock price would want to consider this type of combination plan.

SAR/Stock Option Plans

Q 8:19   What is a tandem SAR/stock option plan?

This type of tandem plan grants the executive SARs that are attached to nonqualified stock options. Most companies grant one SAR for each stock option granted. The exercise of one SAR cancels out one stock option. The real value of this type of tandem plan is the opportunity it offers the executive to exercise SARs to raise the cash necessary to then exercise/purchase stock options and pay the required income tax. With this plan, even insiders are allowed to pay the option exercise price by using the increase in the value of the company shares, which decreases the amount of personnel investment required.

Under Section 16 of the SEC rules, the SAR for insiders is subject to the requirement of Section 16(b), which requires insiders to avoid any combination of purchase or sale for a six-month period. Section 16(b)3 allows insiders to exercise the SAR during the "window period" (third to fourth working day following release of quarterly earnings) and then to use this cash six months later to purchase the stock options.

Some companies set the option price of the tandem SAR higher than the exercise price of the stock option to encourage the executive to exercise the option rather than the SAR.

Example 1. Executive A is an executive of Altoona Corporation and participates in their long-term incentive plan. On January 15, 1993, he receives 1,000 SARs with a $10 base price, attached to 1,000 nonqualified stock options with a $10 option price. The current market value of the stock is $10. Five years later in January 1998, the current market value of Altoona stock has risen to $30. If A takes all of the SARs, he will receive $20,000 ($20 in stock appreciation × 1,000 SARs). If he were to exercise all of his stock options he would also receive $20,000 ($20 in appreciation × 1,000 shares).

Example 2. Executive B is an executive of Altoona Corporation and also participates in their long-term incentive plan. On January 15, 1993 she receives 1,000 SARs with a $10 base price attached to 1,000 nonqualified stock options with a $10 option price. The current market value of the stock is $10. Five years later in January 1998, the current market value of Altoona stock has risen to $30. If B exercises 500 of the SARs, she would receive $10,000 ($20 in appreciation × 500 shares). She can then use the $10,000 in cash to exercise the remaining 500 nonqualified stock option shares which have an option price of $5,000 ($10 × 500 shares). B still has $5,000 remaining in cash to use for meeting her ordinary income tax obligations.

Q 8:20   What is a parallel SAR/stock option plan?

This type of plan grants the executive a fixed number of stock appreciation rights and a separate number of nonqualified stock options. The exercise of one form of long-term incentive does not cancel any shares in the other because these are stand-alone grants.

Q 8:21   How prevalent are SAR/stock option plans?

These plans have historically appeared as tandem plans, with almost one-third of the publicly traded companies using them during the 1980s. These plans are not as popular in the 1990s because of the significant changes in SEC Section 16 rules. Specifically, insiders have considerably more flexibility to exercise stock options and then immediately to sell the underlying securities without violating the short-swing liability of Section 16(b). The 1991 SEC regulations provide for the stock option grant to be a purchase event. Therefore, once the insider exercises the shares, typically three to four years after grant, there is no requirement at that time for the insider to hold the shares. Companies are also not using these combination plans as frequently because, in practice, executives were exercising the SARs and letting the stock options rights expire. Thus company objectives of stock ownership were not being achieved. The plans were becoming long-term cash plans.

Q 8:22   What is the accounting impact of combination SAR/stock option plans?

The accounting requirements of the SAR will prevail with respect to tandem SAR/stock option plans, and there would be an accounting charge throughout the award period. A company can select either FAS 28 or FAS 123. If FAS 28 is selected, the earnings charge is equal to the number of vested shares of the SAR multiplied by the stock appreciation per share. If FAS 123 is selected, the earnings charge is determined at the time of grant and is equal to the "fair value" of the SAR, which is then accrued over the vesting period. For an explanation of fair value calculations, see Q 1:49.

With a parallel SAR/stock option plan, the same is true in that the SAR is subject to an accounting charge as just described. The stock option is subject to either FAS 123 or APB 25. (See Q 1:45.) The company must select one of these; however, if it has already selected

FAS 123 for the SAR, it must also use it to calculate the earnings charge for the stock option.

Q 8:23 What is the tax treatment of combination SAR/stock option plans?

There is no tax impact to the company or to the executive at the time of the grant. When the executive receives income from either the SAR or the stock option, the executive will be taxed at ordinary income rates and the company will receive a tax deduction equal to the value or appreciation received by the executive.

If the SAR is payable in stock, then the executive would receive capital gains treatment on future appreciation after the exercise of the SAR. If the shares are held for at least one year, then the capital gains tax rate would apply. The same would be true upon the exercise and purchase of the nonqualified stock option.

Chapter 9

Executive Benefit Plans

Various tax reform measures have caused significant cutbacks in the tax-favored treatment of certain employer-provided retirement benefits and perquisites. In response to these limitations, companies are implementing specialized executive programs to compensate for regulatory limitations and to respond to competitive recruiting pressures. Nonqualified retirement plans allow executive retirement benefits to be provided on a selective confidential basis up to virtually any level of compensation commensurate with the executives contribution to the company. The plan might be designed to resemble a defined benefit, defined contribution, or 401(k) type of benefit that incorporates executive pre-tax income deferrals and matching contributions at the employer's option. Split-dollar life insurance plans provide life insurance benefits, executive cash value accumulation, and postretirement paid-up insurance at little or no cost to the executive. The life insurance benefit is particularly attractive to senior executives seeking ways to protect wealth (generated by stock options or other equity incentives) from estate tax rates as high as 55 percent. Group insurance disadvantages such as inflated cost for life insurance coverage exceeding $50,000, lack of permanence and non-portability are primary reasons that executive split-dollar plans are so widely accepted today. Executive disability insurance plans are being used to provide higher coverage levels than typical group long-term disability coverage limits, offering tax advantages to the company and the executive alike. Employers are thus able to provide benefit plans for top management that are competitive with peer companies. This chapter covers the ERISA and general tax issues of executive benefit plans, as well as plan design and competitive practices.

General Considerations   9-2
Nonqualified Retirement Plans   9-3
Funding Arrangements   9-17
Insurance-related Nonqualified Deferred Compensation Plans   9-20
Split-Dollar Life Insurance   9-23
Executive Disability Income Insurance   9-26
ERISA Considerations   9-27
Top-Hat Plans or SERPs   9-28
Excess Benefit Plans   9-33
Nonqualified Plans in Nonprofit Organizations   9-37
Tax Considerations   9-39

General Considerations

Q 9:1   Why are executive benefit plans so important?

Recruiting and retaining uniquely skilled executives is a vital component of corporate management. In today's rugged business environment it is now commonplace for competitors to seek valuable people with years of training and experience from peer companies. The seniority and abilities of a key executive represent an immeasurable investment of someone's time and money. It is no secret that meaningful retirement, death, and disability benefits tied to continuous employment are crucial elements in attracting and "handcuffing" key executives to a company along with traditional compensation items. As a matter of fact, executives today expect and require these benefits as a condition of continued employment. If these benefits were not provided by the employer the executive would need additional cash compensation to purchase them.

Q 9:2   How do traditional benefit programs fail executives?

Unfortunately, traditional benefit programs such as 401(k) and qualified retirement plans, group life insurance, and group disability income protection have been restricted and severely limited by federal legislation. Numerous statistical studies indicate that executives typically need approximately 60 to 70 percent of final pay in order to maintain their standard of living after retirement. Without company benefits and tax-advantaged methods to accumulate funds, this goal is typically unattainable.

Q 9:3   How do these executive benefit programs fit into overall compensation?

They are usually considered to be long-term incentives. Instead of cash, the company provides insurance, investment, or retirement benefits to relieve the executive of having to acquire the benefits personally with after-tax dollars. The flexibility and confidentiality of these plans present an excellent opportunity to replace benefit packages that would be lost by individuals the company wishes to recruit.

Executive benefit plans are also a tool used by companies to retain recruited executives. Such plans are often designed so the executive who leaves stands to lose all or part of the plan benefits.

Nonqualified Retirement Plans

Q 9:4   What is deferred compensation?

Deferred compensation refers to the process of delaying receipt of income and its taxation to a later date. A nonqualified compensation agreement that postpones payment of compensation until a later time, typically until after retirement, is needed for this purpose.

Q 9:5   What are the three primary approaches for deferring compensation?

One approach involves an agreement between the executive and the company for the executive to give up some portion of his current compensation in exchange for the company's promise to make a deferred payment sometime in the future. Typically the executive defers some portion of his annual compensation. To encourage the executive to make this deferral, many companies have offered a guaranteed investment return that is higher than the executive can hope to obtain on his own, in recent years it has become more common to offer investment options that mirror the 401(k) plan.

The second approach is for the company to provide an additional benefit to the executive. This second approach does not involve any real income deferral on the part of the executive but does involve the company's promise to make additional payments to the executive at some time in the future.

A third approach is a company match on any compensation the executive elects to defer. In this approach the investment options and the match will generally mirror the 401(k) plan.

Deferred compensation as used herein refers to each of these somewhat different approaches.

Q 9:6   What is a nonqualified deferred compensation plan?

A nonqualified deferred compensation plan is a plan that is not subject to most of ERISA and does not receive favorable tax treatment under the Internal Revenue Code (the "Code"). Because these plans are not subject to the restrictive provisions of ERISA or the Code, they can be designed to cover selected executives. These plans cannot be available to the rank and file employees without subjecting the plan to ERISA coverage. The trade-off for this flexibility is that nonqualified benefit plans result in income recognition when the employee's right to the benefit vests rather than deferring recognition of the income to the time of the distribution, as would be the case with a qualified plan.

Q 9:7   How does a nonqualified deferred compensation plan differ from a qualified plan?

Nonqualified plans do not qualify for the special tax treatment afforded to plans that meet the qualification requirements contained in Code Section 401(a). This favorable tax treatment for qualified plans includes a current deduction for the employer for its contributions, and tax deferral for the employee on their contributions and tax-free build-up of investment income until distribution.

Q 9:8 What do nonqualified deferred compensation plans typically provide?

Because a nonqualified deferred compensation plan is usually tailored to one executive or a small group of executives, these plans vary greatly in what they provide. Typically, these plans provide for postretirement payments to the executive, postretirement and preretirement death benefits, and preretirement disability payments. Some of the plans provide for payments prior to retirement. Except in the case of Code Section 457 plans, there is no restriction on the amount to be deferred. And because a nonqualified plan is not attempting to satisfy Internal Revenue Service (IRS) regulations, the plan can be highly discriminatory as to who is covered and what benefits are provided.

Q 9:9 What is the rationale for creating nonqualified deferred compensation plans for executives?

The Tax Reform Act of 1986 (TRA '86) imposed a series of limitations on the benefit levels that highly paid executives can receive. Chief among these limitations were:

1. Capping individual 401(k) plan contributions at $7,000. This figure is adjusted annually to reflect the movement of the consumer price index. The current maximum in 1997 is $9,500.

2. Freezing the Code Section 415 limits on deferred compensation plans.

3. Limiting to $200,000 the earnings that can be included in the calculations of qualified retirement plan benefits. This was indexed to inflation and is now $235,840; however, OBRA changed this to a maximum of $150,000. (See Q 9:10.)

4. Toughening the antidiscrimination testing for 401(k) plans and other benefits.

5. Levying a 15 percent excise tax on excess distributions from tax-qualified retirement plans.

All of these limitations produce a form of reverse discrimination because they cap a benefit or the accrual of a benefit. Many companies have therefore been spurred to develop alternative nonqualified deferred compensation plans that could be used to ensure that executives who were adversely impacted by these provisions would be made whole.

Q 9:10   What changes did the Omnibus Reconciliation Act of 1993 (OBRA) add to the regulatory limits of qualified plans?

This act went into effect in 1994, but the full effect of the additional limitations imposed by the act did not impact organizations until 1995. The primary additional limitation is that the amount of compensation for any individual executive, that can be used by a company in determining the company's contribution to the executive's pension each year, was changed from $235,840 to $150,000 and would be indexed for inflation, but there would be no raises except in $10,000 increments (the limit for 1997 is $160,000).

Beyond obviously limiting a company's contribution to a defined benefit or defined contribution pension plan for an executive, this new limitation also impacts 401(k) contributions.

Example. An executive earns $235,840; the maximum contribution to a 401(k) plan is $9,500 for 1997 (per TRA '86 and OBRA). The executive wants to contribute $9,500 to the 401(k) plan. Under provisions of the Code the average deferral percentage of the "highly compensated employee" (HCE) group (as defined under the Code) cannot exceed the average deferral percentage of the "nonhighly compensated employees" (NHCE) by more than the greater of the lesser of two times the average deferral percentage of the NHCE and the average deferral percentage plus two percentage points, or the average deferral plus 1.25 percent.

Under the above example this executive is now contributing 5.94 percent of compensation to the 401(k) plan for purposes of discrimination testing ($9,500 ÷ $160,000 = 5.94 percent). In reality the executive is contributing 4.03 percent of his total compensation. The NHCE's average deferral must exceed 4.66 percent to meet discrimination requirements of the Code.

The 401(k) plan must meet all discrimination requirements or a disqualification of the company's tax deduction on all company contributions to the plan could occur and the tax deferral of the contributions will be denied. This will necessitate the refund of all contributions and the amendment of their participants income tax returns for all years in which the plan is disqualified.

The other problem created by OBRA with respect to executive compensation is that the $150,000 limit is indexed to inflation, but only if the increments are $10,000, rounded down. For example, if the inflation percentage in 1995 were 6 percent, then 6% × $150,000 = $9,000. Since $9,000 is less than $10,000, there would be no adjustment in the $150,000 for 1996. Due to the composite inflation since OBRA, the compensation limit was raised to $160,000 for 1997 and thereafter.

Q 9:11 What are the typical objectives of the executive in deferring income under a nonqualified deferred compensation plan?

The executive typically defers compensation to provide for future financial commitments and to lower current taxable income. Deferral of compensation is a method of systematic tax-deferred savings. This makes sense for a highly paid employee, who is at the highest marginal tax rate to defer income, particularly in today's business environment.

Q 9:12 What are the typical objectives of the company in providing a deferral program?

The primary reasons for providing deferred compensation plans to executives is the need for companies to attract and retain executives. Competition for executives forces companies to try to develop compensation plans that will be attractive to executives; as qualified plans become more and more restricted as to how much in benefits an executive can receive, the executives are asking for plans that will supplement the companies' retirement plans. Companies also need these plans to attract the key executives they wish to hire away from other companies. These plans can be used to replace qualified plan benefits that a desired executive must give up if he leaves before vesting.

Q 9:13   Who can generally benefit under a nonqualified deferred compensation plan?

Typically, nonqualified deferred compensation plans are designed to benefit the following:

1. Key executives;

2. A select group of management or highly compensated employees; and

3. Employees whose benefits ordinarily would be limited under Code Section 415, which limits benefits for defined contribution plans to the lesser of $30,000 (or, if greater, one-fourth of the dollar limitation applicable to defined benefit plans) or 25 percent of compensation, and limits benefits for defined benefit plans to the lesser of $120,000 (indexed for cost-of-living increases) or 100 percent of a participant's average compensation for her highest three consecutive years.

A nonqualified deferred compensation plan may also be designed to benefit employees who do not satisfy the requirements for participating in a qualified plan or to award employees for their services; however, the use of a nonqualified deferred compensation plan for a broad cross-section of employees could cause the plan to come under the requirements of ERISA.

Q 9:14   Are there different types of nonqualified deferred compensation plans?

Yes, there are several types of nonqualified deferred compensation plans. These include:

1. A "top-hat" plan (sometimes referred to as a supplemental executive retirement plan or SERP), which is generally an unfunded plan maintained by an employer primarily to provide deferred compensation for a select group of management or highly compensated employees.

Example. Company A needs to attract a number of new executives who will typically give up retirement benefits from their current employers in order to join Company A. Therefore, Company A offers a "top-hat" plan that provides these executives with a minimum benefit from a combination of the company's defined pension benefit plan and the nonqualified deferred compensation plan of 30 percent of final average pay (as defined in the plan), if the executive stays employed with the company until age 62 or after.

2. An excess benefit plan, which is a plan maintained by an employer solely for the purpose of providing benefits for select employees in excess of the limitations on contributions and benefits imposed by Code Section 415 on plans to which that section applies, without regard to whether the plan is funded.

Example. Company B has a number of executives that can only contribute 3 percent of compensation to a 401(k) plan if the plan is to meet the Code discrimination requirements and avoid disqualification of the company's tax deduction on company contributions. Other non-executives can contribute up to 7 percent of compensation. Therefore, the company offers executives the opportunity to contribute an additional 4 percent of compensation (after-tax compensation) to a nonqualified excess benefit plan that is administered separately from the qualified 401(k) plan.

3. A plan for governmental or tax-exempt employers under Code Section 457, which is an unfunded plan that provides for annual deferrals of the lesser of $7,500 or one-third of includable compensation (unless a $15,000 catch-up provision applies).

Example. A YMCA wishes to allow its executive director to contribute 10 percent of compensation to its qualified pension plan. The executive director has compensation of $90,000, and therefore wants to contribute $9,000 ($90,000 × 10% = 9,000). Section 457 allows for a maximum contribution of $7,500. The YMCA decides to establish a Section 457 plan that will allow the executive director to contribute an additional (after tax) $1,500 ($9,000 − $7,500 = $1,500) each year. The YMCA could also decide to match this contribution, annually, based on specific performance measures established annually.

Q 9:15   How are nonqualified and qualified plans treated for tax purposes?

A nonqualified deferred compensation plan does not satisfy the requirements contained in Code Section 401(a) and, as a result, does not receive the favorable tax treatment afforded plans that do satisfy those requirements. An employer contributing to a nonqualified plan will be entitled to a deduction in the year in which the amount attributable to the contribution is includable in the gross income of the participating employees, which may not be until some future date.

When a plan does satisfy the requirements under Code Section 401(a) and qualifies for the favorable tax treatment, the employer will receive an immediate tax deduction for the amount it contributes to the plan for that particular year. An employee participating in a qualified plan is not required to pay income tax on amounts contributed by the employer on her behalf to the plan until she receives these amounts at some later date. Also, the tax on the earnings on the contributions made to a qualified plan is deferred until the earnings are distributed.

Distributions. Plans that satisfy the requirements under Code Section 401(a) and qualify for favorable tax treatment with respect to contributions also qualify for favorable tax treatment at the time these amounts are distributed. When distributions are made from a qualified plan to a participating employee, the amounts distributed may be rolled over to another qualified plan or to an individual retirement account. These distributions may also be eligible for special tax treatment under the income averaging rules.

Q 9:16   What is an example of the tax treatment on company contributions to a nonqualified plan?

Say, for example, that Company A implements a nonqualified supplemental retirement plan for its senior executives. The plan is intended to make up for Code regulations that limit the executive and the company contributions (match) to a 401(k) plan. Any amount that the company matches or contributes to the SERP, in any given year, will be a charge or deduction to the income statement for purposes of financial reporting; however, in calculating earnings for purposes of determining the company's tax obligation that same year, the company contribution to the SERP cannot be taken as a deduction or charge to the income statement. This is shown in Chart 9-1:

Chart 9-1

Assumptions: Company *A* contributes $10,000 to an executive's SERP account in 1995 and in three additional years (1996 through 1998). The executive retires in 1999.

Accounting Income Statement

	1995–98	1999
Company income	$100,000	$100,000
SERP contribution	$ 10,000	-0-
Company taxable income	$ 90,000	$100,000

Tax Income Statement

	1995–98	1999
Company income	$100,000	$100,000
SERP contributions	-0-	$ 40,000
Company taxable income	$100,000	$ 60,000

Q 9:17 What is an example of the tax treatment on company contributions to a qualified plan?

Company B implements a qualified 401(k) retirement plan for its senior executives and other employees. The plan is intended to provide all employees with an opportunity to establish retirement income from both their own contributions and from company contributions. Any amount that the company matches/contributes to the plan, in any given year, will be a charge or deduction to the income statement for purposes of financial reporting, and for purposes of determining the company's tax obligation that same year, the company contribution to the plan can also be taken as a deduction or charge to the income statement. This is shown in Chart 9-2:

Chart 9-2

Assumptions: Company *B* contributes $10,000 to an executive's 401(k) account in 1995 and in three additional years (1996 through 1998). The executive retires in 1999.

Accounting Income Statement

	1995–98	1999
Company income	$100,000	$100,000
401(k) contribution	$ 10,000	–0–
Company taxable income	$ 90,000	$100,000

Tax Income Statement

	1995–98	1999
Company income	$100,000	$100,000
401(k) contributions	$ 10,000	–0–
Company taxable income	$ 90,000	$100,000

Q 9:18   Are contributions to a funded plan treated differently than contributions to an unfunded plan?

Yes. Generally, contributions to an unfunded plan are not deductible by an employer and are not includable in an employee's income until some future date when the benefits are distributed or made available to the employee. A contribution to a funded plan is generally deductible by the employer and is included in an employee's income not in the year the contribution is made, but in the year it is not subject to substantial risk of forfeiture.

Q 9:19   What questions need to be answered by a company in determining the appropriateness of a deferred compensation plan?

Deferred compensation is not always the appropriate ingredient in an executive compensation program because deferred compensation is not suited for every executive. In determining whether a deferred compensation plan is appropriate for a given situation, the following questions need to be answered:

1. Is it possible that a qualified plan is more valuable to the company as a tool for retaining middle level employees?

2. Do the requirements of the Employee Retirement Income Security Act burden the plan with so many details that a nonqualified plan is more suitable?

3. Does the executive for whose benefit the plan is being considered have a competitive current level of compensation?

4. Do the requirements of the Code lessen the tax benefits of a qualified plan or burden the plan with so many restrictions that a nonqualified plan is more beneficial?

5. Will the anticipated tax benefit be offset by loss of social security income?

6. What is the level of executive confidence regarding the company's ability or future willingness to pay?

7. Does the company have a need to provide a better retirement plan or a "golden handcuff"?

8. Is the executive in question a major stockholder?

Q 9:20 When are deferred compensation arrangements subject to FICA and FUTA taxes?

Amounts deferred under a nonqualified deferred compensation plan are subject to Federal Insurance Contributions Act (FICA) tax when the services are completely performed or when the executive's right to such amounts is no longer subject to substantial risk of forfeiture. Most executives would prefer to have amounts that are deferred to be taxed immediately under FICA. At that time their salaries are probably already over the social security taxable wage base and the amounts deferred would escape FICA taxes.

If the amounts deferred are subject to a substantial risk of forfeiture, then the executive will be taxed when the risk lapses. If the deferred compensation payments vest upon retirement, then the present value of the payments expected under the deferred compensation plan will be taxable under FICA in the year of retirement, assuming the social security wage base has not been exceeded.

The rules concerning withholding under the Federal Unemployment Tax Act (FUTA) are similar to those under FICA.

Q 9:21 What are the general ERISA requirements for a nonqualified deferred compensation plan?

Title 1 of ERISA contains most of the nontax requirements for nonqualified deferred compensation plans as well as employee retirement plans. Title 1 defines an employee pension plan as any plan, fund, or program established by a company that provides retirement income for employees, or results in a deferral of income by employees for periods extending to termination of employment or beyond. Because deferred compensation agreements delay payment of some of an executive's compensation until a later time (usually retirement), deferred compensation plans (unless specifically exempted) must comply with the government requirements. Fully exempted plans are governmental plans, church plans, and unfunded excess benefit plans.

Unfunded deferred compensation plans maintained by a company primarily to provide deferred compensation for a select group of management or highly compensated employees must only comply with the reporting and disclosure provisions of Title 1. Note, however, that funded deferred compensation plans must meet all the requirements of Title 1.

ERISA requires each deferred compensation plan to provide for a claim procedure for participants and beneficiaries. There is no requirement to provide the plan document or a summary plan description (SPD) to the Department of Labor (DOL) or IRS for an unfunded nonqualified deferred compensation plan.

Q 9:22 What are the general reporting and disclosure requirements for a nonqualified deferred compensation plan?

Almost all deferred compensation plans must comply with the reporting and disclosure provisions of Title 1 of ERISA. A nonexempt deferred compensation plan must file a plan description with the DOL every five years and furnish a summary plan description to each covered executive or beneficiary. The SPD must be updated every five years if there have been plan changes or every ten years if there have been no plan changes. For unfunded or insured deferred compensation plans maintained by a company primarily to provide deferred compensation for a select group of management or highly compensated employees, the administrator can satisfy the reporting and disclosure provisions by filing, within 120 days, a general statement about the plan with the DOL.

Q 9:23 What are the general participation, vesting, and funding requirements for a nonqualified deferred compensation plan?

Unfunded deferred compensation plans maintained by a company for the purpose of providing deferred compensation for a select group of management or highly compensated employees are excluded from the participation, vesting, and funding requirements of ERISA.

Q 9:24 What are the general fiduciary issues for a nonqualified deferred compensation plan?

Unfunded deferred compensation plans maintained by the company primarily for the purpose of providing deferred compensation for a select group of management or highly compensated employees are excluded from the fiduciary responsibilities provisions of ERISA.

Q 9:25 Is plan termination insurance needed for a nonqualified plan?

Unfunded deferred compensation plans maintained by the company primarily for the purpose of providing deferred compensation for a select group of management or highly compensated employees are excluded from ERISA provisions covering plan termination insurance.

Q 9:26 Is a nonqualified deferred compensation plan a security subject to SEC registration?

Prior to 1995 the SEC was granting no-action letters permitting nonqualified deferred compensation plans to be implemented without registration under the 1933 Securities Act. The staff never gave out the supporting rationale, but it was generally understood that either these plans were not securities or there was no offer of sale involved in their establishment.

The Securities Act of 1933 prohibits the offer or sale of securities unless the registration has been filed or an exemption is available. The SEC recently announced at a meeting of the American Benefit Association's Employee Benefits Committee that it considered all nonqualified deferred compensation plans as potentially registrable, subject to certain exemptions and it would be issuing a formal statement to that effect sometime in the near future.

The current registration exemptions are as follows:

1. Section 3(a)(2), for qualified plans

2. Section 3(a)(11), for securities offered and sold only to persons resident within a single state (the so-called intra-state exemption).

3. Section 3(b), for certain small offerings

4. Section 4(2), for transactions not involving a public offer

Section 3(b) would appear to provide a safe harbor for most nonqualified deferred compensation plans, because their aggregate offering price would most likely be $5 million or less or there would generally be 35 or fewer participants.

Most small nonqualified deferred compensation plans will satisfy the statutory and regulatory exemptions and will not therefore be subject to registration; however, it remains to be seen whether the plans provided in larger organizations would be subject to registration and therefore would have to be analyzed carefully to determine if statutory exemption would be available.

If a plan should have registered but did not do so, and there was no fraud involved, the penalty would be slight, if anything; the main penalty would be to trigger a one-year recision right in the hands of participants. This would largely be an academic exercise: Participants in the nonqualified deferred compensation plans are voluntary participants, and it would not serve for them to cancel their participation in the plan. There is one problem with this: The IRS may construe that the right of recision may trigger a constructive receipt problem for income tax purposes for the plan participants. The other area of concern would be that regardless of how slight the penalties may be, if any, for the failure to register a plan that the SEC finds should have been registered, the corporation would have to report that there has been a securities violation. This may negatively influence investors, since they would not understand the real details of what was involved. This situation appears to be reaching a critical stage; therefore, employers should be cautious in implementing these plans and should review plans that are currently in place to determine the consequences of non-registration versus registration.

Funding Arrangements

Q 9:27   What is a rabbi escrow agreement?

A rabbi escrow agreement or an escrow account is another informal way of funding unfunded deferred compensation plans. Under this approach, a company guarantees deferred compensation amounts by creating an escrow fund with a financial institution as escrow agent. The company makes contributions to the account in an amount determined to be adequate to fund the benefits provided in the deferred compensation plan. As long as the assets in the account remain subject to the claims of the company's general creditors, the contributions to the account will not be includable in the executives income. Income earned from the investment of the escrow fund can either be paid to the company or be applied toward the company's obligation. The income is taxable to the company. In all other respects, this arrangement has the same general provisions and tax consequences as the "rabbi trust" (see Q 9:28).

Q 9:28   What is a rabbi trust?

A rabbi trust is an irrevocable trust into which assets earmarked for benefit liabilities are contributed. Trust assets typically are protected for use in meeting the benefit liabilities, but they must remain accessible to the company's general creditors in the event of bankruptcy or insolvency. The contributions and earnings are not taxable to the executives, and the company does not get a deduction for its contributions. The earnings from the trusts' investments are taxable to the company.

The general creditors' access to the trust assets in the event of bankruptcy or insolvency creates an element of risk for the executives. This uncertainty is the biggest drawback of rabbi trusts; however, companies that have installed rabbi trusts tend to view the bankruptcy and insolvency risk as minimal and to consider the rabbi trust as a safety net for benefits in the case of a takeover.

The primary use of rabbi trusts continues to be to fund nonqualified retirement programs, although they can be used for voluntary deferred arrangements. The appeal of the rabbi trust as a funding vehicle is that when properly structured, it will successfully defer income for the executive while protecting the benefit from all but general creditors. If the trust is not, however, designed in accordance with provisions accepted by the IRS, it runs the risk that the executives may be deemed in constructive receipt of trust assets at the time the trust is funded.

The IRS has issued only general principles relating to these arrangements, although the concept was initially approved by the IRS in a 1980 private letter ruling. Under this ruling, a congregation contributed amounts into an irrevocable trust it established for the benefit of its rabbi (hence the term rabbi trust). The IRS ruled that because the assets were subject to the general creditors of the congregation, the rabbi was not in constructive receipt of the contributions to the trust. Additional private letter rulings reinforced this concept. Because private letter rulings are meant to apply to specific situations, it is prudent, however, for a company to request a private letter ruling that will ensure the validity of the arrangement.

In summary, the advantage of a rabbi trust is that it secures the promise to pay deferred compensation and therefore insures that a new company owner and/or new company management cannot change the company's obligation to pay the vested deferred amounts. If the company goes into bankruptcy, the company creditors can use deferred funds in a rabbi trust to pay company debts. The disadvantage of the rabbi trust is that it does not guarantee the payment of deferred funds, but it does postpone the executives payment of income tax on the deferred funds. Companies that use rabbi trusts do so to protect deferred compensation during a merger, restructuring, or acquisition when there can be changes in company ownership and company management.

Q 9:29   What is a secular trust?

Secular trusts or Code Section 402(b) trusts fund benefit obligations on a current basis; assets are secured until the time of distribution to the beneficiary. Because the assets are not available to general creditors, the funds in the secular trust are taxable income to the beneficiaries. When properly structured, the secular trust can provide the same after-tax benefit as a rabbi trust while costing the company less. This is due to the generally lower tax rates to which individuals are subject and the fact that the company can gross-up an executive's income to pay the tax liability attributable to the annual funding requirement. (The gross-up process is described in Q 10:31 for excise taxes.)

In summary, the advantage of a secular trust is that it secures the payment of deferred compensation, as well as the promise to pay deferred compensation; however, this benefit carries a significant disadvantage in that the secular trust is taxable income to the executive. The amount of taxable income to the executive each year is determined by the extent to which the executive is vested in any amounts in the trust each year. For example, if the executive is vested in 10 percent of the deferred compensation of $100,000 in a secular trust in the first year of deferral, then that executive has taxable income of $10,000 that year.

Q 9:30   What are the major distinctions between a secular trust and a rabbi trust?

The major differences between a secular and rabbi trust is that while creditors can claim assets held in a rabbi trust, money held in a secular trust cannot be reached by creditors; and assets in a rabbi trust are not taxable income to the participants while in the trust, whereas assets in a secular trust are taxed to the participant when contributed and as income is earned.

Q 9:31   Can life insurance also be used by an employer to fulfill its promise to an employee?

Yes, a company may purchase insurance policies to fund its promise. These policies are referred to as corporate-owned life insurance (COLI). A COLI contract generally covers the lives of several employees, and the financial interest that the employer seeks to "insure" generally is determined by the contracted benefits the corporation is obligated to pay on the death of the covered employee. A corporation can in many cases reduce the cost of the plan by using properly designed and priced life insurance contracts.

Insurance-Related Nonqualified Deferred Compensation Plans

Q 9:32   How is life insurance used by an employer to fulfill its promise to an employee?

A corporation will generally purchase specially designed cash value (universal or variable) life insurance policies on individual employees. The cash value in these life insurance policies generates an investment income that is generally exempt from current income tax (i.e., the inside buildup). The ability of a corporation to borrow against the cash value to pay future premiums and deduct the interest has been eliminated for all future contracts and is being phased out for all policies in force as of the end of 1996.

The employer is the owner and beneficiary of the policies and pays the premiums. The employer may pay benefits to the employee with funds obtained from withdrawing up to their basis in the policies and then if necessary borrowing against the cash value of the policies. Note interest on loans from an insurance policy will not be deductible on loans over $50,000 after 1996.

The employer must accrue for the future liabilities of plan, but can offset these liabilities with the increases in the cash value and the accruals for the future tax deductions. The employer does not get to take a current tax deduction for the contributions made to the plan but can accrue for the projected tax deductions that will be available when the benefits are paid.

If the policies are structured correctly and the performance of the policies' investment accounts meets or exceeds the plan assumptions, the policies will have sufficient cash value to fund the benefit payments and the interest on the loans, and maintain the policies for the life of the insured.

The policies must be kept in force for the life of the insured to prevent a taxable event to the company. If the policy is surrendered before the death of the insured, all cash value in excess of the basis in the policy, including loans, will be taxable income to the owner of the policy. If the policy is held until the death of the insured, all proceeds of the policy will be received income tax free, including the cancellation of the loans, by the owner of the policy.

Q 9:33   Can life insurance other than COLI be utilized to fund nonqualified deferred compensation programs?

Yes, it is possible to use the same concept without the company owning the insurance contract. The executive can own an insurance contract such that the benefit at retirement will be equal to a targeted amount of supplemental retirement income. Under this concept, there are two ways to provide these benefits. One, the executive would reach an agreement with the company to have the company pay the premium by providing the executive with taxable income (grossed-up for taxes if desirable; see Q 10:31) in an amount equal to the required premium on the insurance contract. Two, the executive would enter into a slightly different agreement. The executive and the company would "split" the life insurance policy. This is called a "split-dollar" plan. The company would agree to pay the premium in return for a collateral assignment of a portion of the cash value equal to the companys premium payments. The employee would pay the term cost of the life insurance (PS-58 costs) annually. Upon retirement or death of the insured the company could bonus out the portion of the cash value it owns if it so chooses.

In either case contributions would continue during the executive's career. If the executive terminates or is terminated, the company no longer has any obligation to pay the premium; the executive can, however, continue premium payments on his own or can structure arrangements with a later employer to cover the premium cost. Therefore, these methods have portability for the executive.

Q 9:34 What is the difference between COLI and "retail" life insurance contracts?

COLI is a specially designed life insurance contract designed for use in funding unfunded nonqualified deferred compensation plans and keyman insurance coverage. COLI will generally have more liberal underwriting requirements and may even have guaranteed issue provisions if the group is large enough. Unlike "retail" cash value life insurance policies, COLI will generally have significant amounts of cash value in the first year and will always have more cash value than a retail policy with the same investment provisions.

Q 9:35 What are the advantages of using employee-owned life insurance to fund nonqualified deferred compensation benefits?

From the company's perspective, the advantages are as follows:

1. The company incurs no annual accrual on its balance sheet. Therefore, the deferred compensation obligation is neither an asset nor a liability to the company.

2. The company either receives a tax deduction for the amount of the premium since this amount is accounted for as taxable income to the executive, or, if a split dollar plan is used, the company will get a refund of all of the premium payments it has made upon termination of employment or death of the employee.

3. If the executive terminates, the executive could continue any premium payments on her own. Thus the executive is motivated to remain with the company.

Advantages to the executive are as follows:

1. The deferred compensation plan is "secured" through the insurance contract without the complexity of a rabbi or secular trust.

2. The perquisite is "portable" to the executive: The executive can continue paying premiums on her own or make arrangements with a new employer to cover the premium cost.

3. Because an insurance contract is the funding mechanism, some of the deferred compensation payments to the executive from the insurance contract are received income tax free.

Split-Dollar Life Insurance

Q 9:36 What is split-dollar life insurance?

It is not a unique kind of life insurance policy, but an arrangement by two parties jointly to purchase a permanent, cash-value life insurance policy: someone who needs the permanent life insurance benefit and someone with the means of paying the premiums. Split dollar is utilized by most business entities today. This traditionally means an executive will enjoy the benefits and the employer will pay the premiums, although there are differing variations. For purposes of this chapter, we describe the arrangement most typically used.

Q 9:37 How is split dollar treated under ERISA?

Split dollar may be provided for any employee, shareholder, or director of the company. It is considered a welfare benefit plan under ERISA, but is not subject to participation, reporting, or funding requirements. The benefit may be fully discriminatory and confidential.

Q 9:38 How does the policy splitting occur?

The components of the policy are its premium, cash value, and death benefit. Premiums are split with the executive paying the "term insurance cost" of the insurance death benefit provided (as described by Revenue Ruling 64-328) and the employer paying the remainder. The death benefit and cash value are first allocated to the employer, up to the amount of its cumulative premium outlay, with the balance allocated to the executive or the executives designated beneficiary.

Q 9:39   Must the executive actually pay his part of the premium?

Either the executive directly pays the term cost of the coverage or this amount must be included on the executives W-2 as additional taxable income. Employers often "gross up" this added income so the executive has zero net "out of pocket" cost for the coverage.

Q 9:40   How is the policy split accomplished?

With "collateral assignment" split dollar, the policy is owned by the executive and an assignment is executed in favor of the employer, entitling it to a death benefit or cash value allocation equal to its cumulative premium outlay. All excess death benefits and cash values belong to the executive or his beneficiary by virtue of his ownership rights in the policy.

With "endorsement" split dollar, the policy is owned by the employer and the death benefit is allocated to the executive through an endorsement agreement. All cash values are owned by the employer. Tax authority for split dollar rests primarily in Revenue Rulings 64-328 and 66-110.

Q 9:41   What happens when the executive retires?

The policy is typically "rolled out" from the employer to the executive. The executive may receive a paid-up life insurance benefit, cash values, or retirement benefit. The amount of postretirement benefit depends on whether the employer elects to recover its premium outlay or to award its share of the policy to the executive, which would be taxable as bonus compensation and deductible to the company. Policy values are typically withdrawn to cover tax costs.

Q 9:42   What are common split-dollar applications?

Split-dollar plans are often used to replace or supplement group term life insurance plans on a more tax-efficient basis, to provide large amounts of coverage for estate tax protection and to reduce asset risk in nonqualified retirement plans.

Q 9:43   What problems do executives experience in group term life insurance plans?

Although the first $50,000 of noncontributory group term life insurance is not income taxable to the employee or estate taxable to his estate, many employers want to provide higher noncontributory coverage amounts to executives. However, the excess coverage over $50,000 is income taxed to the executive, regardless of the actual cost to the employer, at an inflated rate determined by IRS Group Term Table I. For example, the employer might pay $100 per month for $500,000 coverage for an executive. However, the executive is forced to pay income tax on $150 per month of additional income, resulting in $648 additional tax liability per year for this benefit (assuming an individual tax rate of 36%). Group term coverage also typically terminates at retirement, is not portable, and provides no cash values.

Q 9:44   Why is split dollar effective in replacing group term coverage?

Split-dollar coverage provides significant amounts of coverage to executives at a fraction of the income tax cost of group term. The coverage is portable if the executive decides to terminate prior to normal retirement age (split-dollar agreements typically provide for a buyout of the policy from the employer under such circumstances). At retirement, the executive typically has coverage paid up for life with cash values.

Q 9:45   Why is split dollar useful in estate planning?

When an executive forms an irrevocable life insurance trust to purchase an insurance policy on himself or jointly on himself and his spouse (second-to-die coverage), amounts must be gifted to the trust each year that may far exceed the executive's annual gift exclusion ($10,000 per beneficiary per spouse). Split dollar allows large amounts of coverage to be owned by the trust with the annual gifts valued at the "term costs" of the coverage instead of the entire policy premium. This greatly enhances the already considerable leverage afforded by life insurance trust.

Q 9:46   How can split dollar enhance a nonqualified retirement plan?

Under most circumstances, nonqualified plans are informally funded with an asset, perhaps corporate-owned life insurance, that may be held by a rabbi trust for enhanced security. The asset is still subject to confiscation by corporate creditors in the event of bankruptcy of the employer. Split dollar allows the executive to own the policy and the cash value exceeding the premiums paid by the employer so that the asset risk is more balanced. Only the premiums, that portion of cash value representing "principal" assigned to the employer, are subject to credit risk instead of the entire cash value.

Executive Disability Income Insurance

Q 9:47   How does an executive disability income insurance plan work?

Group long-term disability (LTD) plans typically cap benefits at a percentage of income, usually 50 to 60 percent, and a dollar limit, usually $5,000 per month. Many plans insure only salary and exclude bonuses. This causes highly compensated executives to be underinsured. Executive disability income plans consist of individual policies issued on the executives in addition to the LTD plan. This builds insurance to an appropriate percentage level, usually 80 percent of compensation.

Q 9:48   What legal framework should exist to minimize taxation of executive disability plans?

If the employer does not establish a "sick pay plan," the benefits paid to the executive could be considered "ad hoc" compensation to the executive and taxed as a dividend. This is easily avoidable by incorporating a written plan authorizing payments to disabled executives. Many experts consider the existence of an insurance policy sufficient precedent for a sick pay plan.

Q 9:49   How are benefits taxed to the executive?

Taxation of executive disability income benefits depend on whether premiums are paid by the employer or the executive. If the employer pays premiums, the benefits will be taxable as ordinary income to the executive when received. If the executive pays the premiums, the benefits will be income tax-free.

Q 9:50   How are premiums taxed to the executive and the employer?

If the employer pays disability insurance premiums, they may be tax-deducted by the employer as ordinary business expense but not taxed to the executive. This results in taxable income benefits. If the employer pays premiums and includes them in the executives taxable income, they are taxable to the executive but benefits are tax-free.

Q 9:51   Are executive disability premiums more expensive than LTD?

Individual executive disability insurance policies are typically noncancelable and guaranteed renewable to age 65. In other words, the premiums may not be increased and the policy has to be renewed as long as premiums are paid. Policies typically offer extra features not available in LTD plans and depending on the number of executives in a plan, may be eligible for significant discounts.

Q 9:52   Do executive disability income plan have to be funded by the employer?

Typically, senior management plans are funded by the employer. Many plans being installed today on second and third tier management groups are offered on a contributory basis through payroll deduction, sometimes with a partial employer contribution.

ERISA Considerations

Q 9:53   For purposes of ERISA Title I, is a nonqualified deferred compensation plan generally considered funded or unfunded?

Nonqualified deferred compensation plans generally are "unfunded" plans because they are merely promises by the employer to pay the employee compensation at some future date; however, a nonqualified deferred compensation plan may also be a "funded" plan. This occurs when a fund is created by an employer who irrevocably sets aside an amount with a third party for the benefit of an employee.

Q 9:54   What is the difference between a funded and an unfunded plan?

Whether or not a plan is "funded" or "unfunded" generally requires an examination of the surrounding facts and circumstances.

Funded Plans. A plan usually will be considered funded if an amount is irrevocably placed with a third party for the benefit of an employee and neither the employer nor its creditors has any interest in this amount.

Unfunded Plans. An unfunded plan is merely an unsecured promise by an employer to pay compensation to an employee at some future date. The employer may set aside assets in order to fulfill its promise to the employee, but the set-aside assets must remain part of the employer's general assets and subject to the claims of the employer's creditors. The employer's promise may not be secured in any way. The participant may rely only on the credit of the employer and generally has no rights to the assets other than as a general unsecured creditor.

Q 9:55   For purposes of ERISA Title I, are plans affected by whether or not they are considered funded or unfunded?

Yes. If a plan is funded, the plan will have to satisfy the requirements contained in Title I of ERISA, which pertains to participation and vesting, funding, and fiduciary requirements. If a plan is unfunded, the plan may be exempt from these requirements.

Top-Hat Plans or SERPs

Q 9:56   What is a top-hat plan?

A top-hat plan or SERP is a nonqualified retirement plan used to provide additional or supplemental benefits to an employer's key employees. Under ERISA, as amended, a top-hat plan is generally defined as an unfunded nonqualified deferred compensation plan maintained "primarily for the purpose of providing deferred compensation for a select group of management or highly compensated employees."

Q 9:57 Why would an employer establish a top-hat plan?

Employers establish top-hat plans to provide additional compensation to certain employees. Prior to TRA '86, employers established top-hat plans to allow key executives to defer compensation which could then compound income tax deferred until retirement when, presumably, their tax rates would be substantially lower. Under TRA '86, tax rates were reduced and the various tax brackets were essentially eliminated, which in turn eliminated a significant benefit to deferring an executive's compensation; however, since Congress has increased the current ordinary income tax rates, the benefits achieved by deferring compensation until the recipient is in a lower tax bracket will again be significant.

Other reasons still exist for employers to establish top-hat plans. One reason is that there are significant limitations on contributions that are allowed under a qualified plan. Top-hat plans can avoid the limitations on (1) annual contributions, (2) the amount of compensation benefits can be based upon, and (3) the amount that can be paid out per year without incurring additional taxes.

These plans are also exempt from ERISA rules on vesting, participation, eligibility, reporting and discrimination.

Top-hat plans may be established to provide the following:

1. A pension supplement to attract older executives where the years of service factor in a qualified retirement plan would limit such an employee's benefits;

2. Funds to allow an executive to retire early without losing benefits;

3. An inducement for an executive to remain with the employer;

4. A generous benefit package to attract desired executives; and

5. Avoidance of the 10-percent tax under Code Section 72(t) on distributions made from qualified plans to an executive who is not 59½ years old.

Q 9:58 Does an employer inadvertently create a top-hat plan that is subject to ERISA requirements when it provides benefits to one executive under an employment contract?

Generally no. Benefits provided to one executive under an individual employment contract will ordinarily not be considered a top-hat plan. In two DOL advisory opinions, the DOL ruled that contractual arrangements with individual executives were merely employment contracts and not "employee pension benefit plans" as defined by ERISA and, therefore, not subject to the requirements of ERISA.

Q 9:59 How does the employer pay the benefits provided by a top-hat plan?

An employer generally pays the benefits provided under a top-hat plan out of its general assets at the time the payments become due pursuant to the terms of the plan. The executive must rely solely on the employer's promise to pay these benefits and assumes the risk that these benefits may not be paid if there is an unfriendly change in the management of the employer or a change in the employer's financial situation. For example, if the employer becomes insolvent, the participating employees may not receive any benefits. In addition, if the employer is acquired in a hostile takeover, the new management team may terminate the plan and limit the benefits to be paid to the accrued or vested benefits.

Q 9:60 Can employer assurances be made that future benefits will be paid without subjecting employees to current taxation?

Yes. Top-hat plans have adopted a number of informal funding arrangements to address the issue of employer assurances. They include:

1. *Corporate-Owned Life Insurance.* A COLI policy on the life of a key executive is one method of funding the obligations provided by a top-hat plan that avoids current taxation if certain conditions are met. Under this arrangement, the tax-deferred cash value build-up and the tax-free receipt of death proceeds make the use of an insurance policy an attractive funding vehicle because the policy will provide death benefits in the event the executive dies, or a cash value that the plan can borrow against in order to provide benefits to an executive on retirement. The cash value of an insurance policy used by a top-hat plan, however, will still be subject to claims of the employer's creditors; and the existence of an insurance policy will not guarantee that the promised benefits will actually be paid.

2. *Rabbi Trust.* In general, the rabbi trust is an irrevocable trust that may be used to hold the assets of a top-hat plan (see Chapter 4). Typically, the rabbi trust protects an executive by providing a measure of security that the benefits promised under the top-hat plan will be paid because the assets held in the trust are not available to a corporate raider or subject to the discretion of management. In order to avoid current taxation, however, assets held in the rabbi trust remain subject to the claims of the employer's creditors in the event of the employer's insolvency or bankruptcy.

3. *Third-Party Guarantee.* In this arrangement, a third party guarantees payment of the benefits promised under the top-hat plan in the event the employer defaults. The IRS has ruled that there are no current tax consequences to the employee if the guarantor's promise to pay is unsecured and unfunded. This arrangement will provide adequate assurances to the employee that the benefits will be paid only if the guarantor is financially sound.

4. *Surety Bonds.* Executives can purchase a surety bond to ensure that the benefits provided by a top-hat plan will be paid. The IRS has ruled that the purchase of a financial surety bond by the executive to protect the executive's future deferred compensation payments may not, by itself, cause the deferred amounts to be included in the executive's income either at the time the executive purchased the bond or at the time the executive paid the premiums thereon. The IRS informally

indicated, however, that when surety bonds are used to protect an unfunded, unsecured promise to pay, the surety bonds may be treated as taxable property under the economic benefit doctrine.

Q 9:61   Are top-hat plans subject to the requirements under Title I of ERISA?

Yes, if funded; however, if a plan maintained by an employer primarily for the purpose of providing deferred compensation for a select group of management or highly compensated employees is unfunded, the plan is exempt from certain requirements of ERISA Title I.

Q 9:62   Is a top-hat plan a funded or unfunded plan for purposes of Title I of ERISA?

A top-hat plan is generally defined as an unfunded plan under ERISA Sections 201(2), 301(a)(3), and 401(a)(1), and generally will be unfunded if plan benefits are payable out of the employer's general assets and any participant in the plan has no greater rights in these assets than a general unsecured creditor.

Conversely, a plan will generally be considered funded if the assets are segregated or otherwise set aside and are identified as a source to which participants may look for the payment of their benefits.

Q 9:63   Are contributions to an unfunded top-hat plan treated differently than contributions to a funded top-hat plan?

Yes. Contributions to an unfunded top-hat plan are generally not deductible by an employer and are not includable in an employee's income until the benefits are actually distributed or made available to the employee. Employer contributions to a funded top-hat plan are, however, generally deductible by the employer and includable in the employee's income in the year the contribution is made. Note that contributions made to a funded top-hat plan that are subject to a substantial risk of forfeiture will generally not be deductible to an employer or includable in the employee's income until the benefits vest and are not subject to a substantial risk of forfeiture.

Q 9:64 What is an example of a supplemental executive retirement plan?

A company wants to hire Executive A; however, the executive will be losing retirement benefits upon leaving the former employer. In order to attract the executive to the company, a SERP is provided such that the minimum benefit to the executive will be 30 percent of final average pay provided that the executive is employed for ten years until age 65 (current age 55). The company's qualified retirement plan would provide the executive with a benefit of 15 percent of final average pay.

Assuming that Executive A has a final average pay of $300,000, the qualified plan will produce a benefit of $24,000 ($160,000 × 15%). The SERP has guaranteed a benefit of $90,000 (30% × $300,000). The qualified benefits would be paid to the executive at age 65, and the additional $66,000 of retirement benefit ($90,000 – $24,000 = $66,000) would be provided by the company to the executive in the form of a SERP payment.

Executive B is a long-term executive with the same company and is eligible for a 60 percent retirement benefit (2% of final average pay × 30 years of service). Assume that Executive B also has final average pay of $300,000. Executive B is therefore eligible for a pension of $180,000 (60% × $300,000). The maximum benefit allowed under ERISA from a qualified plan that year is $125,000. If the company had provided this executive with a SERP that insured that the normal plan benefit would have been paid, upon retirement Executive B would have received $125,000 from the qualified retirement plan and $55,000 from the SERP.

Excess Benefit Plans

Q 9:65 What is an excess benefit plan?

An excess benefit plan is a nonqualified deferred compensation plan "maintained by an employer solely for the purpose of providing benefits for certain employees in excess of the limitations on contributions and benefits imposed by Code Section 415." In simplified terms, an excess benefit plan either takes the place of a more rigid qualified plan governed by ERISA or supplements the qualified plan to provide more benefits to the participants. In addition, not only may an excess benefit plan be a separate and distinct plan itself, it may also be a separable part of a tax-qualified plan.

Q 9:66   What is the main difference between a SERP and an excess benefit plan?

A SERP is limited in the number of employees that may be participants without subjecting the plan to ERISA coverage. An excess benefit plan can cover a greater number of employees without incurring ERISA coverage providing the excess benefits are limited to benefits covered by Code Section 415 limits.

Q 9:67   How does a plan qualify as an excess benefit plan?

In order to qualify as an excess benefit plan, the sole purpose of the nonqualified plan must be limited to providing benefits to participants in excess of the limitations imposed by Code Section 415.

Q 9:68   Why would an employer establish an excess benefit plan?

An employer may be interested in establishing an excess benefit plan for several reasons, including:

1. Attracting certain personnel through the additional benefits provided by such plans;
2. Retaining certain employees by making the excess benefit plan a disincentive for any employee contemplating resignation;
3. Providing employees with an excess benefit plan as an incentive for better service and increased productivity;
4. Creating goodwill between the employer and the participants in the excess benefit plan;
5. Encouraging early retirement for some highly paid employees by providing them with increased benefits; and

6. Making up for the limitations in qualified plans that discriminate against higher paid employees.

Q 9:69 Are there benefits to establishing an excess benefit plan?

Yes. Because an excess benefit plan is not generally governed by a strict statutory or regulatory framework (although funded excess benefit plans must meet certain ERISA requirements), an excess benefit plan offers greater flexibility because it can be drafted to meet the specific needs of the employer. An excess benefit plan is ordinarily established in concert with a qualified deferred compensation plan with the excess benefit plan providing supplemental benefits to certain employees in addition to the benefits provided under the qualified plan.

Finally, another example of the flexibility of an excess benefits plan is that it need not be based upon the number of years of service of the participant. Employees often need to be assured of receiving compensation in future years, and an excess benefit plan allows employers to provide their employees with such compensation.

Q 9:70 Are there limitations in establishing an excess benefit plan?

Yes. The major limitations in establishing an unfunded excess benefit plan relate to the tenuous position of the participant. The participant holds the status of a general, unsecured creditor with regard to the excess benefit plan benefits; as a result, the participant may not have any comfort that she will ever receive any benefits under the plan, especially if the employer is not well-capitalized.

A second limitation relating to an unfunded excess benefit plan is that, unlike a qualified deferred compensation plan, the employer who establishes such an excess benefit plan generally does not receive an income tax deduction for its contributions until the contributions are actually distributed or made available to the participants, which can often be years in the future.

A third major limitation on the use of an excess benefit plan is that an excess benefit plan is expressly limited to a plan maintained solely for providing benefits to the plan participants in excess of the limitations imposed by Code Section 415. The term "solely" has not been clearly defined. As a result, the employer must make certain that the sole purpose for establishing the excess benefit plan is to provide benefits in excess of the limitations contained in Code Section 415 to protect the status of the plan as an excess benefit plan. (If the plan ceases to be considered an excess benefit plan, it may be considered a top-hat plan but it must satisfy the requirements applicable to top-hat plans.)

Q 9:71   Is an excess benefit plan subject to the ERISA Title I requirements?

An excess benefit plan may be subject to certain requirements under Title I of ERISA depending upon whether the plan is funded or unfunded. An excess benefit plan is defined in ERISA Section 3(36) as a plan maintained by an employer solely for the purpose of providing benefits for certain employees in excess of the limitations on contributions and benefits imposed by Code Section 415, without regard to whether the plan is funded. If the plan is unfunded, the plan is exempt from the requirements under Title I of ERISA. If the plan is funded, the plan is subject to certain requirements under ERISA.

Q 9:72   Is an excess benefit plan subject to the participation, vesting, and funding requirements imposed by Title I of ERISA?

No. An excess benefit plan, whether funded or unfunded, is not subject to the participation and vesting rules of Part 2 of Title I of ERISA and the funding rules of Part 3 of Title I.

Q 9:73   Is an excess benefit plan subject to the reporting and disclosure requirements imposed by Title I of ERISA?

It depends on whether the plan is funded or unfunded. A funded excess benefit plan will be subject to the reporting and disclosure requirements under Part 1 of Title I of ERISA; an unfunded excess benefit plan will not.

Q 9:74   What is an example of an excess benefit plan?

Assume that a company has a 401(k) plan in effect that allows employees to contribute up to 10 percent of their compensation up to the 415 limits (pre-tax under the terms of the 401(k)), with an employer match of employees contributions up to 6 percent of covered compensation dollar-for-dollar by the employer. An executive with a salary of $200,000 wishes to contribute 10 percent of her base salary ($20,000) into the 401(k); however, due to the 415 limits she can only contribute the lesser of (1) $9,500, (2) 10 percent of $160,000 covered compensation, or (3) the percentage of compensation allowed by the discrimination test. The company will match her allowed contribution up to 6 percent of her covered compensation ($9,500), but not the remaining $10,600. Assume that during the given year the maximum amount that any employee can contribute to the 401(k), per qualified plan regulations, is $9,500. Therefore, the qualified 401(k) plan would have (during the given year) $9,500 of the executive's own contribution, matched by $9,500 from the employer.

A Section 415 excess plan could be developed such that it included the remaining executive contribution, in this example $10,600 ($20,000 minus the $9,500 in the 401(k) plan) plus the remaining employer contribution, which is $2,500 (6% of $200,000 = $12,000 minus $9,500 already contributed to the 401(k)). The total amount contributed for the executive in this year to the 401(k) plan and the excess benefit plan would thus be $32,000, $20,000 of which was contributed by the executive ($200,000 × 10%) and $12,000 contributed by the employer ($20,000 × 6%).

	401(k)	*415 Excess*	*Plan Total*
Employee	$ 9,500	$10,500	$20,000
Employer	$ 9,500	$ 2,500	$12,000
TOTAL	$19,000	$13,000	$32,000

Nonqualified Plans in Nonprofit Organizations

Q 9:75   What is a Code Section 457 deferred plan?

Code Section 457 covers nonqualified deferral plans for not-for-profit organizations. This section describes the requirements that must be met in order to avoid immediate taxation to the executive for the deferred monies. These specific regulations for a nonqualified plan are often overlooked because in the profit sector, nonqualified plan implies no guidelines on permissible amounts of deferral.

The maximum amount that can be deferred under this provision for any taxable year cannot exceed $7,500 or 33 percent of the executive's compensation. (This number is occasionally updated by the IRS). During the last three years prior to normal retirement age, the maximum amount is the lesser of $15,000 or the sum of the maximum amounts that could have been deferred but were not. The Code Section 457 maximums are reduced by any amounts deferred under qualified plans.

Compensation can be deferred for any calendar month as long as the decision is made prior to that month. All amounts of compensation deferred under this type of plan and all income from those amounts have to remain solely the property of the company and subject to the claims of creditors.

Q 9:76 What is an example of a Code Section 457 plan?

A tax-exempt organization wishes to provide its top three executives with a supplemental retirement benefit in addition to the company's 401(k) plan. The supplement is to be funded by both employee and employer. The organization creates an executive benefit that is technically a welfare benefit plan subject to ERISA, and structures the benefit as a "bona fide" severance program, with benefits payable at termination or retirement. This structure avoids application of Section 457 provisions.

The plan is funded by the executive and employer, each contributing 10 percent of total cash compensation each year. All contributions are secured by a rabbi trust. The targeted benefit is to double total cash compensation at termination. Once the maximum benefit is achieved, these funds can be invested until the executive's termination or retirement. Should severance occur, any accrued benefits would be paid to the executive; otherwise, the welfare/severance benefit accrues and serves as a supplemental retirement if the executive remains in employment until the normal retirement date.

Tax Considerations

Q 9:77 How are employers who establish funded excess benefit plans treated for tax purposes?

The employer generally is entitled to deduct contributions made pursuant to the provisions of a funded plan in the year in which the contributions are made. In an unfunded plan, the employer cannot deduct contributions until they are included in the participating employee's income (i.e., when paid).

In addition, the employer must maintain separate accounts for funded plans covering more than one participant in order to be entitled to a deduction.

Q 9:78 How are employees who benefit from excess benefit plans treated for tax purposes?

The tax treatment to the employee depends upon whether the excess benefit plan is unfunded or funded. If unfunded, no tax liability occurs to the employee until payments are received. If funded, there is tax liability to the employee to the extent vesting in future benefits occurs each taxable year.

Q 9:79 Are contributions made pursuant to a nonqualified deferred compensation plan includable in an employee's income under the constructive receipt doctrine?

Generally no. If the employee's control over the contributions is subject to substantial limitations, then contributions to a nonqualified deferred compensation plan should not be subject to the constructive receipt doctrine. Generally, a taxpayer includes the amount of any item of gross income in his gross income for the taxable year in which he receives it, unless, under the taxpayer's method of accounting, it is properly included in a different period. Generally, the employee, as a cash method taxpayer, includes amounts in gross income when they are actually or constructively received.

Q 9:80 Are contributions made pursuant to a nonqualified deferred compensation plan includable in the employee's income under the economic benefit doctrine?

Generally no. If contributions are made, or amounts set aside in accordance with a nonqualified deferred compensation plan are subject to the claims of the employer's general creditors, then such contributions or amounts should not be subject to the economic benefit doctrine. If, on the other hand, contributions to the plan are protected from the employer's creditors and the rights of the participating employees to the benefits provided under the plan are nonforfeitable, the economic benefit doctrine should apply and the contributions should be includable in the participating employee's income.

Q 9:81 How does Code Section 83 tax property transfers to an employee in exchange for the performance of services?

In general, Code Section 83 provides rules for the taxation of property transferred to an employee in connection with the performance of services. This property is generally not taxable to an employee until it has been transferred to, or becomes substantially vested in, the employee. The application of Code Section 83 can be broken down as follows:

1. *What is a transfer of property?* A transfer of property occurs when a person acquires a beneficial ownership interest in the property.

2. *When is property substantially vested?* Property is substantially vested for purposes of Code Section 83 when it is either transferable or not subject to a substantial risk of forfeiture. A substantial risk of forfeiture exists when rights in property that are transferred are conditioned either upon the future performance, or nonperformance, of substantial services by any person, or the occurrence of a condition related to a purpose of the transfer.

3. *When are property rights transferable?* The rights of an employee in property are transferable if the employee can transfer any interest in the property to any person other than the

transferor of the property, but only if the transferee's rights in the property are not subject to a substantial risk of forfeiture.

4. *What is property?* The term "property" includes real and personal property other than money or an unfunded and unsecured promise to pay money in the future. The term also includes a beneficial interest in assets, including money, that are transferred or set aside from the claims of creditors of the transferor.

If the contributions under a nonqualified deferred compensation plan are subject to the claims of the employer's general creditors, then such contributions do not meet the definition of property. Therefore, there can be no transfer of property within the meaning of Code Section 83. If, on the other hand, contributions under a nonqualified deferred compensation plan are not available either to the employer or the employer's general creditors, and the participating employees are fully vested in the contributions, then there is a transfer of property within the meaning of Code Section 83, and the employee is subject to tax on the transferred amount.

Chapter 10

Perquisites and Other Benefits

Executive perquisites are those benefits that are above and beyond what is available to all employees. Although executive perquisites and other benefits have lost most of their tax advantages, companies continue to use them primarily as a status symbol. Perquisites include such benefits as first-class air travel, a company-provided automobile, a luncheon or dining club membership, a country club membership, and tax and financial counseling. Non-traditional benefits such as employment contracts and golden parachute agreements are considered executive perquisites as well. This chapter covers the common perquisites that are offered to executives, highlighting important tax and accounting considerations.

General Considerations 10-2
Reimbursement 10-3
Memberships and Other Common Perquisites 10-5
Employment Agreements 10-9
Severance Agreements 10-12

General Considerations

Q 10:1   What is an executive perquisite?

An executive perquisite, or fringe benefit, is any enhancement of employment beyond basic salary and benefits. Perquisites take up where benefits leave off. An executive usually considers perquisites to include such things as expense accounts or reimbursement for travel and entertainment costs; however, to the extent that these expenses are reasonable and related to a necessary business purpose, they are technically not fringe benefits. These are expenses that may be deductible by the corporation as legitimate business expenses and that may be reimbursed to the executive without being considered income. Perquisites are special benefits that give the executive status, while assisting the executive in conducting job responsibilities. Examples are company cars, financial planning, supplemental retirement and/or life insurance, first-class travel, company planes, expense accounts for customer entertainment, laptop computers, cellular phones, and country and/or luncheon club memberships.

Q 10:2   What is the tax treatment of executive perquisites?

Reasonable expenses incurred by an executive that are related to a recurring business purpose may be reimbursed without creating compensation income to the executive. (See Qs 10:5 and 10:6 for special rules relating to travel and entertainment expenses.) Perquisites are generally deemed to be compensation, with their value therefore taxable as compensation to the executive, unless they meet certain conditions that will allow them to be accorded preferred tax treatment.

Section 132 of the Internal Revenue Code (Code) sets up certain categories of perquisites that will be accorded preferred tax treatment; that is, any of the following benefits will not be included in the employee's income:

- Services that the employer offers to nonemployees in its usual business, where the employer incurs no additional cost in providing the service to the employee, as long as the benefit is not available only to the company's most highly compensated employees

- Employee discounts on merchandise or services that the employer offers to nonemployees in its usual business, up to the amount of the employer's usual profit (in the case of merchandise) or 20 percent (in the case of services), as long as the benefit is not available only to the company's most highly compensated employees

- Any property or services provided to the executive that would be deductible by the executive as a business or trade expense if the executive had paid for such property or services

- Property or services where the accounting for such property or services would be unreasonable or administratively impracticable, for example, Christmas hams or turkeys

Note, however, that for a Subchapter S corporation, fringe benefits granted to an employee who owns 2 percent or more of the company's stock are generally not accorded preferred tax treatment, since those people are treated as partners.

Q 10:3   What is the accounting treatment of executive perquisites?

Where executive perquisites are treated as compensation to the executive, the company can deduct the cost of the benefits as a compensation expense. The company is, however, also subject to the employer's share of any employment taxes that may be due. Where perquisites are not compensation to the executive because they are reasonable and related to a necessary business purpose, they are deductible by the company as a business expense.

Reimbursement

Q 10:4   What expenses can a company generally reimburse an executive for without creating income to the executive?

Generally, a company can reimburse an executive for her out-of-pocket expenses and deduct the reimbursed amounts as a business expense as long as the expense is an ordinary and necessary cost, bearing a sufficient relationship to the company's business and reasonable in amount.

Q 10:5 What are the special rules relating to the reimbursement of travel expenses?

The rules that determine whether travel expenses will be deductible are extremely complex. Simply stated, in order to be fully deductible by a company, travel expenses must be incurred while away from home in pursuit of the company's business; if this is the case, then travel expense includes not only transportation fares, but also the cost of meals and lodging, and related expenditures, although not entertainment expenses. Travel expenses must be carefully documented by the company, and thus by the executive; substantiation must be given for all expenses, and for each expense the company must be able to state the amount, the date and place incurred, and the destination and business purpose of the trip. Effective January 1, 1994, travel by spouses on business trips is not deductible unless the spouse is also an employee of the company, and the trip had a business purpose.

Q 10:6 What are the special rules relating to the reimbursement of entertainment expenses?

In addition to the general rule requiring that the expense be reasonable, ordinary, and necessary, entertainment expenses must be either "directly related to" or "associated with" the active conduct of the company's business. An expense is "directly related" to a company's business if it involved an active discussion aimed at obtaining immediate revenue (as opposed to mere goodwill), or occurred in a clear business setting such as a hospitality room. An expense is "associated with" a company's business if it is associated with the active conduct of the company's business and precedes or follows a substantial and bona fide business discussion. Entertainment expenses, like travel expenses, must be carefully substantiated so that the company is able to state the amount, the date and place incurred, the persons entertained (including relevant business associations), type of entertainment and its business purpose or benefit, and the nature of any business discussion or activity that took place for each expense. In 1997, a company's deductible portion of business entertainment expenses is limited to 50 percent, unless the entertainment was a company picnic, Christmas party, or sporting event organized to benefit a tax-exempt organization. Deductions in this case are 100 percent.

Q 10:7   How common are expense accounts and how are they treated for tax and accounting purposes?

Expense accounts are quite common. Most surveys indicate that all companies provide expense reimbursement, and many also provide a fixed expense account. The amount of the expense reimbursement or the fixed account is deductible to the company, and will not be taxable income to the executive if all expenses were business-related, and if the executive submits receipts to the company.

Memberships and Other Common Perquisites

Q 10:8   How common are club membership payments and how are they treated for tax and accounting purposes?

Club membership payments are one of the most common executive perquisites, although this is expected to change. Under current tax rules, such payments are not deductible to the company. Specific business expenses that occur at a club location (e.g., business meetings or luncheons) are 100 percent deductible as ordinary business; however, if a company pays club fees, dues, initiation etc., on behalf of an executive, then these amounts are imputed income on the executive's W-2, and there is no deduction allowed for the company.

Q 10:9   How common are company car programs, and how are they treated for tax and accounting purposes?

Company car programs are one of the most common executive perquisites. Company car costs are deductible by the company, and are not imputed income to the executive, if they are directly attributable to its business. Commuting costs and other personal use of a company car is not a deductible expense to the company, and it will constitute imputed income to the executive.

> **Example.** A company provides its executives with leased cars of their choice, up to a maximum monthly amount of $800. Executive A leases a car for $800 and drives the car 20,000 miles in one year. If 70 percent of this mileage is personal usage, then the amount of income computed in that executive's W-2 during the tax year will be $6,720 (70% × $800 = $560 per month × 12 months = $6,720).

In addition, if the company provides the executive with operating costs (e.g., gasoline, oil, other maintenance), these amounts would also be added to the executive's income on the same basis (70 percent of the total cost would be computed in the executive's W-2).

Sample company car provisions in executive employment contracts are provided in Appendix D at the back of this book.

Q 10:10   How common are home offices, computers, and car phones, and how are they treated for tax and accounting purposes?

Surveys indicate home computers and car phones are among the fastest growing perquisites during the past few years. The IRS allows an individual to deduct home office expenses only if it is the primary place of business, and is used as a place for meetings with clients, customers, patients, etc. The cost of home computers is deductible to the executive under an accelerated depreciation table if the computer is used over 50 percent for business, and if the home computer is for the convenience of the employer. This same principle applies to the one-time cost of installing a car phone, and to ongoing monthly fees and calls. Any personal calls are imputed income to the executive, along with a pro-rated portion of the monthly service fee.

Q 10:11   Can a hiring bonus be provided as a perquisite?

A hiring bonus is a one-time payment used by companies to entice an executive into accepting employment by compensating her for concerns that are not related to specific job qualifications or experience. Such concerns include compensating executives for relocating into less desirable geographic locations or for accepting a lower initial base salary, to offset the loss of annual incentives or unvested stock awards, or simply for agreeing to change positions.

Example. A company wants to attract a new executive; however, that executive will be losing a $10,000 annual bonus and $12,000 in "paper profits" on unvested stock option shares. The executive has requested that the company make up lost payments of $22,000.

In addition to normal employment provisions, the company provides the executive with a front-end grant of 1,000 restricted shares with a current market value of $20 per share, and a two-year restriction period, with 50 percent of the shares vesting after one year and 100 percent fully vested after two years.

The company has therefore provided the executive with an opportunity to make up lost payments, by approximately matching the amount of these payments with a restricted stock grant. The vesting provision of the restricted stock grant was designed to equal the vesting period of the stock option shares lost by the executive. In addition, anticipated growth in the company stock will raise the value of the restricted shares so that it will equal or exceed the total lost payment of the executive.

Q 10:12   Is supplemental life insurance a taxable perquisite to the executive?

The cost of company-provided life insurance is taxable income to the executive unless the insurance is provided under a group-term policy. Under a group-term policy, the benefit is tax-free only up to $50,000 of coverage. The cost of additional insurance is taxable income to the executive and the amount of this taxable income is not the amount the company actually pays for the coverage but is the amount based on an IRS table of coverage or "uniform premiums."

Q 10:13   What is split-dollar life insurance?

Split-dollar life insurance is a form of executive compensation that has been popular for many years. It is an arrangement that provides for the company and the executive to "split" the cost of the executive's life insurance. The advantage of the split-dollar approach is that it allows the company to provide the executive with life insurance at a minimal cost to the executive. While there are several variations on the split-dollar approach, the typical approach involves a situation where the company receives all of the rights under the policy except the right to designate the beneficiary. The company and the executive agree to split the premium cost although the actual split depends on both the insurance product and the level of desired spending. Typically, the company pays the great majority or all of the premium and, at the time of the executive's death, the company receives an amount equal to the cash surrender value of the policy; the balance of the proceeds goes to the beneficiary that was designated by the executive.

Q 10:14   Can a company take out additional insurance on an executive with itself as the beneficiary?

Yes. This is often called key-man insurance. It is not an executive perquisite, however, because only the company benefits from the insurance, not the executive.

Q 10:15   Are company planes and first class air travel common perquisites?

These perquisites are typically used by large companies only, because they are costly. As long as there is no personal use, the expense does not represent taxable income to the executive. They are always fully deductible to the company as a business expense, or as compensation to the executive (i.e., imputed income).

Q 10:16   What is the financial planning perquisite?

With the financial planning perquisite, the company agrees to pay outside consultants, up to a specified maximum, for personal financial planning services for executives. These services typically cover income tax planning and preparation, investment advice, guidance on obtaining the full advantage of compensation and executive benefits, retirement counseling, and estate planning.

In most cases, the IRS treats the fee paid by the company as taxable income to the executive. To the extent that the fee is paid for tax counsel or in connection with the preparation of tax returns, or for investment counsel in connection with investments held for income production, this fee may, however, be deductible by the executive. Where this is not the case, some companies "gross-up" the executive's compensation to cover any additional tax liability (see Q 10:31 for an explanation of the gross-up process).

Q 10:17 How common is it to offer low-interest or interest-free loans to executives?

Prior to the Tax Reform Act of 1984 (TRA '84), interest-free loans were a common executive perquisite. Currently, these are rarely used. Loans of over $10,000 are subject to regulations. With certain exceptions, if a company grants a loan in excess of $10,000 to an executive, the executive must report as taxable income the difference between the established federal rate and the actual interest charged by the company on the loan.

From a tax point of view, the entire compensation portion of a below-market loan is taxable to the employee and deductible to the company each year.

The same is true for residential/house purchase loans to executives or non-executives during a company relocation. If the company provides an interest-free or low-interest loan, then the executive will have imputed income.

Employment Agreements

Q 10:18 What are the advantages of giving an executive an employment agreement?

Employment agreements are considered a perquisite because, from the executive's perspective, they guarantee employment during the term of the agreement. The primary advantage to a company of giving an executive an employment agreement is the resulting opportunity to include a restrictive covenant, that is, an agreement by the executive not to work for any other employer.

Q 10:19   Are there disadvantages of giving an executive an employment agreement?

The primary disadvantage from the company's perspective of entering into an employment agreement with an executive is the resulting obligation to employ that executive in the agreed position during the full term of the agreement, even though the executive's performance may deteriorate during the term. From the executive's perspective, it prohibits him from seeking a better job opportunity elsewhere.

Q 10:20   What is an example of an executive employment agreement?

Typical employment contracts define both executive and company employment responsibilities. For example, the executive would thereby agree to the following conditions: (1) to devote all working time exclusively to the performance of any services assigned by the company; (2) to work only at specified company locations; (3) to abstain from rendering any labor or service to any other person, firm, or corporation during the term of the employment agreement; and (4) to keep all work-related information (any information on the company, its business, or its products or services) confidential. Companies may also state on the agreement that working for or with competitors is prohibited for a specified period after employment is terminated; however, this is difficult to enforce unless compensation is provided in exchange for the noncompetition agreement.

For its part, the company will typically agree to employ the executive for a specified time period (typically one to three years) at a specified salary, with, in some cases, a targeted bonus opportunity and/or a targeted stock award/long-term performance grant. Companies may also indicate executive eligibility for specific benefits and/or perquisites.

A cancellation clause will also be included in these contracts indicating that a minimum notice period may be provided by either party to cancel a contract. This notice period is normally six months or more, recognizing that the purpose of the employment contract is to create a commitment that is long-term, not short-term. The time period of the cancellation clause will normally tie in administratively to the renewal date of any employment contract. For example, if an employment contract was for three years with a six-month cancellation clause, then six months prior to the completion of the three-year employment contract a new contract would typically be negotiated. As an alternative, it is possible to have an "evergreen" provision in the contract to state that the employment contract is automatically renewed every year unless the cancellation clause (six months' notice) is enacted by either party.

Sample executive employment contracts are provided in Appendix D at the back of this book.

Q 10:21   How enforceable is a contractual agreement with regard to a fixed term of employment?

A contractual agreement with regard to a fixed term of employment is not specifically enforceable against the executive. If the executive quits, the company is not likely to go to court to enforce the agreement, because a court will not require an employee to continue to provide services against his will (although the corporation would be entitled to cease making payments under the agreement). The fixed term of employment is enforceable, however, against the employer company in the sense that the company must continue to fulfill its payment obligations as set forth in the agreement throughout the term of the agreement, even if it involuntarily terminates the executive. Generally, the only way a company can terminate an employment agreement before its expiration is if the executive has engaged in the kind of conduct that allows the corporation to terminate for "cause." Often the agreement itself will define the meaning of cause, and the most typical definitions include a material breach by the executive of the provisions of the agreement or conviction of a felony-type crime (e.g., stealing, embezzlement). Where cause is not defined, the company must rely on its state's common law rules concerning what conduct constitutes cause.

Planning Tip. Employers and employees should consider an employment contract provision that allows either party to cancel the contract with 90 days' (or more) notice. It can also be beneficial to both parties to have an involuntary termination provision in the employment contract that allows the company to make this decision provided it guarantees the employee some minimum severance (e.g., six or more months' salary, bonus, and benefits continuation).

Sample employment termination provisions in executive employment agreements are provided in Appendix D at the back of this book.

Q 10:22   How enforceable is a noncompetitive agreement?

A noncompetitive agreement must be reasonable in order to be enforced, and reasonableness is measured by the extent of the restriction and the length of time it covers. Each of these variables is measured differently in each state. As a whole, a restriction that prohibits the executive from engaging in the employer's business is generally disfavored by the courts. A restriction against soliciting company clients or employees is, however, more likely to be enforced.

Companies may make an alternative arrangement by paying terminated executives a specified amount (i.e., a severance payment) during a period of nonemployment in lieu of allowing them to work for competitors. Most court rulings have in fact supported this type of noncompetition agreement.

Sample noncompetition provisions in executive employment contracts are located in Appendix C at the back of this book.

Severance Agreements

Q 10:23   Is severance compensation an employee perquisite?

Severance compensation is an executive perquisite in much the same way as is an employment agreement, because it gives the executive a guarantee of certain payments in the event her employment is terminated by the company. These can also be provided as contracts in the same way as employment agreements. Severance compensation paid to a top-level executive because of termination resulting from a change in control will be governed by the rules affecting golden parachutes even if the severance agreement makes no reference to the change in control.

Sample severance provisions in executive employment contracts are provided in Appendix C at the back of this book.

Q 10:24   What is a golden parachute?

A golden parachute is an agreement that provides a generous severance package to top executives in the event of a change in control of the company, such as resulting from a takeover or merger. A golden parachute can be either "single trigger" or "double trigger." A single trigger agreement allows the executive to receive the stated severance benefits even if he voluntarily leaves following a change in control; the change in control is therefore the only "trigger" necessary to assure the executive of benefits if he wants them. A double trigger agreement requires that the executive's employment be terminated by the new management following the change in control, either directly or through an adverse change in working conditions that amounts to a constructive termination.

Q 10:25   What is an example of a golden parachute provision?

A company provides executives with a "change of control" golden parachute such that if control of the company changes and if the executive is involuntarily terminated within two years of the change of control (double trigger provision), then the executive will be provided with the following severance payments:

1. An amount equalling one year's base salary, that is, the salary that was in effect at the time of involuntary termination (alternatively, the highest base salary in effect during the last five years);

2. The higher of the previous year's incentive award or the highest incentive award during the past five years;

3. All vested and unvested amounts from long-term stock awards and/or performance plan awards;

4. Payment of one year's country club dues and one additional financial plan review with the executive's financial planning consultant;

5. Payment of company car expenses for a period of one year with the option to purchase the car at the wholesale blue book value; or

6. Provision of an office, and payment of secretarial services in that office for a period of one year.

Assume that the total value of the above severance package is $500,000. The company would then calculate the "base period" compensation (average W-2 pay during the last five years). If this amount were $200,000, then the executive would not be subject to any excess parachute payment since the amount of the parachute ($500,000) does not exceed 2.99 times this base amount (2.99 × $200,000 = $598,000). (See Q 10:29 for an explanation of the factor 2.99.)

If the base period amount had been $150,000, an excess parachute payment would be due because the amount of the parachute ($500,000) exceeds 2.99 times the base amount of $150,000 ($448,500). In this case, the executive would owe a 20 percent excise tax, and it would be based on the amount of parachute payment beyond the base amount, which equals $500,000 minus $150,000, or $350,000. The excise tax would be 20 percent of $350,000 ($70,000), and this would be paid in addition to ordinary income tax rates.

Q 10:26 What constitutes a change in control?

The severance agreement will generally define the term "change in control." Its primary elements are usually the acquisition of a stated percentage of voting stock, generally between 20 percent and 50 percent, and a change in a majority of the Board of Directors.

Q 10:27   Why do companies provide golden parachutes?

Many companies feel that parachute programs are appropriate because they encourage key personnel, who might otherwise resign for fear of losing their positions in the event of a takeover, to remain with the company. These companies also argue that it is in the best interest of the company and its shareholders, employees, and customers that it not be taken over and that golden parachute programs reduce the likelihood that such a takeover will occur. But in the event a takeover does occur, the golden parachute provides a sufficient assurance of continuity of income to motivate the executive to negotiate the best deal possible for shareholders. In either event, companies continue to treat payments under golden parachute contracts as an ordinary and necessary trade or business expense.

Q 10:28   Are there criticisms of golden parachute programs?

Yes. Many individuals, including government officials, feel that in many instances golden parachute contracts do little but assist an entrenched management team to remain in control and/or provide corporate funds to subsidize officers and other highly paid executives who leave after the takeover, when that is the time they are most needed. In fact, the government has concluded that a tax penalty should be exacted in certain situations in order to prevent the tax law from being used as a subsidy for entrenched management or other highly compensated executives (see Q 10:29).

Q 10:29   What penalties has the government imposed on golden parachutes?

A payment to an officer, director, or highly compensated individual will be deemed to be a parachute payment if it is contingent upon a change in control of the corporation and the total present value of all such contingent compensation exceeds 299 percent of the "base amount," that is, the individual's average annual compensation during the five tax years immediately prior to the change in control. For these purposes, an executive is a highly compensated individual if he is among the highest paid 1 percent of the employees or, if less, one of the highest paid 250 employees of the company.

Once it has been established that a parachute payment exists, the corporation will not be entitled to deduct the part of the payment that constitutes an "excess parachute payment" (see Q 10:30) and the individual receiving the payment will be subject to a 20 percent excise tax on the excess, in addition to all other ordinary income tax obligations.

The parachute provisions do not apply to "small business corporations," which are corporations that have elected subchapter S status or are eligible to do so, nor to closely held corporations whose stock is not readily tradeable and whose stockholders have approved the severance agreements by more than a 75 percent vote with "adequate disclosure" of all material facts. For nonpublic corporations, the reason for adopting parachute agreements is not as compelling because management generally controls more than a majority of the stock and it is unlikely that the company will find itself in a hostile takeover situation.

Q 10:30 What is an excess parachute payment?

An excess parachute payment is any payment that exceeds the base amount. The distinction between a parachute payment and an excess parachute payment is an important one because while a parachute payment exists if payments aggregate to more than three times the base amount, once a parachute payment is found to exist, all payments above the base amount are deemed to be excess.

Q 10:31 Is there any way to avoid the negative tax impact of the excess parachute payment?

Yes. Limit parachute payments to 299 percent of the base amount. Another alternative is to "gross-up" the executive for the tax burden of the excise tax. In the gross-up process, the company pays tax on incremental income to the executive. The process is as follows: any amounts added as income to an employee's W-2 are taxable, and the company pays this tax. The company adds the amount of this tax payment as further income on the employee's W-2 (which makes the tax payment taxable as income) and pays the tax owed for this tax payment.

At the other extreme, companies can install a "fail-safe" provision in their severance compensation agreements, in the form of a paragraph that states that any amounts that may be paid to an executive that would otherwise be parachute payments should be treated as a loan by the company, repayable by the executive.

Chapter 11

Building a Total Compensation Strategy

There are five elements to executive compensation: base salary, benefits, short-term incentives, long-term incentives, and perquisites. Each of these elements has complex tax, accounting, and regulatory considerations. In addition, companies change, as do the purposes of these elements of executive compensation. For these reasons, companies find that they need to develop a strategy on how each of these elements should be used. This chapter provides information on the compensation, benefit, and other factors to be considered in developing the appropriate mix of executive compensation and on the overall total compensation strategy for a company. The chapter also identifies specific subjects that should be included under each element of executive compensation discussed in a strategy statement, and provides examples of strategy statements.

General Considerations 11-2
Compensation Factors 11-3
Benefit Factors 11-6
Other Factors 11-9
Determining the Mix 11-10
Developing a Total Strategy 11-14
Approval and Implementation 11-15
Example of Strategy Statements 11-17

General Considerations

Q 11:1   What is a total compensation strategy?

A total compensation strategy serves as a statement of the business value of and philosophy behind a company's compensation and benefit programs. The statement identifies the purpose of all executive compensation programs and establishes parameters that guide the utilization of those programs within the organization (see Q 1:1).

Q 11:2   What elements of executive compensation are included in a total compensation strategy statement?

The five elements of executive compensation are base salary, short-term incentives, long-term incentives, benefits, and perquisites (see Q 1:1). Total compensation strategy statements address all of these executive compensation elements.

Q 11:3   What are the business purposes of a total compensation strategy?

Total compensation strategies give organizations the opportunity to accomplish the following:

1. Evaluate the cost of executive compensation programs to the company versus the value of executive compensation to company executives;

2. Compare executive compensation costs in the company with similar costs in other companies;

3. Identify how executive compensation programs are supporting business goals;

4. Identify how executive compensation programs are supporting human resource goals;

5. Define competitive labor markets and establish a targeted competitive level of executive pay appropriate for the company;

6. Identify where changes or enhancements to executive compensation programs are required in support of changing business and human resources objectives;

7. Determine measures of key performance (for use in executive compensation programs) that drive business success;

8. Identify primary areas of executive activity and behavior that are required for business success;

9. Identify where executive compensation programs may need to differ by company business unit; and

10. Determine all communication necessary to convey to executives (and non-executives) the company's executive compensation philosophy, executive compensation program roles and purposes, and individual plan objectives.

Compensation Factors

Q 11:4   What factors determine a total compensation strategy?

In building a total compensation strategy, the company should review the following factors: its basic philosophy; mission and vision; business plans; life cycle; internal factors such as organizational structure, business processes and systems, and work force demographics; external factors such as tax and accounting regulations, industry regulations, and competitive environment.

Q 11:5   How does a company's philosophy affect its total compensation strategy?

A company's business philosophy encompasses its basic values and beliefs. It defines the environment in which a total compensation strategy will be administered. For example, a management style that focuses on short-term gains needs a total compensation strategy that emphasizes short-term incentives. Companies with a highly delegative and informal management style need a total compensation strategy that emphasizes team performance from short-term and long-term incentive compensation programs. Companies with a paternalistic philosophy might place a heavier emphasis on salary and benefits.

Q 11:6 How can a company's mission or vision statement affect its total compensation strategy?

A company's mission statement identifies the purpose of the organization, while a vision statement is best described as a tangible image that should guide the company's executives as they implement the company mission. These terms will frequently set the company's philosophy and culture as well as its total compensation strategy. For example, a well-known consumer products company has a statement that its vision is to be the number one consumer products company in the world. In contrast, another leading U.S. company has a mission statement of service to humanity. These mission statements affect both company culture and total compensation strategy as follows:

Mission	Culture	Total Compensation Strategy
Best consumer product company in the world	Risk-taking, aggressive, and high degree of change	Heavy emphasis on incentive compensation and high pay levels
Service to humanity	Paternalistic, heavy emphasis on planning and controlled, profitable growth	Typical mix of incentive compensation elements, high base salary and benefits

Q 11:7 How can a company's business plan affect a total compensation strategy?

The business strategies and plans of any company will directly affect a total compensation strategy. For example, a company that has short-term concerns such as cash flow, short-term debt, or reorganization following a merger would likely place significant emphasis on short-term incentives in its total compensation strategy. In contrast, a company that has just made a major capital investment would likely emphasize long-term incentives in its total compensation strategy. Another example is a company that is planning a number of mergers and company reorganizations that could result in significant employee turnover. This company would likely focus its total compensation strategy on benefits and perquisites.

Business plans also contain key performance measures that should be utilized in executive compensation plans and total compensation strategies (see Qs 4:29–4:34).

Q 11:8   How can a company's life cycle affect its total compensation strategy?

A company life cycle is commonly expressed as one of three stages: growth, maturity, and decline. A small growth company without a lot of cash might establish a total compensation strategy that emphasizes long-term income in the form of stock options, because from a cost perspective, stock options are not charged to a company's earnings. A mature company with sufficient cash that has applied more extensive and varied performance measures might establish a total compensation strategy that emphasizes performance-based short-term or long-term incentives. Similarly, a company in a cycle of decline would probably emphasize benefits and perquisites.

Q 11:9   How do internal factors affect a company's total compensation strategy?

Like business plans, internal factors have a direct impact on the development of a total compensation strategy. Organizational structure is one such factor: A decentralized company with various strategic business units must decide if these units should have similar or different total compensation strategies.

Quality management programs (e.g., quality circles) are a major internal factor for many companies. The teamwork and team building required in these organizations will frequently drive a total compensation strategy that emphasizes profit sharing in both short- and long-term incentive plans.

Other internal factors are the number of policies and procedures in an organization, and the sophistication of its financial reporting methods. When these internal factors are present in an organization, they will usually drive performance-based incentive plans (both short- and long-term).

The demographics of a company's executive work force can also drive a total compensation strategy. For example, if there is a shortage of executives in the labor market, long-term incentive plans (like restricted stock) could be a major element of executive compensation in the total compensation strategy. If many executives are approaching retirement age, this factor could drive the use of benefit or perquisite enhancements as the major emphasis of the total compensation strategy.

Q 11:10 How do external factors affect a company's total compensation strategy?

Highly regulated industries such as utility companies, transportation companies, and nonprofit organizations typically have not adopted a total compensation strategy with a heavy emphasis on incentive compensation (both short- and long-term). These companies would typically adopt a total compensation strategy that emphasizes salary and benefits.

On the other hand, companies under heavy external competitive threat can use total compensation strategy statements to emphasize the achievement of immediate short-term business goals.

Another external factor is the constant change in tax and accounting regulations, which can direct total compensation strategies, particularly with respect to long-term income. For example, major tax law changes historically have caused companies to restructure long-term income in the form of stock awards that emphasize either capital gains or ordinary income tax, whichever is most favorable at the time.

Benefit Factors

Q 11:11 What benefit programs should be included in a total compensation strategy statement?

Total compensation strategy statements should include provisions for health care benefits and costs, retirement, capital accumulation plans, and life and disability insurance. These four benefit programs are affected by changing business conditions and thus can affect a company's total compensation strategy. Other benefits, such as holidays, vacations, and time off with pay, usually do not vary with business conditions and business priorities and therefore are not included in a total compensation strategy statement.

Q 11:12   How can health care plan benefits and costs affect a total compensation strategy statement?

The decade of the 1990s has already seen an unparalleled focus on health care cost containment. The current 20 percent annual growth in health costs represents an excellent reason for companies to develop a total compensation strategy. One such health care strategy may be to maintain the current employer/employee cost responsibility ratio at 60 percent for employer and 40 percent for employee during the next three years. Another example would be for a company to establish employer health care cost levels such that benefits are at or below 10 percent of the average monthly payroll costs for full-time active employees.

Self-insurance is another key strategy with respect to health care plans. While many companies have adopted this strategy as a means of cost control, this may not be appropriate for companies with low cash flow amounts. Therefore, any self-insurance strategy should also be included in a company's total compensation strategy statement as a means of establishing both direction and cost parameters for this important element of health care.

Q 11:13   How can retirement benefits affect a company's total compensation strategy statement?

Retirement benefits for executives include those from a defined benefit or defined contribution pension plan plus those retirement benefits from any nonqualified plan or supplemental executive retirement plan (see Q 9:31). A total compensation strategy statement should identify the desired level of executive retirement benefit, in recognition of required costs. For example, the total retirement benefit for executives from a qualified and nonqualified plan can be targeted for 20 percent of final average pay, if retirement occurs at age 60, after 20 years of service.

There are other important dimensions of a retirement benefit strategy. Prior retirement benefits from another employer should be considered for inclusion in the targeted retirement benefit for executives. The integration of targeted retirement benefits with those provided by the government (in the form of social security) should also be referenced in a total compensation strategy statement.

Q 11:14   How can life insurance and disability insurance affect a company's total compensation strategy statement?

Any consideration of life insurance in a total compensation strategy should be focused primarily on the level of supplemental life insurance to be either provided to executives by the company or purchased by the executive. For example, a company may provide life insurance for non-executives in an amount equal to base salary and for executives in an amount double that of base salary, since the surviving spouse of an executive will generally require greater income replacement upon the executive's death. A similar issue exists for disability insurance; however, in most companies the executive benefit involves a higher maximum dollar amount of disability income protection provided by the company's disability plan rather than the provision of additional disability insurance. This is accomplished by establishing a minimum percentage of income protection for executives so that they can receive a similar value from the disability plan. For example, a typical disability plan might provide 50 percent of base salary up to $1,500 per month. For executives, the total compensation strategy may be to provide 50 percent of base salary with no maximum, or with a maximum of $3,000 per month rather than $1,500 per month.

Q 11:15   How can capital accumulation plans affect a company's total compensation strategy statement?

Like retirement benefits, capital accumulation plans include any tax qualified plan benefit (e.g., a 401 (k) plan with a company matching 50 percent of the employee contribution up to a maximum of 6 percent of base salary), plus any nonqualified plan benefit, also known as an Internal Revenue Code (the Code) Section 415 excess plan (see Q 9:40). The U.S. government, through its ERISA requirements, sets the maximum contribution that companies can make to a qualified plan. Companies can use their total compensation strategy statement to identify and evaluate the amount and cost of any excess benefit plan that can generally restore the company contributions or matching amounts to the level prescribed by the qualified plan but restricted by Code Section 415. This same strategy issue applies to capital accumulation plans such as profit sharing plans or ESOPs. As with other benefit plan issues, the inclusion of company strategies in a total compensation strategy statement disciplines a company to deal with both the benefit and cost implications appropriate for its business.

Other Factors

Q 11:16 Can total compensation strategies vary by company business unit?

Yes. This can be most appropriate in large companies that are in more than one business. The factors that determine a total compensation strategy (see Q 11:4) will indicate whether strategies should differ among company business units. For example, a parent company may establish a business strategy of growth in another industry. The business characteristics, level of risk taking, and the time span for product/service development may differ significantly between the existing and contemplated industries; thus, total compensation strategies will differ as well.

Example. A regional utility company wants to expand its business into other states so that it can purchase additional power from these states for use during peak usage periods. The department responsible for this expansion has business characteristics similar to the real estate industry in that it has an aggressive and deal-oriented environment, quite unlike the utility industry, which is more stable, cautiously aggressive, and highly regulated. These different business characteristics will drive different total compensation strategies. The expanded department may have a total compensation strategy that uses incentive compensation extensively while the parent company may have a total compensation strategy that focuses more on long-term income programs.

Q 11:17   Can total compensation strategies be developed for international businesses?

Yes. The integration of compensation and benefits is most critical in companies with international operations because government-mandated benefits differ significantly from country to country. Business strategies for international companies or business units of a multinational company can also vary significantly from those in the United States. Companies should consider comparing (1) the total compensation levels among countries where they have international operations and (2) the competitiveness of total compensation levels within each of those countries.

Measuring international compensation and benefit levels is considerably more difficult for the following reasons: (1) many different programs exist; (2) ability to measure total compensation varies between countries; (3) a greater knowledge of benefit accounting and tax laws is required for the measurement of total compensation (e.g., benefit cost determination can vary significantly depending on who pays what and how); (4) compensation cost analysis can vary depending on the evaluation methods used for stock-related plans. While these factors can also apply in a comparison of U.S. companies, the complexity is multiplied when conducting total compensation analyses for international businesses.

Determining the Mix

Q 11:18   How can a company determine the proper mix of executive compensation elements in a total compensation strategy statement?

After reviewing the factors determining a total compensation strategy (see Qs 11:4–11:10) companies will typically identify target amounts for each element of executive compensation and express them as a percentage of base salary.

For example:

Compensation Element	Percentage of Base Salary
Annual incentive award	30
Long-term incentive award	35
Benefits	40
Perquisites	5
TOTAL	110%

Under this example, an additional 110 percent of base salary can be earned from other elements of executive compensation. This percentage will vary by position in an organization. Higher-level jobs will typically have a higher percentage of annual incentive and long-term incentive award potential plus perquisites, while benefits will remain relatively constant. The logic behind higher amounts of incentive is that higher-level jobs with greater responsibility should have greater total compensation dependent upon performance. Companies typically believe, as well, that higher-level positions with greater responsibility require more perquisites such as complex financial planning assistance and greater use of business clubs.

Q 11:19   How should companies define competitive labor markets?

Many companies will develop a list of labor market competitors who are either in the same or similar businesses or who represent companies from which employees can be recruited. An important factor in this determination is to ensure that competitor companies are not necessarily limited to those organizations that market the same product or service. For instance, human resources talent can be found outside of the direct competition; therefore, a total compensation strategy needs to be flexible.

Labor markets for executive positions are national. Surveys show very little total compensation differences based on location. Thus, geography should not be a primary factor in defining competitive labor markets (see Q 1:16).

Q 11:20   Should all companies establish a total compensation strategy to pay at the 50th percentile of labor market competitors?

No, but companies should start at this point. If a company's business environment is high growth, and a number of new employees are being recruited from outside the company, then a company's total compensation strategy might appropriately be to pay above the 50th percentile of competitors. This strategy should be applied equally to current as well as new employees.

A company's total compensation strategy may be to pay below the 50th percentile in certain situations: if the supply of executives may exceed the demand; actual pay levels of executives may be well above the market median; or company performance may be far below expected levels and profit may be threatened. This decision should be reviewed annually to determine whether it remains appropriate.

Q 11:21   How can a company decide on the type of short-term incentive?

A simple method to determine the best type of short-term incentive for a company is to compare the six types of short-term incentive (discretionary, percentage of profit, growth, performance target, peer comparison, and matrix plan) described in Chapter 4 to the factors that determine a total compensation strategy as described in Q 11:4. Once a company has evaluated the factors that determine a total compensation strategy, it can use this information to decide on the type of short-term incentive. An example of this is shown in Chart 11-1, which first lists the six types of short-term incentive (horizontally) and then lists (vertically) the factors that determine the total compensation strategy (in this example, only the life cycle factor is shown). In the first example, a decision is made concerning the application of a discretionary plan to the small company that is in the growth life cycle. In this case, where there is little sophistication in measuring performance, the discretionary plan fits the growth company's life cycle very well and a YES is entered into that column. The same conclusion is reached with respect to the percentage of profit plan type, and the growth plan type. On the other hand, the performance target, peer company comparison, and matrix plan concepts all require the use of sophisticated performance measures, and a NO is entered into these categories to indicate that they are not the best plan type given this company's growth life cycle characteristics. The second example in Chart 11-1 is a large company in a mature life cycle, with stable cash flow and a high ability to measure performance. In this case, the growth, performance target, peer company, and matrix plan types are assigned a YES, indicating that these concepts would work well in this business environment. The discretionary and percentage of profit plan types are assigned a NO.

If companies will prepare a similar analysis to that shown in Chart 11-1 for all six factors that determine a total compensation strategy, then the best plan type can emerge from this analysis and guide the company in its selection process.

Chart 11-1. Short-Term Incentive Selection

	Discretionary	Percentage of Profit	Growth	Performance Target	Peer Comparison	Matrix Plan
Growth Life Cycle	YES	YES	YES	NO	NO	NO
Mature Life Cycle	NO	NO	YES	YES	YES	YES

Q 11:22 How can companies decide on the best type of long-term incentive?

A similar analysis as that described in Question 11:21 for short-term incentives can be used in selecting the long-term incentives. The various types of long-term incentives described in Chapters 5 through 8 can be compared to the factors that determine a total compensation strategy, so that a judgment can be made for the plan type that best fits each strategy factor. An example of this is shown in Chart 11-2, which compares three long-term stock award alternatives (nonqualified stock options, restricted stock, and stock appreciation rights) to three specific business objectives (low cost, executive ownership, and long-term stock appreciation). From this specific comparison, the nonqualified stock option, which does not have any charge to the company's income statement, emerges as the best form of long-term income if the primary business objective is low cost. With respect to achieving executive ownership, the restricted stock alternative emerges as the best alternative because it is the only one of the three that provides for immediate ownership at the time of grant. With respect to the third business objective of long-term stock appreciation, the chart indicates that the nonqualified stock option and the stock appreciation right are the best alternatives since the value of both is dependent upon stock appreciation.

Chart 11-2. Long-Term Incentive Selection

Business Objective	Nonqualified Stock Option	Restricted Stock	Stock Appreciation Right
Low cost	YES	NO	NO
Executive ownership	NO	YES	NO
Stock appreciation	YES	NO	YES

Any method used to determine the best type of long-term incentive requires a judgment call and follows a two-step process: (1) identifying business concerns that need to be supported with a total compensation strategy, and (2) identifying the plan types that can be utilized in a total compensation strategy in direct support of business objectives.

Developing a Total Strategy

Q 11:23 What should be included in a total compensation strategy statement?

A total compensation strategy should include statements that address the following:

1. A description of the company's total compensation philosophy as it applies to each element of total compensation. For example, will compensation plans be "pay for performance," or will they remain relatively constant from year to year; will benefit plans be "cost sharing" or will the employer pay most costs?

2. The purpose of each element of total compensation (base salary, annual bonus, long-term incentive, perquisites, and

benefits), and, where possible, a specific reference as to how the element(s) support company business and/or human resource objectives.

3. The structure of each element of executive compensation. For example, will long-term plans be stock-based or performance-based; will health care plans be self-insured?

4. The targeted levels of labor market competitiveness for each element of total compensation by strategic business unit or major department, as appropriate. For example, maintain salary and bonus levels that are at the 50th percentile for a select group of competitive companies.

5. The criteria for communication of the company's executive compensation program, to include what should be communicated, and to whom communication should occur (e.g., executives, non-executives, members of the Board of Directors).

Approval and Implementation

Q 11:24 Who should approve a total compensation strategy?

Companies with a board compensation committee should use these directors to approve a compensation strategy (see Q 2:23). Outside directors on a board compensation committee will typically have the responsibility of approving the design of executive compensation programs and strategies, and of approving individual stock plans for officers. Companies without a board compensation committee would typically have the CEO approve a total compensation strategy.

Q 11:25 How should a total compensation strategy be communicated to executives?

There are two key events related to the communication of a total compensation strategy to executives. The first of these is the full communication of the strategy statement itself through group or individual meetings. Simple discussion of the entire total compensation strategy document is the most simple and effective way to

accomplish this communication. Elaborate video or slide presenta-
tions are not necessary. Each executive should be given a copy of the
strategy statement for reference throughout the year. The value that
can be realized from communicating a total compensation strategy is
as follows:

1. A certain level of expectation is established with respect to the
   purpose of each element of executive compensation.

2. The priorities of each element of executive compensation are
   clarified, which helps bring focus to the individual activities
   and efforts of each executive.

3. The value of the amount of total compensation (both financial
   and nonfinancial) to the individual executive is established,
   along with the contributions that are required of each executive.

The second event in communicating total compensation strategies
is to inform each executive at the end of each year of her major
accomplishments and actual earnings for that year. This can be
accomplished with an individual executive compensation statement
showing the following information:

1. Base salary earned.

2. Annual incentive amounts paid.

3. Long-term income awards granted that year, plus the number
   of shares and the value of all shares that have vested from
   previous year grants.

4. Perquisite values expressed as either amounts actually used
   and added to the executive's W-2 or expressed as typical
   executive usage (e.g., club memberships, first-class air travel,
   and company car expenses paid).

5. Benefit program values—typically, a summary from a company's benefit statement. If a company does not use a benefit
   statement, the value of company payments for health care,
   retirement plans, life/disability insurance, and capital accumulation should be added to the individual executive compensation statement.

Many companies develop excellent total compensation strategy
statements but do not realize their full value because they fail to
communicate the objectives of the programs as well as the results.

Ongoing communication of a company's total compensation strategy enables it to receive a full value from this business activity.

Another dimension in communicating total compensation strategy is that other constituencies—for example, shareholders and non-executives—could benefit from knowledge of the company's total compensation strategy. However, communication to these other constituencies can be a double-edged sword. On the one hand, any communication is subject to criticism, and on the other hand, the absence of communication can sometimes create incorrect conclusions about company executive compensation programs. Any communication to shareholders or non-executives should therefore be conducted only if the value far exceeds the potential for criticism.

Examples of Strategy Statements

Q 11:26   What is an example of a total compensation strategy statement for a small company?

A small company might have the following total compensation strategy statement:

1. Our company's total compensation philosophy for executive positions will be performance-driven. We believe that individual executive performance can have a direct impact on company success. We will therefore emphasize incentive compensation opportunities as we provide executives with the following elements of total compensation:

   - Base salary in payment for the performance of ongoing job responsibilities
   - Short-term incentives, annual reward opportunities for accomplishing specific, key objectives in the annual business plan
   - A long-term income plan in the form of stock options
   - Perquisites that overcome the limits imposed by the government
   - A level of benefit programs equal to those provided by competitors.

2. Base salary and benefits will be established at or below the 50th percentile of the general industry. Benefit costs will be shared by employer and employee, with 60 percent paid by the employer, 40 percent by the employee. Incentive compensation will be established at the 75th percentile of the general industry.

3. Stock awards will be approximately double those of general industries. This is critical if we are to attract the new executives required by our company to achieve growth objectives.

4. Perquisites will be significantly below competitive practice and will be limited to supplemental retirement and supplemental life insurance for officers.

5. All executives will receive copies of this total compensation strategy statement.

Q 11:27   What is an example of a total compensation strategy statement for a large company?

A large company total compensation strategy statement might look like the following:

1. The foundation of our corporate executive compensation philosophy will be to pay above labor market averages if company performance is above labor market averages. Each company division will also develop its own strategy statement, consistent with the concepts in this corporate philosophy statement.

2. Total cash compensation (base salary plus annual bonus) will be targeted for the 50th percentile of selected peer companies in the outside labor market, with incentive compensation opportunities having significant upside potential such that high performance could bring total cash compensation to the 75th percentile of selected peer companies. The annual incentive award will be based on both company and individual performance.

3. Long-term income will be in the form of:

   • Competitive stock option grants, giving executives the same opportunity as our shareholders to purchase company shares. Incentive stock options will be utilized to the maximum extent possible, as long as the capital gains tax remains favorable. The level of stock option grants will be at the 50th percentile of our selected peer company group.

- Performance share grants, annually rewarding executives for accomplishing results in the three-year strategic plan. All goals in this plan will be approved by the board compensation committee. The combined value of stock options and performance shares are intended to place our total compensation between the 60th and 75th percentile if all performance goals are achieved.

4. Perquisites will be provided if they accomplish the following:

- Allow executives to allocate more time to the job and less to conducting personal affairs

- Assist executives in accomplishing job responsibilities

- Make up benefits lost due to regulatory limits on qualified benefits. The following perquisites meet this criteria: club memberships, financial planning assistance, first-class air travel, supplemental retirement plan, and Code Section 415 excess plan benefits associated with our savings and thrift plan.

5. Benefits will be the same as those typical of our selected peer company group. We will self-insure health care, disability, and life insurance up to a maximum amount, and insure above that point. Our retirement plan will be a defined contribution plan and will be integrated into our 401(k) savings plan.

6. The company will conduct annual meetings with executives to communicate the total compensation strategy. An annual statement will also be provided to each executive indicating their individual value from our total compensation programs.

7. Each company division will use this corporate total compensation strategy to prepare its own strategy statement and submit it to the CEO for approval.

Q 11:28   What is an example of a total compensation strategy statement in an entrepreneurial, high-growth company?

Entrepreneurial companies would typically have a total compensation strategy statement similar to the following:

1. The overall strategy of our company's executive compensation is that individual wealth can be created when company growth occurs. We will achieve this by providing our executives with three to four times the amount of stock ownership that is provided to similar jobs in other businesses. The factors that drive success of this company are growth in customers and revenue and growth in earnings. When this occurs, stock price will increase significantly and executive compensation will increase significantly.

2. Base salary and annual bonus levels will be below the 50th percentile of the labor market until pre-tax income exceeds $1 million. Our strategy will then be to increase our total cash compensation toward but not over the 50th percentile.

3. Long-term income will have no maximum or targeted labor market position, because executives will be treated like entrepreneurs and share in the capital created by stock growth, just like the original company shareholders.

4. Perquisites will be kept at a minimum except where they have a direct business value. Policies that fit this definition are first-class air travel, club memberships and fees (grossed-up for tax purposes), customer outings, meals, and entertainment.

5. Benefits will focus on protecting the executive and family from catastrophic events. Therefore, we will have competitive in-hospital coverage, disability insurance, and life insurance. Coverage of occasional doctor visits, dental exams, retirement, etc. will be below competitive averages.

6. Formal communication programs of our executive compensation strategy are unnecessary because of the informal culture of our organization and the free access of all executives to compensation data. We do expect, however, that our executives will respect the need for the confidentiality of compensation information on non-executive people.

Chapter 12

Small Company Considerations

Small companies typically have quite different executive compensation plans from those of large companies. One reason is that they often have less cash to spend on plan funding. Small companies therefore use different types of long-term incentives—specifically, stock option plans—to overcome their limited cash flow. This chapter provides specific information on how small companies, particularly family-owned businesses, structure their executive compensation to support the unique characteristics of their environment.

The Small Business Job Protection Act of 1996, signed into law on August 20, 1996, is major new legislation providing tax relief and new savings opportunities for small businesses and the self-employed. Key provisions are discussed generally in this chapter and will be covered in further detail in future supplements.

General Considerations 12-2
New Venture Businesses 12-10

General Considerations

Q 12:1 How does the mix of executive compensation elements differ in small companies?

Small companies tend to allocate more total compensation dollars to long-term incentives than do large companies. This is because unlike base salary and bonuses, which require cash flow and are a business expense, long-term incentives (specifically stock options) presently require neither company cash flow nor a charge to company earnings (if stock options are granted at fair market value at the time of grant).

As a result, small companies incur less compensation expense by using stock options (see Chart 12-1). In fact, surveys show that small companies provide three to four times the number of shares to executive compensation plans, as a percentage of total shares outstanding, than do large companies (15 percent versus 5 percent of total shares outstanding over five years, according to a survey by Management Performance Int'l Inc.).

Charts and discussions in Chapter 1 provide more survey information on the differences in the mix of total compensation between small companies and large companies.

Chart 12-1. Compensation Expenses of Executive Pay

Form of Compensation	Business Expense	Cash Flow Required
Base salary	Yes	Yes
Cash bonus	Yes	Yes
Bonus deferred or paid in stock	Yes	No
Stock options	No	No
Restricted stock	Yes	No
Performance plan	Yes	No

Q 12:2   How do small companies with less sophisticated business performance measures establish annual incentives?

Target performance plans, discussed in Question 4:15, use financial and nonfinancial goal achievement as the basis for the annual incentive plan payment. Since small companies do not always have sophisticated business performance measures, and if performance fluctuates significantly from year to year, they will find other types of annual incentive plans more suitable.

Growth improvement plans (see Q 4:12) are often chosen because annual incentive payments can logically be tied to growth in factors such as the number of customers, accounts, sales, or assets. The plan assumption is that as growth occurs on these factors, earnings (however defined) will also improve. Discretionary bonus plans (see Q 4:24) are also most commonly used because under these plans the company chief executive officer (CEO) can determine the appropriate bonus award given the performance of each individual executive as well as the company's overall ability to pay.

Q 12:3   How can small companies with a small human resources staff determine appropriate compensation levels?

Two sources provide general information on actual compensation levels. *The Officer Compensation Report* (Panel Publishers, 1994) provides multi-industry total cash compensation (salary plus bonus) and long-term income compensation levels for more than 12 key executive positions. Large consulting firms also publish executive compensation surveys.

Q 12:4   What form of long-term incentive is most appropriate for small companies?

From a cost perspective, stock options (see Qs 6:9 and 6:11) are best for small companies, because they require no charge to the company's income statement and bring cash to the company when the executive purchases the shares. Private companies can use phantom shares (see Q 7:28) or book value shares to avoid dilution of stock.

A number of long-term incentive plans are useful motivators, and can further company business objectives. Company net worth (equity) can best be built by a plan that measures increases in book value (earnings divided by equity). If the objective is to build executive stock ownership, restricted stock (see Q 7:30) can provide this immediately while motivating executives to remain with the company until the restrictions have been met. A performance plan (see 7:46) is best used to reward executives for the achievement of long-term business goals under their direct control.

The most motivating long-term incentive plan is one that provides immediate value in terms of growth and personal net worth to the executive, has a high potential value, and requires little or no cost to the executive. The restricted stock plan comes closest to all of these objectives.

As shown in Chart 12-2, stock options are the most popular form of long-term incentive in small companies, as they are in large companies. This parallels a similar survey shown in Chart 6-1. Book value plans are widely used in the small company because they reward executives for building the net worth of the company, while phantom stock plans are also used extensively in the small company because they motivate the executive to build company stock price without having to use actual shares and thus dilute the stock holdings of current shareholders.

Chart 12-2. Popular Forms of Long-Term Incentive

Plan type	Prevalence*
Stock options	87%
Restricted stock	22%
Performance plans	14%
Phantom stock plans	43%
Book value plans	28%

*Totals are greater than 100% because companies use more than one form of long-term incentive.

Source: HR Management, Inc. 1995 Survey on the Prevalence of Long-Term Incentive Plans in the Small Company.

Q 12:5 How can small companies attract high-quality people without offering competitive base salary and bonus amounts?

By providing significantly greater amounts of long-term incentives in the form of stock options, small companies can offer a competitive total compensation package. Chart 12-3 contrasts small and large company compensation packages.

As shown in Chart 12-3, this small company offers considerably less base salary and benefits but significantly greater long-term incentive potential via 150,000 shares rather than 15,000 shares.

The other attractive recruitment tool for small companies is the typically greater scope of accountability offered the executive. For example, a chief financial officer (CFO) in a small company may also be responsible for the human resources and public relations areas. In a large company the CFO would be a separate position from that of chief personnel officer and chief public relations officer.

Chart 12-3. Sample Small and Large Company Employment Offers

Executive Compensation	Company with Sales at $50 million	Company with Sales at $5 billion
Base salary	$100,000	$400,000
Annual incentive	$ 25,000	$200,000
Long-term incentive	$150,000 s/o shares at $3 per share	15,000 s/o shares at $30 per share
Benefits	25% of base salary	35% of base salary
Perquisites	Company car	Car + club membership + financial planning

While the breadth of knowledge and accountability is higher in small company executive jobs, the complexity of business operations in a large company requires a greater depth of knowledge and accountability. Depending upon how this issue is presented to the executive, it can be a good recruiting tool.

Another attractive recruitment tool for small companies is often found in the nonprofit sector. Many nonprofit organizations emphasize the job satisfaction realized from doing a job that also enables one to fulfill a social responsibility. For example, a position in a YMCA or a day care facility for the elderly can provide a double reward to the executive (i.e., both job satisfaction and the satisfaction of answering a societal need). The well-known for-profit ice cream company Ben & Jerry's highlighted the same issue in recruiting a new chief executive officer.

In addition, the recently enacted Small Business Job Protection Act of 1996 (SBJPA) and other new legislation provide tax relief and new savings opportunities for small businesses and the self-employed. With the new legislation, small businesses and the self-employed can set up pension plans that are simpler, less costly, and free of many of the rules associated with current plans (e.g., certain nondiscrimination rules and reporting requirements). Certain contribution ceilings and distribution penalties have been waived or eliminated for some top-paid employees as well. Such changes will result in additional recruitment incentives for small companies. Details will be covered in future supplements as the effects of the new legislation are seen in practice.

Q 12:6 How can small companies offer competitive executive retirement plans without incurring significant costs?

Several types of nonqualified plans for executives, such as the nonqualified supplemental executive retirement plan discussed in Question 9:39, 401(k) benefit plans discussed in Question 9:48, and Internal Revenue Code (Code) Section 457 plans for nonprofit companies discussed in Question 9:50 are useful for small companies. Because these plans need not be provided to non-executive employees, they can keep costs down.

Another advantage of these plans is that benefits can be tied to the achievement of specified company performance goals. For example, a 401(k) arrangement may provide matching funds to the executive subject to that executive's achieving a 10 percent increase in company earnings during the fiscal year. Nonfinancial goals can be used for this same purpose.

Q 12:7   When and how do family-owned companies provide stock to non-family members?

During a successful start-up or threshold phase of business growth, many entrepreneurial family-owned companies decide to provide additional stock ownership to family and non-family executives. This serves primarily to retain key executives to lead the company into future successful growth and development phases. There are six key ways to deliver stock ownership:

- Book value (Q 6:41)
- Phantom shares (Q 7:20)
- Restricted stock (Q 7:30)
- Stock options (Q 6:6, 6:14)
- Performance shares (Q 7:46)
- Nonqualified profit sharing (Q 4:9)

Individual awards are determined as a percentage of a predetermined target award or as a predetermined pro rata share of incremental profit.

Q 12:8   What total compensation strategies are used in small companies?

As discussed in Qs 12:4 and 12:6, small companies tend to use a higher number of stock option shares (as a percentage of the total shares outstanding) and lower levels of base salary and annual bonus than is the case in large companies. This concept is shown in the following table, which shows how company size can drive total compensation strategy.

Compensation Element	Small Companies	Medium Companies	Large Companies
Base salary	Low	Low	Average
Annual bonus	Low	Average	Average
Long-term/stock plans	Very high	High	Average
Benefits/perquisites	Average	Average	Average

Small companies use a strategy weighted in favor of long-term incentives because they can offer generous levels of potential award without any negative impact on the company income statement. Then if the small company goes public, executives can exercise the stock options and sell them on the stock market, where there is no negative impact on company cash flow. If the company remains private, most plans will require the executive to sell the shares back to the company. When this occurs, the company is, hopefully, in a better cash flow position than it was at the time the stock option was granted. Many private companies will structure plans so that they can control when the executive is allowed to sell shares back to the company.

Q 12:9   How do small, high-growth companies establish competitive values on executives when their companies are doubling in size every one or two years?

As discussed in Q 12:8, companies offer generous levels of stock options to reward executives for the rapid growth of an organization. With respect to total cash compensation, however, small companies are at a disadvantage if they establish targeted levels based on current revenues, because executive pay levels are scope-sensitive. As company sales increase, compensation also increases.

Example. A company has current sales of $20 million, but projects sales at $60 million in three years. The company needs to hire a new executive. If it establishes targeted total cash compensation at the $20 million sales level, then the executive could be paid below median market levels when the company reaches $60 million, unless pay increases were significant. The 1994 *Officer Compensation Report* (Panel Publishers/Aspen Publishers, Inc.) shows that the median base salary of a chief executive officer in a company with sales of $20 million is $170,000, while the same job in a company with sales of $60 million is $223,500, a difference of 31.5 percent.

Companies can overcome this problem by using projected sales when establishing targeted total cash compensation levels in high-growth companies.

Planning Tip. A good standard to use in establishing pay levels for the small, high-growth company is to use company sales that are projected for up to three years beyond the current date. For example, the company described in the Example above could use the three-year projected sales of $60 million to establish the targeted base salary level of its chief executive officer.

Q 12:10 Are design issues for annual incentive compensation plans different in the small company?

No, the design issues are the same, but the solutions to these design issues may be different.

Eligibility. In a large company, the number of executives that are offered participation in the annual incentive plan is approximately 0.5 percent to 1.0 percent of total employment. In a small company, the number of executives offered participation in the annual incentive plan is 5-10 percent of total employment.

Performance measures. Most medium and large companies use annual performance goals that are contained in the annual business plan (i.e., a performance-based plan that uses projected results at year-end). Most small companies review performance by looking back and making a judgment on what actually happened versus what should have happened (i.e., a discretionary plan).

Q 12:11 How are executive benefits and perquisites different in the small company?

Panel Publishers' *Report on Executive Perquisites and Benefits* provides survey data on the prevalence of these plans in small companies. The most frequent perquisites are a supplemental executive retirement plan and a company car, in addition to regular benefits of health, dental, life, and disability insurance, plus a 401(k) plan. Regulatory maximums on the amount of pre-tax employee contributions and tax-deductible company contributions to a 401(k) plan previously limited the value of such a plan to executives; therefore, the supplemental executive retirement plan (SERP) or excess plan had significant value (see Q 9:48). The recent SBJPA eliminated contribution ceilings for top-paid employees in some 401(k) plans.

The immediate effect of the new rules will be discussed in a future supplement.

New Venture Businesses

Q 12:12   How is incentive compensation structured in new venture businesses?

The most common definition of a new venture business is that it is a division or wholly owned subsidiary of a larger company, and that it operates in an industry that is not the same as the core business of the parent/owner. The financing for the new venture typically comes from the parent company or primary shareholder/owner. An example was the General Mills restaurant business, which was a separate venture from its core business of cereal and other store-bought foods. In this case, the restaurant venture became very successful and grew into a second core business for the company.

In new venture businesses, executive compensation can be structured in the same manner as in all other businesses, or the annual and long-term incentives can be combined and targeted payouts linked to the accomplishment of "milestone" objectives.

Example. A manufacturing company has a new venture into computer software. The software division has a new product that it wants to put into a regional test market and then market nationally. The test market phase will take two to two and one-half years (Milestone 1). The rollout nationally will take an additional three years (Milestone 2). The company can combine targeted income for each executive position from the short-term incentive plans and the long-term incentive plan and provide payment when and if each milestone is achieved. The company can also develop a payout schedule so that if one or both of the milestones are achieved in advance of the scheduled date, then a greater amount of incentive compensation is paid. Correspondingly, if one or both of the milestones are achieved, but well after the scheduled date, then less than the target incentive is paid.

Q 12:13   How are base salary and benefits structured in new venture businesses?

New venture companies typically have base salary, benefits, and perquisites that parallel parent company or general industry norms. In some situations, these companies must employ executives who can manage a business that will be five to ten times its current size in a short time (i.e., two to three years). New venture companies use two techniques to attract and retain key executives into this type of dynamic business environment:

1. Follow small company practices and project sales for the next three years, then establish base salary under the assumption that those sales will be achieved (see Q 12:9).

2. Link base salary increases to the successful accomplishment of the milestones.

Chapter 13

Board of Directors' Compensation

Public attention has intensified on the roles, responsibilities, and performance of company boards of directors. Director positions are becoming more difficult to fill, given the increased liability and time demands associated with corporate governance. This in turn has increased the importance of director compensation. Both the amounts and forms of compensation have changed significantly over the past several years. Amounts paid for the most common forms of director compensation—meeting fees and annual retainers—are increasing, as is the prevalence of stock-based plans and retirement plans for directors. This chapter covers current trends and issues in board compensation.

General Considerations 13-2
Outside vs. Inside Directors 13-3
Compensation Methods 13-6
Other Benefits 13-8

General Considerations

Q 13:1   How does a company choose the members of its board of directors?

Directors of a company do not apply; they are asked to serve. When they agree, they are then elected by the stockholders of that company. In private companies, the major stockholders usually function as executive officers and directors. In public companies, stock ownership plays a much smaller factor in the election of officers and there are a number of "outside" directors, as well as "inside" directors.

Q 13:2   What is the role of a company board of directors?

Members of a company board of directors share responsibilities such as the following:

1. Representing shareholders in ensuring that the activities of the business properly fulfill the company's objectives of providing a product or service to society, providing employment, and providing appropriate financial returns to shareholders.
2. Providing the chief executive officer (CEO) with advice and counsel on the strategic direction of the corporation.
3. Within their areas of expertise, providing other senior executives of the company with advice on specific company programs and activities (for example, financial statements, public relations activities, legal advice and counsel, employment relations).
4. Overseeing the activities of the company's auditors and financial department and the board audit committee. In this capacity, directors would typically review and endorse company investment policy, payment of dividends, and general utilization of financial resources.
5. Through a board compensation committee, approving the design of executive compensation programs, the appointment of key officers, specific compensation increases, stock awards, and other forms of remuneration for top executives.
6. Evaluating company products and services.

As policy makers and strategic planners, members of a company's board of directors play an extremely critical role in today's business environment. They are no longer "rubber stamps" to internal management policies. The number of organizational changes such as reorganizations, mergers, restructurings, and recapitalizations that have occurred in recent years has significantly increased the role of directors, as well as their compensation.

Outside vs. Inside Directors

Q 13:3 Why would a company choose to have outside directors?

As discussed in Chapter 2, an employee benefit plan must be administered by disinterested directors in order to take advantage of the Securities Exchange Commission (SEC) Rule 16b-3 exemption, which provides that grants of stock options and other securities under a plan to insiders will not be deemed to be purchases of those securities for purposes of determining Section 16(b) liability. In order to be disinterested, a director cannot be or have been granted or awarded stock or options under any discretionary company plan while acting as a director or for one year prior to becoming a director. Companies do not want to exclude their top management from participating in benefit plans in order to meet the "disinterested" standard, because they are the very people that companies most desire to motivate and retain through the use of the mechanism of executive compensation. Therefore, a company will ask people who do not work for the company—well-qualified "outsiders"—to sit on its board of directors and will pay them a special retainer and per-meeting fees.

Even for privately held companies for whom the Section 16 exemption is not relevant, disinterested directors are useful as a mechanism to insulate the company against shareholder derivative challenges to the amounts or types of executive compensation paid because courts apply the business judgment rule to the compensation decisions made by disinterested directors. Specifically, courts will assume that the disinterested directors used their best business judgment in deciding on the compensation paid.

Q 13:4 What are the typical compensation elements for directors?

Most companies compensate their directors with some combination of annual retainers for their services and additional fees for their attendance at actual committee meetings and meetings of the board. Many companies have also established certain special stock plans for their directors, and others give directors retirement benefits after a minimum period of service. Few provide directors with other benefits merely for serving as directors. For example:

Outside Director Compensation in a Small Company:

Annual retainer	$ 5,000
Committee fees ($500 per meeting × 10 meetings)	$ 5,000
TOTAL	$10,000*

*Plus reimbursement of all necessary expenses for meeting attendance.

Outside Director Compensation in a Large Company:

Annual retainer	$20,000
Committee fee ($1,000 per meeting × 10 meetings)	$10,000
TOTAL	$30,000*

*Plus some or all of the following benefits:

1. Retirement benefit equal to the amount of the annual retainer to be paid for the lesser of ten years or the total number of years of board service, upon reaching the retirement age of 70;

2. A one-time stock option grant of 1,000 shares of company stock with the same plan provisions (e.g., vesting, award period) as that provided to key executives; and

3. Reimbursement of all necessary expenses for attendance at company board meetings and committee meetings.

Q 13:5   Are inside directors compensated specifically for their activities as directors?

Directors who are also executive officers of a corporation are usually not given additional compensation such as annual retainers or meeting fees for acting as directors, although many companies adjust the base salaries of their executives who also serve on the board.

Q 13:6   How much do outside directors receive for their services?

The size of retainer and meeting fees paid to "outside" directors varies greatly from company to company. Unfortunately, it is statistically impossible to isolate the factors that determine the level of compensation accorded to directors, although the size of the company in question is one indicator. The average retainer in a small company is between $1,000 and $5,000, while the average retainer in a large company is $15,000 to $20,000. Typical board meeting fees range from $250 to $500 per meeting in a small company and $1,000 to $1,500 per meeting in a large company. Statistically, this means that the average director receives less than 5 percent of the compensation paid to a CEO of a Fortune 500 company. However, directors spend considerably less time on company matters than the CEO. A key factor in determining compensation can be the hourly rate of the director versus the hourly rate of the CEO. In most companies the hourly rate of the CEO would be higher because the responsibility of the job is greater than that of any individual director.

Most large companies also provide an additional retainer and/or meeting fees for service on a committee of the board. A typical committee retainer ranges between $2,000 and $5,000, while typical committee meeting fees run between $1,000 and $1,500 per meeting.

Note that the director may elect to defer receipt of these fees until a future date as agreed with the company. Similarly, the company may wish to pay the outside director his retainer in the form of stock options or restricted stock.

Compensation Methods

Q 13:7   How is director income taxed?

Directors are taxed on the amounts paid to them by the company, as on all other income. Outside directors are not, however, considered employees of the company; therefore, the company need not withhold taxes and social security payments from their fees. Instead, a director's income is considered self-employment income. This is the case regardless of whether she receives a retainer or fees for attending meetings or serving on committees.

Q 13:8   What methods are used in deferring compensation for directors?

There are two principal methods a company will use in deferring compensation of its board members. The most common method is simply to defer payment of the retainer and annual fees—as well as the taxes on such compensation—until a future date, which is typically retirement from the board or some other event. Another method is to allow a director to invest his deferred compensation in units of phantom stock, with the dividends credited on the purchased units being reinvested in additional units.

Q 13:9   In what types of performance-based plans do directors participate?

Under the new Section 16 rules, which are much more liberal than the old rules, a director's disinterested status will not be affected by her (1) merely being eligible to participate in a plan, (2) participation in a nondiscretionary plan, (3) participation in a participant-directed exempt plan, or (4) election to receive the annual retainer fee in securities.

A growing number of companies are offering their directors the opportunity to participate in capital accumulation plans. The company's rationale for doing this is similar to its motives for adopting plans for its officers and employees, which is to provide incentives to people who are performing services for the company by giving them the chance to participate in the growth that their performance and decisions may cause.

Stock options granted to outside directors are subject to the same tax rules as options granted to regular employees.

Q 13:10 How are stock options used in compensating directors?

Some companies offer directors the option to receive their annual retainer in the form of stock. In such a case, the fee is equal to the amount of the "spread" of a discounted stock option, the anticipated spread of an option granted at fair market value, or the grant value of restricted stock shares. For example, instead of paying a $10,000 fee to a director, a company could grant that director options to purchase 500 shares of stock with a market value of $12,500 ($25 per share) at a discount of $5 per share ($20 per share purchase price × 500 shares = $10,000), or grant the director 400 restricted shares (typically a three- to five-year restriction) also with a value of $10,000 (400 × $25 per share market value).

There are several significant benefits to using discounted stock options. The director is taxed on the compensation element (the amount of the spread), yet that director has effectively invested in stock using pre-tax dollars. Using the example above, assume that the director involved is in the 31 percent federal income tax bracket and a 10 percent state income tax bracket. If that director receives the $10,000 retainer in cash, only $5,900 would remain after taxes. Taking that $5,900 plus the additional $2,500 paid to exercise the options, the director would be able to purchase a total of only $8,400 in company stock. On the other hand, by choosing to receive discounted stock options, the director receives $12,500 in stock, for which a total of $6,600 (the $2,500 exercise price plus taxes of $4,100) is paid. As for the company, it has not only saved the cash it would have had to pay the director but it will also receive cash when the director exercises the option. In addition, the company has succeeded in giving the director a personal interest in the company that is more closely aligned with the interests of the company's stockholders.

Q 13:11　How do the Section 16 rules apply to directors' options?

Directors are insiders. The decision to receive the annual fee or retainer in the form of options is considered a purchase for purposes of SEC Section 16 and is matchable against any sale by that director of company securities within the six months before or after that purchase.

Q 13:12　Do companies provide "regular" stock plans for directors?

Yes. Many companies allow their directors to participate in restricted stock plans and tie the vesting of the stock to years of service on the board. Remember, though, that a director is not disinterested as to any plan in which he participates.

Q 13:13　Can tandem SARs/stock options be granted to directors?

Yes. Tandem SARs/stock options may be granted to directors; the SARs will be taxed in the same manner as if they were granted to company executives.

Other Benefits

Q 13:14　What other benefits are typically provided to directors?

Most publicly traded companies will provide outside directors with liability insurance and expense reimbursement, while others may also provide additional benefits such as medical insurance, life insurance, or retirement plans. The rationale for providing limited benefits, simply stated, is that the outside directors are not employees of the company but were asked to be directors as a result of their corporate expertise in their primary jobs, which provide them with the coverage they require.

Q 13:15   Do companies provide retirement benefits for their directors?

Many companies choose to provide directors with a special retirement plan. Companies usually make the benefit payable at age 65 or the normal retirement date, which is often later than age 65.

A typical retirement plan for an outside director would include provisions such as:

- A minimum service requirement for eligibility
- Increasing benefit levels based on the number of years, over the minimum number, served as a director
- A maximum benefit level equal to a specified percentage, often approaching 100 percent, of the retainer
- Forfeiture of rights if the director competes with or otherwise harms the company

Q 13:16   Can Keogh plans be utilized by outside board members?

Outside directors are considered to be self-employed, independent contractors and therefore are eligible to create a tax-qualified retirement plan (i.e., Keogh plan). They can contribute a portion of their fees to the plan. Larger deductions are available in some cases. Investment income on the amount contributed builds up tax-deferred with the director paying tax only as she receives payment.

Q 13:17   Can Keogh plans be utilized by insider board members?

Even where a company chooses to pay its inside directors special fees for serving as directors, Internal Revenue Service regulations prevent an insider board member (who is not considered a self-employed individual) from participating in a Keogh plan.

Q 13:18   What are some new trends in board of director compensation?

The most significant new trend for outside directors (other than those included in this chapter, such as retirement benefits and stock awards) is a benefit called the "legacy" grant. Legacy grants involve the promise of the company to pay, on the outside director's behalf, upon his death a substantial amount to a charitable organization specified by that director. The legacy grant is funded via the life insurance benefit concept, with the intent being that all or part of the legacy amount is funded by the cash value of the life insurance. For example, a company may offer an outside director the opportunity to provide a legacy grant of $250,000 to an educational institution or a nonprofit charity of her own choice, upon death. The company would then take out a life insurance policy on the executive, with the charity as the beneficiary, and fund payments/premiums with the cash value of the policy. Upon payment, the company and the former director would receive a rather significant public relations value from the activity.

The legacy grant concept is a significant recruiting tool for companies, helping them attract high quality directors to their organization.

Q 13:19   Do outside directors get perquisites?

Yes, many of the programs previously described in this chapter are good examples: legacy grants, life insurance, retirement, access to deferred compensation investments used by the company, and so forth. In addition, these directors often can travel first class or in company planes, are given liberal expense accounts, can use company products or services (if applicable), receive the same Christmas gifts that the company provides to its customers, and can be invited to company outings at various resorts or sporting events with all expenses paid.

Chapter 14

Executive Compensation in the Not-For-Profit Organization

There are a number of differences in the structure of executive compensation programs at the not-for-profit (or nonprofit) organization. The purpose of these organizations differs from that of the for-profit company, so it follows that the purposes and methods used to establish executive pay can also vary significantly.

General Considerations 14-1
Base Salary 14-6
Annual Incentives 14-7
Long-Term Incentives 14-9
Perquisites 14-10

General Considerations

Q 14:1 What is a not-for-profit company?

Not-for-profit companies are organizations that do not exist for the purpose of creating profit or "value for shareholders" and are defined in the various Internal Revenue Code (Code) sections as generally including the following:

501(c)(3) Organizations: Hospitals, religious and charitable organizations

501(c)(4) Organizations: Civic leagues or associations

501(c)(5) Organizations: Labor or agricultural organizations

501(c)(6) Organizations: Chambers of commerce, boards of trade, and business associations

501(c)(14) Organizations: Credit unions

Q 14:2 How does the mix of executive compensation elements differ in a not-for-profit company?

Executives of not-for-profit companies receive quite different compensation packages than do their counterparts in for-profit companies. Following are some of the compensation elements for nonprofit company executives:

1. Base salary: Typically, higher levels
2. Annual incentive: Typically, lower levels
3. Long-term incentive programs: Few if any such programs
4. Perquisites: Not as common
5. Benefits: Equal to or greater than those in for-profit companies

The reason for these differences in the mix of total compensation is threefold: Not-for-profits (1) are more regulated; (2) operate a personal service business where their purpose is to meet human needs rather than produce a product for profit; and (3) focus primarily on quality of service, not financial return to shareholders.

Q 14:3 How do the business objectives of executive compensation plans differ in a not-for-profit company?

Chart 14-1 shows how the different business objectives of nonprofit and for-profit companies can affect their determination of executive compensation elements. Although base salary and benefits tend to serve the same purposes in both organizations, annual incentive plans, long-term incentive plans, and perquisites can be very different. As can be seen from Chart 14-1, annual incentive plans typically have completely different performance measures in not-for-profit and for-profit organizations. While long-term incentive plans are not typically used in the not-for-profit company, they could have a useful business purpose and should be considered.

Chart 14-1

	For-Profit Company	*Not-for-Profit Company*
Base salary	Established by labor market, based on job value	Same
Annual incentive	Rewards for achieving additional profit	Rewards for achieving expense control
Long-term incentive	Additional rewards for achieving additional profit or stock growth	Rarely used because most organizations are not publicly owned
Benefits	Protection against financial hardship due to illness	Same
Perquisites	Convey status to senior executives	Not needed (e.g., country clubs rarely used to conduct business)

Example. A YMCA has a building campaign with two phases: Phase I is to raise money, and Phase II is the actual construction. Goals are established for both phases. A long-term incentive plan is established using the goals for Phase II:

1. Minimum goal: Meet building schedule with costs exceeding estimates by up to 5 percent.

2. Target goal: Meet building schedule within cost estimates.

3. Maximum goal: Meet building schedule under cost estimates.

If any of these goals is met, an incentive payout will be made as follows: $5,000 for achieving the minimum goal, $10,000 for the target goal, and $15,000 for the maximum.

Q 14:4　Does the size of the organization affect executive compensation in a not-for-profit organization?

Yes, two not-for-profit executives with the same position accountability but in different size organizations will likely have different total compensation. For example, a hospital administrator in a 100-bed hospital will make less total compensation than a hospital administrator with similar job responsibilities in a 1,000-bed hospital. The reason is a belief that the position in the 1,000-bed hospital has more complexity and a greater magnitude of accountability and impact on the organization. The same is true of an executive director in a YMCA with a $1 million budget versus the same job with a budget of $10 million. The director with the $10 million budget will make more total compensation.

Q 14:5　Does the type of not-for-profit organization affect the level of executive compensation?

Yes. For example, the executive director of a United Way agency will typically have a higher level of total compensation than the executive director of another similar organization. The reasons for this are size (see Q 14:4) and the fact that the primary comparisons of executive compensation in a not-for-profit organization are against other similar not-for-profits. In this example, executive compensation in other non-United Way agencies is not as relevant. The same is true when reviewing total compensation of a hospital administrator versus an executive director of a United Way agency. The primary labor market comparisons for the hospital administrator will be to other hospital administrators.

Another factor is that in for-profit companies, profit margins drive varying levels of executive compensation; that is, the industries with a higher profit margin tend to have higher levels of executive compensation. Profit margins do not drive executive compensation in not-for-profits because there is no profit. Of course, fundraising could be substituted for profit in driving executive pay levels in nonprofit organizations. (The higher the amount of funds raised, the higher the level of executive pay.)

Q 14:6 Does geographical location affect executive compensation in the not-for-profit company?

In contrast to the for-profit company, where geographical differences are rare, the not-for-profit organization will find that executive compensation is affected by geography. A not-for-profit executive does not typically transfer at the request of the organization, so there is no reason for these organizations to establish executive pay on the basis of a national labor market. A not-for-profit executive tends to be employed from the local labor market; therefore, local pay levels are a major factor in executive compensation along with size of the not-for-profit organization. (See Q 14:4.)

Q 14:7 What is the impact of recent legislation on not-for-profit organizations?

Of immediate effect is the Taxpayer Bill of Rights, which cracks down on wayward tax-exempt organizations engaging in questionable financial practices with respect to employee compensation and private inurement from funds meant to benefit the organization. The bill poses an excise tax on excess benefit transactions on or after September 14, 1995.

Excess benefit transactions are non-fair-market-value transactions, unreasonable compensation, or some transaction violating the prohibition on private inurement. Compensation is considered reasonable if approved by an independent board of directors or trustees (1) composed entirely of individuals not related to or in control of those persons exercising substantial authority over the organization's affairs, (2) who obtained and relied upon appropriate data regarding compensation levels at similar organizations, or (3) who adequately documented the basis for the compensation determination.

As for private inurement, organizations are eligible as tax-exempt only if no part of their net earnings inure to the benefit of any private shareholder or individual.

The Small Business Job Protection Act of 1996 (SBJPA) also has an effect on tax-exempt organizations, especially those with less than 100 employees. Under the SBJPA, after December 31, 1996, tax-exempt organizations can establish 401(k) plans for their employees. In addition, the definition of compensation is expanded to include elective deferrals (to calculate limits on qualified plan contributions and benefits). Effective for years beginning after December 31, 1997, compensation includes elective contributions to nonqualified deferred compensation plans of tax-exempt employers and state or local government (Section 457) plans.

Under the new act, tax-exempt organizations that qualify as small businesses (under 100 employees) can set up pension plans that are simpler, less costly, and free of many of the burdensome rules and regulations associated with current plan. This improves access for all taxpayers to retirement savings plans.

The true effects of the new legislation are yet to be felt. Company response to the new laws will be reported in future supplements as events unfold.

Base Salary

Q 14:8   How are base salary ranges established in not-for-profit companies?

The number of labor market surveys continues to increase in the not-for-profit industry, and these surveys serve as the primary basis for establishing competitive base salary ranges on executive as well as non-executive positions. Survey data are reported as averages (weighted averages) or in trend lines that compare total cash compensation (base salary plus annual incentive, if any) to a measure of scope such as annual budget or number of hospital beds.

Not-for-profit organizations use a second technique of internal job evaluation to drive decisions on base salary ranges. (See Q 3:3 for a description of internal job evaluation methods.) As is the case with the for-profit companies, the not-for-profits encounter discrepancies between results from internal job evaluation and results from the use of external labor market surveys. When this occurs, the first step is to review all assumptions to ensure that they are correct, then either to use broad salary ranges to accommodate different results on job values or to recognize that the ultimate criterion for valuing any job is its worth on the labor market.

Q 14:9 Are merit increases to base salary used in not-for-profit companies?

Yes. Merit increases are an important issue for executive and non-executive positions in a not-for-profit company because base salary is frequently the primary form of direct compensation. Also, merit increases can drive the value of indirect compensation plans like life or disability, which have benefits determined as a multiple of base salary. As discussed in Q 14:2, not-for-profit organizations tend to have lower annual incentive compensation and little long-term incentive compensation; thus, merit increases are a primary way to motivate executives.

Annual Incentives

Q 14:10 What is the prevalence of annual incentive plans in not-for-profit companies?

Annual incentive plans are not as prevalent in nonprofits as in for-profit companies. When such plans are provided, the amount of incentive is typically less in the not-for-profit organization. As shown in Chart 14-2, approximately 65 percent of nonprofits surveyed used some form of annual incentive plan in 1994; compare this to the 96 percent used in for-profit companies. It is relevant to note, however, that the 65 percent usage of annual incentive plans in nonprofits represents a 13 percent increase during the last three years.

Chart 14-2. Prevalence of Annual Incentive Compensation Plans

	Percentage of Companies with Annual Incentive Compensation Plans	
	1991	*1994*
For-profit companies	92	96
Not-for-profit companies	52	65

Q 14:11 Does the size of the annual incentive award in the not-for-profit company differ from that in the for-profit company?

Yes. As shown on Chart 14-3, the award for a chief executive officer in a for-profit company will typically be 20-25 percent higher than the similar position in a not-for-profit company. The same is true for other executive positions.

Chart 14-3. Average Size of Annual Incentive Awards

	Targeted annual incentive for CEO
For-profit companies	50% of base salary
Not-for-profit companies	40% of base salary

As indicated in Q 14:7, more not-for-profit organizations are surveying total cash compensation (base salary plus annual incentive). As a result, the current trend toward increased usage of this executive compensation element is expected to continue. As more not-for-profits observe that annual incentive plans are the norm, more new plans will be implemented.

Q 14:12 What performance measures are typically used in the annual incentive plans of not-for-profit companies?

Performance measures are qualitative and quantitative. The most common qualitative measure is patient/user service evaluations or ratings, while the most common quantitative measure is budget/expense control. Other performance measures in not-for-profit companies are similar to those in for-profit companies. These are discussed in Qs 4:36, 4:37, and 4:42.

Q 14:13 How is eligibility determined for annual incentive plans in not-for-profit companies?

Typically, eligibility is granted only to the chief executive officer or executive director and key department heads or officers who report directly to the senior executive.

Q 14:14   What regulations guide incentive compensation plans for the not-for-profit company?

Code Section 403(b) describes tax-deferred annuities that can be used by schools and Code Section 501(c)(3) organizations (e.g., the YMCA and other United Way agencies). A tax-deferred plan under Code Section 403(b) is essentially the same as the 401(k) retirement plan used by for-profit companies.

Code Section 457 is the primary regulation covering the not-for-profit company. It establishes limitations on the amount of deferred compensation for executives in not-for-profit organizations. The 457 plan described in Qs 9:49 and 9:50 is essentially a top-hat plan that picks up where a 403(b) plan leaves off. In other words, it allows the not-for-profit organization to have a SERP (supplemental executive retirement plan) that enables company executives to overcome regulatory limits (in the 401(k) and 403(b) plans) and to build an adequate retirement income.

The SBJPA has made certain changes to Code Section 457, particularly as it relates to elective contributions made after December 31, 1997. These changes will be discussed in a future supplement.

Long-Term Incentives

Q 14:15   What types of long-term incentive plans are prevalent in not-for-profit companies?

As with for-profit companies, the most common form of long-term incentive in not-for-profit companies is the stock option. The phantom equity plan is the second most common form of long-term incentive plan. As shown in Chart 14-4, few not-for-profit companies use any form of long-term incentive.

Chart 14-4. Long-Term Incentives in Not-for-Profit Companies

Form of Long-Term Incentive	Prevalence in Not-for-Profit Companies
Stock options	34%
Phantom stock	26%
Performance shares	18%

Perquisites

Q 14:16   What types of perquisites are prevalent in not-for-profit companies?

Few, if any, perquisites are used in not-for-profit companies. For this reason, the subject is rarely included in a survey. Favorable parking, full payment at association meetings, free attendance at fund-raising events such as dinners or golf outings, and free or preferential use of the not-for-profit company facilities are common. Typical perquisites in a for-profit company, such as a company car, club memberships, first-class air travel, or financial planning, are not needed in not-for-profits, since in most cases their facilities are local.

The one perquisite that is used by a small number of not-for-profits is the Section 457 plan referenced in Q 14:13. These are sometimes established as combination severance/supplemental retirement plans. Such a severance pay plan is not subject to the Section 457 prescribed limitations on company contributions.

Q 14:17   What are the requirements of a SERP for executives in a not-for-profit organization?

The Internal Revuenue Code uses the term "bona fide severance plan," which can be used by the not-for-profit company as a SERP. IRS notices provide some guidance on requirements that need to be met if a bona fide severance plan is to be used as a SERP:

1. The plan must be limited to a few select individuals.

2. Company benefits are limited to twice the amount of the final year's compensation.

3. Individual executives can make their own contributions.

4. No distributions are permitted until termination (voluntary or involuntary).

These plans may or may not be placed in a rabbi trust.

For additional guidance, the services of a qualified professional should be obtained.

Chapter 15

Special Early Retirement Programs

A company that needs to reduce staff or reorganize may offer certain employees the opportunity to retire early. Generally, early retirement arrangements are made available only to those employees who meet specified age and service requirements (such as age 55 with 20 years of service). Such arrangements also typically allow retirement benefits to be initiated earlier than specified in the existing retirement plan. This chapter discusses early retirement arrangements, explaining their rationale and detailing associated benefits, agreements by employees in exchange for early retirement, consequences for company and employee, and investment and ERISA implications.

Future supplements to this work will update this information as well as discuss recent major legislation with some effect on early retirement arrangements. For example, future updates will cover the waiver for 1997 through 1999 of the 15 percent excise tax on excess distributions from qualified plans, tax-sheltered annuities, and IRAs, as well as certain taxes eliminated or reduced on 401(k) lump-sum distributions.

Q 15:1   What are special early retirement programs?

Also known as early retirement "window periods," early retirement programs are one-time opportunities for employees to elect retirement at a younger age than normally specified in a company's pension plan. The employee must make this election during a designated period (window period) and is typically eligible for retirement benefits per plan formulas or at an enhanced benefit level. The special election will also typically allow for the retirement benefit to be initiated at a time that is earlier than the normal retirement age in the plan (e.g., age 50 rather than age 60).

> **Example 1.** A company offers employees an opportunity to retire early under the company's pension plan at age 55 (rather than age 60) if they have 20 years of service. Retirement benefits are started immediately based on the pension plan's normal formula.

> **Example 2.** A company offers an enhanced early retirement benefit to any employee who elects normal early retirement under existing plan provisions at age 55 with 20 years of service. The enhanced benefit is that no actuarial reduction will be applied to the employee's retirement calculation as normally would be the case under the plan for any early retirement election.

These programs can be applied to qualified pension plans or to non-qualified special executive retirement plans (SERPs).

Q 15:2   Why do companies offer special early retirement programs?

Typically, such plans are offered because of a reorganization and/or downsizing of the company's operations, which creates the need for fewer employees. The automation of work processes or the discontinuation of company products/services can also create the need for companies to use these programs.

As competition increases in a business, companies are finding that they need to conduct their business in different and more efficient ways. Sometimes this results in the need for fewer employees. Rather than lay off or terminate employees, companies offer special early retirement programs, so that longer service employees can pursue other employment or non-employment career interests.

Q 15:3   Do companies offer special severance programs with special early retirement programs?

Yes. Companies typically do this as encouragement and motivation for employees to accept the program, particularly if the purpose of the program is to downsize the work force. In many early retirements, the employee is required to find another position or adjust to a new career or lifestyle. There is a need to help the employee bridge this gap by providing him with the time and financial support to make the adjustment. Most employees who accept these programs decide either to look for another position or to start their own businesses.

Example. An eligible executive is provided with a one-year continuation of base salary if a special early retirement program is accepted.

Q 15:4   What are the typical severance benefits used with a special early retirement program?

A review of numerous early retirement program provisions shows that companies will normally provide special early retirement program participants with one of two special benefits whenever severance is provided as part of an early retirement program:

1. Additional eligibility for the company's regular severance program. (Severance is not normally given to retirees.)
2. An enhanced severance program that is a one-time program with more favorable benefits than the company's regular severance program.

Q 15:5   How do companies fund the costs of these programs?

Companies will take a one-time charge to earnings in the year that the special program is provided. This charge is then shown on their balance sheet as an accrued liability. Estimates are required on the number of employees who will accept the program, and actual acceptance is then reviewed after the fact to ensure that accrued funds are sufficient. Adjustments could be required after final costs are calculated.

Q 15:6 What, if any, are the negative consequences to companies that implement special early retirement programs, and how can these consequences be handled?

One important consideration is the possibility that the company will lose a large number of executives or non-executives who have crucial skills, or will lose all or most of its managers in a given department because they are offered and accept the program.

> **Example.** A company offers a special early retirement program to employees age 55 and with 20 years of service. The finance department has five executives eligible for the program: the chief financial officer, the treasurer, the controller, the tax executive, and the information services executive. All accept the program.

Companies must evaluate the potential consequences of special early retirement programs before they offer them, so that they can avoid a negative impact on company operations. A company can offset this potential negative impact either by evaluating the qualifications of replacement candidates within the organization or by structuring the special program so that there is time to find replacement candidates from outside the company. It is also possible that a reorganization or downsizing will result in the elimination of certain executive positions; these executives can be given eligibility in the program.

Another possible situation is that certain jobs, vacated by the acceptance of a special early retirement program, could be combined or even eliminated after the company knows which executives accept the program. These pivotal issues should all be evaluated before a program is offered.

Q 15:7 Are there any negative consequences to employees who accept a special early retirement program?

Yes. An employee, especially an executive, might have a pension plan that pays a lump-sum benefit. Such an individual who wishes to accept early retirement must also consider whether current investments and investment strategy need to be revised. The risk for growth of these funds into continued or future retirement income would be transferred to the individual at early retirement.

Another factor is that these early retirement programs rarely provide individuals with their full amount of required retirement income, particularly when there is no eligibility for social security benefits. Thus executives will typically need to develop supplemental amounts of retirement income and/or secure another job until they begin full retirement. These programs require a great deal of personal financial planning before an individual can decide whether to accept or reject early retirement.

Q 15:8   What are the ERISA implications of a special early retirement program under a qualified plan?

A company will want to maintain the qualified status of its employee retirement plan and thereby be able to take a tax deduction in the year that it makes a contribution to the employee pension plan. To accomplish this, the company must meet the requirements of ERISA. A number of issues must be considered by companies who are considering a special early retirement program within their qualified pension plan:

1. *Plan amendment.* Typically, companies will need to amend their qualified plans in order to offer a special early retirement program, because under regular plan provisions, the special program is not authorized. The amendment will simply allow for a subsidized benefit during the early retirement period.

   Example 1. A special early retirement may be at age 55 rather than age 65. Therefore, a special contribution must be allowed under the plan to fund the special/earlier benefit. An amendment is required in the plan.

   Example 2. A qualified plan allows for an early retirement at age 55 with an actuarial reduction in retirement benefits. A special early retirement offers early retirement at age 55 with no actuarial reduction. This requires a plan amendment.

2. *Disclosure.* The special early retirement opportunity must be communicated to all plan participants. This does not present a problem prospectively; however, it can be a problem retrospectively.

Example. An executive decides to take early retirement with actuarial reduction under normal plan provisions at age 55 with 20 years of service in March of a given year. The company announces a special enhanced early retirement benefit with no actuarial reduction in September of the same year. The employee can claim that the company was "considering" the enhancement in March, but failed to communicate this to the employee. The employee could bring a lawsuit against the retirement plan administrators claiming that they did not fulfill their obligation of communicating planned changes in the early retirement provision of the qualified pension plan.

3. *Discrimination as to benefits.* ERISA requires that a qualified plan not discriminate with respect to "highly compensated employees" (as defined in ERISA) versus lower-paid employees. If most of the employees who are eligible for a special early retirement program are highly paid executives, then the special program could be offering benefits that discriminate in favor of the executives.

Another dimension of this section in the ERISA regulations is the acceptance of a special early retirement program. If most of the employees who accept the special program are lower-paid employees, then the plan could no longer meet the discrimination requirements of ERISA, since there may be too many highly paid employees who continue in the pension plans.

Example 1. A company offers pension plan participants the opportunity to accept a special early retirement program if they are age 55 with 20 years of service. Most of the employees who fit this definition are highly paid executives. This plan could be in violation of the ERISA regulations on discrimination.

Example 2. A company offers pension plan participants the opportunity to accept a special early retirement program if they are age 55 with 20 years of service. Most of the employees who accept this offer are highly paid executives. This plan could be in violation of the ERISA regulations on discrimination after the acceptances.

4. *Partial termination of a plan.* Another ERISA problem that can be triggered by a special early retirement program is that if too many participants accept early retirement, then the plan can

be deemed terminated, and those "affected participants" (who accept the early retirement) must be given full vesting of accrued benefits under the qualified pension plan. This ERISA regulation seems redundant since the provisions of most special early retirement programs typically include full vesting of accrued benefits anyway.

Example. A company offers pension plan participants a special early retirement program with a benefit equal to their accrued pension with no actuarial reduction, if they have reached age 55 and have 20 years of service. The vesting requirement in the company's plan is five years of service. Even if this plan is deemed to be partially terminated, the company has no problem: Because eligibility for early retirement is only after 20 years of service, those who elect the special benefit are already fully vested (five years of service).

Q 15:9 Do companies require employees who elect a special early retirement to sign non-compete and/or non-litigation agreements?

Yes, in return for special retirement and/or special severance benefits, employees will typically be asked to sign an agreement that prohibits them from taking a similar position with direct competitors and using any company confidential information that the employee had access to during employment. These agreements will also include a provision that prohibits the employee from filing a lawsuit against the company for any reason. The reason for these agreements is simply that companies believe they are giving the employee some special consideration/benefit and expect some special consideration in return.

Q 15:10 Do companies provide medical benefits with a special early retirement program?

The company's existing plan language on the availability of benefits to retirees will typically be used for any special program. In other words, an early retiree is a retiree and is eligible for any retiree medical benefits.

If severance is given with the special early retirement program, then the benefits of an active employee will normally be continued during the severance period, and the employee will then be switched to the retiree medical coverage at the end of the severance period.

Chapter 16

U. S. Executives Working Overseas

This chapter defines and shows sample policies of the various types of executive expatriate compensation programs to include foreign service premiums; housing, cost of living, relocation, and education allowances; language training; home leave; company cars; and other perquisites typical for executives on overseas assignment. The critical issue of tax equalization is described, including definitions of hypothetical home country tax and home country tax withholding, and how these programs help the executive cope with double taxation (home country and foreign country) while working overseas. The final section of the chapter discusses questions on special compensation to include protection from currency fluctuation, stock appreciation rights, and other forms of long-term income while on overseas assignment, and "net-to-net" compensation plans.

General Considerations 16-2
Tax Considerations 16-9
Special Compensation 16-16

General Considerations

Q 16:1   What is an executive expatriate?

The term "expatriate" refers to an individual who is assigned to a position located outside of his home country. Home country typically refers to the country of natural (by birth) citizenship, and is typically the current place of residence for the individual. An executive expatriate is considered an officer or key manager within a company and will normally be provided with special allowance or benefits/perquisites that are equal to or greater than those provided to non-executive expatriates. For example, the executive expatriate may be given a higher housing allowance or better company car than the non-executive expatriate.

Q 16:2   What are the typical elements of an executive expatriate compensation package?

Executive compensation packages vary by company size and company culture. Typically, the larger the company the more structured the expatriate package. The smaller the company the more expatriate benefits are determined by negotiation. Company culture is a factor because it will drive the level of expatriate benefit. For example, a paternalistic company with a "family" environment will tend to ensure that the executive expatriate is reimbursed dollar for dollar for any extra costs, while a large company will establish expatriate allowances from tables and not try to achieve any dollar-for-dollar reimbursement. The most common strategy is to "keep the executive expatriate whole" in comparison to other similar executives who are not on overseas assignment.

A good definition of the term "keep whole" is that the executive expatriate will "neither gain nor lose total compensation because of the overseas assignment."

Given these general parameters, the most common elements in an executive expatriate program are as follows:

- Foreign service premium (and, on occasion, a hardship allowance)
- Cost of living allowance

- Housing allowance
- Relocation allowance
- Education allowance
- Language training
- Home leave
- Tax equalization
- Company car
- Club membership
- Supplemental medical

Q 16:3   What is a foreign service premium?

A foreign service premium is a percentage of base salary, 5 to 15 percent, that is provided to the executive expatriate during the duration of the overseas assignment, but it does not continue after repatriation back to the home country. It is intended to motivate the executive to accept the relocation to the foreign country (particularly if there is a "career risk" of being out-of-sight, out-of-mind of the top officers in the company), and to help the executive maintain a higher standard of living in the foreign country—typically the overseas executive will need to increase the amount of customer and/or employee entertaining.

Q 16:4   What is a hardship allowance?

A hardship allowance is provided in addition to a foreign service premium in those countries where the standard of living is considerably below that of the home country. The hardship premium is typically 10 to 15 percent of base salary and is provided for the duration of the overseas assignment. Like the foreign service premium, the hardship allowance discontinues upon repatriation back to the home country.

Q 16:5   What is a cost of living allowance?

A cost of living allowance (COLA) is designed to offset additional costs incurred by the executive expatriate in the overseas country.

The allowance is determined from published tables (e.g., ORC in New York City, AIRINC in Washington, D.C., Runzheimer in Rochester, Wisconsin, and similar organizations). The tables measure "spendable income," which includes goods and services such as food, clothing, recreation, insurance, and transportation. Spendable income does not include income that the executive expatriate uses for such things as housing, education, or taxes.

Spendable income tables compare the price of goods and services in the executive's home country versus those in the overseas country and establishes the difference, which is then provided to the executive tax-free in a monthly allowance. If the tables show that the price of goods and services is lower in the overseas country, then there is no allowance.

Because prices continually change, these tables are updated monthly; it is possible that the allowance could vary from month to month. For example, the costs of food and clothing could be increasing more rapidly in the executive's home country than in the overseas country, which could cause the tables to show a smaller difference in spendable income, which then lowers the cost-of-living allowance. Employee relations problems can, however, result if the executive suddenly has a lower allowance and less money to spend on goods and services; therefore, most companies will not implement monthly table changes until there is a significant difference (i.e., 4 to 5 percent), and they will give the expatriate two to three months' advance notice. Another common practice is to review the cost of living tables quarterly or semi-annually and make adjustments only two to four times a year, again with significant notice.

The term "tax free" means that if a cost-of-living allowance results in additional taxable income to the executive (which it typically does), any increase in tax owed by the executive (in either the home country or the overseas country) is paid for by the company. This calculation is included in the company's tax equalization policy (see Q 16:12).

Cost-of-living allowances are typically calculated in home company currency but paid in the overseas country's local currency since the allowance is normally spent at the overseas location. This can present a problem to the executive expatriate if the currency exchange rate between the home country and the overseas country becomes unfavorable (i.e., the home country currency exchange rate produces less of a cost-of-living allowance simply due to the fluctuating values of currency). Companies may therefore have exchange rate protection if the COLA tables are only published in home country currency (see Q 16:14).

Q 16:6   What is a housing allowance?

The concept of the housing allowance is to reimburse the executive expatriate for the difference between "assumed monthly housing costs at the home country" (monthly mortgage payment), and the actual monthly housing costs at the overseas country, with a maximum established for the overseas housing costs. Tables are published by firms like ORC, AIRINC, and Runzheimer (see Q 16:5). There is the obvious potential of a debate between the executive expatriate and the company on what the maximum housing costs should be at the overseas country. Companies need to establish a policy on this issue before they offer the overseas assignment to the executive expatriate.

The assumed monthly housing costs at the home country are established in the tables by analyzing the executive's level of income, home country location, and number of persons in the family who live in the current home. This number will often be close to the amount of foreign service premium.

Example. An executive with a base salary of $150,000 from the United States is given an overseas assignment in England. The executive is told she will receive a 10% foreign service premium ($15,000 annually or $1,250 per month). In addition, the executive is provided with a housing allowance at the overseas location in the amount of 50,000 pounds sterling per year or 4,167 pounds sterling per month minus assumed monthly housing costs in the home country of $1,200 (determined from tables). Under current currency exchange rates, the $1,200 is equal to approximately 720 pounds sterling. Therefore, the executive's housing allowance is 3,447 pounds sterling (4,167 – 720 = 3447).

In this example, the executive expatriate would probably use the 3,447 pounds sterling housing allowance and most of the foreign service premium to pay for housing at the overseas location. Note that the hypothetical housing cost of $1,200 is approximately equal to the foreign service premium of $1,250.

Thus, an alternative approach to the combination of foreign service premium and housing allowance is simply to combine the two and provide the executive expatriate with free housing at the overseas location, but with a maximum.

Example. An executive with a base salary of $150,000 from the United States is given an overseas assignment in England. The executive is told he will receive free housing at the new assignment but that the maximum payment by the company for this housing will be 50,000 pounds sterling per year, or 4,167 pounds sterling per month. The company pays no foreign service premium, but reimburses the executive the full amount of the monthly housing allowance of 4,167 pounds sterling. The result is free housing at the overseas location.

Q 16:7 Do executive expatriates receive reimbursement of any home sale or other relocation costs when they take an overseas assignment?

Yes, home sale benefits are typically the same as that provided for relocations with home sale within the home country, plus there are some additional reimbursements provided for expenses that are unique to international relocations.

Companies with a relocation policy that includes home sales will typically reimburse employees for costs associated with the home sale, such as real estate costs and closing costs, and in some large companies will even have loss-on-sale protection programs. For example, if the appraised value of the home is less than the amount that the employee paid for the home, the company will reimburse the difference or some percentage of the difference.

Other typical reimbursements in company relocation policies include:

- Home-finding trip for executive and spouse to the overseas location
- Shipment costs of all household belongings

- Business class air travel for the family to the overseas location
- Storage of some furniture during the overseas assignment
- Temporary living expenses for the employee and family prior to arrival of household goods
- Shipment of pets and/or other special handling items (e.g., art work, statues)
- Miscellaneous expense allowance (e.g., one month's salary for use in fixing up the new home)

In the case of an executive expatriate who leases an apartment, the company would pay for any fees associated with lease termination.

Companies that do not have a relocation policy will need to determine whether they will provide (or negotiate) the reimbursement of these standard relocation costs.

Other typical reimbursements unique to international relocations are:

1. *Protection against capital gains tax upon sale of home.* The typical criteria for this reimbursement are:
   a. The protection only applies on the difference between the purchase price and sale price of the executive's current home.
   b. The minimum waiting period applicable to the sale of capital assets is met.
   c. The home is the executive expatriate's primary residence.
2. *Costs/fees associated with the rental of the executive's principal residence during the overseas assignment.* This is normally in lieu of any other home sale assistance from the company.
3. *Appliance allowance for the new home at the overseas location.* This is frequently necessary because the electric systems at the overseas location are different from those in the executive's home country; therefore, the executive's current appliances will not work at the new location.
4. *Costs/fees associated with passports, visa, work permits, etc.* Such costs are normally a business expense.

All of the reimbursements under a home sale/relocation for executive expatriates are part of the tax equalization program provided by the company.

Q 16:8   What is a home rental program?

An executive expatriate who decides not to sell his primary residence may either leave the home unoccupied or rent it. If it is left unoccupied, he may want to pay someone to maintain the home (e.g., cutting the grass, providing pest control, periodic inside-home inspections, and repairs). Most companies will reimburse the executive for these costs.

In the case of home rental, the executive expatriate will contract with a home management firm to rent the home, and would be reimbursed for rental fees, outside maintenance, and inside repairs. There is normally a limit for these costs such as one or two months' rent value per year.

Q 16:9   What is an education allowance?

When an executive expatriate relocates her family to an overseas location, the children need to be enrolled in a school with an educational curriculum similar to that in the home country. These schools may be private and have tuition fees or similar fees for books, labs, etc. Any cost associated with maintaining the child's educational advancement as it would have been in the home country are reimbursed by the company under an education allowance program.

Q 16:10   What is language training?

This is a common reimbursement to an executive expatriate for all costs incurred while learning the language at the new overseas location. It applies to the executive and his family as well. Costs for the executive are a business expense, while costs for the family can either be business (particularly if the spouse is expected to entertain local customers or employees) or part of the relocation program, which is designed to help the family adapt to the new culture and environment.

Q 16:11   What is home leave?

Home leave is intended to allow the executive expatriate and family to reunite ties with family and friends back at the home country. It is normally provided in conjunction with vacation, and reimburses the executive for all travel costs (business class airfare), plus car rental and hotel and meals for any non-vacation days. When home leave is taken, there is frequently a business day or two to visit the company home office in the home country. One trip per year is the norm, and all expatriate allowances are maintained during the home leave.

Some expatriates have children attending college while the executive is on overseas assignment. In these situations, companies will allow three or four return trips home for the student-child at major holidays and semester breaks.

Executive expatriates will often wish to combine tour packages with their home leave (e.g., one week at an island resort that is on the way back to the home country). In these cases, companies will provide reimbursement up to the cost of a round-trip business class airline ticket for the executive and family.

Example. The round-trip business class airfare for an executive expatriate and family is $4,000. The executive wishes to have the family take a resort island tour package in combination with round-trip coach airfare while on home leave. The cost for executive and family is $5,000. The company would reimburse the executive for $4,000.

Home leave may subject the executive to additional tax liability. If this is the case, most companies will assume this additional tax liability.

Tax Considerations

Q 16:12   What is tax equalization?

The objective of a tax equalization policy is to insure that the executive expatriate will pay the same federal and state tax while on overseas assignment as would have been paid if the executive had been paid the same direct compensation (excluding expatriate program allowances) and stayed working in the home country (i.e., the executive expatriate will neither gain nor lose as the result of the overseas assignment). Companies will use international CPA firms to calculate the following:

1. *Hypothetical home country income.* The amount of income that the executive expatriate would have had if he or she had worked and lived in the home country during the previous tax year. It includes the following:

   - Base salary
   - Annual incentive
   - Long-term incentives/stock awards that were an ordinary income tax event to the executive that year
   - Imputed income on home country perquisites, supplemental life insurance, etc.
   - Capital gains and capital losses incurred by the executive that year in the home country
   - Exemptions allowed by home country tax laws
   - Itemized or standard deduction amounts allowed under home country tax laws
   - Any other income or deduction normally taken by the executive under home country tax laws (e.g., gains or losses from rental of a second home, dividends)

   Any allowances or reimbursements provided by the company under the executive expatriate program are excluded.

2. *Hypothetical home country tax.* This calculation represents the amount of federal and state tax that the executive expatriate would have paid had she lived in the home country during each year of the overseas assignment. The hypothetical tax does not include any allowances or reimbursements provided under the expatriate compensation program.

3. *Hypothetical home country withholding tax.* An estimate of the deductions to the executive expatriate's income that would be required to offset the hypothetical tax calculated from the hypothetical income, this is based on the withholding allowances outlined in the home country tax law.

The amount of hypothetical withholding tax is made equal to the hypothetical tax, which then becomes the actual tax obligation of the executive expatriate each year of the overseas assignment. Any actual tax obligations beyond this amount will be reimbursed to the executive.

4. *Foreign taxes.* Foreign taxes levied on the executive expatriate in the overseas country (or any other country where business is conducted by the executive) will also be paid by the company. Executive expatriates may be subject to "double taxation" from both home country and overseas country on the same income. Companies will typically pay any foreign country tax assessed to the executive expatriate.

One way to summarize is as follows:

Actual U.S. tax to be paid by executive
Actual foreign tax to be paid by executive
= Amount company reimburses or pays for executive

The company is taking on significant financial support for the executive; therefore, it will require the executive to maintain adequate and accurate financial records. Home country or overseas country tax obligations incurred by the spouse are typically the responsibility of the executive and spouse.

Q 16:13 What is tax-free income?

This refers to the company practice of tax gross-up, and is designed to insure that the executive does not pay any additional taxes due to the allowances and reimbursements provided by the expatriate program.

For example, if an executive is provided with a $2,000 per month housing allowance, she will have $24,000 added to annual income and will be required to pay taxes (federal and state if applicable) on this amount. Under a tax gross-up (or tax-free) policy, the company will calculate the amount of this tax given the executive (e.g., adjusted gross income, exemptions, deductions) and pay this amount to tax authorities on behalf of the executive. This tax gross-up amount also becomes additional income to the executive, and the company will perform the same calculation on this amount and pay the tax on behalf of the executive (also known as the tax on the tax). In some cases there is a tax gross-up on a tax gross-up. Most companies will have to limit the tax gross-up calculation to two or three times. The overall effect of the tax gross-up is that allowances or reimbursements under the expatriate program are tax free.

Q 16:14 What is spendable income?

These are items that an expatriate purchases with disposable income or income that is left after paying/allocating income to federal and state taxes, housing costs, benefits, and personal savings. It is used to establish a cost-of-living allowance for the executive expatriate. Spendable income includes the following:

- Food—both at home and away from home
- Clothing
- Recreation
- Personal care
- Commuting and transportation
- Household furnishings and maintenance
- Alcohol/tobacco
- Medical expenses outside of insured plan reimbursement

The process used to measure these items is as follows:

1. Spendable income is identified by level of base salary.
2. On-site surveys are taken at the home country and the overseas country by pricing a "market basket" of representative items in each of the above categories.
3. An index is developed, typically with the home country location considered 100% and the overseas country as some percentage of 100%, e.g., 110%.
4. The index is multiplied by the amount of spendable income to determine the executive expatriate's cost of living allowance.
5. The allowance is then converted to local currency used in the overseas country.

Where the index is less in the overseas country, there is simply no supplemental allowance given to the expatriate (see Q 16:5).

Q 16:15   What are foreign earned income exclusions?

A U.S. resident must pay an income tax on payments made for services rendered in the United States and, if a non-resident, on payments made for performing services outside of the United States If the foreign country where the services are performed also levies an income tax, then there is double taxation; however, the United States allows taxpayers to elect and claim a credit or deduction on their U.S. income tax form for foreign earned income paid or accrued during the tax year if they meet certain criteria:

1. The taxpayer is a U.S. citizen who has a foreign tax home, defined as a principal place of employment.

2. The U.S. citizen is a bona fide resident of the foreign country, generally meaning that the executive must reside in the foreign country for an entire taxable year.

Example. A U.S. executive moves to Germany in July 1996. Can she claim a deduction for foreign earned income in 1996? The answer is no, but if the executive remains in Germany through 1997, she can file an amended return for 1996 to claim a deduction, because she became a bona fide resident during 1997. The executive was also a bona fide resident during 1997 and can claim a deduction for foreign earned income for this year as well.

The maximum amount of this foreign earned income deduction is $70,000 per taxable year. The term "earned income" refers to salaries, bonuses, overseas premiums and allowances, home leave payments, and tax equalization payments.

In addition, executive expatriates can deduct "reasonable" housing allowances, up to $30,000 per year, that exceed a base housing amount equal to 16 percent of the salary of a U.S. government employee, GS-14, step 1.

The amount of foreign earned income excluded from an executive expatriate's U.S. income cannot exceed the total foreign income earned.

Example. An executive expatriate has foreign earned income as follows:

Base salary	$100,000
Bonus	$ 25,000
Housing allowance	$ 40,000
COLA allowance	$ 10,000
Other allowances	$ 10,000
Total foreign earned income	$185,000
Foreign earned income exclusion	($70,000)
Housing exclusion ($40,000 minus base housing amount of $10,000)	($30,000)
Total foreign income exclusion	($100,000)

Q 16:16   How can executive expatriates avoid taxes when on overseas assignment?

Tax evasion is against the law, but tax avoidance is not. There are three primary methods used by expatriates to avoid taxation:

1. Reclassifying executive expatriate allowances;
2. Changing the country that pays income to the executive expatriate; and
3. Deferring executive expatriate income.

Reclassifying allowances. These actions have the effect of providing the executive expatriate with the same benefit or allowance, but in a different form that is allowed by the local country. Some experts in this field have said that it simply means "calling it something different," but in fact the benefit received is coming from a completely different source.

Example 1. Companies can own or lease housing, and then provide it to the executive expatriate, rather than a housing allowance. In many countries this action results in preferential or lower taxation from the overseas country and the United States.

Example 2. In some overseas countries, allowances for things such as education or home leave are not taxable by the overseas country if paid directly by the company rather than as an allowance to the executive.

Changing the country that pays the income. Many overseas countries determine taxation on the basis of the number of days spent working in their country. This leads to a practice of paying the executive expatriate in Country *A*, only for the time he worked in Country *A*. Other names for these payments are "offshore payments" or "dual contracts."

Example 1. An executive expatriate with an overseas residence in Japan spends 25 percent of his working days in other southeast Asian countries. The home country of the executive expatriate provides 75 percent of all compensation to the executive while he is located in Japan, and 25 percent of all compensation is paid "offshore" or outside of Japan. Therefore, 25 percent of this income is not taxed in Japan.

Example 2. An executive expatriate has two employment contracts with her company. Under these dual contracts, one provides payment for all employment services provided in the United Kingdom and the other provides payment for all services worked in European countries.

Deferring income. The timing of compensation provided to executive expatriates can have significant impact on taxation costs. In particular, annual bonus and long-term stock payments, if deferred, can save company costs on tax equalization.

Example 1. An executive expatriate defers annual bonus earned during a three-year assignment overseas. The company saves significant tax gross-up expenses.

Example 2. An executive borrows funds needed to pay foreign taxes while on an overseas assignment. Under this loan-bonus plan, the executive is given a bonus to pay back the loan after she returns to the United States. The bonus includes interest charges on the loan. The company has again saved significant tax gross-up expenses.

Note: Specific tax laws of the United States and the overseas countries must be carefully analyzed before these ideas are implemented. It is recommended that CPA firms be used for counsel and advice.

Q 16:17   Can an executive expatriate avoid capital gains tax on the sale of a home while on overseas assignment?

Yes, an exemption or "suspension" of capital gains is available for the period the executive is overseas, if certain conditions are met:

1. The home was the executive's primary residence.

2. Reinvestment of the capital gain from the sale occurs within the required time period after the executive returns to the United States.

3. Occupancy of a new home occurs within the required time period after the executive returns to the United States.

4. The total time period from sale to repurchase does not exceed the maximum time period for the exemption.

Vacation homes do not qualify under these provisions.

Special Compensation

Q 16:18   Are executive expatriates protected against currency fluctuations?

This is one of the most volatile issues for executive expatriate programs. An executive receiving additional income as the result of currency fluctuation tends to view this as a natural right; however, if currency fluctuation results in less income, the executive will complain loudly and tell the company that there is an obligation to make up the loss.

The many allowances available to executive expatriates (e.g., housing, cost of living, education) can all be paid in the foreign currency of the overseas country. But if any portion is paid in U.S. currency, the problem begins.

Companies take one of three positions on this issue:

1. Limit currency fluctuations to a specific percentage change each month or quarter (e.g., 1 percent).

2. Establish a fixed exchange formula at the beginning of the overseas assignment and keep it throughout the assignment.

3. Explain to the executive expatriate at the beginning of the overseas assignment that fluctuation will occur, and that no action will be taken by the company.

Alternative 1 seems the most reasonable to both the company and the executive expatriate, especially if it is also agreed that all allowances will be reviewed and reestablished each year if currency fluctuations change total direct compensation by more than 5 percent in any given year. This establishes a level playing field and maintains the balance sheet concept of having the executive expatriate neither gain nor lose in total compensation due to the overseas assignment.

Q 16:19   What is a completion bonus?

This is a bonus paid to an executive expatriate after he completes the overseas assignment and has returned to the United States. This is frequently used when the executive expatriate is asked to take a lateral career move to an overseas assignment that will broaden his knowledge and experience, or situations when the executive expatriate is asked to take an assignment in an undesirable area, which might also provide a hardship allowance. (A completion bonus can also be used in lieu of a hardship allowance.)

Q 16:20   Can stock options be granted to executive expatriate?

Yes, however, some foreign countries tax these transactions at the time of grant, even though no stock ownership has occurred. (A stock option is the right to purchase shares of company stock in the future.)

Another problem with stock options is that if the expatriate exercises them while overseas, there is the possibility of double taxation (foreign tax on the proceeds plus U.S. tax) and the potential cost of tax equalization. The exercise terms of existing stock option grants held by an executive expatriate are an important consideration prior to the move overseas. Most companies will let the executive exercise any existing stock options while overseas; however, they will issue stock appreciation rights during the period of the overseas assignment.

Surveys by large CPA firms and large compensation consulting firms indicate that the majority of companies in the United States use stock appreciation rights for expatriates and foreign national executives.

Q 16:21   What are free-standing stock appreciation rights?

Stock appreciation rights (SARs) are the rights to stock appreciation over a base price, during a fixed number of years, after some vesting period has been met. The term "free standing" means that the SARs are not attached to a stock option, but stand alone.

Example: Free-Standing SAR. An executive expatriate on a four-year overseas assignment is given rights to the stock appreciation of 1,000 shares of company stock during the four-year period. The executive must hold the rights for one year prior to exercise. The base price at the time of grant is $20.

Three years later, the stock has a value of $50 and the executive exercises the right to the stock appreciation. The executive is paid $30,000 minus appropriate taxes ($50 − $20 = $30; $30 × 1,000 shares = $30,000)

Example: SAR Attached to Stock Option. An executive expatriate on a four-year overseas assignment is given 1,000 stock option shares with 1,000 stock appreciation rights attached to these shares. They are in tandem, in that the executive can exercise either the stock option or the stock appreciation right. There is a one-year holding or vesting period. The base price at the time of grant is $20.

Three years later, the stock has a value of $50, and the executive exercises 600 of the stock appreciation rights. The executive is paid $18,000 ($50 − $20 = $30; $30 × 600 = $18,000). The executive has 400 remaining shares of stock options or stock appreciation rights.

Q 16:22   Can long-term bonus plans be used for executive expatriates?

Yes, and they would be structured in the same way as similar plans for U.S.-based executives (see Q 7:39 and Q 7:46). The only difference is that performance measures would be based on the overseas business unit objectives rather than U.S. business unit objectives. Some companies will also require the executive to defer any amounts earned from the long-term plan until the executive returns to the United States from the overseas assignment, so that the company can save significant costs on tax equalization and duplicate taxes (foreign and United States).

Q 16:23   Can annual incentive plans be used for executive expatriates?

Yes, and they would be structured in the same way as similar plans for U.S.-based executives except with respect to the form of payment. The earned bonus can be paid in (1) local currency, (2) home country currency, or (3) a split payment of local and home country currency.

The tax implications of any "split payment" should be evaluated before a decision is made to use this alternative. Some companies will give the executive the choice of the form of currency, so that the executive can take advantage of current currency exchange rates.

Q 16:24   What kind of medical benefits are provided to executive expatriates?

Most companies will maintain the executive's eligibility in the home country medical plan. Under the balance sheet concept, the executive expatriate should neither gain nor lose in compensation during the overseas assignment; however, many overseas countries will have statutory benefits that the executive expatriate must be granted. If this is the case, the home country medical plan is the "floor," or the minimum coverage provided. The executive selects the medical coverage used, and the company coordinates benefits so that there is no duplication of benefits paid.

Another alternative to accommodate statutory benefits at the overseas location is for the country to provide local private medical care that "clones" the company's medical plan. This will also achieve the concept of equality of medical care for the executive expatriate while overseas.

Large companies will often join an international medical plan that has member health facilities in multiple cities throughout the world. Executive expatriates can then use these facilities while living or traveling overseas.

Q 16:25   What happens to an executive expatriate's pension plan while on overseas assignment?

Companies will continue making contributions to an executive's pension plan on the same basis as if the executive were still in the home country.

Many overseas countries have statutory retirement plans that require a company or executive contribution. Companies will make these contributions, and most will ensure that the total amount contributed by the executive while overseas is the same as if the executive were in the home country. This element of company cost is an important part of the decision on using expatriates.

If the executive should be overseas long enough to have qualified for a pension payment at retirement age from the overseas statutory pension plan, then companies will coordinate benefits with the home country pension plan so that the executive neither gains nor loses in the amount of pension due.

Q 16:26   How are life insurance and disability established for executive expatriates?

These benefits are kept at the same level that would exist if the executive were still in the home country. For example, if an executive has a disability plan that provides 60 percent payment of base salary upon disability, then this same benefit would apply to an overseas disability. The more important issue to the company is the length of the disability. The company is still providing allowances to an executive expatriate and, hopefully, the executive will be returning to work very soon. If not, the executive will probably be repatriated.

Q 16:27   What perquisites are provided to executive expatriates?

This varies by the level of executive as well as the overseas country where the executive is assigned. The one rule of thumb that applies is simply that, all factors being equal, the executive in the overseas assignment will have greater perquisites than if he were in the home country, particularly if the home country is the United States. This is the one exception to the balance sheet concept. For example, it is standard practice for an executive in most overseas countries to be given a company car, while this is not the case in the United States. In addition, the overseas executive is frequently there to develop business and, therefore, is given a more liberal expense account than in the home country.

This issue must be determined on an individual case basis, taking into account the local norms and the level and business purpose of the overseas assignment.

Q 16:28 What is done for executive expatriates upon repatriation?

Typically, companies will bring executives back to their home country and provide them with similar relocation benefits as they had when taking the expatriate assignment. These include:

- Home-finding trip for the executive and spouse
- Shipment of all household belongings
- Business class air travel for executive and family
- Temporary living expenses for executive and family prior to arrival of household goods; this also includes extended rental of an automobile, since cars are normally shipped separately from household goods and take longer on an international relocation
- Delivery/shipment of any household goods kept in storage
- Shipment of any special handling items like pets or art work
- Miscellaneous expense allowance (typically one month's base salary)

For executives who seek an apartment, many companies will also pay for any security deposits or up-front fees required of a new lease. Executives who purchase a new home will also receive reimbursement of any closing costs on the purchase.

Q 16:29 What special compensation is provided to an executive expatriate who takes a second overseas assignment?

The first issue that must be addressed in these situations is whether the executive should be reclassified from expatriate to international employee. General practice is for a company to classify all employees as "international" if they have been working outside of their home country for five years and if there is no future plan to repatriate the employee.

An executive who takes a second assignment as an expatriate would be provided with the same program in the new overseas location as was provided in the first location. Housing, COLA, and education allowances may be different in the new location, but the executive is still given the same expatriate support programs

If an executive is reclassified as an international employee, then the common practice is to provide one of two compensation methods: the "net to net" compensation program and the "modified home country balance sheet program." (These concepts may have different names in some companies, but the theory is the same.)

The modified home country balance sheet approach is a first step in "disconnecting" the executive expatriate from a full expatriate compensation program. As foreign service assignments of the executive continue, the second step is adoption by the company of a net to net compensation program.

Q 16:30   What are the elements of a net to net compensation program?

The following eight elements are normally found in a net to net compensation program:

1. Base salary is in local currency and is established by awarding the executive an actual base salary equal to the same salary range position previously held by the executive in the home country. For example, an executive with a 110 percent compensation ratio in the home country would have a 100 percent compensation ratio in the new overseas country's salary range assigned to their position. The compensation ratio is the percentage relationship of actual base salary to the salary range midpoint, with the midpoint equalling 100 percent.

2. No foreign service premium would be paid.

3. A fixed housing allowance would be provided. (Said another way, free housing up to a maximum.)

4. A COLA would be provided based on a comparison of the old location to the new location. (Published tables are typically used from ORC, AIRINC, etc.)

5. Tax protection (not tax equalization) is provided. Tax protection means that the company will compare net income after deducting taxes and add the housing and COLA allowances in the home country or country where the executive was previously assigned, to net income in the new country after the same deductions and additions. (Hence the basis of the term "net to net.") The executive is responsible for her own taxes but may receive a reimbursement from the tax protection program if taxes in the new overseas country would result in a substantial reduction of net income.

6. Educational and language allowances are negotiable and depend on the individual situation of the executive. There is no reliable survey data on company practices in this area.

7. Companies may maintain a "phantom home country base salary" for pension plan purposes, and, if so, ongoing company contributions would be made to this retirement benefit. In these cases, upon retirement, any retirement income earned in a foreign country would be deducted from the retirement income that the executive earns from the home country. Some large companies have an "offshore pension plan" that clones the home country pension plan and is specifically for international employees who may have multiple overseas assignments during their career, and multiple pensions. The offshore plan establishes a minimum retirement, typically tied to final average pay and years of service, and then consolidates all executive pension amounts to avoid duplication of payments.

8. Medical, insurance, and disability are normally provided to the executive expatriate per normal practice of the new overseas country. Large companies may develop offshore medical plans or use an international medical plan with numerous facilities around the world in order to provide the executive with a minimum benefit level.

Q 16:31   What are the typical elements of a modified home country balance sheet compensation program?

Six elements typically constitute a modified home country balance sheet compensation program:

1. Base salary is paid in local currency and is established using compensation ratio comparisons of former location to new location, as described in the net to net compensation program.

2. No foreign service premium is paid.

3. A fixed housing allowance is provided (i.e., free housing as with the net to net compensation program).

4. A COLA is provided (from tables) based on a comparison of living costs in the executive expatriate's home country vs. current overseas location.

5. Tax equalization is provided to the executive expatriate.

6. All other allowances and benefits/pension are per the company's regular executive expatriate compensation program.

Q 16:32   Is there a checklist of issues that should be considered by a company and/or executive in developing an executive expatriate compensation program?

This is a useful tool, and such a list would include the following:

Pre-Assignment

- Education regarding the history, government, language, weather, economy, living standard, location, and culture of the overseas country
- Compensation program of similar executive positions in the overseas country or in similar countries
- Term of overseas assignment
- Business objective of executive expatriate position and repatriation plans
- Legal documents required, for example, passports, visa, work permits, drivers license, letters of credit, letters of competency
- Medical requirements, for example, vaccinations and statutory medical/pension plans in the new country

- Compensation and allowances, and the source (i.e., ORC COLA tables)
- Pre-assignment visit by executive and spouse to examine housing, appliances, food/sanitation standards, clothing styles, availability of personal services, medical facilities, educational facilities, recreational facilities, religious and social opportunities, and servants
- Local transportation, shopping, telephone service, currency, and miscellaneous issues like spousal employment or anything specific to the individual executive and family

Starting the Overseas Assignment

- Decision and implementation of home sale vs. home rental
- Language training
- Children's education registration at new location
- Full documentation of pay, allowance, benefits, vacations, home leave, tax equalization, special short-term or long-term incentive plans, automobile purchase or shipment, and perquisites
- Necessary documents such as visas, business cards, change of address notices, revised wills
- Relocation plan to include shipment of household goods, family travel, temporary living location, and home sale
- Development of new banking relationships and enrollment into new medical facilities
- Purchase of new appliances
- Assimilation plan at work and in the home so that all the family gets acclimated to the new environment in a satisfactory manner.

International assignments are challenging but they can also be exciting, educational, and rewarding for all executives.

Chapter 17

Executive Compensation in the Public Sector

Executive compensation programs in public sector organizations (e.g., schools, governments) are being reviewed at many locations as the result of board of director interest in improving the organization while, at the same time, controlling executive compensation costs. Tenure-based pay systems are being replaced by performance-based pay systems. Annual incentive plans and supplemental retirement plans are new ideas to public sector organizations and can be useful tools in attracting, retaining, and motivating executives. This chapter answers questions on current differences between public and private sector base salary, performance management, incentives, benefits, and perquisites.

The Small Business Job Protection Act of 1996 and other recent legislation has an effect on executive compensation in public companies. Relevant provisions will be discussed in a future supplement.

Q 17:1 What is the driving philosophy behind executive compensation in the public sector versus that in the private sector?

In the private sector, the driving philosophy is pay for performance. Additionally, executives have a significant amount of compensation at risk or subject to the achievement of performance goals.

There are varying opinions on how well this is done, but the philosophy and intent of executive pay is clear.

In the public sector, the driving philosophy is tenure-based; that is, the longer you occupy a position, the higher the pay.

This is the cause of great debate. Merit pay systems have been tried in both government and schools, but are still not widely used, except in the federal government where some higher level civilian employees are under merit pay. Critics claim that the absence of performance-based pay for executives results in an absence of accountability, which leads to mediocrity and poor quality.

The opposing argument is that public sector executives are clearly accountable to school boards, or elected officials, and the public will not stand for poor quality.

Q 17:2   How is base salary different in the public sector organization than in the private sector organization?

Many jobs in the public sector have no counterpart in the private sector that can be used for comparison (e.g., director–road maintenance, superintendent of schools); however, there are many jobs in the public sector that are similar to others in the private sector, such as director of accounting or personnel.

When jobs are similar, the base salary levels in the public sector tend to be different from the private sector for two reasons:

1. The labor market definition is typically more limited in the public sector than in the private sector.
2. The salary ranges used in the public sector are broader than those in the private sector.

Labor Market Definition. Government organizations tend to market price their jobs against other government organizations. Schools tend to market price their jobs by comparing to other schools. Public sector organizations use a more limited labor market because not all labor market organizations have jobs that are similar to their own. This tends to perpetuate industry practice or, as some would say, makes it incestuous, because labor market pricing of jobs is only conducted within the industry.

Salary Ranges. The tenure-based pay philosophy in the public sector results in automatic step increases each year (based on tenure). These step increases require a broad salary range because there are so many steps (in some cases 15 or 20 steps with a 3 to 4 percent pay increase per step). The result is broader salary ranges. A recent survey by the human resource consulting firm of HR Management, Inc. showed a typical public sector organization salary range for executive positions to be 70 percent. The same number in the private sector, per the American Compensation Association, is 40 to 50 percent (see Q 17:5).

This factor produces an interesting characteristic of public sector base salary levels. At the low end of the salary range, actual base salary rates are significantly lower than those in the total labor market (although they parallel those of other organizations in the public sector labor market). At the high end of the salary range, actual base salary levels are significantly above those in the total labor market (although they parallel those of other organizations in the public sector labor market).

Q 17:3 Are job evaluation systems used for executive positions in public sector organizations?

Yes, the same job evaluations used in the private sector are adopted/modified for public sector organizations. The descriptions used in each job evaluation factor are simply modified. For example, the descriptions in a common job evaluation factor of "interactions with others" are compared for a private corporation and public sector (school) organization in the following chart:

Level	Private Sector Description	Public Sector Description
1	Other employees	Department employees
2	Vendors & suppliers	Professional associations
3	Customers	Students
4	Directors & officers	County administrators
5	Board of directors	Members of school board

Q 17:4   Can merit increases to base salary work for executive positions in public sector organizations?

Yes, but such merit increases are rare because, in most cases, public sector jobs are unique and hard to measure. Take, for example, a superintendent of curriculum development or a county sheriff. What performance measures are appropriate for curriculum development? Measures like student grades or SAT scores are affected by other variables, and there are few if any national evaluations on the quality of curriculums. The same is true for a county sheriff. Most performance measures selected will also be affected by many other factors.

Most public sector positions have been granted "tenure-based" salary increases for years. Public organizations have little experience with performance evaluation programs, which are the basis for merit pay increases. For these reasons merit pay has little use.

The few public sector organizations that have tried merit pay have used performance measures like the following:

Position Title	Performance Measure
School Teacher	1. Teaching skills (measured by observation)
	2. Student test scores (national tests)
	3. Peer ratings by other teachers
	4. Teacher scores on continuous education courses
Police Officer	1. Knowledge of the law (measured via tests)
	2. Number of crime prevention programs in department/geographic area
	3. Opinion survey of public safety in department/geographic area
	4. Crime rate in department/geographic area

The disadvantages of a tenure-based pay increase (discussed in Q 17:5) can be overcome with a merit increase system; however, a new set of challenges must be met if merit pay is to be more effective. The major challenge is the selection of performance measures.

Q 17:5   What are the advantages and disadvantages of tenure-based pay increase systems?

Tenure-based pay increase systems use tenure as the basis for an annual pay increase. An example follows:

Position: Director of Accounting

Years of Experience	1	2	3	4	5	6	7	8
Compensation (in $ thousands)	$40.0	$41.6	$43.3	$45.0	$46.8	$48.7	$50.6	$52.6

Years of Experience	9	10	11	12	13	14	15	16
Compensation (in $ thousands)	$54.7	$56.9	$59.2	$61.6	$64.1	$66.7	$69.4	$72.2

The difference between the rate at Year 1 and Year 16 is 80 percent. This is unusually broad versus typical private sector practice, which, according to the American Compensation Association, would be 30 to 40 percent for non-executive positions and 50 percent for executive positions. (See Q 17:2). This quantitative analysis shows the first disadvantage of tenure-based pay systems, as shown in the following chart:

Tenure-Based Pay Increase Systems

Advantages	*Disadvantages*
1. Retention of executives.	1. At the higher steps, pay is well above the labor market, resulting in higher annual costs.
2. Costs are predictable.	2. Pay levels and cost escalate each year regardless of performance.
3. Less administrative time and cost without the need to measure performance.	3. Executives have less motivation to perform because there is no financial incentive tied to the achievement of work results.

Q 17:6   Why do public sector organizations prefer a tenure-based pay increase system?

Many executive positions in the public sector report to an elected official, and elected officials frequently change. Whenever there is change, new attitudes and opinions on compensation can occur, resulting in an irregular pay system. To avoid this, the tenure-based pay system was developed. It has eliminated discretionary judgments on pay increase by the elected executives (who come and go) and was intended to stabilize the compensation of the non-elected executive.

Most would agree that this objective has been achieved; however, because of the disadvantages suggested in Q 17:5 (i.e., high pay levels vs. the labor market, automatic escalating costs each year, and the absence of any focus on performance achievement), many school boards and county/state officials have been prompted to look for alternative solutions. The few government organizations and school districts that have implemented merit pay for higher level executives (with modest success) have found that they require significant time to train executives in goal setting, coaching/counseling, completing the performance evaluation form, and discussing performance results with employees. Private sector corporations have reached the same conclusion.

The question becomes: Does the extra training effort make merit pay increase systems more effective than tenure-based pay increase systems? The answer simply depends on the level of achievement of the organization. If an organization (public or private) is experiencing high performance, a change in pay increase systems will probably have little value to the organization. If the organization, however, is experiencing mediocre or below average performance, then a change in pay increase systems can have a positive effect on the organization.

Q 17:7   Are salary ranges used in the public sector?

Yes, but salary ranges found in the public sector are typically different from those found in the private sector. They contain numerous steps and are, therefore, broader in length.

Example. Assume that the labor market value for the executive position of chief financial officer in a $100 million sales company is $75,000 per year. In a private sector company the salary range would typically be as follows:

Private Sector Salary Range

Minimum	Midpoint	Maximum
$60,000	$75,000	$90,000

Assume as well that the labor market value for the executive position of chief financial officer in a county school district is $75,000. In this public sector organization, the salary range would typically be as follows:

Public Sector Salary Range

Step 1	Step 2	Step 3	Step 4	Step 5
$54,100	$56,300	$58,600	$60,900	$63,300

Step 6	Step 7	Step 8	Step 9	Step 10
$65,800	$68,400	$71,100	$73,900	$76,900

Step 11	Step 12	Step 13	Step 14	Step 15
$80,000	$83,200	$86,500	$90,000	$93,600

Q 17:8 Are annual incentives used in public sector organizations?

Generally, no. There are some special award programs that pay a lump-sum bonus for some extraordinary/outstanding performance, but the public sector does not make use of incentive compensation for executives. Many believe that, like many not-for-profit organizations, the public sector is missing a great opportunity to motivate executives with an annual incentive plan; however, since these organizations rarely have a merit increase system on which to base pay, they also have no performance measures or performance evaluation system within the organization. Performance measures are an essential requirement of any incentive compensation plan.

Q 17:9　Are long-term performance plans or stock award plans used in public organizations?

There is no stock, nor are there stockholders, in public sector organizations. As discussed in previous questions, because there is rarely any ability to measure performance in these organizations annually or over the long term, these plans rarely exist. The significant payments from stock plans (and other forms of long-term compensation) to private sector executives are certainly a big advantage with respect to total compensation for these executives.

Q 17:10　Are insured benefits in the public sector better than those in private companies?

HR Management, Inc. analyzed the benefit plans in 25 public sector organizations and 25 private sector organizations. There were no significant differences in the level of benefit coverage. With respect to executive cost, the public sector organizations charged their executives less than the private sector organization for approximately the same level of insured benefit coverage.

This is not surprising, since private corporations have been more aggressive in passing on insured benefit plan cost increases to all employees. This has been accomplished through new cafeteria benefit plans that allow employees to select the level of benefit and associated cost, and by more aggressive use of managed care organizations like HMOs and PPOs (health maintenance organizations and preferred provider organizations).

Private companies have also been experiencing more downsizing and merger acquisition activity than public sector organizations. Thus the public sector has maintained a higher level of "career employment" and "status quo" than private companies, where organization tenure and loyalty have changed significantly. The organization and the executive in the private sector are more independent in today's business environment. This facilitates a different strategy on benefit costs.

Q 17:11   Are retirement plans in the public sector better than those in private companies?

The same survey mentioned in Q 17:10 also reviewed retirement plans. There were no significant differences in eligible retirement benefits between public and private sector organizations; however, public sector executives had an average tenure greater than that for private company executives. This is consistent with the tenure-driven compensation systems used in the public organization.

A significantly greater number of executives in private companies had eligibility for supplemental retirement plans than in the public sector where these plans are rarely used.

Q 17:12   Can supplemental retirement plans be used in public sector organizations?

Yes, but they rarely are used for the following reasons:

1. Public sector executives are not paid compensation at the level of many billion-dollar private companies (i.e., $250,000 to $1,000,000); therefore, the regulatory maximum in retirement plans rarely affects the public sector executive as it can affect the private sector executive. Supplemental executive retirement plans (SERPs) were initially developed because ERISA limits the amount of retirement that can be paid to any individual in a qualified pension plan. (Qualified here means that annual organization contributions to a retirement plan qualify for a tax deduction.) This is an important issue for for-profit private companies.

2. Private companies are not tenure-driven. In addition, they frequently want executives to retire early so that they can get new ideas into the organization. For executives of such companies there is a business need for a SERP, which is not the case in most public sector organizations.

One can easily conclude that in public sector organizations there is an organizational and motivational value to executives in considering performance-driven base pay and annual incentive plans; however, this is not the case with SERPs. They are rare in public sector organizations because there is little need for them.

Q 17:13   Are public sector organizations subject to Title VII of the Civil Rights Act of 1964, the Fair Labor Standards Act, Americans with Disabilities Act, Age Discrimination in Employment Act, or other such regulations?

Yes, but over the years such regulations have had little impact on public sector executives. Equal pay is rarely an issue because of the tenure-driven nature of public sector pay systems. All executives are automatically treated equally. The tenure-driven philosophy also results in many older executives in the public sector. Public sector organizations also have shown over the years that they do an excellent job in adhering to the race, sex, and national origin provisions of Title VII.

Q 17:14   Do public sector executives have perquisites?

Yes, but not anywhere close to the level of the private company executive. The most popular perquisites in the private sector are first-class air travel, cellular phones, company cars, club memberships, financial planning, and supplemental executive retirement plans, all of which are rarely provided to any public sector executive. The absence of SERPs for public sector executives is discussed in Q 17:12.

Q 17:15   How can compensation plans be used to attract high-quality executives into the public sector?

The downsizing and restructuring that have occurred in private companies during the past 10 years has resulted in the availability of a number of high-quality executives who could make valuable contributions in public sector organizations. But these executives typically have been trained in, and have developed, work methods in performance-driven organizations rather than in tenure-driven organizations; therefore, they rarely consider the public sector.

A change in the compensation plans of public sector organizations can attract these executives. These changes are:

1. Smaller salary ranges with fewer automatic step increases

2. The use of performance-based pay increases in lieu of step increases once a median labor market base pay rate is reached (or immediately used at the time of initial employment)

3. Annual incentive compensation that is determined from achievement of annual performance goals

These compensation plan changes could also have an extremely positive impact on current executives in the public sector, since the changes can motivate them to achieve goals that are critical to a high-quality public organization.

Chapter 18

Compensation for Temporary Executives

As a result of numerous corporate restructuring, downsizing, mergers/divestitures, and other such changes in today's business environment, we have available an ever-growing number of unemployed executives who are over age 50, with extensive knowledge and ability. At the same time, companies are showing more interest in using independent contractors to fulfill-short-term and/or project work at the executive and non-executive level. These factors have contributed to a significant increase in the use of temporary executives at both public and private companies, and the emergence of recruiting firms that deal exclusively with the placement of temporary executives. This chapter explains the various legal and practical issues relevant to this expanding executive labor market and the creative compensation packages that are being offered participating executives.

In recent years a number of companies have come under increased scrutiny for the use of independent contractors to avoid having to pay for benefits such as health insurance. Under laws recently enacted, this scrutiny is becoming more relaxed, as are excise taxes on excess distributions for people currently at regulatory maximums. These new provisions and their implications will be discussed in a future supplement.

Q 18:1   What is a temporary executive?

A temporary executive does not have a permanent job, and takes employment on temporary assignments from a temporary employment firm. The executive is an employee of the temporary employment firm, and has FICA and other tax withheld from his paycheck. The temporary employment firm finds suitable temporary work for the executive, and bills the company that uses the executive. A portion of this billing is kept by the temporary employment firm, and a portion is given to the executive.

Most temporary executives are employed in offices rather than in production/operations or technical support positions, as shown below.

Types of Employment for Temporary Executives

1.	Office Work: (Includes management, advisory board, financial, legal, MIS, human resources, public, and government relations projects)	60%
2.	Production and Operations Work: (Includes traffic, inventory, warehousing, distribution, and scheduling projects)	5%
3.	Technical Work: (Includes sales, marketing, engineering, research, and similar occupations)	35%

Source: HR Management, Inc.

Q 18:2   Are temporary executives independent contractors?

No, not as long as they are on the payroll of the temporary employment firm. An independent contractor is an executive who works for himself and is responsible for his own FICA and tax withholding. Independent contractors must estimate their earnings, and file quarterly tax payments on IRS Form 1040ES and other appropriate state tax forms. Independent contractors may or may not be incorporated.

The independent contractor will bill the company directly for her employment services and will receive a Form 1099 annually from the company which summarizes taxable income paid to the executive.

Q 18:3   What are the advantages and disadvantages of being an independent contractor to the executive?

An independent contractor will perform project- or task-oriented services in her area of expertise for any employer. Advantages and disadvantages are as follows:

Advantages	*Disadvantages*
1. There is no "middleman," so the independent contractor can charge less, and earn more.	1. The independent contractor must take all of the legal and financial risk of being an employer.
2. There is the security of a job during the contract period and help in finding the next temporary assignment.	2. All taxes and office costs must be absorbed by the independent contractor, as well as health insurance costs.
3. Most firms will provide benefits after a minimum service period.	3. The independent contractor finds it difficult to sell and perform services.
4. The independent contractor can turn down undesirable work.	4. The independent contractor has irregular needs because of unpredictable staff work load demands.

Q 18:4   What are the advantages and disadvantages of independent contractors to a company?

More and more companies are benefiting from contacts with temporary executives, whether as independent contractors or as staff members of a temporary employment firm. The advantages and disadvantages are as follows:

Advantages	*Disadvantages*
1. Can add or subtract to payroll as needed by business familiar with company conditions.	1. Temporary executives are not procedures.
2. Company can avoid severance during a downsizing.	2. Temporary executives do not understand the company's culture and decision making process.
3. There is access to multiskilled executives.	3. Loyalty may not be as high as with a permanent executive who has long tenure with the company.
4. Hiring and training costs lower.	
5. Costs (including benefits) are not any greater for the temporary executive.	
6. Temporary executives can bring fresh ideas to company problems.	

Q 18:5 What is the difference between a short-term and long-term temporary assignment?

A short-term assignment is typically one month to one year. A long-term assignment is typically one year or more.

Q 18:6 What is outsourcing?

Outsourcing is the use of an outside firm or non-employees to accomplish the types of projects formerly done in-house by employees. Executive responsibilities can be outsourced. For this purpose, a company may decide to use a temporary executive who is either an independent contractor or an employee of a temporary employment firm, for an employment period that may be short or long term.

Outsourcing can also involve the use of leased executives. Leased executives are full-time employees of a leased employee company, but are dedicated to, and who work for, another client company. The leased employee receives all benefits from the leased employee company and has all FICA and tax withholding administered by them. In this regard the leased employee firm is similar to a temporary employee firm except that leased employees tend to be on permanent assignment to the client company.

Q 18:7   What are other alternatives to outsourcing?

Companies may use their own employees on a part-time or flextime basis. Part-time refers to the use of an executive for a fixed number of hours per day or week that is well under the normal-40-hour work week. For example, a part-time executive may work from 1 to 5 p.m. every day, or the same hours only on the last week of the month to assist in the preparation of month-end financial reports.

Flextime executives tend to work longer hours than a part-time executive but typically the hours will be either before or after the normal business hours. For example, a flextime executive may work 2 to 8 p.m. or 6 a.m. to 12 p.m.

Q 18:8   How do temporary executives obtain an assignment?

If the executive is with a temporary firm, the firm will normally have an assignment manager who is responsible for understanding the executive's experience and abilities, and for finding a company that needs these abilities.

A temporary executive who is an independent contractor must rely on reputation and personal contacts to find a use for his services. Many such executives will develop "referral representatives," that is, people in the business community who are aware of the executive's abilities or who have known the executive for a long time, and can refer the executive's name to companies in the business community, whether it be local, national, or international.

Q 18:9   How is base salary determined for temporary executives?

This will depend on the number of hours that the executive is asked to work per day. If the executive is working normal daily hours, the base salary could be expressed as a monthly rate and would be similar to the monthly rate that the executive would be paid if she were a permanent employee of the company. If the executive is not working normal hours and is an independent contractor who is hired to perform a specific project, the base salary will typically be expressed as an hourly rate.

Another factor affecting the base salary is whether the executive is an independent contractor or an employee of a temporary employee firm. If an employee, the firm will charge a base salary plus a fee to cover its costs. If an independent contractor, the executive could also add selling and administrative costs to the fee.

Example 1. An executive who was previously making $12,000 per month ($120,000 per year) takes early retirement. He decides to do consulting as an independent contractor. Soon after, he is hired by another company as a temporary employee for a period of six months to fill in for an executive who is having surgery. The temporary executive will be using his primary skills in his area of expertise, and will be working normal work hours during the period of employment. The executive charges the company $14,400 per month. He determines this fee by adding 20% to his competitive labor value of $12,000 ($12,000 × 1.2 = $14,400).

Example 2. An executive who was previously making $12,000 per month ($120,000 per year) takes early retirement. She decides to work for a temporary employment firm. Soon after, she gets an assignment as a temporary employee for a period of six months to fill in for an executive who is having surgery. The temporary executive will be using her primary skills in her area of expertise, and will be working normal hours during this period. The executive's temporary firm charges the company $15,000 and pays the executive $12,000. The remaining $3,000 is retained by the temporary employment firm to cover its costs.

In both of the previous examples the fees included a base salary that paralleled the temporary executive's former rate and labor market value. Additional costs to the executive and/or temporary employment firm were passed on to the company; however, the company did not incur any more costs than it would have if the executive were its own employee because the company is not paying for, or contributing to, the executive's benefit costs.

Another example of base salary costs is the executive who is on project work or an hourly fee structure. Hourly rates are essentially established by supply and demand and labor market factors. Executive hourly rates could parallel business consultant rates, which vary from $200 to $1,000 per hour in most cases, or they could be less, depending on the nature of the work.

> **Example 3.** An executive who is an independent contractor is hired by a company to help it implement a new product inventory system. The executive has already done this kind of work for other companies and can estimate the number of hours to do the task with reasonable accuracy. The executive's fees are $200 per hour, with the estimated number of hours at 120. If the executive accomplishes the project after the 120 hours, the total fees would be $24,000 ($200 × 120 hours = $24,000).

It is common for compensation to be defined in a contract between the company and the temporary executive or his or her temporary employment firm.

Q 18:10　Are temporary executives provided with incentive compensation?

They can be. If incentive compensation is provided, it is normally defined in the temporary executive's contract, along with the performance goals (if any) that will be used to determine payment. Most temporary executives receive incentive compensation while employed full-time by a company, which can be a basis for determining the potential size of an incentive award for temporary executives.

An alternative is to obtain labor market compensation surveys and identify competitive amounts of incentive compensation paid to similar positions. If the nature of the temporary work is project work, incentive compensation would typically be built into the hourly fee or be defined as an add on, particularly if it was based on the work being performed in advance of the estimated time or on some quality standard.

Another type of incentive compensation provided to executives as well as non-executives who perform temporary work is the longevity or tenure bonus. Such bonuses are normally given by a temporary employment firm. For example, if an executive stays with the temporary employment firm for one year, the firm may grant him a lump-sum bonus in order to retain his services in the future.

Some temporary employment firms will also give "merit increases" to executives if they stay for a fixed period of time (e.g., one year). The motivation is simply retention of that executive's service.

Q 18:11   Are temporary executives provided with stock awards?

It would be rare for a temporary executive to receive any stock or other long-term award. Long term in most businesses is defined as three to four years, and it would be rare for any company to have a temporary in place for this long.

Q 18:12   Are temporary executives provided with perquisites?

No, these are not part of the compensation of a temporary executive.

Q 18:13   What insured benefits are provided to temporary executives?

Independent contractors must provide their own benefits. An executive employee with a temporary employment firm will typically be given a low level of medical benefits (e.g., reimbursement of 50 to 60 percent of costs after a high deductible, for example, $1,000, has been met), provided that a minimum number of hours have been worked (e.g., 1,000 hours). Temporary employment firms are not obligated to give benefits, but this is a tool for them to retain good employees.

In all cases there will be a coordination of benefits with other benefit coverage that the executive or spouse is eligible to receive.

Q 18:14   Are temporary executives provided with retirement benefits?

No, it is rare for a temporary employment firm to provide executives with retirement plan eligibility. The only exception is if the executive works full-time on some long-term assignment. Then the requirements of the federal law, ERISA, state that an employee with 1,000 hours must be granted eligibility for any pension plan that is available to other employees.

Q 18:15   Are temporary executives subject to federal regulations on equal pay, age, etc.?

Yes, the provisions of Title VII of the Civil Rights Act of 1964, and the Americans with Disabilities Act, and other antidiscrimination laws all apply to temporary employees. Executives who are full-time employees are not frequently impacted by these laws, and the same is true in their status as temporary employees.

Q 18:16   Can temporary executives be placed on an overseas assignment?

Yes. If this occurs, the executive would typically be on a short-term assignment and would receive reimbursement of all travel and living costs. It would be rare for a temporary executive to be an expatriate, as discussed in chapter 16.

Q 18:17   Can temporary executives be converted to full-time status?

Yes, this occurs often, and the executive's compensation will need to be converted into the company's ongoing total compensation programs. A temporary employment firm will normally require that the executive be employed with it and with the client company for a minimum employment period before it will agree to converting the executive to full-time status with the client company.

Chapter 19

Economic Value-Added

Economic value-added (EVA) is one of the hottest new ideas in executive compensation. Large human resource consulting firms report that use of this performance measure has almost tripled during the last three years from 5 percent to 12 percent. As a performance-based alternative to traditional accounting measures, it is being used in both large and small businesses.

The consulting firm of Stern Stewart is given credit for creating the idea, but many variations are being used. In small companies a simple definition is more popular than the sophisticated formula that started the use of the concept. This chapter gives the answers to a number of questions on EVA definitions and then on implementation issues.

General Considerations   19-1
Implementation   19-6

General Considerations

Q 19:1   What is the definition of economic value-added?

There are multiple definitions of economic value-added (EVA). The most common is found in Q 5:9, which states a calculation of net after-tax operating profit (NOPAT) minus the cost of capital. The cost of capital is capital employed in the business, multiplied by the cost of employing this capital, typically defined as normal investor expectations of an investment return (e.g., a treasury-bill interest rate of 5 to 6 percent) plus a premium that is required to attract an investor to buy a company's stock (e.g., another 5 to 6 percent). If NOPAT in a company is $15 million, capital employed is $100 million, and the cost of capital is 10 percent, then EVA is $5 million ($100 million $\times$ 10 = $10 million. $15 million – $10 million = $5 million).

Some small- to medium-size companies (like Valmont Industries in Valley, Nebraska) that use an EVA performance measure have elected a more simple calculation such as NOPAT minus a fixed 10 percent cost of capital assumption. To the extent this number increases each year, the company is adding economic value to the business. An even simpler definition of EVA is net income minus payments on long-term debt plus dividends.

Larger companies (like The Coca-Cola Company) that use an EVA performance measure have elected a more sophisticated calculation such as NOPAT minus [cash plus inventory plus (accounts receivable minus accounts payable) plus non-current assets], times the cost capital. Cost of capital is determined by taking a normal investment return expected by an investor, plus a premium return, multiplied by a beta factor that measures the extent to which the company's stock performance follows normal stock market highs and lows. The resulting percentage is then multiplied by capital to get the cost of capital. NOPAT must exceed the cost of capital in order to have EVA. To the extent EVA increases each year, the company is adding economic value to the business.

As seen in the Coca-Cola example the EVA concept is to earn a return (in NOPAT) that is in excess of the company's cost of capital. To many this is a sound concept.

Q 19:2 Why are companies using economic value-added?

The primary reasons are:

1. It is a tool for strategic business decision making. When a company is evaluating possible acquisitions, mergers, divestitures, spin-offs, etc., it can calculate current economic value

and estimated economic value after the business transaction. If the transaction results in less economic value, then the planned venture should be changed or dropped.

2. It focuses executives on performance factors that drive increases in the value of the company. Traditional incentive plans use performance measures that are accounting measures, and these may or may not drive increases in the value of the company.

3. EVA plans typically provide executives with an uncapped percentage of the incremental EVA; therefore, there is no need to estimate levels of performance against accounting-based goals. Many non-EVA incentives use goals that may be easy to meet or unrealistic to achieve. This is not an issue with EVA plans.

4. Large consulting firms have conducted studies that show EVA as a better driver of company stock price than traditional accounting measures. Therefore shareholder value can be directly enhanced by EVA plans. These studies focus on the fact that companies must produce greater profit from the capital they employ if they want to attract investors. EVA focuses on this exact issue.

Q 19:3   What are the disadvantages of economic value-added?

The primary disadvantages are:

1. The original concept of EVA was complicated (i.e., calculating cost of capital with a beta factor), and executives did not understand this new performance measure as well as they understood accounting measures. Moreover, members on the board compensation committee in companies also did not understand the calculation. In fact, research at the University of Chicago has suggested that the beta factor used in many EVA plans is no longer an accurate predictor of shareholder returns. The capital asset pricing model (CAPM) is often used by companies in calculating the cost of capital, and its validity is being debated in academic circles.

2. Some compensation planners dispute the fact that EVA has a better correlation to shareholder value. They claim that accounting measures like earnings per share and return on capital

can also drive shareholder value as well as EVA. They further state that all performance measures are subject to the vagaries of the stock market and shareholder value is driven by stock market and overall economic conditions in the country as well as measures of company performance.

3. There are some highly publicized examples of EVA plans that did not work. One of these is AT&T, where *Fortune* magazine in September 1993 stated that the company was a leading example of the success of EVA incentive plans. Shortly thereafter the company announced a major downsizing; and cost-reduction programs and financial results, including stock price, were well below projections and previous levels of company performance.

4. Few executives have an impact on the cost of capital. Moreover, it is difficult for a large company to change its capital structure. Even if it were able to do so, only a few people would be involved in that decision, i.e., the chief executive officer, chief financial officer, and possibly the chairman of the board's finance committee.

Q 19:4   How do companies use EVA plans?

Once companies determine an EVA formula, they will in most cases assign eligible executives with their pro-rata portion of any incremental value in EVA. In this regard EVA incentive plans are similar to profit sharing incentive plans. The one major difference with EVA plans is that a portion of the earned pro-rata incentive is typically deferred. This deferral is mandatory and is typically until retirement or termination. Part of the EVA plan is therefore used as a supplemental retirement plan for executives.

The other key feature of EVA plans is that the amount earned by executives is "uncapped." The greater the increase in EVA, the greater the incentive earned by the executives.

An example of how EVA plans are used is as follows:

Example. Company A defines EVA as net operating profit after taxes minus a fixed 15 percent cost of capital. Currently NOPAT is $60 million, so EVA is $51 million ($60 × 15% = $9; $60 – $9 =

$51). The company has 15 eligible executives, and it will provide them with 20 percent of any incremental EVA. The pro-rata portions of incremental EVA are as follows:

Title	No.	% EVA
Chief Executive Officer	1	3%
Senior Vice Presidents	3	2% each (Total of 6%)
Vice Presidents	11	1% each (Total of 11%)
Total:		20%

One-half is paid currently and one-half is deferred.

Actual EVA in the first year of the plan is $61 million, or an increase of $10 million. Actual payments to each executive would total 20 percent of $10 million ($2 million), and would be as follows:

Title	No.	Current Payment	Deferred Payment
Chief Executive Officer	1	$ 150,000	$ 150,000
Senior Vice Presidents (each)	3	$ 100,000	$ 100,000
Vice Presidents (each)	11	$ 50,000	$ 50,000
Total:		$1,000,000	$1,000,000

Q 19:5 Can executives really have an impact on the cost of capital?

Costs of capital calculations are developed from capital asset pricing models, which factor in interest rates, the stock performance of peer companies, expected rates of return, discounted cash flow, etc., all of which are highly sophisticated calculations. Therefore, the true line of sight or focus of executives in an EVA plan is NOPAT, since few impact or understand the cost of capital calculations. Most executive compensation experts will agree that executives impact earnings, the relationship of receivables and payables, cash flow, inventory, etc., all of which are a part of most EVA calculations. One can therefore argue that it is not really important that executives understand the cost of capital, provided it does not change dramatically from year to year.

Q 19:6   Can EVA be used in divisions or SBUs?

Yes, the EVA performance measure is as valid for executives in a strategic business unit as it is for a group of corporate officers. Capital can be defined as those assets that are clearly influenced by a division executive and the same is true for the earnings definition.

Q 19:7   Can EVA be correlated to shareholder value?

Many EVA consultants, especially those at Stern Stewart, would say yes. In fact, Stern Stewart has published an analysis of both economic value-added and market value-added (MVA) by Fortune 1000 companies. In order to calculate market value-added, they combined a company's debt and market value of its stock, then subtracted the capital that had been invested in the company. The result is market value-added (or negative market value). To calculate economic value-added, they took a company's net after-tax operating profit minus the cost of capital employed in the business. (See Q 19:1 for an explanation of the cost of capital.) A comparison of MVA to EVA should show that both are positive, because a positive EVA will drive market value up. This is one way to correlate EVA with shareholder value.

Some companies in the Stern Stewart analyses had a market value that was positive, but EVA was negative. In these cases, investors obviously looked past the negative EVA and saw a good future for the company.

Implementation

Q 19:8   What steps are required to implement an EVA plan?

There are six steps as follows:

1. *Define Earnings.* In most cases this is operating income or profit after taxes. This type of earnings definition can be used in both corporate and division organizations.

2. *Define Capital.* For a corporate organization, this could be shareholder equity plus long-term borrowing. For a division, it

could be inventory, accounts receivable, assets employed in the manufacturing process.

3. *Define the Cost of Capital.* A fixed percentage can be used. In the Stern Stewart analysis of Fortune 1000 companies, the median cost of capital was approximately 10 percent with a range of 7 to 15 percent. The more sophisticated approach is to use a beta factor (the extent to which a company's stock price follows the patterns of the stock market) and multiply it by normal and premium returns expected of an investor.

4. *Make a Current EVA Calculation.* This establishes the base, and is typically accomplished by multiplying the cost of capital (a percentage) by capital and determining the amount of NOPAT (or a similar earnings figure) that exceeds (if any) capital costs. This base is then used as a performance measure in executive incentive plans.

5. *Determine Eligibility and Payment Criteria.* Each executive is assigned a percentage of the amount of increase in EVA. If the plan has executives and non-executives, then a fixed percentage of salary could be used and correlated to specified increases in EVA. Typically there is no cap or maximum on potential payments from the plan, although where executives only are defined as participants, it is common to have part of the earned incentive paid in current cash and part deferred.

6. *Assign Plan Administration Accountabilities.* The board compensation committee is typically the plan administrator and approves all payments for executives (and others, if any). Plan calculations are normally delegated to a financial executive, while plan communication and the maintenance of participant accounts are normally delegated to a financial or human resource manager.

Q 19:9   Can stock options be linked to EVA?

Yes, but few companies follow this practice since EVA is an incentive plan while a stock option is a reward based on position/responsibility level, i.e., the higher the executive's position, the greater her potential impact on the business, and the higher the number of stock options. In addition, stock options are intended to reward executives over a long time period (four to five years) and therefore have a retention value to companies. Few companies make stock option grants based on performance in an incentive plan or merit pay plan, because these plans address different business purposes in an organization.

Q 19:10   How do companies link EVA to executive compensation?

EVA plans are frequently combination annual and long-term incentive plans in organizations. This decision is driven by the amount of EVA that should be made available for distribution to executives. Consider the following example.

Example. Assume that EVA in a company is $50 million, and the company is willing to pay 20% of any increase in the EVA. Further assume that the company believes a 10% increase in EVA is reasonable. This means that, if achieved, the EVA incentive would provide a $1 million fund for participants ($50 million × 10% = $5 million × 20% = $1 million).

Further assume that there are 14 executives eligible for the EVA plan and that targeted annual and long-term incentive compensation for these executives is as follows:

Title	No.	Targeted Annual Incentive	Targeted Long-Term Incentive
Chief Executive Officer	1	$150,000	$150,000
Senior Vice President	3	$300,000	$300,000
Vice President	10	$500,000	$500,000
Totals:	14	$950,000	$950,000

Since the company has targeted $950,000 for its annual incentive and $950,000 for its long-term incentive, the EVA plan might be an annual incentive plan only, in this company, unless the company's board believed that there was significant underperformance in the business and that long-term incentives should not be earned until EVA was improved.

In the previous example, the EVA plan would probably be used as an annual incentive plan, and a stock option or other stock award plan would be the company's long-term incentive plan. The final decision in linking EVA to executive compensation is to decide if all or a part of the incentive should be deferred. If a company uses EVA as both an annual and long-term incentive plan, it would likely have some mandatory deferral of amounts earned, i.e., part paid currently, part deferred to retirement, termination, or some future or longer-term vesting or payment date. If a company uses EVA as its annual incentive only, it would likely have deferral as a voluntary alternative.

Q 19:11 How are EVA plans communicated to executives?

Carefully. EVA plans are like any other executive incentive plan in that their success will largely depend on the effectiveness of their communication to eligible executives. A participant's outline should be provided to executives, stating the purpose of the plan, all definitions of the EVA performance measures, planned feedback to participants on year-to-date achievement, examples of potential compensation that can be earned from the plan, payment procedures in the event of a change of job, termination, disability, etc., and plan administrative accountabilities.

Q 19:12 Can EVA plans apply to non-executives?

Yes, but it is best to implement plans with broad eligibility in phases. For example, grant eligibility to executives in phase one (the first year or two) and, if successful, grant eligibility to other managerial positions in phase two, and, if successful, grant eligibility to non-managerial professional positions in phase three, etc. By doing this, an organization is managing the plans's success and effectiveness.

Q 19:13 What is an example of a successful EVA plan?

SPX Corporation, an auto supplier, has an EVA plan that has helped the company go from a net income loss to a positive net income. The company has publicly stated that EVA is a "change accelerator." Its plan extends to over 4,000 employees, and the chief executive officer recently earned nearly $2 million dollars from the plan.

SPX's EVA formula is a standard operating profit after taxes minus a theoretical cost of capital designed to "mirror" the kind of return investors would expect from their investment. The plan was communicated to company personnel, who were told that if profits increased, they would all share in this success. The incentive plan was designed to provide above-average competitive compensation, for non-executive positions, if earned, and to be part of competitive compensation (if earned) for executives.

The chief executive earned an annual bonus of $920,000 in 1996 and "banked" another $1,050,000 in deferred compensation due to significant increases in net income and the fact that the EVA plan focused employees on finding ways to increase net income without spending additional capital.

Q 19:14 What is an example of an unsuccessful EVA plan?

A division of CSX Corporation, a major transportation company, implemented EVA and did an excellent job of explaining to managers how an improvement in net income could increase EVA and increase their bonuses. Unfortunately, the division managers did a fantastic job of increasing sales and net income by adding business, but at a cost of neglecting service to some major current customers, and these customers went elsewhere for their transportation needs. There was no deferred compensation element to the plan; it was all current compensation. The plan has since been changed.

Chapter 20

Trends in Executive Compensation

This chapter will be continuously updated to describe new ideas and trends in the field of executive compensation. Topics will include regulatory issues, media issues, new types of compensation, and modifications being implemented on current pay programs.

Total Cash Compensation 20-1
Long-Term Compensation 20-5
Outside Directors 20-8
Regulations 20-9

Total Cash Compensation

Q 20:1 How are base salary levels changing for executive positions in large companies?

The increases in top officer base salary levels (i.e., the top five highest paid executives) continue to rise faster than that of other executives and non-executives. The American Compensation Association annual salary budget survey for 1996 to 1997 reports that the average increase for executives is 4.3 percent projected for 1997 while the similar statistic for exempt and non-exempt employees is 4.1 percent. Large human resource consulting firms report average officer salary increases to be between 6 percent and 8 percent. A review of 100 public company proxies selected at random shows an average increase for the top five officers of 8 percent.

Q 20:2 Is the $1 million cap on the deductibility of executive pay having any influence on the base salary levels of the top five officers in public companies?

A review of the proxies in 100 large public companies clearly leads one to conclude that the $1 million cap is having little if any impact on the base salary levels of top executives in public companies. For example, the chief executive officers of Allied Signal and Kodak both have annual base salary levels of $2 million, while the chief executive officer of General Electric has an annual base salary of $2.3 million. These companies can only deduct $1 million of this compensation expense when calculating the amount of corporate income that is subject to corporate taxes because base salary is not "performance-based." Annual and long-term incentive payments and most stock award plans are typically exempt from the $1 million cap in public companies because they meet the Code Section 162(m) definitions of performance-based pay, which is excluded from the cap.

There are some exceptions to this general trend in companies like IBP, Inc, where the chief executive has had the same base salary of $1 million for three years. Also, the former chief executive officer of Bell South, John Clendenin, actually had his base salary go down over a three-year period (although his annual bonus increased significantly during the same period). In the Clendenin example, overall cash compensation increased, although it was clearly performance-based, which was the intent of the IRS when they adopted the $1 million cap on the deductibility of executive pay.

Q 20:3 How are base salary levels for executives changing in small companies?

The pattern of base pay increase in small companies is similar to that in large companies. A review of 50 small company proxies also shows that the top five executives have average increases that exceed those of other executives and all non-executive positions.

Q 20:4   Are there any new ideas in base salary administration for executives?

Yes, one is the trading of base salary for stock options. Mr. Richard Manoogian of Masco Corporation took a base salary of $1.00 and an annual bonus of $0 in 1996 but got board compensation committee approval of 1 million stock options. Moreover, the stock options are performance-based in that the exercise price is $41 while the stock price at the time of grant was $27.875. This is similar to the Disney World stock option grant to new Chief Executive Officer Michael Eisner (i.e., 1 million stock option shares with an exercise price that was well beyond the price at the time of grant); however, Mr. Eisner's base salary and bonus were not $1.

Q 20:5   How are annual bonus levels changing for executives?

Executive bonus awards as a percentage of base salary are increasing significantly. A review of 100 public company proxies selected at random shows that the average bonus as a percentage of base salary is 110 percent. This is a significant trend. If a similar analysis were done five years ago, the average bonus as a percentage of base salary would have been slightly over 50 percent. This suggests that companies are putting significantly greater leverage into their annual bonus payout schedules, i.e., the higher the performance, the higher the increase in the bonus percentage.

It follows that the dollar amount of annual bonus awards is also increasing significantly. Examples of some of the highest bonus award levels paid during 1996 in the large billion dollar companies is as follows:

Company	CEO Bonus	Bonus % of Base Salary
General Electric Company	$4.0 million	174%
IBP, Inc.	$3.7 million	372%
The Coca-Cola Company	$3.5 million	204%
Allied Signal, Inc.	$2.8 million	140%
Monsanto Corporation	$2.1 million	172%
Rockwell Int'l. Corp.	$2.0 million	220%

Bonus levels of $1 million are common in large companies for the chief executive officer and other top four executive positions.

Q 20:6   How are bonus payout schedules changing?

There is greater leverage in today's annual incentive plan payout schedules than in previous payout schedules with more gradual accrual of incentive fund dollars. With a steeper payout accrual once the targeted performance is achieved, the payout schedule has more leverage.

A specific example of greater leverage in a corporation's annual incentive is the Rockwell International Corporation plan where specified corporate positions have multiple performance measures in their annual incentive plan. These measures are earnings per share, return on equity, operating cash flow, and shareholder return. These performance measures are weighted by the board compensation committee in determining the amount of actual incentive to be paid to each eligible executive. The most recent Rockwell proxy states that "the range of actual incentive compensation for individual executive positions, as a percentage of target, ranged from 121% to 240%."

Another way that annual incentive payouts are changing is the increasing use of discretionary award criteria by board compensation committees. An example is The Coca-Cola Company, which states in its recent proxy that the chief executive officer

> earned an annual incentive award of $3,500,000 for 1996, of which $2,587,000 was made under the Executive Performance Incentive Plan and $913,999 as a discretionary award. The total award which falls in the 4th quartile of historical competitive standards, was made in consideration of the Company's outstanding performance, the high strategic vision that guided the Coca-Cola business system so successfully through a year of profound changes in competitive positions in the soft drink industry in key markets around the world.

Public company board compensation committees are required to state the executive compensation philosophy of the company, and the reasons for the annual incentive award of the chief executive officer. This is a provision in the Securities Exchange Commission proxy reporting regulations.

Q 20:7   What changes are occurring in the mix of base salary and annual incentive for executive positions?

There is a greater percentage of total cash compensation being earned by executives from their company's annual incentive plan. Part of the reason for this is the greater leverage in incentive plan payout schedules discussed in Q 20:6. When incentives are earned, they are higher than in previous years, in both percentage and real dollars.

The other reason is that board compensation committees are enforcing a higher level of pay for performance. For example, a review of 350 public company proxies showed that nearly 20 percent of all chief executives had a lower bonus (or zero) in 1996 than in 1995. Therefore, there is a greater tendency to pay less (or zero) in poor performing years but more in high performing years. The net result is higher overall annual incentives for executives.

Long-Term Compensation

Q 20:8   How are stock award levels changing for executive positions?

The size of stock option awards continues a prior trend of increasing significantly. The average stock option (defined as stock price times number of shares) grant to company chief executive officers in large companies is between $4 million and $6 million (depending on the mix of companies selected in the analysis). A typical NYSE-listed company would have a stock price of $40. If a chief executive officer is granted $4 million in stock options, the number of shares is 100,000 ($4 million divided by $40 = 100,000). Thus, if company stock price goes up $1, the CEO has a gain of $100,000.

Large human resource consulting firms report that option values for chief executive officers range from 1.5 to 4.5. For example, the chief executive officer of ConAgra, Inc. has been given approximately 35,000 stock options for each of the last three years. With a recent stock price of $40, this executive has an annual option value of $1.4 million (35,000 × $40.00 = $1,400,000). The base salary of the chief executive officer is $900,000. This results in an option value of 1.6 ($1,400,000 divided by $900,000 = 1.55 rounded to 1.6).

Jumbo stock option grants also continue as a major precedent in executive compensation. An example is the chief executive of Allied Signal, who in 1994 received 1,800,000 stock option shares. The 1996 proxy of the company reports that these options plus previous option shares have a potential value that is just under $80 million. The Coca-Cola Company proxy reports that its chief executive officer has unexercised in-the-money options with a value of $112 million. These are examples of jumbo grants.

The size and number of restricted stock awards is also increasing significantly. The use of restricted stock, as reported in most any industry market survey, has increased from 25 percent usage five years ago to 40 to 50 percent usage today (depending on the survey selected). Most of these awards are one-time grants. For example, the chief executive officer of Honeywell, Inc. received a restricted stock grant of $2,245,203 in 1993; the restrictions lapse in 9 years or sooner if performance goals are met. The chief executive officer of Campbell Soup Company received a restricted stock award of $2,846,765 in 1995; these are also tied to the attainment of financial goals. More of the restricted stock grants to executives are performance-based as shown in these examples.

Q 20:9 Does the use of performance-based stock options continue as a trend?

Yes, examples are Dupont, BankAmerica, and Disney World, who use performance options. At BankAmerica these are called "premium options" and the performance feature is that the exercise price is higher than the grant price, i.e., the price at grant was $108 per share and the exercise price is $144 per share, 33.3 percent higher. A similar provision is used in Dupont where the exercise price is 20 percent over the grant price.

At Disney World, the chief executive officer received 3 million performance options and 5 million regular (non-performance) options. A member of the Disney Board estimated that if stock price at the company increased 15 percent, the chief executive officer would have options valued at over $1 billion.

Q 20:10 Have non-compete clauses been used in stock award plans?

Yes, IBM is the high-profile example of this concept. It required an ex-executive to give back the gain from a stock option that was exercised just before the executive voluntarily resigned to take a position with Digital Equipment Corporation. The executive had signed a non-compete agreement that stipulated if a stock option is exercised within six months of a voluntary termination, the executive would have to return the gain to the company. This particular case was settled but no details have been released. Clearly, there was one concerned executive when IBM decided to enforce the non-compete stock option agreement.

Q 20:11 Are economic value-added plans continuing as a trend?

Yes. See Chapter 19. EVA plans are one of the hottest new ideas in executive compensation. Compaq Computer Corporation made the following quarterly press release in 1997: "Compaq's first quarter earnings increase 66 percent: EVA more than triples." At SPX Corporation, the chief executive officer credits EVA as an important part of his turnaround strategy. He publicly stated to the Wall Street Journal, "When linked to compensation, EVA is a change accelerator."

There are many different definitions of EVA, but advocates believe that this performance measure produces a more direct link between company and executive performance and shareholder value. Traditional accounting measures are not as effective. The prevalence of EVA is around 25 percent in most surveys, indicating that most companies still use financial performance measures. This is an issue that many executive compensation planners are investigating for use in their company or are closely tracking.

Outside Directors

Q 20:12   How are remuneration levels changing for outside directors?

They are increasing. As shown in Chart 20-2, the median total compensation over a three-year period increased 23 percent in large companies (from $43,500 to $53,500) and 16.7 percent in small companies (from $21,000 to $24,500).

Chart 20-2a: Large Companies.

Year	Median Annual Retainer	Median Committee Retainer	Median Board Retainer	Median Committee Meeting Fee	Median Total Fee	Cash Compensation
1993	$30,000	N/A	$1,000	$1,000	$43,500
1996	$37,000	$4,500	$1,200	$1,200	$53,500

Chart 20-2b: Small Companies.

Year	Median Annual Retainer	Median Committee Retainer	Median Board Retainer	Median Committee Meeting Fee	Median Total Fee	Cash Compensation
1993	$15,000	N/A	$750	$750	$21,000
1996	$18,500	N/A	$750	$750	$24,500

These significant increases parallel continuous increases in the responsibility levels and time commitments required of today's outside directors.

Q 20:13   Are retirement plans still prevalent for outside directors?

No. Retirement plans for outside directors are decreasing in large numbers. This is a major trend in outside director remuneration. In 1993, 60 percent of all large companies surveyed had some form of retirement plan for outside directors. In 1996, the number was down to 30 percent. A review of 100 public companies selected at random shows that 26 percent eliminated retirement plans just in 1996. Some are replacing them with deferred compensation plans and/or restricted stock/stock options, but the guaranteed defined benefit plan is becoming a pay plan of the past for outside directors.

Q 20:14 Do outside directors still receive stock awards?

Yes, and the use of stock awards for outside directors is increasing significantly. In 1996, 72 percent of large companies surveyed provided some form of stock award for their outside directors. In 1993, the corresponding number was 40 percent. The value of these awards is in addition to the cash compensation increase discussed in Q 20:12. An example of a large company plan is the Quaker Oats Company, which gives each outside director 800 shares of the company's common stock on January 1 of each year. At $40 per share this is a value of $32,000 on top of annual retainer, meeting fees, etc.

Small companies also are using stock awards. Cryolife, Inc., a small publicly held biotechnology company, provides each outside director with a modest $500 fee for each board. If the company has six board meetings in a year, total fees are $3,000. In addition the company provides each outside director with 4,000 stock option shares each year. During a recent 12-month period, the company's stock advanced $5 per share, which is a potential value of $20,000 (4,000 × $5 = $20,000) for each outside director.

The use of stock as a major remuneration program for outside directors clearly assists companies in aligning the interests of outside directors with those of shareholders.

Regulations

Q 20:15 How have companies reacted to FAS 123 on the accounting for stock options?

The reaction has been as expected, with companies electing not to use FAS 123, which results in a charge to earnings. Companies are following APB 25, which does not create a charge to income statements for stock options, provided the stock option is granted at 100 percent of fair market value (or greater), and provided there is no variable performance criteria that could make the executive ineligible to exercise the option. FAS 123 also requires that companies that elect APB 25 (rather than calculate a charge to earnings under FAS 123) must show the impact of company stock options on net income and earnings per share.

An example of a company that uses APB 25 is the Raytheon Company. In its annual report, notes to the financial statement, the company states its use of APB 25 and then shows net income and earnings per share both as reported in the financial statements and as they would have appeared had the company taken a charge to its earnings for stock options. The difference during 1996 was ten cents per share or 3.1 percent.

Q 20:16   **How do executive compensation levels compare to company performance graphs that are displayed, per SEC regulations, in public company proxies?**

As shown in Chart 20-3, the correlation of company performance and executive pay is close. Depending on how one interprets the information in Chart 20-3, approximately 75 to 85 percent of all public companies surveyed had a correlation between the two variables.

Chart 20-3. Correlations of Executive Pay and Company Performance in 100 1996 Proxies

Executive Pay Down	Executive Pay Up
Company Performance Down	Company Performance Up
35%	40%
Executive Pay Down	Executive Pay Up
Company Performance Up	Company Performance Down
10%	15%

While comparable information is not available for previous years, most expect that in a typical year of the past, the correlation would not have been as great when there was no reporting of this type of comparison.

In the 15 percent of those cases in Chart 20-3 where executive pay was up while company performance was down, it is likely that board compensation committee members in those companies would take a close look at executive pay and respond appropriately to the inconsistency.

Q 20:17 What is the new bill in Congress that is intended to further limit the tax deduction companies can take on stock options?

Senators Carl Levin and John McCain have introduced a bill (S.576) that would result in a further limitation on company tax deductions for stock options. It would limit the tax deduction to the amount that the company charges to its earnings. Therefore, if a company elects APB 25, as shown with the Raytheon company, in Q 20:15, then such a company would have no tax deduction on exercised stock options (as they now do under IRS regulations) since there is no earnings charge. Incentive stock options do not have a tax deduction, unless they are disqualified by the executive (the executive does not hold the stock for one year after exercise before selling), but nonqualified stock options do permit the company to take a tax deduction equal to the amount of appreciation received by the executive at the time of exercise (when the executive is required to pay ordinary income tax).

The proposed bill would impact executive stock option plans, as it contains exemptions for what is called broad-based plans that provide stock options to all employees. While there is no indication of any level of support for the bill, it should obviously be tracked by executive compensation planners.

Q 20:18 Will the proposed changes in capital gains tax rates effect executive compensation?

Yes, they are expected to result in greater use of incentive stock options. The current proposal is to reduce the capital gains tax rate from 28 percent to 20 percent. The incentive stock option provides the opportunity for capital gains tax rates if the option is held and not sold for at least one year after exercise. When this occurs, the full appreciation is taxed at capital gains rates to the executive.

There are two negatives to incentive stock options. The first is that there is no tax deduction to the company when the executive is subject to capital gains tax. The second is that the statutory requirements of the incentive stock option limit the annual vesting to $100,000 (i.e., the option value of stock price times number of shares cannot exceed $100,000). Therefore, an executive cannot be made eligible to exercise more than the $100,000 option value in any given year. However, this vesting limit is cumulative, i.e., after five years it is $500,000.

There are other ways to take advantage of a lower capital gains tax:

1. Executives should exercise stock options as soon as possible. Upon exercise, the executive owns the capital asset. Any capital asset, if held for one year, is subject to capital gains tax.

2. Companies can pay incentive compensation (annual and long-term) in stock. Again, when paid, the executive owns a capital asset; if held for one year before sale, it is subject to capital gains.

3. Companies can use reload features on stock awards, both stock options and restricted stock. The reload feature simply gives the executive another grant of options when he or she exercises any given number of shares, or another grant of restricted stock whenever restrictions lapse on a current grant. Both techniques can result in stock ownership, and the capital gains tax applies if the stock is held for one year before sale.

Q 20:19   Will more executives be subject to the alternative minimum tax if ISO use increases due to a lower capital gains tax?

Probably yes, because the AMT applies to preference income, and the "paper gain" from the exercise of an incentive stock option is subject to the AMT calculation. The AMT was designed to close a loophole of tax shelters and other tax-deductible items that offer preferential treatment under the Internal Revenue Code. The AMT requires taxpayers to calculate ordinary income tax as well as to also make an alternative minimum tax calculation and then pay the higher of the two tax calculations. Under the AMT, the value of the paper gain on an incentive stock option is added to income (it is not under the ordinary income tax calculation), and the AMT does not allow as many deductions as the ordinary income tax calculation.

If the use of incentive stock options increases, as expected, with lower capital gains tax rates, companies will need to assess the impact of AMT on their executives.

Appendix A

IRS Model Rabbi Trust Arrangement

Revenue Procedure 92-64 [1992-2 CB 422] provides the following model rabbi trust investment for plan sponsors to use. Using this model agreement, or parts of it, may reduce the number of occasions when the plan sponsor finds it necessary to seek private letter rulings from the Internal Revenue Service.

[¶40,096] Rev Proc 92-64, 1992-2 CB 422.—"Rabbi trust" arrangements

——Section 1. Purpose

This revenue procedure contains a model grantor trust for use in executive compensation arrangements that are popularly referred to as "rabbi trust" arrangements. This revenue procedure also provides guidance for requesting rulings on nonqualified deferred compensation plans that use such trusts.

——Section 2. Background

The Internal Revenue Service receives and responds to many requests for rulings on the federal income tax consequences of trusts established in connection with unfunded deferred compensation arrangements. In many of these requests, the trust instruments are very similar. Consequently, in order to aid taxpayers and to expedite the processing of ruling requests on these arrangements, this revenue procedure provides a model trust instrument that plan sponsors may use.

——Section 3. Scope and Objective

The model trust provided in this revenue procedure is intended to serve as a safe harbor for taxpayers that adopt and maintain grantor trusts in connection with unfunded deferred compensation arrangements. If the model trust is used in accordance with this revenue procedure, an employee will not be in constructive receipt of income or incur an economic benefit solely on account of the adaptation or maintenance of the trust. However, the desired tax effect will be achieved only if the nonqualified deferred compensation arrangement effectively defers compensation. Thus, no inference may be drawn by reason of adoption of the model trust concerning constructive receipt or economic benefit issues that may be present in the underlying nonqualified deferred compensation plan. In addition, the use of the model trust does not change the rules generally applicable under section 6321 of the Code with respect to the attachment of a federal tax lien to a taxpayer's property and rights to property.

The Service will continue to rule on unfunded deferred compensation plans that do not use a trust, on unfunded deferred compensation plans that use the model trust, and, where the model trust is used, generally, on the issue of whether a trust constitutes a grantor trust within the meaning of subpart E, part I, subchapter J, subtitle A of the Internal Revenue Code of 1986. However, rulings will not be issued on unfunded deferred compensation arrangements that use a trust other than the model trust, except in rare and unusual circumstances.

Taxpayers that adopt the model trust and wish to obtain a ruling on the underlying nonqualified deferred compensation plan, must include a representation that the plan, as amended, is not inconsistent with the terms of the trust and must follow the guidelines outlined in Section 4 of this revenue procedure and Revenue Procedure 92-65, this Bulletin. Rulings issued on such deferred compensation arrangements will continue to provide that the Service expresses no opinion as to the consequences of the arrangement under Title I of the Employee Retirement Income Security Act of 1974 ("ERISA"). The Department of Labor has advised that whether a "top hat" or excess benefit plan is funded or unfunded depends upon all of the facts and circumstances. However, it is the DOL's view that such plans will not fail to be "unfunded" for purposes of sections 4(b)(5), 201(2), 301(a)(3), and 401(a)(1) of ERISA solely because there is maintained in connection with such a plan a trust which conforms to the model trust described in Section 5 of this revenue procedure.

In addition, rulings issued on deferred compensation arrangements using the model trust will provide that the Service expresses no opinion on the consequences under subchapter C of chapter 1 of subtitle A of the Code or under sections 1501 through 1504 on the trust's acquisition, holding, sale or disposition of stock of the grantor.

——Section 4. Guidance Regarding Trusts

01. A private letter ruling on a nonqualified deferred compensation arrangement using a grantor trust subject to the claims of the employer's creditors will be issued only if the trust conforms to the model language contained in Section 5 of this revenue procedure. The model language must be adopted verbatim, except where substitute language is expressly permitted.

The request for a ruling must be accompanied by a representation that the trust conforms to the model trust language contained in this revenue procedure, including the order in which sections of the model trust language appear, and that the trust adopted does not contain any inconsistent language, in substituted portions or elsewhere, that conflicts with the model trust language. Of course, provisions may be renumbered if appropriate, language in brackets may be omitted, and blanks may be completed. In addition, the taxpayer may add sections to the model language provided that such additions are not inconsistent with the model language. Finally, the submission must also include a copy of the trust on which all substituted or additional language is either underlined or otherwise clearly marked and on which the location of the required investment authority language is indicated.

02.   The request for a ruling must contain a representation that the trust is a valid trust under state law and that all of the material terms and provisions of the trust, including the creditors' rights clause, are enforceable under the appropriate state laws.

03.   The trustee of the trust must be an independent third party that may be granted corporate trustee powers under state law, such as a bank trust department or other similar party.

——Section 5. Model Provisions

01.   The model trust language in this section contains all provisions necessary for operation of the trust except describing the trustee's investment powers. Provisions agreed to by the parties should be used to describe investment powers. The trustee must be given some investment discretion, such as the authority to invest within broad guidelines established by the parties (e.g., invest in government securities, bonds with specific ratings, or stocks of the Fortune 500 companies).

The model trust language contains a number of optional provisions, which are printed in italics and marked as "OPTIONAL." The taxpayer may substitute language of its choice for any optional provision, provided that the substituted language is not inconsistent with the language of the model trust. The model trust language also contains several alternative provisions, which are printed in italics and marked as "ALTERNATIVE." The taxpayer must choose one of these alternatives. Items in brackets are explanatory.

02.   The text of the model trust follows.

TRUST UNDER _____ PLAN

OPTIONAL

(a)   This Agreement made this _____ day of _____, by and between _____ Company) and _____ (Trustee);

OPTIONAL

(b)   *WHEREAS, Company has adopted the nonqualified deferred compensation Plan(s) as listed in Appendix .*

OPTIONAL

(c)   WHEREAS, Company has incurred or expects to incur liability under the terms of such Plan(s) with respect to the individuals participating such Plan(s);

(d)   WHEREAS, Company wishes to establish a trust (hereinafter called "Trust") and to contribute to the Trust assets that shall be held therein, subject to the claims of Company's creditors in the event of Company's Insolvency, as herein defined, until paid to Plan participants and their beneficiaries in such manner and at such times as specified in the Plan(s);

(e)   WHEREAS, it is the intention of the parties that this Trust shall constitute an unfunded arrangement and shall not affect the status of the Plan(s) as an unfunded plan maintained for the purpose of providing deferred compensation for a select group of management or highly compensated employees for purposes of Title I of the Employee Retirement Income Security Act of 1974;

(f)   WHEREAS, it is the intention of Company to make contributions to the Trust to provide itself with a source of funds to assist it in the meeting of its liabilities under the Plan(s);

NOW, THEREFORE, the parties do hereby establish the Trust and agree that the Trust shall be compromised, held and disposed of as follows:

Section 1.   *Establishment Of Trust*

(a)   Company hereby deposits with Trustee in trust _____ [insert amount deposited], which shall become the principal of the Trust to be held, administered and disposed of by Trustee as provided in this Trust Agreement.

ALTERNATIVES—Select one provision.

(b)   The Trust hereby established shall be revocable by Company.

(b)   The Trust hereby established shall be irrevocable.

(b)   The Trust hereby established is revocable by Company; it shall become irrevocable upon a Change of Control, as defined herein.

(b)   The Trust shall become irrevocable _____ [insert number] days following the issuance of a favorable private letter ruling regarding the Trust from the Internal Revenue Service.

(b)   The Trust shall become irrevocable upon approval by the Board of Directors.

(c)   The Trust is intended to be a grantor trust, of which Company is the grantor, within the meaning of subpart E, part I, subchapter J, chapter 1, subtitle A of the Internal Revenue Code of 1986, as amended, and shall be construed accordingly.

(d)   The principal of the Trust, and any earnings thereon shall be held separate and apart from other funds of Company and shall be used exclusively for the uses and purposes of Plan participants and general creditors as herein set forth. Plan participants and their beneficiaries shall have no preferred claim on, or any beneficial ownership interest in, any assets of the Trust. Any rights created under the Plan(s) and this Trust Agreement shall be mere unsecured contractual rights of Plan participants and their beneficiaries against Company. Any assets held by the Trust will be subject to the claims of Company's general creditors under federal and state law in the event of Insolvency, as defined in Section 3(a) herein.

ALTERNATIVES—Select one or more provisions, as appropriate.

(e)   Company, in its sole discretion, may at any time, or from time to time, make additional deposits of cash or other property in trust with Trustee to augment the principal to be held, administered and disposed of by Trustee as provided in this Trust Agreement. Neither Trustee nor any Plan participant or beneficiary shall have any right to compel such additional deposits.

(e)   Upon a Change of Control, Company shall, as soon as possible, but in no event longer than ____ [fill in blank] days following the Change of Control, as defined herein, make an irrevocable contribution to the Trust in an amount that is sufficient to pay each Plan participant or beneficiary the benefits to which Plan participants or their beneficiaries would be entitled pursuant to the terms of the Plan(s) as of the date on which the Change of Control occurred.

(e)   Within ____ [fill in blank] days following the end of the Plan year(s), ending after the Trust has become irrevocable pursuant to

Section 1(b) hereof, Company shall be required to irrevocably deposit additional cash or other property to the Trust in an amount sufficient to pay each Plan participant or beneficiary the benefits payable pursuant to the terms of the Plan(s) as of the close of the Plan year(s).

Section 2. *Payments to Plan Participants and Their Beneficiaries.*

(a) Company shall deliver to Trustee a schedule (the "Payment Schedule") that indicates the amounts payable in respect of each Plan participant (and his or her beneficiaries), that provides a formula or other instructions acceptable to Trustee for determining the amounts so payable, the form in which such amount is to be paid (as provided for or available under the Plan(s)), and the time of commencement for payment of such amounts. Except as otherwise provided herein, Trustee shall make payments to the Plan participants and their beneficiaries in accordance with such Payment Schedule. The Trustee shall make provisions for the reporting and withholding of any federal, state, or local taxes that may be required to be withheld with respect to the payment of benefits pursuant to the terms of the Plan(s) and shall pay amounts withheld to the appropriate taxing authorities or determine that such amounts have been reported, withheld and paid by Company.

(b) The entitlement of a Plan participant or his or her beneficiaries to benefits under the plan(s) shall be determined by Company or such party as it shall designate under the Plan(s), and any claim for such benefits shall be considered and reviewed under the procedures set out in the Plan(s).

(c) Company may make payment of benefits directly to Plan participants or their beneficiaries as they become due under the terms of the Plan(s). Company shall notify beneficiaries as they become due under the terms of the Plan(s). Company shall notify Trustee of its decision to make payment of benefits directly prior to the time amounts are payable to participants or their beneficiaries. In addition, if the principal of the Trust, and any earnings thereon, are not sufficient to make payments of benefits in accordance with the terms of the Plan(s), Company shall make the balance of each such payment as it falls due. Trustee shall notify company where principal and earnings are not sufficient.

Section 3. *Trustee Responsibility Regarding Payments to Trust Beneficiary When Company is Insolvent.*

(a)   Trustee shall cease payment of benefits to Plan participants and their beneficiaries if the Company is Insolvent. Company shall be considered "Insolvent" for purposes of this Trust Agreement if (i) Company is unable to pay its debts as they become due, or (ii) Company is subject to a pending proceeding as a debtor under the United States Bankruptcy Code.

OPTIONAL

, or (iii) Company is determined to be insolvent by _____
[insert names of applicable federal and/or state regulatory agency].

(b)   At all times during the continuance of this trust, as provided in Section 1 (d) hereof, the principal and income of the Trust shall be subject to claims of general creditors of Company under federal and state law as set forth below.

(1)   The Board of Directors and the Chief Executive Officer [or substitute the title of the highest ranking officer of the Company] of Company shall have the duty to inform Trustee in writing of Company's Insolvency. If a person claiming to be a creditor of Company alleges in writing to Trustee that Company has become Insolvent, Trustee shall determine whether Company is Insolvent and, pending such determination, Trustee shall discontinue payment of benefits to Plan participants or their beneficiaries.

(2)   Unless Trustee has actual knowledge of Company's Insolvency, or has received notice from Company or a person claiming to be a creditor alleging that company is Insolvent, Trustee shall have no duty to inquire whether Company Is Insolvent. Trustee may in all events rely on such evidence concerning Company's solvency as may be furnished to Trustee and that provides Trustee with a reasonable basis for making a determination concerning Company's solvency.

(3)   If at any time Trustee has determined that Company is Insolvent, Trustee shall discontinue payments to Plan participants or their beneficiaries and shall hold the assets of the Trust for the benefit of Company's general creditors. Nothing in this Trust Agreement shall in any way diminish any rights of Plan participants or their

beneficiaries to pursue their rights as general creditors of Company with respect to benefits due under the Plan(s) or otherwise.

(4)   Trustee shall resume the payment of benefits to Plan participants or their beneficiaries in accordance with Section 2 of this Trust Agreement only after Trustee has determined that Company is not Insolvent (or is no longer Insolvent).

(c)   Provided that there are sufficient assets, if trustee discontinues the payment of benefits from the Trust pursuant to Section 3(b) hereof and subsequently resumes such payments, the first payment following such discontinuance shall include the aggregate amount of all payments due to Plan participants or their beneficiaries under the terms of the Plan(s) for the period of such discontinuance, less the aggregate amount of any payments made to Plan participants or their beneficiaries by Company in lieu of the payments provided for hereunder during any such period of discontinuance.

Section 4.   *Payments to Company.*

[The following need not be included if the first alternative under 1(b) is selected.]

Except as provided in Section 3 hereof, after the Trust has become irrevocable, Company shall have no right or power to direct Trustee to return to Company or to divert to others any of the Trust assets before all payment of benefits have been made to Plan participants and their beneficiaries pursuant to the terms of the Plan(s).

Section 5.   *Investment Authority.*

ALTERNATIVES—Select one provision, as appropriate

(a)   In no event may Trustee invest in securities (including stock or rights to acquire stock) or obligations issued by Company, other than a de minimis amount held in common investment vehicles in which Trustee invests. All rights associated with assets of the Trust shall be exercised by Trustee or the person designated by Trustee, and shall in no event be exercisable by or rest with Plan participants.

(a)   Trustee may invest in securities (including stock or rights to acquire stock) or obligations issued by Company. All rights associated

with assets of the Trust shall be exercised by Trustee or the person designated by Trustee, and shall in no event be exercisable by or rest with Plan participants.

OPTIONAL

except that voting rights with respect to Trust assets will be exercised by Company.

OPTIONAL

, except that dividend rights with respect to Trust assets will rest with Company.

OPTIONAL

Company shall have the right, at anytime, and from time to time in its sole discretion, to substitute assets of equal fair market value for any asset held by the Trust.

[If the second Alternative 5(a) is selected, the trust must provide either (1) that the trust is revocable under Alternative 1(b), or (2) the following provision must be included in the Trust]:

"Company shall have the right at anytime, and from time to time in its sole discretion, to substitute assets of equal fair market value for any asset held by the Trust. This right is exercisable by Company in a nonfiduciary capacity without the approval or consent of any person in a fiduciary capacity."

Section 6. *Disposition of Income.*

ALTERNATIVES—Select one provision.

(a)   During the term of this Trust, all income received by the Trust, net of expenses and taxes, shall be accumulated and reinvested.

(a)   During the term of this trust, or ___ [insert amount] part of the income received by the Trust, net of expenses and taxes, shall be returned to Company.

Section 7.   *Accounting by Trustee.*

OPTIONAL

Trustee shall keep accurate and detailed records of all investments, receipts, disbursements, and all other transactions required to be made, including such specific records as shall be agreed upon in writing between Company and Trustee. Within ___ [insert number] days following the close of each calendar year and within ___ [insert number] days after the removal or resignation of Trustee, Trustee shall deliver to Company a written account of its administration of the Trust during such year or during the period from the close of the last preceding year to the date of such removal or resignation, setting forth all investments, receipts, disbursements and other transactions effected by it, including a description of all securities and investments purchased and sold with the cost or net proceeds of such purchases or sales (accrued interest paid or receivable being separate), and showing all cash, securities and other property held in the Trust at the end of such year or as of the date of such removal or resignation, as the case may be.

Section 8.   *Responsibility of Trustee.*

OPTIONAL

(a)   Trustee shall act with the care, skill, prudence and diligence under the circumstances then prevailing that a prudent person acting in like capacity and familiar with such matters would use in the conduct of an enterprise of a like character and with like aims, provided, however, that Trustee shall incur no liability to any person for any action taken pursuant to a direction, request or approval given by Company which is contemplated by and in conformity with, the terms of the Plan(s) or this Trust and is given in writing by Company. In the event of a dispute between Company and a party, Trustee may apply to a court of competent jurisdiction to resolve the dispute.

OPTIONAL

(b)   If Trustee undertakes or defends any litigation arising in connection with this Trust, Company agrees to indemnify Trustee against Trustee's costs, expenses and liabilities (including, without

limitation, attorneys' fees and expenses) relating thereto and to be primarily liable for such payments. If company does not pay such costs, expenses and liabilities in a reasonably timely manner, Trustee may obtain payment from the Trust.

OPTIONAL

(c) Trustee may consult with legal counsel (who may also be counsel for Company generally) with respect to any of its duties or obligations hereunder.

OPTIONAL

(d) Trustee may hire agents, accountants, actuaries, investment advisors, financial consultants or other professionals to assist it in performing any of its duties or obligations hereunder.

(e) Trustee shall have, without exclusion, all powers conferred on Trustees by applicable law, unless expressly provided otherwise herein, provided, however, that if an insurance policy is held as an asset of the Trust, Trustee shall have no power to name a beneficiary of the policy other than the Trust, to assign the policy (as distinct from conversion of the policy to a different form) other than to a successor Trustee, or to loan to any person the proceeds of any borrowing against such policy.

OPTIONAL

(f) However, notwithstanding the provisions of Section 8(e) above, Trustee may loan to Company the proceeds of any borrowing against an insurance policy held as an asset of the Trust.

(g) Notwithstanding any powers granted to Trustee pursuant to this Trust Agreement or to applicable law, Trustee shall not have any power that could give this Trust the objective of carrying on a business and dividing the gains therefrom, within the meaning of section 301.7701-2 of the Procedure and Administrative Regulations promulgated pursuant to the Internal Revenue Code.

Section 9. *Compensation and Expenses of Trustee.*

OPTIONAL

Company shall pay all administrative and Trustee's fees and expenses. If not so paid, the fees and expenses shall be paid from the Trust.

Section 10. *Resignation and Removal of Trustee.*

(a) Trustee may resign at any time by written notice to Company, which shall be effective ___ [insert number] days after receipt of such notice unless Company and Trustee agree otherwise.

OPTIONAL

(b) Trustee may be removed by Company on ___ [insert number] days notice or upon shorter notice accepted by Trustee.

OPTIONAL

(c) Upon a Change of Control, as defined herein, Trustee may not be removed by Company for ___ [insert number] year(s).

OPTIONAL

(d) If Trustee resigns within ___ [insert number] year(s) after a Change of Control, as defined herein, Company shall apply to a court of competent jurisdiction for the appointment of a successor Trustee or for instructions.

OPTIONAL

(e) If Trustee resigns or is removed within ___ [insert number] year(s) of a Change of Control, as defined herein, Trustee shall select a successor Trustee in accordance with the provisions of Section 11(b) hereof prior to the effective date of Trustee's resignation or removal.

(f) Upon resignation or removal of Trustee and appointment of a successor Trustee, all assets shall subsequently be transferred to the successor Trustee. The transfer shall be completed within ___ [insert number days after receipt of notice of resignation, removal or transfer, unless Company extends the time limit.

(g)   If Trustee resigns or is removed, a successor shall be appointed, in accordance with Section 11 hereof, by the effective date of resignation or removal under paragraph(s) (a) [or (b)] of this section. If no such appointment has been made, Trustee may apply to a court of competent jurisdiction for appointment of a successor or for instructions. All expenses of Trustee in connection with the proceeding shall be allowed as administrative expenses of the Trust.

Section 11.   *Appointment of Successor.*

OPTIONAL

(a)   If Trustee resigns [or is removed] in accordance with Section 10(a) [or (b)] hereof, Company may appoint any third party, such as a bank trust department or other party that may be granted corporate trustee powers under state law, as a successor to replace Trustee upon resignation or removal. The appointment shall be effective when accepted in writing by the new Trustee, who shall have all of the rights and powers of the former Trustee, including ownership rights in the Trust assets. The former Trustee shall execute any instrument necessary or reasonably requested by Company or the successor Trustee to evidence the transfer.

OPTIONAL

(b)   If Trustee resigns or is removed pursuant to the provisions of Section 10(e) hereof and selects a successor Trustee, Trustee may appoint any third party such as a bank trust department or other party that may be granted corporate trustee powers under state law. The appointment of a successor Trustee shall be effective when accepted in writing by the new Trustee. The new Trustee shall have all rights and powers of the former Trustee, including ownership rights in Trust assets. The former Trustee shall execute any instrument necessary or reasonably requested by the successor Trustee to evidence the transfer.

OPTIONAL

(c)   The successor Trustee need not examine the records and acts of any prior Trustee and may retain or dispose of existing Trust assets, subject to Sections 7 and 8 hereof. The successor Trustee shall not be responsible for and Company shall indemnify and defend the succes-

sor Trustee from any claim or liability resulting from any action or inaction or any prior Trustee or from any other past event, or any condition existing at the time it becomes successor Trustee.

Section 12. *Amendment or Termination.*

(a)   This Trust Agreement may be amended by a written instrument executed by Trustee and Company. [Unless the first alternative under 1(b) is selected, the following sentence must be included.] Notwithstanding the foregoing, no such amendment shall conflict with the terms of the Plan(s) or shall make the Trust revocable after it has become irrevocable in accordance with Section 1(b) hereof.

(b)   The Trust shall not terminate until the date on which Plan participants and their beneficiaries are no longer entitled to benefits pursuant to the terms of the Plan(s) [unless the second alternative under 1(b) is selected, the following must be included:], "unless sooner revoked in accordance with Section 1(b) hereof." Upon termination of the Trust any assets remaining in the Trust shall be returned to Company.

OPTIONAL

(c)   Upon written approval of participants or beneficiaries entitled to payment of benefits pursuant to the terms of the Plan(s), Company may terminate this Trust prior to the time all benefit payments under the Plan(s) have been made. All assets in the Trust at termination shall be returned to Company.

OPTIONAL

(d)   Section(s) ___ [insert number(s)] of this Trust Agreement may not be amended by Company for ___ [insert number] year(s) following a Change of Control, as defined herein.

Section 13. *Miscellaneous.*

(a)   Any provisions of this Trust Agreement prohibited by law shall be ineffective to the extent of any such prohibition, without invalidating the remaining provisions hereof.

(b)   Benefits payable to Plan participants and their beneficiaries under this Trust Agreement may not be anticipated, assigned (either at law or in equity), alienated, pledged, encumbered or subjected to attachment, garnishment, levy, execution or other legal or equitable process.

(c)   This Trust Agreement shall be governed by and construed in accordance with the laws of _____ .

OPTIONAL

(d)   For purposes of this Trust, Change of Control shall mean; [insert objective definition such as: "the purchase or other acquisition by any person, entity or group of persons, within the meaning of section 13(d) or 14(d) of the Securities Exchange Act of 1934 ("Act"), or any comparable successor provisions, of beneficial ownership (within the meaning of Rule 13d-3 promulgated under the Act) of 30 percent or more of either the outstanding shares of common stock or the combined voting power of Company's then outstanding voting securities entitled to vote generally, or the approval by the stockholders of Company of a reorganization, merger, or consolidation, in each case, with respect to which persons who were stockholders of Company immediately prior to such reorganization, merger or consolidation do not, immediately thereafter, own more than 50 percent of the combined voting power entitled to vote generally in the election of directors of the reorganized, merged or consolidated Company's then outstanding securities, or a liquidation or dissolution of Company or of the sale of all or substantially all of Company's assets"].

Section 14.   *Effective Date.*

The effective date of this Trust Agreement shall be _____, 19__ .

——Section 6. Effective Date

01.   This revenue procedure is effective on July 28, 1992.

02.   Ruling requests with respect to grantor trusts used in executive compensation arrangements and subject of the claims of the employer's creditors that are submitted to the Service subsequent to

the effective date of this revenue procedure must comply with the terms of this revenue procedure.

03. This revenue procedure does not affect any private letter rulings that were issued prior to the effective date. If a plan or trust that was the subject of such a ruling is amended, and such amendments affect the rights of participants or other creditors, such ruling will generally not remain in effect.

——Section 7. Public Comment

Written comments, including suggested language, concerning the model trust provision contained in this revenue procedure may be sent to the Internal Revenue Service, Office of the Associate Chief Counsel (Employee Benefits and Exempt Organizations), Attention: CC:EE:1:1, Room 5201, P.O. 7604, Ben Franklin Station, Washington, D.C. 20044.

Drafting Information

The principal author of this revenue procedure is Catherine Livingston Fernandez of the Office of the Associate Chief Counsel (Employee Benefits and Exempt Organizations). For further information regarding this revenue procedure, contact Ms. Fernandez at (202) 622-6030 (not a toll-free number).

[¶40,097] Rev Proc 92-65, 1992-33 IRB 16—Rulings on unfunded deferred compensation arrangements. [Rev Proc 71-19, 1971-1 CB 698, amplified.]

——Section 1. Purpose

01. The purpose of the Revenue Procedure is to set forth the conditions, or circumstances, under which the Internal Revenue Service will issue advance rulings concerning the application of the doctrine of constructive receipt to unfunded deferred compensation arrangements and to amplify Rev. Proc. 71-19, 1971-1 C.B. 698.

——Section 2. Background

In 1960, the Service issued Rev. Rul 60-31, 1960-1 C.B. 174, concerning the application of the doctrine of constructive receipt to certain deferred compensation arrangements. Rev. Rul. 60-31, was modified by Rev. Rul. 64-279, 1964-2 C.B. 121, and Rev. Rul. 70-435, 1970-2 C.B. 100. The conditions under which the Service would issue advance rulings on unfunded deferred compensation arrangements, were originally published in Rev. Proc. 71-19, 1971-1 C.B. 698.

——Section 3. Scope and Objective

01.   In each request for a ruling involving the deferral of compensation, the Service will determine whether the doctrine of constructive receipt is applicable on a case by case basis. The Service will ordinarily issue rulings regarding unfunded deferred compensation arrangements only if the requirements of Rev. Proc. 71-19 are met and, in addition, the arrangement meets the following guidelines.

(a)   Section 3.01 of Rev. Proc. 71-19 states that, if the plan provides for an election to defer payment of compensation, such election must be made before the beginning of the period of service for which the compensation is payable, regardless of the existence in the plan of forfeiture provisions. The period of service for purposes of this requirement generally has been regarded by the Service as the employee's taxable year for cash basis, calendar year taxpayers. Rev. Rul. 68-86, 1968-1 C.B. 184; Rev. Rul. 69-650, 1969-2 C.B. 106; Rev. Rul. 71-419, 1971-2 C.B. 220. There are two exceptions to this general requirement, as follows:

(1)   In the year in which the plan is first implemented, the eligible participant may make an election to defer compensation for services to be performed subsequent to the election within 30 days after the date the plan is effective for eligible employees.

(2)   In the first year in which a participant becomes eligible to participate in the plan, the newly eligible participant may make an election to defer compensation for services to be performed subsequent to the election within 30 days after the date the employee becomes eligible.

(b) The plan must define the time and method for payment of deferred compensation for each event (such as termination of employment, regular retirement, disability retirement or death) that entitles a participant to receive benefits. The plan may specify the date of payment or provide that payments will begin within 30 days after the occurrence of a stated event.

(c) The plan may provide for payment of benefits in the case of an "unforeseeable emergency." "Unforeseeable emergency" must be defined in the plan as an unanticipated emergency that is caused by an event beyond the control of the participant or beneficiary and that would result in severe financial hardship to the individual if early withdrawal were not permitted. The plan must further provide that any early withdrawal approved by the employer is limited to the amount necessary to meet the emergency. Language similar to that described in section 1.457-2(h)(4) and (5) of the Income Tax Regulations may be used.

(d) The plan must provide that participants have the status of general unsecured creditors of the employer and that the plan constitutes a mere promise by the employer to make any benefit payments in the future. If the plan refers to a trust, the plan must also provide that any trust created by the employer and any assets held by the trust to assist it in meeting its obligations under the plan will conform to the terms of the model trust as described in Revenue Procedure 92-64, this Bulletin. Finally, the plan must state that it is the intention of the parties that the arrangements be unfunded for tax purposes and for purposes of Title I of ERISA.

(e) The plan must provide that a participant's rights to benefit payments under the plan are not subject in any manner to anticipation, alienation, sale, transfer, assignment, pledge, encumbrance, attachment, or garnishment by creditors of the participant or the participant's beneficiary.

——Section 4. Procedure

The general procedures of Rev. Proc. 92-1, 1992-1 I.R.B. 9, relating to the issuance of ruling and determination letters, and Rev. Proc. 71-19, 1971-1 C.B. 698, apply to requests relating to unfunded deferred compensation arrangements to the extent they are not covered by this revenue procedure.

——**Section 5. Effect On Other Revenue Procedures**

Rev. Proc. 71-19, 1971-1 C.B. 698, is hereby amplified to set forth the conditions under which the Service will issue advance rulings on unfunded deferred compensation plans.

——**Section 6. Effective Date**

The revenue procedure is effective on July 28, 1992.

Drafting Information

The principal author of this revenue procedure is Catherine Livingston Fernandez of the Office of the Assistant Chief Counsel, (Employee Benefits and Exempt Organizations). For further information regarding this revenue procedure contact Ms. Fernandez at (202) 622-6030 (not a toll-free call).

Appendix B

Sample Compensation Agreements

Three sample compensation plans, presented for consideration at a recent meeting of shareholders of Eastman Kodak Company and included in the proxy statement, are provided for your information, and to bring to life some of the related issues covered in this book. The first plan is a long-term compensation plan; the second plan is a management variable compensation plan; and the third plan is a wage dividend plan.

PLAN 1: 1995 OMNIBUS LONG-TERM COMPENSATION PLAN

ARTICLE 1—PURPOSE AND TERM OF PLAN

1.1 Purpose

The purpose of the Plan is to provide motivation to selected Employees of the Company to put forth maximum efforts toward the continued growth, profitability, and success of the Company by providing incentives to such Employees through the ownership and performance of the Common Stock of Kodak. Toward this objective, the Committee may grant stock options, stock appreciation rights, Stock Awards, performance units, performance shares, Performance

Awards, Common Stock and/or other incentive Awards to Employees of the Company on the terms and subject to the conditions set forth in the Plan.

1.2 Term

The plan shall become effective as of February 1, 1995, subject to its approval by Kodak's shareholders at the 1995 Annual Meeting of the Shareholders. No Awards shall be exercisable or payable before approval of the Plan has been obtained from Kodak's shareholders. Awards shall not be granted pursuant to the Plan after December 31, 1999; except that the Committee may grant Awards after such date in recognition of performance for Performance Cycles commencing prior to such date.

ARTICLE 2—DEFINITIONS

2.1 Approved Reason

"Approval Reason" means a reason for terminating employment with the Company which, in the opinion of the Committee, is in the best interest of the Company.

2.2 Award

"Award" means any form of stock option, stock appreciation right, Stock Award, performance unit, performance share, Performance Award, shares of Common Stock under the Performance Stock Program, or other incentive Award granted under the Plan, whether singly, in combination, or in tandem, to a Participant by the Committee pursuant to such terms, conditions, restrictions and/or limitations, if any, as the Committee may establish by the Award Notice or otherwise.

2.3 Award Notice

"Award Notice" means a written notice from the Company to a Participant that establishes the terms, conditions, restrictions, and/or limitations applicable to an Award in addition to those established by this Plan and by the Committee's exercise of its administrative powers.

2.4 Award Payment Date

"Award Payment Date" means, for a Performance Cycle, the date the Awards for such Performance Cycle shall be paid to Participants. The Award Payment Date for a Performance Cycle shall occur as soon as administratively possible following the completion of the certification required pursuant to Subsection 13.5(c).

2.5 Board

"Board" means the Board of Directors of Kodak.

2.6 Cause

"Cause" means (a) the willful and continued failure by an Employee to substantially perform his or her duties with his or her employer after written warnings identifying the lack of substantial performance are delivered to the Employee by his or her employer to specifically identify the manner in which the employer believes that the Employee has not substantially performed his or her duties, or (b) the willful engaging by an Employee in illegal conduct which is materially and demonstrably injurious to Kodak or a Subsidiary.

2.7 CEO

"CEO" means the Chief Executive Officer of Kodak.

2.8 Change In Control

"Change In Control" means a Change In Control of Kodak of a nature that would be required to be reported (assuming such event has not been "previously reported") in response to Item 1(a) of the Current Report on Form 8-K, as in effect on August 1, 1989, pursuant to Section 13 or 15 (d) of the Exchange Act; provided that, without limitation, a Change In Control shall be deemed to have occurred at such time as (i) any "person" within the meaning of Section 14(d) of the Exchange Act, other than Kodak, a Subsidiary, or any employee benefit plan(s) sponsored by Kodak or any Subsidiary, is or has become the "beneficial owner," as defined in Rule 13d-3 under the Exchange Act, directly or indirectly, of 25% or more of the combined voting power of the outstanding securities of kodak ordinarily having the right to vote at the election of directors, or (ii) individuals who constitute the Board on January 1, 1995 (the "Incumbent Board") have ceased for any reason to constitute at least a majority thereof, provided that any person becoming a director subsequent to January 1, 1995 whose election, or nomination for election by Kodak's shareholders, was approved by a vote of at least three quarters (3/4) of the directors comprising the incumbent Board (either by a specific bote or by approval of the proxy statement of Kodak in which such person is named as a nominee for director without objection to such nomination) shall be, for purposes of this Plan, considered as though such person were a member of the Incumbent Board.

2.9 Change In Control Price

"Change In Control Price" means the highest closing price per share paid for the purchase of Common Stock on the New York Stock Exchange during the ninety (90) day period ending on the date the Change In Control occurs.

2.10 Change In Ownership

"Change In Ownership" means a Change In Control which results directly or indirectly in Kodak's Common Stock ceasing to be actively traded on the New York Stock Exchange.

2.11 Code

"Code" means the Internal Revenue Code of 1986, as amended from time to time, including regulations thereunder and successor provisions and regulations thereto.

2.12 Committee

"Committee" means the Executive Compensation and Development Committee of the Board, or such other Board committee as may be designated by the Board to administer the Plan; provided that the Committee shall consist of three or more directors, all of whom are both a "disinterested person" within the meaning of Rule 16b-3 under the Exchange Act and an "outside director" within the meaning of the definition of such term as contained in Proposed Treasury Regulation Section 1.162-27(e)(3), or any successor definition adopted.

2.13 Common Stock

"Common Stock" means Common Stock, $2.50 par value share, of Kodak which may be newly issued or treasury stock.

2.14 Company

"Company" means Kodak and its Subsidiaries.

2.15 Covered Employee

"Covered Employee" means an Employee who is a "Covered Employee" within the meaning of Section 162(m) of the Code.

2.16 Disability

"Disability" means a disability under the terms of any long-term disability plan maintained by the Company.

2.17 Effective Date

"Effective Date" means the date an Award is determined to be effective by the Committee upon its grant of such Award.

2.18 Employee

"Employee" means either: (a) a salaried employee of Kodak; or (b) a salaried employee of a Subsidiary.

2.19 Exchange Act

"Exchange Act" means the Securities and Exchange Act of 1934, as amended from time to time, including rules thereunder and successor provision and rules thereto.

2.20 Key Employee

"Key Employee" means a senior level Employee who holds a position of responsibility in a managerial, administrative, or professional capacity.

2.21 Kodak

"Kodak" means Eastman Kodak Company.

2.22   Negative Discretion

"Negative Discretion" means the discretion authorized by the Plan to be applied by the Committee in determining the size of an Award for a Performance Period or Performance Cycle if, in the Committee's sole judgment, such application is appropriate. Negative Discretion may only be used by the Committee to eliminate or reduce the size of an Award. By way of example and not by way of limitation, in no event shall any discretionary authority granted to the Committee by the Plan, including, but not limited to Negative Discretion, be used to: (a) grant Awards for a Performance Period or Performance Cycle if the Performance Goals for such Performance Period or Performance Cycle have not been attained; or (b) increase an Award above the maximum amount payable under Sections 7.5, 8.6, 9.6 or 13.6 of the Plan.

2.23   Participant

"Participant" means either any Employee to whom an Award has been granted by the Committee under the Plan or a Key Employee who, for a Performance Cycle, has been selected to participate in the Performance Stock Program.

2.24   Performance Award

"Performance Award" means the Stock Awards, Performance units and Performance Shares granted to Covered Employees pursuant to Article 7. All Performance Awards are intended to qualify as "Performance-Based Compensation" under Section 162(m) of the Code.

2.25   Performance Criteria

"Performance Criteria" means the one or more criteria that the Committee shall select for purposes of establishing the Performance Goal(s) for a Performance Period or Performance Cycle. The Performance Criteria that will be used to established such Performance Goal(s) shall be limited to the following: return on assets, return on capital, shareholders returns, profit margin, earnings per share, net earnings, operating earnings, Common Stock price per share, and sales or market share. To the extent required by Section 162(m) of the Code, the Committee shall, within the first 90 days of a Performance Period or Performance Cycle (or, if longer, within the maximum period allowed under Section 162(m) of the Code), define in an objective fashion the manner of calculating the Performance Criteria it selects to use for such Performance Period or Performance Cycle.

2.26 Performance Cycle

"Performance Cycle" means the one or more periods of time, which may be of varying and overlapping durations, as the Committee may select, over which the attainment of one or more Performance Goals will be measured for the purpose of determining a Participant's right to and the payment of an Award under the Performance Stock Program.

2.27 Performance Formula

"Performance Formula" means, for a Performance Period or Performance Cycle, the one or more objective formulas applied against the relevant Performance Goals to determine, with regards to the Award of a particular Participant, whether all, some portion but less than all, or none of the Award has been earned for the Performance Period or Performance Cycle. In the case of an Award under the Performance Stock Program, in the event the Performance Goals for a Performance Cycle are achieved, the Performance Formula shall determine what percentage of the Participant's Target Award for the Performance Cycle will be earned.

2.28 Performance Goals

"Performance Goals" means, for a Performance Period or Performance Cycle, the one or more goals established by the Committee for the Performance Period or Performance Cycle based upon the Performance Criteria. The Committee is authorized at any time during the first 90 days of a Performance Period or Performance Cycle, or at any time thereafter (but only to the extent the exercise of such authority after the first 90 days of a Performance Period or Performance Cycle wold not cause the Awards granted to the Covered Employees for the Performance Period or Performance Cycle to fail to qualify as "Performance-Based Compensation" under Section 162(m) of the Code), in its sole and absolute discretion, to adjust or modify the calculation of a Performance Goal for such Performance

Cycle in order to prevent the dilution or enlargement of the rights of Participants, (a) in the event of, or in anticipation of, any unusual or extraordinary corporate item, transaction, event or development; (b) in recognition of, or in anticipation of, any other unusual or nonrecurring events affecting the Company, or the financial statements of the Company, or in response to, or in anticipation of, changes in applicable laws, regulations, accounting principles, or business conditions; and (c) in view of the Committee's assessment of the business strategy of the Company, performance of comparable organizations, economic and business conditions, and any other circumstances deemed relevant.

2.29   Performance Period

"Performance Period" means the one or more periods of time, which may be of varying and overlapping durations, as the Committee may select, over which the attainment of one or more Performance Goals will be measured for the purpose of determining a Participant's right to and the payment of a Performance Award.

2.30   Performance Stock Program

"Performance Stock Program" means the program established under Article 13 of the Plan pursuant to which selected Key Employee receive Awards for a Performance Cycle in the form of shares of Common Stock based upon attainment of Performance Goals for such Performance Cycle. All awards granted to Covered Employees under the Performance Stock Program are intended to qualify as "Performance-based Compensation" under Section 162(m) of the Code.

2.31   Plan

"Plan" means the Eastman Kodak Company 1995 Omnibus Long-Term Compensation Plan.

2.32   Retirement

"Retirement" means, for all Plan purposes other than Article 18, a termination of employment from the Company on or after attainment of age 60 which constitutes a retirement under any defined benefit pension plan maintained by the Company which is either a tax-qualified plan under Section 401(a) of the Code or is identified in writing by the Committee as a defined benefit pension plan. For purposes of Article 18, "Retirement" means retirement under any defined benefit pension plan maintained by the Company which is either tax-qualified plan under Section 401(a) of the Code or is identified in writing by the Committee as a defined benefit pension plan.

2.33 Stock Award

"Stock Award" means an Award granted pursuant to Article 10 in the form of shares of Common Stock, restricted shares of Common Stock, and/or Units of Common Stock.

2.34 Subsidiary

"Subsidiary" means a corporation or other business entity in which Kodak directly or indirectly has an ownership interest of 80 percent or more.

2.35 Target Award

"Target Award" means, for a Performance Cycle, the target Award amount, expressed as a number of shares of Common Stock, established for each wage grade by the Committee for the Performance Cycle. The fact, however, that a Target Award is established for a Participant's wage grade shall not in any manner entitle the Participant to receive an Award for such Performance Cycle.

2.36 Unit

"Unit" means a bookkeeping entry used by the Company to record and account for the grant of the following Awards until such time as the Award is paid, canceled, forfeited or terminated, as the case may be: Units of Common Stock, performance units, and performance shares which are expressed in terms of Units of Common Stock.

ARTICLE 3—ELIGIBILITY

3.1 In General

Subject to Section 3.2, all Employees are eligible to participate in the Plan. The Committee shall select, from time to time, Participants from those Employees who, in the opinion of the Committee, can further the Plan's purposes. Once a Participant is so selected, the Committee shall determine the type or types of Awards to be made to the Participant and shall establish in the related Award Notices the terms, conditions, restrictions and/or limitations, if any, applicable to the Awards in addition to those set forth in this Plan and the administrative rules and regulations issued by the Committee.

3.2 Performance Stock Program

Only Key Employees shall be eligible to participate in the Performance Stock Program.

ARTICLE 4—PLAN ADMINISTRATOR

4.1 Responsibility

The Committee shall have total and exclusive responsibility to control, operate, manage and administer the Plan in accordance with its terms.

4.2 Authority of the Committee

The Committee shall have all the authority that may be necessary or helpful to enable it to discharge its responsibilities with respect to the Plan. Without limiting the generality of the preceding sentence, the Committee shall have the exclusive right to: (a) interpret the Plan; (b) determine eligibility for participation in the Plan; (c) decide all questions concerning eligibility for and the amount of Awards payable under the Plan; (d) construe any ambiguous provision of the Plan; (e) correct any default; (f) supply any omission; (g) reconcile any inconsistency; (h) issue administrative guidelines as an aid to administer the Plan and make changes in such guidelines as it from time to time deems proper; (i) make regulations for carrying out the Plan and make changes in such regulations as it from time to time deems proper; (j) determine whether Awards should be granted singly, in combination or in tandem; (k) to the extent permitted under the Plan, grant waivers of Plan terms, conditions, restrictions, and limitations; (1) accelerate the vesting, exercise, or payment of an Award or the Common Stock of an Award when such action or actions would be in the best interest of the Company; (m) establish such other types of Awards, besides those specifically enumerated in Article 5 hereof, which the Committee determines are consistent with the Plan's purpose; (n) subject to Section 8.2, grant Awards in replacement of Awards previously granted under this Plan or any other executive compensation plan of the Company; and (o) establish and administer the Performance Goals and certify whether, and to what extent, they have been attained; and (p) take any and all other action it deems necessary or advisable for the proper operation or administration of the Plan.

4.3 Discretionary Authority

The Committee shall have full discretionary authority in all matters related to the discharge of its responsibilities and the exercise of its authority under the Plan including, without limitation, its construction of the terms of the Plan and its determination of eligibility for participation and Awards under the Plan. It is the intent of Plan that the decisions of the Committee and its action with respect to the Plan shall be final, binding and conclusive upon all persons having or claiming to have any right or interest in or under the Plan.

4.4 Section 162(m) of the Code

With regards to all Covered Employees, the Plan shall, for all purposes, be interpreted and construed in accordance with Section 162(m) of the Code.

4.5 Action by the Committee

The Committee may act only by a majority of its members. Any determination of the Committee may be made, without a meeting, by a writing or writings signed by all of the members of the Committee. In addition, the Committee may authorize any one or more of its number to execute and deliver documents on behalf of the Committee.

4.6 Delegation of Authority

The Committee may delegate some or all of its authority under the Plan to any person or persons provided that any such delegation be in writing; provided, however, that only the Committee may select and grant Awards to Participants who are subject to Section 16 of the Exchange Act or are Covered Employees.

ARTICLE 5—FORM OF AWARDS

5.1 In General

Awards may, at the Committee's sole discretion, be paid in the form of Performance Awards pursuant to Article 7, stock options pursuant to Article 8, stock appreciation rights pursuant to Article 9, Stock Awards pursuant to Article 10, performance units pursuant to Article 11, performance shares pursuant to Article 12, shares of Common Stock pursuant to Article 13, any form established by the Committee pursuant to Subsection 4.2(m), or a combination thereof. All Awards shall be subject to the terms, conditions, restrictions and limitations of the Plan. The Committee may, in its sole judgment, subject an Award to such other terms, conditions, restrictions and/or limitations (including, but not limited to, the time and conditions of exercise and restrictions on transferability and vesting), provided they are not inconsistent with the terms of the Plan. Awards under a particular Article of the Plan need not be uniform and Awards under two or more Articles may be combined into a single Award Notice. Any combination of Awards may be granted at one time and on more than one occasion to the same Employee. For purposes of the Plan, the value of any Award granted in the form of Common Stock shall be the mean between the high and low at which the Common Stock trades on the New York Stock Exchange as of the date of the grant's Effective Date.

5.2 Foreign Jurisdictions

Awards may be granted, without amending the Plan, to Participants who are foreign nationals or employed outside the United States or both, on such terms and conditions different from those specified in the Plan as may, in the judgment of the Committee, be necessary or desirable to further the purposes of the Plan or to accommodate differences in local law, tax policy or custom. Moreover, the Committee may approve such supplements to or alternative versions of the Plan as it may consider necessary or appropriate for such purposes without thereby affecting the terms of the Plan as in effect for any other purpose; provided, however, no such supplement or alternative version shall: (a) increase the limitations contained in Sections 7.5, 8.6, 9.6 and 13.6; (b) increase the number of available shares under Section 6.1; or (c) cause the Plan to cease to satisfy any conditions of Rule 16b-3 under the Exchange Act or, with respect to Covered Employees, Section 162(m) of the Code.

ARTICLE 6—SHARES SUBJECT TO PLAN

6.1 Available Shares

The maximum number of shares of Common Stock, $2.50 par value per share, of Kodak which shall be available for grant of Awards under the Plan (including incentive stock options) during its term shall not exceed 16,000,000. (Such amount shall be subject to adjustment as provided in Section 6.2.) Any shares of Common Stock related to Awards which terminate by expiration, forfeiture, cancellation or otherwise without the issuance of such shares, are settled in cash in lieu of Common Stock, or are exchanged with the Committee's permission for Awards not involving Common Stock, shall not be available again for grant under the Plan. Moreover, shares of Common Stock with respect to which an SAR has been exercised and paid in cash shall not again be eligible for grant under the Plan. The maximum number of shares available for issuance under the Plan shall not be reduced to reflect any dividends or dividend equivalent that are reinvested into additional shares of Common Stock or credited as additional performance shares. The shares of Common Stock available for issuance under the Plan may be authorized and unissued shares or treasury shares.

6.2 Adjustment to Shares

(a) In General. The provisions of this Subsection 6.2(a) are subject to the limitation contained in Subsection 6.2(b). If there is any change in the number of outstanding shares of Common Stock through the declaration of stock dividends, stock splits or the like, the number of shares available for Awards, the shares subject to any Award and the option prices or exercise prices of Awards shall be automatically adjusted. If there is any change in the number of outstanding shares of Common Stock through any change in the capital account of Kodak, or through a merger, consolidation, separation (including a spin-off or other distribution of stock or property), reorganization (whether or not such reorganization comes within the meaning of such term in Section 368(a) of the Code) or partial or complete liquidation, the Committee shall make appropriate adjustments in the maximum number of shares of Common Stock which may be issued under the Plan and any adjustments and/or modifications to outstanding Awards as it, in its sole discretion, deems appropriate. In the event of any other change in the capital structure or in the Common Stock of Kodak, the Committee shall also be authorized to make such appropriate adjustments in the maximum number of shares of Common Stock available for issuance under the Plan and any adjustments and/or modifications to outstanding Awards as it, in its sole discretion, deems appropriate. The maximum number of shares available for issuance under the Plan shall be automatically adjusted to the extent necessary to reflect any dividend equivalents paid in the form of Common Stock.

(b) Covered Employees. In no event shall the Award of any Participant who is a Covered Employee be adjusted pursuant to Subsection 6.2(a) to the extent it would cause such Award to fail to qualify as "Performance-Based Compensation" under Section 162(m) of the Code.

6.3 Maximum Number of Shares for Stock Awards, Performance Units and Performance Shares

From the maximum number of shares available for issuance under the Plan under Section 6.1, the maximum number of shares of Common Stock, $2.50 par value per share, which shall be available for Awards granted in the form of Stock Awards, performance units or performance shares (including those issued in the form of Performance Awards) under the Plan during its term shall be 5,000,000.

ARTICLE 7—PERFORMANCE AWARDS

7.1 Purpose

For purposes of grants issued to Covered Employees, the provisions of this Article 7 shall apply in addition to and, where necessary, in lieu of the provisions of Articles 10, 11 and 12. The purpose of this Article is to provide the Committee the ability to qualify the Stock Awards authorized under Article 10, the performance units under

Article 11, and the performance shares under Article 12 as "Performance-Based Compensation" under Section 162(m) of the Code. The provisions of this Article 7 shall have control over any contrary provision contained in Articles 10, 11, or 12.

7.2 Eligibility

Only Covered Employees shall be eligible to receive Performance Awards. The Committee will, in its sole discretion, designate within the first 90 days of a Performance Period (or, if longer, within the maximum period allowed under Section 162(m) of the Code) which Covered Employees will be Participants for such period. However, designation of a Covered Employee as a Participant for a Performance Period shall not in any manner entitle the Participant to receive an Award for the period. The determination as to whether or not such Participant becomes entitled to an Award for such Performance Period shall be decided solely in accordance with the provisions of this Article 7. Moreover, designation of a Covered Employee as a Participant for a particular Performance Period shall not require designation of such Covered Employee as a Participant in any subsequent Performance Period and designation of one Covered Employee as a Participant shall not require designation of any other Covered Employee as a Participant in such period or in any other period.

7.3 Discretion of Committee with Respect to Performance Awards

With regards to a particular Performance Period, the Committee shall have full discretion to select the length of such Performance Period, the type(s) of Performance Awards to be issued, the Performance Criteria that will be used to establish the Performance Goal(s), the kind(s) and/or level(s) of the Performance Goal(s), whether the Performance Goal(s) is (are) to apply to the Company, Kodak, a Subsidiary, or any one or more subunits of the foregoing, and the Performance Formula. Within the first 90 days of a Performance Period (or, if longer, within the maximum period allowed under Section 162(m) of the Code), the Committee shall, with regards to the Performance Awards to be issued for such Performance Period, exercise its discretion with respect to each of the matters enumerated in the immediately preceding sentence of this Section 7.3 and record the same in writing.

7.4   Payment of Performance Awards

(a) Condition to Receipt of Performance Award. Unless otherwise provided in the relevant Award Notice, a Participant must be employed by the Company on the last day of a Performance Period to be eligible for a Performance Award for such Performance Period.

(b) Limitation. A Participant shall be eligible to receive a Performance Award for a Performance Period only to the extent that: (1) the Performance Goals for such Period are achieved; and (2) and the Performance Formula as applied against such Performance Goals determines that all or some portion of such Participant's Performance Award has been earned for the Performance Period.

(c) Certification. Following the completion of a Performance Period, the Committee shall meet to review and certify in writing whether, and to what extent, the Performance Goals for the Performance Period have been achieved and, if so, to also calculate and certify in writing the amount of the Performance Awards earned for the period based upon the Performance Formula. The Committee shall then determine the actual size of each Participant's Performance Award for the Performance Period and, in so doing, shall apply Negative Discretion, if and when it deems appropriate.

(d) Negative Discretion. In determining the actual size of an individual Performance Award for a Performance Period, the Committee may reduce or eliminate the amount of the Performance Award earned under the Performance Formula for the Performance Period through the use of Negative Discretion, if in its sole judgment, such reduction or elimination is appropriate.

(e) Timing of Award Payments. The Awards granted for a Performance Period shall be paid to Participants as soon as administratively possible following completion of the certifications required by Subsection 7.4(c).

(f) Noncompetition. No Participant shall receive payment for an Award if, subsequent to the commencement of a Performance Period and prior to the date the Awards for such period are paid, the

Participant engages in any of the conduct prohibited under Section 14.3.

7.5 Maximum Award Payable

Notwithstanding any provision contained in the Plan to the contrary, the maximum Performance Award payable to any one Participant under the Plan for a Performance Period is 50,000 shares of Common Stock or, in the event the Performance Award is paid in cash, the equivalent cash value thereof on the Performance Award's Effective Date.

ARTICLE 8—STOCK OPTIONS

8.1 In General

Awards may be granted to Employees in the form of stock options. These stock options may be incentive stock options within the meaning of Section 422 of the Code or nonqualified stock options (i.e., stock options which are not incentive stock options), or a combination of both. All Awards under the Plan issued to Covered Employees in the form of stock options shall qualify as "Performance-Based Compensation" under Section 162(m) of the Code.

8.2 Terms and Conditions of Stock Options

An option shall be exercisable in whole or in such installments and at such times as may be determined by the Committee. The price at which Common Stock may be purchased upon exercise of a stock option shall be not less than 100% of the fair market value of the Common Stock, as determined by the Committee, on the Effective Date of the option's grant. Moreover, all options shall not expire later than 10 years from the Effective Date of the Option's grant. Stock options shall not be repriced, i.e., there shall be no grant of a stock option(s) to a Participant in exchange for a Participant's agreement to cancellation of a higher-priced stock option(s) that was previously granted to such Participant.

8.3 Restrictions Relating to Incentive Stock Options

Stock options issued in the form of incentive stock options shall, in addition to being subject to the terms and conditions of Section

8.2, comply with Section 422 of the Code. Accordingly, the aggregate fair market value (determined at the time the option was granted) of the Common Stock with respect to which incentive stock options are exercisable for the first time by a Participant during any calendar year (under this Plan or any other plan of the Company) shall not exceed $100,000 (or such other limit as may be required by the Code). From the maximum number of shares available for issuance under the Plan under Section 6.1, the number of shares of Common Stock that shall be available for incentive stock options granted under the Plan is 16,000,000.

8.4   Additional Terms and Conditions

The Committee may, by way of the Award Notice or otherwise, establish such other terms, conditions, restrictions and/or limitations, if any, of any stock option Award, provided they are not inconsistent with the Plan.

8.5   Exercise

Upon exercise, the option price of a stock option may be paid in cash, shares of Common Stock, a combination of the foregoing, or such other consideration as the Committee may deem appropriate. The Committee shall establish appropriate methods for accepting Common Stock, whether restricted or unrestricted, and may impose such conditions as it deems appropriate on the use of such Common Stock to exercise a stock option. Subject to Section 19.9, stock options Awarded under the Plan may be exercised by way of the Company's broker-assisted stock option exercise program, provided such program is available at the time of the option exercise. The Committee may permit a Participant to satisfy any amounts required to be withheld under applicable Federal, state and local tax laws, in effect from time to time, by electing to have the Company withhold a portion of the shares of Common Stock to be delivered for the payment of such taxes.

8.6   Maximum Award Payable

Notwithstanding any provision contained in the Plan to the contrary, the maximum number of shares for which stock options may be granted under the Plan to any one Participant for a Performance Period is 200,000 shares of Common Stock.

ARTICLE 9—STOCK APPRECIATION RIGHTS

9.1   In General

Award may be granted to Employees in the form of stock appreciation rights ("SARs"). An SAR may be granted in tandem with all or a portion of a related stock option under the Plan ("Tandem SARs"), or may be granted separately ("Freestanding SARs"). A Tandem SAR may be granted either at the time of the grant of the related stock option or at any time thereafter during the term of the stock option. SARs shall entitle the recipient to receive a payment equal to the appreciation in market value of a stated number of shares of Common Stock from the exercise price to the market value on the date of exercise. All Awards under the Plan issued to Covered Employees in the form of an SAR shall qualify as "Performance-Based Compensation" under Section 162(m) of the Code.

9.2   Terms and Conditions of Tandem SARs

A Tandem SAR shall be exercisable to the extent, and only to the extent, that the related stock option is exercisable, and the "exercisable price" of such an SAR (the base from which the value of the SAR is measured at its exercise) shall be the option price under the related stock option. However, at no time shall a Tandem SAR be issued if the option price of its related stock options less than the fair market value of the Common Stock, as determined by the Committee, on the Effective Date of the Tandem SAR's grant. If a related stock option is exercised as to some or all of the shares covered by the Award, the related Tandem SAR, if any, shall be canceled automatically to the extent of the number of shares covered by the stock option exercise. Upon exercise of a Tandem SAR as to some or all of the shares covered by the Award, the related stock option shall be canceled automatically to the extent of the number of shares covered by such exercise, and such shares shall not again be eligible for grant in accordance with Section 6.1. Moreover, all Tandem SARs shall not expire later than 10 years from the Effective Date of the SARs grant.

9.3 Term and Conditions of Freestanding SARs

Freestanding SARs shall be exercisable in whole or in such install-ments and at such times as may be determined by the Committee. The exercise price of a Freestanding SAR shall be not less than 100% of the fair market value of the Common Stock, as determined by the Committee, on the Effective Date of the Freestanding SAR's grant. Moreover, all Freestanding SARs shall expire no later than 10 years from the Effective Date of the Freestanding SAR's grant.

9.4 Deemed Exercise

The Committee may provide that an SAR shall be deemed to be exercised at the close of business on the scheduled expiration date of such SAR if at such time the SAR by its terms remains exercisable and, if so exercised, would result in a payment to the holder of such SAR.

9.5 Additional Terms and Conditions

The Committee may, by way of the Award Notice or otherwise, determine such other terms, conditions, restrictions and/or limita-tions, if any, of any SAR Award, provided they are not inconsistent with the Plan.

9.6 Maximum Award Payable

Notwithstanding any provision contained in the Plan to the con-trary, the maximum number of shares for which SARs may be granted under the Plan to any one Participant for a Performance Period is 200,000 shares of Common Stock.

ARTICLE 10—STOCK AWARDS

10.1 Grants

Awards may be granted in the form of Stock Awards. Stock Awards shall be Awarded in such numbers and at such times during the term of the Plan as the Committee shall determine.

10.2   Award Restrictions

Stock Awards shall be subject to such terms, conditions, restrictions, and/or limitations, if any, as the Committee deems appropriate including, but not by way of limitation, restrictions on transferability and continued employment; provided, however, they are not inconsistent with the Plan. The Committee may modify or accelerate the delivery of a Stock Award under such circumstances as it deems appropriate.

10.3   Rights as Shareholders

During the period in which any restricted shares of Common Stock are subject to the restrictions imposed under Section 10.2, the Committee may, in its sole discretion, grant to the Participant to whom such restricted shares have been Awarded all or any of the rights of a shareholder with respect to such shares, including, but not by way of limitation, the right to vote such shares and, pursuant to Article 15, the right to receive dividends.

10.4   Evidence of Award

Any stock Award granted under the Plan may be evidence in such manner as the Committee deems appropriate, including, without limitation, book-entry registration or issuance of a stock certificate or certificates.

ARTICLE 11—PERFORMANCE UNITS

11.1   Grants

Awards may be granted in the form of performance units. Performance units, as that term is used in this Plan, shall refer to Units valued by reference to designated criteria established by the Committee, other than Common Stock.

11.2   Performance Criteria

Performance units shall be contingent on the attainment during a Common Stock of certain performance objectives. The length of the Common Stock, the performance objectives to be achieved during the Common Stock, and the measure of whether and to what degree such objectives have been attained shall be conclusively determined by the Committee in the exercise of its absolute discretion. Performance objectives may be revised by the Committee, at such times as it deems appropriate during the Common Stock, in order to take into consideration any unforeseen events or changes in circumstances.

11.3 Additional Terms and Conditions

The Committee may, by way of the Award Notice or otherwise, determine such other terms, conditions, restrictions, and/or limitations, if any, of any Award of performance units, provided they are not inconsistent with the Plan.

ARTICLE 12—PERFORMANCE SHARES

12.1 Grants

Awards may be granted in the form of performance shares. Performance shares, as that term is used in this Plan, shall refer to shares of Common Stock or Units which are expressed in terms of Common Stock.

12.2 Performance Criteria

Performance units shall be contingent on the attainment during a Common Stock of certain performance objectives. The length of the Common Stock, the performance objectives to be achieved during the Common Stock, and the measure of whether and to what degree such objectives have been attained shall be conclusively determined by the Committee in the exercise of its absolute discretion. Performance objectives may be revised by the Committee, at such times as it deems appropriate during the Common Stock, in order to take into consideration any unforeseen events or changes in circumstances.

12.3 Additional Terms and Conditions

The Committee may, by way of the Award Notice or otherwise, determine such other terms, conditions, restrictions, and/or limitations, if any, of any Award of performance units, provided they are not inconsistent with the Plan.

ARTICLE 13—PERFORMANCE STOCK PROGRAM

13.1 Purpose

The purposes of the Performance Stock Program are: (a) to promote the interests of the Company and its shareholders by providing a means to acquire a proprietary interest in the Company to selected Key Employees who are in a position to make a substantial contribution to the continued progress and success of the Company; (b) to attract and retain qualified individuals to serve as Employees in those positions; (c) to enhance long-term performance of the Company by linking a meaningful portion of the compensation of selected Key Employees to the achievement of specific long-term financial objectives of the Company; and (d) to motivate and reward selected Key Employees to undertake actions to increase the price of the Common Stock.

13.2 Eligibility

Any Key Employee is eligible to participate in the Performance Stock Program. Within the first 90 days of a Performance Cycle (or, if longer, within the maximum period allowed under Section 162(m) of the Code), the CEO will recommend to the Committee, and from such recommendations the Committee will select, those Key Employees who will be Participants for such Performance Cycle. However, designation of a Key Employee as a Participant for a Performance Cycle shall not in any manner entitle the Participant to receive payment of an Award for the cycle. The determination as to whether or not such Participant becomes entitled to payment of an Award for such Performance Cycle shall be decided solely in accordance with the provisions of this Article 13. Moreover, designation of a Key Employee as a Participant for a particular Performance Cycle shall not require designation of such Key Employee as a Participant in any subsequent Performance Cycle and designation of one Key Employee as a Participant shall not require designation of any other Key Employee as a Participant in such Performance Cycle or in any other Performance Cycle.

13.3 Description of Awards

Awards granted under the Performance Stock Program provide Participants with the opportunity to earn shares of Common Stock, subject to the terms and conditions of Section 13.8 below. Each Award granted under the Plan for a Performance Cycle shall consist of a Target Award expressed as fixed number of shares of Common Stock. In the event the Performance Goals for the Performance Cycle are achieved, the Performance Formula shall determine, with regards to a particular Participant, what percentage of the Participant's Target Award for the Performance Cycle will be earned. All of the Awards issued under the Performance Stock Program to Covered Employees are intended to qualify as "Performance-Based Compensation" under Section 162(m) of the Code.

13.4 Procedure for Determining Awards

Within the first 90 days of Performance Cycle (or, if longer, within the maximum period allowed under Section 162(m) of the Code), the Committee shall establish in writing for such Performance Cycle the following: the specific Performance Criteria that will be used to establish the Performance Goal(s), the kind(s) and/or level(s) of the Performance Goal(s), whether the Performance Goal(s) is(are) to apply to the Company, Kodak, a Subsidiary,or any one or more subunits of the foregoing, the amount of the Target Awards, and the Performance Formula.

13.5 Payment of Awards

(a) Condition to Receipt of Awards. Except as provided in Section 13.7, a Participant must be employed by the Company on the Performance Cycle's Award Payment Date to be eligible for an award for such Performance Cycle.

(b) Limitation. A Participant shall be eligible to receive an Award for a Performance Cycle only if: (1) the Performance Goals for such cycle are achieved; and (2) the Performance Formula as applied against such Performance Goals determines that all or some portion of the Participant's Target Award has been earned for the Performance Period.

(c) Certification. Following the completion of a Performance Cycle, the Committee shall meet to review and certify in writing whether, and to what extent, the Performance Goals for the Performance Cycle have been achieved. If the Committee certifies that the Performance Goals have been achieved, it shall, based upon application of the Performance Formula to the Performance Goals for such cycle, also calculate and certify in writing for each Participant what percentage of the Participant's Target Award has been earned for the cycle. The Committee shall then determine the actual size of each Participant's Award for the Performance Cycle and, in so doing, shall apply Negative Discretion, if and when it deems appropriate.

(d) Negative Discretion. In determining the actual size of an individual Award to be paid for a Performance Cycle, the Committee may, through the use of Negative Discretion, reduce or eliminate the amount of the Award earned under the Performance Formula for the Performance Cycle, if in its sole judgment, such reduction or elimination is appropriate.

(e) Timing of Award Payments. The Awards granted by the Committee for a Performance Cycle shall be paid to Participants on the Award Payment Date for such Performance Cycle.

(f) New Participants. Participants who are employed by the Company after the Committee's selection of Participants for the Performance Cycle, as well as Key Employees who are selected by the Committee to be Participants after such date, shall, in the event Awards are paid for the Performance Cycle, only be entitled to a pro rata Award. The amount of the pro rata Award shall be determined by multiplying the Award the Participant would have otherwise been paid if he or she had been a Participant for the entire Performance Cycle by a fraction the numerator of which is the number of full months he or she was eligible to participate in the Performance Stock Program during the Performance Cycle over the total number of full months in the Performance Cycle. For purposes of this calculation, a partial month of participation shall: (1) be treated as a full month of participation to the extent a Participant participates in the Performance Stock Program on 15 or more days of such month; and (2) not to be taken into consideration to the extent the Participant participates in the Performance Stock Program for less than 15 days of such month.

(g) Noncompetition. No Participant shall receive payment for an Award if, subsequent to the commencement of the Performance Cycle and prior to the Award Payment Date for such cycle, the Participant engages in the conduct prohibited under Section 14.3.

13.6 Maximum Award Payable

Notwithstanding any provision contained in the Plan to the contrary, the maximum Award payable to any one Participant under the Plan for a Performance Cycle is 50,000 shares of Common Stock.

13.7 Termination of Employment During Performance Cycle

In the event a Participant terminates employment due to Death, Disability, Retirement or Termination of Employment for an Approved Reason prior to the Award Payment Date for a Performance Cycle, the Participant shall receive, if Awards are paid for such Performance Cycle and if he or she complies with the requirements of Subsection 13.5(g) through the Award Payment Date, a pro rata Award. The amount of the pro rata Award shall be determined by multiplying the Award the Participant would have otherwise been paid if he or she had been a Participant through the Award Payment Date for the Performance Cycle by a fraction, the numerator of which is the number of full months he or she was a Participant during such Performance Cycle over the total number of full months in the Performance Cycle. For purposes of this calculation, a partial month of participation shall: (1) be treated as a full month of participation to the extent a Participant participates in the Performance Stock Program on 15 or more days of such month; and (2) not be taken into consideration to the extent the Participant participates in the Performance Stock Program for less than 15 days of such month. Such pro rata Award shall be paid in the form of shares of Common Stock, not subject to any restrictions, limitations or escrow requirements. In the event of Disability, Retirement or Termination for an Approved Reason, the pro rata Award shall be paid directly to the Participant and, in the event of death, to the Participant's estate.

13.8 Awards

On the Award Payment Date for a Performance Cycle, the Committee shall issue to each Participant the Award, in the form of shares of Common Stock, he or she has earned for such Performance Cycle. Such shares of Common Stock shall be subject to such terms, conditions, limitations and restrictions as the Committee, in its sole judgment, determines.

ARTICLE 14—PAYMENT OF AWARDS

14.1   In General

Absent a Plan provision to the contrary, payment of Awards may, at the discretion of the Committee, be made in cash, Common Stock, a combination of cash and Common Stock, or any other form of property as the Committee shall determine. In addition, payment of Awards may include such terms, conditions, restrictions and/or limitations, if any, as the Committee deems appropriate, including, in the case of Awards paid in the form of Common Stock, restrictions on transfer and forfeiture provisions; provided, however, such terms, conditions, restrictions and/or limitations are not inconsistent with the Plan. Further, payment of Awards may be made in the form of a lump sum or installments, as determined by the Committee.

14.2   Termination of Employment

If a participant's employment with the Company terminates for a reason other than death, Disability, Retirement, or any Approved Reason, all unexercised, unearned, and/or unpaid Awards, including but not by way of limitation, Awards earned but not yet paid, all unpaid dividends and dividend equivalents, and all interest accrued on the foregoing shall be canceled or forfeited, as the case may be, unless the Participant's Award Notice provides otherwise. The Committee shall, notwithstanding Section 4.4 and 19.11 to the contrary, have the authority to promulgate rules and regulations to determine the treatment of an Award under the Plan in the event of the Participant's death, Disability, Retirement or Termination for an Approved Reason, provided, however, in the case of Awards issued under the Restricted Stock Program, such rules and regulations are consistent with Section 13.7.

14.3   Noncompetition

Unless the Award Notice specifies otherwise, a Participant shall forfeit all unexercised, unearned, and/or unpaid Awards, including, but not by way of limitation, Awards earned but not yet paid, all unpaid dividends and dividend equivalents, and all interest, if any, and accrued on the foregoing if, (i) in the opinion of the Committee, the Participant, without the prior written consent of Kodak, engages directly or indirectly in any manner or capacity as principal, agent, partner, officer, director, stockholder, employee or otherwise, in any business or activity competitive with the business conducted by Kodak or any Subsidiary; (ii) at any time divulge to any person or any entity other than the Company any trade secrets, methods, processes or the proprietary or confidential information of the Company; or (iii) the Participant performs any act or engages in any activity which in the opinion of the CEO is inimical to the best interests of the Company. For purposes of this Section 14.3, a Participant shall not be deemed a stockholder if the Participant's record and beneficial ownership amount to not more than 1% of the outstanding capital stock of any company subject to the periodic and other reporting requirements of the Exchange Act.

ARTICLE 15—DIVIDEND AND DIVIDEND EQUIVALENT

If an Award is granted in the form of a Stock Award, stock option, or performance share, or in the form of any other stock-based grant, the Committee may choose, at the time of the grant of the Award or any time thereafter up to the time of the Award's payment, to include as part of such Award an entitlement to receive dividends or dividend equivalents, subject to such terms, conditions, restrictions and/or limitations, if any, as the Committee establish. Dividends and dividend equivalents shall be paid in such form and manner (i.e., lump sum or installments), and at such time(s) as the Committee shall determine. All dividends or dividend equivalents which are not paid currently may, at the Committee's discretion, accrue interest, be reinvested into additional shares of Common Stock or, in the case of dividends or dividend equivalents credited in connection with performance shares, be credited as additional performance shares and paid to the Participant if and when, and to the extent that, payment is made pursuant to such Award. The total number of shares available for grant under Section 6.1 shall not be reduced to reflect any dividends or dividend equivalents that are reinvested into additional shares of Common Stock or credited as additional performance shares.

ARTICLE 16—DEFERRAL OF AWARDS

At the discretion of the Committee, payment of any Award, dividend, or dividend equivalent, or any portion thereof, may be deferred by a Participant until such time as the Committee may establish. All such deferrals shall be accomplished by the delivery of a written, irrevocable election by the Participant prior to the time established by the Committee for such purpose, on a form provided by the Company. Further, all deferrals shall be made in accordance with administrative guidelines established by the Committee to ensure that such deferrals comply with all applicable requirements of the Code. Deferred payments shall be paid in a lump sum or installments, as determined by the Committee. Deferred Awards may also be credited with interest, at such rates to be determined by the Committee, and, with respect to those deferred Awards denominated in the form of Common Stock, with dividends or dividend equivalents.

ARTICLE 17—CHANGE IN OWNERSHIP

17.1 Background

Notwithstanding any provision contained in the Plan, including, but not limited to, Sections 4.4 and 19.11, the provisions of this Article 17 shall control over any contrary provision. Upon a change In Ownership: (i) the terms of this Article 17 shall immediately become operative, without further action or consent by any person or entity; (ii) all terms conditions, restrictions, and limitations in effect on any unexercised, unearned, unpaid, and/or deferred Award, or any other outstanding Award, shall immediately lapse as of the date of such event; (iii) no other terms, conditions restrictions and/or limitations shall be imposed upon any Awards on or after such date, and in no circumstance shall in an Award be forfeited on or after such date; and (iv) except in those instances where a prorated Award is required to be paid under this Article 17, all unexercised, unvested, unearned, and/or unpaid Awards or any other outstanding Awards shall automatically become one hundred percent (100%) vested immediately.

17.2 Dividends and Dividend Equivalents

Upon a Change in Ownership, all unpaid dividends and dividend equivalents and all interest accrued thereon, if any, shall be treated and paid under this Article 17 in the identical manner and time as the Award under which such dividends or dividend equivalents have been credited. For example, if upon a Change In Ownership, an

Award under this Article 17 is to be paid in a prorated fashion, all unpaid dividends and dividend equivalents with respect to such Award shall be paid according to the same formula used to determine the amount of such prorated Award.

17.3   Treatment of Performance Units and Performance Shares

If a Change In Ownership occurs during the term of one or more Common Stocks for which the Committee has granted performance units and/or performance shares (including those issued as Performance Awards under Article 7), the term of each such Common Stock (hereinafter a "current Common Stock") and each completed Common Stock for which the Committee has not on or before such date made a determination as to whether and to what degree the performance objectives for such period have been attained (hereinafter a "completed Common Stock"), it shall be assumed that the performance objectives have been attained at a level of one hundred percent (100%) or the equivalent thereof.

A Participant in one or more "current Common Stock" shall be considered to have earned and, therefore, be entitled to receive, a prorated portion of the Awards previously granted to him for each such Common Stock. Such prorated portion shall be determined by multiplying the number of performance shares or performance units, as the case may be, granted to the Participant by a fraction, the numerator of which is the total number of whole months that have elapsed since the beginning of the Common Stock, and the denominator of which is the total number of full months in such Common Stock. For purposes of this calculation, a partial month shall be treated as a full month to the extent 15 or more days in such month have elapsed.

A Participant in one or more "completed Common Stocks" shall be a considered to have earned and, therefore, be entitled to receive all the performance shares or performance units, as the case may be, previously granted to him during each such Common Stock.

17.4   Treatment of Awards under Performance Stock Program

Upon a Change In Ownership, any Participant of the Performance Stock Program, whether or not he or she is still employed by the Company, shall be paid, as soon as practicable but in no event later than 90 days after the Change in Ownership, a pro rata Award for each Performance Cycle in which the Participant was selected to participate and during which the Change in Ownership occurs. The amount of the pro rata Award shall be determined by multiplying the Target Award for such Performance Cycle for Participants in the same wage grade as the Participant by a fraction, the numerator of which shall be the number of full months in the Performance Cycle prior to the date of the change in Ownership and the denominator of which shall be the total number of full months in the Performance Cycle. For purpose of this calculation, a partial month shall be treated as a full month to the extent 15 or more days in such month have elapsed. To the extent Target Awards have not yet been established for the Performance Cycle, the Target Award for the immediately preceding Performance Cycle shall be used.

17.5   Valuation of Awards

Upon a Change In Ownership, all outstanding Units of Common Stock, Freestanding SARs, stock options (including incentive stock options), Stock Awards (including those issued as Performance Awards under Article 7), performance shares (including those earned as a result of the application of Section 17.3), and all other outstanding stock-based Awards (including those earned as a result of the application of Section 17.4 and those granted by the Committee pursuant to its authority under Subsection 4.2(m) hereof), shall be valued and cashed out on the basis of the Change In Control Price.

17.6   Payment of Awards

Upon a Change In Ownership, any Participant, whether or not he or she is still employed by the Company, shall be paid, in a single lump-sum cash payment, as soon as practicable, but no later that 90 days after the Change In Ownership, all of his or her Units of Common Stock, Freestanding SARs, stock option (including incentive stock options), Stock Awards (including those issued as Performance Awards under Article 7), performance units and shares (including those earned as a result of the application of Section 17.3), all other outstanding stock-based Awards (including those earned as a result of the application of Section 17.4 and those granted by the Committee pursuant to its authority under Subsection 4.2(m) hereof), and all other outstanding Awards.

17.7 Deferred Awards

Upon a Change In Ownership, all Awards deferred by a Participant under Article 16 hereof, but for which he or she has not received payment as of such date, shall be paid in a single lump-sum cash payment as soon as practicable, but in no event later than 90 days after the Change In Ownership. For purposes of making such payment, the value of all Awards which are stock based shall be determined by the Change In Control Price.

17.8 Section 16 of Exchange Act

Notwithstanding anything contained in this Article 17 to the contrary, any Participant who, on the date of the Change In Ownership, holds any stock options or Freestanding SARs that have not been outstanding for a period of at least six months from their date of grant and who on such date is required to report under Section 16 of the Exchange Act shall not be paid such Award until the first day next following the end of such six-month period.

17.9 Miscellaneous

Upon a Change In Ownership, (i) the provisions of Sections 14.2, 14.3 and 19.3 hereof shall become null and void and of no further force and effect; and (ii) no action, including, but not by way of limitation, the amendment, suspension, or termination of the Plan, shall be taken which would affect the rights of any Participant or the operation of the Plan with respect to any Award to which the Participant may have become entitled hereunder on or prior to the date of such action or as a result of such Change In Ownership.

ARTICLE 18—CHANGE IN CONTROL

18.1 Background

Notwithstanding any provisions contained in the Plan, including, but not limited to, Section 4.4 and 19.11, the provisions of this Article 18 shall control over any contrary provision. All Participants shall be eligible for the treatment afforded by this Article if their employment terminated within two years following a Change In Control, unless the termination is due to (i) Death, (ii) Disability, (iii) Cause, (iv) Resignation other than (A) resignation from a declined reassignment to a job that is not reasonably equivalent in responsibility or compensation (as defined in Kodak's Termination Allowance Plan), or that is not in the same geographic area (as defined in Kodak's Termination Allowance Plan), or (B) resignation within 30 days following a reduction in base pay, or (v) Retirement.

18.2   Vesting and Lapse of Restrictions

If a participant is eligible for treatment under this Article 18, (i) all of the terms, conditions, restrictions, and limitations in effect on any of his or her unexercised, unearned, unpaid and/or deferred Awards shall immediately lapse as of the date of his or her termination of employment; (ii) no other terms, conditions, restrictions and/or limitations shall be imposed upon any of his or her Awards on or after such date, and in no event shall any of his or her Awards be forfeited on or after such date; and (iii) except in those instances where a prorated Award is required to be paid under this Article 18, all of his or her unexercised, unvested, unearned and/or unpaid Awards shall automatically become one hundred percent (100%) vested immediately upon his or her termination of employment.

18.3   Dividends and Dividend Equivalents

If a Participant is eligible for treatment under this Article 18, all of his or her unpaid dividends and dividend equivalents and all interest accrued thereon, if any, shall be treated and paid under this Article 18 in the identical manner and time as the Award under which such dividends or dividend equivalents have been credited.

18.4   Treatment of Performance Units and Performance Shares

If a Participant holding either performance units or performance shares (including those issued a Performance Awards under Article 7) is terminated under the conditions described in Section 18.1 above, the provisions of this Section 18.4 shall determine the manner in which such performance units and/or performance shares shall be paid to the Participant. For purposes of making such payment, each "current Common Stock," as that term is defined in Section 17.3, shall be treated as terminating upon the date of the Participant's termination of employment, and for each such "current Common Stock" and each "completed Common Stock," as the term is defined in Section 17.3, it shall be assumed that the performance objectives have been attained at a level of one hundred percent (100%) or the equivalent thereof. If the Participant is participating in one or more "current Common Stocks," he or she shall be considered to have earned and, therefore, be entitled to receive that prorated portion of the Awards previously granted to him for each such performance period, as determined in accordance with the formula established in Section 17.3 hereof. A Participant in one or more "completed Common Stock" shall be considered to have earned and, therefore, be entitled to receive all the performance shares and performance units previously granted to him during each Common Stock.

18.5   Treatment of Awards under Performance Stock Program

If a Participant of the Performance Stock Program is eligible for treatment under this Article 18, he or she shall be paid, as soon as practicable but in no event later than 90 days after the date of his or her termination of employment, a pro rata Award for each Performance Cycle in which the Participant was selected to participate and during which the Change in Ownership occurs. The amount of the pro rata Award shall be determined by multiplying the Target Award for such Performance Cycle for Participants in the same wage grade as the Participant by a fraction, the numerator of which shall be the number of full months in the Performance Cycle prior to the date of his of her termination of employment and the denominator of which shall be the total number of full months in the Performance Cycle. For purposes of this calculation, a partial month shall be treated as a full month to the extent 15 or more days in such month have elapsed. To the extent Target Awards have not yet been established for the Performance Cycle, the Target Awards for the immediately preceding Performance Cycle shall be used.

18.6   Valuation of Awards

If a Participant is eligible for treatment under this Article 18, his or her Awards shall be valued and cashed out in accordance with the provisions of Section 17.5.

18.7   Payment of Awards

If a Participant is eligible for treatment under this Article 18, he or she shall be paid, in a single lump-sum cash payment, as soon as practicable but in no event later than 90 days after the date of his or her termination of employment, all of his or her Units of Common Stock, Freestanding SARs, stock options (including incentive stock options), Stock Awards (including those issued as Performance Awards under Article 7), performance units and shares (including those earned as a result of the application of Section 18.4 above), all other outstanding stock-based Awards (including those earned as a result of the application of Section 18.5 above and those granted by the Committee pursuant to its authority under Subsection 4.2(m) hereof), and all other outstanding Awards.

18.8   Deferred Awards

If a Participant is eligible for treatment under this Article 18, all of his or her deferred Awards for which payment has not been received as of the date of his or her termination of employment shall be paid to the Participant in a single lump-sum cash payment as soon as practicable, but in no event later than 90 days after the date of the Participant's termination. For purposes of making such payment, the value of all Awards which are stock based shall be determined by the Change In Control Price.

18.9   Section 16 of Exchange Act

Notwithstanding anything contained in this Article 18 to the contrary, any Participant who, on the date of his or her termination of employment under the conditions described in Section 18.1, holds any stock options or Freestanding SARs that have been outstanding for a period of at least six months from their date of grant and who on the date of such termination is required to report under Section 16 of the Exchange Act shall not be paid such Award until the first business day next following the end of such six-month period.

18.10   Miscellaneous

Upon a Change In Control, (i) the provision of Sections 14.2, 14.3, and 19.3 hereof shall become null and void and of no force and effect insofar as they apply to a Participant who has been terminated under the conditions described in Section 18.1 above; and (ii) no action, including, but not by way of limitation, the amendment, suspension or termination of the Plan, shall be taken which would affect the rights of any Participant or the operation of the Plan with respect to any Award to which the Participant may have become entitled hereunder on or prior to the date of the Change In Control or to which he or she may become entitled as a result of such Change In Control.

18.11   Legal Fees

Kodak shall pay all legal fees and related expenses incurred by a Participant in seeking to obtain or enforce any payment benefit of right he or she may be entitled to under the Plan after a Change In Control; provided, however, the Participant shall be required to repay any such amounts to Kodak to the extent a court of competent jurisdiction issues a final and non-appealable order setting forth the determination that the position taken by the Participant was frivolous or advanced in bad faith.

ARTICLE 19—MISCELLANEOUS

19.1   Nonassignability

No Awards or any other payment under the Plan shall be subject in any manner alienation, anticipation, sale, transfer (except by will or the laws of descent and distribution), assignment, pledge, or encumbrance, nor shall any Award be payable to or exercisable by anyone other than the Participant to whom it was granted.

19.2   Withholding Taxes

The Company shall be entitled to deduct from any payment under the Plan, regardless of the form of such payment, the amount of all applicable income and employment taxes required by law to be withheld with respect to such payment or may require the Participant to pay to it such tax prior to and as a condition of the making of such payment. In accordance with any applicable administrative guidelines it establishes, the Committee may allow a Participant to pay the amount of taxes required by law to be withheld from an Award by withholding from any payment of Common Stock due as a result of such Award, or by permitting the Participation to deliver to the Company, shares of Common Stock having a fair market value, as determined by the Committee, equal to the amount of such required withholding taxes.

19.3 Amendments to Awards

The Committee may at any time unilaterally amend any unexercised, unearned, or unpaid Award, including, but not by way of limitation, Awards earned but not yet paid, to the extent it deems appropriate; provided, however, that any such amendment which, in the opinion of the Committee, is adverse to the Participant shall require the Participant's consent.

19.4 Regulatory Approvals and Listings

Notwithstanding anything contained in this Plan to the contrary, the Company shall have no obligation to issue or deliver certificates of Common Stock evidencing Stock Awards or any other Award resulting in the payment of Common Stock prior to (i) the obtaining of any approval from any governmental agency which the Company shall, in its sole discretion, determine to be necessary or advisable, (ii) the admission of such shares to listing on the stock exchange on which the Common Stock may be listed, and (iii) the completion of any registration or other qualification of said shares under any state or Federal law or ruling of any governmental body which the Company shall, in its sole discretion, determine to be necessary or advisable.

19.5 No Right to Continued Employment or Grants

Participation in the Plan shall not give any Employee any right to remain in the employ of Kodak or any Subsidiary. Kodak or, in the case of employment with a Subsidiary, the Subsidiary, reserves the right to terminate any Employee at any time. Further, the adoption of this Plan shall not be deemed to give any Employee or any other individual any right to be selected as a Participant or to be granted an Award.

19.6 Amendment/Termination

The Committee may suspend or terminate the Plan at any time with or without prior notice. In addition, the Committee may, from time to time and with or without prior notice, amend the Plan in any manner, but may not without shareholder approval adopt any amendment which would require the vote of the shareholders of Kodak pursuant to Section 16 of the Exchange Act or Section 162(m) of the Code, but only insofar as such amendment affects Covered Employees.

19.7 Governing Law

The Plan shall be governed by and construed in accordance with the laws of the State of New York, except as superseded by applicable Federal Law.

19.8 No Right, Title, or Interest in Company Assets

No Participant shall have any rights as a shareholder as a result of participation in the Plan until the date of issuance of a stock certificate in his or her name, and, in the case of restricted shares of Common Stock, such rights are granted to the Participant under the Plan. To the extent any person acquires a right to receive payments from the Company under the Plan, such rights shall be no greater than the rights in or against any specific assets of the Company. All of the Awards granted under the Plan shall be unfunded.

19.9 Section 16 of the Exchange Act

In order to avoid any Exchange Act violations, the Committee may, from time to time, impose additional restrictions upon an Award, including but not limited to, restrictions regarding tax withholdings and restrictions regarding the Participant's ability to exercise Awards under the company's broker-assisted exercise program.

19.10 No Guarantee of Tax Consequences

No person connected with the Plan in any capacity, including but not limited to, Kodak and its Subsidiaries and their directors, officers, agents and employees makes any representation, commitment, or guarantee that any tax treatment, including, but not limited to, Federal, state and local income, estate and gift tax treatment, will be applicable with respect to amounts deferred under the Plan, or paid to or for the benefit of a Participant under the Plan, or that such tax treatment will apply to or be available to a Participant on account of participation in the Plan.

19.11 Compliance with Section 162(m)

If any provision of the Plan, other than the application of those contained in Articles 17 and 18 hereof, would cause the Awards granted to a Covered Person not to qualify as "Performance-Based Compensation" under Section 162(m) of the Code, that provision, insofar as it pertains to the Covered Person, shall be severed from, and shall be deemed not to be a part of, this Plan, but the other provisions hereof shall remain in full force and effect.

19.12 Other Benefits

No Award granted under the Plan shall be considered compensation for purposes of computing benefits under any retirement plan of the Company nor affect any benefits or compensation under any other benefit or compensation plan of the Company now or subsequently in effect.

PLAN 2: MANAGEMENT VARIABLE COMPENSATION PLAN

ARTICLE 1—PURPOSE, EFFECTIVE DATE, AND TERM OF PLAN

1.1 Purpose

The purposes of the Plan are to provide an annual incentive to Key Employees of the Company to put forth maximum efforts toward the continued growth and success of the Company, to encourage such Key Employees to remain in the employ of the Company, to assist the Company in attracting and motivating new Key Employees on a competitive basis, and to endeavor to qualify the Awards granted to Covered Employees under the Plan as "Performance-Based Compensation as defined in Section 162(m) of the Code. The Plan is intended to apply to Key Employees of the Company in the United States and throughout the world.

1.2 Effective Date

The Plan shall be effective as of January 1, 1995, subject to approval by Kodak's shareholders at the 1995 Annual Meeting of the Shareholders of Kodak.

1.3 Term

Awards shall not be granted pursuant to the Plan after December 31, 1999; provided, however, the Committee may grant Awards after such date in recognition of performance for a Performance Period completed on or prior to such date.

ARTICLE 2—DEFINITIONS

2.1 Actual Award Pool

"Actual Award Pool" means, for a Performance Period, the amount determined in accordance with Section 6.4.

2.2 Average Net Assets

"Average Net Assets" means, for the Performance Period, the simple average of the Company's Net Assets for each of the following five fiscal quarters of the Company: the four fiscal quarters of the Performance Period and the fiscal quarter immediately preceding the Performance Period. For purposes of this calculation, Net Assets for a fiscal quarter shall be determined as of the end of such quarter.

2.3 Award

"Award" means the compensation granted to a Participant by the Committee for a Performance Period pursuant to Articles 6 and 7 or the compensation granted to a Key Employee by the Committee pursuant to Article 9. All Awards shall be issued in the form(s) specified by Article 5.

2.4 Award Payment Date

"Award Payment Date" means, for each Performance Period, the date that the amount of the Award for that Performance Period shall be paid to the Participant under Article 7, without regard to any election to defer receipt of the Award made by the Participant under Article 8 of the Plan.

2.5 Board

"Board" means the Board of Directors of Kodak.

2.6 Carryforward Amount

"Carryforward" means, for a Performance Period, that portion, if any, or all of the difference, if any, between the Maximum Award for such Performance Period and the sum of all Awards paid under the Plan for such Performance Period, which the Committee elects to add to the Carryforward Amount.

2.7 Cause

"Cause" means (a) the willful and continued failure by a Key Employee to substantially perform his or her duties with his or her employer after written warnings identifying the lack of substantial performance are delivered to the Key Employee by his or her employer to specifically identify the manner in which the employer believes that the Key Employee has not substantially performed his or her duties; or (b) the willful engaging by a Key employee in illegal conduct which is materially and demonstrably injurious to the Company.

2.8 CEO

"CEO" means the Chief Executive Officer of Kodak.

2.9 Change in Control

"Change In Control" means a Change In Control of Kodak of a nature that would be required to be reported (assuming such event has not been "previously reported") in response to Item 1(a) of the Current Report on Form 8-K, as in effect on August 1, 1989, pursuant to Section 12 or 15(d) of the Exchange Act; provided that, without limitation, a Change In Control shall be deemed to have occurred at such time as (i) any "person" within the meaning of Section 13(d) of the Exchange Act, other than Kodak, a Subsidiary, or any employee benefit plan(s) sponsored by Kodak or any Subsidiary, is or has become the "beneficial owner," as defined in Rule 12d-3 under the Exchange Act, directly or indirectly, of 25% or more of the combined voting power of the outstanding securities of Kodak ordinarily having the right to vote at the election of directors, or (ii) individuals who constitute the Board on January 1, 1995 (the "Incumbent Board") have ceased for any reason to constitute at least a majority thereof, provided that any person becoming a director subsequent to January

1, 1995 whose election, or nomination for election by Kodak's shareholders, was approved by a vote of at least three-quarters (3/4) of the directors comprising the Incumbent Board (either by a specific vote or by approval of the proxy statement of Kodak in which such person is named as a nominee for director without objection to such nomination) shall be, for purposes of this Plan, considered as though such person were a member of the Incumbent Board.

2.10 Change In Ownership

"Change In Ownership" means a Change In Control which results directly or indirectly in Kodak's Common Stock ceasing to be actively traded on the New York Stock Exchange.

2.11 Code

"Code" means the Internal Revenue Code of 1986, as amended from time to time, including regulations thereunder and successor provisions and regulations thereto.

2.12 Committee

"Committee" means the Executive Compensation and Development Committee of the Board, or such other Board committee as may be designated by the Board to administer the Plan; provided that the Committee shall consist of three or more directors, all of whom are both a "disinterested person" within the meaning of Rule 16b-3 under the Exchange Act and an "outside director" within the meaning of the definition of such term as contained in Proposed Treasury Regulation Section 1.162-27(e)(3), or any successor definition adopted.

2.13 Common Stock

"Common Stock" means the Common Stock, $2.50 par value per share, of Kodak which may be newly issued or treasury stock.

2.14 Company

"Company" means Kodak and its Subsidiaries.

2.15   Covered Employee

"Covered Employee" means a Key Employee who is a "Covered Employee" within the meaning of Section 162(m) of the Code.

2.16   Disability

"Disability" means a disability under the terms of any long-term disability plan maintained by the Company.

2.17   Effective Date

"Effective Date" means the date an Award is determined to be effective by the Committee upon its grant of such Award.

2.18   Exchange Act

"Exchange Act" means the Securities Exchange Act of 1934, as amended form time to time, including rules thereunder and successor provisions and rules thereto.

2.19   Key Employee

"Key Employee" means either: (1) a salaried employee of the Company in wage grade 48 or above, or the equivalent thereof; or (2) a salaried employee of the Company who holds a position of responsibility in a managerial, administrative, or professional capacity and is in wage grade 43 or above.

2.20   Kodak

"Kodak" means Eastman Kodak Company.

2.21   Maximum Award

"Maximum Award" means, for a Performance Period, the dollar amount calculated in accordance with Section 6.2 by applying the Performance Formula for such Performance Period against the Performance Goals for the same Performance Period.

2.22   Maximum Award Pool

"Maximum Award Pool" means, for a Performance Period, the dollar amount calculated in accordance with Section 6.3(b) by adding the Maximum Award for the Performance Period with the Carryforward Amount.

2.23 Negative Discretion

"Negative Discretion" means the discretion granted to the Committee pursuant to Section 6.3(e) to reduce or eliminate the Maximum Award Pool or a portion of the Maximum Award Pool Allocated to a Covered Employee.

2.24 Net Assets

"Net Assets" means the Company's consolidated Total Shareholders' Equity and Borrowings (both short-term and long-term) as reported in its audited consolidated financial statements. The Committee is authorized at any time during the first 90 days of a Performance Period, or at any time thereafter in its sole and absolute discretion, to adjust or modify the calculation of Net Assets for such Performance Period in order to prevent the dilution or enlargement of the rights of Participants, (a) in the event of, or in anticipation of, any unusual or extraordinary corporate time, transaction, event or development; (b) in recognition of, or in anticipation of, any other unusual or nonrecurring events affecting the Company, or the financial statements of the Company, or in response to, or in anticipation of, changes in applicable laws, regulations, accounting principles, or business conditions; and (c) in view of the Committee's assessment of the business strategy of the Company, performance of comparable organizations, economic and business conditions, and any other circumstances deemed relevant. However, if and to the extent the exercise of such authority after the first 90 days of a Performance Period would cause the Awards granted to the Covered Employees for the Performance Period to fail to qualify as "Performance-Based Compensation" under Section 162(m) of the Code, then such authority shall only be exercised with respect to those Participants who are not Covered Employees.

2.25 Net Income

"Net Income" means, for a Performance Period, the Company's consolidated Net Earnings (Loss) before Cumulative Effect of Changes in Accounting Principle for the Performance Period as reported in its audited consolidated financial statements. The Committee is authorized at any time during the first 90 days of a Performance Period, or at any time thereafter in its sole and absolute discretion, to adjust or modify the calculation of Net Income for such Performance Period in order to prevent the dilution or enlargement of the rights of Participants, (a) in the event of, or in anticipation of, any dividend or other distribution (whether in the form of cash, securities or other property), recapitalization, restructuring, reorganization, merger, consolidation, spin off, combination, repurchase, share exchange, liquidation, dissolution, or other similar corporate transaction, event or development; (b) in recognition of, or in anticipation of, any other unusual or nonrecurring event affecting the Company, or the financial statements of the Company, or in response to, or in anticipation of, changes in applicable laws, regulations, accounting principles, or business conditions; (c) in recognition of, or in anticipation of, any other extraordinary gains or losses; and (d) in view of the Committee's assessment of the business strategy of the Company, performance of comparable organizations, economic and business conditions, and any other circumstances deemed relevant. However, if and to the extent the exercise of such authority after the first 90 days of a Performance Period would cause the Awards granted to the Covered Employees for the Performance Period to fail to qualify as "Performance-Based Compensation" under Section 162(m) of the Code, then such authority shall only be exercised with respect to those Participants who are not Covered Employees.

2.26 Participant

"Participant," means either (a) for a Performance Period, a Key Employee who is designated to participate in the Plan for the Performance Period pursuant to Article 3; or (b) for purposes of Article 9, a Key Employee who is granted an Award pursuant to such Article.

2.27 Performance Criteria

"Performance Criteria" means the stated business criterion upon which the Performance Goals for a Performance Period are based as required pursuant to Proposed Treasury Regulation Section 1.162-27(e)(4)(iii). For purpose of the Plan, RONA shall be the Performance Criterion.

2.28 Performance Formula

"Performance Formula" means, for a Performance Period, the one or more objective formulas applied against the Performance Goals to determine whether all, some portion but less than all, or none of the Awards have been earned for the Performance Period. The dollar amount obtained through application of the Performance Formula shall be the Maximum Award. The Performance Formula for a Performance Period shall be established in writing by the Committee within the first 90 days of the Performance Period (or, if later, within the maximum period allowed pursuant to Section 162(m) of the Code).

2.29 Performance Goals

"Performance Goals" means, for a Performing Period, the one or more goals for the Performance Period established by the Committee in writing within the first 90 days of the Performance Period (or, if longer, within the maximum period allowed pursuant to Section 162(m) of the Code) based upon the Performance Criterion. The Committee is authorized at any time during the first 90 days of a Performance Period, or at any time thereafter in its sole and absolute discretion, to adjust or modify the calculation of a Performance Goal for such Performance Period in order to prevent the dilution or enlargement of the rights of Participants, (a) in the event of, or in anticipation of, any unusual or extraordinary corporate item, transaction, event, or development; (b) in recognition of, or in anticipation of any other unusual or nonrecurring events affecting the Company, or the financial statements of the Company, or in response to, or in anticipation of, changes in applicable laws, regulations, accounting principles, or business conditions; and (c) in view of the Committee's assessment of the business strategy of the Company, performance of comparable organizations, economic and business conditions, and any other circumstances deemed relevant. However, to the extent the exercise of such authority after the first 90 days of a Performance Period would cause the Awards granted to the Covered Employees for the Performance Period to fail to qualify as "Performance-Based Compensation" under Section 162(m) of the Code, then such authority shall only be exercised with respect to those Participants who are not Covered Employees.

2.30 Performance Period

"Performance Period" means Kodak's fiscal year or any other period designated by the Committee with respect to which an Award may be granted.

2.31 Plan

"Plan" means the Management Variable Compensation Plan.

2.32 Retirement

"Retirement" means retirement under any defined benefit pension plan maintained by the Company which is either a tax-qualified plan under Section 401(a) of the Code or is identified in writing by the Committee as a defined benefit pension plan.

2.33 RONA

"RONA" means, for a Performance Period, Return on Net Assets for the Performance Period. RONA shall be calculated by dividing Net Income for the Performance Period by Average Net Assets for the same period.

2.34 Subsidiary

"Subsidiary" means a subsidiary which is majority owned by Kodak and reported in Kodak's audited consolidated financial statements.

2.35 Target Award

"Target Award" means, for a Performance Period, the target Award amounts established for each wage grade by the Committee for the Performance Period. The Target Awards shall serve only as a guideline in making Awards under the Plan. Depending upon the Committee's exercise of its discretion pursuant to Section 6.4(c), but subject to Section 6.5, a Participant may receive an Award for a Performance Period which may be more or less than the Target Award for his or her wage grade for that Performance Period. Moreover, the fact that a Target Award is established for a Participant's wage grade for a Performance Period shall not in any manner entitle the Participant to receive an Award for such period.

ARTICLE 3—ELIGIBILITY

All Key Employees are eligible to participate in the Plan. the Committee will, in its sole discretion, designate within the first 90 days of a Performance Period which Key Employees will be Participants for such Performance Period. However, the fact that a Key Employee is a Participant for a Performance Period shall not in any manner entitle such Participant to receive an Award for the period. The determination as to whether or not such Participant shall be paid an Award for such Performance Period shall be decided solely in accordance with the provisions of Articles 6 and 7 hereof.

ARTICLE 4—PLAN ADMINISTRATION

4.1 Responsibility

The Committee shall have total and exclusive responsibility to control, operate, manage, and administer the Plan in accordance with its terms.

4.2 Authority of the Committee

The Committee shall have all the authority that may be necessary or helpful to enable it to discharge its responsibilities with respect to the Plan. Without limiting the generality of the preceding sentence, the Committee shall have the exclusive right: to interpret the Plan, to determine eligibility for participation in the Plan, to decide all questions concerning eligibility for and the amount of Awards payable under the Plan, to establish and administer the Performance Goals and certify whether, and to what extent, they are attained, to construe any ambiguous provision of the Plan, to correct any default, to supply any omission, to reconcile any inconsistency, to issue administrative guidelines as an aid to administer the Plan, to make regulations for carrying out the Plan and to make changes in such regulations as they from time to time deem proper, and to decide any and all questions arising in the administration, interpretation, and application of the Plan. In addition, in order to enable Key Employees who are foreign nationals or are employed outside the United States or both to receive Awards under the Plan, the Committee may adopt such amendments, procedures, regulations, subplans, and the like as are necessary or advisable, in the opinion of the Committee, to effectuate the purposes of the Plan.

4.3   Discretionary Authority

The Committee shall have full discretionary authority in all matters related to the discharge of its responsibilities and the exercise of its authority under the Plan including, without limitation, its construction of the terms of the Plan and its determination of eligibility for participation and Awards under the Plan. It is the intent of the Plan that the decisions of the Committee and its action with respect to the Plan shall be final, binding, and conclusive upon all persons having or claiming to have any right or interest in or under the Plan.

4.4   Section 162(m) of the Code

With regard to all Covered Employees, the Plan shall for all purposes be interpreted and construed in accordance with Section 162(m) of the Code.

4.5   Delegation of Authority

Except to the extent prohibited by law, the Committee may delegate some or all of its authority under the Plan to any person or persons provided that any such delegation be in writing; provided, however, only the Committee may select and grant Awards to Participants who are Covered Employees.

ARTICLE 5—FORM OF AWARDS

Awards may at the Committee's sole discretion be paid in cash, Common Stock, or a combination thereof. The Committee may, in its sole judgment, subject an Award to such terms, conditions, restrictions and/or limitations (including, but not limited to, restrictions on transferability and vesting), provided they are not inconsistent with the terms of the Plan. For purposes of the Plan, the value of any Award granted in the form of Common Stock shall be the mean between the high and low at which the Common Stock trades on the New York Stock Exchange as of the date of the grant's Effective Date.

ARTICLE 6—DETERMINATION OF AWARDS FOR A PERFORM-ANCE PERIOD

6.1 Procedure for Determining Awards

As detailed below in the succeeding Sections of this Article 6, the procedure for determining Awards for a Performance Period entails the following: (a) determination of Maximum Award; (b) determination of Maximum Award Pool; (c) determination of Actual Award Pool; and (d) allocation of Actual Award Pool among individual Participants. Upon completion of this process, any Awards earned for the Performance Period shall be paid in accordance with Article 7.

6.2 Determination of Maximum Award

(a) Purpose of Maximum Award. The Maximum Award for a Performance Period is an addend in the calculation of the Maximum Award Pool for such Performance Period.

(b) Calculation of Maximum Award. The Maximum Award for a Performance Period is the dollar amount obtained by applying the Performance Formula for such Performance Period against the Performance Goals for the same Performance Period.

6.3 Determination of Maximum Award Pool

(a) Purpose of Maximum Award Pool. The Maximum Award Pool, for a Performance Period, serves as the basis for calculating the maximum amount of Awards that may be granted to all Participants for such Performance Period.

(b) Calculation of Maximum Award Pool. The Maximum Award Pool for a Performance Period shall be calculated by adding the Maximum Award for such Performance Period with the Carryforward Amount.

(c) Limitation. The total of all Awards granted for a Performance Period shall not exceed the amount of the Maximum Award Pool for such Performance Period.

(d) Allocation of Maximum Award Pool to Covered Employees. Within the first 90 days of a Performance Period (or, if longer, within the maximum period allowed under Section 162(m) of the Code), the Committee shall allocate in writing, or establish in writing an objective means of allocating, on behalf of each Covered Person, a portion or the Maximum Award Pool (not to exceed the amount set forth in Section 6.5(a)) to be granted for such Performance Period in the event the Performance Goals for such period are attained.

(e) Negative Discretion. The Committee is authorized at any time during or after a Performance Period, in its sole and absolute discretion, to reduce or eliminate the Maximum Award Pool for the Performance Period, for any reason, based on such factors, indicia, standards, goals, and/or measures it determines in the exercise of its sole discretion. Similarly, the Committee is authorized at any time during or after a Performance Period, in its sole and absolute discretion, to reduce or eliminate the portion of the Maximum Award Pool allocated to any Covered Employee for the Performance Period, for any reason.

6.4   Determination of Actual Award Pool

(a) Purpose of Actual Award Pool. The Actual Award Pool for a Performance Period determines the aggregate amount of all the Awards that are to be issued under the Plan for such Performance Period.

(b) Establishment of Actual Award Pool. The Actual Award Pool for a Performance Period shall be the Maximum Award Pool for such period after adjustment, if any, by the Committee through Negative Discretion. Thus, to the extent the Committee elects for a Performance Period not to exercise Negative Discretion with respect to the Maximum Award Pool, the Actual Award Pool for the Performance Period shall be the Maximum Award Pool for such period.

(c) Allocation of Actual Award Pool to Individual Participants. The portion of the Actual Award Pool that will be Awarded to any individual Participant will be determined by the Committee, in its sole and absolute discretion, based on such factors, indicia, standards, goals, and measures which it determines in the exercise of its sole discretion. By way of illustration, and not by way of limitation, the Committee may, but shall not be required to, consider: (1) the Participant's position and level of responsibility, individual merit, contribution to the success of the Company and Target Award; (2) the performance of the Company or the organizational unit of the Participant based upon attainment of financial and other performance criteria and goals; and (3) business unit, division or department achievements.

(d) Adjustment to Carryforward Amount. To the extent the sum of all Awards paid for a Performance Period exceeds the Maximum Award for such period, the Carryforward Amount shall be reduced by an amount equal to such difference.

6.5   Limitations on Awards to Covered Employees

The provisions of this Section 6.5 shall have control over any Plan provision to the contrary.

(a) Maximum Award Payable to Covered Employees. The maximum Award payable to any Covered Employee under the Plan for a Performance Period shall be $4,000,000.

(b) Attainment of Performance Goals. The Performance Goals for a Performance Period must be achieved in order for a Covered Employee to receive an Award for such Performance Period.

(c) Allocation of Actual Award Pool. The portion of the Actual Award Pool allocated to a Covered Employee by the Committee pursuant to Section 6.4(c) shall not exceed the portion of the Maximum Award Pool allocated to such Covered Employee under Section 6.3(d).

ARTICLE 7—PAYMENT OF AWARDS FOR A PERFORMANCE PERIOD

7.1   Certification

(a) In General. Following the completion of each Performance Period, the Committee shall meet to review and certify in writing whether, and to what extent, the Performance Goals for the Performance Period have been achieved.

(b) Performance Goals Achieved. If the Committee certifies that the Performance Goals have been achieved, it shall, based upon application of the Performance Formula to the Performance Goals for such period, calculate and certify in writing the amount of: (i) the Maximum Award; (ii) the Maximum Award Pool; and (iii) the Maximum Award Pool to be allocated to each Covered Employee in accordance with Section 6.3(d). Upon completion of these written certifications, the Committee shall determine the amount of the Actual Award Pool for the Performance Period.

(c) Performance Goals Not Achieved. In the event the Performance Goals for a Performance Period are not achieved, the limitation contained in Section 6.5(b) shall apply to the Covered Employees. Further, any Awards granted for the Performance Period must be paid from the Carryforward Amount which shall be reduced to reflect the amount of such Awards.

7.2   Election of Form of Award

Prior to or coincident with its calculation of the amount of the Actual Award Pool for a Performance Period, the Committee shall, in its sole discretion, determine the form(s) in which to grant Awards under the Plan for such period.

7.3   Timing of Award Payments

Unless deferred pursuant to Article 8 hereof, the Awards granted for a Performance Period shall be paid to Participants on the Award Payment Date for such Performance Period, which date shall occur as soon as administratively practicable following the completion of the procedure described in Section 7.1.

ARTICLE 8—DEFERRAL OF AWARDS

At the discretion of the Committee, a Participant may, subject to such terms and conditions as the Committee may determine, elect to defer payment of all or any part of any Award which the Participant might earn with respect to a Performance Period by complying with such procedures as the Committee may prescribe. Any Award, or portion thereof, upon which such an election is made shall be deferred into, and subject to the terms, conditions and requirements of, the Eastman Kodak Employees' Savings and Investment Plan, 1982 Eastman Kodak Company Executive Deferred Compensation Plan or such other applicable deferred compensation plan of the Company.

ARTICLE 9—ADDITIONAL AWARDS

9.1 In General

In addition to the Awards that are authorized to be granted under Article 6 and paid under Article 7 for a Performance Period, the Committee may, in its sole judgment, form time to time grant Awards under the Plan from the Carryforward Amount.

9.2 Eligibility

All Key Employees, other than those who are Covered Employees, are eligible to receive the Awards authorized to be granted under this Article 9.

9.3 Form of Awards

Any Award granted by the Committee pursuant to the provisions of this Article 9 shall be issued in one or more of the forms permitted under Article 5 of the Plan.

9.4 Terms and Conditions

The Committee shall, by way of an Award notice or otherwise, establish the terms, conditions, restrictions and/or limitations that will apply to an Award issued pursuant to this Article 9; provided, however, such terms, conditions, restrictions and limitations are not inconsistent with the terms of the Plan.

9.5 Carryforward Amount

Upon the issuance of any Award under this Article 9, the Carryforward Amount shall be immediately reduced by an amount equal to the value of such Award.

ARTICLE 10—CHANGE IN OWNERSHIP

10.1 Background

Notwithstanding any provision contained in the Plan, including but not limited to Sections 1.1, 4.4, and 13.10, the provisions of this Article 10 shall have control over any contrary provision. Upon a Change in Ownership: (a) the terms of this Article 10 shall immediately become operative, without further action or consent by any person or entity: (b) all terms, conditions, restrictions and limitations in effect on any unpaid and/or deferred Award shall immediately lapse as of the date of such event; (c) no other terms, conditions, restrictions and/or limitations shall be imposed upon any Awards on or after such date, and in no event shall an Award be forfeited on or after such date; and (d) except where a prorated Award is required to be paid under this Article 10, all unvested and/or unpaid Awards or any other outstanding Awards shall automatically become one hundred percent (100%) vested immediately.

10.2 Payment of Awards

Upon a Change in Ownership, any Key Employee, whether or not he or she is still employed by the Company, shall be paid, as soon as practicable but in no event later than 90 days after the Change in Ownership, the Awards set forth in (a) and (b) below:

(a) All of the Key Employee's unpaid and/or deferred Awards; and

(b) A pro rata Award for the Performance Period in which the Change in Ownership occurs. The amount of the pro rata Award shall be determined by multiplying the Target Award for such Performance Period for Participants in the same wage grade as the Key Employee by a fraction, the numerator of which shall be the number of full months in the Performance Period prior to the date of the Change in Ownership and the denominator of which shall be the total number of full months in the Performance Period. For purposes of this calculation, a partial month shall be treated as a full month to the extent of 15 or more days in such month have elapsed. To the extent Target Awards have not yet been established for the Performance Period, the Target Awards for the immediately preceding Performance Period shall be used. The pro rata Awards shall be paid to the Key Employee in the form of a lump-sum cash payment.

10.3 Miscellaneous

Upon a Change In Ownership, no action, including, but not by way of limitation, the amendment, suspension, or termination of the Plan, shall be taken which would affect the rights of any Key Employee or the operation of the Plan with respect to any Award to which the Key Employee may have become entitled hereunder on or prior to the date of such action or as a result of such Change In Ownership.

ARTICLE 11—CHANGE IN CONTROL

11.1 Background

Notwithstanding any provision contained in the Plan, including, but not limited to, Sections 1.1, 4.4, and 13.10, the provisions of this Article 11 shall control over any contrary provision. All Key Employees shall be eligible for the treatment afforded by this Article 11 if their employment with the Company terminates within two years following a Change In Control, unless the termination is due to (a) death; (b) Disability; (c) Cause; (d) resignation other than (1) resignation from a declined reassignment to a job that is not reasonably equivalent in responsibility or compensation (as defined in Kodak's Termination Allowance Plan), or that is not in the same geographic area (as defined in Kodak's Termination Allowance Plan), or (2) resignation within thirty days of a reduction in base pay; or (e) retirement.

11.2 Vesting and Lapse of Restrictions

If a Key Employee qualifies for treatment under Section 11.1, his or her Awards shall be treated in the manner described in Subsections 10.1(b) and (c). Further, except where a prorated Award is required to be paid under this Article 11, all of the Key Employee's unvested and/or unpaid Awards shall automatically become one hundred percent (100%) vested immediately.

11.3 Payment of Awards

If a Key Employee qualifies for treatment under Section 11.1, he or she shall be paid, as soon as practicable but in no event later than 90 days after his or her termination of employment, the Awards set forth in (a) and (b) below:

(a) All of the Key Employee's unpaid and/or deferred Awards; and

(b) A pro rata Award for the Performance Period in which his or her termination of employment occurs. The amount of the pro rata Award shall be determined by multiplying the Target Award for such Performance Period for Participants in the same wage grade as the Key Employee by a fraction, the numerator of which shall be the number of full months in the Performance Period prior to the date of the Key Employee's termination of employment and the denominator of which shall be the total number of full months in the Performance Period. For purposes of this calculation, a partial month shall be treated as a full month to the extent 15 or more days in such month have elapsed. To the extent Target Awards have not yet been established for the Performance Period, the Target Awards for the immediately preceding Performance Period shall be used. The pro rata Awards shall be paid to the Key Employee in the form of a lump-sum cash payment.

11.4 Miscellaneous

Upon a Change In Control, no action, including, but not by way of limitation, the amendment, suspension, or termination of the Plan, shall be taken which would affect the rights of any Key Employee or the operation of the Plan with respect to any Award to which the Key Employee may have become entitled hereunder prior to the date of the Change In Control or to which he or she may become entitled as a result of such Change In Control.

ARTICLE 12—SHARES SUBJECT TO THE PLAN

12.1 Available Shares

Subject to adjustment as provided in Subsection 12.2 below, the maximum number of shares of Common Stock, $2.50 par value per share, of the Company which shall be available for grant of Awards under the Plan during its term shall not exceed 1,000,000. Any shares of Common Stock related to Awards which terminate by expiration, forfeiture, cancellation or otherwise without the issuance of such shares, are settled in cash in lieu of Common Stock, or are exchanged with the Committee's permission for Awards not involving Common Stock, shall not be available again for grant under the Plan. The shares of Common Stock available for issuance under the Plan may be authorized and unissued shares or treasury shares.

12.2 Adjustment of Shares Available

(a) In General. The provisions of this Subsection 12.2 (a) are subject to the limitation contained in Subsection 12.2(b). If there is any change in the number of outstanding shares of Common Stock through the declaration of stock dividends, stock splits or the like, the number of shares available for Awards and the shares subject to any Award shall be automatically adjusted. If there is any change in the number of outstanding shares of Common Stock through any change in the capital account of Kodak, or through a merger, consolidation, separation (including a spin off or other distribution of stock or property) reorganization (whether or not such reorganization comes within the definition of such term in Section 368(a) of the Code) or partial or complete liquidation, the Committee shall make appropriate adjustments in the maximum number of shares of Common Stock which may be issued under the Plan and any adjustments and/or modifications to outstanding Awards as it, in its sole discretion, deems appropriate. In the event of any other change in the capital structure or in the Common Stock of the Company, the Committee shall also be authorized to make such appropriate adjustments in the maximum number of shares of Common Stock available for issuance under the Plan and any adjustments and/or modifications to outstanding Awards as it, in its sole discretion, deems appropriate.

(b) Covered Employees. In no event shall the Award of any Participant who is a Covered Employee be adjusted pursuant to Subsection 12.2(a) to the extent it would cause such Award to fail to qualify as "Performance-Based Compensation" under Section 162(m) of the Code.

ARTICLE 13—MISCELLANEOUS

13.1 Nonassignability

No Awards under the Plan shall be subject in any manner to alienation, anticipation, sale, transfer (except by will or the laws of descent and distribution), assignment, pledge, or encumbrance, nor shall any Award be payable to anyone other than the Participant to whom it was granted.

13.2 Withholding Taxes

The Company shall be entitled to deduct from any payment under the Plan, regardless of the form of such payment, the amount of all applicable income and employment taxes required by law to be withheld with respect to such payment or may require the Participant to pay to it such tax prior to and as a condition of the making of such payment. In accordance with any applicable administrative guidelines it establishes, the Committee may allow a Participant to pay the amount of taxes required by law to be withheld from an Award by withholding from any payment of Common Stock due as a result of such Award, or by permitting the Participant to deliver to the Company, shares of Common Stock having a fair market value, as determined by the Committee, equal to the amount of such required withholding taxes.

13.3 Amendments to Awards

The Committee may at any time unilaterally amend any unearned, deferred or unpaid Award, including, but not by way of limitation, Awards earned but not yet paid, to the extent it deems appropriate; provided, however, that any such amendment which, in the opinion of the Committee, is adverse to the Participant shall require the Participant's consent.

13.4 Regulatory Approvals and Listings

Notwithstanding anything contained in this Plan to the contrary, the Company shall have no obligation to issue or deliver certificates of Common Stock evidencing Awards or any other Award resulting in the payment of Common Stock prior to (a) the obtaining of any approval from any governmental agency which the Company shall, in its sole discretion, determine to be necessary or advisable, (b) the admission of such shares to listing on the stock exchange on which the Common Stock may be listed, and (c) the completion of any registration or other qualification of said shares under any state or Federal law or ruling of any governmental body which the Company shall, in its sole discretion, determine to be necessary or advisable.

13.5 No Right to Continued Employment or Grants

Participation in the Plan shall not give any Key Employee any right to remain in the employ of the Company. Kodak or, in the case of employment with a Subsidiary, the Subsidiary, reserves the right to terminate any Key Employee at any time. Further, the adoption of this Plan shall not be deemed to give any Key Employee or any other individual any right to be selected as a Participant or to be granted an Award.

13.6 Amendment/Termination

The Committee may suspend or terminate the Plan at any time with or without prior notice. In addition, the Committee may, form time to time and with or without prior notice, amend the Plan in any manner, but may not without shareholder approval adopt any amendment which would require the vote of the shareholders of Kodak pursuant to Section 16 of the Exchange Act or Section 162(m) of the Code, but only insofar as such amendment affects Covered Employees.

13.7 Governing Law

The Plan shall be governed by and construed in accordance with the laws of the State of New York, except as superseded by applicable Federal Law.

13.8 No Right, Title, or Interest in Company Assets

No Participant shall have any rights as a shareholder as a result of participant in the Plan until the date of issuance of a stock certificate in his or her name, and, in the case of restricted shares of Common Stock, such rights are granted to the Participant under the Plan. To the extent any person acquires a right to receive payments from the Company under this Plan, such rights shall be no greater than the rights of an unsecured creditor of the Company and the Participant shall not have any rights in or against any specific assets of the Company. All of the Awards granted under the Plan shall be unfunded.

13.9 No Guarantee of Tax Consequences

No person connected with the Plan in any capacity, including, but not limited to, Kodak and its Subsidiaries and their directors, officers, agents and employees, makes any representation, commitment, or guarantee that any tax treatment, including, but not limited to, Federal, state and local income, estate and gift tax treatment, will be applicable with respect to amounts deferred under the Plan, or paid to or for the benefit of a Participant under the Plan, or that such tax treatment will apply to or be available to a Participant on account of participation in the Plan.

13.10   Compliance with Section 162(m)

If any provision of the Plan would cause the Awards granted to a Covered Person not to constitute qualified "Performance-Based Compensation" under Section 162(m) of the Code, that provision, insofar as it pertains to the Covered Person, shall be severed from, and shall be deemed not to be part of, this Plan, but the other provisions hereof shall remain in full force and effort.

PLAN 3: WAGE DIVIDEND PLAN

ARTICLE 1—PURPOSE, EFFECTIVE DATE, AND TERM OF PLAN

1.1   Purpose

The purpose of the Plan is to assist the Company in attracting, motivating and retaining its Employees by rewarding Employees for their contributions to the Company's growth and success, provided Company performance meets or exceeds established Performance Goals, and to endeavor to qualify the Awards granted to Covered Employees under the Plan as "Performance-Based Compensation" as defined in Section 162(m) of the Code.

1.2   Effective Date

The Plan shall be effective as of January 1, 1995, subject to approval by Kodak's shareholders at the 1995 Annual Meeting of the Shareholders of Kodak.

1.3   Term

Awards shall not be granted pursuant to the Plan after December 31, 1999: provided, however, the Committee may grant Awards after such date in recognition of performance for a Performance Period completed on or prior to such date.

ARTICLE 2—DEFINITIONS

2.1 Average Net Assets

"Average Net Assets" means, for the Performance Period, the simple average of the Company's Net Assets for each of the following five fiscal quarters of the Company: the four fiscal quarters of the Performance Period and the fiscal quarter immediately preceding the Performance Period. For purpose of this calculation, Net Assets for a fiscal quarter shall be determined as of the end of such quarter.

2.2 Award

"Award" means the compensation payable to a Participant by the Committee for a Performance Period pursuant to Article 7. All Awards shall be issued in one or more of the forms specified by Article 5.

2.3 Award Payment Date

"Award Payment Date" means, for each Performance Period, the date that the Awards, if any, for the Performance Period shall be paid to Participants pursuant to Article 7, without regard to any election to defer receipt of an Award made under Article 8 of the Plan.

2.4 Board

"Board" means the Board of Directors of Kodak.

2.5 Code

"Code" means the Internal Revenue Code of 1986, as amended from time to time, including regulations thereunder and successor provisions and regulations thereto.

2.6 Committee

"Committee" means the Executive Compensation and Development Committee of the Board, or such other Board committee as may be designated by the Board to administer the Plan, provided, however, that the Committee shall consist of three or more directors, all of whom are both a "disinterested person" within the meaning of Rule 16b-3 under the Exchange Act and an "outside director" within the meaning of the definition of such term as contained in Proposed

Treasury Regulation Section 1.162-27(e)(3), or any successor definition subsequently adopted.

2.7 Common Stock

"Common Stock" means the Common Stock, $2.50 par value per share, of Kodak which may be newly issued or treasury stock.

2.8 Company

"Company" means Kodak and its Subsidiaries.

2.9 Covered Employee

"Covered Employee" means an Employee who is a "Covered Employee" within the meaning of Section 162(m) of the Code.

2.10 Effective Date

"Effective Date" means the date an Award is determined to be effective by the Committee upon its grant of such Award.

2.11 Employee

"Employee" means, for a Performance Period, any person employed by the Company during such Performance Period and compensated for services in the form of an hourly wage or salary, provided, however, that Limited Service Employees are not Employees.

By the way of example, and not by way of limitation, the term "Employee" does not include independent contractors or leased employees (within the meaning of Section 414(n) of the Code).

2.12 Exchange Act

"Exchange Act" means the Securities Exchange Act of 1934, as amended from time to time, including rules thereunder and successor provisions and rules thereto.

2.13 Kodak

"Kodak" means Eastman Kodak Company.

2.14 Limited Service Employee

"Limited Service Employee" means a person who is hired by the Company for the specific purpose of meeting short-term needs of 900 hours or less in any consecutive 12 month period and who is designated as a Limited Service Employee when hired.

2.15 Negative Discretion

"Negative Discretion" means the discretion authorized by the Plan to be applied by the Committee in determining the size of the Award to be paid to a Covered Employee for a Performance Period if, in the Committee's sole judgment, such application is appropriate. Negative Discretion may only be used by the Committee to eliminate or reduce the size of the Award earned by a Covered Employee pursuant to the Performance Formula. By way of example, and not by way of limitation, in no event shall any discretionary authority granted to the Committee by the Plan, including, but not limited to Negative Discretion, be used to (a) grant an Award to a Covered Employee for a Performance Period if the Performance Goals for such Performance Period have not been attained; or (b) increase an Award to a Covered Employee above the maximum payable under Section 6.2(b) of the Plan.

2.16 Net Assets

"Net Assets" means the Company's consolidated Total Shareholders' Equity and Borrowings (both short-term and long-term) as reported in its audited consolidated financial statements. The Committee is authorized at any time during the first 90 days of a Performance Period, or at any time thereafter in its sole and absolute discretion, to adjust or modify the calculation of Net Assets for such Performance Period in order to prevent the dilution or enlargement of the rights of Participants, (a) in the event of, or in anticipation of, any unusual or extraordinary corporate item, transaction, event or development; (b) in recognition of, or in anticipation of, any other unusual or nonrecurring events affecting the Company, or the financial statements of the Company, or in response to, or in anticipation of, changes in applicable laws, regulations, accounting principles, or business conditions; and (c) in view of the Committee's assessment of the business strategy of the Company, performance of comparable organizations, economic and business conditions, and any other circumstances deemed relevant. However, if and to the extent the exercise of such authority after the first 90 days of a Performance Period would cause the Awards granted to the Covered Employees for the Performance Period to fail to qualify as "Performance-Based Compensation" under Section 162(m) of the Code, then such authority shall only be exercised with respect to those Participants who are not Covered Employees.

2.17 Net Income

"Net Income" means, for a Performance Period, the Company's consolidation Net Earning (Loss) before Cumulative Effect of Changes in Accounting Principle for the Performance Period as reported in its audited consolidated financial statements. The Committee is authorized at any time during the first 90 days of a Performance Period, or at any time thereafter in its sole an absolute discretion, to adjust or modify the calculation of Net Income for such Performance Period in order to prevent the dilution or enlargement of the rights of Participants (a) in the event of, or in anticipation of, any dividend or other distribution (whether in the form of cash, securities or other property), recapitalization, restructuring, reorganization, merger, consolidation, spin off, combination, repurchase, shares exchange, liquidation, dissolution, or other similar corporate transaction, event or development; (b) in recognition of, or in anticipation of, any other unusual or nonrecurring event affecting the Company, or the financial statements of the Company, or in response to, or in anticipation of, changes in applicable laws, regulations, accounting principles, or business conditions, (c) in recognition of, or in anticipation of, any other extraordinary gains or losses; and (d) in view of the Committee's assessment of the business strategy of the Company, performance of comparable organizations, economic and business conditions, and any other circumstances deemed relevant. However, if and to the extent the exercise of such authority after the first 90 days of a Performance Period would cause the Awards granted to the Covered Employees for the Performance Period to fail to qualify as "Performance-Based Compensation" under Section 162(m) of the Code, then such authority shall only be exercised with respect to those Participants who are not Covered Employees.

2.18 Participant

"Participant" means, for a Performance Period, an Employee who is designated to participate in the Plan pursuant to Section 3.2.

2.19 Participation Rules

"Participation Rules" means, for a Performance Period, the rules established by the Committee in accordance with Section 3.2 pursuant to which the Committee shall determine which Employees will be Participants for such Performance Period.

2.20 Performance Criterion

"Performance Criterion" means the stated business criterion upon which the Performance Goals for a Performance Period are based as required pursuant to Proposed Treasury Regulation Section 1.162-27(e)(4)(iii). For purposes of the Plan, RONA shall be the Performance Criterion.

2.21 Performance Formula

"Performance Formula" means, for a Performance Period, the one or more objective formulas applied against the Performance Goals to determine which Awards have been earned for the Performance Period and, if so, the amount of such Awards. The Performance Formula for a Performance Period shall be established in writing by the Committee within the first 90 days of the Performance Period (or, if later, within the maximum period allowed pursuant to Section 162(m) of the Code).

2.22 Performance Goals

"Performance Goals" means, for a Performance Period, the one or more goals for the Performance Period established by the Committee in writing within the first 90 days of the Performance Period (or, if later, within the maximum period allowed pursuant to Section 162(m) of the Code) based upon the Performance Criterion. The Committee is authorized at any time during the first 90 days of a Performance Period, or at any time thereafter in its sole and absolute discretion, to adjust or modify the calculation of a Performance Goal for such Performance Period in order to prevent the dilution or enlargement of the rights of Participants, (a) in the event of, or in anticipation of, any unusual or extraordinary corporate item, transaction, event or development; (b) in recognition of, or in anticipation of, any other unusual or nonrecurring events affecting the Company, or the financial statements of the Company, or in response to, or in anticipation of, changes in applicable laws, regulations, accounting principles, or business conditions; and (c) in view of the Committee's assessment of the business strategy of the Company, performance of comparable organizations, economic and business conditions, and any other circumstances deemed relevant. However, if and to the extent the exercise of such authority after the first 90 days of a Performance Period would cause the Awards granted to the Covered Employees for the Performance Period to fail to qualify as "Performance-Based Compensation" under Section 162(m) of the Code, such authority shall only be exercised with respect to those Participants who are not Covered Employees.

2.23 Performance Period

"Performance Period" means Kodak's fiscal year.

2.24 Plan

"Plan" means the Wage Dividend Plan.

2.25 RONA

"RONA" means, for a Performance Period, Return on Net Assets for the Performance Period. RONA shall be calculated by dividing Net Income for the Performance Period by Average Net Assets for the same period.

2.26 Stock Equivalent

"Stock Equivalent" means an Award under Article 5 that is valued in whole or in part by reference to, or is payable in or is otherwise based on Common Stock.

2.27 Subsidiary

"Subsidiary" means a subsidiary which is majority owned by Kodak and reported in Kodak's audited consolidated financial statements.

ARTICLE 3—ELIGIBILITY AND PARTICIPATION

3.1 Eligibility

All Employees are eligible to participate in the Plan. However, the fact that a person if an Employee for a Performance Period shall not in any manner entitle such Employee to be eligible for an Award for the Performance Period. In order to be eligible for an Award for a Performance Period, the Employee must be designated as a Participant for such Performance Period by the Committee in accordance with Section 3.2 below.

3.2 Participation

Through the adoption of written Participation Rules within the first 90 days of a Performance Period, the Committee will, in its sole discretion, designate those Employees who will be Participants for such Performance Period. Pursuant to the Participation Rules for a Performance Period, the Committee may condition the receipt of Awards upon satisfaction of such preconditions and/or requirements as it, in its sole discretion, determines. The fact that an Employee is a Participant for a Performance Period shall not in any manner entitle such Participant to receive an Award for the Performance Period. The determination as to whether or not such Participant shall be paid an Award for such Performance Period shall be decided solely in accordance with the provisions of Article 7 hereof.

ARTICLE 4—PLAN ADMINISTRATION

4.1 Responsibility

The Committee shall have total and exclusive responsibility to control, operate, manage, and administer the Plan in accordance with its terms.

4.2 Authority of the Committee

The Committee shall have all the authority that may be necessary or helpful to enable it to discharge its responsibilities with respect to the Plan. Without limiting the generality of the preceding sentence, the Committee shall have the exclusive right: to interpret the Plan, to determine eligibility for participation in the Plan, to decide all questions concerning eligibility for and the amount of Awards payable under the Plan, to establish and administer the Performance Goals and certify whether, and to what extent, they are attained, to construe any ambiguous provision of the Plan, to correct any default, to supply any omission, to reconcile any inconsistency, to issue administrative guidelines as an aid to administer the Plan, to make regulations for carrying out the Plan and to make changes in such regulations as they from time to time deem proper, and to decide any and all questions arising in the administration, interpretation, and application of the Plan. In addition, in order to enable Employees who are foreign nationals or are employed outside the United States or both to receive Awards under the Plan, the Committee may adopt such amendments, procedures, regulations, subplans, and the like as are necessary or advisable, in the opinion of the Committee, to effectuate the purposes of the Plan.

4.3 Discretionary Authority

The Committee shall have full discretionary authority in all matters related to the discharge of its responsibilities and the exercise of its authority under the Plan including, without limitation, its construction of the terms of the Plan and its determination of eligibility for participation and Awards under the Plan. It is the intent of Kodak that the decisions of the Committee and its action with respect to the Plan shall be final, binding, and conclusive upon all persons having or claiming to have any right or interest in or under the Plan.

4.4 Section 162(m) of the Code

With regard to all Covered Employees, the Plan shall for all purposes be interpreted and construed in accordance with Section 162(m) of the Code.

4.5   Delegation of Authority

Except to the extent prohibited by law, the Committee may delegate some or all of its authority under the Plan to any person or persons provided that any such delegation be in writing.

ARTICLE 5—FORM OF AWARDS

Awards may at the Committee's sole discretion be issued and paid in cash, Common Stock, Stock Equivalents, or a combination thereof. Awards paid in the form of Common Stock or Stock Equivalent shall be issued for no consideration. The Committee may, in its sole judgment, subject an Award to such terms, conditions, restrictions and/or limitations (including, but not limited to, restrictions on transferability and vesting), provided they are not inconsistent with the terms of the Plan. For purposes of the Plan, the value of any Award granted in the form of Common Stock shall be the mean between the high and low at which the Common Stock trades on the New York Stock Exchange as of the date of the grant's Effective Date. To the extent Awards are granted in Common Stock or Stock Equivalents, such payments shall count against the number of available shares reserved under Section 9.1.

ARTICLE 6—DETERMINATION OF AWARDS FOR A PERFORMANCE PERIOD

6.1   Procedure for Determining Awards

Within the first 90 days of a Performance Period (or, if later, within the maximum period allowed under Section 162(m) of the Code), the Committee shall establish in writing for such Performance Period: (a) the Participation Rules; (b) the Performance Goal(s); and (c) and the Performance Formula.

6.2   Limitations on Awards

The provisions of this Section 6.2 shall control over any Plan provision to the contrary.

(a) General Limitation. Participants in the Plan for a Performance Period shall be eligible to receive Awards for such Performance Period only if: (1) the Performance Goals for such Performance

Period are achieved; and (2) the Performance Formula as applied against such Performance Goals determines that Awards have been earned for the Performance Period.

(b) Maximum Award Payable to Covered Employees. The maximum Award payable to any Covered Employee under the Plan for a Performance Period shall be $700,000.

ARTICLE 7—PAYMENT OF AWARDS FOR A PERFORMANCE PERIOD

7.1 Certification

Following the completion of each Performance Period, the Committee shall meet to review and certify in writing whether, and to what extent, the Performance Goals for the Performance Period have been achieved. If the Committee certifies that such Performance Goals have been achieved, it shall, based upon the Performance Formula, (i) calculate and certify in writing the amount of the Award earned by each Covered Employee; (ii) determine the actual size of the Award to be paid to each Covered Employee for the Performance Period by applying Negative Discretion, if and when it deems appropriate; and (iii) calculate the size of the Awards to be paid for the Performance Period to all other Participants.

7.2 Election of Form of Award

Prior to or coincident with its performance of the certifications required by Section 7.1, the Committee shall, in its sole discretion, determine the form(s) in which to grant Awards under the Plan for such period.

7.3 Negative Discretion

In determining the actual size of the Award to be paid to a Covered Employee for a Performance Period, the Committee may, through the use of Negative Discretion, reduce or eliminate the amount of the Award earned under the Performance Formula for the Performance Period, if, in its sole judgment, such reduction or elimination is appropriate.

7.4 Timing of Award Payments

Unless deferred pursuant to Article 8 hereof, the Award granted for a Performance Period shall be paid to Participants on the Award Payment Date for such Performance Period, which date shall occur as soon as administratively practicable following the completion of the procedure described in Section 7.1.

ARTICLE 8—DEFERRAL OF AWARDS

At the discretion of the Committee, a Participant may, subject to such terms, conditions, and limitations as the Committee may determine, elect to defer payment of all or a portion of the Award that would otherwise be paid to the Participant with respect to a Performance Period by complying with such procedures as the Committee may prescribe. Any award, or portion thereof, upon which such an election is made shall be deferred into, and subject to the terms, conditions, and requirements of the Eastman Kodak Employees' Savings and Investment Plan, the 1982 Eastman Kodak Company Executive Deferred Compensation Plan, or successor plans thereto.

ARTICLE 9—SHARES SUBJECT TO THE PLAN

9.1 Available Shares

Subject to adjustment as provided in Section 9.2 below, the maximum number of shares of Common Stock, $2.50 par value per share, of the Company shall be available for grant of Awards under the Plan during its term and shall not exceed 4,000,000. Any shares of Common Stock related to Awards which are terminated by expiration, forfeiture, cancellation or otherwise without the issuance of such shares, or are settled in cash in lieu of Common Stock, or are exchanged with the Committee's permission for Awards not involving Common Stock, shall not be available again for grant under the Plan. The shares of Common Stock available for issuance under the Plan may be authorized and unissued shares or treasury shares.

9.2 Adjustment of Shares Available

(a) In General. The provisions of this Subsection 9.2(a) are subject to the limitation contained in Subsection 9.2(b). If there is any change in the number of outstanding shares of Common Stock through the declaration of stock dividends, stock splits or the like, the number of shares available for Awards and the shares subject to any Award shall be automatically adjusted. If there is any change in the number of outstanding shares of Common Stock through any change in the capital account of Kodak, or through merger, consolidation, separation (including a spin-off or other distribution of stock or property), reorganization (whether or not such reorganization comes within the definition of such term in Section 368(a) of the Code), or partial or complete liquidation, the Committee shall make appropriate adjustments in the maximum number of shares of Common Stock which may be issued under the Plan and any adjustment and/or modifications to outstanding Awards as it, in its sole discretion, deems appropriate. In the event of any other change in the capital structure or in the Common Stock of the Company, the Committee shall also be authorized to make such appropriate adjustments in the maximum number of shares of Common Stock available for issuance under the Plan and any adjustments and/or modifications to outstanding Awards as it, in its sole discretion, deems appropriate.

(b) Covered Employees. In no event shall the Award of any Participant who is a Covered Employee be adjusted pursuant to Subsection 9.2(a) to the extent it would cause such Award to fail to qualify as "Performance-Based Compensation" under Section 162(m) of the Code.

ARTICLE 10—MISCELLANEOUS

10.1 Nonassignability

No Awards under the Plan shall be subject in any manner to alienation, anticipation, sale, transfer (except by will or the laws of descent and distribution), assignment, pledge, or encumbrance. Further, except in the case of an Award payable to a deceased Participant, no Award shall be payable to anyone other than the Participant to whom it was granted. In the case of an Award payable to a deceased Participant, the Committee shall, in the exercise of its sole and absolute discretion, determine the party to whom such Award shall be paid.

10.2 Withholding Taxes

The Company shall be entitled to deduct from any payment under the Plan, regardless of the form of such payment, the amount of all applicable income and employment taxes required by law to be withheld with respect to such payment or may require the Participant to pay to it such tax prior to and as a condition of the making of such payment. In accordance with any applicable administrative guidelines it establishes, the Committee may allow a Participant to pay the amount of taxes required by law to be withheld from an Award by withholding from any payment of Common Stock due as a result of such Award, or by permitting the Participant to deliver to the Company, shares of Common Stock having a fair market value, as determined by the Committee, equal to the amount of such required withholding taxes.

10.3 Regulatory Approvals and Listings

Notwithstanding anything contained in this Plan to the contrary, the Company shall have no obligation to issue, deliver, pay, credit or otherwise acknowledge any Award resulting in the payment of Common Stock prior to (a) the obtaining of any approval from any governmental agency which the Company shall, in its sole discretion, determine to be necessary or advisable, (b) the admission of such shares to listing on the stock exchange on which the Common Stock may be listed, and (c) the completion of any registration or other qualification of said shares under any state or Federal law or ruling of any governmental body which the Company shall, in its sole discretion, determine to be necessary or advisable.

10.4 No Right to Continued Employment or Grants

Participation in the Plan shall not give any Employee any right to remain in the employ of the Company. Kodak or, in the case of employment with a Subsidiary, the Subsidiary, reserves the right to terminate any Employee at any time. Further, the adoption of this Plan shall not be deemed to give any Employee any right to be selected as a Participant or to be granted an Award.

10.5   Amendment/Termination

The Committee may suspend or terminate the Plan at any time with or without prior notice. In addition, the Committee may, from time to time and with or without prior notice, amend the Plan in any manner, but may not without shareholder approval adopt any amendment which would require the vote of the shareholders of Kodak pursuant to Section 16 of the Exchange Act or Section 162(m) of the Code, but only insofar as such amendment affects Covered Employees.

10.6   Governing Law

The Plan shall be governed by and construed in accordance with the laws of the State of New York, except as superseded by applicable Federal Law.

10.7   No Right, Title, or Interest in Company Assets

In the case of Awards payable in the form of Common Stock or Awards resulting in the payment of Common Stock, no Participant shall have any rights as a shareholder as a result of participation in the Plan until the date of issuance of a stock certificate in his or her name or, in the event such Common Stock is issued in book entry form, until Kodak's transfer agent provides valid written notification thereof to the Participant, and, in the case of restricted shares of Common Stock, such rights are granted to the Participant under the Plan. To the extent any person acquires a right to receive payments from the Company under this Plan, such rights shall be no greater than the rights of an unsecured creditor of the Company and the Participant shall not have any rights in or against any specific assets of the Company. All of the Awards granted under the Plan shall be unfunded.

10.8   No Guarantee of Tax Consequences

No person connected with the Plan in any capacity, including, but not limited to, Kodak and its Subsidiaries and their directors, officers, agents and employees makes any representation, commitment, or guarantee that any tax treatment, including, but not limited to, Federal, state and local income, estate and gift tax treatment, will be applicable with respect to amounts deferred under the Plan, or paid to or for the benefit of a Participant under the Plan, or that such tax treatment will apply to or be available to a Participant on account of participation in the Plan.

10.9 Compliance with Section 162(m)

If any provision of the Plan would cause the Awards granted to a Covered Person not to constitute qualified "Performance-Based Compensation" under Section 162(m) of the Code, that provision, insofar as it pertains to the Covered Person, shall be severed from, and shall be deemed not to be a part of, this Plan, but the other provisions hereof shall remain in full force and effect.

10.10 Compliance with Exchange Act

With respect to Participants who are subject to the Section 16 of the Exchange Act, transactions under this Plan are intended to comply with applicable conditions of Rule 16b-3 or its successors under the Exchange Act. To the extent any provision of the Plan or action by the Committee fails to so comply, it shall, but only insofar as it pertains to Participants who are subject to Section 16 of the Exchange Act, be deemed null and void, to the extent permitted by law and deemed advisable by the Committee.

DEFINITIVE COPY

(CORPORATE LOGO OMITTED)

EASTMAN KODAK COMPANY

This Proxy is Solicited on behalf of the Board of Directors.

Appendix C

Sample Severance and Noncompetition Agreement

The following Securities and Exchange Commission-filed document, which has been provided by the Bombay Company, may be used for top officers.

Dear _____:

The Board of Directors (the "Board") of The Bombay Company, Inc. (the "Company") recognizes that you have made and are expected to make a substantial contribution to the profitability, growth, and financial strength of the Company. In addition, the Board has determined that it is appropriate to induce you to enter into an agreement (the "Agreement") with the Company containing certain post-employment restrictions and providing for the continuation of certain benefits and income to you in the event you leave the employ of the Company.

1. *Term of Agreement; Termination Date.* The term of this Agreement is three years, commencing on the date of execution by both parties. At the end of the first year, which shall be the anniversary of the effective date hereof (the "Anniversary Date") and thereafter upon each Anniversary Date, this Agreement will be automatically renewed for an additional year, unless the Company has delivered to you a notice that it does not wish to renew the Agreement at least 30 days prior to such Anniversary Date. Upon notice of nonrenewal, you are entitled to the protection of this Agreement for the remaining

term of the Agreement, subject to all other provisions of this Agreement.

2. *Compensation upon Termination of Employment.* As set forth herein, your employment with the Company may be terminated prior to the expiration of the term specified in Section 1 of this Agreement. However, the provisions of Sections 2 through 18 will continue in full force and effect regardless of whether you continue to be employed by the Company and regardless of the reason your employment is terminated.

(a) *Termination for Cause.* Your employment may be terminated by the Company for Cause, evidenced by a duly adopted resolution of the Board. Unless made subject to an arbitration proceeding as set forth below, such termination will be effective immediately upon delivery to you of a Notice of Termination. "Notice of Termination" means a notice, timely delivered, which indicates the specific provisions in this Agreement relied upon for termination. It will set forth in reasonable detail the facts and circumstances claimed provide a basis for termination of your employment under the provisions so indicated. If the Company terminates you for Cause, you are entitled to receive your Base Salary and Calculated Bonus to the termination date as specified in the Notice of Termination (the "Termination Date"). "Calculated Bonus" means your bonus calculated based upon Company performance (the elements, criteria and formula of which shall be determined by the executive bonus plan for the fiscal year as approved by the Board) on a year-to-date basis through the Termination Date, the computation of which shall be made by the Company consistent with generally accepted accounting practices and past practices.

"Cause" means (i) the willful and continued failure by you to perform your duties with the Company (other than failure resulting from incapacity due to physical or mental illness) after a written demand for substantial performance is delivered to you by the Board which specifically identifies the manner in which the Board believes that you have not substantially performed your duties; (ii) a final, nonappealable determination by a court that you committed an act of dishonesty, fraud, or willful misconduct involving the Company; (iii) your conviction of any felony; or (iv) the material breach by you of any provision of this Agreement. For purposes of this definition of

"Cause," no act, or failure to act, on your part will be considered "willful" unless done, or omitted to be done, by you not in good faith and without reasonable belief that this action or omission was in the best interest of the Company.

In the event there is a dispute over the basis for a termination for Cause pursuant to (i) or (iv) in the preceeding paragraph, and provided you request in writing to the Company within 7 days following the Date of Termination, the dispute will be made the subject of compulsory arbitration, which you agree will be final, binding and nonappealable absent gross fraud or misconduct by one or more of the arbitrators. You agree that such arbitration will be in accordance with the rules and procedures of the American Arbitration Association, by three arbitrators designated by such Association, will be held in Fort Worth, Texas unless mutually agreed to the contrary, and shall be held within 90 days following the Date of Termination. You shall continue to be paid your normal compensation and receive normal benefits during the pendency of the arbitration. If the arbitration decision concludes that Cause did not exist for the termination, then the termination shall automatically become a termination other than for Cause, and the compensation specified in this Agreement shall commence. If arbitration is selected, then for purposes of this Agreement, the Date of Termination shall become the date of the arbitration decision.

"Base Salary" means your annual base salary, payable bi-weekly in accordance with Company policy, plus any increases in salary as established in the executive compensation program approved by the Board for a given fiscal year.

(b) *Mutual Consent.* At any time during the term of this Agreement, the parties hereto may terminate your employment by mutual consent. Such termination by mutual consent must be in writing, signed by both parties, and must set forth the mutual agreement of the parties regarding the terms and conditions for the continuation of income or benefits payments, if any, from the Company to you.

(c) *Termination by You.* You may terminate your employment with the Company. In the event that you do so, termination will be effective (i) for voluntary resignation, thirty days after you deliver a Notice of Termination or comparable notice to the Company; (ii) for

"Good Reason" (defined below), on the tenth day after you deliver a Notice of Termination to the Company, specifying in detail the reasons therefor, provided the Company has not, during such ten day period, cured the event or events causing such "Good Reason"; or (iii) for the Company's material breach of this Agreement, on the thirtieth day after written notice to the Company of such alleged breach, provided the Company has not, during such thirty day period, cured such breach. In the event you voluntarily resign, you are entitled to receive your Base Salary and Calculated Bonus to the Termination Date.

"Good Reason" means any of the following:

(i) without your express written consent, the assignment to you of material duties inconsistent with or the removal of material duties normal to your position, responsibilities and status with the Company, a material adverse change in your reporting responsibilities, titles or offices, or your removal from or any failure to re-elect you to any of such positions, except in connection with the termination of your employment for Cause or termination by you other than for Good Reason;

(ii) any reduction by the Company in your level of Base Salary and Target Bonus as in effect on the date hereof, which is inconsistent with a broad-based compensation reduction involving all or substantially all corporate and divisional officers of the Company and their equivalents;

"Target Bonus" means the amount of bonus dollars you would receive pursuant to the executive bonus plan if the Company achieved its planned objectives set forth in the annual business plan, as approved by the Board for a given fiscal year.

(iii) the Company's requiring you to be based anywhere other than the Company's corporate offices in Fort Worth, Texas, except for required travel on the Company's business to an extent substantially consistent with your present business travel obligations, or, if you consent to any relocation, the failure by the Company to pay (or reimburse you) for all reasonable moving expenses incurred by you relating to a change of your principal residence in connection with such relocation and to indemnify you against any loss (defined as the difference between the actual sale price of such residence and the higher of (A) your aggregate investment in such residence or (B) the fair market value of such residence as determined by a real estate appraiser mutually acceptable to both parties) realized on the sale of your principal residence in connection with any such change of residence;

(iv)   any failure of the Company to obtain, in accordance with Section 12 of this Agreement, the assumption of the agreement to perform this Agreement by any successor to the Company; or

(v)   any purported termination of your employment which is not effected pursuant to a properly delivered Notice of Termination; for purposes of this Agreement, no such purported termination shall be effective.

(d)   *Termination Without Cause; Good Reason.* If the Company terminates your employment other than for Cause, or if you terminate your employment for Good Reason or because of the material breach by the Company of this Agreement which is not timely cured, then the Company agrees to make payments and provide the following benefits:

(i)   The Company agrees to pay you your Base Salary for a period of 24 months following the Termination Date, provided, however, if you obtain New Employment (as defined below) any compensation attributed to such employment shall reduce the required payments herein on a dollar for dollar basis after the completion of 12 months following the Termination Date, such payment period hereinafter called the "Continuation Period." For fiscal years beginning subsequent to the Termination, Date but during the Continuation Period, you shall be paid, on a pro rata basis, your Target Bonus as set by the Board of Directors for such subsequent year. The payments described in this Section 2(d)(i) shall be defined as "Continuance Amount(s)." The Continuance Amount will be paid in installments in accordance with the regular payroll of the Company, and each installment will be subject to regular payroll deductions and all applicable taxes.

"New Employment" means your acceptance of a compensated position of employment with another person, entity or organization, or the creation or establishment of a business causing you to be self-employed during the Continuation Period. If you accept employment during the Continuation Period with a level of compensation or attributed earnings less than the Continuance Amount, then the Company shall, on a monthly basis, pay any discrepancy between your compensation or earnings and the Continuance Amount until the earlier of (i) the final day of the Continuation Period, or (ii) the discrepancy no longer exists. For purposes of this Section 2(d)(i), compensation or earnings from New Employment shall include, but not be limited to, any sign-on bonuses, other bonuses, guarantees or value given to you in connection with the employment. You agree to provide the Company appropriate documentation describing the employment and establishing the discrepancy, the failure of which shall serve to excuse any future payment by the Company under this Section 2(d)(i). The Company shall have the right to determine, in its sole discretion, acting reasonably, the value of the compensation or earnings for purposes of satisfying any discrepancy.

(ii)   Within 45 days following the Termination Date, you will also receive, in a lump sum, your bonus for the fiscal year during which the termination occurred, based on the greater of either (i) your prorated Target Bonus to the Date of Termination or (ii) your Calculated Bonus.

(iii)   The Company also agrees that you will be entitled to continue to participate in the Company's group health plan (medical, dental, and basic life insurance) on the same terms as other Company employees until the earlier of: (i) the expiration of the Continuation Period or (ii) your eligibility for similar plans by a subsequent employer. In accordance with the plan's provisions, your coverage will cease on the Termination Date under the Key Executive Disability Plan and the Family Security Plan. Anything to the contrary notwithstanding, the Company will have no obligation to continue to maintain during the Continuation Period any plan solely as a result of the provisions of this Agreement.

(iv) Any front-loaded stock options previously granted to you under any stock option plan of the Company will vest as of the Termination Date, provided the date of grant is at least 12 months prior to the Termination Date, in the following proportionate amount: the numerator being the number of months elapsed since the date of the grant of the option and the denominator being 24. All other outstanding stock options granted to you at least 12 months prior to the Termination Date under any of the Company's stock option plans will automatically be accelerated and fully vested as of the Termination Date. For options granted under the 1986 Stock Option Plan, you will be entitled to continue to hold these options and to exercise them for a period of three months after the Termination Date, after which period such options will expire and be cancelled. Upon completion of three months following the Date of Termination, you shall be granted a cash-only stock appreciation right (SAR) for each stock option exercised during the three month period, exercisable by you at any time during the following 21 months for any stock appreciation from the date of exercise of the option to the date of exercise of the SAR. Your exercise of the SAR shall be by written notice to the Company, which notice shall be irrevocable when given and shall be based upon the closing price of the Company's Common Stock on the date of the notice. Upon receipt of the notice, which shall specify the number of rights being exercised and the cash value of such rights, the Company shall redeem the rights tendered and shall become obligated to pay to you the value of the SAR exercised. The Company may, at its option, pay such amount in equal quarterly payments over a period of 12 months following its receipt of your notice. Any SAR not exercised in accordance with this Agreement within the time period required shall expire and be cancelled, and shall only be transferable to the extent that the underlying stock option was transferable. Notwithstanding the three month exercise period set forth above, in the event the Company elects to amend any existing stock option plan or adopts a new stock option plan which would permit a post termination exercise period greater than three months, then you shall, for any options granted under such amended or new plan, be entitled to exercise the options for the full period allowed, provided, however, in such event, the SAR grant shall be reduced for such options such that for any option granted, the combined exercise period and SAR period shall not exceed 24 months. Upon written request, the Company may consent to provide you registration rights (which consent may not be unreasonably withheld) whereby you could register some or all of the shares of the Company's common stock owned by you.

(v) Additionally, your participation in and the Company's contributions for you in the Stock Purchase Program, Employee 401(k) Savings and Stock Ownership Plan, Supplemental Stock Program (or similar plans adopted for the Company's executives subsequent to this Agreement) will cease on the Termination Date. The Company agrees to provide you, however, a cash payment equal to (A) the amount of such contribution not previously paid or credited to you attributable to the portion of your Base Salary (in effect on the Termination Date) that accrues up to and including the Termination Date and any bonus accrued as of the Termination Date, which will be payable in one lump sum, and (B) the amount of the Company's contribution attributable to the Continuance Amount payable to you under subparagraph (i) above, to which you are entitled under this Agreement, and which the Company will pay monthly as long as such Continuance Amount is required to be made to you by the Company.

(e) *Withholdings From Payment/Offset.* Any payments made by the Company to you under this Section 2 will be subject to all applicable local, state, federal or foreign taxes, including income tax, withholding tax, and social security tax. Further, to the extent you have, on the Termination Date, any outstanding debts or financial obligations to the Company, the Company shall be entitled to set off against payments due you hereunder for such debts or obligations.

(f) *Parachute Payments.* Notwithstanding any other provision to the contrary herein, payments made pursuant to this Agreement shall be reduced to the extent necessary to prevent such payments from constituting "excess parachute payments" within the meaning of Section 280G(b) of the Internal Revenue Code of 1986, as amended, if, and only if, the Board of Directors determines that such reduction will have the likely effect of increasing your after-tax benefit. Such determination, and the determination of any reduction pursuant to this paragraph, shall be based upon the opinion of the Company's outside counsel or a nationally recognized accounting firm selected by the Company.

(g) *Payments After Death.* All payments of Continuance Amounts shall cease upon the latter of your death or the expiration of the twelfth month after the Termination Date. Any such payments after your death that may be due hereunder will be paid to your named beneficiary provided to the Company in connection with this Agreement, or if no such designation has been made by you, then to your executors, administrators, heirs, personal representatives, successors, or assigns, as the case may be.

3. *Additional Perquisites.* Upon termination of your employment with the Company for any reason other than for Cause or mutual agreement, the Company agrees to provide you with executive outplacement services up to a maximum expense of $20,000 or 10% of your Base Salary, whichever is greater. Additionally, the Company will continue to pay, for a period of one year after the Termination Date or until you obtain New Employment (whichever occurs first), all of your club membership dues to the same extent to which dues were previously paid by the Company. For a period of 45 days following the Termination Date, you will have the opportunity to purchase, for the lesser of fair market or book value, the automobile which the Company provided to you. Any car allowance you previously received, however, will cease immediately on the Termination Date.

4. *Conditions Applicable to Severance Benefits.* In consideration of the payments and benefits provided to you hereunder by the Company, you agree as follows:

(a) *No Competing Employment.* You agree that during the term of your employment and for a period commencing on the Termination Date (or the date a court of competent jurisdiction enters a final judgment enforcing this provision, whichever is later), and ending on the second anniversary thereof, you will not, directly or indirectly, either as an employee, employer, consultant, agent, principal, partner, stockholder, corporate officer, director, or in any other individual or representative capacity, work for, engage or participate in any business which is a Direct Competitor with the Company (as defined below) within the United States, Canada or other country where the Company conducts business as of the Termination Date, provided, however, that you may own, directly or indirectly, solely as an investment, securities of any entity that is registered under the Securities Exchange Act of 1934, as amended, if you (a) are not a controlling person of, or a member of a group which controls such entity or (b) do not, directly or indirectly, own 5% or more of any class of securities of such entity. You represent to the Company that the enforcement of this restriction would not be unduly burdensome to you. If a court of competent jurisdiction determines that this Section 4 meets the requirements of Section 15.50(1) of the Texas Business & Commerce Code ("TBCC") but not the requirements of Section 15.50(2) of the TBCC, then the Company and you each agree that the Company is deemed to have requested reformation by such court pursuant to Section 15.51(c) of the TBCC.

For the purposes of this Section 4, "Direct Competitor" shall mean any of the following: (i) any business that is principally engaged in, or any subsidiary, division, operating unit or department within another business in which such subsidiary, division, operating unit or department is principally engaged in the wholesale, mail order or retail sale of traditional-style or country-style home furniture, whether such operation is conducted in shopping malls, strip centers, free standing locations or through mail order catalogs; and (ii) any business that is the same or substantially similar to any new business unit developed or being developed by, or entity acquired by the Company after the effective date of this Agreement and prior to the Termination Date. "Being developed" as used herein shall mean either (i) the expenditure of $25,000 or more directly in connection with the business or concept being developed or (ii) a Board resolution approving the development of the business.

(b) *Confidentiality.* You will not disclose to any person at any time during or following your employment, any proprietary information, trade secrets, systems, manuals, confidential reports or lists of vendors, suppliers, manufacturers or clients, the nature and type of product design and development or services rendered by the Company, or equipment and methods used by the Company (the "Confidential Information"). Notwithstanding the foregoing, Confidential Information will *not* be deemed to include information which (i) is or becomes available to the public other than as a result of disclosure by you in violation of this Section 4(b) or (ii) you are required to disclose under any applicable laws, regulations or directives or any governmental agency, tribunal or authority having jurisdiction in the matter or under subpoena or other process of law.

You agree that all Confidential Information is and will remain the exclusive property of the Company. Upon termination of your employment for any reason, you agree to return to the Company all Confidential Information (including any copies or reproductions thereof), and any other property belonging to the Company, that is in your possession or control. You agree to provide the Company with written verification that all of the Confidential Information provided to you has been returned to the Company, that all memoranda, notes or other documents in any way relating to the Confidential Information and the business affairs of the Company have either been returned to the Company or destroyed and that you have not retained any copies of such Confidential Information, memoranda or notes.

(c) *No Interference.* You will not, for a period commencing upon the Termination Date and ending upon the second anniversary thereof, either directly or indirectly, (i) make known to any person, firm or corporation the names and addresses of any of the vendors, suppliers or manufacturers of the Company or other proprietary contacts of the Company within the specialty retailing industry or any other information pertaining to such persons; (ii) call on, solicit, or take away, or attempt to call on, solicit, or take away any of the employees of the Company whether for you or for any other person, firm or corporation; or (iii) call on, solicit, or take away, or attempt to call on, solicit, or take away any customer, vendor, supplier, or manufacturer of the Company which has, within the current or previous fiscal year, produced goods for, or provided services to the Company in an amount in excess of 2% of the Company's total purchases of resale merchandise (at cost), whether for you or for any other person, firm or corporation.

You will not make or publish, or cause to be made or published, any written or oral statements which may cause damage, financial or otherwise, to the Company, including, but not limited to, damage to the Company's goodwill.

(d) *Use of Name.* After the Termination Date, you shall be indefinitely restricted and forbidden from using the names "Bombay", "Alex & Ivy" or any other names being used by the Company as of the Termination Date, or any other names deceptively similar thereto in any venture in which you are or may become directly or indirectly involved.

(e) *Equitable Remedies.* You acknowledge that a breach of any of the covenants contained in Sections 4(a) through 4(d) may result in material irreparable injury to the Company for which there is no adequate remedy at law and that it will not be possible to measure precisely damages for such injuries. You agree that, in the event of such a breach threat thereof, the Company shall be entitled, in addition to any other rights or remedies it may have, to obtain a temporary restraining order and/or a preliminary or permanent injunction enjoining or restraining you from engaging activities prohibited by Sections 4(a) through 4(d).

The parties to this Agreement agree that the limitations contained in this Section 4 with respect to geographic area, duration, and scope of activity are reasonable. However, if any court of competent jurisdiction shall determine that the geographic area, duration, or scope of activity of any restriction contained in this Section 4 is unenforceable, it is the intention of the parties that such restrictive covenant set forth herein shall not thereby be terminated but shall be deemed amended to the extent required to render it valid and enforceable.

You agree that the representations and covenants contained in this Section 4 pertaining to you shall be construed as ancillary to and independent of any other provision of this Agreement, and the existence of any claim or cause of action you may have against the Company or any officer, director, or stockholder of the Company, whether predicated on this Agreement or otherwise, shall not constitute a defense to the enforcement by the Company of the covenants contained in this Section 4.

5. *Consulting.* Except in the event of voluntary resignation, for a period of 90 days following the Termination Date, you shall be available, on a reasonable basis, to the Company for up to 5 days for the purpose of providing consultation to the Company's management and performing other transition assignments. The Company shall reimburse you for reasonable travel and other business expenses incurred by you at the Company's request during such period, but no additional compensation shall be payable to you for such services.

6. *Nonpayment Upon Breach.* Notwithstanding anything in this Agreement to the contrary, at any time after the Termination Date, if you, by any action or omission to act, breach any covenant, agreement, condition or obligation contained herein, the Company is entitled to cease making any payments and cease providing any of the benefits to you as contemplated in this Agreement.

7. *Legal Fees and Expenses.* The Company will pay the reasonable legal fees and expenses that you may incur as a result of the Company's contesting the validity, enforceability or your interpretation of this Agreement. If the Company is the successful party to such action, however, the Company has no obligation to pay such legal fees and expenses incurred by you. If the Company is required to pay your reasonable legal fees and expenses, the Company will promptly pay such expenses upon your submission to the Company of invoices or other written evidence of the legal fees or expenses incurred by you.

8. *Mediation; Arbitration.* Notwithstanding anything herein to the contrary, if a dispute or disagreement arises out of or in connection with this Agreement, prior to submission of the controversy to arbitration or for resolution by a court of competent jurisdiction, the parties hereto shall submit the controversy to mediation in a proceeding to be conducted in Fort Worth, Texas.

9. *Period of Limitations.* No legal action shall be brought and no cause of action shall be asserted by or on behalf of the Company or any affiliate of the Company against you, your spouse, heirs, executors, or personal or legal representatives after the expiration of two years from the date of accrual of such cause of action, and any claim or cause of action of the Company or its affiliate shall be extinguished and deemed released unless asserted by the timely filing of a legal action within such two-year period, provided, however, that if any shorter period of limitations is otherwise applicable to any such cause of action such shorter period shall govern.

10. *Nonexclusivity.* Your rights hereunder shall be in addition to any other rights you may have under the Company's Bylaws, the Delaware General Corporation Law, or otherwise.

11. *Amendments.* No supplement, modification or amendment of this Agreement shall be binding unless executed in writing by both

of the parties hereto. No waiver of any of the provisions of this Agreement shall be deemed or shall constitute a waiver of any other provisions hereof (whether or not similar), nor shall such waiver constitute a continuing waiver.

12. *Binding Effect; Assignment.* Except as provided otherwise herein, this Agreement shall be binding upon and inure to the benefit of and be enforceable by the parties hereto and their respective successors and assigns, including any direct or indirect successor by purchase, merger, consolidation or otherwise to all or substantially all of the business or assets of the Company, provided, however, you hereby acknowledge that this Agreement is a personal services contract and that you will not be entitled to assign any rights or obligations hereunder. The Company will require and cause any successor (whether direct or indirect by purchase, merger, consolidation or otherwise) to all, substantially all, or a substantial part, of the business or assets of the Company, by written agreement in form and substance satisfactory to you, expressly to assume and agree to perform this Agreement in the same manner and to the same extent that the Company would be required to perform if no such succession had taken place.

13. *Severability.* The provisions of this Agreement shall be severable if any of the provisions hereof are held by a *court* of competent jurisdiction to be invalid, void or otherwise unenforceable, and the remaining provisions shall remain enforceable to the fullest extent permitted by law.

14. *Governing Law.* This Agreement shall be governed by and construed and enforced in accordance with the laws of the State of Texas applicable to contracts made and to be performed in such state without giving effect to the principles of conflicts of laws. Subject to the provisions of this Agreement regarding mediation, the appropriate state or federal court located in Fort Worth, Texas shall have exclusive jurisdiction over all matters arising under this Agreement and will be the proper forum in which to adjudicate those matters.

15. *Notices.* All notices and communications which are required by this Agreement, or which may be given pursuant to this Agreement, shall be in writing and shall be transmitted to the following addresses:

The Bombay Company, Inc.
550 Bailey Avenue, Suite 700
Fort Worth, Texas 76107

Attn: Michael J. Veitenheimer

Either party may change the address to which such notices and communications shall be sent by written notice to the other party.

16. *Multiple Counterparts.* This Agreement may be executed in any number of counterparts, all of which taken together shall constitute one and the same document, and each of which shall be deemed an original, and any of the parties hereto may execute this Agreement by signing any of the counterparts.

17. *Legal Counsel.* The Company and its legal counsel have prepared this Agreement. You hereby acknowledge that you have had the opportunity to consult with and seek the advice of independent legal counsel of your choice regarding the terms of this Agreement and its subject matter.

18. *Entire Agreement.* This Agreement sets forth the entire agreement and understanding of the parties relating to the subject matter hereof, and supersedes all prior agreements, arrangements and understandings, written or oral, relating to the subject matter hereof.

Very truly yours,

THE BOMBAY COMPANY, INC.

By:_____

ACCEPTED AND AGREED as of
the ___ day of ___ , 199_.

Appendix D

Sample Employment Agreements

Four sample employment agreements are provided here for your information. Many clauses in these agreements provide sample language for related issues of executive compensation found within this book.

The first employment agreement that follows was drafted pursuant to a merger. The second agreement is between a company and a sole shareholder. The third agreement was drafted pursuant to an asset purchased. The fourth agreement is between a company and its president.

These forms have been provided by Julie M. Edmond, Esq., a partner in the law firm of Shea & Gardner, Washington, DC.

SAMPLE EMPLOYMENT AGREEMENT I: PURSUANT TO A MERGER

EMPLOYMENT AGREEMENT, dated September 19_, by and between _____ a ___ corporation (the "Company") and _____ (the "Executive").

The Executive was a shareholder of _____, a Corporation (_____), and was its President and the Chairman of its Board of Directors. Pursuant to an Agreement and Plan of Merger, dated September __, 19_ (the "Merger Agreement"), by and among _____ (the "Buyer"), the Company, the Executive, and the other stockholders of _____, was merged into the Company. The Buyer was and is the sole stockholder of the Company. This Agreement is being entered into pursuant to paragraph 7(b) of the Merger Agreement.

In consideration of the foregoing, and of the mutual covenants and agreements hereinafter set forth, the parties hereto agree as follows:

1. *Employment, Duties, and Acceptance.*

1.1 *Employment by the Company.* The Company hereby employs the Executive for the term provided in Section 2 (the "Term") to render exclusive and full-time services to the Company as President thereof and, in connection therewith, to perform the duties provided in Section 1.4 (the "Duties").

1.2 *Acceptance of Employment by the Executive.* The Executive hereby accepts such employment and agrees to perform the Duties for the Company. The Executive shall devote his entire working time and his best efforts to the business of the Company during the Term.

1.3 *Place of Employment.* The Executive's principal place of employment shall be in _____, subject to such reasonable travel, not in excess of that customary in the past, as the performance of the Duties may require.

1.4 *Duties.* The Executive shall hold the position and title, and exercise the responsibilities, of President of the Company. The Executive shall have the right and obligation, in his capacity as President, to perform the duties of the President as are described in the By-Laws of the Company and such other duties as may be assigned to him by the Board of Directors of the Company, in accordance with the policies and procedures promulgated for operating companies owned by the Buyer. The Executive shall report solely to the Chief Executive Officer of the Buyer, in his capacity as a member of the Board of Directors of the Buyer.

2. *Term of Employment and Other Employment.*

2.1 *Term of Employment.* The Term of the Executive's employment under this Agreement shall commence on the date of this Agreement and shall end on the third anniversary date thereof, unless extended as provided in this Section 2. The Company shall have the option, on the third anniversary date, to extend the Term of the Executive's employment until the fourth anniversary date; and, if the Company shall exercise such option, it shall on the fourth anniversary date have the option to extend the Term of such employment until the fifth anniversary date. The Company shall exercise such options by notifying the Executive in writing at least thirty (30) days prior to the corresponding anniversary date. On or after the third anniversary date or, if the Company shall exercise the first (or first and second) option(s) noted above, after the fourth (or fifth) anniversary date, as the case may be, the Executive's employment under this Agreement shall continue until terminated by either party. Such termination, if by the Executive, shall be only upon at least 90 days' prior written notice. Such termination, if by the Company, shall be by written notice; *provided, however,* notwithstanding the date of such termination, the Company shall continue to pay the Executive's salary for a period of one year following such date. The Term of such employment, as extended or continued, shall be treated for all purposes hereunder as the Term. Notwithstanding the foregoing, the termination of the Executive's employment under this Agreement, as provided elsewhere herein, shall end the Term.

2.2   *Other Employment.* In the event that the employment of the Executive is terminated by the Company pursuant to Section 2.1, the Executive shall have no obligation to accept employment offered to him by others, and the Company shall not interpose any defense against the payment of amounts due under Section 2.1 based on the refusal of the Executive to seek or accept any such employment, *provided, however,* if the Executive shall accept such employment, the Company may offset the amount of any compensation received from such employment from the amount otherwise due under Section 2.1.

3.   *Compensation.*

3.1   *Salary.* As compensation for all services to be rendered pursuant to this Employment Agreement, the Company shall pay the Executive during the Term a salary of at least $___ per annum and such additional compensation as may be provided for in this Section 3. All of the Executive's compensation shall be payable in accordance with the payroll policies of the Company as from time to time in effect, less such appropriate deductions as shall be required to be withheld by applicable law and regulations, or by written election of the Executive.

3.2 *Bonus.* The Company shall pay to the Executive a bonus of $___ over the first three years of the Term. The Company shall place such bonus in a special expense fund earmarked for the Executive's exclusive discretionary use within ten (10) days after the date of this Agreement. The Executive shall have the right to apply all or part of this fund as he deems appropriate over the Term, except that he shall apply no more than $___ of such fund over the first year of the Term, and no more than one-half (1/2) of the remaining balance at the completion of the first year of the Term over the second year of the Term. In addition, the Executive and up to four (4) other executives of the Company shall be entitled to participate in a management incentive plan to be established for the calendar year 1986, and for each year thereafter during the Term, as the Board of Directors of the Company shall provide. Such plan shall be established on a basis similar to that provided in bonus programs adopted by other companies owned by the Buyer.

3.3 *Participation in Employee Benefit Plans.* The Executive shall be permitted during the Term, to the extent eligible, to participate in any group life, medical, or disability insurance plan, health program, dental program, pension plan or similar benefit plan, stock option plan thrift plan, or other fringe benefit plan of the Company, which participation shall be on a basis that is at least equivalent to that which is then made available to other executives of the Company.

3.4 *Expenses.* Subject to such policies as may from time to time be established by the Board of Directors of the Company, the Company shall pay or reimburse the Executive for all reasonable expenses actually incurred or paid by the Executive during the Term in the performance of his Duties upon presentation of expense statements or vouchers or such other supporting information as the Company may require.

3.5 *Salary Adjustments.* Effective October 1, 19_, and thereafter during the Term effective on every succeeding October 1, the annual salary of the Executive then in effect shall be reviewed by the Board of Directors of the Company in accordance with generally applied normal corporate policy and practice.

3.6 *Paid Vacation.* During each year of the Term of this Agreement, the Executive shall be entitled to four (4) weeks vacation, during which vacation period he shall continue to receive the salary and other compensation provided in this Section 3.

3.7 *Interest Free Loan.* The parties hereto acknowledge that the Executive has received an unsecured interest free loan from the Company in the amount of $___. The Executive shall repay to the Company within ten (10) days after the date of this Agreement the full amount of such loan, as well as the full amount of any and all other unpaid loans received by the Executive from the predecessor of the Company.

3.8 *Insurance.* The Company shall provide life insurance for the Executive on a basis similar to that on which it is provided to executives in other companies owned by the Buyer. The Company shall have the option to maintain a key-employee life insurance policy on the life of the Executive and may elect to continue as that insurance policy the insurance policy upon the life of the Executive in the amount of $___ of which the Company is currently the owner and partial beneficiary, *provided, however,* the Executive shall have the option for thirty (30) days after the date of this Agreement to purchase that policy from the Company for a sum equal to the current cash surrender value of that policy.

3.9 *Car.* The Company shall continue to make available to the Executive, until the second anniversary date of this Agreement, the _____ more fully identified by the copy of the Registration Statement previously delivered to the Buyer, currently being used by the Executive. On the second anniversary date of this Agreement, and on every third anniversary of that date during the Term, the car shall be replaced by an _____ 4-door sedan or other car of equivalent cost, as normally provided by the Buyer to equivalent executives of its U.S. subsidiaries, which car shall be made available to the Executive by the Company (by lease) for his full time use, *provided, however,* the Executive shall have the option on the second anniversary date of this Agreement and on every third anniversary of that date during the Term of applying the payments to be made by the Company for the lease of such car to the lease of a higher-priced car, the additional cost of the lease of such higher-priced car to be paid from the bonus provided in Section 3.2 or from the Executive's personal funds at his option, and such higher-priced car to be made available to the Executive for his full time use. The Executive shall have the option to purchase each car replaced under this Section for its estimated end-of-term wholesale value as reflected in the Agreement for the lease of such car. The Company shall be responsible for the maintenance of the car that it makes available to the Executive for his use, shall maintain full casualty and personal liability insurance with respect to such car, and shall provide the Executive, free of charge, with parking space at a parking garage near the corporate headquarters of the Company.

4.   *Termination.*

4.1   *Termination upon Death.* The Executive's employment under this Agreement shall terminate upon the Executive's death, subject to the Company's continuing obligation to make payment of salary or other compensation to the Executive's legal representatives to the extent then generally provided in the compensation programs of other companies owned by the Buyer. Such payments shall not affect any other amounts payable as insurance or other death benefits under any plan or arrangement then in force and effect with respect to the Executive.

4.2   *Termination upon Disability.*

(a)   If, during the Term of his employment, the Executive becomes physically or mentally disabled, so that the Executive is unable substantially to perform his duties hereunder, the Company may terminate his employment after a period of disability determined on the same basis as that generally applied by the Buyer with respect to the termination of the employment of executives of other companies owned by the Buyer on grounds of physical or mental disability.

(b)   During the first half of the period of disability that must pass before the Company may terminate the Executive's employment under subsection (a) above, the Company shall continue to pay the Executive the full amount of his annual salary (as then in effect) and any bonus that may have accrued. Thereafter, and until the termination of his employment, the Company shall pay the Executive fifty percent (50%) of his annual salary (as then in effect) and of any bonus that may have accrued. Any amounts payable as disability benefits under any plan or arrangement then in force and effect with respect to the Executive shall be deducted from the payments provided for in this subsection (b). Nothing in this Section 4.2 shall be deemed to extend the Term of this Agreement.

(c)   In case of any disagreement between the Executive and the Board of Directors of the Company as to whether the Executive is disabled so as to permit the Company to terminate the Executive's employment hereunder in accordance with this Section 4.2, the question of such disability shall be submitted for determination to an impartial and reputable physician selected either by mutual agreement of the Executive and the Company or, failing such agreement, at the request of the Company by the then President of the Medical Society of _____ (or by such Society under the procedures it may have for such selection), and such determination of the question of such disability by such physician shall be final and binding on the Executive and the Company. The Company shall pay the fees and expenses of such physician.

4.3   *Termination for Cause.* The Board of Directors of the Company shall have the right to terminate the Executive's employment and discharge him for cause, which shall mean and be limited to the following events:

(a)   An act or acts of dishonesty on the part of the Executive intended or reasonably likely to result directly or indirectly in substantial gain or personal enrichment at the expense of the Company or any of its subsidiaries, or the commission of a felony under the laws of the State of New York (other than a Class E felony);

(b)   A determination by a licensed physician in New York State that the Executive is a chronic alcoholic or a narcotics addict (as that term is defined under the Mental Hygiene Law of the State of New York, as amended, or any successor statute). The Executive shall submit to an examination by such licensed physician upon the reasonable request of the Company;

(c)   An act or omission which constitutes a substantial failure to perform his Duties hereunder, *provided, however,* no discharge shall be deemed for cause under this subsection (c) unless the Executive shall have first received written notice from the Board of Directors of the Company advising the Executive of the specific acts or omissions alleged to constitute a substantial failure to perform his Duties hereunder, and such failure continues after the Executive shall have had a reasonable opportunity to correct the acts so complained of;

(d)   A determination by the Company that the Executive actually knew that the Merger Agreement contained a material misrepresentation or breach of warranty at the Effective Date.

Upon termination of his employment for cause, as provided herein, the Company shall pay the Executive his annual salary (as then in effect) accrued up to the last day of the month in which such termination occurs.

5.   *Protection of Confidential Information; Non-competition.*

5.1   In view of the fact that the Executive's work as an employee of the Company hereunder will bring him into close contact with many confidential affairs of the Company, including information about costs, profits, sales, trade secrets, and other information not readily available to the public (hereinafter collectively referred to as "confidential matters"), the Executive agrees to keep secret all confidential matters of the Company and not to disclose them to anyone outside of the Company or otherwise use his knowledge of them for his own benefit, either during or after his employment with the Company.

5.2   The parties incorporate herein by reference the restrictive covenant contained in Section 13 of the Merger Agreement as it applies to the Executive, *provided, however,* the restrictive covenant contained therein shall not apply to the Executive if he shall voluntarily terminate his employment during the Term because of a breach of this Agreement by the Company.

5.3   If the Executive commits a breach, or threatens to commit a breach, of any of the provisions of this Section 5, the Company shall have the following rights and remedies:

(a)   The right and remedy to have the provisions of this Section 5 specifically enforced by any court having equity jurisdiction, it being acknowledged and agreed that any such breach or threatened breach will cause irreparable injury to the Company and that money damages will not provide an adequate remedy to the Company; and

(b)   The right and remedy to require the Executive to account for and pay over to the Company all compensation, profits, monies, accruals, increments, or other benefits (hereinafter collectively referred to as the "Benefits") derived or received by the Executive as the result of any transactions constituting a breach of any of the provisions of this Section 5, the Executive hereby agreeing to account for and pay over the Benefits to the Company.

5.4   If any covenant contained in this Section 5, or any part thereof, is held to be unenforceable because of the duration of such covenant or the area covered thereby, the parties agree that the court making such determination shall have the power to reduce the duration and/or area of such covenant and, in its reduced form, said covenant shall then be enforceable.

6.   *Indemnification.* The Company shall indemnify the Executive to the full extent authorized by law in the event he is made or threatened to be made a party to any action, suit or proceeding, whether criminal, civil, administrative or investigative, by reason of the fact that he is or was a director, officer or employee of the Company or any predecessor of the Company or serves or served any other enterprise as a director, officer or employee at the request of the Company or any predecessor of the Company.

7.   *Other Provisions.*

7.1   *Notices.* Any notice or other communication required or permitted hereunder shall be in writing and shall be delivered personally, telegraphed, telexed, sent by facsimile transmission, or sent by certified, registered, or express mail, postage prepaid. Any such notice shall be deemed given when so delivered personally, telegraphed, telexed, or sent by facsimile transmission or, if mailed, two days after the date of deposit in the United States mails addressed as follows:

(i) if to the Company, to:

Attention: The Board of Directors

with a copy to:

Attention:

(ii) if to the Executive, to:

with a copy to:

Attention:

7.2 *Entire Aqreement.* This Agreement, and any other agreements incorporated therein by reference, sets forth the entire agreement and understanding of the parties relating to the subject matter hereof, and supersedes all prior agreements (including the Employment Agreement, dated March ___ 19_ between the Company and the Executive), arrangements, and understandings, written or oral, relating to the subject matter hereof.

7.3 *Waivers and Amendments.* This Agreement may be amended, superseded, cancelled, renewed, or extended, and the terms hereof may be waived, only by a written instrument signed by the parties or, in the case of a waiver, by the party waiving compliance. No delay on the part of any party in exercising any right, power, or privilege hereunder shall operate as a waiver thereof, nor shall any waiver on the part of any party of any such right, power, or privilege, nor any single or partial exercise of any such right, power, or privilege, preclude any other or further exercise thereof or the exercise of any other such right, powers, or privilege.

7.4 *Governing Law.* This Agreement shall be governed by and construed in accordance with the laws of the State of New York applicable to agreements made and to be performed entirely within such State.

7.5 *Assignment.* The provisions of this Agreement shall be binding upon and inure to the benefit of the parties hereto and their respective heirs, legal representatives, successors, and assigns. This Agreement, and the Executive's rights and obligations hereunder, may not be assigned by the Executive. The Company may assign this

Agreement and its rights, together with its obligations hereunder, in connection with any sale, transfer, or other disposition of all or substantially all of its respective assets or business, whether by merger, consolidation, or otherwise.

7.6 *Headings.* The headings in this Agreement are for reference only and shall not affect the interpretation of this Agreement.

IN WITNESS WHEREOF, the parties have executed this Agreement the date first above written.

ATTEST: By: _____

By: _____

                           By: _____

SAMPLE EMPLOYMENT AGREEMENT II: WITH SOLE SHAREHOLDER

EMPLOYMENT AGREEMENT, dated ___, 19_ by and between _____ a corporation (the "Company"), and _____ (the "Executive").

The Executive is the sole shareholder of the Company, its President and the Chairman of its Board of Directors. Pursuant to an Agreement of even date herewith (the "Acquisition Agreement"), by and between the Executive and _____, 100% of the issued and outstanding capital shares of the Company will be acquired by _____. This Agreement is being entered into pursuant to paragraph 5(b) of the Acquisition Agreement.

In consideration of the foregoing, and of the mutual covenants and agreements hereinafter set forth, the parties hereto agree as follows:

1. *Employment, Duties and Acceptance.*

1.1 *Employment by the Company.* The Company hereby employs the Executive for the term provided in Article 2 (the "Term") to render exclusive and full-time services to the Company as President and, in connection therewith, to perform the duties provided in Section 1.4 (the "Duties").

1.2 *Acceptance of Employment by the Executive.* The Executive hereby accepts such employment and agrees to perform the Duties diligently to the best of his abilities and in the best interests of the Company. The Executive shall devote his entire working time and his best efforts to the business of the Company during the Term.

1.3 *Place of Employment.* The Executive's principal place of employment shall be at _____ or such other location in the Washington, DC metropolitan area as the Company may designate upon reasonable notice to the Executive. The Company may direct the Executive to engage in such reasonable travel as the performance of the Duties may require.

1.4 *Duties.* The Executive shall hold the position and title, and exercise the responsibilities, of President. The Executive shall have the right and obligation, in his capacity as President, to perform the duties of that office to the extent they are described in the By-laws of the Company, as well as such other duties as from time to time may be assigned to him by the Company.

2. *Term of Employment.* The Term of the Executive's employment under this Agreement shall commence on the day of this Agreement and shall end on the third anniversary date thereof, unless extended as provided in this Article 2. The Company shall have the option, on the third anniversary date, to extend the Term of the Executive's employment until the fourth anniversary date; and, if the Company shall exercise such option, it shall on the fourth anniversary date have the option to extend the Term of such employment until the fifth anniversary date. The Company shall exercise such options by notifying the Executive in writing at least ninety (90) days prior to the corresponding anniversary date. On or after the third anniversary date or, if the Company shall exercise the first (or first and second) option(s) noted above, after the fourth (or fifth) anniversary date, as the case may be, the Executive's employment under this Agreement shall continue until terminated by either party. Such termination, if by the Executive, shall be only upon at least 30 days' prior written notice. Such termination, if by the Company, shall be only upon at least 30 days' prior written notice. The period of such employment, as extended or continued, shall be treated for all purposes hereunder as the Term. Notwithstanding the foregoing, the Executive's employment under this Agreement may be terminated as provided elsewhere herein, and such termination shall end the Term.

3. Compensation.

3.1 *Salary.* As compensation for all services to be rendered pursuant to this Agreement, the Company shall pay the Executive during the Term a salary of at least $___ per annum. All of the Executive's compensation shall be payable in accordance with the payroll policies of the Company as from time to time in effect, less such appropriate deductions as shall be required to be withheld by applicable law and regulations, or by written election of the Executive if agreed to by the Company.

3.2 *Participation in Employee Benefit Plans.* The Executive shall be permitted during the Term, to the extent eligible, to participate in any group life, medical, or disability insurance plan, health program, dental program, profit-sharing or pension or similar benefit plan, thrift plan, or other fringe benefit plan of the Company, participation shall be on a basis that is at least equivalent to that which is then made available to other executives of the Company. The Company shall continue to provide the Executive with the car that the Company now leases and provides for his use. The Company shall pay for the upkeep, maintenance, repair, normal operating expenses, and parking at the office for such automobile as well as all taxes associated with its registration and use. Upon expiration of the current lease of such automobile by the Company, the Company will provide the Executive with the use of an automobile pursuant to the Company's normal and usual policy then in effect.

3.3 *Incentive Plan.* The Executive shall be eligible to participate in Buyer's Senior Management Incentive Plan, starting with the 19_ Plan *pro rata,* in accordance with its terms and conditions.

3.4 *Expenses.* Subject to such policies as may from time to time be established by the Company, the Company shall pay or reimburse the Executive for all reasonable expenses actually incurred or paid by the Executive during the Term in the performance of his Duties upon presentation of expense statements or vouchers or such other supporting information as the Company may require.

3.5 *Salary Adjustment.* Effective June 1, 19_ and thereafter during the Term effective on every succeeding June 1, the annual salary of the Executive then in effect shall be reviewed by the President of Buyer in accordance with generally applied normal corporate policy and practice; except, however, the Executive's compensation shall not be less than $___ per annum as provided in Section 3.1 hereof.

3.6 *Paid Vacation.* During each year of the Term of this Agreement, the Executive shall be entitled to a vacation of the greater of twenty (20) working days or the time allowed under the Company's policies and practices then in effect, in addition to other holidays designated by the Company, during which vacation period he shall continue to receive the salary and other compensation provided in this Article 3. Such paid vacation must be taken at a time and in a manner consistent with his Duties.

4. *Termination of Employment.*

4.1 *Termination upon Death.* The Executive's employment under this Agreement shall terminate upon the Executive's death. The Company shall continue to make payment of salary or other compensation to the Executive's legal representatives in accordance with the Company's general policies and practices then in effect.

4.2 *Termination upon Disability.*

(a) If, during the Term of his employment, the Executive becomes physically or mentally disabled, so that he is unable substantially to perform his duties hereunder, the Company may terminate his employment after a period of disability determined on the same basis as that generally applied by the Company with respect to the termination of the employment of executives of the Company on grounds of physical or mental disability.

(b) In the case of any disagreement between the Executive and the Company as to whether the Executive is disabled so as to permit the Company to terminate the Executive's employment hereunder in accordance with this Section 4.2, the question of such disability shall be submitted for determination to an impartial and reputable physician selected by the mutual agreement of the Executive (or his legal representative) and the Company. Failing such agreement, the Company shall request a physician referral from the Medical Society of _____ and the Executive and the Company hereby agree in advance to accept the first name provided in that referral. The determination of the question of disability by such physician selected consistent with this subsection (b) shall be final and binding on the Executive and the Company. The Company shall pay the fees and expenses of such physician.

(c) If, with respect to the first ninety (90) days of the period during which the Executive suffers a disability of the kind described in subsection (a) above, the total amount of payment received by the Executive pursuant to sick leave and similar practices and policies generally followed by the Company is less than 100% of the amount of the salary that the Executive would have received with respect to the same period, the Company shall pay him the difference.

4.3 *Termination for Cause.* The Company may terminate the Executive's ernployment for cause. "Termination for cause" shall mean discharge from employment for committing an unlawful, deceitful or fraudulent act, for knowingly withholding from the Company's Board of Directors information material to the Company's interests, for knowingly making any misrepresentation to the Company's Board of Directors regarding a matter material to the Company's interests, for knowingly failing to carry out the instructions of the Company's Board of Directors, or for knowingly failing to abide by or to enforce any material policy or procedure of the Company. Upon termination of his employment for cause, as provided herein, the Company shall pay the Executive his salary (as then in effect) accrued up to the last date of the month in which such termination occurs.

5. *Confidentiality and Proprietary Materials.*

5.1 *Confidentiality.* The Executive shall not at any time during his employment with the Company or at any time after the termination of the same for any reason (including expiration of the Term) disclose, impart, divulge, or otherwise reveal in any manner whatsoever, directly or indirectly, in writing or orally, whether by counsel, discussion, recommendation, suggestion, or otherwise, any "Protected Information" except in the course of the proper discharge of his Duties or as expressly authorized by the Company's Board of Directors.

(a) As used in this Agreement "Protected Information" means any confidential or proprietary information (in whatever form recorded) about the Company, any Affiliate of the Company, or any customer or client of the Company or any such Affiliate, that the Executive has obtained, had access to, or gained knowledge of in the course of his employment with the Company. An Affiliate of the Company is any entity controlling, controlled by, or under common control with, the Company. Protected Information shall include, without limitation:

(i) Information concerning or relating to properties, organization, operations, procedures, plans, projects, programs, products, processes, systems, profitability, finances, and business relationships and opportunities;

(ii) Any trade secret or other similar information including, without limitation, the identity of customers or clients, customer or client lists, mailing lists, software programs, databases, coding information, standard forms, market analysis and strategies, and pricing and cost information, except to the extent that such information is lawfully and readily available to the general public;

(iii) Information relating to any litigation including, without limitation, attorney work product and any data, documents, or other information that may be subject to the attorney-client privilege.

(b) As used in this Agreement, the phrase "any Customer or Prospective Customer of the Company" means any person or entity (including, without limitation, any department, agency, or bureau of the federal or any state or local government) with whom the Company currently is doing business, is engaged in negotiations, to whom the Company has submitted a bid, or from whom the Corporation is otherwise seeking to obtain or renew a contract, *provided* that in the event of any termination of the Executive's employment with the Company, the phrase shall apply to any person or entity who was a Customer or Prospective Customer of the Company during the two years prior to the date of such termination. Promptly upon the Executive's written request made within thirty (30) days of termination of his employment with the Company, the Company shall give him a list of its Customers and Prospective Customers as defined herein.

(c) The Executive will not, without the prior express written consent of the Company's Board of Directors, use any Protected Information for his own benefit or the benefit of any person or entity other than the Company.

(d) Upon termination of employment with the Company for any reason, including the expiration of the Term, the Executive shall return all books, records, lists, computer programs, documents, notes, and other materials of any kind and in any form whatsoever, including all copies thereof, which contain any Protected Information (hereinafter "Protected Materials"). All Protected Materials shall be returned whether initially (i) furnished by the Company or any

Affiliate of the Company, or any Customer or Prospective Customer of the Company or any such Affiliate, (ii) prepared by the Executive or any officer, director, employee, or agent of the Company, any Affiliate of the Company, or any Customer or Prospective Customer of the Company or any such Affiliate, or (iii) otherwise obtained in the course of the Executive's employment with the Company.

5.2   *Proprietary Materials.* All discoveries made, inventions created, and all ideas, concepts, designs, formulas, proposals, projects, programs, products, processes, systems, techniques, and improvements of whatever kind conceived or developed by the Executive directly or indirectly, alone or jointly with others, in the course of employment with the Company, whether during normal business hours or otherwise (hereinafter "Proprietary Materials"), shall be and remain the sole and exclusive property of the Company. The Executive shall fully and promptly disclose to the Company all such Proprietary Materials, together with all information and data necessary to impart a full understanding of the same. Upon request and without further compensation from the Company, but at the Company's expense, the Executive will (i) execute, acknowledge, and deliver all such papers and instruments as the Company may deem necessary in order for it to perfect, secure, and maintain all rights, title, and interest in and to any Proprietary Materials, including, without limitation, any and all patent, copyright, trademark, and trade secrets rights and protections in the same, and (ii) aid and assist the Company in any litigation involving the maintenance or establishment of such rights and protections, including, if necessary, testifying on behalf of the Company.

5.3   *Enforcement.* The Executive agrees that, having regard to the importance of the Duties hereunder and his position in relation to the Company's business, the obligations undertaken by him in this Article 5 are reasonable and necessary for the protection of the legitimate interests of the Company and do not work harshly upon him. If the Executive commits a breach, or threatens to commit a breach, or any of the provisions of this Article 5, the Company shall have the following rights and remedies:

(a)   the right and remedy to have the provisions of this Article 5 specifically enforced by any court having equity jurisdiction, it being acknowledged and agreed that any such breach or threatened breach will cause irreparable injury to the Company and that money damages will not provide an adequate remedy to the Company; and

(b) the right and remedy to require the Executive to account for and pay over to the Company all compensation, profits, monies, accruals, increments, or other benefits (hereinafter collectively referred to as the "Benefits") derived or received by the Executive as the result of any transactions constituting a breach of any of the provisions of this Article 5, the Executive hereby agreeing to account for and pay over the Benefits to the Company.

6. *Indemnification.* The Company shall indemnify the Executive to the full extent authorized by law in the event he is made or threatened to be made a party to any action, suit, or proceeding, whether criminal, civil, administrative or investigative, by reason of the fact that he is or was a director, officer, or employee of the Company or serves or served any other enterprise as a director, officer, or employee at the request of the Company.

7. *Other Provisions.*

7.1 *Notices.* Any notice or other communication required or permitted hereunder shall be in writing and shall be delivered personally, telegraphed, telexed, sent by facsimile transmission, or sent by certified, registered, or express mail, postage prepaid. Any such notice shall be deemed given when so delivered personally, telegraphed, telexed, or sent by facsimile transmission or, if mailed, three days after the date of deposit in the United States mails addressed as follows:

(i) if to the Company, to:

with a copy to:

(ii) if to the Executive, to:

Copy to:

7.2 *Entire Agreement.* This Agreement and any other agreements incorporated herein by reference set forth the entire agreement and understanding of the parties relating to the subject matter hereof, and supersede all prior agreements, arrangements, and understandings, written or oral, relating to the subject matter hereof.

7.3 *Waivers and Amendments.* This Agreement may be amended, superseded, cancelled, renewed, or extended, and the terms hereof may be waived, only by a written instrument signed by the parties or, in the case of a waiver, by the party waiving compliance. No delay on the part of any party in exercising any right, power, or privilege hereunder shall operate as a waiver thereof, nor shall any waiver on the part of such party of any such right, power, or privilege, nor any single or partial exercise of any such right, power, or privilege, preclude any other or further exercise thereof or the exercise of any other such right, power, or privilege.

7.4 *Governing Law.* This Agreement shall be governed by and construed in accordance with the laws of the State of _____ without regard to its conflict of laws rules.

7.5 *Assignment.* The provisions of this Agreement shall be binding upon and inure to the benefit of the parties hereto and their respective heirs, legal representatives, successors, and assigns. This Agreement, and the Executive's rights and obligations hereunder, may not be assigned by the Executive. The Company may assign this Agreement and its rights, together with its obligations, hereunder, in connection with any sale, transfer, or other disposition of all or substantially all of its respective assets or business, whether by merger, consolidation, or otherwise.

7.6 *Headings.* The headings in this Agreement are for reference only and shall not affect its interpretation.

7.7 *Severability.* In the event that one or more of the provisions contained in this Agreement, or any part thereof, shall be determined to be invalid, illegal, or unenforceable in any respect under any applicable statute or rule of law, only such provision(s) shall be considered invalid, illegal, or unenforceable (and then only to the extent of such invalidity, illegality, or unenforceability), and the rest of the provisions shall remain in full force and effect. The Executive agrees that if any provision contained herein shall be adjudged to be invalid, illegal, or unenforceable for any reason, but would be adjudged to be valid, legal, and enforceable if part of the wording thereof were deleted and/or the time period thereof and/or the geographic area thereof were reduced, the said provision shall apply with such modification(s) as may be necessary to make it valid, legal, and enforceable.

IN WITNESS WHEREOF, the parties have executed this Agreement the date first above written.

ATTEST:

By:_____   By:_____
WITNESS:

By:_____   By:_____

GUARANTY
_____ hereby guaranties the payment by the Company of the compensation of the Executive pursuant to Article 3 of the foregoing Employment Agreement.
ATTEST:

By:_____   By:_____
[Corporate Seal]

SAMPLE EMPLOYMENT AGREEMENT III:
PURSUANT TO ASSET PURCHASED

This EMPLOYMENT AGREEMENT (this "Agreement") is made as of the ___ of November 1993, by and between _____ corporation with principal offices located at _____ (the "Company"), and _____ ("Executive").

WHEREAS, the Company and _____ corporation have entered into an Asset Purchase Agreement as of _____ (the "Purchase Agreement"), pursuant to which the Company is acquiring and _____ is selling substantially all of _____ assets; and

WHEREAS, Executive is the majority shareholder of _____ and is presently serving as President of _____ and it is a condition precedent to the closing of the Purchase Agreement that Executive and the Company enter into an employment agreement satisfactory to each and that Executive enter into a covenant not to compete with the Company; and

WHEREAS, the Company and Executive desire to enter into such an employment agreement and such a covenant not to compete subject to the terms and conditions set forth herein;

NOW, THEREFORE, in consideration of the foregoing premises and of the mutual covenants and agreements hereinafter set forth, the receipt and sufficiency of which are hereby acknowledged, the Company and Executive hereby agree as follows:

Section 1. *Employment.* The Company agrees to employ Executive, subject to the terms and conditions of this Agreement, to render full-time services to the Company as Vice President and Director of the Company's _____ Division/Operation. Executive agrees to such employment and agrees to perform the duties provided in Section 3 with reasonable diligence to the best of his abillties and in the best interests of the Company. Executive may continue, in his free time, to engage in private business transactions and provide minimal services on behalf of _____, *provided, however,* that Executive shall not engage in any business or perform any services in any capacity whatsoever in violation of Section 7 hereof.

Section 2. *Term.* The term of Executive's employment by the Company under this Agreement shall be for a period of three years commencing on the date hereof, and shall thereafter automatically be renewed on a year-to-year basis unless terminated by either party by 90 days' prior written notice to the other party. Notwithstanding the foregoing, Executive's employment under this Agreement may be terminated as hereinafter provided.

Section 3. *Duties.* Executive shall hold the positions and titles, and exercise the responsibilities, of Vice President and Director of the Company's _____ Division/Operation. Executive shall have such powers and duties as may from time to time be prescribed by the Company or its Board of Directors or mutually agreed upon by the Company and Executive. During his employment hereunder, Executive shall devote his full time, skill and efforts to the performance of his duties and the business and affairs of the Company as is customary for a person in his positions and/or with his duties and responsibilities at a comparable company and shall use his reasonable best efforts to advance the best interests of the Company at all times. Executive may engage in other private business transactions so long as they are not in violation of Section 7 hereof and so long as they do not affect Executive's full-time performance of his duties hereunder.

Section 4. *Place of Performance.* Executive shall perform his duties hereunder at _____ the headquarters of the Company's _____ Division/Operation, or at such other location mutually agreed upon by the parties, *provided, however,* that the Company may reasonably require Executive to travel and render services in different locations from time to time incident to the performance of such duties.

Section 5. *Compensation.* The Company agrees to pay Executive the following compensation for all services rendered by Executive to the Company:

(a) *Salary:* The Company shall pay Executive an annual salary of ___ Dollars ($___). Such salary shall be subject to withholding by the Company on account of payroll taxes and similar matters as are required by applicable law, rule or regulation of any appropriate govemmental authority, and shall be payable in accordance wlth the payroll policies of the Company from time to time in effect (such payments are, as of the date of this Agreement, made in bi-weekly installments).

(b) *Incentive Plan:* Executive shall receive incentive compensation up to a maximum annual award of ___ payable within 60 days after the end of each calendar year during the term of Executive's employment by the Company. Such incentive compensation will be based upon performance in relation to stated performance goals mutually agreed upon by the Company and Executive in Executive's annually reviewed incentive plan.

(c) *Bonus:* The Company shall establish a bonus pool constituting ten percent (10%) of the before tax profit (as determined by contract accounting in accordance with GAAP) earned on (i) any contract resulting from a ___ proposal or bid for any of the following seven contracts: (A) ___, (B) ___, (C) ___, (D) ___, (E) ___, (F) ___, or (G) ___, which are each identified in Schedule A attached hereto and (ii) each of the following four contracts for which the Company and _____ have jointly bid in 1993 or for which the Company, through its _____ Division/Operation, may bid or re-bid in the remainder of 1993 or in 1994: (A) ___, (B) ___, (C) ___, and (D) ___, which are each identified in Schedule A attached hereto. Executive shall allocate such bonus pool in any manner he deems advisable to one or more employee(s), including Executive, of the Company's _____ Division/Operation, *provided, however,* that, in the event of Executive's death, the entire applicable bonus pool shall be paid to his estate. Bonus payments shall be made by the Company directly to the employee(s) specified by Executive, subject to such withholding described above as required by law, and shall be income only to the employee(s) actually receiving such payments. Such bonus payments shall continue until the end of the pertinent initial contract and any exercised options on such contract, shall not be calculated or made based on any follow-on contracts, and shall be contingent upon Executive's continued compliance with the material terms of this Agreement. The share of before tax profit to be paid into the bonus pool shall be determined by the Company's accountant on or before the 60th day following the last day of each fiscal year of the Company during the term of this Agreement, and a written statement by the Company's chief financial officer, certifying such amount, shall be delivered to Executive on or before each such date. Payment of the amount due to the bonus pool shall be made by the Company on or before the 75th day following the last day of each such fiscal year of the Company, subject to such withholding described above as may be required by law.

(d) *Expenses:* The Company shall pay the reasonable expenses incurred by Executive (within limits that may be established by the Board of Directors of the Company, which limits shall not be unreasonable) in the performance of his duties hereunder (or shall reimburse Executive on account of such expenses paid directly by Executive) promptly upon the submission to the Company by Executive of appropriate vouchers prepared in accordance with Company rules and applicable regulation of the Internal Revenue Service.

(e) *Vacation:* Executive shall be entitled to a certain number of paid vacation days in each calendar year in accordance with the vacation policies and practices of the Company as determined by the Board of Directors of the Company, but not less than 15 business days in any calendar year, prorated appropriately on account of any calendar year during which Executive renders services hereunder for less than the entire such year. In addition, Executive shall be entitled to take, at any time reasonably acceptable to the Company during the term of his employment by the Company, up to thirty working days of paid vacation accrued while working for _____. Executive shall also be entitled to all paid holidays given by the Company to its senior executive employees. If, at the time of the termination (for any reason) of his employment with the Company, Executive has accrued but unused vacation time Executive shall be compensated for such time based upon his salary.

(f) *Other Benefits:* Executive shall be permitted, during the term of his employment with the Company, to participate in any group life, medical or disabillty insurance plan or program, profit-sharing or pension or similar benefit plan, or other fringe benefit plan of the Company as the Company may from time to time establish and in which Executive would be entitled to participate pursuant to the terms the thererof, *provided, however,* that the Company's medical plan shall cover any pre-existing condition of Executive or his dependents that was covered under Executive's medical plan in effect immediately prior to the date of this Agreement and providing that any known existing condition has been disclosed in a confidential letter to the Company's health plan administrator, _____ prior to the date of this Agreement. The foregoing, however, shall not be construed to require the Company to establish any such plans or to prevent the Company from modifying or terminating such plans once established, and no such action or lack thereof shall affect this Agreement.

Section 6. *Confidential Information and Proprietary Materials.*

(a) *Confidentiality:* (i) Executive shall not at any time during his employment with the Company or at any time after the termination of the same for any reason (including expiration of the term of Executive's employment hereunder) disclose, impart, divulge, or otherwise reveal in any manner whatsoever, directly or indirectly, in writing or orally, whether by counsel, discussion, recommendation, suggestion, or otherwise, any "Protected Information" except in the course of the proper discharge of his duties hereunder or as expressly authorized by the Company's Board of Directors.

(ii) As used in this Agreement, "Protected Information" means any confidential or proprietary information (in whatever form recorded) about the Company, any subsidiary of the Company, or any Customer or Prospective Customer of the Company or any subsidiary of the Company, that Executive has obtained, had aceess to, or gained knowledge of in the course of his employment with the Company or any subsidiary of the Company. Protected Information shall include, without limitation, except as provided in Subsection (vi) below:

(A) Information concerning or relating to properties, organization, personnel, operations, procedures, plans, projects, programs, products, processes, systems, profitability, finances, and business relationships and opportunities, except to the extent that such information is lawfully available to the public;

(B) Any trade secret or other similar information including, without limitation, the identity of customers or clients, customer or client lists, mailing lists, software programs, engineering or technical data, databases, coding information, market analysis and strategies, processes, systems, plans, projects, programs, and pricing and cost information, except to the extent that such information is lawfully available to the public; and

(C)   Information relating to any litigation including, without limitation, any attorney work-product and any data, documents, or other information that may be subject to the attorney-client privilege.

(iii)   As used in this Agreement, the phrase "any Customer or Prospective Customer of the Company or any subsidiary of the Company" means any person or entity (including, without limitation, any department, agency, or bureau of the federal or any state or local or foreign govemment) with whom the Company or any subsidiary of the Company currently is doing business or is engaged in negotiations, to whom the Company, or any subsidiary of the Company has submitted a bid or made a presentation, or from whom the Company or any subsidiary of the Company has sought to or is otherwise seeking to obtain or renew a contract, *provided, however,* that in the event of any termination of Executive's employment with the Company, the phrase shall also apply to any person or entity who was a Customer or Prospective Customer of the Company or any subsidiary of the Company during the one year prior to the date of such termination.

(iv)   Executive will not, without the prior express written consent of the Company's Board of Directors, use any Protected Information for his own benefit or the benefit of any person or entity other than the Company or any subsidiary of the Company.

(v)   Upon termination of Executive's employment with the Company for any reason, Executive shall return all books, records, lists, computer programs, documents, notes, and other materials of any kind and in any form whatsoever, including all copies thereof, which contain any Protected Information (hereinafter "Protected Materials"). All Protected Materials shall be returned whether initially (A) furnished by the Company or any subsidiary of the Company, or any Customer or Prospective Customer of the Company or any subsidiary of the Company; (B) prepared by Executive or any officer, director, employee, or agent of the Company, any subsidiary of the Company, or any Customer or Prospective Customer of the Company or any subsidiary of the Company; or (C) otherwise obtained in the course of Executive's employment with the Company.

(vi)   The term "Protected Infommation" shall not include information (A) available to the pubiic, (B) disclosed with the prior approval of the Company or its customers, (C) made available to a third party by the Company without restriction, or (D) ordered to be disclosed by a court or administrative agency of competent jurisdiction.

(b) *Proprietary Materials:* Unless offered to the Company by Executive and refused by the Company, all discoveries made, inventions created, and all ideas, concepts, designs, formulas, proposals, projects, programs, products, processes, systems, techniques, and improvements of whatever kind conceived or developed by Executive directly or indirectly, alone or jointly with others, during the term of his employment with the Company, whether during normal business hours or otherwise (hereinafter "Proprietary Materials"), shall be and remain the sole and exclusive property of the Company. Executive shall fully and promptly disclose to the Company all such Proprietary Materials, together with all information and data necessary to impart a full understanding of the same. Upon request and without further compensation from the Company, but at the Company's expense, Executive will (i) execute, acknowledge, and deliver all such papers and instruments as the Company may reasonably deem necessary in order for it to perfect, secure, and maintain all rights, title, and interest in and to any Proprietary Materials, including, without limitation, any and all patent, copyright, trademark, and trade secrets rights and protections in the same; and (ii) aid and assist the Company in any litigation involving the maintenance or establishment of such rights and protections, including, if necessary, testifying on behalf of the Company during his term of employment by the Company.

Section 7. *Non-Competition.* (a)   In conjunction with and as an integral component of the sale to the Company under the Purchase Agreement of the Assets (as defined in the Purchase Agreement) and _____ business relating to such Assets, Executive agrees that during the period of Executive's employment by the Company (including any extensions of the original three year term) or for a period of three (3) years beginning on the date hereof, whichever is longer, Executive will not, directly or indirectly:

(i)   within any state, district, city, town, or marketing area in the United States or any foreign country in which the Company or any subsidiary of the Company is doing business or is qualified to do business, own, manage, operate, control, consult for, perform services for, be employed by or participate in the ownership, management, operation or control of, or be connected in any manner with or have any interest in, any person, firm, company or other entity engaged in any business of the type and character engaged in and competitive with that conducted by the Company or any subsidiary of the Company, *provided, however,* that Executive may become a member of professional organizations and societies and serve on the Board of Directors of one or more companies. If he first obtains the consent of the Company to such membership or services, and *provided, further,* that Executive may maintain ownership of any number of shares of the capital stock of _____ and provide minimal services on behalf of _____ so long as (A) ___ sole business activity consists of performing the existing work under and follow-on to ___ existing Contract and ___ does not actively pursue any other business, and (B) Executive has no active role in the day-to-day management of business of _____. The Executive may continue to direct the use and investment of the assets of _____. Executive shall exercise his best efforts to ensure that _____ and Executive act in conformity with this subsection 7(a)(i). For these purposes, ownership of securities of not in excess of 1% of any class of securities of a company whose stock is publicly traded shall not be considered to be competition with the Company or any subsidiary of the Company; or

(ii)   persuade or attempt to persuade any Customer or Prospective Customer of the Company or any subsidiary of the Company not to hire the Company or any Subsidiary of the Company, or to hire another company, or

(iii)   without the advance consent of the Company, persuade or attempt to persuade any employee of the Company or any subsidiary of the Company to leave the Company's or any such subsidiary's employ, or to become employed by any person, firm or company other than the Company or any subsidiary of the Company.

(b)   In exchange for Executive's non-competition covenants contained in this Section 7, the Company shall pay Executive ___ Dollars ($___ per year in calendar years 1994, 1995, and 1996, payable as follows: (A) the 1994 payment shall be made in full on December 29, 1993; and (B) the 1995 and 1996 payments shall be made in eight quarterly installments of ___ Dollars ($___ each on the last day of March, June, September, and December of 1995 and 1996, *provided, however,* that any such payments may be offset against any amounts payable to the Company by _____ and Executive under Section 6.2, Indemnification, of the Purchase Agreement as a result of any failure on the part of _____ or Executive to pay any applicable taxes payable prior to the closing of the Purchase Agreement.

(c)   Executive acknowledges and recognizes that this covenant not to compete is ancillary to the sale to the Company by _____ of the Assets and _____ business related to the Assets, and that such covenant contain reasonable limitations as to time, geographical area and scope of activity to be restrained necessary to protect the Company's business interests.

Section 8. *Termination.*

(a)   *Termination After Original Three-Year Term:* Beginning three years after the date of this Agreement, either Executive or the Company may terminate Executive's employment by the Company under this Agreement upon 90 days' prior written notice to the other.

(b)   *Termination Upon Death:* Executive's employment under this Agreement shall terminate upon Executive's death.

(c)   *Termination Upon Disability:*

(i)   If, during the term of his employment hereunder, Executive becomes physically or mentally disabled, so that he is unable to substantially perform his duties hereunder even with reasonable accommodation, the Company may terminate his employment after a period of disability determined on the same basis as that generally applied by the Company with respect to the termination of the employment of executives of the Company on grounds of physical or mental disability.

(ii)   In case of any disagreement between Executive and the Company as to whether Executive is disabled so as to permit the Company to terminate Executive's employment hereunder in accordance with this subsection 8(c), the question of such disability shall be submitted for determination to an impartial and reputable physician selected by the mutual agreement of Executive (or his legal representative) and the Company. Failing such agreement, the Company shall request a physician referral from the _____, and Executive and the Company hereby agree in advance to accept the first name provided in that referral. The determination of the question of disability by such physician selected consistent with this subsection (ii) shall be final and binding on Executive and the Company. The Company shall pay the fees and expenses of such physician.

(d) *Termination for Cause:* The Company may terminate Executive's employment for cause. Termination for "cause" shall include discharge from employment for (i) failing or refusing to perform his duties in material breach of this Agreement, including, but not limited to, violating any of the provisions of Section 6 or 7 hereof, (ii) committing a deceitful or fraudulent act in connection with his employment, (iii) conviction of any crime or offense (other than a minor misdemeanor or motor vehicle violation) in connection with his employment, (iv) conviction of any felony, (v) knowingly and intentionally withholding from any officer or agent of the Company information material to the Company's interests, (vi) knowingly and intentionally making any material misrepresentation to any officer or agent of the Company, or (vii) knowingly and intentionally failing to carry out the instructions of the Company's Board of Directors or senior executive officers, or (viii) knowingly and intentionally failing to abide by or to enforce any policy or procedure of the Company, which failure would normally be considered grounds for dismissal of any employee of the Company. Any disputes regarding the Company's termination of Executive under this subsection 8(d) shall be submitted to binding arbitration pursuant to Section 12 hereof. No amounts otherwise payable by the Company to the Executive under this Agreement shall be withheld by the Company during the first thirty (30) days after termination of Executive's employment for cause under this subsection 8(d); upon the expiration of such thirty-day period, the Company may withhold payments in accordance with subsection 8(e)(iii) hereof unless Executive has initiated an arbitration proceeding in which case the Company shall not withhold any amounts otherwise payable to Executive under this Agreement until completion of the arbitration, and the arbitration panel's issuance of a ruling in favor of the Company, *provided, however,* that any payments made subsequent to the termination may be recoverable by the Company if the arbitration panel finds in the Company's favor.

(e) Payments Upon Termination:

(i) If Executive elects to terminate Executive's employment pursuant to subsection 8(a) hereof, (A) the Company shall pay Executive his salary and all other compensation set forth in Section 5 hereof accrued up to the date such termination occurs and (B) the Company shall pay the payments for his non-competition covenants set forth in subsection 7(b) hereof and (C) Executive shall have no right to receive any compensation from the Company for any period subsequent to the date of such termination. If the Company elects to terminate Executive's employment pursuant to subsection 8(a) hereof, (A) the Company shall pay Executive his salary and all other compensation set forth in Section 5 hereof accrued up to the date such termination occurs, (B) the Company shall continue to pay Executive and/or his designee(s) the bonus compensation to which they are entitled under subsection 5(c) hereof, (C) the Company shall pay the payments for his non-competition covenants set forth in subsection 7(b) hereof, and (D) Executive shall have no right to receive any other compensation from the Company for any period subsequent to the date of such termination.

(ii) In the event of termination of Executive's employment under subsection 8(b) or 8(c) hereof, (A) the Company shall pay Executive or, if applicable, his estate, his salary and all other compensation set forth in Section 5 hereof accrued up to the date such termination occurs and (B) the Company shall continue to pay Executive or, if appiicable, his estate the payments for his non-competition covenants set forth in subsection 7(b) hereof on the schedule set forth in such sections so long as no provision of Section 6 or 7 of this Agreement is violated. In the event of the Executive's death, the Company shall continue to pay to his estate the bonus in subsection 5(c) contingent upon the ability to obtain a Term Life Insurance Policy on the Executive, payable to the Company for a mutually agreed upon face value amount. If the total bonus pursuant to subsection 5(c) is less than 50% of the face amount of this policy, the difference will be paid to the Executive's estate from the proceeds of the policy. The Company and the Executive will equally share the cost of this insurance. If the Executive becomes disabled as defined in subsection 8(c) of this agreement, the Company will continue to pay the Bonus Payments listed in subsection 5(c) of this agreement.

(iii) If the Company terminates Executive's employment under subsection 8(d) hereof, (A) the Company shall pay Executive his salary and all other compensation set forth in Section 5 hereof accrued up to the date such termination occurs; (B) the Company shall continue to pay Executive the amounts due him for his non-competition covenants on the schedule set forth in subsection 7(b) hereof so long as Executive continues to abide by all the material terms of Sections 6 and 7 of this Agreement, *provided, however,* that Executive shall receive no such payments for his non-competition covenants if the Company terminates his employment under subsection 8(d)(ii) or 8(d)(iii) hereof; and (C) Executive shall have no right to receive any compensation, including, but not limited to, any bonus under subsection 5(c) hereof (other than non-competition payments under subsection 8(d)(iii)(B) hereof) from the Company for any period subsequent to the date of such termination.

(f) *Non-exclusive Rights:* The Company's right of termination shall be in addition to and shall not affect its rights and remedies under Sections 6, 7, and 12 of this Agreement, and such rights and remedies under such Sections shall survive termination of this Agreement and Executive's employment.

Section 9. *Notice.* Any notice or other communication required or permitted hereunder shall be in writing and shall be sufficiently given if delivered in person or sent by telex, telecopy, registered or certified mail with postage prepaid, Federal Express or Express Mail, addressed as follows:

(a) If to Executive, to:

(b) If to the Company, to:

Such addresses and numbers may be changed by written notice. Such notice or communication shall be deemed to have been given as of the date so delivered in person or sent by telex or telecopier wlth receipt confirmed, or as of two days after the date mailed, registered or certified, postage prepaid or sent by Federal Express or Express Mail.

Section 10. *Entire Agreement.* This Agreement and the Purchase Agreement set forth the entire agreement and understanding of the parties relating to the subject matter hereof, and supersede all prior agreements, arrangements, and understandings, written or oral, relating to the subject matter hereof.

Section 11. *Waivers and Amendments.* This Agreement may be amended, superseded, canceled, renewed, or extended, and the terms hereof may be waived, only by a written instrument signed by Executive and, on behalf of the Company, by an officer other than Executive specifically designated by the Board of Directors of the Company or, in the case of a waiver, by such party waiving compliance. No delay on the part of any party in exercising any right, power, or privilege hereunder shall operate as a waiver thereof, nor shall any waiver on the part of such party of any such right, power, or privilege, preclude any other or further exercise thereof or the exercise of any other such right, power, or privilege.

Section 12. *Enforcement, Arbitration, and Governing Law.*

(a)   It is the desire and intent of the Company and Executive that the provisions of this Agreement shall be enforced to the fullest extent permissible under the laws and public policies applied in each jurisdiction in which enforcement is sought. If any particular provision or portion of this Agreement shall be adjudicated to be invalid or unenforceable, this Agreement shall be deemed amended to delete therefrom such provision or portion adjudicated to be invalid or unenforceable. Executive agrees that, having regard to the importance of his duties hereunder and his position in relation to the Company's business, the obligations undertaken by him in this Agreement including, but not limited to, the obligations in Sections 6 and 7 hereof, are reasonable and necessary for the protection of the legitimate interests of the Company and do not work harshly upon him.

(b)   All disputes relating or in any way connected to this Agreement shall be submitted to binding arbitration in lieu of all other remedies available at law or in equity. Any matter submtted to arbitration shall be arbitrated in _____ or in such other location as shall be mutually agreed upon by the Company and Executive, in accordance with the commercial Arbitration Rules of the American Arbitration Association ("AAA") then in effect. The arbitration shall be conducted by a tripartite tribunal with the Company and Executive each selecting one arbitrator with technical expertise in the area of dispute and such two arbitrators selecting a third, mutually agreeable, neutral arbitrator who shall act as chair of the tribunal. If either the Company or Executive fails to select an arbitrator, the AAA shall appoint an arbitrator on such party's behalf. The arbitration panel may order specific performance of any provision of this Agreement and a court may order injunctive relief to make such agreements effective. Notwithstanding the foregoing, the parties agree that, upon application thereto, a court of competent jurisdiction may issue preliminary injunctive relief to preserve the status quo or otherwise enforce or provide for the effectiveness of the terms and conditions of this Agreement pending the outcome of the arbitration hereunder. The decision rendered by the arbitrators shall be final and binding upon all parties to this Agreement, and judgment upon that award may be entered in any court having jurisdiction thereof and may be enforced by either party to the arbitration. The tribunal shall determine which party to the arbitration shall bear the cost of the arbitration or the proportion of such cost that each party shall bear, and the prevailing party shall have his or its attorneys' fees paid by the non-prevailing party.

(c) The interpretation and construction of this Agreement and all matters relating thereto shall be governed by the laws of the State (excluding its conflict of laws rules) applicable to agreements executed and to be performed solely within such State.

(d) Subject to the arbitration requirements of subsection 12(b), any appropriate judicial proceeding brought against any of the parties to this Agreement may be brought in the courts of the State _____ or in the United States District Court for the _____ and, by execution and delivery of this Agreement, each of the parties hereto expressly consents to the jurisdiction of such courts, waives any defense of inconvenient forum, and irrevocably agrees to be bound by any judgment rendered thereby in connection with this Agreement. The parties consent to service of process by registered mail, return receipt requested. The foregoing consents to jurisdiction shall not constitute general consents to service of process in the State of

Texas for any purpose except as provided above and shall not be deemed to confer rights on any person other than the respective parties to this Agreement. The prevailing party in any such judicial proceeding shall have his or its attomeys' fees paid by the non-prevailing party.

Section 13. *Parties and Assignment.* The provisions of this Agreement shall be binding upon and inure to the benefit of the parties hereto and their respective heirs, legal representatives, successors, and assigns. This Agreement, and Executive's rights and obligations hereunder, may not be assigned by Executive. The Company may assign this Agreement and its rights, together with its obligations, hereunder, in connection with any sale, transfer, or other disposition of all or substantially all of the assets or business of the Company whether by merger, consolidation, or otherwise.

Section 14. *Headings.* The headings in this Agreement are for reference only and shall not affect its integration.

Section 15. *Severability.* In the event that one or more of the provisions contained in this Agreement, or any part thereof, shall be determined to be invalid, illegal, or unenforceable in any respect under any applicable statute or rule of law, only such provision(s) shall be considered invalid, illegal, or unenforceable (and then only to the extent of such invalidity, illegality, or unenforceability), and the rest of the provisions shall remain in full force and effect. Executive agrees that if any provision contained herein shall be adjudged to be invalid, illegal, or unenforceable for any reason, but would be adjudged to be valid, legal, and enforceable if part of the wording thereof were deleted and/or the time period there and/or the geographic area thereof were reduced, the said provision shall apply with such modification(s) as may be necessary to make it valid, legal, and enforceable.

Section 16. *Counterparts.* This Agreement may be signed in separate counterparts, each of which shall be deemed an original and both of which together shall constitute one and the same instrument.

Section 17. *Effective Date.* This Agreement shall be effective as of the Closing (as defined in the Purchase Agreement) of the Purchase Agreement, and shall be null, void, and of no effect if such Closing does not take place.

IN WITNESS WHEREOF, this Agreement has been duly executed and delivered by Executive and by the duly authorized officer of the Company as of the date first above written.

[Corporate Seal]

Attest:

By:_____   By:_____
        Secretary   Executive Vice President
                                        Chief Financial Officer

SCHEDULE A

CONTRACTS

——————————

——————————

——————————

——————————

——————————

——————————

——————————

——————————

——————————

——————————

SAMPLE EMPLOYMENT AGREEMENT IV: WITH A COMPANY PRESIDENT

EMPLOYMENT AGREEMENT, dated March 19_, by and between _____ a ___ corporation (the "Company") and _____ (the "Executive").

In consideration of the mutual covenants and agreements hereinafter set forth, the parties hereto agree as follows:

1. *Employment, Duties and Acceptance.*

1.1 *Employment by the Company.* The Company hereby employs the Executive for the term provided in Article 2 (the "Term") to render exclusive and full-time services to the Company as President and, in connection therewith, to perform the duties provided in Section 1.4 (the "Duties").

1.2 *Acceptance of Employment by the Executive.* The Executive hereby accepts such employment and agrees to perform the Duties diligently to the best of his abilities and in the best interests of the Company. The Executive shall devote his entire working time and his best efforts to the business of the Company during the Term.

1.3 *Place of Employment.* The Executive's principal place of employment shall be at _____ or such other location in the Washington metropolitan area as the Company may designate upon reasonable notice to the Executive. The Company may direct the Executive to engage in such reasonable travel performance as the Duties may require.

1.4 *Duties.* The Executive shall hold the position and title, and exercise the responsibilities, of President. The Executive shall have the right and obligation, in his capacity as President, to perform the duties of that office to the extent they are described in the By-Laws of the Company, as well as such other duties as from time to time may be assigned to him by the Company.

2. *Term of Employment.* The Executive's employment under this Agreement shall commence on January 1, 19_, and shall continue

until terminated by either party. The period of such employment shall be treated for all purposes hereunder as the Term. The Executive's employment may be terminated by the Company as provided elsewhere in this Agreement or by the Executive upon at least 90 days' prior written notice. Termination of the Executive's employment hereunder shall end the Term.

3. *Compensation.*

3.1 *Salary.* As compensation for all services to be rendered pursuant to this Agreement, the Company shall pay the Executive during the Term a salary of at least $___ per annum. All of the Executive's compensation shall be payable in accordance with the payroll policies of the Company as from time to time in effect, less such appropriate deductions as shall be required to be withheld by applicable law and regulations, or by written election of the Executive if agreed to by the Company.

3.2 *Participation in Employee Benefit Plans.* The Executive shall be permitted during the Term, to the extent eligible, to participate in any group life, medical, or disability insurance plan, health program, dental program, profit-sharing or pension or similar benefit plan, thrift plan, or other fringe benefit plan of the Company, which participation shall be on a basis that is at least equivalent to that which is then made available to other executives of the Company.

3.3 *Car.* The company shall make available to the Executive for his full-time use a car leased by the Company that is at least as expensive as the cars then normally provided to Presidents of other operating companies owned by _____. The Company shall be responsible for the maintenance of such car, shall maintain full casualty and personal liability insurance with respect to such car, and shall provide the Executive, free of charge, with a parking space within reasonable walking distance of the Company's principal offices at _____.

3.4 *Incentive Plan.* The Executive shall be eligible to participate in the Company's Management Incentive Plan in accordance with its terms and conditions.

3.5 *Expenses.* Subject to such policies as may from time to time be established by the Company, the Company shall pay or reimburse the Executive for all reasonable expenses actually incurred or paid by the Executive during the Term in the performance of his Duties upon presentation of expense statements or vouchers or such other supporting information as the Company may require.

3.6 *Salary Adjustment.* Effective January 1, 19_, and thereafter during the Term effective on every succeeding January 1, the annual salary of the Executive then in effect shall be reviewed by the Board of Directors of the Company in accordance with generally applied normal corporate policy and practice.

3.7 *Paid Vacation.* The Executive shall be entitled to a vacation of twenty (20) working days during 19_ and, during each subsequent year of the Term of this Agreement, the time allowed under the Company's policies and practices then in effect, in each case in addition to other holidays designated by the Company. During each such vacation period the Executive shall continue to receive the salary and other compensation provided in this Article 3. Such paid vacation must be taken at a time and in a manner consistent with his Duties.

4. *Termination of Employment.*

4.1 *Termination upon Death.* The Executive's employment under this Agreement shall terminate upon the Executive's death. The Company shall continue to make payment of salary or other compensation to the Executive's legal representatives in accordance with the Company's general policies and practices then in effect.

4.2 *Termination upon Disability.*

(a) If, during the Term of his employment, the Executive becomes physically or mentally disabled, so that he is unable substantially to perform his duties hereunder, the Company may terminate his employment after a period of disability determined on the same basis as that generally applied by the Company with respect to the termination of the employment of executives of the Company on the grounds of physical or mental disability.

(b) In case of any disagreement between the Executive and the Company as to whether the Executive is disabled so as to permit the Company to terminate the Executive's employment hereunder in accordance with this Section 4.2, the question of such disability shall be submitted for determination to an impartial and reputable physician selected by the mutual agreement of the Executive (or his legal representative) and the Company. Failing such agreement, the Company shall request a physician referral from the Medical Society of the City _____ and the Executive and the Company hereby agree in advance to accept the first name provided in that referral. The determination of the question of disability by such physician selected consistent with this subsection (b) shall be final and binding on the Executive and the Company. The Company shall pay the fees and expenses of such physician.

(c)   If, with respect to the first ninety (90) days of the period during which the Executive suffers a disability of the kind described in subsection (a) above, the total amount of payments received by the Executive pursuant to sick leave and similar practices and policies generally followed by the Company is less than 100% of the amount of the salary that the Executive would have received with respect to the same period, the Company shall pay him the difference.

4.3   *Termination for Cause.* The Company may terminate the Executive's employment for cause. "Termination for cause" shall mean discharge from employment for committing an unlawful, deceitful or fraudulent act, for knowingly withholding from the Company's Board of Directors information material to the Company's interest, for knowingly making any misrepresentation to the Company's Board of Directors regarding a matter material to the Company's interests, for knowingly failing to carry out the instructions of the Company's Board of Directors, or for knowingly failing to abide by or to enforce any material policy or procedure of the Company. Upon termination of his employment for cause, as provided herein, the Company shall pay the Executive his salary (as then in effect) accrued up to the last date of the month in which such termination occurs.

4.4   *Termination by the Board of Directors.* The Company may terminate the Executive's employment other than for cause or disability upon resolution by the Board of Directors in its sole discretion. The Company shall give at least ninety (90) days' prior written notice of such termination. Upon termination of his employment, as provided in this Section 4.4, other than for cause or disability:

(a) The Company shall pay the Executive as severance an amount equal to his annualized salary at the time his employment with the Company ends. The Company shall pay this severance amount within thirty (30) days after the date the Executive's employment ends.

(b) The Company shall provide to the Executive, at the Company's expense, for the period of one year from the date the Executive's employment with the Company ends, such health (including dental), life and long-term disability insurance coverage then generally provided to employees of the Company. The insurance coverage that the Executive would otherwise receive pursuant to this subparagraph shall be reduced by an amount equal to any insurance coverage received by the Executive in connection with other employment performed by the Executive during the one year period following the end of his employment with the Company.

(c) The Company shall obtain professional outplacement services for the Executive, at the Company's expense, to be performed by a nationally recognized outplacement firm.

(d) The Company shall provide to the Executive clear title to his supplemental retirement insurance contract releasing him from the requirement to repay any portion of the gain or company paid premium. Additionally, the Company will make one annual premium payment for the year following the Executive's termination and cover all tax consequences resulting from these actions.

(e) The Company shall continue to provide the Executive, at the Company's expense, for the period of one year from the date the Executive's employment with the Company's ends, with the use of his leased car and be responsible for the maintenance of such car, and shall provide the Executive, free of charge, with a parking space within reasonable walking distance of the Company's principal offices.

5. *Confidential Information Restrictive Covenant.*

5.1 *Confidential Information.* In view of the fact that the Executive's work as an employee of the Company hereunder will bring him into close contact with many confidential affairs of the Company, including information about costs, profits, sales, trade secrets, and other information not readily available to the public (hereinafter collectively referred to as "confidential matters"), the Executive agrees to keep secret all confidential matters of the Company and not to disclose them to anyone outside of the Company or otherwise use his knowledge of them for his own benefit, either during or after his employment with the Company.

5.2 *Restrictive Covenant.* During the Term and for one (1) year after the termination of the Executive's employment with the Company for any reason, the Executive shall not, unless acting with the Company's prior written consent or as an officer, employee or agent of the Company, or of any corporation controlled by, controlling, or under common control with the Company, (i) induce or attempt to induce any client or prospective client of the Company to cease doing business with, or not to do business with the Company; or (ii) induce or attempt to induce any officer or employee of the Company to terminate his or her employment with the Company.

5.3 *Proprietary Materials.* All discoveries made, inventions created, and all ideas, concepts, designs, formulas, proposals, projects, progress, products, processes, systems, techniques, and improvements of whatever kind conceived or developed by the Executive directly or indirectly, alone or jointly with others, in the course of employment with the Company, whether during normal business hours or otherwise (hereinafter "Proprietary Materials"), shall be and remain the sole and exclusive property of the Company. The Executive shall fully and promptly disclose to the Company all such Proprietary Materials, together with all information and data necessary to impart a full understanding of the same. Upon request and without further compensation from the Company, but at the Company's expense, the Executive will (i) execute, acknowledge, and deliver all such papers and instruments as the Company may deem neeessary in order for it to perfect, secure, and maintain all rights, title, and interest in and to any Proprietary Materials, including, without limitation, any and all patent, copyright, trademark, and trade secrets rights and protections in the same, and (ii) aid and assist the Company in any litigation involving the maintenance or establishment of such rights and protections, including, if necessary, testifying on behalf of the Company.

5.4   *Remedies.* If the Executive commits a breach, or threatens to commit a breach, of any of the provisions of this Article 5, the Company shall have the following rights and remedies:

(a)   The right and remedy to have the provisions of this Article 5 specifically enforced by any court having equity jurisdiction, it being acknowledged and agreed that any such breach or threatened breach will cause irreparable injury to the Company and that money damages will not provide an adequate remedy to the Company; and

(b)   The right and remedy to require the Executive to account for and pay over to the Company all compensation, profits, monies, accruals, increments, or other benefits (hereinafter collectively referred to as the "Benefits") derived or received by the Executive as the result of any transactions constituting a breach of any of the provisions of this Article 5, the Executive hereby agreeing to account for and pay over the Benefits to the Company.

5.5   *Judicial Modification.* If any covenant contained in this Article 5, or any part thereof, is held to be unenforceable because of the duration of such covenant or the area covered thereby, the parties agree that the court making such determination shall have the power to reduce the duration and/or area of such covenant and, in its reduced form, said covenant shall then be enforceable.

6.   *Indemnification.* The Company shall indemnify the Executive to the full extent authorized by law in the event he is made or threatened to be made a party to any action, suit, or proceeding, whether criminal, civil, administrative or investigative, by reason of the fact that he is or was a director, officer, or employee of the Company or serves or served any other enterprise as a director, officer, or employee at the request of the Company.

7.   *Other Provisions.*

7.1   *Notices.* Any notice or other communication required or permitted hereunder shall be in writing and shall be delivered personally, telegraphed, telexed, sent by facsimile transmission, or sent by certified, registered, or express mail, postage prepaid. Any such notice shall be deemed given when so delivered personally, telegraphed, telexed, or sent by facsimile transmission or, if mailed, three days after the date of deposit in the United States mails addressed as follows:

    (a) if to the Company, to:

    with a copy to:

    (b) if to the Executive, to:

    7.2 *Entire Agreement.* This Agreement and any other agreements incorporated herein by reference set forth the entire agreement and understanding of the parties relating to the subject matter hereof, and supersede all prior agreements, arrangements, and understandings, written or oral, relating to the subject matter hereof.

    7.3 *Waivers and Amendments.* This Agreement may be amended, superseded, cancelled, renewed, or extended, and the terms hereof may be waived, only by a written instrument signed by the parties or, in the party waiving compliance. No delay on the part of any party in exercising any right, power, or privilege hereunder shall operate as a waiver thereof, nor shall any waiver on the part of such party of any such right, power, or privilege, nor any single or partial exercise of any such right, power, or privilege, preclude any other or further exercise thereof or the exercise of any other such right, power, or privilege.

    7.4 *Governing Law.* This Agreement shall be governed by and construed in accordance with the laws of the State of _____ without regard to its conflict of laws rules.

    7.5 *Assignment.* The provisions of this Agreement shall be binding upon and inure to the benefit of the parties hereto and their respective heirs, legal representatives, successors, and assigns. This Agreement, and the Executive's rights and obligations hereunder, may not be assigned by the Executive. The Company may assign this Agreement and its rights, together with its obligations, hereunder, in connection with any sale, transfer, or other disposition of all or substantially all of its respective assets or business, whether by merger, consolidation, or otherwise.

7.6 *Headings.* The headings in this Agreement are for reference only and shall not affect its interpretation.

7.7 *Severability.* In the event that one or more of the provisions contained in this Agreement, or any part thereof, shall be determined to be invalid, illegal, or unenforceable in any respect under any applicable statute or law, only such provision(s) shall be considered invalid, illegal, or unenforceable (and then only to the extent of such invalidity, illegality, or unenforceability), and the rest of the provisions shall remain in full force and effect. The Executive agrees that if any provision contained herein shall be adjudged to be invalid, illegal, or unenforceable for any reason, but would be adjudged to be valid, legal, and enforceable if part of the wording thereof were deleted and/or the time period thereof and/or the geographic area thereof were reduced, the said provision shall apply with such modification(s) as say be necessary to make it valid, legal, and enforceable.

IN WITNESS WHEREOF, the parties have executed this Agreement the date first above written.

ATTEST:

By:_____   By:_____
                                           Director

Witness:

_____   _____

Appendix E

Sample Shareholder-Approved Annual Incentive Compensation Plan

This appendix shows the shareholder-approved annual incentive plan for the company Fortune Brands, Inc. Because this plan provides for payment in cash, it would not require shareholder approval; however, most companies like Fortune Brands, Inc. would still obtain shareholder approval as a means of authorizing plan administration by the board compensation committee.

The stock exchanges require executive compensation plans that pay in stock to be approved by shareholders. In addition, other regulations also require shareholder approval of compensation plans. For example, the Internal Revenue Code Section 162(m) requires that companies with "performance-based" compensation have plans that award this compensation approved by shareholders if they wish to qualify for an exception to the $1 million cap on company tax deductions for any performance-based compensation.

Fortune Brands, Inc. Annual Executive Incentive Compensation Plan

ARTICLE I

GENERAL

SECTION 1.1   Purpose. The purpose of this Annual Executive Incentive Compensation Plan (the "Plan") is to advance the interests of the stockholders of Fortune Brands, Inc. (the "Company") by providing performance-based incentives to senior executives of the company.

SECTION 1.2   Definitions. As used in the Plan, the following terms shall have the following meanings:

(a) "Award" means, for each Participant, a specific dollar amount payable as determined by the Committee pursuant to Section 2.2 of the Plan after application of the Committee's discretion pursuant to Section 2.4(b) of the Plan;

(b) "Board of Directors" means the Board of Directors of the Company;

(c) "Code" means the Internal Revenue Code of 1986, as amended;

(d) "Committee" means the Compensation and Stock Option Committee of the Board of Directors;

(e) "Incentive Pool" means, with respect to each Performance Period, the total amount of dollars available to be paid to all Participants. This amount shall be based on an objective formula established by the Committee in accordance with Section 2.2 of the Plan using one or more of the Performance Measures. It shall be allocated among the Participants in the manner determined by the Committee in accordance with the Plan;

(f) "Participants" means, with respect to each Performance Period, the group of all persons elected to the office of Vice President of the Company or any office senior thereto except any officer covered by an annual incentive compensation plan of any subsidiary of the Company. A person who during part of such Performance Period has held such office shall participate on a proportional basis reflecting the portion of the

Performance Period during which he or she has held such office;

(g) "Performance Period" means performance goals and objectives, which shall be based on any of the following performance criteria, either alone or in any combination, as the Committee may determine: cash flow; cash flow from operations; earnings per Common share; earnings per Common share from continuing operations; income before income taxes; income before income taxes, depreciation, and amortization; income from continuing operations; net asset turnover; net income; operating income; operating margin; return on equity; return on net assets; return on total assets; return on total capital; sales; economic value added; and total return to stockholders. For any Performance Period, Performance Measures may be determined on an absolute basis or relative to internal goals or relative to levels attained in years prior to such Performance Period or related to other companies. For any Performance Period, the Committee shall provide whether and how the Performance Measures shall be adjusted in the event of any or all of the following items: extraordinary, unusual, or non-recurring items; effects of changes in applicable laws, regulations, or accounting principles; effects of currency fluctuations; effects of financing activities (e.g., effect on earnings per share of issuance of convertible debt securities); realized or unrealized gains and losses on securities; expenses, charges, or credits for restructuring initiatives, producing initiatives, or for impaired assets; non-cash items (e.g., amortization, depreciation, or reserves); other non-operating items; writedowns of intangible assets, property, plant, or equipment, investments in business units and securities resulting from the sale of business units; spending for acquisitions; and effects of any recapitalization, reorganization, merger, acquisition, divestiture, consolidation, spin-off, split-off, combination, liquidation, dissolution, sale of assets, or other similar corporate transaction or event; and

(h) "Performance Period" means each consecutive twelve-month period commencing January 1 of each year.

SECTION 1.3 Administration of the Plan. The Plan shall be administered by the Committee; provided, however, that

(i)   The number of directors on the Committee shall not be less than two and

(ii) Each member of the Committee shall be an "outside director" within the meaning of Section 162(m)(4) of the Code. The Committee may adopt its own rules of procedure, and the action of a majority of the Committee, taken at a meeting, or taken without a meeting by unanimous written consent of the members of the Committee, shall constitute action by the Committee. The Committee shall have the power and authority to administer, construe, and interpret the Plan, to make rules for carrying it out and to make changes in such rules.

ARTICLE II

AWARDS

SECTION 2.1   Awards. The Committee may make Awards to Participants with respect to each Performance Period, subject to the terms and conditions set forth in the Plan.

SECTION 2.2   Terms of Awards. Within 90 days after the commencement of each Performance Period (or prior to such later date as permitted by, or such earlier date as required by, Section 162(m) of the Code and the regulations promulgated thereunder), the Committee shall establish in writing for such Performance Period (i) the objective formula for determining the Incentive Pool for the Performance Period (using one or more of the Performance Measures) and (ii) the allocable percentage of the total Incentive Pool to which each Participant shall be entitled, provided that the total of all such percentages for all Participants for any Performance Period shall not exceed 100 percent. The Committee shall cause each Participant to be notified in writing of (i) his or her selection as a Participant and (ii) the formula for determining the Incentive Pool for the Performance Period.

SECTION 2.3   Limitations on Awards. The maximum amount of an Award to any Participant for any Performance Period shall not exceed $2.5 million. No part of the amount of any Incentive Pool for any Performance Period which is not awarded in such performance Period may be carried forward for award in subsequent Performance Periods.

SECTION 2.4   Determination of Awards

(a) The Committee shall, promptly after the date on which all necessary financial or other information for a particular Performance Period becomes available, in the manner required by Section 162(m) of the Code, certify (i) the degree to which each of the Performance Measures has been attained and (ii) with respect to each Participant, the amount of the Participant's Award, if any.

(b) Notwithstanding anything in the Plan to the contrary, the Committee may, in its sole discretion, reduce or eliminate, but not increase, any Award. In exercising its discretion, the Committee may use such objective or subjective factors as it determines to be appropriate in its sole discretion. The determination by the Committee as to the terms of any of the foregoing adjustments shall be conclusive and binding. No part of any potential Award for any Performance Period that is not actually awarded to a Participant because of any reduction permitted by this Section 2.4(b) or required by Section 2.3 shall be available for award to any other Participant whose actual compensation for such period is subject to Section 162(m) of the Code.

(c) After the end of each Performance Period when the amount of each Participant's Award has been determined, the Committee shall cause each Participant to be provided with written notice of the amount of his or her award, if any. Awards shall become payable in cash as promptly as practicable after the certifications described in this Section 2.4 have been made by the Committee.

SECTION 2.5   Deferral of Payment of Awards. Notwithstanding Section 2.4(c), the Committee may, in its sole discretion, upon the request of a Participant, determine that the payment of an Award (or any portion thereof) to the Participant shall be deferred and when such deferred Award shall be paid and over what period of time. The Committee shall have discretion to provide for the payment of an amount equivalent to interest, at such rate or rates fixed by the Committee or based on one or more predetermined investments selected by the Committee, on any such deferred Award.

ARTICLE III

MISCELLANEOUS

SECTION 3.1 Restriction on Transfer. The rights of a Participant with respect to amounts under the Plan shall not be transferable by such participant, otherwise than by will or the laws of descent and distribution.

SECTION 3.2 Tax Withholding. The Company shall have the right to deduct from all payments made under the Plan to a Participant or to a Participant's beneficiary or beneficiaries any federal, state, or local taxes required by law to be withheld with respect to such payments.

SECTION 3.3 Source of Payments. The Company shall not have any obligation to establish any separate fund or trust or other segregation of assets to provide for payments under the Plan. To the extent any person acquires any rights to receive payments hereunder from the Company, such rights shall be no greater than those of an unsecured creditor.

SECTION 3.4 Employment Rights and Other Benefit Programs. The provisions of the Plan shall not give any Participant any right to be retained in the employment of the Company. In the absence of any specific agreement to the contrary, the Plan shall not affect any right of the Company, or of any affiliate of the Company, to terminate, with or without cause, any participant's employment at any time. The Plan shall not replace any contract of employment between the Company and any Participant, but shall be considered a supplement thereto. The Plan is in addition to, and not in lieu of, any other employee benefit plan or program in which any Participant may be or become eligible to participate by reason of employment with the Company.

SECTION 3.5 Amendment and Termination. The Board of Directors may at any time and from time to time alter, amend, suspend, or terminate the Plan in whole or in part. No termination or amendment of the Plan may, without the consent of the Participant to whom an Award has been determined for a completed Performance Period but not yet paid, adversely affect the rights of such participant in such Award, nor shall any amendment increase the amount payable to a Participant for a Performance Period if such amendment is made after the final day of the period for establishing the objective formula for determining the Incentive Pool for the Performance Period set forth in Section 2.2 of the Plan.

SECTION 3.6 Governing Law. The Plan and all rights and Awards hereunder shall be construed in accordance with and governed by the laws of the State of Delaware.

SECTION 3.7 Severability. If any provision of the Plan is or becomes or is deemed to be invalid, illegal, or enforceable in any jurisdiction such provision shall be construed or deemed amended to conform to applicable laws, or if it cannot be so construed or deemed without, in the determination of the Committee, materially altering the purpose or intent of the Plan, such provision shall be stricken as to such jurisdiction, and the remainder of the Plan shall remain in full force and effect.

SECTION 3.8 Effective Date. The Plan shall be effective as of January 1, 1997, subject to the approval thereof by the stockholders of the Company at the 1997 annual meeting of stockholders. Such approval shall meet the requirements of Section 162(m) of the Code and regulations thereunder. If such approval is not obtained, then the Plan shall not be effective and any formula for determining the Incentive Pool for any Performance Period, any percentage thereof to which any person otherwise may be entitled and any notice given pursuant to Section 2.2 of the Plan shall be void *ab initio*.

Appendix F

Sample Compensation Plan for Outside Directors

This plan of the Dupont Company includes the authorization of stock grants plus a deferred compensation program for outside directors.

Dupont Stock Accumulation and Deferred Compensation Plan for Directors

1. PURPOSE OF THE PLAN

The Purpose of the Dupont Stock Accumulation and Deferred Compensation Plan for Directors (the "Plan") is (1) to further identity of interests of members of the Board of Directors of E.I. Dupont de Nemours and Company (the "Company") with those of the Company's stockholders generally through the grant of common stock of the Company (the "Stock"); and, (2) to permit Directors to defer the payment of all or a specified part of their compensation, including any grant of Stock by the Company, for services performed as Directors.

2. ELIGIBILITY

Members of the Board of Directors of the Company who are not employees of the Company or any of its subsidiaries or affiliates and who do not receive a form of compensation for Board services in lieu of customary Director's fees shall be eligible to receive grants of Stock under the Plan. Members of the Board of Directors of the Company who are not employees of the Company or any of its subsidiaries or affiliates shall be eligible under this Plan to defer compensation for services performed as Directors.

3. ADMINISTRATION AND AMENDMENT

The Plan shall be administered by the Compensation and Benefits Committee of the Board of Directors (the "Committee"). The decision of the Committee with respect to any question arising as to the interpretation of this Plan, including the severability of any and all of the provisions thereof, shall be final, conclusive, and binding. The Board of Directors of the Company reserves the right to modify the Plan from time to time, or to repeal the Plan entirely, provided, however, that (1) no modification of the Plan shall operate to annul an election already in effect for the current calendar year or any preceding calendar year; and, (2) to the extent required under Section 16 of the Securities Exchange Act of 1934 ("Exchange Act"), Plan provisions relating to the amount, price, and timing of stock grants and options shall not be amended more than once every six months, except that the foregoing shall not preclude any amendment necessary to conform to changes in the Internal Revenue Code or the Employee Retirement Income Security Act.

The Committee is authorized, subject to the provisions of the Plan, from time to time to establish such rules and regulations as it deems appropriate for the proper administration of the Plan, and to make such determinations and take such steps in connection therewith as it deems necessary or advisable.

4. COMPLIANCE WITH SECTION 16 OF THE EXCHANGE ACT/CHANGE IN LAW

It is the Company's intent that the Plan comply in all aspects with Rule 16b-3 of the Exchange Act, or its successor, and any regulations promulgated thereunder. If any provision of this Plan is found not to be in compliance with such rule and regulations, the provision shall be deemed null and void, and the remaining provisions of the Plan shall continue in full force and effect. All transactions under this Plan shall be executed in accordance with the requirements of Section 16 of the Exchange Act and regulations promulgated thereunder.

The Board of Directors may, in its sole discretion, modify the terms and conditions of this Plan in response to and consistent with any changes in applicable law, rule, or regulation.

5. ANNUAL STOCK GRANT

Effective with the 1996 Annual Meeting and annually thereafter, each Director eligible under Article 2 hereof shall be awarded an annual grant of two hundred (200) shares of Stock following his/her election to the Board of Directors at the Annual Meeting of Stockholders. A Director elected to the Board at a time other than at the Annual Meeting shall receive a grant of two hundred (200) shares of Stock following his/her first attendance at a Board meeting, provided, however, that no Director shall receive more than two hundred (200) shares of Stock in any given calendar year. A Director may use shares of Stock granted hereunder to satisfy withholding taxes related to grants under this Plan in accordance with terms and conditions established by the Committee.

6. ELECTION TO DEFER

On or before December 31 of any year, a Director may elect to defer, until a specified year or retirement as a Director of the Company, the receipt of the Stock granted under Article 5 or the payment of all or a specified part of all fees payable to the Director for services as a Director during the calendar year following the election and succeeding calendar years in the form of cash or stock units, provided, however, that Stock may only be deferred as stock units. Any person who shall become a Director during a calendar year, and who was not a Director of the Company on the preceding December 31, may elect, within thirty days after election to the Board, to defer in the same manner the receipt of the Stock granted under Article 5 or the payment of all or a specified part of fees not yet earned for the remainder of that calendar year and for succeeding calendar years in the form of cash or stock units. Elections shall be made by written notice delivered to the Secretary of the Committee.

7. DIRECTORS' ACCOUNTS

Fees deferred in the form of cash shall be held in the general funds of the Company and shall be credited to an account in the name of the Director. On the first day of each quarter, interest shall be credited to each account calculated on the basis of the cash balance in each account on the first day of each month of the preceding quarter at the Prime Rate of Morgan Guaranty Trust Company of New York (or at such other rate as may be specified by the Committee from time to time) in effect on the first day of each month. Stock granted under Article 5 to be deferred in the form of stock units, or fees to be deferred in the form of stock units, shall be allocated to each Director's account based on the closing price of the Company's common stock as reported on the Composite Tape of the New York Stock Exchange ("Stock Price") on the effective date of the Stock grant or the date the fees would otherwise have been paid. The Company shall not be required to reserve or otherwise set aside shares of common stock for the payment of its obligations hereunder, but shall make available as and when required a sufficient number of shares of common stock to meet the needs of the Plan. An amount equal to any cash dividends (or the fair market value of dividends paid in property other than dividends payable in common stock of the Company) payable on the number of shares represented by the number of stock units in each Director's account will be allocated to each Director's account in the form of stock units based upon the Stock Price on the dividend payment date. Any stock dividends payable on such number of shares will be allocated in the form of stock units. If adjustments are made to outstanding shares of common stock as a result of split-ups, recapitalizations, mergers, consolidations, and the like, an appropriate adjustment will also be made in the number of stock units in a Director's account. Stock units shall not entitle any person to rights of a stockholder unless and until shares of Company common stock have been issued to that person with respect to stock units as provided in Article 8.

8. PAYMENT FROM DIRECTORS' ACCOUNTS

The aggregate amount of Stock granted under Article 5 which has been deferred and deferred fees, together with interest and dividend equivalents accrued thereon, shall be paid in the year specified or after a Director ceases to be a Director of the Company. Amounts deferred to a specified year shall only be paid in a lump sum and shall be paid promptly at the beginning of that specified year. Amounts deferred to retirement shall be paid in a lump sum or, if the Director elects, in substantially equal annual installments over a period of years specified by the Director. The delivery election must be made by written notice delivered to the Secretary of the Committee prior to the date of retirement, and the first installment (or lump sum payment) shall be paid promptly at the beginning of the following calendar year. Subsequent installment shall be paid promptly at the beginning of each succeeding calendar year until the entire amount credited to the Director's account shall have been paid. Amounts credited to a Director's account in cash shall be paid in cash and amounts credited in stock units shall be paid in one share of common stock of the Company for each stock unit, except that a cash payment will be made with any final installment for any fraction of a stock unit remaining in the Director's account. Such fractional share will be valued at the closing Stock Price on the date of settlement.

9. PAYMENT IN EVENT OF DEATH

A Director may file with the Secretary of the Committee a written designation of a beneficiary for his/her account under the Plan on such form as may be prescribed by the Committee, and may, from time to time, amend or revoke such designation. If a Director should die before all deferred amounts credited to the Director's account have been distributed, the balance of any deferred Stock and fees and interest and dividend equivalents then in the Director's account shall be paid promptly to the Director's designated beneficiary. If the Director did not designate a beneficiary, or in the event that the beneficiary designated by the Director shall have predeceased the Director, the balance in the Director's account shall be paid promptly to the Director's estate.

10. TERMINATION OF ELECTION

A Director may terminate his/her election to defer payment of fees in cash or stock units by written notice delivered to the Secretary of the Committee. Termination shall become effective as of the end of the calendar year in which notice of termination is given with respect to fees payable for services as a Director during subsequent calendar years. Amounts credited to the account of a Director prior to the effective date of termination shall not be affected thereby and shall be paid only in accordance with Articles 7 and 8.

11. NONASSIGNABILITY

During the Director's lifetime, the right to any deferred stock or fees including interest and dividend equivalents thereon shall not be transferable or assignable.

12. GOVERNING LAW

The validity and construction of the Plan shall be governed by the laws of the State of Delaware.

13. EFFECTIVE DATE

This Plan shall become effective as of January 1, 1996, provided it is approved by stockholders at the Company's 1996 Annual Meeting, and shall continue in full force and effect until terminated by the Board of Directors.

Appendix G

Sample Proposal to Increase the Number of Shares Used in an Executive Compensation Plan

This is a generic example of a proposal to shareholders that requests approval to increase the number of shares used in a company's executive compensation plans. It was developed from similar proposals that were sent to the Digital Equipment Corporation shareholders and The Boeing Company shareholders in 1997.

Proposal to Amend the 1992 Executive Long-Term Incentive Plan by Increasing the Number of Shares Available for Issuance

The Board of Directors recommends that the number of shares available for use in the Company's Executive Long-Term Incentive Plan (the "Plan") be increased thereto by 5,000,000 shares. This recommendation is contained on Page 1 of the Company's 1997 Annual Meeting Proxy and will become effective, if approved by stockholders, on the date of the Annual Meeting of Stockholders this year. The increase in shares is needed to enable the Company to meet the Plan's objectives of (1) attracting and retaining high quality executive talent; and (2) providing executives with ownership of company stock so that their interests efforts, and results are linked to the long-term interests of stockholders.

The Board of Directors recommends a vote FOR approving this amendment to the Executive Long-Term Incentive Plan.

A description of the 1992 Executive Long-Term Incentive Plan follows:

In 1992 the Plan was approved by stockholders, and at that time 5,000,000 shares were authorized for issuance to executives. Since adoption of the Plan, 4,280,000 shares have been issued and/or have been made available for purchase.

The Plan is administered by the Compensation Committee of the Board of Directors (the "Committee"), which is composed of non-employee Directors. They determine eligible participants and the type and level of all awards. The Committee may authorize Incentive Stock Options that comply with the provisions of Section 422 of the Internal Revenue Code and therefore provide Company executives with opportunity for capital gains tax rates; Non-Qualified Stock Options, which do not comply with Section 422 of the Internal Revenue Code and therefore do not provide the Company executives with the opportunity for capital gains tax; Stock Appreciation Rights, Phantom Shares, and Cashless Exercise Rights, which can provide executives with cash and/or cash and stock equal to the appreciation in specified amounts of company stock; Restricted Stock Awards that may contain a tenure and/or performance restriction that the executive must meet in order to take possession of the shares without any restriction on their sale; Performance Shares and Performance-Based Stock Options, which provide the executive either with shares or the opportunity to purchase shares if specified company long-term performance goals are achieved; and Performance Units that provide executives with specified cash and/or stock payments if specified company long-term goals are achieved.

The Board of Directors may terminate or amend the Plan provided that no amendment shall, without stockholder approval, increase the number of shares of Common stock to be offered under the Plan or change the class of employees eligible to participate in the Plan.

Appendix H

Sample Proposal of Shareholder-Approved Performance-Based Compensation Plan as Defined under Section 162(m) of IRS Regulations

This example describes how The Boeing Company presented shareholders with an amendment to their executive compensation plans that describes the performance-based feature of their incentive compensation. Payments from the executive compensation plan are intended to qualify as "performance-based" under IRS Section 162(m) and therefore be tax-deductible to the company even if they exceed $1 million total compensation for any one of the top five executives. (Section 162(m) does not permit a company to take tax deductions on compensation over $1 million for the top five executives [as reported in public company proxies] unless they are performance-based.) By obtaining shareholder approval of the performance measures to be used in the plan, a public company can retain tax deductibility of all compensation paid.

Amendment to the Incentive Compensation Plan for Officers of the Boeing Company

The Board of Directors, subject to approval of the Company's shareholders, has adopted resolutions to amend and restate the Incentive Compensation Plan for Officers and Employees of The Boeing Company and Subsidiaries (the "Incentive Plan"). The Incentive Plan was originally approved by the Company's shareholders in 1947 and was last submitted to shareholders for approval of an amendment and restatement in 1957. The Incentive Plan has subsequently been amended and restated by the Board of Directors. The purpose of the Incentive Plan is to attract, retain, and motivate key employees by recognizing, motivating, and rewarding contributions to the Company and the accomplishment of Company objectives.

The proposed Incentive Plan amendments (the "Incentive Plan Amendments") were prepared primarily to qualify certain payments to employees under the Incentive Plan as performance-based compensation under Section 162(m) of the Code. Section 162(m) provides that compensation in excess of $1 million paid in any year to the chief executive officer and the four other highest paid executive officers of a public company (for purposes of the Incentive Plan, "Covered Employees") will not be deductible by the Corporation for federal income tax purposes unless certain conditions are met. One condition is that the compensation qualify as "performance-based compensation." In addition to other requirements for qualification as performance-based compensation, shareholders must be advised of and approve the material terms of the performance goals under which such compensation is to be paid.

Set forth below is a summary of certain important features of the Incentive Plan and the Incentive Plan Amendments, which summary is qualified in its entirety by reference to the full text of the Incentive Plan, as amended and restated, which is published in the 1997 proxy statement as Attachment #1. The proposed substantive amendments are shown in italics in the Attachment.

The Incentive Plan will continue to be administered by the Compensation Committee. Officers and employees of the Company and its 50-percent-owned subsidiaries who hold executive, administrative, supervisory, technical, or other key positions are eligible to participate in the Incentive Plan. In certain cases, employees in other positions within the Company and certain former employees may receive awards under the Incentive Plan. As of February 24, 1997, approximately 2,000 employees were eligible to participate in the Incentive Plan.

The Incentive Plan provides the Committee with complete discretion to make awards of cash, Boeing common stock, "Boeing Stock Units" (the right to receive Boeing common stock and the dividends thereon at the end of a three-year vesting period), or a combination thereof to employees who are eligible for awards under the Incentive Plan. The Committee may also establish programs under the Incentive Plan to provide for long-term incentive awards to selected senior executives. The long-term incentive program previously in effect under the Plan is currently being phased out. The Committee has authority to establish a long-term incentive program in the future, at which time performance criteria and employee maximums may be specified. The Committee may authorize the chief executive officer of the Company (who may in turn authorize other executive officers of the Company) to make awards under the Incentive Plan to certain eligible employees. Awards under the Incentive Plan may be deferral arrangements, and the Company may deduct from the payment of an award withholdings required by law or amounts owed by the award recipient to the company or to a subsidiary of the Company.

The Incentive Plan Amendments provide that payments to participants in the Incentive Plan are limited each year to an aggregate of 6 percent of "Plan Earnings" for the previous year. Plan Earnings are defined as the net earnings of the Company for the year, as reported by the Company in its consolidated financial statements, adjusted to exclude income tax, certain non-recurring and extraordinary items, the Company Share Value Trust, and the Incentive Plan. The amount paid to Covered Employees under the Incentive Plan Amendments is limited to 1 percent of Plan Earnings, with a maximum of 0.3 percent of Plan Earnings for the chief executive officer, 0.2 percent of Plan Earnings for the second most highly compensated Covered Employee and 0.167 percent of Plan Earnings for each of the other three Covered Employees. The Committee has the discretion to reduce amounts awarded to Covered Employees below these maximum levels, but does not have the discretion to increase the amount awarded to a Covered Employee beyond the maximum levels of compensation established by the Incentive Plan. Prior to the Incentive Plan Amendments, the Incentive Plan provided that the Company's Board of Directors could set aside each year for awards under the Incentive Plan a fund in an amount not in excess of 6 percent of "profit subject to the plan" for such year, as such term was defined in the Incentive Plan, and that no person could receive from the fund for any one-year awards in excess of 5 percent of the fund.

The Incentive Plan Amendments provide that the Incentive Plan may be amended by a majority vote of the Company shareholders or Board of Directors, except that the Company's shareholders must approve any amendment that would increase the number of shares available for issuance under the Incentive Plan, change the performance criterion or goal governing the amount that may be paid to Covered Employees, or change the requirements for amending the Incentive Plan. Prior to the Incentive Plan Amendments, a two-thirds vote by the Company's shareholders or Board of Directors was required to amend the Incentive Plan, with shareholder approval required for any amendment that would increase the amount that could be set aside for any year, increase the percentage of the Incentive Plan fund set aside for any year that could be awarded to one participant, or change the requirements for amending the Incentive Plan.

The Incentive Plan Amendments identify the total of 5 million shares of Boeing common stock that continue to be available under the Incentive Plan and may be used for making awards under the Incentive Plan. Prior to the Incentive Plan Amendments, an aggregate share limit was not required to be stated under the Incentive Plan.

The Board of Directors Unanimously Recommends a Vote FOR this Amendment.

Attachment 1

Incentive Compensation Plan for Officers and Employees of The Boeing Company and Subsidiaries (As Amended and Restated)

1. Definitions. As used in this plan (the "Plan"), the following terms have the meanings set forth below:

"Board of Directors" means the Board of Directors of The Boeing Company;

"BSU" means Boeing Stock Unit, as described in Section 5.2;

"Common Stock" means the common stock of The Boeing Company;

"Company" means The Boeing Company;

"Committee" means the Compensation Committee of the Board of Directors;

"Covered Employee" means each of (i) an employee of the Company who on the last day of the year with respect to which an award is made is (or serves in the capacity of) the Company's Chief Executive Officer and (ii) the four most highly compensated executive officers of the Company, other than the Company's Chief Executive Officer, whose total compensation for that year is reported to Company's shareholders in accordance with the provisions of the Securities Exchange Act of 1934, as amended;

"Earnings Credit BSUs" has the meaning given in Section 5.2;

"Exchange" means The New York Stock Exchange;

"Fair Market Value" means, as to a particular day, the mean of the high and low per-share trading prices for the Common Stock as reported for such day in *The Wall Street Journal* or in such other source as the Committee deems reliable;

"Plan Earnings" for a particular year means the net earnings of the Company for such year, as reported on the Company's consolidated financial statement included in its Annual Report on Form 10-K for such year, adjusted to eliminate the following:

(i) Federal and state taxes on income.

(ii) Awards under the Plan,

(ii) Restructuring or similar charges to the extent they are separately disclosed in such annual Report,

(iv) The effect of changes in accounting principles,

(v) The effect on net earnings for the accrued distributable appreciation of the Company's Share Value Program, and

(vi) "extraordinary items" determined under generally accepted accounting principles;

"Subsidiary" means any corporation or association more than 50 percent of the voting securities of which are owned directly or indirectly by the Company or by one or more of its other Subsidiaries and the accounts of which are customarily consolidated with those of the Company for the purpose of reporting to stockholders.

2. Committee. The Committee shall have full power and authority to administer the Plan, and to construe and interpret its terms and provisions. Decisions of the Committee shall be final and binding upon all parties.

3. Eligibility.

3.1 Key Employees. Officers and employees of the Company and its Subsidiaries who hold executive, administrative, supervisory, technical, or other key positions shall be eligible for participation under the Plan, and participants shall for the most part be selected from among Company or of a Subsidiary who is not also an officer or employee of the Company or of a Subsidiary shall be eligible for participation under the Plan.

3.2 Special Contributors; Former Employees. Awards may also be made under the Plan to employees not holding executive, administrative, supervisory, technical, or other key positions who have, nevertheless, made a substantial contribution to the success of the

Company and its Subsidiaries. In addition, a former employee who has either:

(a) Retired under the employee retirement plan of the Company or of a Subsidiary or,

(b) Left the service of the company or of a Subsidiary to enter the armed services and, who would have been eligible for an award but for such retirement or termination of service, may be eligible for an award for the year in which such employee retires or so leaves the service of the Company or of a Subsidiary. In the case of a former employee who would have been eligible for an award but for death, an award may be granted to the surviving spouse or children or to the estate of such former employee, as the Committee may determine in its sole discretion.

4. Making Awards.

4.1. Committee Authority. The Committee shall make awards, subject to the limitations herein, to such individuals within the eligible group and in such amounts and at such times as, in the Committee's judgment, shall best serve the interest of the Company and its Subsidiaries at that time, taking into account each individual's job performance and contributions to the success of the Company and its Subsidiaries.

Except as provided in Section 4.2, the Committee shall have complete discretion in determining to whom awards under the Plan shall be made and when awards shall be paid, including whether all or any portion of any award shall be paid in installments over two or more years, provided, however, in making awards the Committee shall request and consider the recommendations of the Chief Executive Officer of the Company and others whom it may designate.

4.2 Delegation of Award-Making Authority and Award Recommendations. The Committee may, at such times or times as it elects, authorize the Chief Executive Officer of the Company who in turn may authorize other executives of the Company to make additional awards subject to the limitations herein provided, in amounts not exceeding an aggregate amount and under conditions determined by the Committee. In making recommendations to the Committee and in making awards authorized by the Committee, the Chief Executive

Officer of the Company shall request and consider the recommendations of other officers and supervisory employees of the Company and its Subsidiaries.

4.3 Forms of Awards. Awards may be made entirely in cash, in Common Stock, in stock units, or on any combination thereof as determined by the Committee, provided, however, awards made by the Chief Executive Officer or authorized executives of the Company shall be made only in cash or Common Stock or a combination thereof.

4.4 Limits on awards.

4.4.1 Limit on the Number of Shares Awarded. Not more than five million (5,000,000) shares of Common Stock may be used for the purpose of making awards under the Plan. The number of shares awarded under the Plan in any one year shall be consistent with the total number of shares identified in this Section 4.4 being available over the projected twenty-year minimum life of the Plan.

4.4.2 Annual Limit on Value of Awards. The aggregate value of all awards granted under the Plan (including awards granted under Section 4.5 to Covered Employees) in any one calendar year shall not exceed 6 percent of Plan Earnings for the previous year.

4.5 Awards to Covered Employees. Notwithstanding any other provisions of this Section 4, any award under the Plan to a Covered Employee must satisfy the requirements of this Section 4.5. The purpose of this Section 4.5 is to ensure compliance by this Plan with the requirements of Section 162(m) of the Internal Revenue Code of 1986, as amended, related to performance-based compensation. Covered Employees status is determined for the year with respect to which the award is made, rather than the year of payment.

Awards to Covered Employees are subject to:

(a) Approval of this Plan and of the criterion stated in Section 4.4.1 by the shareholders of the Company;

(b) The maximum amount that may be awarded to any Covered Employee under the Plan for any year as stated in Section 4.5.1; and

(c) Approval by the Committee.

4.5.1 Criterion; Maximum Awards. The maximum potential awards under the Plan to Covered Employees for any year shall be the respective percentages of Plan Earnings for such year as follows:

Covered Employee	*Maximum Potential Award as* Percentage of Plan Earnings
Chief Executive Officer	Three-tenths of one percent (0.3%)
The most highly compensated Covered Employee other than the Chief Executive Officer	Two-tenths of one percent (0.2%)
Each other Covered Employee	One-sixth of one percent (0.167%)
Total	One Percent

4.5.2 Shareholder Approval of Performance Goal. The criterion established in Section 4.5.1 on which awards under the Plan are based shall first apply in the year 1997, but such criterion and any awards based thereon shall be conditional upon a vote of the shareholders of the Company approving the Plan and the criterion and performance goal stated herein.

4.5.3 Approval; Committee Discretion. The Committee shall make a determination in writing as to whether the Covered Employees have met the performance goal for the year. The Committee may, in its sole discretion, reduce amounts of awards to all or any of the Covered Employees from the maximum potential awards allocated by application of Section 4.5.1. No such reduction shall increase the amount of the award payable to any other Covered Employee. The Committee shall determine the amount of any reduction in a Covered Employee's award on the basis of such factors as it deems relevant, and it shall not be required to establish any allocation or weighting component with respect to the factors it considers. The Committee shall have no discretion to increase an award above the amount determined by application of Section 4.5.1.

5. Certain Types of Awards

5.1 Long-Term Incentive Program. Subject to the other terms and conditions of this Plan, the Committee may make awards, in capital stock of the Company or otherwise, to selected senior executives within the eligible group pursuant to a program adopted by the Committee providing for long-term incentive awards; and the Committee may in connection therewith reduce other awards under the Plan to such executives.

5.2 BSUs. Subject to other terms and conditions of the Plan, the Committee may direct that all or part of an award shall be made in the form of BSUs. BSU awards shall be subject to the following terms and conditions:

5.2.1 Calculation of Award Amount. A participant shall be credited with BSUs equal in number to either:

(i)   The number of shares specified in the grant of the award, or

(ii) The number of shares of Common Stock that could be purchased with the BSU portion of an award otherwise denominated in cash, based on the Fair Market Value of such stock on the day of the award (or on the next business day on which the Exchange is open, if the Exchange is closed on the day of the award) excluding commissions, taxes, and other charges. Such number shall be carried to two decimal places.

For purposes of the Plan, a "participant" includes an employee or former employee having a BSU account under the Plan; and the number of BSUs in a participant's account shall be appropriately adjusted to reflect stock splits, stock dividends and other like adjustments in the Common Stock.

5.2.2 Participant Accounts. The Company shall maintain accounts for each participant to whom BSUs have been credited, and shall annually report to each participant his or her BSU account balance.

5.2.3 Vesting of BSU Awards. BSUs shall vest three years after the date the award is made or (if earlier) on the date the participant dies, retires, is laid off, or becomes disabled and entitled to Disability Retirement Income under the Company's employee retirement plan or under comparable provisions of a Subsidiary's retirement plan.

5.2.4 Earnings Credit on BSU Awards. Each participant's BSU account shall be credited with Earnings Credit BSUs equal in number to the number of shares of Common Stock that could be purchased with cash dividends that would be payable on the number of shares of Common Stock that equals the number of BSUs in each participant's account. Determination of the number of shares so credited shall be made in the manner described in Section 5.2.1 as to cash-denominated awards, as of each dividend payment date for the Common Stock. Participants shall be notified annually of the number of Earnings Credit BSUs in their accounts. Earnings Credit BSUs shall vest at the same time as the BSUs with which they are associated.

5.2.5 Forfeiture of Non-Vested BSU Awards. If a participant's employment with the Company or a Subsidiary terminates prior to the expiration of three years from the date an award is made, for any reason other than death, retirement, layoff, or disability, the participant's BSUs from such award shall be forfeited and canceled. Earnings Credit BSUs shall be forfeited and canceled along with the BSUs with which they are associated.

5.2.6 BSU Awards Payable in Cash or Stock. Distributions from a participant's BSU account shall be made as soon as reasonably possible after the vesting date of the BSUs. In the absence of an election to the contrary by the participant, distributions shall be in cash. A cash distribution shall equal the cash value, on the date as of which the distribution is calculated (which shall be the vesting date, unless some other date is prescribed by the Committee), of that number of whole shares of Common Stock equal to the whole number of vested BSUs in the participant's account on such date, based on the Fair Market Value of such stock on that date (or on the next day on which the Exchange is open, if the Exchange is closed on the date as of which the distribution is calculated). Any distribution in stock shall be in whole shares of Common Stock equal in number to the whole number of vested BSUs in the participant's account, adjusted in accordance with Section 5.2.7. No fractional shares shall be distributed, and any account balance remaining after a stock distribution shall be added to the required withholdings provided for in Section 5.2.7.

5.2.7 Deferral of BSU Awards. Participants may elect to defer distribution of vested BSUs through the Company's Deferred Compensation Plan. Such deferral elections must be made in the manner and at the times prescribed in that plan.

6. Distribution of Awards

6.1 Terms; Deferred Payment. Distribution of awards shall be governed by the terms and conditions applicable to such awards, as determined by the Committee or its delegate. An award, the payment of which is to be deferred pursuant to the terms of an employment agreement, shall be paid as provided by the terms of such agreement. Awards or portions thereof deferred pursuant to the Company's Deferred Compensation Plan or other deferral arrangement shall be paid as provided in such plan or arrangement. Any other awards the payment of which has been deferred, in whole or in part, shall be paid as determined by the Committee.

6.2 Deductions. The Company shall deduct from the payment of each award any withholdings required by law or required by Section 5.2.6; and the Company may deduct any amounts due from the recipient to the Company or a Subsidiary.

6.3 Notice; Distribution Date. The Committee or its delegates shall advise participants of their awards under the Plan, and shall fix the distribution date or dates for such awards. Awards shall be paid on the distribution date or as soon thereafter as reasonably possible. The number of shares of stock to be issued in payment of awards otherwise denominated in cash shall be determined based on the closing trading price per share of the Common Stock as reported for the business day immediately preceding the applicable distribution date in *The Wall Street Journal* or in such other source as the Committee deems reliable.

7. Repeal; Amendments. The Plan and any and all provisions hereof may be repealed or amended either:

(a) By the affirmative vote of the holders of record of a majority of the shares of stock present in person or by proxy and entitled to vote at any meeting of the shareholders of the Company at which a quorum is present if the notice of such meeting sets forth the form of the proposal for such repeal or amendment or a summary thereof, or

(b) The affirmative vote of a majority of the Board of Directors at any meeting if the notice of such meeting sets forth the form of the proposal for such repeal or amendment or a summary thereof, provided, however, that the Company's shareholders must approve, by a vote meeting the requirements of clause (a) above, any amendment that would:

   (i) Amend Section 4.4.1 so as to increase the number of shares available for issuance under the Plan, or

(ii) Amend Section 4.5.1 so as to change the criterion or goal governing the amount which may be awarded to any Covered Employee or the formula used to determine such amount, or

(iii) Change the definition of Covered Employee, or

(iv) Amend this Section 7.

No repeal or amendment of the Plan shall operate to annul or modify any award previously made under the Plan.

8. Nonassignability. No awards authorized or made pursuant to the Plan shall be subject in any manner to anticipation, alienation, sale, transfer, assignment, pledge, encumbrance, charge, execution, attachment, garnishment, or any other legal process, and any attempt to subject an award to any of the foregoing shall be void.

Index

[References are to question numbers.]

A

Accounting considerations
accounting statements containing
compensation expenses, 1:44
annual incentives, 4:8
APB 25, 1:45–1:48, 1:54
book value appreciation rights, 7:14
book value purchase plans, 6:43
club membership, 10:8
combination performance
share/stock option plans, 8:7
company car programs, 10:9
compensation forms, 1:43
convertible debentures, 6:50
EPS calculations, 1:52, 1:53
executive perquisites, 10:3
expense accounts, 10:7
fair value calculation models, 1:50
FAS 123, 1:45–1:49, 1:51, 20:15
FASB stock option regulations, 1:54,
20:15
fundamental issues, 1:43–1:54
home offices, computers, car
phones, 10:10
ISOs, 6:9
long-term incentive plans, 5:25
nonstatutory stock options, 6:16

option reloads, 6:38
performance-based stock options,
6:64
performance share plans, 7:48
performance unit plans, 7:41
phantom stock plans, 7:23
premium stock options, 6:33
restricted stock grants, 7:32
restricted stock/stock option plan
combination, 8:14
SARs, 7:7
SAR/stock option plans, 8:22
stock awards, 1:45
stock options, FAS 123, 1:54, 20:15
Accumulation. *See* Capital
Administration of plan. *See* Plan administration
Alternative minimum tax
defined, 1:42
increase in ISO rates from lower
capital gains tax, 20:19
ISO, 6:8, 20:19
Amendment
long-term incentive plan, 5:58
Annual incentives
accounting treatment, 4:8
appropriateness, 1:20

[References are to question numbers.]

Annual incentives (*cont'd*)
  characteristics of appropriate organizations, 1:21
  defined, 4:1
  eligibility, 4:4
  establishing, small company, 12:2
  for expatriates, 16:23
  funding incentive plans, 4:57–4:65
  general considerations, 4:1–4:9
  vs. long-term incentives, 1:23, 1:29
  market competition, 3:9
  meeting needs of executives and company, 1:3
  nonprofit organization, 14:10–14:14
  payment forms, 4:5
  pensionable, 4:6
  performance maximums, 4:54
  performance measures, 4:35–4:48
  performance standards, 4:49–4:56
  plan design, 4:10–4:34, 12:10
  prevalence, 4:2
  public sector, 17:8
  rationale, 4:3
  shareholder approval, 4:9
  short-term vs. long-term performance, 1:22
  tax impact, 4:7
Annual salary increase. *See* Salary increases
APB 25. *See* Accounting considerations
Appreciation plans
  book value appreciation rights, 7:13–7:17
  defined, 7:1
  examples, 7:2
  generally, 7:1, 7:2
  stock appreciation rights, 7:3–7:12
Appreciation right. *See* Stock
Approval
  total compensation strategy, 11:24
Assets. *See also* Return on assets
  sample employment agreement, Appendix D

Award
  long-term incentive
    plan design, 5:29
      salary multiple approach, 5:30
      targeted income approach, 5:31
    performance plan
      tax effect, 5:45
    performance unit plans, 7:43
  size
    annual incentive plans, 4:57
    nonprofit organization annual incentive, 14:11
  stock
    accounting, 1:45
    changes in levels, 20:8
    non-compete clauses, 20:10
    outside directors, 20:14
    public sector, 17:9
    temporary executives, 18:11

B

Banding. *See* Salary banding; other increases
Base salary
  above average, 3:10
  administration, new ideas, 20:4
  change in levels
    large company, 20:1
    public company, 20:2
    small company, 20:3
  change in mix with annual incentives, 20:7
  establishing, 3:1, 3:2
  determining total compensation mix, 1:18
  fundamental issues, 1:16–1:18
  geographic location, 1:16
  job evaluation, 3:3–3:10
  market competition, 3:9
  merit increase, nonprofit organization, 14:9

Index

needs of executives vs. those of company, 1:2
new venture businesses, 12:13
vs. other total compensation elements, 1:17
public companies, 17:2
range
    alternatives to, 3:13
    nonprofit organization, 14:8
salary banding; other increases, 3:13–3:16
salary increases, 3:11, 3:12
small company considerations, 12:5
temporary executives, 18:9
Benefits. *See also* Excess benefit plans; Executive benefit plans
costs, total compensation strategy statement, 11:12
insured, temporary executives, 18:13
new venture businesses, 12:13
programs, total compensation strategy statement, 11:11
retirement
    temporary executives, 18:14
    total compensation strategy statement, 11:13
satisfying executive needs, 1:4
Black-Scholes option pricing model, 1:45, 1:47, 1:49, 1:50, 5:26
Board of directors compensation
choosing board members, 13:1
compensation methods, 13:7–13:13
deferred compensation, 13:8
general considerations, 13:1, 13:2
Keogh plans, 13:16, 13:17
other benefits, 13:14–13:19
outside vs. inside directors, 13:3–13:6
performance-based plans, 13:9
perquisites, 13:19
retirement benefits, 13:15
role, 13:2
stock options, 13:10–13:13
taxation of income, 13:7

trends, 13:18
remuneration levels, 20:12
retirement plan prevalence, 20:13
stock awards, 20:14
Bonus
annual, trends, 20:5
completion, 16:19
hiring bonus, as perquisite, 10:11
payout schedules, trends, 20:6
plans, long-term, for expatriates, 16:22
small company considerations, 12:5
Book value appreciation rights
accounting impact, 7:14
advantages, 7:16
defined, 7:13
disadvantages, 7:17
tax treatment, 7:15
Book value purchase plans
accounting impact, 6:43
advantages, 6:45
appropriate companies, 6:47
defined, 6:42
disadvantages, 6:46
tax treatment, 6:44
Building a total compensation strategy. *See* Total compensation
Business plan
total compensation strategy, 11:7
Business unit
affecting total compensation strategies, 11:16
strategic, use of EVA, 19:6
Buy-back agreement
example, 2:9

C

Capital. *See also* Return on capital
accumulation
    plans, total compensation strategy statement, 11:15
    stock-based, 2:6
costs, effect of executives on, 19:5

[References are to question numbers.]

Capital (*cont'd*)
  gains
    avoiding, expatriates, 16:17
    changes in rates, 20:18, 20:19
    defined, 1:37
    rationale for favorable treatment,
      1:38
Car programs. *See* Memberships and
  other common perquisites
Cash compensation
  total, 1:6
  trends, 20:1–20:7
Cashless exercise
  cashless option exercise defined,
    5:51
  vs. SAR, 7:6
Checklist
  executive expatriate compensation
    program, 16:32
Classification system, 3:5
Closely held company
  defined, 2:3
  privately held company as, 2:4
Club membership. *See* Memberships
  and other common perquisites
Code Section 162(m)
  clarifications by IRS in 1996, 1:34
  company response to pay caps, 1:34
Code Section 457 deferred plan
  defined, 9:75
  example, 9:76
Code Section 83
  Code Section 83(b) election, de-
    fined, 5:48
  tax property transfer, 9:81
COLI
  vs. retail life insurance contracts,
    9:34
  tax considerations, 10:12
Combination long-term plans. *See*
  Long-term incentive plans
Communications
  EVA, 19:11
  total compensation strategy, 11:25

Company car programs. *See* Memberships and other common perquisites
Company merger. *See* Merger
Company performance
  effect on total compensation, 1:14
  graph requirement, 2:31
Company philosophy. *See* Corporate
  philosophy
Company plane. *See* Memberships
  and other common perquisites
Company size. *See* Size of company
Comparison of plans. *See* Plan comparisons
Compensation
  agreements, sample, Appendix B
  compensation committee, defined,
    2:25
  philosophy. *See* Corporate philoso-
    phy
Competitive market. *See* Market competition
Completion bonus
  defined, 16:19
Computers. *See* Memberships and
  other common perquisites
Constructive receipt
  and long-term incentives, 5:39, 5:46
  nonqualified deferred compensation
    plan contributions, 9:79
Contributions
  funded vs. unfunded top-hat plan,
    9:63
  nonqualified deferred compensation
    plan
      constructive receipt, 9:79
      economic benefit doctrine, 9:80
Convertible debentures
  accounting impact, 6:50
  advantages, 6:53
  appropriate companies, 6:55
  defined, 6:48
  disadvantages, 6:54
  EPS impact, 6:52
  shareholder approval, 6:49

Index

tax treatment, 6:51

Corporate level
classification, 3:5, 3:6
effect on total compensation, 1:10
performance measures, 4:45
ranking, 3:4

Corporate philosophy
compensation method chosen, 1:27
plan design, 5:27
primary disadvantage of long-term performance plans, 5:28
total compensation strategy, 11:5

Cost of living allowance, 16:5

Costs
benefits, total compensation strategy statement, 11:12
of capital, effect of executives on, 19:5
retirement plans
small company considerations, 12:6
special early retirement programs, 15:5

Currency fluctuation
expatriate protection, 16:18

D

Debentures. *See* Convertible debentures

Deferred compensation
board of directors, 13:8
constructive receipt, 5:46
defined, 9:4
integration during company merger, 5:61, 5:62
nonqualified deferred compensation plan, 9:6–9:26, 9:79
primary approaches, 9:5

Design. *See* Plan design

Dilution
incentive stock options, 6:10
nonqualified stock option, 6:17

Directors. *See* Board of directors compensation

Disability. *See also* Executive disability income insurance plans
executive disability income insurance plans
funding, 9:52
operation, 9:47
premium rates, 9:51
tax considerations, 9:48–9:50
total compensation strategy statement, 11:14
for expatriates, 16:26

Disclosure
excess benefit plans, 9:73
FAS 123, 1:51
nonqualified deferred compensation plan, 9:22
proxy statement
information charts, 2:27
long-term incentive, 5:59
other information, 2:28

Discounted stock options
accounting impact, 6:26
advantages, 6:27
defined, 6:23
depth of discount, 6:29
disadvantages, 6:28
prevalence, 6:24
tax treatment, 6:25

Discretionary plan
advantages, 4:28
defined, 4:27
disadvantages, 4:29

Dividends
phantom stock plans, 7:21
sample wage dividend plan, Appendix B

E

Early retirement. *See* Special early retirement programs

[References are to question numbers.]

Earnings per share
calculations
and definition, 4:38
FASB guidelines, 1:52, 1:53
and convertible debentures, 6:52
incentive stock option, 6:10
Economic benefit doctrine
defined, 5:47
nonqualified deferred compensation
plan contributions, 9:80
Economic pay increases, 3:13
Economic value added
communicating to executives, 19:11
correlation to shareholder value,
19:7
defined, 5:9, 19:1
disadvantages, 19:3
effect of executives on cost of capital, 19:5
example of successful EVA plan,
19:13
example of unsuccessful EVA plan,
19:14
implementation, 19:8
link to executive compensation,
19:10
linking stock options, 19:9
non-executives, 19:12
plan implementation, 5:10
plan trends, 20:11
rationale for using, 19:2
use, 19:4
use in business divisions or SBUs,
19:6
**Economic value/shareholder value
plans**
vs. performance plans, 5:23
vs. stock plans, 5:22
Education allowance, 16:9
Election
Code Section 83(b), 5:48
S corporation status, 2:12, 2:13
Section 83(b), and restricted stock
grant, 7:34

Emerging company. *See* Start-up company
Employee-owned life insurance, 9:35
Employment agreements
advantages, 10:18
company president, Appendix D
disadvantages, 10:19
enforceability of contract term, 10:21
example, 10:20
noncompetition, 10:22
pursuant to merger, Appendix D
sample, Appendix D
with sole shareholder, Appendix D
Entertainment expense
reimbursement, 10:6
Entrepreneurial company
total compensation strategy statement, 11:28
Equity. *See* Return on equity
ERISA considerations
excess benefit plans, 9:71–9:73
funded vs. unfunded plan, 9:54, 9:55
nonqualified deferred compensation
plan, 9:53, 9:55
special early retirement program,
15:8
split-dollar life insurance, 9:37
top-hat plan, 9:58, 9:61–9:63
Estate planning
split-dollar life insurance, 9:45
EVA. *See* Economic value added
Excess benefit plans
benefits, 9:69
defined, 9:65
ERISA requirements, 9:71–9:73
example, 9:74
limitations, 9:70
plan qualification, 9:67
rationale, 9:68
vs. SERP, 9:66
tax considerations, 9:77, 9:78

[References are to question numbers.]

Excess parachute payment. *See* Golden parachute
Executive benefit plans
  ERISA considerations, 9:53–9:55
  excess benefit plans, 9:65–9:74
  executive disability income insurance, 9:47–9:52
  failure of traditional benefit programs, 9:2
  funding arrangements, 9:27–9:31
  general considerations, 9:1–9:3
  importance, 9:1
  insurance-related nonqualified deferred compensation plans, 9:32–9:35
  nonqualified plans in nonprofit organizations, 9:75, 9:76
  nonqualified retirement plans, 9:4–9:26
  overall compensation, 9:3
  split-dollar life insurance, 9:36–9:46
  tax considerations, 9:77–9:81
  top-hat plans or SERPs, 9:56–9:64
Executive disability income insurance plans. *See* Disability
Executive performance
  effect on total compensation, 1:15
Expatriates
  annual incentives, 4:30
  cost of living allowance, 16:5
  defined, 16:1
  education allowance, 16:9
  foreign service premium, 16:3
  general considerations, 16:1–16:11
  hardship allowance, 16:4
  home leave, 16:11
  home rental program, 16:8
  housing allowance, 16:6
  language training, 16:10
  reimbursement, home sale or other relocation costs, 16:7
  special compensation
    annual incentive plans, 16:23
    checklist, 16:32

    completion bonus, 16:19
    currency fluctuation, 16:18
    free-standing stock appreciation rights, 16:21
    home country balance sheet compensation program, 16:31
    life insurance and disability, 16:26
    long-term bonus plans, 16:22
    medical benefits, 16:24
    net to net compensation program, 16:30
    pension plan, 16:25
    perquisites, 16:27
    repatriation, 16:28
    second assignment, 16:29
    stock options, 16:20
  tax considerations
    avoiding taxes, 16:16, 16:17
    foreign earned income exclusions, 16:15
    spendable income, 16:14
    tax equalization, 16:12
    tax-free income, 16:13
  temporary executives, 18:16
  typical compensation elements, 16:2
Expenses
  accounting statements, 1:44
  expense accounts. *See* Perquisites and other benefits; Reimbursement

F

Factor comparison, 3:7
Fair value calculation. *See* Valuation
Family-owned company
  stock provision to non-family members, 12:7
FAS 123. *See* Accounting considerations
FASB
  EPS calculations, 1:52, 1:53
  FAS 123, 1:45–1:49, 1:51
  stock option regulations, 1:54

Fees
board of directors, 13:6
FICA
deferred compensation arrangements, 9:20
Fiduciary issues
nonqualified deferred compensation plan, 9:24
Financial institutions
performance measures, 4:47
Financial performance measures
in annual incentive plans, 4:37
Financial planning perquisites, 10:16
First class travel. *See* Memberships and other common perquisites
Foreign earned income exclusions. *See* Tax considerations
Foreign service premium, 16:3
Forfeiture. *See* Substantial risk of forfeiture
Free-standing stock appreciation rights, 16:21
Full-value plans
choice, 7:19
defined, 7:18
generally, 7:18, 7:19
performance share plans, 7:46–7:48
performance unit plans, 7:39–7:45
phantom stock plans, 7:20–7:29
restricted stock grants, 7:30–7:38
Fundamental concepts
accounting considerations, 1:43–1:54
base salary, 1:16–1:18
incentive plans, 1:19–1:30
tax considerations, 1:31–1:42
total compensation issues, 1:1–1:15
Funding arrangements
annual incentive plans
factors driving amounts, 4:58
maximums or caps, 4:65
participant method, 4:62–4:64
pool method, 4:59–4:62
size of award, 4:57
excess benefit plans, 9:72

executive disability income insurance plans, 9:52
funded plan
contributions, 9:18
excess benefit plans, taxation, 9:77
top-hat plan, 9:62, 9:63
vs. unfunded plan, 9:54, 9:55, 9:63
life insurance, 9:31
nonqualified deferred compensation plan, 9:23
nonqualified deferred compensation plan, 9:53
rabbi escrow agreement, defined, 9:27
rabbi trust
defined, 9:28
vs. secular trust, 9:30
secular trust
defined, 9:29
vs. rabbi trust, 9:30
special early retirement programs, 15:5
top-hat plans or SERPs, 9:62
FUTA
deferred compensation arrangements, 9:20

G

Geographic location
effect on base salary, 1:16
Golden parachute
criticisms, 10:28
defined, 10:24
example, 10:25
excess
avoiding negative tax impact, 10:31
defined, 10:30
penalties, 10:29
rationale, 10:27

[References are to question numbers.]

Group term life. *See* Life insurance

Growth company
total compensation strategy statement, 11:28

Growth or improvement plan
advantages, 4:16
disadvantages, 4:17
operation, 4:15

Guidelines
EPS calculations, 1:52, 1:53
incentive plan design, 1:24

H

Hardship allowance, 16:4

High-growth company
competitive values despite growth, 12:9
total compensation strategy statement, 11:28

Hiring bonus. *See* Bonus

Home leave, 16:11

Home office. *See* Memberships and other common perquisites

Home rental program, 16:8

Housing allowance, 16:6

I

Incentives
annual
accounting treatment, 4:8
appropriateness, 1:20
change in mix with base salary, 20:7
characteristics of appropriate organizations, 1:21
defined, 4:1
eligibility, 4:4
establishing, small company, 12:2
for expatriates, 16:23
funding incentive plans, 4:57–4:65

general considerations, 4:1–4:9
vs. long-term incentives, 1:23, 1:29
market competition, 3:9
meeting needs of executives and company, 1:3
nonprofit organization, 14:10–14:14
payment forms, 4:5
pensionable, 4:6
performance maximums, 4:54
performance measures, 4:35–4:48
performance standards, 4:49–4:56
plan design, 4:10–4:34, 12:10
prevalence, 4:2
public sector, 17:8
rationale, 4:3
shareholder approval, 4:9
short-term vs. long-term performance, 1:22
tax impact, 4:7
eligibility, 1:25
fundamental issues, 1:19–1:30
guidelines for plan design, 1:24
long-term incentives
vs. annual, 1:23, 1:29
common forms in private companies, 2:7
determining, 11:22
meeting needs of executives and company, 1:3
negative effect of not providing in privately held company, 2:10
nonprofit organizations, 14:15
performance plan vs. other long-term incentives, 5:19
small company, 12:4
stock-based plan vs. other long-term incentives, 5:20
new venture businesses, 12:13
rationale, 1:19
short-term incentive, determining, 11:21
stock plans, 1:30
temporary executives, 18:10

[References are to question numbers.]

Incentive stock options
accounting impact, 6:9
advantages, 6:12
alternative minimum tax, 20:19
AMT effect on tax treatment, 6:8
defined, 6:6
disadvantages, 6:13
fully diluted EPS, 6:10
vs. nonstatutory stock options, 6:22
prevalence, 6:11
tax treatment, 6:7

Income
ordinary, 1:36

Independent contractor
temporary executives, 18:2–18:4

Indexed stock options
defined, 6:65

Industry type
effect on total compensation, 1:11

Insurance. *See also* Executive disability income insurance plans; Life insurance
insurance-related nonqualified deferred compensation plans
COLI vs. retail life insurance, 9:34
employee-owned life insurance, 9:35
funding with life insurance other than COLI, 9:33
life insurance to fund promise, 9:32
key man, 10:14
plan termination, nonqualified deferred compensation plan, 9:25
public sector, 17:10
temporary executives, 18:13

International business
total compensation strategies, 11:17

IRS
clarifications to Code Section 162(m), 1:34

J

Job evaluation
base salary above average classification system, 3:5
defined, 3:3
factor comparison, 3:7
labor market values, 3:8
market competition, base salary and annual incentive, 3:9
point factor approach, 3:6
public vs. private companies, 17:3
ranking system, 3:4

Junior stock plans
advantages, 6:57
defined, 6:56
disadvantages, 6:58
prevalence, 6:59

K

Keogh plans
board of directors, 13:16, 13:17

Key man insurance, 10:14

L

Language training
expatriates, 16:10

Level within the corporation. *See* Corporate level

Life cycle
total compensation strategy, 11:8

Life insurance
for expatriates, 16:26
funding promise, 9:31–9:35
insurance-related nonqualified deferred compensation plans, 9:31–9:35
split-dollar
common applications, 9:42
defined, 9:36, 10:13

[References are to question numbers.]

enhancing nonqualified retirement plan, 9:46
ERISA, 9:37
estate planning, 9:45
executive payment of part of premium, 9:39
policy splitting, 9:38–9:40
problems of group term life insurance plans, 9:43
replacing group coverage, 9:44
retirement, 9:41
supplemental, as perquisite, 10:12
total compensation strategy statement, 11:14
Loans. *See* Memberships and other
common perquisites
Local nationals
annual incentives, 4:31
Long-term bonus plans. *See* Bonus
Long-term compensation plan
sample, Appendix B
trends
changes in stock award levels, 20:8
economic value-added plans,
20:11
non-compete clauses in stock
award plans, 20:10
use of performance-based stock
options, 20:9
Long-term incentive plans
appreciation plans, 7:1–7:17
characteristics, 5:2
combination long-term plans
common compensation combinations, 8:5
general considerations, 8:1–8:5
parallel plans, 8:2, 8:3, 8:4
performance share/stock option
plans, 8:6–8:11
restricted stock/stock option
plans, 8:12–8:18
SAR/stock option plans, 8:19–8:23
tandem plans, 8:1, 8:3, 8:4
compensation philosophy, 5:27, 5:28

considerations, 5:6
currently emerging, 5:8
defined, 5:1
economic value-added
defined, 5:9
implementation, 5:10
eligibility, 5:3
exercising a stock option, 5:49–5:56
full-value plans, 7:18–7:48
general considerations, 5:1–5:14
long-term performance plan, defined, 5:13
objectives, 1:28
omnibus plan, 5:38
plan administration, 5:57–5:62
plan comparisons
basic accounting issues, 5:25
Black-Scholes option pricing
model, 5:26
getting executives to own stock,
5:21
performance plan vs. other long-
term incentives, 5:19
shareholder value/economic
value plans vs. performance
plans, 5:23
shareholder value/economic
value plans vs. stock plans, 5:22
stock-based plans vs. other long-
term incentives, 5:20
stock option plan vs. long-term
performance plan, 5:15, 5:17
stock option plan vs. restricted
share plan, 5:16, 5:18
tax rules, 5:24
plan design, 5:29–5:31
prevalence, 5:4
principal types, 5:7
rationale, 5:5
shareholder value
defined, 5:11
plan operation, 5:12
stock options, 5:14, 5:32–5:37
tax considerations, 5:39–5:48

[*References are to question numbers.*]

Long-term incentives
vs. annual, 1:23, 1:29
common forms in private companies, 2:7
determining, 11:22
meeting needs of executives and company, 1:3
negative effect of not providing in privately held company, 2:10
nonprofit organizations, 14:15
performance plan vs. other long-term incentives, 5:19
small company, 12:4
stock-based plan vs. other long-term incentives, 5:20

Long-term performance plan
defined, 5:13
primary disadvantage, 5:28
public sector executive compensation, 17:9
stock option plan vs, 5:15, 5:17

Look back approach, 4:52
Look forward approach, 4:50

M

Management variable compensation plan
sample, Appendix B

Managers. *See* Mid-level managers

Manufacturing organization
performance measures, 4:46

Market competition
determining, 11:19
effect on total compensation, 1:12
50th percentile strategy, 11:20
high-growth company, 12:9
valuing executives, 3:8

Matrix plan
advantages, 4:25
disadvantages, 4:26
key features, 4:24

Measures. *See* Performance

Medical benefits
for expatriates, 16:24
special early retirement programs, 15:10

Memberships and other common perquisites
club membership payments, 10:8
company car programs, 10:9
company phone and first class air travel, 10:15
financial planning, 10:16
hiring bonus, 10:11
home offices, computers, car phones, 10:10
key man insurance, 10:14
loans to executives, 10:17
split-dollar life insurance, defined, 10:13
supplemental life insurance, 10:12
travel expenses, reimbursement, 10:5
use, 10:8

Merger
long-term incentive plan administration, 5:60
deferred compensation integration, 5:61, 5:62
sample employment agreement, Appendix D
short-term incentive plan integration, 4:34

Merit increase
nonprofit organization, 14:9
public companies, 17:4

Merit pay
alternatives, 3:13

Mid-level managers
annual incentives, 4:33

Mission statement
total compensation strategy, 11:6

Model agreement
rabbi trust, Appendix A

[References are to question numbers.]

Models
  fair value determination, 1:50
Modified home country balance sheet compensation program, 16:31

N

Net to net compensation program
  elements, 16:30
New ventures. *See* Start-up company
Noncompete agreement
  enforceability, 10:22
  sample, Appendix C
  special early retirement conditions, 15:9
  stock award plans, 20:10
Non-litigation agreements
  special early retirement conditions, 15:9
Nonprofit organizations
  annual incentives
    award size, 14:11
    eligibility, 14:13
    performance measures, 14:12
    prevalence, 14:10
    regulations, 14:14
  base salary, 14:8, 14:9
  business objectives, 14:3
  company size, 14:4
  compensation mix, 14:2
  defined, 14:1
  general considerations, 14:1–14:7
  geographical location, 14:6
  long-term incentives, 14:15
  nonqualified plans, 9:75, 9:76
  perquisites, 14:16, 14:17
  recent legislation, 14:7
  type of organization, 14:5
Nonqualified deferred compensation plan
  appropriateness, 9:19
  beneficiary, 9:13
  constructive receipt, 9:79

  contributions to funded vs. unfunded plan, 9:18
  defined, 9:6
  economic benefit doctrine, 9:80
  ERISA requirements, 9:21
  fiduciary issues, 9:24
  insurance-related, 9:32–9:35
  OBRA changes, 9:10
  participation, vesting, and funding, 9:23
  vs. qualified plan, 9:7
  rationale, 9:9
  reporting and disclosure, 9:22
  SEC registration, 9:26
  tax considerations, 9:15–9:18, 9:20
  termination insurance, 9:25
  types, 9:14
  typical benefits, 9:8
  typical company objectives, 9:12
  typical objectives of deferring income, 9:11
Nonqualified plans
  in nonprofit organizations, 9:75, 9:76
  nonqualified retirement plans
    deferred compensation, 9:4–9:26
    split dollar enhancement, 9:46
Nonstatutory stock options
  accounting treatment, 6:16
  advantages, 6:19
  calculating dilution, 6:17
  defined, 6:14
  disadvantages, 6:20
  vs. ISOs, 6:22
  offsetting withholding burden, 6:21
  prevalence, 6:15
  tax treatment, 6:18

O

Omnibus plan
  defined, 5:38

Omnibus Reconciliation Act of 1993 (OBRA)
changes, 9:10
Option reloads
accounting impact, 6:38
advantages, 6:40
defined, 6:37
disadvantages, 6:41
tax treatment, 6:39
Options. *See* Stock
Ordinary income
defined, 1:36
Outsourcing
alternatives, 18:7
defined, 18:6
Overseas executives. *See* Expatriates

P

Parallel grant
restricted share and stock option shares, 8:13
Parallel plans
advantages, 8:3
defined, 8:2
disadvantages, 8:4
parallel SAR/stock option plan defined, 8:20
Participant method, incentive pools
advantages, 4:63
disadvantages, 4:64
use of method, 4:62
Pay limits
company response, 1:35
Peer company performance plan
advantages, 4:22
disadvantages, 4:23
operation, 4:21
Peer group approach
performance comparison, 4:51
Pension plan
expatriate, 16:25

Percentage of profits approach
performance standards, 4:53
Performance. *See also* Matrix plan; Performance plans
company performance
effect on total compensation, 1:14
graph requirement, 2:31
executive performance
effect on total compensation, 1:15
graphs, regulations, 20:16
measures
annual incentive plans, 4:35–4:48
nonprofit organization annual incentive, 14:12
performance unit plans, 7:40
small company, 12:2
performance-based stock options
accounting treatment, 6:64
advantages, 6:61
defined, 6:60
disadvantages, 6:62
indexed stock option defined, 6:65
tax consequences, 6:63
trends, 20:9
standards, annual incentives
appropriateness, 4:56
basic, 4:49
look back approach, 4:52
look forward approach, 4:50
peer group approach, 4:51
percentage of profits, 4:53
performance maximums for annual incentive plans, 4:54
threshold performance level, 4:55
Performance plans
award, tax effect, 5:45
long-term, public sector, 17:9
vs. other long-term incentives, 5:19
board of directors, 13:9
peer company performance plan, 4:21–4:23
performance share plan
accounting treatment, 7:48

[References are to question numbers.]

defined, 7:46
stock option plan combination,
8:6–8:11
tax treatment, 7:47
performance unit plans
accounting impact, 7:41
advantages, 7:44
defined, 7:39
disadvantages, 7:45
establishing performance measures, 7:40
tax treatment, 7:42
typical award period, 7:43
shareholder value/economic value
plans vs, 5:23
target performance plan
advantages, 4:19
disadvantages, 4:20
operation, 4:18
Perquisites and other benefits. *See
also* Executive benefit plans
board of directors, 13:19
employment agreements, 10:18–
10:22
executive perquisites
accounting treatment, 10:3
defined, 10:1
tax treatment, 10:2
expatriate, 16:27
general considerations, 10:1–10:3
memberships and other common
perquisites, 10:8–10:17
nonprofit organizations, 14:16
public sector executive compensation, 17:14
reimbursement, 10:4–10:7
satisfying executive needs, 1:4
SERP, nonprofit organizations, 14:17
severance agreements, 10:23–10:31
small company, 12:11
temporary executives, 18:12
Phantom stock plans
accounting impact, 7:23
advantages, 7:25

appropriate companies, 7:28
defined, 7:20
disadvantages, 7:26
dividends, 7:21
prevalence, 7:22
shadow stock plan defined, 7:29
tax treatment, 7:24
vesting, 7:27
Philosophy. *See* Corporate philosophy
Phone benefits. *See* Memberships and
other common perquisites
**Plan administration, long-term in-
centive plans**
amending, 5:58
base salary, recent changes, 20:4
instituting, 5:57
merger, 5:60, 5:61
proxy statements, 5:59
Plan comparisons
basic accounting issues, 5:25
Black-Scholes option pricing model,
5:26
getting executives to own stock, 5:21
performance plan vs. other long-
term incentives, 5:19
shareholder value/economic value
plans
vs. performance plans, 5:23
vs. stock plans, 5:22
stock-based plans vs. other long-
term incentives, 5:20
stock option plan
vs. long-term performance plan,
5:15, 5:17
vs. restricted share plan, 5:16, 5:18
tax rules, 5:24
Plan design
annual incentives
basic plan designs, 4:11
company merger, 4:34
discretionary plan, 4:27–4:29
executives vs. mid-level managers, 4:33
expatriates, 4:30

[References are to question numbers.]

Plan design *(cont'd)*
annual incentives *(cont'd)*
growth or improvement plan,
4:15–4:17
key issues, 4:10
local nationals, 4:31
matrix plan, 4:24–4:26
new ventures/start-ups, 4:32
peer company performance plan,
4:21–4:23
profit sharing plan, 4:12–4:14
small company, 12:10
target performance plan, 4:18–
4:20
compensation philosophy, 5:27
determining amount of long-term incentive payout or grant, 5:29
incentive plans, guidelines, 1:24
salary multiple approach in determining size of long-term incentives, 5:30
targeted income approach, 5:31
Plan termination. *See* Termination of
plan
Planning
tax rate considerations, 1:39
Point factor approach, 3:6
Policy splitting. *See* Life insurance
Pool method, incentive funds
advantages, 4:60
disadvantages, 4:61
operation, 4:59
participant method, 4:62–4:64
Premium. *See* Executive disability income insurance plans; Life insurance; Premium stock options
Premium stock options
accounting impact, 6:33
advantages, 6:35
defined, 6:30
disadvantages, 6:36
establishing premium, 6:31
prevalence, 6:32
tax treatment, 6:34

President of company
sample employment agreement, Appendix D
**Private vs. public company consid-
erations**
closely held company, 2:3, 2:4
executive compensation program
differences, 2:5
general considerations, 2:1–2:5
private or privately held company,
defined, 2:2
proxy rules, 2:23–2:32
public or publicly traded company
change in base salary levels, 20:2
defined, 2:1
future value of stock options, 2:29
S corporations, 2:11–2:14
SEC regulations, 2:15–2:22
stock-based plans, 2:6–2:10
Profit sharing plan
advantages, 4:13
disadvantages, 4:14
operation, 4:12
Proxy rules
board compensation committee,
2:25
change in treatment of executive
compensation, 2:32
company performance graph, 2:31
disclosure information charts, 2:27
effect of reporting requirements,
2:24
future value of stock options, 2:29
media/shareholder reaction to stock
option exercise, 2:30
other proxy statement disclosures,
2:28
performance graphs, 20:16
regulatory base and effective dates,
2:26
shareholder proxy and proxy statement defined, 2:23
Proxy statement
defined, 2:23

[References are to question numbers.]

long-term incentive information, 5:59

other proxy statement disclosures, 2:28

Public company. *See* Private vs. public company considerations

Public sector executive compensation
annual incentives, 17:8
base salary, 17:2
insured benefits, 17:10
job evaluation systems, 17:3
long-term performance plans, 17:9
merit increases, 17:4
perquisites, 17:14
vs. private sector programs, 17:1
recruitment, 17:15
regulations, 17:13
retirement plans, 17:11
salary ranges, 17:7
stock award plans, 17:9
supplemental retirement plans, 17:12
tenure-based pay increase systems, 17:5, 17:6

Purchase plans
book value purchase plans, 6:42–6:47
convertible debentures, 6:48–6:55
defined, 6:1
differences between types, 6:3
discounted stock options, 6:23–6:29
general considerations, 6:1–6:5
incentive stock options, 6:6–6:13
junior stock plans, 6:56–6:59
nonstatutory stock options, 6:14–6:22
option reloads, 6:37–6:41
performance-based stock options, 6:60–6:65
premium stock options, 6:30–6:36
stock option exercise
setting prices, 6:4
typical exercise period, 6:5

types, 6:2

Pyramiding stock swap. *See* Stock

Q

Qualified plan
ERISA considerations, special early retirement program, 15:8
vs. nonqualified deferred compensation plan, 9:7
OBRA changes, 9:10
tax treatment, 9:17

R

Rabbi escrow agreement
defined, 9:27
Rabbi trust
defined, 9:28
model agreement, Appendix A
vs. secular trust, 9:30
Range banding, 3:13
Ranking system, 3:4
Recruitment
and public sector, 17:15
Registration. *See* SEC registration
Regulation T
defined, 5:52
Reimbursement
entertainment expense, 10:6
expense accounts, tax and accounting, 10:7
expenses, 10:4
travel, 10:5
Reloads. *See* Option reloads
Relocation costs
reimbursement, 16:7
Remuneration. *See* Total remuneration
Rental
home rental program, expatriate benefit, 16:8

[References are to question numbers.]

Reporting
excess benefit plans, 9:73
nonqualified deferred compensation plan, 9:22
proxy rules, 2:23–2:32
Responsibility
effect on total compensation, 1:9
Restricted share plan
stock option plan vs, 5:16, 5:18
Restricted stock grants
accounting impact, 7:32
advantages, 7:36
appropriate companies, 7:38
defined, 7:30
disadvantages, 7:37
prevalence, 7:31
Section 83(b) election, 7:34
tax considerations, 5:44, 7:33
vesting, 7:35
Restricted stock plans
stock option plan combination, 8:12–8:18
Retirement benefits
board of directors, 13:15
temporary executives, 18:14
total compensation strategy statement, 11:13
Retirement plans
prevalence, outside directors, 20:13
public sector executive compensation, 17:11
Return on assets
definition and calculation, 4:39
Return on capital
calculation, 4:41
Return on equity
calculation, 4:40

S

Salary banding; other increases
alternatives to base salary ranges and merit pay, 3:13

economic pay increases, 3:13, 3:16
negative experiences, 3:15
positive experiences, 3:14
Salary increases
inflation, 3:12
motivating effect, 3:11
Salary multiple approach, 5:30
Salary ranges
public sector, 17:7
Sale of home
reimbursement, 16:7
Sample compensation agreements, Appendix B
S corporation
defined, 2:11
election, 2:12, 2:13
unreasonable compensation, 2:14
SEC registration
nonqualified deferred compensation plan, 9:26
SEC regulations
Securities Act of 1933, 2:15, 2:17
Securities Exchange Act of 1934, 2:16, 2:18–2:22
SEC Section 16
actions needed to benefit, 2:21
basic rules, 2:18
board of directors options, 13:11
clarifications, 2:22
major changes, 2:19
paying for stock, 5:50
SARs, 7:4
significant effects, 2:20
Section 83(b) election
effect on restricted stock grant, 7:34
Secular trust
defined, 9:29
vs. rabbi trust, 9:30
Securities Act of 1933
avoiding application, 2:17
generally, 2:15
Securities Exchange Act of 1934
generally, 2:16
Section 16 rules, 2:18–2:22

Index

SERP (supplemental executive retirement plans). *See* Top-hat plans or SERPs

Service company
performance measures, 4:48

Severance agreement
change in control, 10:26
golden parachute, 10:24–10:29
as perquisite, 10:23
sample, Appendix C
special early retirement programs, 15:3, 15:4

Shadow stock plan. *See* Phantom stock plans

Shareholder. *See also* Proxy rules
approval
annual incentives, 4:9
convertible debentures, 6:49
sample employment agreement, Appendix D
shareholder value
correlation of EVA, 19:7
defined, 5:11
/economic value plans, vs. performance plans, 5:23
/economic value plans, vs. stock plans, 5:22
operation, 5:12

Short-term incentive. *See* Incentives

Size of award
nonprofit organization annual incentive, 14:11

Size of company
effect on total compensation, 1:13
large company
changes in base salary levels, 20:1
total compensation strategy statement, 11:27
nonprofit organization, 14:4
small company
annual incentive plan design, 12:10
changes in base salary levels, 20:3

competition and cost-containment, 12:6
establishing annual incentives, 12:2
executive benefits and perquisites, 12:11
family-owned companies, 12:7
general considerations, 12:1–12:11
less sophisticated business performance measures, 12:2
long-term incentives, 12:4
mix of compensation elements, 12:1
new venture businesses, 12:12, 12:13
recruitment without competitive salary and bonus, 12:5
small, high-growth companies and competitive values, 12:9
small human resources staff, 12:3
total compensation strategies, 12:8
total compensation strategy statement, 11:26

Small company. *See* Size of company

Special early retirement programs
defined, 15:1
ERISA implications, 15:8
funding, 15:5
medical benefits, 15:10
negative consequences
to companies, 15:6
to employees, 15:7
non-compete or non-litigation agreements, 15:9
rationale, 15:2
severance, 15:3, 15:4

Spendable income, 16:14

Split-dollar life insurance. *See* Life insurance

Standards. *See* Performance

Start-up company
base salary and benefits, 12:13
compensation programs, 1:26

[References are to question numbers.]

Start-up company (*cont'd*)
  incentive compensation, 12:12
  incentive plans, 4:32
Stock
  awards
    accounting, 1:45
    changes in levels, 20:8
    non-compete clauses, 20:10
    outside directors, 20:14
    public sector, 17:9
    temporary executives, 18:11
  Black-Scholes option pricing model, 5:26
  from family-owned company to non-family members, 12:7
  getting executives to own stock, 5:21
  option exercise
    cashless option exercise, 5:51
    exercise period, 6:5
    negative reaction, 2:30
    paying the exercise price, 5:49
    pyramiding stock swap exercise, 5:54
    Regulation T, 5:52
    Section 16 rules, 5:50
    setting exercise price, 6:4
    stock swap, 5:53
  options. *See also* Incentive stock options; Nonstatutory stock options
    board of directors compensation, 13:10
    conditions, 5:35, 5:36
    deduction limits, 20:17
    discounted, 6:23–6:29
    exercise period, 5:33
    to expatriates, 16:20
    FAS 123 accounting, 20:15
    FASB regulations, 1:54
    future value, 2:29
    incentive, 6:6–6:13
    link to EVA, 19:9
    nonstatutory, 6:14–6:22
    option reloads, 6:37–6:41

  performance-based, 6:60–6:65, 20:9
  premium, 6:30–6:36
  rationale of using stock-based plans, 5:34
  reserved shares, 5:37
  tax considerations, 5:42
  types, 5:32
plans
  board of directors, 13:10–13:13
  buy-back agreement, example, 2:9
  FAS 123, 1:48
  incentive plans, 1:30
  long-term incentive, 2:7, 2:10
  vs. other long-term incentives, 5:20
  performance share/stock option plan combination, 8:6–8:11
  phantom stock, 7:20–7:29
  privately held companies, 2:6
  problems with use in private companies, 2:8
  rationale, 5:34
  restricted stock grants, 7:30–7:38
  restricted stock plan/stock option plan combination, 8:12–8:18
  SAR/stock option plan combinations, 8:19–8:23
  shareholder value/economic value plans vs, 5:22
stock appreciation rights
  accounting impact, 7:7
  advantages, 7:10
  appropriate company, 7:12
  vs. cashless exercise, 7:6
  combined with stock options, board of directors compensation, 13:13
  defined, 7:3
  disadvantages, 7:11
  free-standing, 16:21
  prevalence, 7:5
  SEC Section 16 rules, 7:4
  tandem SAR/stock option plans, 8:19–8:23

tax considerations, 5:43, 7:8
vesting, 7:9
stock option plan
defined, 5:15
vs. long-term performance plan,
5:15, 5:17
performance share plan combination, 8:6–8:11
vs. restricted share plan, 5:16, 5:18
restricted stock plan combination, 8:12–8:18
SAR plan combination, 8:19–8:23
stock swap
defined, 5:53
drawbacks, 5:56
pyramiding stock swap exercise,
5:54–5:56
tax considerations, 5:55
Strategic business unit
use of EVA, 19:6
Substantial risk of forfeiture
long-term incentives, 5:40, 5:41
**Supplemental executive retirement
plan (SERP).** *See* Top-hat plans or
SERPs
Supplemental life insurance
as perquisite, 10:12
Supply and demand. *See* Market competition
Swap. *See* Stock

T

Tandem plans. *See also* Long-term incentive plans
advantages, 8:3
defined, 8:1
disadvantages, 8:4
restricted stock/stock option plan,
defined, 8:12
SAR/stock option plan
defined, 8:19
to directors, 13:13

Targeted income approach
plan design, 5:31
Target performance plan
advantages, 4:19
disadvantages, 4:20
operation, 4:18
Tax considerations
alternative minimum tax, 1:42
annual incentives, 4:7
board of directors compensation,
13:7
book value appreciation rights, 7:15
book value purchase plans, 6:44
capital gains, 1:37, 1:38, 20:18,
20:19
club membership, 10:8
Code Section 83 tax property transfers, 9:81
Code Section 162(m), 1:34, 1:35
COLI, 10:12
combination performance
share/stock option plans, 8:8
company car programs, 10:9
compensation forms, 1:31
compensation planning, 1:39
congressional pay limits, 1:35
convertible debentures, 6:51
effective tax rate, 1:40
excess benefit plans, 9:77, 9:78
excess parachute payment, 10:31
executive disability income insurance plans, 9:48–9:50
executive perquisites, 10:2
expatriates
avoiding taxes, 16:16, 16:17
equalization, 16:12
foreign earned income exclusions, 16:15
spendable income, 16:14
tax-free income, 16;13
expense accounts, 10:7
fundamental issues, 1:31–1:42
home offices, computers, car
phones, 10:10

Tax considerations *(cont'd)*
ISOs, 6:7, 6:8
long-term incentive plans, 5:24
Code Section 83(b) election, 5:48
constructive receipt, 5:39, 5:46
deferred compensation, 5:46
economic benefit theory, 5:47
performance plan award, 5:45
restricted stock grant, 5:44
stock appreciation right, 5:43
stock option, 5:42
substantial risk of forfeiture, 5:40,
5:41
marginal tax rate, 1:41
nonqualified and qualified plans,
9:15, 9:16
nonqualified deferred compensation
plan contributions, 9:79, 9:80
nonstatutory stock options, 6:18
option reloads, 6:39
ordinary income, 1:36
performance-based stock options,
6:63
performance share plans, 7:47
performance unit plans, 7:42
phantom stock plans, 7:24
premium stock options, 6:34
pyramiding exercise, 5:55
restricted stock grants, 7:33
restricted stock/stock option plan
combination, 8:15
SARs, 7:8
SAR/stock option plans, 8:23
stock options, 8:23, 20:17
combination performance
share/stock option plans, 8:8
ISOs, 6:7, 6:8
long-term incentive plans, 5:42
nonstatutory, 6:18
option reloads, 6:39
performance-based, 6:63
premium, 6:34
restricted stock/stock option plan
combination, 8:15

SAR/stock option plans, 8:23
stock swap, 5:55
unreasonable compensation, 1:32,
1:33
Temporary executives
alternatives to outsourcing, 18:7
as independent contractors, 18:2
advantages and disadvantages,
18:3, 18:4
base salary, 18:9
conversion to full-time status, 18:17
defined, 18:1
incentive compensation, 18:10
insured benefits, 18:13
obtaining an assignment, 18:8
outsourcing, 18:6, 18:7
overseas assignment, 18:16
perquisites, 18:12
regulations, 18:15
retirement benefits, 18:14
short-term vs. long-term assignment, 18:5
stock awards, 18:11
Tenure-based pay increases, 17:5,
17:6
Termination of plan
insurance, for nonqualified deferred
compensation plan, 9:25
Top-hat plans or SERPs
SERPS
example, 9:64
vs. excess benefit plan, 9:66
nonprofit organizations, 14:17
public sector, 17:12
top hat plan
benefit payment, 9:59
defined, 9:56
ERISA requirements, 9:61–9:63
funding, 9:62, 9:63
future benefit payment, 9:60
inadvertent creation, 9:58
reason for establishing, 9:57
Total compensation
annual and long-term incentives, 1:3

[References are to question numbers.]

base salary, 1:2
  determining mix of elements, 1:18
  vs. other elements, 1:17
benefits and perquisites, 1:4
cash, 1:6, 20:1–20:7
company performance, 1:15
company size, 1:13
corporate level, 1:10
defined, 1:7
executive performance, 1:14
executive responsibility, 1:9
factors, 1:8
industry type, 1:11
small company strategies, 12:8
strategy building
  approval and implementation, 11:24, 11:25
  benefit factors, 11:11–11:15
  business purposes, 11:3
  compensation factors, 11:4–11:10
  determining the mix, 11:18–11:22
  developing a total strategy, 11:23
  elements of executive compensation, 11:2
  examples of strategy statements, 11:26–11:28
  external factors, 11:10
  general considerations, 11:1–11:3
  internal factors, 11:9
  other factors, 11:16, 11:17
  total compensation strategy defined, 11:1
supply and demand, 1:12
total cash compensation, 1:6
total compensation defined, 1:7
total compensation factors, 1:8
total remuneration defined, 1:1
valuation of all compensation elements, 1:5
Total remuneration
defined, 1:1
outside directors, changes in levels, 20:12

Transfers
  property tax, Code Section 83, 9:81
Travel. *See* Memberships and other common perquisites
Trends in executive compensation
  long-term compensation, 20:8–20:11
  outside directors
    remuneration levels, 20:12
    retirement plan prevalence, 20:13
    stock awards, 20:14
  regulations
    alternative minimum tax, 20:19
    capital gains tax rates, 20:18
    FAS 123 on stock option accounting, 20:15
    limiting deductions on stock options, 20:17
    performance graphs, 20:16
  total cash compensation
    change in base salary administration, 20:4
    change in annual bonus levels, 20:5
    change in base salary levels, 20:1–20:3
    change in mix of base salary and annual incentives, 20:7
    change in bonus payout schedules, 20:6

U

Unfunded plan
  contributions, 9:18
  vs. funded plan, 9:54, 9:55, 9:63
  top-hat plan, 9:62, 9:63
U.S. executives working overseas. *See* Expatriates
Unreasonable compensation
  consequences of determination, 1:33
  defined, 1:32
  public vs. private company and S corporation, 2:14

[References are to question numbers.]

V

Valuation
all executive compensation elements, 1:5
economic value added, 19:1–19:14
executive positions, 3:8
fair value
FAS 123, 1:49
models, 1:50
stock option future value, 2:29
Variable compensation plan. *See*
Management variable compensation plan
Venture. *See* Start-up company
Vesting
excess benefit plans, 9:72

nonqualified deferred compensation plan, 9:23
phantom stock plans, 7:27
restricted stock grants, 7:35
SARs, 7:9

W

Wage dividend plan
sample, Appendix B
Withholding
offsetting, nonstatutory stock options, 6:21